ESSENTIALS OF ADVERTISI

SECOND EDITION

ESSENTIALS OF ADVERTISING

SECOND EDITION

LOUIS C. KAUFMAN

HARCOURT BRACE JOVANOVICH, PUBLISHERS

San Diego   New York   Chicago   Austin
London   Sydney   Tokyo   Toronto

ISBN: 0-15-524102-8

Library of Congress Catalog Card Number: 86-70497

Printed in the United States of America

Illustration credits appear on pages 549–552, which constitute a continuation of the copyright page.

TO
THE
STUDENT

I believe two different groups of students will use this text. Those in one group are studying advertising because they have to as part of their major. Students in the second group are studying advertising because they plan a career in that field and want to learn as much as possible about it. It is primarily to this group that my words are directed.

In a survey conducted at the New York Institute of Technology, both advertising executives who did study advertising in college and those who did not (because courses were not available) overwhelmingly recommended it for students wanting a career in advertising.

If you are so hungry to succeed in advertising that you can actually taste it, learning every page of this or any other text will not satisfy you. And it shouldn't. You should start reading the weekly trade media like *Advertising Age* or *ADWEEK*. Soon you'll start to recognize the names of the advertising agencies and the clients and the industry leaders. You'll start to feel you're in advertising, and you'll start to think that way too.

If your school has a marketing or an advertising club, don't merely join it. Be really active, participate in every part of it. If your school does not have a student marketing organization, ask a friendly faculty member to help start one.

If there's an organization of advertising professionals in your area, join as a student member, get involved, attend meetings, and volunteer for the committees.

Membership will introduce you to the advertising professionals in your locality: the advertising managers, whatever their titles may happen to be; the people in the local advertising agencies; those from your local radio, television, or newspapers. One of these days you'll be looking for an internship or perhaps a job, and knowing them will give you a major advantage.

Because advertising is perceived as a glamorous business, many young people want to go into advertising. It's tough to break into advertising, and starting salaries are embarrassingly low. But don't let that stop you. Don't hesitate to start at any menial job. Forty years ago beside me in the mailroom of a leading business advertising agency was a fellow by the name of Fred Poppe. Today he is the C.E.O. of Poppe/Tyson, a leading business oriented ad agency. Hal Heaslip, who today is director of advertising for the Grumman Corporation, was replaced in the mailroom at the Kenyon & Eckhart agency by another beginner named George Simko. Today George Simko is president of one of the three companies that make up D'Arcy, Masius, Benton & Bowles, one of today's mega-agencies.

One excellent way to get the feel of the real world quickly is to begin at a local pennysaver. That will teach you about effective advertising faster than anything else.

In your first dozen years in the advertising business, don't be afraid to move around for a better salary or opportunity. In other kinds of business, it is not uncommon for someone to start with one company and remain there for an entire career. In advertising that's rare. And frankly, it's not to your advantage. Moving around will provide you with a perspective you can never get in a single job. Diversified experience pays off on a résumé.

A career in advertising is never easy, even if your father owns the business. You have to work hard to succeed, especially during the first ten years or so. But then you begin enjoying the priceless pleasure, the satisfaction of seeing the results of your efforts, and that will make it all worthwhile. Sure, there will be times you'll get discouraged. If it becomes unbearable, perhaps you shouldn't be in advertising to begin with.

For the right people, advertising is most demanding. But it is most rewarding and always exciting. Even the most routine assignment can be enjoyable in its way. My career has been 40 years of doing what I always wanted to do — be a part of the advertising business. I've been on the inside of a major corporation as advertising manager of AMF Bowling Products and in agencies such as Grey and Kudner, working with some of the brightest, most talented people in the country. Now I find consulting and teaching to be rewarding in a different way.

My one wish for each of you who wants a career in advertising is that you will feel as pleased with your choice as I have been with mine.

JOHN MAZEY

PREFACE

It has long been my conviction that the art and business of persuasive communication — advertising, for short — is essential to the welfare of the business community itself and to the nation as a whole. That conviction has kept me in the business — as practitioner and teacher — all my working life. I hope this book will transmit to all students some of the excitement I continue to find in the field. I also hope the book makes use of my years in the business and in the classroom to convey the liveliness, the flavor, and the challenge of my profession, both to students interested in a career in advertising and to those taking the course as an elective simply to learn a little about the field.

I have tried to make *Essentials of Advertising* a practical book, organized in a realistic way: Its sequence of chapters corresponds to the decisions and activities of the real world. Thus, media choice precedes creative strategy; budget decisions precede media choice.

The text moves from the pragmatic considerations that underlie the finished ad — marketing intelligence and research (increasingly important today) and the budget (whose constraints affect media choice as well as ad design) — through media, to the final campaign. The media chapters include a full range — from 15-second television commercials to telephone booth posters. There is a chapter on business and farm publications — a rapidly growing segment of the advertising industry that has been relatively neglected — as well as one on outdoor and transit media and another on trade and industrial advertising.

Four chapters are devoted to the creative side of advertising — developing strategies, writing copy, creating art, and choosing appropriate printing processes. In this section, however, the emphasis is not so much on the technical "how to" as on the "why": on deciding and managing and on selecting the best artistic means to achieve the objectives of a particular advertising campaign.

The coordination of all the elements of advertising — budgeting, research, media selection, and creative strategy — is shown in the succeeding chapters on consumer advertising campaigns, retail advertising campaigns, business (trade and industrial) campaigns, and international and service campaigns.

Every chapter contains a brief case history ranging from food to tourism. Each case includes one or more examples of the advertising as well as a description of the objectives. These cases show the media choices and the strategy choices that were made for many different products.

At this point I must acknowledge the wonderful cooperation I enjoyed from agency people and corporate ad managers, who provided details, storyboards, and sample ads for the cases. In this regard, notice the superb illustrations throughout the book, including 73 color plates. They too have been provided through the cooperation of advertising professionals. If I do not acknowledge their contributions individually, it is from fear of omitting someone. People in the advertising business truly are very special. I must also acknowledge the cooperation of the publications in the field from which I obtained tables and charts. Every caption is intended to teach, not merely identify. The captions are an important component of the book.

Since advertising is really a "people business," dependent entirely on the creativity and verve of men and women, there are also 22 profiles of distinguished figures in the advertising business—Raymond Rubicam, David Ogilvy, John Cunningham, and Jerry Della Femina are some of those included. I hope the profiles will enrich the students' appreciation of these personalities and even provide insights into career opportunities.

Each chapter begins with a working vocabulary, a list of real-world terms used every day in the field, that can serve as a framework for class discussion. Each chapter ends with a summary, questions for discussion, and a list of sources and suggestions for further reading.

Along the way, of course, I deal with some of the social aspects and issues of advertising, but as a practitioner I make no secret of my sympathies. How, why, and by whom advertising is policed is the subject of chapter 21.

Many thanks must go to the dedicated people at Harcourt Brace Jovanovich. Like good advertising itself, this book is the result of hard-working, self-effacing people. I must acknowledge the patient and painstaking work of the editor who watched for every detail, every misspelling, and every quotation—Mike McKinley. Thanks is due James Chadwick for his exceptionally attractive design and to Rebecca Lytle and Karen Davidson for their attention to details, especially on the illustration material. I am also grateful to James W. Taylor of California State University, Fullerton, and George Belch of San Diego State University for their suggestions.

I hope that every student who uses *Essentials of Advertising* will not only learn those essentials, but will enjoy learning them.

LOUIS KAUFMAN

TABLE OF CONTENTS

PART 1 SURVEY OF ADVERTISING

1

2

3

PART 2 DECISIONS IN ADVERTISING

PART 3 GUIDE TO ADVERTISING MEDIA

8
Print Media: Newspapers and Consumer Magazines

9
Print Media: Business and Farm Publications

10
The Broadcast Media

PART 5 THE WORLDS OF ADVERTISING

ESSENTIALS OF ADVERTISING

SECOND EDITION

SURVEY OF ADVERTISING

1

◀ Who is it? *The Sweetheart of the Corn*®, in 1907 a symbol for Kellogg's Corn Flakes.

1 THE STORY OF ADVERTISING

Advertising Defined

Advertising Through the Ages

The Ancient Marketplace
Trade and Craft Guilds
The Printed Word
The Explosive Growth of the Newspaper Media
Sandwich Men and Space Brokers
Magazines Accept Advertising
Dawn of the Modern Age
A New Medium — Radio
The Great Depression
How Advertising Won the War

The old trader and his shop were known in the neighbourhood. The talk of the countryside was their sufficient publicity. But the new trader may be at the other side of the mountains or the other side of the world. As he cannot show his face, he must show a placard.

H. G. Wells
The Work, Wealth and Happiness of Mankind

Before we describe what advertising is, we had better be certain we know what it is *not* and what it can not do. Advertising is *not* a science such as chemistry, with laws and rules that, if followed with reasonable precision, will lead to predictable results every time. Advertising is *not* a panacea that can restore a poor product or rejuvenate a declining market; it is *not* a substitute for sound business judgment. Nor is advertising merely the words and pictures that appear in newspapers and in magazines, on billboards and on television screens. These are the means, or the *media,* that advertising uses to communicate information about products, services, and ideas — information designed to persuade people to make buying or action decisions. Advertising *is* the art and business of *persuasive* communication.

Advertising Defined

The most widely accepted definition of advertising is one developed by the American Marketing Association:

Advertising is any form of nonpersonal presentation of goods, services or ideas for action, openly paid for, by an identified sponsor.[1]

Often people are confused about the differences between advertising and personal selling and between advertising and publicity. If we take our definition of advertising apart, however, these differences will become clear:

Any form: This phrase means exactly that — any form of presentation — a sign, an advertisement in a magazine or newspaper, a commercial on radio or television, circulars distributed through the mail or handed out on a street-corner, skywriting, billboards, posters, and matchbooks — the possibilities are limited only by the imagination of the advertiser.

Nonpersonal: This phrase excludes personal selling, which is usually done on a person-to-person or, in some cases (such as a Tupperware party) on a people-to-people basis. If it's in person, it's not advertising.

Goods, services, ideas for action: Most definitions describe the application of advertising to the purchase of goods and services, but neglect the use of advertising by businesses to promote ideas for other forms of action. The United States government, for example, the 26th largest advertiser in the nation in 1984, advertises to recruit men and women for the Army, the Navy, the Air Force, and the Marines. It also uses advertising to try to persuade its citizens to pay their income taxes early and to use ZIP codes. The Red Cross advertises; local hospitals and museums advertise to attract financial contributors. And political candidates advertise to sell themselves — like soap or toothpaste — to the public.

---

[1] *Journal of Marketing,* 12, no. 2 (October 1948), p. 202.

HOW TO TALK TO TEENAGERS ABOUT DRINKING AND DRIVING.

KEEPING OUT OF HARM'S WAY.

Teenagers can get into a lot of trouble with alcohol. Even teenagers who don't drink. Often they aren't aware of the facts.

A new view of the statistics shows where part of the problem lies, and can lead to a better communication between adults and teenagers.

Teenagers are in the high-risk group. People between the ages of 16 and 24 represent only 20 percent of the licensed drivers of our country. But that same group is involved in 42 percent of all the alcohol-related fatal crashes. When you think about that, two tragic things are revealed:

First, not all teenagers killed in such accidents are themselves drunk at the time. Often they have had nothing to drink at all, but are passengers in cars driven by teenagers who have been drinking.

Second, teenagers are often on the roads late at night, especially on weekends, when most crashes involving alcohol occur. They are targets for cars driven by people who have had too much to drink.

Some facts about alcohol you might want to discuss with teenagers are often surprising to adults:

• One can of beer, as well as one four-ounce glass of table wine, and one 1.2-ounce drink of 80-proof liquor are all equally intoxicating. The risk is the same regardless of what you've been drinking.

• The legal definition of intoxication is based on "Blood Alcohol Concentration" or "BAC." If you have a BAC of .10 percent, you are legally drunk in most states. But for drivers or drinkers who are less experienced, a BAC of .05 percent, or sometimes lower, can be dangerous.

• Even relatively low levels of alcohol can reduce your tolerance to injury, increasing the danger in an accident.

Arm your teenagers with the facts and give them time to reflect on them.

If expected to show good judgment, teenagers are more likely to live up to it.

Please discuss the problem of drinking and driving with your teenagers now, and if you think this advertisement will help, ask them to read it.

And keep in mind, that the best way to teach young people—as they may tell you—is by example.

The people of General Motors care, and urge teenagers, and their parents, to give serious thought to the dangers of drinking and driving. It's something we all can do.

This advertisement is part of our continuing effort to give customers useful information about their cars and trucks and the company that builds them.

Chevrolet • Pontiac
Oldsmobile • Buick
Cadillac • GMC Truck

This General Motors advertisement promotes *ideas,* not as a direct effort to sell products, but as a service to the public. The list of General Motors products at the bottom is not meant to sell. General Motors says it cares, and uses such ads to demonstrate its concern.

Companies will also use advertising to promote ideas that are not intended to directly induce the purchase of a product or service. The General Motors ad above was designed to serve the public and promote goodwill.

Openly paid for by an identified sponsor: This means that sponsors of the message must be clearly identified and must acknowledge that they have paid for the use of the media in which the ad appears. Otherwise, the message is considered to be publicity. Publicity is not openly paid for, and the sponsor is not usually

These attractive, informative articles are a sample of the helpful publicity material that manufacturers make available without cost to newspapers and magazines. Because the manufacturer does not pay the media to print these articles, and because the sponsor is not openly identified, they are considered publicity, not advertising.

identified. The publicity organization that prepares the material is paid by the sponsor of the item — but the newspaper, magazine, or radio station that carries it does so free of charge. There is no implication of anything underhanded or manipulative about publicity. It is simply not advertising.

Advertising Through the Ages

The Ancient Marketplace

Although modern advertising as we perceive it today is less than 100 years old, its roots go back a long time in history. The technological developments of the past 50 years have made advertising more extensive and more effective, but the idea behind it — the transmission of information — can be traced back to ancient Greece and Rome.

Over 3,000 years ago criers were used to carry information from the king, or ruler, to the populace. Curiously, the crier's function was then thought to have derived from Hermes, the messenger of the gods and himself god of commerce and theft (an interesting combination?). Later, the criers of Rome performed a variety of services for both the state and private enterprise. An ancient Roman described the job of criers as that of drawing crowds to merchants with goods to sell.

It is not difficult to determine what was sold in this shop, with its wooden sign hanging in front from a wrought iron support.

During this era signs were also used to mark the location of mercantile establishments. An inn in ancient Greece was marked by a pine cone, which stemmed from the practice in those days of coating jugs of wine with pine resin to seal them. The pine cone was also one of the symbols of Dionysius, the god of wine. To this day the Greeks still drink resinated wine — retsina.

Among the signs still legible in the old Roman city of Pompeii (dating from A.D. 79) is that of a cloth merchant, depicting various methods of dyeing cloth. Bookshops fastened announcements of new books to the columns of temples. Perhaps our use of the word *columnist* is derived from the ancient practice of providing information in that fashion?

Trade and Craft Guilds

After the fall of the Roman Empire in the fifth century A.D., advertising practices, whatever they might have been, are lost in obscurity. By the Middle Ages, however, advertising was primarily confined to signs. Frequently, one street of a town would be devoted to a particular trade, and it was the custom to have signs at both ends of the street that depicted that trade. In fact, the names of many streets in Europe and in the United States, such as Baker, Mercer, Haymarket, and Smithfield, are derived from the trade that had once been practiced there.

With time, the emblems of the signs could be seen on the banners carried during a guild procession and on the badges or medallions worn by the members of the guild. By the fourteenth century, signs painted on wood were widespread, suspended from the overhang of houses, swinging from long wrought-iron brackets. They were mostly pictorial, because the population was largely illiterate. Some merchants, envious of the coats of arms of the nobility, tried to incorporate heraldic symbols into their signs whenever possible, but generally the sign was a symbol — a boot, a glove, a bush (for an inn)[2] — easily recognized.

In the thirteenth century, town criers were paid directly by the merchants whose goods they advertised. Later, in the seventeenth century, criers used their talents not so much for advertising as to sell their wares in singsong or even rhyme — "Fuller's earth, Fuller's earth![3] Freshly dug to clean your wool, come and buy, my sacks are full." Many of these cries can still be heard in small

---

[2] There still exists an old saying, "Fine wine needs no bush."
[3] Fuller's earth: an absorbent clay used for removing grease from wool that is being shrunk and thickened by a process known as "fulling."

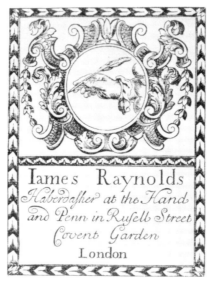

Eighteenth-century business cards. Notice how these three businessmen used illustration — to identify not their products, but their locations.

European towns where fish, produce, or baked goods are sold from wagons in the streets. And how about the American news vendor's cry: "Read all about it"?

The Printed Word

But it was the invention of printing that really revolutionized the possibilities of advertising. Thirty years after Gutenberg issued the first book printed with movable type, the Catholic Church was using printed circulars to advertise the "Grand Pardon de Notre Dame de Reims." By the year 1500, Frankfurt had become the headquarters for book publishers, and Albrecht de Menninger brought out the first book catalog. Albrecht's catalog contained over 200 titles. It is to William Caxton of London that we owe the first book to be printed in the English language. Caxton was a mercer, or cloth merchant, who in his later years turned from the cloth business to the newly discovered art of printing. To advertise his books, he issued handbills. Subsequently, these handbills (only 3 inches by 5 inches) became large posters, which were often pasted to the columns of St. Paul's Cathedral. We are still reminded of this nuisance by the admonition lettered on blank walls: *Post No Bills.*

The Explosive Growth of the Newspaper Media

The seventeenth century marked the development of the newspaper. From the first, these newspapers were simply filled with advertisements. They were issued irregularly, their growth impeded by a scarcity of printers, the lack of an organized postal service, and the social and political climate of that era. The first publication similar to our modern newspaper appeared in Florence in 1597, when the grand duke gave a Florentine printer permission to publish weekly commercial bulletins. By the early 1600s there were gazettes[4] in Basle, Vienna, Frankfurt, Hamburg, Berlin, Amsterdam, and London.

---

[4] Gazette: from the old Venetian word *gazeta,* a coin that was the price of the paper. *Gazeta* is a diminutive of the Italian word *gaza,* a magpie.

At the end of the seventeenth century, a great number of commercial newspapers were being printed in England, all of them filled with quotations for imported goods and other commercial information. One of the most popular subjects of early advertisements was books, since only those few people who could read books could read the advertisements. Later, there appeared offers of marriage, advertisements for travel, and advertisements for the new beverage just becoming popular, imported from China and called *Tcha*. By 1710 there even existed a *frequency rate* — a reduced rate of charge for advertisements run a certain number of times within a given period without change. (See examples of early newspaper mastheads below.)

Meanwhile, the government of King George, ever alert to fund-raising opportunities, levied a heavy tax on "news-papers." Faced with the prospect of raising the price of the newspaper and thereby reducing sales, the publishers instead emphasized the sale of advertising to increase their revenues. Advertising thereby became the *main* source of revenue for the newspapers, and they were filled with announcements of lotteries, rewards for stolen property, and many "indelicate" advertisements regarding lovers' meetings and "help for

Mastheads of some early newspapers. With the exception of *The London Times,* they appear to be weekly papers. In earlier years *The London Times* published only advertisements on its front page. The publishers assumed that readers interested in the news would open the paper to the inside pages.

ladies finding themselves in difficult situations."[5] Of course, critics of that time attacked advertising as so much "puffery."

In the English colonies of North America, the growth of the newspaper industry followed a pattern similar to that of England's press. The first American newspaper, *The Boston Weekly News-Letter,* carried advertisements of sailings from Boston, imported goods, runaway slaves, and sales of slaves. By 1765 there were 25 newspapers in existence when the English imposed a stamp tax that aroused strong opposition among independent-minded colonists. In 1784 the first daily newspaper was issued — *The Pennsylvania Packet and Daily Advertiser.* The paper actually resembled today's pennysaver — that is, it contained far more advertisements than news.[6] The coffeehouses of that period were very instrumental in the development of the newspapers, because they served as clubs for intellectuals and businessmen. Some coffeehouse proprietors sought to build patronage by publishing their own news sheets.

Sandwich Men and Space Brokers

Newspaper advertising was not the only form of advertising that was growing. So many people were reluctant to spend a penny or two to purchase a newspaper that posters were utilized extensively. Bill posters were everywhere. When Dickens described the streets of nineteenth-century London, he included people handing out circulars and carrying signs, particularly the men with signs front and back, whom he dubbed "sandwich men." In fact, by the end of the nineteenth century, people were complaining about the number of advertisements that were to be found in railroad stations, along highways, and in other areas that were accustomed to much traffic. The major impetus for the growth of the advertising business during this period was the Industrial Revolution. Local manufacturers discovered that their ability to produce goods far exceeded the ability of their local markets to absorb them. The need to find and exploit new markets was aided by the rapid development of rail transportation and the extension of public education.

By 1860, there were several advertising agencies in New York City. These were not advertising agencies as we know them today, but really only firms that served as brokers for advertising space. The distinction of being the first advertising agent in the United States goes to Volney B. Palmer, who established his business in 1841. In those days newspapers did not publish rates or circulation figures, and advertising rates were negotiated. It was not until 1912 that the Audit Bureau of Circulation was established as a joint effort by advertisers and newspapers to develop reliable figures on circulation.

During the Civil War one of the first nationwide advertising campaigns was launched. The financier Jay Cooke was charged with managing the government's fund-raising efforts, and he, in turn, enlisted the services of L. F. Shattuck, an advertising agent, to help sell United States war bonds. By advertising the bonds in over 5,000 publications, Shattuck was able to sell $2 billion worth. The bond issue owed its success to advertising.

---

[5] Philippe Schumer, *History of Advertising* (London: Leisure Arts Ltd., 1966), p. 46.

[6] Today's *pennysaver* is usually an 8-to-24-page booklet, consisting almost entirely of advertising by local retailers or services. The penny that is "saved" refers to the cost of a newspaper many years ago. The reader received this little publication free and hence saved a penny. It is a highly localized advertising tool that is often distributed by hanging it in a plastic bag on the doorknob of a house or by mailing it to the house's "resident."

Many of the early posters reflect the absence of the "marketing concept" that is so apparent in today's advertising. Mr. Suchard apparently expected that his name alone would induce people to buy his brand of chocolate.

Magazines Accept Advertising

The years between the end of the Civil War and the beginning of the twentieth century were marked by the growth of drug and patent medicine advertising. For the most part, these advertisements appeared in newspapers, because the magazines of that day were not accepting advertising. A man named James W. Thompson, the founder of the J. Walter Thompson agency, was responsible for persuading American magazines to accept advertising. He then bought up all the space that these magazines made available and resold it, not only to advertisers, but to other advertising agents as well. As late as 1898, Thompson still controlled all the advertising space in most American magazines. Successful publications of this era included such currently popular magazines as *Cosmopolitan* and the *Ladies' Home Journal.*

Dawn of the Modern Age

In 1900, the total volume of advertising in the United States was estimated at $542 million—an 11-fold increase since 1865. The space brokerage days were drawing to a close, and the new advertising agencies were beginning to offer their clients essentially the same services that they perform today—the planning, creation, and implementation of complete advertising campaigns. The media were beginning to officially recognize the function of advertising agencies. When the American Newspaper Publishers Association was founded in 1887, it agreed that general agents should be entitled to a commission, which was to be withheld from advertisers who placed their business directly with a newspaper. In 1901, Curtis Publishing Company would not allow the agent's commission to advertisers who placed ads directly with its magazines.

Meanwhile, advertising theory and practice were growing up. Agencies began to hire established writers and journalists—men who had a flair for expression—to write advertising copy. People in other professions were also

The Chevrolet Motor Company's first advertisement appeared in May 1919. The Chevrolet trademark was prominently featured. Compare this advertisement to a recent one for the same product in color plate 1.

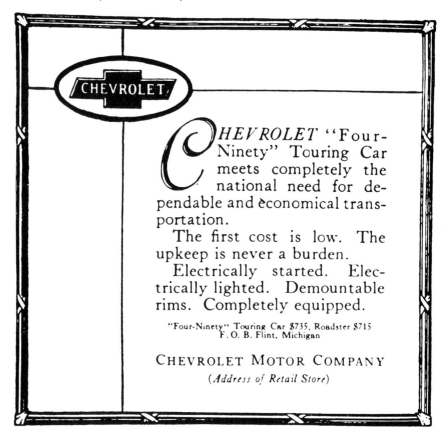

This advertisement is for the 1927 "coach model" Chevrolet. In contrast to the Chevrolet ad of 1919 on the facing page, this advertisement features a prominent illustration of the product.

The 1949 Chevrolet was advertised as "The most Beautiful Buy of all." The Chevrolet trademark is still featured, as well as the slogan, "Quality at Low Cost," which appeared in the 1927 advertisement.

becoming involved. Professors of psychology began to publish articles on the psychological aspects of advertising. Dr. Walter Dill Scott, who went on to become president of Northwestern University, published a series of articles on "Psychology in Advertising" in *Atlantic Monthly* in 1908.

The new approach to advertising that developed in the first two decades of the twentieth century brought sex, science, and romance to reinforce advertising appeals. Testimonials were extremely popular. Dr. Allen Pusey, professor of dermatology at the University of Illinois, helped to create advertisements for Pond's cold creams that were based on scientific facts and backed by testimonials from top stage and screen stars and from socialites. Fleischmann's Yeast promoted its product as an aid to health and adolescent skin care, with an impressive battery of bearded European medical men supplying the scientific background. One of these ads, for example, contained the headline: "'Yeast builds resistance,' says Prof. Doctor Paul Reyher, famous lecturer at the University of Berlin." (See color plate 2 for an example of a modern testimonial ad.)

The first list of advertising agencies was published in 1917 by the National Register Publishing Company. It contained 1,400 agencies, some of which are still in business, while others have merged with, or have been transformed into, some of today's well-known giant agencies. N. W. Ayer, the largest agency in 1917, is still alive and well and close to the top, as is J. Walter Thompson. The story goes that the designation J. Walter Thompson was made by James Walter Thompson, the magazine man, when he learned that

Almost 100 years of advertising history is spanned by these advertisements for Chese-brough-Ponds, Inc. Notice how the appeal and style of the ads have changed over the years. As the consumers have become more sophisticated, so have the ads. From the all-purpose panaceas, the advertising after 1912 turned to a *rational, reason-why* approach. The 1920s saw the development of the testimonial — an endorsement of the product by a famous person. Though still in style, testimonials today are more likely to feature an athlete or entertainer, than royalty. In the 1940s, advertising took on a psychological tone, offering consumers the implicit benefit of beauty and romance. By the 1970s, the Pond's theme was "Beautiful Women of the World" — a broad and sophisticated approach to reach women of every color. The ads appeared in *Woman's Day, Family Circle,* and *Ladies Home Journal,* among others. The theme continued in the 1980s, but with variations (see color plate 3).

there were numerous J. W. Thompsons, but no other J. Walter Thompson.[7] George Batten Co. went on to become Batten, Barton, Durstine & Osborn (BBD&O). H. K. McCann Co. and Erickson Co. ultimately merged to become McCann–Erickson. And so it went; as advertising volume grew, so did the agencies.

A New Medium — Radio

By 1929, radio was well on its way to becoming the most important entertainment medium.[8] An agency in Chicago — Blackett, Sample, Hummert — was the leader in daytime radio. This agency subsequently became Dancer, Fitzgerald, Sample. The concept of the soap opera was launched

---

[7] *Advertising Age* (December 7, 1964), p. 3.
[8] National Carbon Co. sponsored the first regular series of radio entertainments in 1923 with its "Ever-ready Hour."

in 1932, and these programs poured out of radio for the next 20 years, sponsored by advertisers such as General Mills, Sterling Drug, American Home Products, and Procter & Gamble. Daytime radio became an endless succession of 15-minute problems, Monday through Friday, with enormous emotional appeal for millions of Americans. Not until the homey voice of a former Washington taxi driver named Arthur Godfrey announced that it was "Arthur Godfrey Time" did a serious challenge to the "soapers" arise. Although the 1929 figures looked good, the $18 million of network radio billing then looked pretty small compared with the $81 million of 1942.

The Great Depression

When the Great Depression hit, advertising volume dropped from the 1929 high of $3.4 billion to a low in 1933 of $1.3 billion, which was where it had been in 1914. The depression had a more pronounced effect on advertising than just a drop in volume, however. Gimmicks were needed to coax money from empty pockets. Contests, premiums, prizes, and "double-your-money-back" offers were extensively promoted.

Advertisers searched for ways to make their advertising more productive. The Townsend brothers, for example, developed a secret checklist of 27 points against which to appraise all advertising copy for effectiveness. More important than the Townsend formula itself was the trend it signaled among advertisers. The Townsends were the forerunners of the great names in advertising and marketing research, men such as George Gallup, Claude Robinson, Daniel Starch, and A. C. Nielsen. Gallup joined Young & Rubicam in 1932 as its first director of research. After a successful career at that famous agency, Gallup went on to public opinion polling. Later he joined with Claude Robinson to develop the "impact" method of evaluating advertising. Daniel Starch left his job as a professor of psychology to become a director of research at the American Association of Advertising Agencies in 1924. There he developed techniques to study a reader's interest in the editorial and advertising material in a magazine. He left the four A's in 1932 to found Daniel Starch & Staff, now Starch INRA Hooper, Inc.

The depression years also prompted the development of the well-known A. C. Nielsen Co. During this time, Nielsen started compiling the now widely used indexes of food and drug sales by checking drugstores. His idea was to form a permanent sample of stores and to audit the flow of selected merchandise through those stores to secure information on the market shares obtained by various advertisers.

Every year, *Advertising Age,* the leading newspaper in the advertising field, publishes a ▶ list of the nation's leading advertisers. Most of the corporate names are familiar to you. Procter & Gamble continues as the nation's perennial leading advertiser.

The 100 leaders have an average advertising-to-sales ratio of about 3 percent. It is interesting to note the dramatic increase in spending by Beatrice which, in 1982, was in 16th place. Measured advertising includes newspaper, magazine, radio, television, and outdoor advertising. Unmeasured advertising includes cable, direct mail, collateral materials, co-op advertising, trade show promotions, and point-of-purchase and transit advertising. Retail advertising is not included. If local newspaper advertising were included in the measured advertising, Sears would rank number one.

The Leading Advertisers by Rank ($000)* 1984

Rank	Company	Advertising	Rank	Company	Advertising
1.	Procter & Gamble Co.	$872,000	51.	Chesebrough-Pond's	$145,500
2.	General Motors Corp.	763,800	52.	Schering-Plough Corp.	144,300
3.	Sears, Roebuck & Co.	746,937	53.	Campbell Soup Co.	142,000
4.	Beatrice Cos.	680,000	54.	Mars Inc.	139,282
5.	R.J. Reynolds Industries	678,176	55.	Adolph Coors Co.	138,700
6.	Philip Morris Inc.	570,435	56.	Loews Corp.	137,900
7.	American Telephone & Telegraph	563,200	57.	Toyota Motor Sales Corp.	137,900
8.	Ford Motor Co.	559,400	58.	Beecham Group p.l.c.	137,000
9.	K mart Corp.	554,400	59.	UAL Inc.	136,700
10.	McDonald's Corp.	480,000	60.	American Honda Motor Co.	134,700
11.	J.C. Penney Co.	460,000	61.	Time Inc.	133,900
12.	General Foods Corp.	450,000	62.	American Brands	133,000
13.	Warner-Lambert Co.	440,000	63.	Mattel Inc.	132,892
14.	Ralston Purina Co.	428,600	64.	Xerox Corp.	127,583
15.	PepsiCo Inc.	428,172	65.	IC Industries	127,289
16.	American Home Products	412,000	66.	CPC International	123,500
17.	Unilever U.S.	395,700	67.	Levi Strauss & Co.	122,000
18.	International Business Machines	376,000	68.	American Motors Corp.	120,500
19.	Anheuser-Busch Cos.	364,401	69.	Cosmair Inc.	119,500
20.	Coca-Cola Co.	343,300	70.	Jos. E. Seagram & Sons Co.	115,827
21.	Nabisco Brands	334,977	71.	Batus Inc.	113,400
22.	Pillsbury Co.	318,473	72.	AMR Corp.	110,800
23.	Chrysler Corp.	317,400	73.	Clorox Co.	109,600
24.	Eastman Kodak Co.	301,000	74.	Bayer AG	105,296
25.	Johnson & Johnson	300,000	75.	Volkswagen of America	103,000
26.	U.S Government	287,807	76.	Canon Inc.	100,000
27.	American Cyanamid	284,410	77.	Apple Computer	100,000
28.	General Mills	283,400	78.	Union Carbide Corp.	93,000
29.	Dart & Kraft	269,200	79.	E.I. du Pont de Nemours	91,000
30.	Colgate-Palmolive Co.	258,731	80.	Wendy's International	90,833
31.	Bristol-Myers Co.	258,440	81.	S.C. Johnson & Son	90,000
32.	Sara Lee Corp.	258,362	82.	GTE Corp.	89,775
33.	RCA Corp.	239,400	83.	Pfizer Inc.	86,400
34.	H.J. Heinz Co.	227,286	84.	Stroh Brewery Co.	85,200
35.	Kellogg Co.	208,800	85.	Hasbro Inc.	83,691
36.	Revlon Inc.	205,000	86.	Greyhound Corp.	80,200
37.	General Electric	202,400	87.	Kimberly-Clark Corp.	80,000
38.	Tandy Corp.	190,000	88.	Hershey Foods Corp.	79,200
39.	Nestle Enterprises	186,848	89.	MCA Inc.	77,058
40.	Warner Communications	181,749	90.	Grand Metropolitan p.l.c.	76,200
41.	CBS Inc.	179,800	91.	Noxell Corp.	74,200
42.	Mobil Corp.	172,500	92.	Mazda Motor Corp.	71,797
43.	American Express Co.	172,100	93.	Wm. Wrigley Jr. Co.	70,400
44.	ITT Corp.	168,000	94.	American Broadcasting Cos.	68,900
45.	Sterling Drug Co.	166,600	95.	Delta Air Lines	66,900
46.	Gillette Co.	165,673	96.	Trans World Airlines	66,200
47.	Nissan Motor Corp.	164,200	97.	Goodyear Tire & Rubber Co.	64,700
48.	Richardson-Vicks	163,500	98.	Cotter & Co.	63,900
49.	Quaker Oats Co.	161,300	99.	Eastern Airlines	60,800
50.	Gulf & Western Industries	149,249	100.	Van Munching & Co.	58,970

* Figures are a composite of measured and unmeasured advertising.

Source: Reprinted with permission from the September 26, 1985, issue of *Advertising Age.* Copyright © 1985 by Crain Communications, Inc.

Raymond Rubicam

In 1944, at the age of 52, Raymond Rubicam retired as president of the agency that still bears his name — Young & Rubicam International, Inc. It was the pinnacle of a career that spanned 30 years in advertising.

Raymond Rubicam was born in 1892 in Brooklyn, New York. After a brief stint as a reporter for the *Philadelphia Inquirer* in 1916, he joined a small advertising agency in Philadelphia as a copywriter. Three years later, he was hired as a copywriter by N. W. Ayer & Son, Inc., then the largest advertising agency in the United States. While he was at Ayer, he wrote many successful advertisements, including well-known slogans for Steinway pianos ("The instrument of the immortals") and for E. R. Squibb & Sons ("The priceless ingredient of every product is the honor and integrity of its maker"). It was a Steinway executive who gave him the idea of starting his own agency. He teamed up with John Orr Young, then an account man at Ayer, to found Young & Rubicam in 1923.

Under Raymond Rubicam's direction the new agency became known for its work in a new medium — radio. He developed humorous, conversational commercials that other advertisers said would fail and which, in fact, proved to be very popular. He hired such popular radio stars as Jack Benny and Arthur Godfrey to be the spokesmen for Jell-O and Lipton Tea, and he also hired a recent graduate of the University of Iowa to run Young & Rubicam's research department — Dr. George Gallup.

On his retirement, he was the principal stockholder of the agency. He sold his stock to the agency's employees, however, because he wanted the company to belong to men and women who were still active in the advertising business. In 1974 he was elected to the American Advertising Federation's Advertising Hall of Fame, and, in the next year, to the Copywriter's Hall of Fame.

As of 1985, Young & Rubicam had total billings of $3.575 billion. The agency's network covers 23 countries and 32 agencies worldwide. Approximately 34 percent of the agency's billings are overseas. Among their well-known clients are Colgate-Palmolive. Eastman Kodak, General Foods, Johnson & Johnson, and Kentucky Fried Chicken.

How Advertising Won the War

After the attack on Pearl Harbor in 1941, the talents of advertising people turned to helping the war effort. Advertising men set up the War Advertising Council, underwritten by the American Association of Advertising Agencies, the Association of National Advertisers, and four media associations representing newspapers, magazines, radio, and outdoor advertising. Working primarily through the Office of War Information, the council helped promote war bonds. In fact, 85 million people bought small denomination bonds, and $45 billion worth of bonds were in the hands of the public by the end of the war. It was the largest, most extensive advertising campaign ever conducted for any-

CASE HISTORY

Avon Products, Inc.

Avon is the world's largest cosmetics manufacturer and distributor of costume jewelry. Avon's cosmetic products include fragrances, make-up, soap and skin care products, and basic toiletry items. The product is sold to consumers via a network of direct selling representatives. Avon competes with a host of other cosmetic, fragrance, and toiletry products — some of them sold door-to-door, like Avon, and some of them sold through retail outlets.

Avon wanted to increase penetration among potential consumers and to enhance awareness of a specific Avon product — in this case, lipstick — so that consumers would be encouraged to welcome their Avon representative and thus be presented with the full line of Avon products.

A one-month campaign, the largest single promotion in Avon history, was undertaken — Operation Smile. The lipstick product was featured at a special price and a complete synergistic advertising campaign was developed under the theme "Avon, You Make Me Smile." A media "blitz" approach was created to include television and radio, magazine and newspaper supplements, and bus posters. The advertising was coordinated with an all-out effort by the Avon field representatives to call on every home in America.

Was it successful? Indeed it was. Total sales for the one-month period were 40 percent higher than the same period in the previous year. Lipstick sales of 18 million units for the month were double the annual sales for the previous year.

The campaign for Avon was prepared by its advertising agency, N. W. Ayer Incorporated, the oldest advertising agency in the United States, founded in Philadelphia in 1869. In 1985

1. Singers: Spring is springin'

2. up all across the land

3. And the flowers are bloomin'

4. Avon sunny smiles come shinin'

5. It's a time for beauty

6. An Avon smile I love to be seen in / An Avon smile I love to be bein' beautiful

7. Avon you make me smile / Avon you make me smile

8. Spokeswoman: This month, give your Avon Representative your old lipstick and get the most luscious

9. lipstick in America. For 35¢ and a smile. We're out to put Avon on everybody's lips.

10. Singers: You give me lips with smiles so fun and

11. So many shades so fresh so young and You give me spring in style

12. Oh, Avon you make me smile. Avon you make me smile....

it was the 18th largest advertising agency in the United States, with worldwide billings of $826.4 million. It is headquartered in New York, with branches in major American cities, and a network of affiliates all over the world.

Readers and viewers in America have been urged by N. W. Ayer copywriters to "Walk a mile for a Camel"; "Be all you can be" for the U.S. Army; "Watch the Fords go by"; and to celebrate romantic occasions with gifts from DeBeers that equate the endurance of love with the line "A diamond is forever." Ayer is also responsible for the GM slogan "Nobody sweats the details like GM."

thing anywhere.[9] The Advertising Council is still operating, supplying advertising and promotion for public service programs on forest fire prevention and aid to higher education, as well as for such organizations as Radio Free Europe, CARE, and the Peace Corps.

The radio industry experienced tremendous growth during the Second World War. Listener interest was at peak; wages and earnings were up. There was also a severe shortage of paper that limited magazine production. By 1945, radio billings were up to $125 million and peaked at $134 million in 1948. Thereafter, radio billings declined as television became more important.

When the war ended in 1945, total advertising volume in the United States was $2.87 billion, still below the 1929 record level. By 1948, however, advertising volume had surpassed the 1929 level by more than $1 billion, and advertisers were moving cautiously into a new medium — television. From 190,000 sets in use in 1948, the number zoomed to 15.8 million by the end of 1952. By 1955, television had established itself as the most important national advertising medium.

Summary

The American Marketing Association defines advertising as the "nonpersonal presentation of goods, services or ideas for action, openly paid for by an identified sponsor." Although the term *advertising,* as we understand its meaning today, was not used until about 100 years ago, the practice of using advertising for the transmission of information goes back to ancient Greece and Rome. Criers and signs were used to advertise goods and services long before the development of printing. During the Middle Ages, when most people could not read, advertising signs generally consisted of a very explicit illustration of, or a symbol for, what was being advertised. But, as printing techniques were perfected and as industry developed, the written word came to replace the sign.

During the 1600s, newspapers began to appear throughout Europe. Naturally, early colonists in North America brought with them the advertising techniques they were familiar with in Europe. But it was not until the original 13 colonies won independence from England that newspapers and newspaper advertising began to develop fully in the United States. Magazines, for the most part, were late in getting started, and their growth as an advertising medium did not come until after the Civil War. The growth of outdoor advertising had to wait on the expansion of the automobile industry and the improvement of roads. By 1926, radio was available as an advertising medium, adding the power of the human voice to advertising messages it carried.

By the end of the 1920s, advertising was well on its way to becoming a major industry and a major factor in the growth of all American industry, particularly automobiles and packaged foods. As might be expected, the growth in advertising volume brought about the expansion of the advertising agency business. From mere wholesalers of newspaper and magazine space, advertising agencies have evolved into national organizations that combine the talents of writers, artists, musicians, psychologists, and marketing experts, providing the advertiser with an extensive range of sophisticated services.

---

[9] *Advertising Age* (December 7, 1964), p. 10.

1 | **THE STORY OF ADVERTISING**

Advertising volume, slowed in its growth, first by the Great Depression of the 1930s, then by the war years, has, since the end of the Second World War, risen to new peaks.

Questions for Discussion

1. How have technological developments affected the nature of advertising?
2. What interest does the study of advertising have for anyone not planning to enter the field?
3. From current publications, select examples of advertisements that are used to promote:
   a. merchandise
   b. services
   c. ideas
4. If advertising were, for any reason, to be prohibited entirely, what could business do to promote its products?
5. What makes heavy advertising such a basically American practice?
6. In addition to recruitment for the armed forces, what other areas are important in government advertising?
7. Do you find any symbols of royalty or nobility used on products or in their promotions today?

Sources and Suggestions for Further Reading

Elliott, Blanche B. *A History of English Advertising.* London: Business Publications Ltd., 1962.

Foster, G. Allen. *Advertising: Ancient Market Place to Television.* New York: Criterion Books, 1967.

Gloag, John. *Advertising in Modern Life.* London: William Heinemann, Ltd., 1959.

Miller, Clyde R. *The Process of Persuasion.* New York: Crown Publishers Inc., 1946.

Presbrey, Frank. *The History and Development of Advertising.* Garden City: Doubleday, Doran & Company, 1929.

Schumer, Philippe. *History of Advertising.* London: Leisure Arts Ltd., 1966.

Sutphen, Dick. *The Mad Old Ads.* Minneapolis: The Dick Sutphen Studio Inc., 1966.

Watkins, Julian Lewis. *The 100 Greatest Advertisements.* New York: Moore Publishing Co., 1949.

Wood, James Playsted. *The Story of Advertising.* New York: The Ronald Press, 1958.

2 THE MARKETING FOUNDATIONS OF ADVERTISING

Marketing Defined

Elements of the Marketing Mix

The Product
    Product Attributes
    Consumer vs. Industrial Goods
    Convenience Goods
    Shopping Goods
    Specialty Goods
The Price
Channels of Distribution

What Is a Market?

Segmenting the Target Market

Conditions That Affect Marketing Success

The Dynamics of Consumer Tastes
Changes in Social and Cultural Influences
Changing Demographics
Economic Conditions
Legal and Political Climate
Changes in Technology
Competitive Actions

Working Vocabulary _____

marketing concept	convenience goods	market segment
marketing	shopping goods	segmentation analysis
marketing mix	specialty goods	reference group
product	channels of distribution	demographics
consumer goods	market	
industrial goods	target market	

25

This is a world of bustle, of imperfect knowledge, of constantly evolving competitive and other external pressures, and of interrelationships among the company, its ultimate customers, and its middlemen, among elements of its own marketing mix — even among products or services in its line.

The Conference Board, Inc.
Some Guidelines for Advertising Budgeting

The business world in the United States today operates, as it has operated for the past three decades, under what is known as the marketing concept. Quite simply, the **marketing concept** means that for every seller of goods and services, the prime consideration at every step in that organization's functioning is the satisfaction of the prospective customer. Gone forever is the attitude typified by Henry Ford's dictum that his customers

One drive is worth a thousand words.

Ford has indeed come a long way from the Model T. The Thunderbird is sophisticated in design and lets the picture suggest its image and performance to the target market. That market is the younger, upscale buyer, male or female, 25 to 44, concentrated to a large extent in California and the Northeast. Note the clever demonstration of power and ease of handling in the uphill angle. And the caption says it all.

Get it together–Buckle up

Thunderbird
Have you driven a Ford... lately? *Ford*

could have their Model T in any color they liked — as long as it was black. In 1986, the Ford Motor Company not only manufactured 18 different makes of passenger cars but also offered their customers an extensive choice of styles, colors, and optional features for each. Today, most manufacturers are interested in making the products that people want. Retailers try to stock the product assortment that people will demand and to offer their customers special delivery services and convenient evening shopping hours. Both manufacturers and retailers try to design the product and service mix that will assure their customers maximum satisfaction. Satisfied customers will, in turn, assure these businesses of steady demand.

Marketing Defined

Marketing is the process that facilitates the exchange of goods and services between producers and users to the satisfaction of all parties. Note that the word *process* is used to indicate an activity that does not stop. In fact, postsales activity is a very vital part of marketing. The word *consumer* has purposely been omitted from this definition because it has more than one meaning: A steel service supply center is a consumer of steel for a steel rolling mill. A manufacturer of soups is a consumer of the supply center's steel for canning. A homemaker is also called a consumer — of soup — but is in fact "consuming" the steel as well.

Thus, the exchange process involves all of these users and more. The marketing of steel involves the transfer of the sheet steel from the steel mill to the steel supply house to the canner, where it is transformed into a can. That steel, now in the form of a can, goes from the wholesaler of grocery products to the retailer of grocery products to the ultimate purchasers — who buy the soup to feed themselves or their families.

Each step involves an exchange, usually the exchange of money for the specific product. Likewise, each step has to provide satisfaction for both parties to the exchange — a profit and a salable product for the rolling mill, the steel supply center, the cannery, the grocery wholesaler, and the retailer; and a tasteful, nutritious food for the people who eat the soup.

Elements of the Marketing Mix

If you were to examine the activities of the soup manufacturer carefully, you would see that several important marketing decisions were made. The soup canner decided on:

1. the product
2. the price of that product
3. the kinds of outlets through which the product would be sold (the channels of distribution)
4. the promotional activities that will accompany that specific product, at that specific price, through the chosen channels of distribution

These types of decisions, all within the control of the producer, are known as the **marketing mix.** We will examine the first three types of decisions — product, price, and channels of distribution — in this chapter; we will examine the fourth type — promotional activities — in chapter 3.

The Product

In its broadest sense, a **product** is a good or service that an individual or an organization buys in order to obtain a measure of satisfaction. As stated earlier, that satisfaction may range from the profitable, resalable nature of the product to its taste and nutritional value.

Product Attributes   The physical attributes of the product—the taste, the aroma, the color, the texture, and the quantity—are important contributions to consumer satisfaction. But, at the same time, every product has a number of psychic attributes that may be major components in the creation of that satisfaction. Such psychic attributes include the brand name, the style, the design, the exclusivity, and the package. In the selection of such services as restaurants, hairdressers, or retail stores of any kind, customers consider the store's location, reputation, and atmosphere, as well as the quality of its service.

In the case of the soup manufacturer, the soup could have been packaged in a glass container. It could have been dehydrated and packaged in foil as individual servings or in a jar to be portioned out by the spoonful. Each packaging decision would make the product different in the eyes of the ultimate purchaser.

Therefore, in addition to the basic characteristics of the soup product such as taste, aroma, quantity of chicken, consistency, etc., the advertiser of that product must also consider such factors as the design or style of the package, the reputation of the manufacturer, the name chosen for the brand, and the convenience of use.

Consumer vs. Industrial Goods   For reference purposes, marketing people usually distinguish between **consumer goods** and **industrial goods.** To be sure, the industrial purchaser is indeed a consumer, but industrial buying activity is prompted by business or organizational needs, not by personal needs. The consumer that interests us is a person who buys products and services for personal and family use. The words *goods* and *products* are, for our purposes, interchangeable and include services and intangible products.

There are no doctrinal rules for classifying consumer products, but we can gain a better understanding of the advertising implications if we classify goods according to the manner in which the consumer buys them. The advertising manager finds it helpful to group consumer goods in three categories: convenience goods, shopping goods, and specialty goods. Each category has marketing characteristics that help guide the advertising approach.

Convenience Goods   The term **convenience goods** best describes merchandise that has a low unit price and little or no fashion connotation. What goods are included in this category? Groceries, drug sundries (such as toothpaste, shaving cream, deodorant, and mouthwash), hardware products (such as light bulbs and flashlight batteries), inexpensive candy, and cigarettes. Convenience goods are not large in physical size, and consumers generally demonstrate a preference for one brand over another. Convenience goods are usually purchased frequently or with some degree of predictable regularity. The consumer purchases this type of goods when needed, as rapidly as possible, and with the greatest convenience—hence the designation. Any savings the consumer might obtain by "shopping around" are usually not worth the effort.

From the advertising viewpoint, the consumer is familiar with the product and its attributes before setting out to buy it. The retail outlet is of little importance. The package and the brand name are of the utmost importance, as are point-of-purchase displays. Retailers, as a rule, carry several brands of any convenience item, and we cannot expect them to advertise such goods, especially when every retailer carries essentially the same assortment. The bulk of the promotional effort is by the manufacturer. (The retailer will sometimes cooperate with the manufacturer in newspaper advertising of convenience goods; such cooperative advertising is discussed more fully in chapter 19.)

Shopping Goods In contrast to convenience goods, **shopping goods** are those for which consumers are willing to shop around, visiting several stores in order to compare price, quality, and style. Typical shopping goods are women's apparel, men's ready-to-wear clothing, home furnishings, jewelry, and fabrics. In general, shopping goods represent higher unit value than convenience goods. The extent to which consumers will shop around is related to the benefit they believe they will gain from this investment of their time and energy. The consumer does not have extensive product knowledge about shopping goods and seeks to augment that information by visiting different stores and comparing merchandise. Such purchases are made infrequently; otherwise the consumer would be forever busy shopping. (See color plate 4.)

A shopping good — a quality product advertised by the manufacturer to the target market. No price indicated but the presentation suggests a quality product that can be found at your favorite dealer.

Leather perfect.

If we at Rolfs have one minor flaw, it's our insistence on perfection. Take this men's trifold. As with all our wallets, our trained craftsmen cut every piece of leather from the strongest, best looking part of the hide. Then, for added durability, we precisely trim and turn the outer edges. Of course, maintaining the highest standards of American craftsmanship isn't always easy. But it does make it perfectly easy to recognize a Rolfs when you see one.

R O L F S.

Good things last.

LININGS CONTAIN
DUPONT NYLON

West Bend, WI 53095. Available at fine stores throughout the USA and Canada.

A marketing consideration for the manufacturer of shopping goods would be to use fewer retail outlets than the manufacturer of convenience goods. Because customers are willing to shop around, and because such purchases are made infrequently, shopping goods are carried in department stores and large retail outlets. These stores are usually located near each other so that people can make comparisons conveniently. Inasmuch as the manufacturer uses fewer retailers, there is also less use of wholesalers and a more direct relationship with retailers. Above all, the store's name and reputation are important attributes, often more important than the manufacturer's name. The store itself becomes a major factor in the consumer's purchasing decision. This fact will affect the promotional effort, in which retailers provide most of the advertising and display.

Specialty Goods　The consumer's insistence on a specific brand is the distinguishing characteristic of **specialty goods.** Many such goods are the same as shopping goods — expensive wearing apparel, gourmet food products, stereo components, cameras, home appliances, and automobiles. As in the case of convenience goods, the consumer usually has a good deal of information about the particular product before setting out to make a purchase. As in the

Note the words that help define the market for what must be perceived as a quality shoe . . . *traditional* . . . *classics* . . . *elegant.* And for the final touch . . . *custom bootmakers* . . . not mere manufacturers of shoes.

For store listings and illustrated brochure write Alden Shoe Co., Dept. 4N, Middleborough, MA 02346.

case of shopping goods, but unlike convenience goods, the consumer is willing to make a shopping trip (often at some inconvenience) to buy a desired brand —and *that brand only.* (See color plate 5.)

Manufacturers can therefore be more selective in their choice of retail outlets, often confining their product to a single store in a particular area, as a form of franchise. This establishes a close relationship between the manufacturer and the retailer. The retailer will mention the manufacturer's name prominently in local advertising, and the manufacturer often pays for a portion of the retailer's advertising costs. In a similar manner, manufacturers will often name retailers in their national advertising. The interdependence between manufacturer and retailer is close.

The Price

For good or ill, in American society price is frequently used as an index of quality. When making purchases in the absence of other criteria, many people equate quality with price. They assume that if a product or service costs more, it must be better. The reverse is also considered true — if the product costs less, then obviously, it cannot be as good. To a large extent, of course, the manufacturer's pricing decision is closely related to the quality and quantity of the product. A soup manufacturer who is marketing a chicken noodle soup recognizes the demand of the homemaker for that type of soup at a particular price. Obviously, adding more chicken meat to the soup will increase its cost. And, among the various kinds of soup, lobster bisque will be more expensive than chicken noodle. Even among lobster bisques, there will be variations in price, depending upon the quantity and quality of lobster in the can.

Channels of Distribution

The third decision required of manufacturers is the choice of a distribution network through which they will reach the ultimate purchaser — in this example, the homemaker. There are various **channels of distribution** available to the manufacturer of such products. Soup, particularly the chicken noodle soup, could be sold through every type of retail food outlet — from supermarkets to corner grocery stores and delicatessens. The lobster bisque, however, might be more appropriately distributed through gourmet food shops and the gourmet food departments of better department stores. Sales of another type or flavor of soup might be helped by distribution through health food stores.

The distribution decisions made by the manufacturer are contingent upon the nature of the product, the price, the channels that are available, and the practices that are common to the industry. Consider some of the options that are available:

1. *Selling to retailers through wholesalers*
   The manufacturer can sell to merchant wholesalers who will buy in quantity, maintain inventory (taking title to the goods), deliver, extend credit, and provide information and advice. These middlemen are sometimes designated as jobbers, distributors, or full-service wholesalers.
2. *Selling to retailers through agents*
   Agents do not take title to the goods, do not maintain inventory, and do not extend credit. They rarely perform any service other

than selling. They are often designated brokers or manufacturers' representatives, depending on their contractual arrangement with the manufacturer.

3. *Selling directly to retailers*

   Working through their own sales force, manufacturers will sell to a retailer — a business organization that stocks and displays the goods on the premises and sells them, in turn, to consumers. Depending on the nature of the product, manufacturers have a number of choices — independent retailers, chain stores, supermarkets, department stores, discount stores, and vending machines.

4. *Selling directly to the consumer*

   Manufacturers may choose to establish their own retail outlets, to recruit a sales force in the field (as Avon and Fuller Brush do), or to sell through mail order. Each manufacturer will make this decision based on the nature of the product, the market, and the manufacturer's own capabilities.

What Is a Market?

Manufacturers use the word **market** very often. They say they will bring a new product "to market." They use research techniques to learn if there is a "market" for a particular product. A market is people — people with the desire for a product, the willingness to buy it, and the ability to pay for it. Of course, there are many markets: An industry may be a market; the government may be a market; schools may be a market; farmers may be a market. The manufacturers of home appliances are a market for the manufacturers of sheet steel. The Department of Defense is a market for the manufacturers of military hardware. A school system is a market for the publishers of textbooks. Our focus in this text is on consumers as a market.

We are probably very accustomed to finding an adjective in front of the word *market.* We often say "mass market" when we mean very large numbers of people. We say "urban market" when we wish to designate consumers who live in cities. We say "male market" when we wish to define the sex of the consumer. With such adjectives we define more precisely what we mean by a market. We have narrowed the total market — male or female, urban or rural, mass or class — into the most likely prospects for our product. When we have defined those consumers who have a need for our product, a willingness (in our opinion) to buy it, and the ability to pay for it, we have designated our target, or more commonly, our **target market.** Remember this term because we will use it often in preparing our advertising appeal and in selecting our media.

Segmenting the Target Market

To be certain that our marketing effort is directed most efficiently — that is, with a minimum of wasted time, effort, and money — we divide our target market into submarkets, called **market segments.** For example, if we were planning to market lipstick, our target market would be a female market. But "female market" is not an adequate definition. Not all women wear lipstick. For example, girls under the age of twelve generally do not wear lipstick. Our segment, or submarket, would be females over twelve years of age. That narrows the market for us. But even this description is inadequate. Our final

This ad appeared in the business section of the *New York Times.* At first glance the target market appears to be companies that drill for oil. However, placing an ad for that purpose in a New York newspaper would represent a considerable waste of money — there are not many oil wells in Manhattan. The target for this ad is actually the investing public: men and women who are affluent enough to buy the company's stock for their investment portfolios or who are in a position to recommend its purchase by others.

definition would depend upon many different factors, including the price of our lipstick. Lipstick that sells for $5 would appeal to one segment of the market. Lipstick that sells for $1 would appeal to a totally different market segment. These represent logical, identifiable, reasonably homogeneous market segments. They enable us to evaluate the type of package, the preferred channels of distribution, and the appeal and media selection that we would use to market our lipstick. (See color plate 7.)

A similar procedure (called **segmentation analysis**) is used for any product or service. An airline that flies overseas will have two basic consumer segments — the tourist on vacation and the business or government executive traveling on business. The tourists can be further segmented into different submarkets — students off for the summer, first-time travelers, and knowledgeable, sophisticated travelers who have been abroad before. Each segment wants something different from the airline. Can you visualize a different advertising appeal for each segment? And perhaps a different "package"?

Obviously Cunard does not have passenger space on its *Queen Elizabeth 2* for all 6 million tourists who visit Europe each year. Since the air/sea prices for this trip range from $1,600 to $8,000 per couple, Cunard's target market is clearly affluent and interested in the "good life." This advertisement appeared in *Gourmet* magazine. A food publication? Yes, but a food publication that reaches the sophisticated and affluent market segment from which the steamship line expects to find its 42,000 passengers.

Conditions That Affect Marketing Success

For a business to enjoy the full benefit of the marketing concept, that concept must be translated into specific activities. Everything that the company does must be directed toward satisfying the customer and, in the process, making a profit or achieving whatever other measure of success is applicable.

Remember, advertising is not a science. There are no laws or rules that tell the advertiser what specific combination of price, product, and distribution channel, together with the right amount of advertising, will yield a specific sales result. Our inability to devise a formula for success arises from the fact that a number of critical factors in the marketing of a product are beyond our control — factors that can delay or even completely thwart our hoped-for results.

The success of our marketing effort is affected by changes in:

1. consumer tastes
2. social and cultural influences
3. demographics
4. economic conditions
5. the legal and political climate
6. technology
7. the actions of competitors

Let us consider the ways each of these factors affects our marketing, and helps or hinders our advertising plans.

The Dynamics of Consumer Tastes

What makes tastes change? No one really knows for sure. Listen to people talk: "That's what they're all buying." "That's what they're wearing this season." Who are *they*? Perhaps *they* are a **reference group** — a group of people to which a person looks for establishing his or her own attitudes or behavior. Common examples are members of work groups, school groups, or social groups who appear to have a life style worth emulating, such as business or government executives, sports or show business stars. The idea for the advertiser is to create an appeal that suggests to the target market that they can be like the athlete or famous person if they use the particular product.

A brief glance at new products introduced to the market in recent years hardly provides a clue to the direction of consumers' fancies. "Natural" foods such as yogurt have increased in popularity, but so have "junk" foods. Eighty percent of the new products introduced do not succeed.[1] Is it because the marketers are so enamored of their products that they do not bother to find out what the market wants? Not at all.

Here is what frequently happens: After a market study has been carefully made, a manufacturer decides that the time is ripe for the introduction of a new product. The manufacturer gears up for a small production run, has a beautiful package designed, selects the most suitable channel of distribution, advertises, and — nothing happens. In the six months that have elapsed since the development of the manufacturer's brainchild, consumer interests have moved on. The failure of the Edsel provided a multimillion-dollar lesson in the fickleness of consumer tastes.

Changes in Social and Cultural Influences

Much consumer behavior is culturally determined. The old Puritan ethic of hard work, abstinence, and thrift — saving money, paying cash, living within one's means — has been replaced by an "existential" philosophy. Social and cultural fashions have changed in the past 20 years. Marriage and mother-

The target market for this ad is upscale — that is, well educated and affluent — and has an abiding interest in fine foods and restaurants. The market segment thus identified, with interest in the product and the ability to buy it, the advertiser provides the last dollop — a reference group — in this case some of the best-known names in haute cuisine. Note the small picture of the product and the complete absence of "nuts-and-bolts" copy. (See color plate 6 for another Cuisinart ad.)

---

[1] Thomas L. Berg, *Mismarketing* (Garden City, N.Y.:Doubleday & Co., Anchor Books, 1971).

hood are no longer the most important goals of many women. As of 1984, 36 million women — half of all women 18 to 64 years old — were working full-time outside the home. Life styles have been affected. Two-earner couples dine out more often than single-earner couples. Working women have been fueling the boom in catalog shopping, microwave ovens, automatic teller machines, and other goods and services that conserve their free time. For these women, consumer products help them juggle their work and family roles. Over 50

The elderly population is growing by 20 percent during the 1980s, and growth is expected to slow a bit during the 1990s, then rise rapidly in the early decades of the next century. By 2030, one of every five Americans will be 65 or older. The very old segment of the population — people 85 or older — is expected to rise from 9 percent in 1980 to 19 percent in 2040, when one of every 20 Americans will be 85 or older. The sharp increase in numbers of the elderly will mean more conservatively styled clothing, more special salt-free and low-cholesterol foods, more health care products, more travel, more comfortable automobiles. The market for soft drinks, beer, motorcycles, and candy will decline.

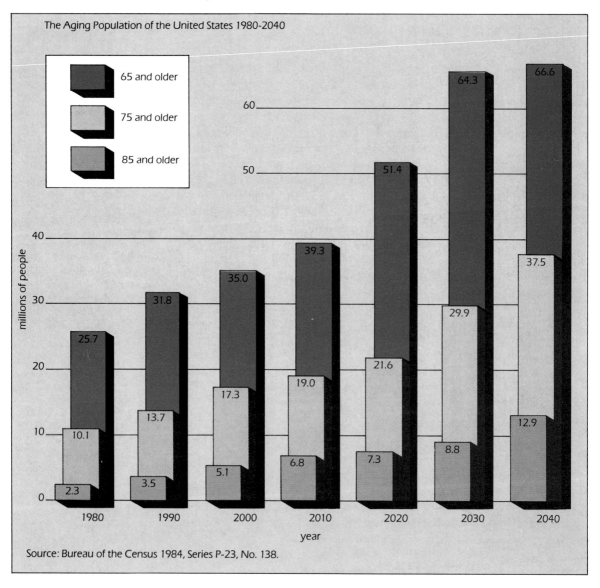

The Aging Population of the United States 1980-2040

Source: Bureau of the Census 1984, Series P-23, No. 138.

percent own a frost-free refrigerator and a dishwasher. They own food processors and home exercise equipment. Other changes have also been dramatic. Thirty-eight percent of working women aged 21 to 24 are college graduates; only 19 percent of their mothers graduated from college. Upscale employed women spend an average of $1,000 a year on fashion — double the average for all women.

The 70s and 80s may go down in marketing history as the decades of the *Yuppies* — young, upwardly mobile professionals, 20 to 39 years old — who have made a contribution to the American economy as well as to our vocabulary. They demand products that permit them to differentiate themselves with snob appeal associated with breeding, graceful living, and culture. These products include gourmet foods and wines, decorator and designer products, painting, sculpture, and performing arts. Yuppies travel. They are familiar with international tastes and products. They want products and services that enhance the physical self and maintain youthfulness — cosmetics, skin care products, hair styling, and exercise facilities. They buy monogrammed and custom-made items to demonstrate self-expression. They love active sports for which they must buy the correct equipment and the proper attire. They love products that represent mobility — all-night restaurants, credit cards, portable telephones. Do life style changes affect our marketing? Indeed they do. (See color plate 8.)

Changing Demographics

As you may have noted, much segmentation analysis is based on observable characteristics of the people who compose our target market. These characteristics are the subject matter of **demographics** — the science of vital social statistics, such as sex, age, income level, marital status, geographic location, and occupation. You can see how the markets for most products are easily segmented by the use of one or more of these characteristics. For certain products, our market is women, but not all women. We may want young women or mature women, single women, married women, or mothers. Doesn't a married woman with two children buy different products than a single woman of the same age? Indeed she does.

You may have noted that we used the word *observable* to describe these characteristics. That means we want to be able to quantify this information, and we can. Census data and other sources provide us with information on the number and location of various segments. Although we have defined the target market as people with the desire for a product and the ability to buy it, we must also determine whether or not enough of these people exist to make our marketing effort profitable.

We must also consider all the changes in the population of the United States that have occurred in the past ten years. People have been moving to the Sunbelt, which means that they spend more time outdoors and therefore buy more patio furniture, barbecue equipment, swimming pools, bathing suits, and suntan lotion and spend less for heavy winter clothing.

The population is also getting older, and older people want more health-care products, more low-cost travel, more trailers, vans, and mobile homes. They want remote control for their television set so they don't have to get up to change channels. Many have moved back into the center city from the suburbs. They don't want automobiles. They do want compact kitchens.

It is easy to understand how economic conditions can affect our marketing results. The most useful, high-quality, well-priced product or service cannot sell well in an area where the unemployment rate is high. The purchase of expensive items — major appliances, for example — represents confidence in the economy. The prospective purchasers expect that they will have their jobs over the payout period. Rising prices coupled with slower economic growth (stagflation) have prompted shifts in consumer spending patterns. Dry cleaning sales are down. Camera sales are up. As the price of meat and fish goes up, so do sales of macaroni and spaghetti products. What area will suffer major strikes or devasting winter storms that will close factories and stores? These events will drastically affect our marketing plans.

PROFILE

Albert D. Lasker

Albert D. Lasker has been called the father of modern advertising. In fact, his story parallels the history of the advertising business itself. In 1898, shortly after graduation from high school in Galveston, Texas, he went to work as an office boy for Lord & Thomas advertising agency in Chicago. Before he was 40, he was earning a million dollars a year and owned the agency, which had become the largest in the United States at that time.

In the early 1900s, most manufacturers considered advertising as merely a way of "keeping your name before the public," but Albert Lasker learned from a copywriter named John E. Kennedy that advertising was really *salesmanship in print.* He came to understand that effective advertising should give its readers reasons why they should buy the goods or services being offered. "Reason why" became the motif of the Lord & Thomas agency, and the "salesmanship in print" school of copywriting Albert Lasker started became the training ground for many writers who went on to form their own successful agencies.

Among the well-known accounts for which Albert Lasker worked were Stokley-Van Camp, California Fruit Exchange (later to become Sunkist), Kimberly-Clark, Pepsodent, and Lucky Strike cigarettes. In 1918, he left management of the Lord & Thomas agency in the hands of a great copywriter named Claude C. Hopkins and went to work for the presidential campaign of Warren G. Harding. He was among the first to bring modern advertising techniques to politics.

In 1923, Albert Lasker resumed active management of Lord & Thomas, and during the next two decades applied his ideas to such modern forms of advertising as the radio commercial. It was Lasker who gave a struggling young comedian named Bob Hope a chance to do a radio show for Pepsodent. Then, in 1942 after 44 years in the advertising business, Albert Lasker decided to retire. He turned the agency over to his three branch managers: Emerson Foote in New York, Fairfax M. Cone in Chicago, and Don Belding in Los Angeles. The new agency was named Foote, Cone & Belding (see profile of Fairfax M. Cone in chapter 3).

From his retirement until his death in 1952, Albert Lasker devoted himself and his wealth to an active life of philanthropy. Author John Gunther called Albert Lasker "one of the most extraordinary personalities of our time."

Legal and Political Climate

New rules and regulations issued by various agencies of the federal government have had a powerful impact on the advertising business. The ban on cigarette advertising on television caused major shifts in cigarette advertisers' media schedules and forced them to reevaluate the use of print media. The ban on cyclamates sent all the soft-drink companies running to find a substitute. Having found that substitute in saccharin, the bottlers once again had their marketing plans upset by the government's contentions regarding that sweetener. The rapid growth of Nutrasweet(R) is the industry's response to the need for a low-calorie, hopefully safe, artificial sweetener. As more states require bottle returns for soft drinks (and beer) there has been more push for larger bottles — to a size of 2 liters, which reduces the number of containers that have to be returned to the supermarket.

Sodium bicarbonate — baking soda — has been around for a long time. Our grandparents probably used it as an antacid or mouthwash. Of course, it is called "baking soda" because it is used as a leavening agent in cakes and breads. But this advertiser has found a new use for sodium bicarbonate and has thereby increased its market.

KELLY, NASON INC.
ADVERTISING

Client: CHURCH & DWIGHT

Product: ARM & HAMMER BAKING SODA

Type: TV

Title: "KITTY PARTY"

Comm'l No.: ZCTB-0237

Length: 30 SECONDS

SFX: MUSIC
1st cat: Lovely party, isn't it?

2nd cat: Yes, but don't you detect an odor?

1st cat: Must be the litter box.

2nd cat: The litter box? Haven't you told our hostess about Arm & Hammer Baking Soda?

It absorbs odor naturally for days and days, so the litter box smells clean.

One part Arm & Hammer...

With three parts cat litter.

The litter lasts longer so she won't have to change it as often.
1st cat: O' Jessica! You're so sophisticated.

SUPER: ARM & HAMMER BAKING SODA. FOR A CLEANER-SMELLING LITTER BOX.

CASE HISTORY

Moussy Alcohol-Free Light Malt Beverage

White Rock has been a popular brand of mixers for over 100 years. For the past 30 years they have also been marketing a full line of fruit-flavored soft drinks. White Rock products are distributed throughout most of the United States with a concentration in New York and New England.

Sales in the soft drink category have been flat for several years. Therefore, White Rock decided to look for new sources of business growth. Recognizing trends toward lighter, healthier products, reduced alcohol consumption, and increased concern over drinking and driving issues, White Rock management saw the potential for a non-alcoholic beer in the United States.

In 1983, White Rock introduced Moussy, an alcohol-free, light malt beverage, imported from Cardinal of Fribourg, Switzerland, one of Europe's oldest and most famous breweries. Moussy is pronounced *Moose-ee* as in Moose. It comes from "La Mousse" meaning the head, or foam, on a glass of beer. Moussy has all the characteristics of an imported beer except alcohol and calorie content, because it is brewed just like traditional beer. The complete elimination of alcohol is achieved through an exclusive distillation process after the brewing process is complete. Other "near beers" stop the fermentation process half way, preventing the production of the alcohol, which often results in a less satisfying taste.

How do you introduce a new product in a new product category? *Solution:* The theme line of Moussy's advertising is "The Drink To Choose When You Choose Not to Drink." This unique positioning allows White Rock to communicate that Moussy is the perfect adult beverage choice for those occasions when alcohol is not appropriate, without condemning alcohol consumption.*

The thrust of their consumer advertising includes a combination of television and radio commercials. In each case, a situation is established where it would be normal for people to have a drink. When circumstances suddenly change, making a drink inappropriate, the character(s) order Moussy.

Additionally, there are several special programs targeted to specific audiences. One is the "On-Premise" program, in which Moussy provides free advertising time to new restaurant accounts. Custom-tailored scripts are written for restaurants in which Moussy's availability at the restaurant is mentioned. Another special program is a public relations program targeted to opinion leaders. The campaign consists of a series of ads that run on the Op-Ed page of the New York Times. The ads are tied to specific holidays or events.

Results: Advertising started in April 1983 in New York. Sales of 240,000 cases in that year exceeded even the most optimistic projections.

In 1984, with advertising only in New York, sales exceeded 1,000,000 cases versus a goal of 600,000 cases. Over 500,000 of the cases were sold in New York.

---

* The Moussy campaign was created by Venet Advertising, Inc., New York. In addition to other clients, Venet is the agency for Pathmark, Drake's Bakery, and Prince Spaghetti, for whom it developed the theme "Wednesday is Prince Spaghetti Day."

MOUSSY
"AIRPLANE"
WHITE ROCK PRODUCTS, INC.

SFX: (PLANE LANDING)

SFX: (CREW ENTERING LOUNGE)

ANNCR: What makes Moussy

the perfect choice for moments like these?

Moussy, brewed in Switzerland, just like a fine imported beer,

is crisp, cold, refreshing -- full-bodied enough to satisfy --

yet incredibly light at only 50 calories.

Moussy is the perfect choice for moments when you'd like a drink,

but not the alcohol or alcohol's calories.

CAPTAIN: C'mon -- we've got a plane to catch.

Flight attendants, prepare for takeoff!

ANNCR: Alcohol-free Moussy. . .the drink to choose when you choose not to drink.

Created by Venet Advertising, Inc.

Marketers and their advertising agencies find it expedient to have copy for their advertisements cleared with their legal staffs to be sure that none of the material contravenes the law. Recent court rulings requiring advertisers to put disclaimers in their present ads have made everyone in the advertising business very circumspect.

Changes in Technology

The development of polyester fiber put many laundries out of business. The permanent-press shirt and the no-iron sheet eliminated the need to send these items to the laundry. The old phonograph has been replaced by complex stereo systems that include Dolby noise suppression, reel-to-reel tape and cassette decks, and laser discs. As products have changed, so have marketing opportunities, for the better for some companies, for the worse for others. The blender has given way to the food processor. New cameras, recreation vehicles, jogging shoes, television games, radial tires — every day scores of new products enter the marketplace, thwarting the plans and expectations of others.

Competitive Actions

Competition is like an enemy skirmish line, always searching for a weakness in your front. Chivas Regal competes with Johnnie Walker and with Teacher's and with all the other well-known brands of Scotch whiskey. Each brand tries to increase its market share. Any marketer has five ways to increase sales:

1. by increasing the frequency of product use
2. by increasing the quantity of purchase
3. by increasing the length of the buying season
4. by taking customers from competitors
5. by increasing the range of the total market

But sometimes the attack comes from an unexpected quarter. Who wants to take business away from brand X Scotch? Brands Y and Z to be sure, but also all the vodkas, gins, and rums. Jose Cuervo tequila woos drinkers of Scotch, vodka, rye, gin, and rum. Trucking companies compete with each other and with railroads and airlines for freight business. Everyone wants a piece of the pie.

Of course, all brands of electric blankets compete with each other; but consider the other competitors as well: a feather comforter, heavy pajamas, an electric space heater, a heavy woolen blanket, or one could even simply turn up the thermostat. The object of the purchase for the consumer is to keep warm on cold winter nights, and any of these products will serve that need. Therefore, they can all be said to compete with the electric blanket.

Summary

Advertising is a tool of marketing, and every advertising decision is influenced by the four components of the *marketing mix*. These four components are: the nature of the product, the price of the product, the channels of distribution that take the product to the consumer from the producer, and the promotional activities, including advertising, that are used to help sell the product.

FCB

DATE: April, 1983
PRODUCER: Coast Productions

CLIENT: S. C. Johnson & Son, Inc. (CP82-1319)
PRODUCT: Raid Line
FILM NO.: JSRD3130
FILM TITLE: "Bug Slides"

FILM LENGTH: :30

1. (MUSIC UNDER)
INSTRUCTOR (VO): Roachus Disgustus.

2. Waspi Dangerosa.

3. Flyus Germspreadum.

4. Fleahopita Biteus...

5. ANNCR (VO): You could spend years learning about bugs,...

6. INSTRUCTOR (VO): Plantium Devourum.

7. ANNCR (VO): ...but all you really need to know...
INSTRUCTOR (VO): Antlovem Picnicia.

8. ANNCR (VO): ...is Raid.
INSTRUCTOR (VO): Insectus Deadicus.

9. BUGS: Insectus Deadicus?!?

10. Raaaiiiddd!!!

11. (SFX: KA-BLOOEY)...

12. ...

13. ANNCR (VO): Raid kills bugs...

14. (SFX: POW!)

15. ...dead.

For more than 28 years RAID has been using the "RAID bug" in building and maintaining a strong number one position in the U.S. insecticide market. The advantages of using animation are numerous and include: (a) instant brand recognition (The RAID bug and "RAID!!" yell are now universally known.), (b) the quick connection of the RAID heritage of efficacy to a diverse and growing line of insecticides, (c) a clear, graphic way to set up a problem and emphasize RAID as a solution to the problem, and (d) avoidance of distasteful, live insects in commercials and print ads for family viewing. In 1983, this TV storyboard was a gold medal winner in national and regional advertising competitions.

Summary

Today, every manufacturer applies the *marketing concept:* the concept that every facet of an organization should be dedicated to satisfying the wants of prospective customers. This concept has led marketers to use *segmentation analysis,* which is the examination of submarkets composed of people with certain attributes who are the most likely purchasers of the product. We call these submarkets our *target market,* and we call the attributes of people that distinguish them as targets or nontargets, *demographics.* Demographic characteristics include sex, age, income level, and other statistical classifications into which we can separate people for advertising purposes.

We are also aware that products, as well as people, can be separated into categories—for example, *consumer products* and *industrial products*—on the basis of the purpose for which they are bought. We can further divide consumer products into categories based on the *behavior* of the people who buy them. These categories are *convenience goods, shopping goods,* and *specialty goods.* Advertising for a consumer product is influenced by the category the product falls under.

Furthermore, as we prepare our advertising and marketing plans, we are well aware that we do not operate in a vacuum. In the real world, decisions are always influenced by forces beyond our control, such as changes in consumer tastes and life-styles, changes in demographics, the activities of competitive products, changes in technologies, and the pervasive activities of government.

Questions for Discussion

1. What is, or should be, the relationship of the marketing mix to the organization's advertising effort?
2. If we could indeed build a better mousetrap, what would we have to do to market it successfully in today's economy?
3. Why would a company with no product to sell to the general public advertise?
4. What marketing changes can you foresee as a result of
   a. smaller families
   b. the return to all-cotton men's shirts
   c. a total ban on advertising for alcoholic beverages
   d. population shifts to the Sunbelt
5. What changes in packaging do you foresee as a result of
   a. an increasing number of working women
   b. a continued trend toward smaller families
6. What products would be affected by changing demographic factors such as
   a. age
   b. family size
   c. educational level
7. How many segments can you identify in the market for
   a. toothpaste
   b. bottled water
   c. shampoo
8. How have the cultural and social changes of the past twenty years affected the marketing of certain products?
9. There have been a few noticeable changes in retailing in recent years. What are some of these changes? How have they affected the marketing of some products?

Sources and Suggestions for Further Reading

"Americans Change: How Demographic Shifts Affect the Economy." *Business Week,* 20 February 1978.

Bartos, Rena. "The Moving Target: The Impact of Women's Employment on Consumer Behavior." *Journal of Marketing* (July 1977).

Berg, Thomas L. *Mismarketing: Case Histories of Marketing Misfires.* Garden City: Doubleday & Co., Anchor Books, 1971.

Bloom, David E., and Sanders D. Korenman. "Spending Habits of American Consumers." *American Demographics,* vol. 8 (March 1986), no. 3.

Crawford, C. Merle. "The Role of Personal Values in Marketing and Consumer Behavior." *Journal of Marketing* (April 1977).

Fannin, Rebecca. "Who's Taking a Licking?" *Marketing & Media Decisions* (June 1986).

Glick, Paul C. "How American Families are Changing." *American Demographics,* vol. 6 (January 1984), no. 1.

Hartley, Robert F. *Marketing Mistakes.* 2nd ed. Columbus, Ohio: Grid Publishing, Inc., 1981.

Henry, Walter A. "Cultural Values Do Correlate with Consumer Behavior." *Journal of Market Research* (May 1976).

"How the Changing Age Mix Changes Markets." *Business Week,* 12 January 1976.

Lazar, William, and John E. Smallwood. "The Changing Demographics of Women." *Journal of Marketing* (July 1977).

Lazar, William. "How Rising Affluence Will Reshape Markets." *American Demographics,* vol. 6 (February 1984), no. 2.

Levitt, Theodore. "Marketing Myopia." *Harvard Business Review 53* (September-October 1975).

McCall, Suzanne H. "Meet the Workwife." *Journal of Marketing* (July 1977).

"Marketing to Blacks." *Special Report, Advertising Age* (December 19, 1985).

"Marketing to the Affluent." *Special Report, Advertising Age* (March 13, 1986).

Rogers, David S., and Howard L. Green. "Changes in Consumer Food Expenditure Patterns." *Journal of Marketing* (April 1978).

Russell, Cheryl. "The New Homemakers." *American Demographics,* vol. 7 (October 1985), no. 10.

Stanley, Thomas J., and George Moschis. "America's Affluent." *American Demographics,* vol. 6 (March 1984), no. 3.

Taylor, Thayer C. "Local Twists of Social Change." *Sales & Marketing Management,* vol. 131 (October 31, 1983), no. 6.

"Wine & Beer Marketing." *Special Report, Advertising Age* (January 31, 1985).

3 THE PROMOTIONAL MIX

The Marketing Plan and Advertising

Marketing Objectives
Factors Influencing the Promotional Mix
    The Nature of the Market
    The Nature of the Product
    The Life Cycle of the Product
    The Advertiser's Financial Capabilities

Advertising as the Main Thrust

The Decision to Advertise
Factors Influencing the Decision to Advertise
    Primary Demand
    Brand Differentiation
    Market Potential
    The Advertising Budget
    The Product Must Be Good
Advertising Objectives
Advertising Redefined
    Retail and National Advertising
    Consumer and Business Advertising
    Institutional and Public-Service Advertising

Working Vocabulary

promotional mix	retail advertising	industrial advertising
marketing plan	mail-order advertising	professional advertising
product's life cycle	national advertising	institutional advertising
primary demand	consumer advertising	public-service advertising
selective demand	business advertising	
appeal	trade advertising	

From the standpoint of the producer, advertising is clearly used because it is thought to be the most efficient marketing technique. If the advertiser knew of a selling tool that promised lower cost or greater return, he'd be irrational to continue advertising.

Herbert Stein
Advertising Is Worth Advertising

As you may recall from the preceding chapter, the marketing mix consists of four elements: the product (which includes the package), the price, the channels of distribution, and the promotion. The subject of this chapter is promotion — or what is more appropriately termed the **promotional mix.** It is a mix because as marketers we select the combination of advertising, publicity, personal selling, and sales promotion that we believe will best assist us in achieving our overall marketing objectives. Promotion, then, is the term that is used to include all four of these marketing activities.

In keeping with a systems approach, an organization should consider all of its promotional efforts as a complete subsystem within the total marketing system. This means that the activities of the sales force, the advertising and publicity programs, and all other promotional efforts must be coordinated. Technically, promotion is an exercise in communication, the purpose being to provide information, persuade, and influence behavior.

The Marketing Plan and Advertising

Successful advertising does not exist in a vacuum. It must be part of an overall marketing program. Among marketing people, few decisions can more significantly affect the growth and profitability of a business than the formulation of the marketing program. The marketing objectives of the company must be determined product-by-product together with the marketing activities that will be necessary to achieve those objectives.

The first step in developing the marketing program is to decide on the **marketing plan** — the foundation on which the company's operating plans are based. The marketing plan integrates the four components of the marketing mix into a single comprehensive program designed to achieve the marketing objectives. Wherever possible, these objectives should be defined in quantitative terms so that progress toward them can be measured. There are dollar goals and nondollar goals. Dollar goals may be specific short-term or long-term financial aims such as increased profitability, sales volume, return on investment, and earnings per share of common stock.

Nondollar goals usually lead to dollar goals. Nondollar goals may include developing the company image, attaining a certain standing or reputation in particular markets, supporting community programs, and winning public approval for company programs.

Marketing Objectives

Marketing objectives should be measurable, attainable, and clear; they should be acceptable to the sales department, to the advertising department, and to the various production and operating departments whose cooperation is critical to the achievement of these goals. Marketing objectives should be flexible, challenging, and consistent with each other. If the objectives satisfy these criteria, we are ready to consider how we can use advertising to help achieve the desired results. A countless number of decisions must be made — should more salespeople be hired? Can product quality be improved? Can the price be reduced? Should the amount of advertising be increased? These decisions are all related to each other. Low prices will do little good unless we tell people about them through advertising.

When top management states a goal explicitly — for example, "increase profits" — this becomes the implicit goal of every division or department of the organization. Advertising cannot be assigned specific communications tasks that are separate from marketing goals. If the job to be done is a goal of advertising, it *automatically* becomes a goal of marketing. Advertising has no goal of its own, but rather a continuing responsibility to help management attain the higher order company goals. For example, can advertising be used to increase distribution? Will advertising increase market share? Will a media change result in more sales? Dozens of questions such as these must be answered for every product.

Advertising's principal task is to make more sales at more profit than would have been made without advertising, just as the job of the sales force is to make more sales at more profit than would have been made without salespeople. In order for advertising to succeed, the product, the price, and the method of distribution must be right. Personal selling and sales promotion strategies must be right. The promotional mix must be right.

Factors Influencing the Promotional Mix

One of the most difficult jobs in marketing is choosing the most effective promotional mix. No one knows exactly how much any one element contributes to the attainment of the sales goals. In general, however, there are four factors that influence management's decision:

1. the nature of the market
2. the nature of the product
3. the life cycle of the product
4. the advertiser's financial capabilities

The Nature of the Market The nature of the market has a tremendous bearing on the promotional mix. For an industrial product such as a utility generator, for which there are relatively few customers, the mix will differ considerably from that used to sell a toaster to hundreds of thousands of homes. The manufacturer of a utility generator can use personal selling efforts very extensively, whereas, for the toaster manufacturer, personal selling efforts to reach the ultimate consumer would be prohibitively costly. In fact, some retailers would not even stock the product unless the manufacturer agreed to do a certain amount of advertising. Thus, the number of prospects, the type of customer, and the geographic distribution of the market must all be considered.

The Nature of the Product Consumer products usually require quite different strategies than do industrial goods. Each strategy is based on the nature of the product. The mix will vary within each category, as well as between categories — capital machinery installations, for example, are not promoted in the same way that industrial raw materials are promoted. Sales of convenience goods rely on a heavy advertising investment and on displays at

Campbell's Soups
S RING- SUMME
1984 SALES BUILDING PROGRAM

TRADE ALLOWANCES

96¢ OFF PER CASE

temporary off-invoice performance allowance on all purchases of these Campbell's Condensed Soups:
Cream of Celery Soup (48/10¾ oz.)
Cream of Chicken Soup (48/10¾ oz.)

HIGH-VOLUME SALES OPPORTUNITY

Both Campbell's Condensed Cream of Celery Soup and Cream of Chicken Soup are ideal products for spring and summer merchandising opportunities:
• Building store traffic
• Displaying with tie-in products
• Featuring in multiple-price specials
• Generating volume sales
• Merchandising recipe and cooking ideas
• Soup and Salad tie-ins
• Soup and Sandwich ideas
• Quick, warm weather meal specials

Plan now to advertise, display and feature Campbell's high-volume soups this Spring and Summer.

HIGH-INTEREST "FUEL FOR FITNESS" OFFERS

U.S.A. "GO FOR THE GOLD" shirt (suggested retail $9.95) Only $4.95 plus 3 labels from any Campbell's Condensed Soups. Shirt features:
• Adult sizes XS to XL—100% comforlon singlet top—polyester/cotton mesh insert—wrinkle-proof/washable—fade resistant

U.S.A. "GO FOR THE GOLD" shorts (suggested retail $9.95) Only $4.95 plus 3 labels from any Campbell's Condensed Soups. Shorts feature:
• Adult sizes XS to L—50% polyester/50% nylon comforlon short with inner lining.
Both of these U.S.A. "Go For The Gold" design items are good values and perfect for warm weather fun and fitness activities.

The Triangle Band™—1 Model 101 (suggested retail $13.99) Only $7.99 and 3 labels from any Campbell's Condensed Soups. Triangle Band™ features:
• 2.2 lbs. per pair (1 kilo.)
• An ankle/wrist band, the most common starter size.
• Adjustable to ankle or wrist

The Triangle Softbell™—2 Model 402 (suggested retail $23.99) Only $14.99 plus 3 labels from any Campbell's Condensed Soups. Triangle Softbell features:
• 12 lbs. per pair (6 lbs. 2.7 kilos each)
• A moderate workout device for men and women
Both of these Triangle Fitness Products are excellent items to help your consumers shape up for the warm weather season.

MERCHANDISING MATERIALS

A complete line of full-color materials designed for Spring and Summer merchandising are available.

(Details on back)

This is a portion of a brochure by Campbell's Soups addressed to grocery retailers. It is not enough for Campbell's to advertise to consumers as part of its "pull" strategy; it helps retailers build sales with "push" promotions like those described in this brochure.

the point of sale, where buying decisions are frequently made. Personal selling activities play a minor role. Many raw materials, however, are unbranded, and the products from competing firms may be equally acceptable. In this case, the persuasive efforts of the field sales force may be the most effective influence.

The Life Cycle of the Product   Strategy decisions for promoting any product are also influenced considerably by the particular phase of the **product's life cycle.** Products go through a cycle in much the same way people do. We start as infants that need to be carefully nurtured; move on through a vigorous, growing youth; into our mature development to a level of stability; then on to old age and decline. So, too, with a product. Its life begins with an introductory stage (infancy); then the product catches on, and there is a period of vigorous growth (youth), followed by its maintenance of a share of a relatively stable market (maturity). When a product's market share shows signs of decline (old age), we have the choice of putting it to sleep (demarketing) or rejuvenating it (improving, repackaging, and developing a different advertising appeal).

In the introductory, or pioneering, stage of this cycle the manufacturer is concerned with the stimulation of primary demand. The objective of promotion during this stage is to inform and educate the potential customers. The advertiser has to tell the market that the product exists, how it may be used, and

3 | THE PROMOTIONAL MIX

COLOR PLATE I

COLOR PLATE I Notice the way the vehicle is placed—level, straight. It suggests stability and reliability—just like the person who owns it. This car is an expression of proud achievement. Thus, Oldsmobile is selling more than a car. It is selling the owner's good judgment for the world to see.

Seve Ballesteros takes the rough with the smooth. Just like his Rolex.

In 1980 America was introduced to a new golfing sensation who seemed to delight in hitting drives far off the fairway, then recovering with a beautiful approach shot to record a birdie.

His style allowed Seve Ballesteros that year to become the youngest player ever to win the Masters. In 1983 he repeated—in characteristic fashion. One stroke behind going into the final round, he shot a birdie, eagle, par and birdie on the first four holes, and breezed to his second title.

His go-for-broke approach to golf has won Seve numerous major tournaments on five continents—including the prestigious British Open twice.

While he is a natural athlete with enormous physical strength, his early introduction to the game in Pedreña, Spain, a tiny fishing village, is also a factor in his success. Seve grew up learning golf with a single iron and frequently played in semidarkness. Such conditions require inventiveness, and that is precisely what makes Ballesteros such a remarkable player today.

While his golf seems to thrive on adversity, his watch is known for its reliability and consistently excellent performance: the Rolex Oyster Day-Date. "I may have good days and bad days," he says, "but this watch only has good days."

The unpredictable Seve Ballesteros. And his entirely predictable Rolex.

ROLEX

Pictured: The Rolex Day-Date Chronometer. Available in 18 kt. gold, with matching bracelet.

Write for brochure. Rolex Watch, U.S.A., Inc., Dept. **747**, Rolex Building, 665 Fifth Avenue, New York, NY 10022-5383. World headquarters in Geneva. Other offices in Canada and major countries around the world.

COLOR PLATE 2

COLOR PLATE 2 A testimonial—but different. The Rolex does not help Ballesteros play better. Such a suggestion would be unbelievable. Instead we have a daring, successful golfer who thrives on unpredictable golf shots but demands stability and reliability in his watch. A Rolex, of course.

COLOR PLATE 3

COLOR PLATE 3 Advertising for Chesebrough-Pond's, Inc., has continued to change with the times (see pages 16 and 17). A recent variation is the theme designed to appeal to the mature woman. Notice how the illustration and the copy are in tune with the times: a mature woman—a business executive who travels widely—keeps her skin young with Pond's. This particular ad appeared in *Modern Maturity*—a relatively new publication aimed at mature men and women. Good advertising. Good marketing.

Hartmann presents the overnight case that means business.

It's a carry-on.

It's a desk.

It's an organizer.

It's a wardrobe.

It's a wonder how you've done without it.

Satisfying your business needs and your personal needs all in one case isn't easy. But, thankfully, Hartmann has designed the Overnight Business Traveler.

It's a briefcase. And—an ingeniously compact piece of luggage. This handsome hybrid combines the most intelligent features of both. All under one Hartmann handle.

It comes in our exclusive Industrial Belting Leather, and in cordovan or chestnut leather. There's also walnut tweed fabric trimmed in belting leather, and 100% nylon packcloth with belting leather or vinyl trim.

The fact that Hartmann has created so wondrous a case should be no wonder. After all, it's a Hartmann.

Send for a list of your nearest Hartmann dealers, Dept.
© 1985 Hartmann Luggage, Hartmann Dr., Lebanon, TN 37087
Du Pont TEFLON® water & stain repeller

We don't cut corners.

Color Plate 4 The overnight case is a shopping good, but how can it be distinguished from similar pieces of luggage? Show them. Tell them. The ad does both. If one picture is worth a thousand words, the artist who designed the ad saved a lot of them. No price is indicated, but this ad suggests a quality product, which is to be found, of course, at your favorite luggage dealer. Do note that the newspaper peeking out of the pocket at the bottom left is—you guessed it—the *Wall Street Journal*.

COLOR PLATE 5 A shopping good? A specialty good? GE positions this new kind of kitchen range as a specialty—as the ad says—unlike ordinary electric and gas ranges. Strong visual impact both with the illustration and the clever play on words with the headline.

COLOR PLATE 6 Cuisinart does not sell a kitchen appliance. It sells convenience, speed, flexibility. It's not just for the special jobs—the big holiday dinners—it's for every day. The mouth-watering illustrations reinforce the copy. What the words don't tell the reader, the illustrations do.

COLOR PLATE 7 How to create a bold, young, ▶ contemporary look for men's shoes? Bold bright colors and an exciting photograph will capture the attention of the target market. Extra impact is added with a two-page spread.

COLOR PLATE 5

COLOR PLATE 6

from Thom McAn

Sara Lee
introduces
the croissant of
croissants.

New Sara Lee Croissants.
You've never tasted anything
more utterly delicious.
Only Sara Lee could bring you
croissants so light. So flaky. So buttery.
So French.
The moment each beautiful bite
melts away in your mouth, you'll know.
Sara Lee has created just about the
lightest, flakiest, butteriest croissants
this side of the Eiffel Tower.

Nobody doesn't like *Sara Lee*

COLOR PLATE 8 The growth of croissants in the bread products category is typical of changing tastes and changing lifestyles. The product logically would be adopted by affluent, educated people who have traveled abroad and experienced this typical French product. In many metropolitan cities, small bakeries in "Yuppie" neighborhoods have been catering to the market. It was a well-considered marketing decision by Sara Lee, as a national distributor, to capitalize on the trend to ethnic and gourmet products.

The advertising support for this introduction consisted of national and local television in addition to a national print campaign in major women's magazines. The television commercial, used on network as well as spots in major metropolitan areas, was chosen one of the best commercials of 1983 by *Advertising Age,* the industry's leading trade magazine.

According to Cathy Abdun-Nur, Director of Retail Marketing/New Products, "The 1983 introduction of Sara Lee Croissants was the most successful in our company's history, with first-year sales three times greater than expected. Our research shows that awareness for the croissant form has increased 50 percent since our brand introduction."

A Genuine Idaho® potato. The first bite of every great steak.

Next time you serve a tender, juicy steak, watch what everybody takes a bite of first. Nine times out of ten, it's the baked potato. So if you want the light, fluffy taste of Genuine Idaho® potatoes, make sure to look for the Grown in Idaho seal on the bag. And you'll start out right from the very first bite.

If you'd like even more ways to start out right with Genuine Idaho potatoes, just write: IPC, Box 1068, Boise, ID 83701.

© Idaho Potato Commission, 1985

Genuine Idaho

GROWN IN IDAHO®

COLOR PLATE 9

COLOR PLATE 9 This ad is one in a campaign in women's magazines to show the versatility of potatoes in complementing so many entrees. However, potatoes being a commodity, the Idaho Potato Commission wants to be sure the homemaker looks for *Idaho* potatoes. As the caption suggests—whatever the entree—everybody takes a forkful of potatoes first. Idaho potatoes, of course.

The Old Raisin Ploy, Part 4:

"My dad's real big.

Mom says it's 'cause
he always ate raisins for snacks.

So I eat raisins, too.

...sure hope she's right."

This usually successful ploy is brought to you by
Raisins from California. Nature's candy.

California Raisin Advisory Board

COLOR PLATE 10 This ad is from a campaign by the raisin growers of California to stimulate primary demand for their product. Each of the individual growers expects to share in the public response to this advertising program. Target market: homemakers with children. The individual producers may also advertise under their own names (Del Monte, Sun Maid) in an effort to stimulate selective demand, that is, to create a preference not merely for raisins, but for a particular brand.

From generation to generation,
diabetes is carried on by the inevitable force of genetic predestination.
But Upjohn is working to change that destiny.

Since the 1950's, the people at Upjohn have been developing medicines to help the diabetic.

But beyond helping people live with disease, we'd like to see everyone living without it.

Through our Chinese hamster colony, the only one in the U.S. devoted solely to diabetes research, we have made significant discoveries about the relationship between diabetes and nutrition.

And recent research has shown that instead of having inadequate insulin levels, many diabetics in fact have inadequate levels of insulin receptors.

So we're working to find ways to increase these receptors in diabetics so their bodies can take full advantage of the insulin which is there.

For nearly 100 years, we've searched for new answers to help improve the quality of life. And searching for more will make our second century of caring even more exciting than the first.

For a free booklet "What You Should Know About Diabetes," write CARING, Department D P.O. Box 2497, Kalamazoo, Michigan 49003.

Upjohn

COLOR PLATE 11 An institutional ad that seeks to build the image of the company. And it does it with art as well as words. The photograph shows three generations of women and relates to the genetic concept under discussion. The brown ink used in the ad, instead of full color, casts a nostalgic (rather than old-fashioned) glow to the scene that ties in well to "a century of caring."

COLOR PLATE 12 Here is an imaginative use of a figure in a billboard. Upright it would appear too small, but at the angle shown, it does not appear awkward and is fitted neatly with the five words of copy. Notice the use of the container, easily recognizable as milk, and the word "milk," legible at a distance and even at an angle. No wasted space and a play on words—"fitness you can drink."

COLOR PLATE 11

COLOR PLATE 12

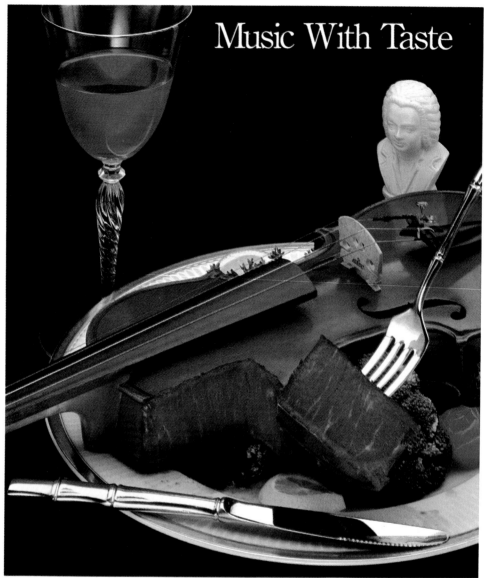

Photo: © Jim Brown, Nashville, TN 615–889-7079

4104 HILLSBORO ROAD   NASHVILLE, TENNESSEE 37215   (615) 298-2200

COLOR PLATE 13

COLOR PLATE 13 No this is not an ad for a music store. J. S. Brock (dig that name and the spelling of m-u-s-i-k) writes musical advertising jingles. It has written for products ranging from bleach (Vivit) to cold cereal (General Mills) to recruitment (U.S. Marines). The ad is clever and creative which is what J. S. Brock is all about. Where would it be located but in Nashville? Where would it advertise but in advertising business publications where this ad appeared?

THE WENDY'S NATIONAL ADVERTISING PROGRAM, INC.

TITLE: "HOT STUFFED II"

LENGTH: 30 SECONDS
COMM'L NO.: WOFH-3373

WHISPER: Ooh.

WHISPER: Hot

WHISPER: Hot, so hot.

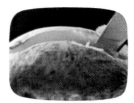

COOL ANNCR: Wendy's baked potatoes are

WHISPER: Hot stuff.

ANNCR: Wendy's stuffs 'em all kinds of ways.
WHISPER: Hot!
ANNCR: Like with cheese.

WHISPER: Oh, what a tease!

ANNCR: Or chili and cheese,

bacon and cheese

broccoli and cheese

WHISPER: Wendy's

ANNCR: Or sour cream and chives.

WHISPER: That makes five.

ANNCR: Wendy's stuffed baked potatoes.

They're hot!

For Wendy's kind of people.
WHISPER: Oooh.

COLOR PLATE 14

COLOR PLATE 14 In November 1983, Wendy's introduced its baked potato promotion as part of a menu diversification. Its commercial featured steaming baked potatoes with a variety of toppings. Jazzy music, dramatic lighting, rhyming lyrics, and sound effects were combined to produce a sales impact that produced a 15 percent sales increase in the first three weeks of the product introduction. By the end of 1984, Wendy's was serving 600,000 potatoes per day. And that's not small potatoes.

My son's the reason we switched to Crest.

I'm going to be involved with my son as much as I can. Whether it's taking the time to teach him to tie his tie the right way, or making sure he brushes with a toothpaste we trust. That's why we switched to Crest. We learned there's no better cavity fighter than the fluoristat in Crest. And that's important to us. And, there are 3 great-tasting flavors to choose from...regular, mint and gel... and that's important to him.

Aren't your kids worth *Crest*? © P & G 1984

COLOR PLATE 15

COLOR PLATE 15 A switch from the usual Mom with child brushing the teeth—this time it's Dad and a powerful statement for black magazines. Note too, that Dad is not throwing a ball or one of his usual and expected activities, but a grown-up activity—tying a tie. The ad has real thought to it. Nor did the designer forget the packages.

COLOR PLATE 16 Competition is keen among business publications as they seek advertisers who want to reach corporate America. *Dun's Business Month* uses a play on words to suggest that its publication reaches more top honchos, described as "the cream." The illustration suggests that the editorial content makes *Dun's* better. That's why the two honchos are looking to see what the other honcho is reading in Dun's.

COLOR PLATE 17 How can you show *"created by the earth ages ago"*? A modern pump? A stainless steel bottling plant? They would lose the image the advertiser wants to project. Show fantasy art: a bottle (strong identification) bursting forth from the planet.

YOU NEED THIS HOT MARKET!

NUMBER 1

BECAUSE TAMPA BAY* LEADS IN FLORIDA**

- 1st in Population
- 1st in Households
- 1st in Effective Buying Power
- 1st in Food Sales
- 1st in Automotive Sales
- 1st in General Merchandise
- 1st in Eating & Drinking Places

The Tampa Tribune is also FIRST in reaching your target audience group. Based on the 1983 Scarborough Newspaper Audience Study compared to the other major newspaper combination in the market, The Tampa Tribune daily delivers:

- 27% more readers in the age of acquisition (25-54 years).
- 22% more adults in the upper income group (35.000 -).
- 41% more adult readers in the top level occupations (Professional and Manager).
- 27% more adult readers with three or more persons in household.
- 89% more adult readers with high food expenditures ($150 plus per week).

The Tampa Bay Market is 21st in the Top 25 U.S. Markets

TO REACH THIS HOT MARKET YOU NEED THE TAMPA TRIBUNE
Morning and Sunday ... the Quality Buy

To maximize your coverage of the Tampa Bay Market include our weekly direct mail product in your schedule:
Contact Joe Gess. General Advertising Manager
P.O. Box 191. Tampa. Florida. 33601-4005 or dial – (813) 272-7447

SOURCES: *The Tampa Bay Market (MSA) consists of these Florida counties — Hillsborough. Hernando. Pasco and Pinellas. **Sales & Marketing Management Survey of Buying Power. 1984

Q The Quality Buy

This ad appeared in an advertising magazine. It tells advertisers and agencies that the newspaper "delivers" the Tampa market — a MSA (Metropolitan Statistical Area; see chapter 5) that covers four counties.

face an agency representing a major cigarette advertiser and a major brewery that marketed brand A beer. If the cigarette company bought a brewery that made brand B beer, the agency would be forced to drop either the cigarette advertising account or the brand A beer account. In fact, for the large agencies, one of the most serious limits to growth comes from client conflict. Advertisers are diversifying into one another's businesses.

Advertising Media

Although we shall examine in close detail all the media available to national advertisers in chapters 7–12, it is only fitting that we consider the scope of the communications industry as part of our examination of the advertising business.

In the United States there are approximately:

6,540 commercial radio stations
3,400 business publications
  446 morning newspapers
1,284 evening newspapers
   29 "all day" newspapers
  772 Sunday newspapers
7,547 weekly newspapers
1,200 consumer magazines
  869 commercial television stations
  283 public television stations
8,123 cable stations
  500 Sunday magazine sections
  280 farm publications
  230 color comic sections

This list includes only the *major media* in which advertisers place the greatest volume of their advertising. Although secondary advertising media represent only a tiny portion of total billings, their range is enormous and includes station posters, matchbooks, car cards, and pennysavers.

The media recognize the value of the advertising agency. The agency relieves the publisher or the broadcaster of the need to prepare advertisements, a service that some media still have to provide for small advertisers. The agency creates more effective advertising and thereby improves the effectiveness of the medium. The agency carries the burden of credit. In short, agencies simplify media's task.

As these ads from an advertising trade publication indicate, advertisers and advertising agencies rely on many ancillary companies to provide the back-up services they need—from creating banners to skywriting advertising messages. (See color plate 13 for an ad promoting an ancillary company specializing in music.)

David Ogilvy

At the age of 38, David Ogilvy founded the advertising agency that was to become Ogilvy & Mather International, the fifth largest agency in the world in 1978, with billings of $1,003.7 million. During his career as an advertising man, David Ogilvy built a reputation as a creator of sophisticated and literate advertising, advertising that his clients also found to be extremely effective. *Time* magazine proclaimed him to be "the most sought after wizard in the advertising business," and *Newsweek* referred to him as "one of the innovative giants of U. S. Advertising."

Born in West Horsley, England, in 1911, David Ogilvy worked as a chef in a Paris Hotel and a stove salesman in Scotland before emigrating to the United States. Soon after arriving in this country, he went to work for Dr. George Gallup's American Institute of Public Opinion, where his first assignment involved measuring the popularity of movie stars and pretesting story ideas for Hollywood motion picture studios. During the Second World War, he joined the British Secret Service and later served as Second Secretary at the British Embassy in Washington.

In the 26 years that he headed Ogilvy & Mather, David Ogilvy produced a great number of successful advertising campaigns. For Hathaway shirts he thought of the idea of featuring a model with a black eyepatch; for Rolls-Royce Corporation he wrote the famous headline: "At 60 miles an hour the loudest noise in this new Rolls-Royce comes from the electric clock"; for Dove soap he stressed the fact that "one quarter percent cleansing cream, Dove will cream your skin while you wash." His other clients have included General Foods, Lever Brothers, Sears Roebuck, IBM, Schweppes, Guinness, and Helena Rubinstein. During this period, he somehow found time to write his best-selling book on the advertising industry: *Confessions of an Advertising Man.*

Now living in semi-retirement in the Chateau de Touffou, a castle in the south of France, David Ogilvy has written his autobiography: *Blood, Brains, and Beer.* In this book, the following advice heads the list of the "Eleven Lessons I Learned on Madison Avenue."

> You can divide advertising people into two groups—the amateurs and the professionals. The amateurs are in the majority. They aren't *students* of advertising. They guess. The Professionals don't guess, so they don't waste so much of their clients' money.

Ancillary Advertising Services

There would be no advertising business if it were not for the services of all the technical experts who provide the *physical* components of advertising. Typographers set the type. Engravers provide engravings or film for publications. Film studios prepare and process film and tape for television commercials. Photography studios take the photographs so essential to the message. Sound studios prepare the transcriptions and tapes for radio commercials. Art studios perform specialized services that are needed from time to time. Printers print the catalogs and brochures designed and prepared by the advertising

CASE HISTORY

Wendy's Old Fashioned Hamburgers

The first Wendy's opened in November 1969, in downtown Columbus, Ohio. It did not begin to franchise until August of 1972. Today, Wendy's International, Inc., headquartered in Dublin, Ohio, operates over 3,300 restaurants in the United States and 16 countries, about one-third of them company owned. Over 175 are located outside the country. System-wide sales in 1984 were $2.42 billion—a remarkable growth in less than 16 years.

Competition in fast-foods is fierce. Burger King, McDonald's, and thousands of small local hamburger restaurants all compete with Wendy's. How can one firm create a distinctive image for itself under such conditions? In 1983, Wendy's adopted an attention-getting, comparative theme, and advertised aggressively. The objective was to heighten consumer awareness of Wendy's. It contrasted its quality and service with its main competitors, naming names. The campaign, developed by Dancer Fitzgerald Sample, was the most effective in Wendy's history and achieved a 30 percent rise in revenues.

"Where's the Beef?" caught on like wildfire. Bumper stickers sprouted on cars. Cartoonists used the theme. A presidential candidate used the phrase in a nationally televised debate. Clara Peller, the octogenarian grandmother, became an American heroine—the consumer who is not afraid to speak up. In May 1984, "Where's the Beef?" won three Clio awards as one of the top commercials of 1983. Clara Peller was awarded Best Performance for a female. (See color plate 14 for a different Wendy's promotion.)

department and the agency. Market research organizations conduct polls and surveys, compile special studies of markets that are of interest to advertisers, and evaluate the effectiveness of advertising campaigns. All these services are part of the advertising business, and all are in the business of advertising.

Summary

Although the person who is responsible for an organization's advertising may have one of several different titles, the functions are generally the same. The advertising manager is responsible for the planning of the advertising, for the selection of the advertising agency, and for the supervision of the advertising program. Some companies employ product managers who direct the advertising of individual products under the supervision of a general advertising

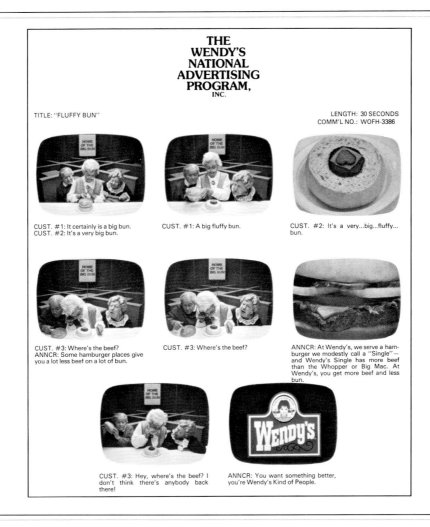

THE
WENDY'S
NATIONAL
ADVERTISING
PROGRAM,
INC.

TITLE: "FLUFFY BUN"

LENGTH: 30 SECONDS
COMM'L NO.: WOFH-3386

CUST. #1: It certainly is a big bun.
CUST. #2: It's a very big bun.

CUST. #1: A big fluffy bun.

CUST. #2: It's a very...big...fluffy... bun.

CUST. #3: Where's the beef?
ANNCR: Some hamburger places give you a lot less beef on a lot of bun.

CUST. #3: Where's the beef?

ANNCR: At Wendy's, we serve a hamburger we modestly call a "Single" — and Wendy's Single has more beef than the Whopper or Big Mac. At Wendy's, you get more beef and less bun.

CUST. #3: Hey, where's the beef? I don't think there's anybody back there!

ANNCR: You want something better, you're Wendy's Kind of People.

manager. Many large advertisers maintain fully staffed advertising departments in addition to employing the services of one or more advertising agencies. There are over 7,000 agencies in the United States, most of them *full-service* organizations that provide complete service for advertisers, including copywriting, art, market research, media analysis and scheduling, and the services of creative people in producing print ads and radio and television commercials. The organization of the agency will depend, for the most part, on the size of the agency. Most operate on a departmentalized basis; others work with a *matrix-type* organization that combines groups of people into teams that provide the talents needed to serve each client. There are also some highly specialized advertising organizations — *boutique agencies* — that provide a very creative, but limited portion of the advertising service, generally art or media or special promotion. For its work, the advertising agency receives a 15 percent commission from most media. Although most agencies work within the standard agency commission arrangement, others work with clients on a fee basis, particularly when a large portion of the advertising consists of low-cost business advertising. Agencies rarely, if ever, work for competing clients at the same time. In fact, one of the limits to agency growth has been the diversification of many large advertisers. As for media, there are more than 12,000 media to choose from in the United States, ranging from radio stations (more than 6,000) to business publications (more than 3,300) and hundreds of other choices in between, from farm magazines to color comic sections.

Questions for Discussion

1. Why would top management insist on participation in the selection of an advertising agency?
2. If you were to consider a fee basis for advertising service, what factors would you have to consider:
    a. if you were the advertiser?
    b. if you were the agency?
3. If you examine the worldwide billings of the leading advertising agencies, what accounts for the remarkable prominence of Japanese advertising agencies?
4. If you were a foreign manufacturer seeking to bring your product to the American market, would you prefer an American advertising agency or one from your own country?
5. What criteria would you set for the selection of an advertising agency? Would the kind of product affect your criteria?

Advertising Industry Reference Guide

Advertising Associations

The Advertising Council, 825 Third Avenue, New York, N.Y. 10022
Advertising Research Foundation (ARF), 3 East 54th Street, New York, N.Y. 10022.
American Association of Advertising Agencies (AAAA), 666 Third Avenue, New York, N.Y. 10017
American Marketing Association (AMA), 250 S. Wacker Drive, Chicago, IL 60606

Media Associations

American Business Press, Inc. (ABP), 205 East 42nd Street, New York, N.Y. 10017
American Newspaper Publishers Association (ANPA), The Newspaper Center, 11600 Sunrise Valley Drive, Reston, VA 22091
Audit Bureau of Circulation (ABC), 900 N. Meacham Road, Schaumburg, IL 60195
Business Publications Audit of Circulation (BPA), 360 Park Avenue South, New York, N.Y. 10010
Direct Mail Marketing Association, 6 East 43rd Street, New York, N.Y. 10017
Magazine Publishers Association (MPA), 575 Lexington Avenue, New York, N.Y. 10022
Radio Advertising Bureau (RAB), 485 Lexington Avenue, New York, N.Y. 10017
Television Bureau of Advertising, 485 Lexington Avenue, New York, N.Y. 10017

Advertising Publications

Advertising Age, 740 Rush Street, Chicago, IL 60611
AdWeek, 820 Second Avenue, New York, N.Y. 10017
Editor and Publisher, 575 Lexington Avenue, New York, N.Y. 10022
Industrial Marketing, 740 Rush Street, Chicago, IL 60611

Marketing & Media Decisions, 1140 Avenue of the Americas, New York, N.Y. 10036

Madison Avenue, 369 Lexington Avenue, N.Y. 10017

Television/Radio Age, 1270 Avenue of the Americas, New York, N.Y. 10020

Journal of Marketing, 250 S. Wacker Drive, Chicago, IL 60606

Sales & Marketing Management, 633 Third Avenue, New York, N.Y. 10017

Reference Books

Standard Directory of Advertisers, National Register Publishing Co., Inc., 3004 Glenview Rd., Wilmette, IL 60091

Sources and Suggestions for Further Reading

Barton, Roger, ed. *Advertising Agency Operations and Management.* New York: McGraw-Hill, 1970.

Donnermuth, William P. *Promotion: Analysis, Creativity and Strategy.* Boston: Kent Publishing Co., 1984.

Faison, Edmund W. J. *Advertising: A Behavioral Approach for Managers.* New York: John Wiley & Sons, 1980.

Hurwood, David L., and Earl L. Bailey. *Advertising, Sales Promotion and Public Relations — Organizational Alternatives.* New York: National Industrial Conference Board, 1968.

Mayer, Martin. *Madison Avenue, U.S.A.* New York: Harper & Row, 1958.

Ogilvy, David. *Blood, Brains, and Beer.* New York: Atheneum, 1978.

Ogilvy, David. *Confessions of an Advertising Man.* New York: Atheneum, 1963.

Ogilvy, David. *Ogilvy on Advertising.* New York: Crown, 1983.

Reeves, Rosser. *Reality in Advertising.* New York: Alfred A. Knopf, 1961.

Sachs, William. *Advertising Management: Its Role in Marketing.* Tulsa, Oklahoma: Penn-Well Publishing Company, 1983.

Stansfield, Richard. *The Dartnell Advertising Manager's Handbook.* Chicago: The Dartnell Corporation, 1969.

Follow the Liters.

With average yearly incomes of $57,000, over 600,000
of Smithsonian's 2,000,000 subscribers buy wine and liquor by the case.
Here's to a market that thirsts for the finer things in life.

Smithsonian

DECISIONS IN ADVERTISING 2

◄ When you address sophisticated people — in this case prospective advertisers and agencies — you can use a clever play on words — and more than once as this ad reveals.

5 MARKETING INTELLIGENCE: STATISTICS BEHIND SALES

The Role of Marketing Intelligence

Objectives for Marketing Intelligence
Taking Aim at Sales Potential

Intelligence Sources

Secondary Data
   External Sources of Secondary Data
   Internal Secondary Data
   Evaluating Secondary Data
Primary Data
Collecting Primary Data
   Observational Method
   Survey Method
Sampling
   Sampling Methods

Motivation Research

Psychographics
Copy Testing
Media Research

Working Vocabulary ———————————————————————

marketing research	unrestricted probability	depth interview
marketing intelligence	sample	focus group
market potential	stratified probability sample	selective perception
sales potential	nonprobability sample	psychographics
secondary data	quota sampling	scales
primary data	motivation research	
panel	projective techniques	

Commercial propaganda or advertising had its genesis in the need of the mass producer to sell goods in large quantities, and competition of other goods forced him to resort to an anonymous market: an aggregation of people scattered geographically, and unknown and unidentified as individuals.

Edmund D. McGarry
The Propaganda Function in Marketing

N o executive would make the decision to purchase a multimillion-dollar computer system without first learning as much about that computer system, and computer systems in general, as possible. So it is with the decision to advertise. For many companies advertising is the single largest expenditure in the operating budget. Executives rely on their company's marketing intelligence system to supply them with the information they need to make intelligent advertising decisions.

The scope of marketing intelligence is very wide. In practice it includes the gathering of information on pricing, product mix, product development, sales quotas, sales-force performance, distribution channels, market forecasts, and market share analyses. But for our purposes, we will simply take an overview of marketing intelligence so that you will understand its place — and its importance — in relation to advertising. It is so important that we will deal with other aspects of it in chapters 14, 18, and 19.

The Role of Marketing Intelligence

The term **marketing research** is often used interchangeably with marketing intelligence, but a distinction does exist. **Marketing intelligence** concentrates on the gathering of as much general marketing information as possible, whereas marketing research is a systematic seeking out of facts related to a *specific* marketing problem. Marketing research is concerned with *nonrecurring problems* and is conducted on a project-by-project basis. Marketing intelligence, on the other hand, is concerned with a *continous flow* of marketing information for use in frequent decision making. Marketing research examines what has already taken place. Marketing intelligence is more *future-oriented*.

Objectives for Marketing Intelligence

A marketing intelligence system is similar in many ways to a military intelligence system. Of course, every country would love to have access to information from spies planted in the innermost circles of enemy governments. But this method of intelligence is more frequently encountered in the pages of novels than in real life. For the most part, an effective marketing intelligence system relies on the routine, systematic collection of data. If we are selling a product to women, we want data on how many women in the United States are prospective customers for our product. Of these women, we might want to know, for example, how many of them are married. We do not need spies to obtain this kind of information — just a methodical approach to the gathering of data and a knowledge of potential sources of information.

If our advertising is to achieve its maximum effectiveness, our message must reach the greatest number of potential customers at the lowest possible cost. To help us achieve this objective, our marketing intelligence system must seek the answers to such questions as: Who are our prospective customers?

Where are they located? What features do they like in our product? What appeals will be most effective in stimulating them to buy? We also need to obtain information on the most effective advertising strategy. When and how often should our advertisements be run? What will be the best media for carrying our message?

Some of these questions can be refined still further. If we use print media, what layout, style of illustration, and size of type will work best? Should our advertisement be in color or in black and white? If we use broadcast media, what program and format will reach the largest audience? What consumer attitudes already exist with regard to the product? Effective marketing intelligence can supply us with the answers to all these questions.

Taking Aim at Sales Potential

In chapter 7 we shall discuss the availability and interpretation of media data. The problems involved in evaluating the effectiveness of any advertising campaign will be investigated in chapter 18. At present, we are going to concentrate on the methods of obtaining intelligence on our markets.

What is the potential market for our product? **Market potential** is the ability of a market to absorb a specific volume of product sales. If we were manufacturers of toothpaste, for example, our market potential would include every user of toothpaste in the world. Can any company ever hope to achieve such a potential? Of course not. Our **sales potential** is merely the portion or share of the total market that we can reasonably hope to persuade to try our toothpaste.

As we stated in an earlier chapter, for a product to justify an advertising investment, that product must have certain attributes. The product must have an identifiable appeal, and it must be capable of being distinguished by advertising. Now we add one more qualification: that the product's sales potential must be worth the cost of its attainment. In addition to providing us with a base for our advertising projections, there are other good reasons to determine sales potential. The sales department needs such information to determine the size of the sales force as well as the quotas and territories to assign to that sales force. The production department will want to know if its manufacturing facilities are adequate.

Returning to our former example, if we examine the total market for toothpaste more closely, we will see that it breaks down into segments for regular toothpaste, toothpaste with fluorides, toothpaste with whiteners, and mint-flavored toothpastes. There are toothpastes for people with sensitive teeth and toothpastes for people with dentures. These are but a few examples of market segments.

If we decide to manufacture fluoride toothpaste, we must depend on our marketing intelligence to tell us: (1) how many people currently use fluoride toothpaste, (2) what brands of fluoride toothpaste they now use, and (3) how many of these potential customers we can reasonably expect to buy our new brand.

Intelligence Sources

There are two basic sources of information for companies or advertising agencies that are seeking marketing intelligence. These sources are: secondary data and primary data.

New Metropolitan Areas by Region

Metropolitan Area	1980 Population	Percent Change 1970–80	Percent White	Percent Black	Percent Hispanic	Percent Other*	1980 Households
NORTHEAST							
Bangor, ME	83,919	5.0	98.0	0.3	0.4	1.7	28,362
Burlington, VT	114,070	16.0	98.6	0.4	0.8	1.0	38,004
Glens Falls, NY	109,649	7.4	98.3	1.1	0.9	0.7	37,307
Newburgh-Middletown, NY	259,603	17.1	91.4	6.2	4.3	2.3	84,251
Portsmth-Dvr-Rch, NH-ME	163,880	15.2	98.1	0.9	0.7	1.0	57,681
Sharon, PA	128,299	0.8	95.4	4.2	0.3	0.4	44,657
State College, PA	112,760	13.6	97.0	1.3	0.7	1.7	36,122
NORTH CENTRAL							
Benton Harbor, MI	171,276	4.5	84.1	14.5	1.2	1.4	60,276
Joplin, MO	127,513	13.0	97.7	0.9	0.7	1.4	48,436
Newark, OH	120,981	12.2	97.7	1.7	0.4	0.6	42,218
Sheboygan, WI	100,935	4.4	98.6	0.3	1.0	1.1	35,484
Wausau, WI	111,270	14.2	99.3	<0.1	0.3	0.7	37,703
SOUTH							
Anderson, SC	133,235	26.3	82.4	17.2	0.6	0.4	46,944
Athens, GA	130,015	20.7	80.9	18.1	1.0	1.0	45,568
Charlottesville, VA	113,568	26.9	83.9	15.0	0.8	1.1	40,241
Cumberland, MD-WV	107,782	0.6	97.7	2.0	0.4	0.4	39,107
Danville, VA	111,789	6.3	69.7	30.0	0.7	0.3	39,658
Florence, SC	110,163	22.9	62.2	37.5	0.8	0.3	35,705
Ft. Walton Beach, FL	109,920	24.6	88.3	8.6	2.3	3.0	37,538
Hagerstown, MD	113,086	8.9	95.1	4.2	0.6	0.7	39,957
Hickory, NC	130,207	18.0	90.8	8.8	0.6	0.4	45,836
Jacksonville, NC	112,784	9.4	75.8	20.2	3.9	4.0	30,307
Ocala, FL	122,488	77.4	82.7	16.6	1.6	0.7	45,458
Rock Hill, SC	106,720	25.2	76.3	22.3	0.6	1.4	34,861
Salisbury-Concord, NC	185,081	12.4	84.5	15.0	0.6	0.5	66,559
Victoria, TX	68,807	28.0	81.1	6.8	30.4	12.1	22,988
WEST							
Bellingham, WA	106,701	30.2	94.6	0.3	1.9	5.1	39,630
Bremerton, WA	146,609	44.1	92.4	1.8	2.6	5.8	52,591
Casper, WY	71,856	40.2	96.6	0.7	3.5	2.7	25,841
Chico, CA	143,851	41.1	93.2	1.2	5.2	5.6	56,904
Medford, OR	132,456	40.1	96.7	0.1	3.0	3.2	49,011
Olympia, WA	124,264	61.6	94.4	0.8	2.1	4.8	46,375
Redding, CA	115,715	49.0	95.7	0.6	3.0	3.7	43,014
Visalia-Tul-Prtvle, CA	245,751	30.5	73.3	1.4	29.8	25.3	80,659
Yuba City, CA	101,979	17.7	83.2	2.7	10.3	14.1	36,313

Source: U.S. Census

* "Other" includes American Indians, Eskimos, Aleuts, Asians, Pacific Islanders.

Readily available secondary data like this help marketers guide their efforts toward the most promising markets. These newly formed SMSAs (Standard Metropolitan Statistical Areas) represent areas for the advertisers to evaluate for media coverage and for retailers to consider for location of new branches. Even social and ethnic information, provided by the U.S. Census, can be used in the promotion of particular products. The data show the substantial ten-year population growths of Ocala, Florida, and Olympia, Washington; the 37.5 percent black population of Florence, South Carolina; and the 30.4 percent Hispanic population of Victoria, Texas.

Top 30 Metropolitan Areas, 1982

Rank	MSA	Pop. (000)	Percent Change	Rank	MSA	Pop. (000)	Percent Change
1.	New York CMSA	17,589	+0.3	15.	Atlanta MSA	2,243	+4.9
2.	Los Angeles CMSA	11,930	+3.8	16.	Baltimore MSA	2,218	+0.8
3.	Chicago CMSA	7,974	+0.5	17.	Minneapolis/St. Paul MSA	2,194	+2.6
4.	Philadelphia CMSA	5,713	+0.6	18.	Seattle/Tacoma CMSA	2,178	+4.1
5.	San Francisco CMSA	5,515	+2.7	19.	San Diego MSA	1,962	+5.4
6.	Detroit/Ann Arbor CMSA	4,630	−2.6	20.	Tampa MSA	1,721	+6.6
7.	Boston/Lawrence CMSA	3,988	+0.4	21.	Denver/Boulder CMSA	1,721	+6.3
8.	Houston/Galveston CMSA	3,458	+11.5	22.	Cincinnati/Hamilton CMSA	1,672	+0.7
9.	Washington, D.C.	3,339	+2.7	23.	Phoenix MSA	1,609	+6.6
10.	Dallas/Fort Worth CMSA	3,143	+7.3	24.	Milwaukee/Racine CMSA	1,572	+0.1
11.	Cleveland/Akron CMSA	2,808	−0.9	25.	Kansas City CMSA	1,454	+1.4
12.	Miami CMSA	2,790	+5.5	26.	Portland CMSA	1,332	+2.6
13.	Pittsburgh CMSA	2,403	−0.9	27.	New Orleans MSA	1,300	+3.5
14.	St. Louis CMSA	2,377	—	28.	Columbus MSA	1,267	+1.8
				29.	Buffalo CMSA	1,218	−2.0
				30.	Norfolk MSA	1,201	+3.5

Source: U.S. Census

In 1983, the SMSA and SCSA (Standard Consolidated Statistical Area) were replaced with new classifications of urban data — the MSA and the CMSA. A MSA (Metropolitan Statistical Area) is a freestanding area with an urban center population of 50,000 and a total population of 100,000 individuals that have a social and economic relationship. A MSA is usually bordered by nonurbanized counties. The CMSA (Consolidated Metropolitan Statistical Area) represents giant cities like New York, Los Angeles, and Chicago, and includes any urbanized county or counties with social and economic ties to the city. Thus, Long Island's Nassau and Suffolk counties are part of the New York City CMSA. Aurora–Elgin is part of the Chicago CMSA.

The figures show a slight growth in areas that had lost population in the 1970–1980 decade but, more importantly, show the continued growth of areas in Texas, Florida, and California. Advertisers must be aware of such population shifts in order to plan effectively.

Secondary Data

A foreign government wouldn't send spies into the United States to obtain information that is published every day in our newspapers. Advertisers, too, know that they can obtain much valuable marketing information from **secondary data** — from records that have been compiled and published by someone else.

External Sources of Secondary Data   The public library is a warehouse of marketing information — most of it provided by the United States government. The Federal Reserve Board, the Department of Commerce, the Department of Agriculture, and the Department of Health and Human Services produce volumes of data on consumers, markets, occupations, and industries. State and county governments provide data on income, housing, education, retail sales, auto registration, alcoholic beverage consumption — the list is almost endless. Publishers of newspapers provide data on retail sales for various segments of their market, trading area, or Standard Metropolitan Statistical Area (SMSA). Trade associations gather much data on their industries and,

The 30 Major Cities of the United States

Rank Order 1980	(1970)	City, State	1980 Population	Population Change 1970–80	Percent Change 1970–1980
1.	(1)	New York, NY	7,015,608	−879,955	−11.1
2.	(2)	Chicago, IL	2,969,570	−399,787	−11.9
3.	(3)	Los Angeles, CA	2,950,010	138,209	4.9
4.	(4)	Philadelphia, PA	1,680,235	−269,761	−13.8
5.	(6)	Houston, TX	1,554,992	321,457	26.1
6.	(5)	Detroit, MI	1,192,222	−321,841	−21.3
7.	(8)	Dallas, TX	901,450	57,049	6.8
8.	(15)	San Diego, CA	870,006	172,535	24.7
9.	(7)	Baltimore, MD	783,320	−122,467	−13.5
10.	(14)	San Antonio, TX	783,296	129,143	19.7
11.	(20)	Phoenix, AZ	781,443	197,140	33.7
12.	(11)	Indianapolis, IN	695,040	−34,728	−4.8
13.	(13)	San Francisco, CA	674,063	−41,611	−5.8
14.	(17)	Memphis, TN	644,838	20,850	3.3
15.	(9)	Washington, DC	635,185	−121,483	−16.1
16.	(12)	Milwaukee, WI	632,989	−84,383	−11.8
17.	(29)	San Jose, CA	625,763	165,850	36.1
18.	(10)	Cleveland, OH	572,532	−178,347	−23.8
19.	(16)	Boston, MA	562,118	−78,953	−12.3
20.	(21)	Columbus, OH	561,943	21,918	4.1
21.	(19)	New Orleans, LA	556,913	−36,558	−6.2
22.	(23)	Jacksonville, FL	541,269	37,004	7.3
23.	(22)	Seattle, WA	491,897	−38,934	−7.3
24.	(25)	Denver, CO	488,765	−25,913	−5.0
25.	(18)	St. Louis, MO	448,640	−173,596	−27.9
26.	(26)	Kansas City, MO	446,562	−60,768	−12.0
27.	(31)	Nashville, TN	439,599	13,570	3.2
28.	(45)	El Paso, TX	424,522	102,261	31.7
29.	(24)	Pittsburgh, PA	423,962	−96,127	−18.5
30.	(27)	Atlanta, GA	422,293	−72,746	−14.7

Source: U.S. Census

Note the dramatic population shifts that have taken place over the ten-year span between collections of census data. An examination of changes shows how important it is to continually evaluate the advertising effort. San Diego, California, jumped from 15th place to 8th place with a 25 percent increase in population. San Jose, also in California, jumped from 29th place to 17th place with a 36 percent increase. During the same time span, Detroit experienced a 21 percent loss of population and St. Louis a 28 percent loss.

although most is reserved for their members, in many instances it is made available to interested advertisers. Magazine publishers and television and radio stations are constantly conducting surveys to determine the reading or viewing habits of their audiences, as well as their eating and drinking habits, income and educational levels, and other demographic details. They are always eager to supply advertisers and their agencies with this information.

Internal Secondary Data   A well-organized business routinely accumulates substantial amounts of information that an efficient marketing intelligence system can utilize. The sales records of the company, carefully studied, can be a mine of valuable information. From them, researchers can determine,

The 30 Counties That Gained the Most Population, 1970–1980

County	City	State	Pop. Gain 1970–1980	1980 Pop.	Percent Change 1970–1980
1. Harris	Houston	TX	667,632	2,409,544	38.3
2. Maricopa	Phoenix	AZ	540,508	1,508,030	55.9
3. Orange	Anaheim-St. Anna	CA	511,184	1,931,570	36.0
4. San Diego	San Diego	CA	503,992	1,861,846	37.1
5. Los Angeles	Los Angeles	CA	445,582	7,477,657	6.3
6. Broward	Ft. Lauderdale	FL	393,943	1,014,043	63.5
7. Dade	Miami	FL	358,187	1,625,979	28.3
8. Santa Clara	San Jose	CA	230,357	1,295,071	21.6
9. Dallas	Dallas	TX	229,228	1,556,549	17.3
10. Palm Beach	W. Palm Beach	FL	224,372	573,125	64.3
11. San Bernardino	San Bernardino	CA	209,085	893,157	30.6
12. Pinellas	St. Petersburg	FL	206,080	728,409	39.5
13. Riverside	Riverside	CA	204,849	663,923	44.6
14. Clark	Las Vegas	NV	188,528	461,816	69.0
15. Pima	Tucson	AZ	179,596	531,263	51.1
16. Du Page	Chicago	IL	166,295	658,177	33.8
17. Salt Lake	Salt Lake City	UT	160,459	619,066	35.0
18. Suffolk	New York City	NY	159,281	1,284,231	14.2
19. Bexar	San Antonio	TX	158,340	988,800	19.1
20. Hillsborough	Tampa	FL	156,695	646,960	32.0
21. Ventura	Santa Barbara	CA	153,469	529,899	40.8
22. Sacramento	Sacramento	CA	151,883	783,381	24.1
23. Tarrant	Fort Worth	TX	144,563	860,880	20.2
24. Fairfax	Washington, D.C.	VA	141,880	596,901	31.2
25. Jefferson	Denver	CO	138,710	371,741	59.5
26. Ocean	Atlantic City	NJ	137,568	346,038	66.0
27. Honolulu	Honolulu	HI	133,698	762,874	21.2
28. Arapahoe	Denver	CO	131,479	293,621	81.1
29. Orange	Orlando	FL	127,349	471,660	37.0
30. Travis	Austin	TX	123,819	419,335	41.9

Source: U.S. Census

The county is widely used to establish territories because it is a clearly defined and unchanging geographical area for which statistics are available from many sources. Although the geographical borders of a county may remain permanent, its population characteristics do not. Management must be aware of the population shifts in order to maintain adequate evaluation and control of sales potential, particularly when potential is related to population size.

among other things, the season in which the company's sales peak, the regions of the country that offer the best markets for the company's product, and the channels of distribution that are the most effective. Of course, the amount of information collected will vary from company to company, but certainly there will be enough basic data to provide an important foundation for future advertising decisions.

Evaluating Secondary Data Although the use of secondary data offers savings in time and cost, a word of caution is warranted. Before basing important marketing decisions on such data, we should ask ourselves a number of questions that will help us evaluate the material.

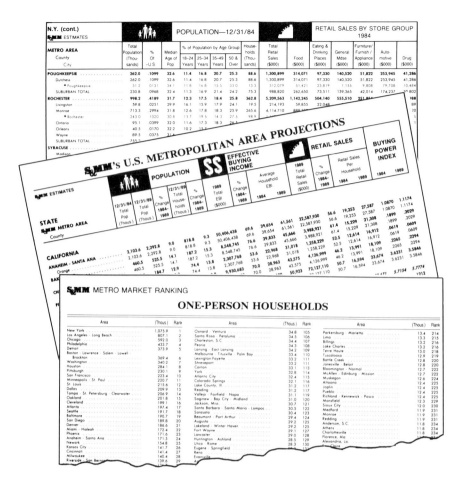

Sales & Marketing Management's "Survey of Buying Power," published in July and October each year, is an excellent source of market information. The July issue includes up-to-the-minute estimates of demographic factors by region, state, metropolitan areas, counties, and cities. The October issue rearranges the data in terms of television and newspaper markets to help make media/market evaluations. As may be seen from these representative pages, we can find population data, income data, retail sales for various categories of goods, and other importat market facts.

1. *Under what conditions was the data gathered?*
   The data compiled by a well-known market research company offers a greater level of reliability than, for example, statistics quickly assembled by a local chamber of commerce.

2. *Who financed it?*
   Not that anyone would knowingly provide incorrect data, but sometimes a company or business or organization commissions a study to prove that its interpretation of the facts is the correct one. It is simply good business to find out who paid for the data search.

3. *When was the data gathered?*
   We live in a very dynamic world. Last year's figures may be stale, if not suspect. Data gathered five or ten years ago may be all but valueless.

4. *How are the terms defined?*

    A report describing sales of *fresh fruit* is not at all clear. What does "fresh" mean? Not cooked? Is it the same as raw fruit? Are frozen strawberries fresh because they have not been cooked? And what fruits have been included in the study? Apples? Peaches? Does "part-time" employment mean five hours a week or twenty-five hours a week? You see the difficulty.

5. *Was the sample adequate?*

    By "adequate" we mean large enough, representative of the market, randomly selected, or whatever other criteria we value in sampling. We will have more to say about sampling later in this chapter.

Primary Data

When the information we seek is not available from secondary sources — perhaps because it is so specialized that we are the only people interested in it — we must go out and collect the data for ourselves. **Primary data,** as the name implies, is firsthand information, collected according to plan by our procedure and, generally, for our private use. If we want to know, for example, how many females between the ages of 12 and 18 live in Florida, the chances are good that such data have already been compiled. If we want to know what percentage of these females is black and what percentage white, that information, too, should not be difficult to find. But, suppose we want to know how many of them make their own clothes? (Perhaps we are interested in selling them sewing machines or clothing patterns, or perhaps we want to open a chain of fabric stores.) This type of information is not usually available from secondary sources — not from the government, not from a trade association, not from a syndicated service. Therefore, we must obtain our own data.

There are many different ways we could go about gathering the information we want. We always begin our search by obtaining all the related secondary data available. Once we have done this, our next step is to take a sample of our total potential market or universe (in this case, all young women 12 to 18 years old) and find out what percentage of this sample consists of women who sew their own clothes. We could conduct the survey of our sample by questionnaire, by telephone, or through personal interviews at the local high schools. Each of these methods has advantages and limitations. The formulation of the questionnaire and the selection of the sample demand specialized skills. For that reason, we might want to contract with a market research organization to do the survey for us. Of course, if we did undertake such a survey, we would want, at the same time, to gather additional data about our market. We might want to ask the young women in our sample what kind of fabrics they buy, how often they sew, how many garments they make in a year, and what makes of sewing machines they own. Such information, when gathered and assembled, is very valuable and we would keep it for our exclusive use. But it will be costly to obtain.

Collecting Primary Data

Observational Method   The simplest method of gathering primary data is to have a trained observer watch what takes place when a consumer purchases our product. The observer then records particular aspects of the

This ad is an announcement for an interesting new development in marketing research — tracking eye movement. For example, an advertiser might want to know if a new package stands out on the shelf. Is it more visible than competitive packages? Which area of the package catches the eye of the consumer first? The illustration? The name? Which part of an ad does the reader notice first? This company tracks the eye movements of respondents and then interviews them to measure the impact of the message and the brand image conveyed.

consumer's purchase behavior. How do consumers select a particular type of packaged food? Do they scan all the shelves or do they go straight to the brand they want? Do they read the information on the package to check for weight or contents?

The observer may then gather additional information by conducting a

```
6a.  Do you, yourself, use a toothpaste for brushing your teeth?

         Yes  ( )  (ASK Q. 6)    No   ( )  (SKIP TO Q. 7a)

  b.  What brand of toothpaste did you use the last time for brushing your
      teeth?  (RECORD ANSWER BELOW)

  c.  What other brands, if any, do you use quite regularly?  (RECORD ANSWER
      BELOW)

  d.  Are there any other brands of toothpaste that any members of your family
      consider to be their regular brands?

         Yes  ( )  (ASK Q. 6e)    No   ( )  (SKIP TO Q. 7a)

  e.  What are these brands?  (RECORD ANSWER BELOW)
```

| | Q. 6b | Q. 6c | Q. 6e |
| | | | Other Family Members |
	Last Time	Quite Regularly	Quite Regularly
Aim	( )	( )	( )
Close-Up Green	( )	( )	( )
Close-Up Red	( )	( )	( )
Colgate	( )	( )	( )
Crest Regular	( )	( )	( )
Crest Mint	( )	( )	( )
Gleem II	( )	( )	( )
Macleans Regular	( )	( )	( )
Macleans Spearmint	( )	( )	( )
Peak	( )	( )	( )
Pearl Drops	( )	( )	( )
Pepsodent	( )	( )	( )
Plus White	( )	( )	( )
Ultra Brite Regular	( )	( )	( )
Ultra Brite Mint	( )	( )	( )
Other (SPECIFY)	_____	_____	_____
None other		( )	( )

The illustration shows a portion of a research questionnaire designed to collect primary data through personal interviews. The interviewer seeks to determine the brand preferences of toothpaste users.

personal interview with the customers after they have made their selection. There are many other observational techniques that may be used. Some of them involve nothing more than counting the number of people entering a store or department during a specified period of time, or using a mechanical counter to record the number of cars that pass a given point each day.

But the observational method provides only overt behavioral information. We do not learn why consumers do something, only that they do it. Any other conclusions must be inferred.

Survey Method   Surveys may be classified by the procedure used to gather the data. These procedures include the personal interview, mail survey, and telephone survey.

The personal interview is the most costly of all survey procedures. But if it's successful, it can provide us with information critical to the success of our advertising program. We can use personal interviews to obtain information on the consumers' knowledge of our product, their attitudes toward it, their life-styles, and many demographic details. Large amounts of information can be collected in a short time, but the cost of the survey will be ten to twenty times greater than a mail survey.

A *mail survey* typically employs the use of a self-administered questionnaire; the subject answers the questions without help from an interviewer. The procedure is simple and the cost is far less than a personally administered questionnaire. The major drawback of a mail survey is the amount of time required to gather the information. It takes time to get the mailing out, time for the respondent to complete the questionnaire, and then more time for the questionnaire to be returned. In some cases, the time required to complete a mail survey can be as long as two months. Another drawback is the poor rate of return. Many people simply do not take the time to answer and return the questionnaire. Finally, a mail survey generally elicits only very limited types of information.

The *diary* is another form of questionnaire. The subjects of the study are given a diary in which they record their behavior. In some cases they are asked to record their supermarket purchases or their product use. In other cases, they record their reading and/or viewing habits. In this way, we can learn about the consumption of certain products, their frequency of purchase, and frequency of use. We can detect shifts in taste. *A media exposure diary* might provide information about which programs television viewers watch. If the diarists have been carefully selected, the results of such a survey can be projected onto the relevant market.

Obviously, the diary method of survey also has its limitations: It is very expensive; it requires two to three months for completion; and it is difficult to control. Because of the cost and time involved, there are a number of market research organizations that maintain a continuous diary-information service. They in turn make this information available, for a fee, to advertisers and advertising agencies. Most major consumer advertisers make use of diary information.

Somewhere between the personal interview and the mail survey lies the *telephone interview.* The costs are lower than those for personal interviews, but higher than those for a mail survey. The interviews can be completed very quickly. Much valuable information can be elicited on the telephone — demographic characteristics, attitudes, and intentions. The amount of such information is restricted, however, because it is difficult to complete a long, detailed interview over the telephone.

Some market research organizations make use of large groups of people that represent cross sections of the entire population of the United States. These groups are known as **panels** and provide a continuous source of consumer purchasing behavior information that the research organization makes available to its subscribers. Sometimes an individual advertiser sets up a panel, but it is difficult to maintain the active participation of its members. To purchase this information from a research firm is, in the long run, cheaper and faster.

Sampling

A *sample* is a small, but representative, portion of the total. We cut off a small piece of a wheel of cheese in order to *sample* the whole wheel. We receive a small tube of toothpaste in the mail to encourage us to *sample* that brand of toothpaste. We assume that the little bite of cheese or the half ounce of toothpaste will tell us whether or not we like the product well enough to buy it on our own.

This marketing research company offers a very large panel of 150,000 households. By mail or telephone it can reach and obtain information from households with selected demographic characteristics — as the ad says, from people with money in the bank to those who love cruises.

It is not necessary to eat a whole wheel of Swiss cheese to see if we like it. Nor is it necessary to brush our teeth with an entire tube of one brand of toothpaste to see if we like its taste. We predicate our decisions to purchase (or not to purchase) on the assumption that the sample truly represents the entire product. But we must take pains to ensure that the sample we are using is truly representative of the product that interests us. Basing decisions on personal samples ("I asked my brother") or on gut reactions ("It *looked* like good cheese") is very dangerous.

In marketing intelligence, sampling is one step in the establishment of a system intended to obtain the most accurate information on our target market as efficiently and as economically as possible. The scope of the information desired and the expense of gathering that information are the important considerations. Let us turn our attention now to the two most crucial aspects of sampling as described above.

Is the sample representative of the target market?

The question is: How do we define "representative"? Our target population may have a specified income level or it may have only a typical income range. Or we may want information on a certain age group — over 18, perhaps, or 18 to 34. Such *parameters,* or boundaries, of our sample would depend on the nature of the market and would affect our sampling procedure.

Is the sample accurate and reliable?

If we are going to base important advertising decisions on the results of our sample, we must really plan to obtain dependable results.

It is not unlikely that two samples, using the same procedures, could produce two sets of widely differing data. To rely on *either* set of data would be unwise. The reliability of the sample — the amount of confidence we have in it — depends on two things: the sampling procedure applied and, even more important, the size of the sample. A sample of 1,000 will produce more reliable results than a sample of 200. And, it will be more expensive. The importance of the advertising decision that will later be based on the results of the sample should be the guide to determining the size of the sample. Time, too, is a factor. There is no need to obtain a degree of accuracy that is not warranted by the risk involved in making a particular decision. Data that arrive too late to be useful serve no purpose regardless of their accuracy. Data must be fresh to be valuable.

Sampling Methods Our first step, of course, is to define the population from which the sample is to be drawn. This definition must be clear and complete. We must state the attributes of the target population in terms that are as precise as possible. Once we have specified the demographic characteristics of our target population, we can then decide on the method to use for extracting the sample.

An **unrestricted probability sample** is a sample chosen at random in which every member of the population has an equal chance of being selected. If we were using an unrestricted probability sample to determine the average weight of all the male students at our school, we would choose the students for our sample at random. We could pick the first 100 male students who cross the campus or every nth student who crosses the campus until we have 100. By using random selection we expect, according to the laws of probability, to get a normal distribution of weights in our sample. It is possible that by chance we could pick the fattest 100 men on our campus. It is equally possible that we could draw the skinniest 100. But it is likely that the characteristics of our random sample will cluster around the true mean. We can, in fact, predict our probable error mathematically.

We can obtain more accurate data by using a *restricted,* or **stratified probability sample.** In this sampling method we first divide, or stratify, our population into subgroups and then apply an unrestricted sample to each of the subgroups. For example, we might want to specify that our sample of 100 students consists of equal numbers of freshmen, sophomores, juniors, and seniors, or we might want to have numbers proportionate to the percentage these groups represent in the total school population. It is more than likely that freshmen would compose the largest percentage of the student population, with the percentages declining for each higher category. A stratified sample of this kind will make our data more accurate (and at no extra cost).

We encountered an example of a **nonprobability sample** in a different context when we described how research firms use consumer panels to obtain marketing data. They cannot use either random selection *or* a stratified sample to get as wide a cross section, or as representative a panel, as they need. Instead, they use *purposive selection.* They select one household, in Indiana for example, with a predetermined level of income and of a specified family size. Then they add similar households in other areas of the country to their sample. To this mix, they then add some households with no children, also carefully chosen from different areas of the country, some households with higher and lower income levels and so on, for other demographic characteristics. By carefully selecting their "sample" they can, with as few as 1,000 households, project the purchase behavior of the rest of the American population. This technique is called **quota sampling,** because the research firm has specified a *quota* for each household category. This method is widely used in market studies because it is faster and less expensive than a *probability sample.*

Another form of purposive selection is the *judgment* sample. In this procedure, the criteria for selection are specified and population members are sought, who, in the *judgment* of the individual conducting the study, represent the criteria. The procedure is obviously not scientific, but there are situations in which such judgment might be used. If a member of a panel were to drop out, the research director or supervisor might select a replacement who, *in his or her judgment,* had the same attributes. If advertisers wanted to study the attitude of retail store owners carrying their products and wanted to draw a sample for such purpose, the research director might set up criteria that would describe the types of stores (by dollar sales, location, lines of merchandise, number of employees, and so on). Then, by examining a list of stores, he or she could select the retailers that in *his or her judgment* met the criteria. Of course, the individual exercising that judgment is expected to avoid prejudice and personal whim. The method is efficient, and it does avoid the chances, present in a random selection, of drawing a misrepresentative sample from the target population.

Motivation Research

The data we have gathered thus far are all demographic, that is, they have recorded only such information as age, marital status, income, family size, place and type of residence, car ownership, and other similar attributes of our target population. But demographic information alone may be insufficient for the development of advertising strategy and copy. Although our research may

Murray Hill Center provides focus group facilities. On assignment by an advertiser or agency, six to ten people of specified demographic characteristics will be assembled in a pleasant room. Under the guidance of a skilled moderator, these people will discuss the product category of interest to the advertiser. Out of the focus group's relaxed discussion, the advertiser may learn more about consumers' attitudes and perceptions of a product and brands. The researchers observe the discussion through a one-way mirror. The entire session may be videotaped for later review and analysis.

MURRAY HILL CENTER

Qualitative Research Facility

Beautiful. Efficient.
Competitively Priced.

205 Lexington Avenue
New York, New York 10016
212 889 4777

United States Testing Company's 12 Permanent Mall Centers

★ Seattle

Milwaukee ★
Chicago ★
Philadelphia ★

★ Colorado Springs

★ Wichita

★ St. Louis

★ Los Angeles
★ Mission Viejo

Augusta ★

Houston ★

Daytona Beach ★

You can connect with up to 12 fully **owned** and **operated** central locations with just one call to our Chicago headquarters.

The same call can also connect you with . . .

- Three focus group facilities — Chicago, St. Louis, Colorado Springs
- Experts in advertising claim substantiation research
- Our expanded WATS center

Interviewing Center Facilities

- Full Kitchens Including Freezers and Microwaves
- T-Scope Equipment
- Controlled Track Lighting
- Flexible Display Areas
- Slide and Film Projection
- 3/4″ Cassette VTRs

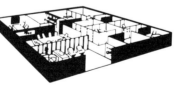

UNITED STATES TESTING COMPANY, INC.

Corporate Headquarters
300 Marquardt Drive
Wheeling, IL 60090
(312) 520-3600

Client Service Office
1415 Park Avenue
Hoboken, NJ 07030
(201) 792-2400

The mall interview catches the consumer in the shopping environment where he or she can be asked to taste products, or to express an opinion regarding product use, packaging, or advertising. A facility with a full kitchen enables prompt, fresh preparation of food products under conditions that resemble home situations.

describe a potential user of our product as a woman between the ages of 30 and 35, with 2.3 children, living in a home with 5.4 rooms and 2.1 baths, with 0.6 dogs and 1.58 automobiles, we do not meet many women like this in real life. Moreover, after our product has been on the market for some time, we may discover that Mrs. A., 32 years old, 3 children, buys our product and, in fact, is quite "brand loyal"—she buys 32 units of our product every month. Meanwhile, Mrs. B., 32 years old, 3 children, buys only 7 units of our product each month; and Mrs. C., also 32 years old, 3 children, same education and income level as Mrs. A. and Mrs. B., does not buy our product at all — in fact, will not even try it. Why? Obviously, the notion that we will know our target market after we have segmented it by means of clearly discernible demographics is deceiving.

In order to understand the consumers in our target market better — to understand what makes the difference between users of our product and non-users, between heavy users and light users — we must begin to probe the *reasons why* they buy particular products. This is the subject matter of **motivation research.** By applying the techniques of psychology, sociology, and anthropology, motivation researchers attempt to explain *what makes consumers react to various products and different appeals.* In many cases the consumers themselves are not aware of the reasons for their reactions, or they are unwilling to reveal them. Under carefully controlled conditions, however, researchers may be able to obtain information on the whys of people's purchasing behavior by using projective techniques and depth interviews.

Projective techniques are based on the idea that, although individuals may be unable or unwilling to describe their own feelings in a particular situation, they may do so *indirectly* by ascribing to others the emotions or attitudes that underlie their own reactions to a product, idea, or situation. The procedures used include the Thematic Apperception Test (TAT), picture-association test, word association and sentence completion tests, and other psychological devices calculated to get the respondent to *act out* the idea.

In **depth interviewing,** researchers encourage respondents to freely express their ideas on subjects that are important to the area being researched. The procedure is slow and expensive. Some researchers use a **focus-group** interview, working with a group of five or six consumers who will speed the process and perhaps even generate more information as a result of their interaction with each other.

Psychographics

Every day each of us is bombarded by a tremendous number of advertising messages; yet at the end of the day we will remember only one or two of these appeals. The others will have vanished from our consciousness as if we had never seen or heard them. We have protected ourselves from being overwhelmed by this flood of product information by a process psychologists describe as **selective perception.** Unconsciously, we filter out words and symbols that we deem unimportant, while allowing those words and symbols we consider important to pass through.

As advertisers, once we understand what motivates consumers in our target market to buy, we must supply the copywriters and artists who create our advertising message with detailed information on the words, signs, and symbols that effectively stimulate this purchasing behavior. Otherwise, there is a very real danger that the personal values of our creative staff will dominate the advertisements they create. As a result, our advertising may impress the advertising community but leave the consumer unaffected.

In the attempt to supply creative personnel with all the information they need to create effective advertising, advertising agencies and research firms have developed methods of obtaining psychographic data. **Psychographics** refers to the development of psychological profiles of several different types of "typical" consumers and their life-styles. A consumer's *life-style* is a distinctive pattern of activities, interests, and opinions that often cannot be deduced from other demographic data.

Psychographics had its origins in motivation research and later attempts by psychological researchers to relate these personality variables to product choice. Psychographics may serve to explain and predict consumer behavior when demographic and socioeconomic analyses are not sufficient. Psychographic variables may include *self-concept, life-style, attitudes, interests, and perception of product attributes.* The first national probability sample study of psychographics conducted by *Holiday* magazine showed a strong positive correlation between life-style and self-concept. People who went out often were also heavy buyers of new products. They thought of themselves as more imaginative and more outgoing than others.[1]

The measurement of personality traits is very complex. A trait is a relatively enduring tendency in an individual to respond a certain way in all situations.[2] To measure these traits, researchers administer interviews, tests, scales, and, when possible, direct observation of an individual's behavior.

Scales are psychological tests that are generally divided into three types: agreement-disagreement (or approve-disapprove), rank order, and forced choice.[3] In the *agree-disagree scale* the subject reports his or her reaction to each item by agreeing or disagreeing. Typical items might be:

I believe it is very important to keep the house spotless.
I believe it is necessary to place the needs of the children before
     my own. (See color plate 15 for an ad appealing to this attitude.)

The *rank-order* scale is one in which the subject is asked to rank all the items in a series of value concepts. Typical statements might be:

a comfortable life
a sense of accomplishment
equality
freedom
social recognition

The *forced-choice* method requires the subject to choose among alternatives that appear (on the surface) equally favorable or unfavorable. In this way the

[1] Emanuel Denby, "Psychographics and from Whence It Came," *Life Style and Psychographics,* ed. William D. Wells (Chicago: American Marketing Association, 1974), p. 15.
[2] Fred N. Kerlinger, *Foundations of Behavioral Research,* 2d ed. (New York: Holt, Rinehart and Winston, Inc., 1973), p. 494.
[3] For detailed information on personality scales and tests, *see Mental Measurements Yearbook,* 8th ed., ed. O. Buros (Highland Park, N.J.: Gryphon Press, 1978). For much valuable information on the subject of attitudes and behavioral research, *see* Kerlinger, *Behavioral Research;* and M. Rokeach, *Beliefs, Attitudes, and Values* (San Francisco: Jossey-Bass, 1968).

TEST

ROUGH COMMERCIALS

Rough commercials are not the same as finished commercials. Unlike other services that test rough commercials "also" (with a system designed for finished commercials), we test rough commercials *only*. In the past 8 years, we have tested almost 3000 rough commercials for most major ad agencies and 41 of the top 100 advertisers. Rough commercial norms are available.

We are the only service that undertakes both production *and* testing. This gives us a unique insight into the relationship between executional elements and test scores.

WHY DO ROUGH COMMERCIALS NEED A SPECIAL TEST?

Rough commercials are primarily tested to assess their ability to convey the message, compare alternatives and expose major negatives. This calls for a test that provides detailed diagnostics to improve the commercial before going into final production.

Recall scores, which are often used to evaluate finished commercials, cannot always be used for roughs because executional elements which generate recall are often missing at this stage.

WHAT DO WE TEST FOR?

Our test is specifically designed for rough commercials. The key measures are communications, relevance and persuasion. We also provide scores for product uniqueness, competitive strength, and commercial likes and dislikes.

Our system provides more in-depth informa- tion than any syndicated service because the data is derived from viewers who base their responses on what they just saw in the commercial — not a sub sample who "claim" to recall the commercial 30 minutes to 72 hours later.

HOW DO WE TEST?

We test commercials with your target audience through one-on-one interviews at a location of your choice.

It is a monadic test where the respondent is exposed to your commercial without any surrounding program material or clutter. Forced exposure to only one commercial focuses the respondent's attention and provides in-depth reactions to judge and even improve the execution.

WHAT ELSE DO WE DO?

Testing Rough Magazine Advertisements. Our magazine-in-a-folder is available in five different levels of "finish" to test rough magazine advertisements.

Campaign Monitor. A syndicated service to track the performace of television campaigns. It addresses itself to issues of longer term effectiveness and is used to measure penetration and wearout.

Outstanding Campaigns Research. For the past seven years we have been tracking Outstanding Television Campaigns. These lists appear regularly in national media.

Video Production. Complete color studio and sound stage with editing/duplication facilities for animatics, photomatics, and live roughs.

VIDEO STORYBOARD TESTS

107 EAST 31ST STREET, NEW YORK N.Y. 10016, (212) 689-0207

The cost of airing a 30-second commercial on prime time (7 to 11 PM) is around $118,840. The cost of production for a commercial may range upward from $30,000. Together, the preparation and broadcast add up to a large investment. Before making that investment the advertiser can have its "rough" commercials tested — with measures of relevance and persuasion — to assess their ability to convey the message. In addition, this firm will also test magazine ads in rough form.

preference value of the items is determined. For example, the subject may be asked to choose between two paired statements such as:

getting ahead in the world
enjoying the pleasure of the moment

In some forced-choice scales four statements are presented for which the subject indicates high preference or low preference. For example:

conscientious
agreeable
responsive
sensitive

The subject chooses two high-preference words and two low-preference words. Of the four words, two are irrelevant. The subject cannot tell which of the words are irrelevant and which are discriminant of a trait.

Copy Testing

Although we will deal with the problem of measuring advertising effectiveness in a later chapter, it is appropriate at this point to consider the *pretesting* of copy. By pretesting we mean we are testing before the advertisement goes into a magazine or on the air.

Many different methods of pretesting have been developed. We can have rough television commercials, called animatics, shot from a series of drawings of the scenes we want to show. A videotape of the drawings, accompanied by a sound track, can help researchers evaluate the commercial's effectiveness. We

PROFILE

Ernest Dichter

Dr. Ernest Dichter is internationally recognized as the leading exponent and practitioner in the field of motivational research. He is founder of the Institute of Motivational Research and founder and president of Ernest Dichter Associates International, Ltd.

Born and educated in Austria, Dr. Dichter received a Ph.D. in Psychology from the University of Vienna. In 1938, he came to the United States and joined the J. Stirling Getchell advertising agency, where he introduced a new approach in selling Plymouth automobiles for Chrysler Corporation. He found that when married couples were asked who made the decision to buy a car, the men answered, "I did." But when further questioned about how they arrived at a particular choice, the men began to use the plural pronoun "we" in their explanations. This led Dichter to suggest that Chrysler aim some of its advertising at the real decision makers in car buying — women.

Dr. Dichter has developed many psychological and sociological techniques to study consumer buying habits. He introduced depth interviewing into marketing research and adapted numerous clinical techniques to consumer testing. He is the author of numerous books and articles on market research, including *Handbook of Consumer Motivation* and *Motivating Human Behavior.*

His approach to marketing and motivational research is keen and penetrating and he brings a sense of excitement to his work. As he has said:

Any good detective can show you what proper motivational research is. "What's the motive?" Columbo always asks. There must be a motive. He does motivational research. The motive is greed or jealousy or whatever. . . . We do the same thing.

Mr. Goodwrench

Since the early 1960s, General Motors' share of the multi-billion dollar market for automobile replacement parts had been shrinking steadily. Two market research surveys, one commissioned by the National Automobile Dealers Association and one by General Motors itself, indicated that the owners of GM automobiles were not returning to their GM dealers for parts and service. In fact, 72 percent of all GM car owners were going to other companies for parts and service within three years of buying their new cars. In the summer of 1974, the General Motors Parts Division invited 25 of its key dealers to discuss their common problem: stiff competition for service business.

The result was a new marketing program, arrived at with the help of the GM Corporate Service Section and General Motors' advertising agency, D'Arcy-MacManus & Masius. The object of the program was to fight back against Sears, Ward's, K-Mart, and other retailers who had moved into the profitable replacement market for shocks, brakes, and tune-up kits.

The market survey commissioned by the National Automobile Dealers Association had been made by the Harvard Business School, and it cited four main reasons for customer dissatisfaction with dealer service. First, owners said they were treated with indifference. Second, they complained that service work was often not done right the first time. The third reason that they gave was inconvenience — inconvenient service hours, lack of quick service, and lack of alternate transportation. The fourth reason was the belief that GM dealer service was more expensive than that of other companies.

The General Motors Parts Division set up a program that they hoped would increase dealer

service and parts volume by building the belief among GM car owners that GM dealers would provide the best parts and service for their cars. At the same time, the program aimed at instilling an attitude of pride in workmanship among GM dealer personnel to improve the quality of service.

The campaign was centered around a trade character — Mr. Goodwrench — a friendly, believable spokesman who, it was hoped, would help improve the image of GM dealers. The concept was tested by research teams in Minneapolis and Orlando. The research teams found that the GM spokesman was accepted as a me-

chanic whose appearance, as judged by consumer panels, promised experience, friendliness, and trustworthiness.

The next step was advertising in the test cities. Advertisements were placed on television and radio, and in newspapers. The object was to reach 95 percent of all homes in the trading areas as often as possible. Results were very positive — every dealership noted an increase in service business. There was also a noticeable improvement among dealership personnel in their attitude toward their work.

GM used the same advertising strategy in their roll-out (launch) plan, and on March 1, 1977, Mr. Goodwrench was introduced nationally. Ads were placed in *Time, Newsweek, U.S. News and World Report,* and *Sports Illustrated.* Sunday supplements such as *Parade* and *Family Weekly* were used in over 450 Sunday papers. Sixty-second commercials were aired on 1,988 radio stations. Mr. Goodwrench appeared on every television network — ABC, NBC, and CBS — over 646 stations.

How is Mr. Goodwrench doing? Extremely well. In fact, 9 out of 10 GM car maintainers are aware of Mr. Goodwrench. And awareness has been maintained above the 80 percent level since 1980. Research shows that the customer knows who Mr. Goodwrench is.

How is this accomplished? Partly through excellent creative strategy. Good ads have personality. Mr. Goodwrench humanizes the sale of automotive products and services and makes the advertising work harder — by making it easier for the public to remember.

Consistent media exposure also contributes to the maintenance of high awareness levels. Mr. Goodwrench advertising appears in national magazines and on television throughout the year. Magazine ads are read year round in publications such as *Newsweek, Time, Sports Illustrated,* and *Reader's Digest.* Mr. Goodwrench television commercials are aired on major networks featuring college football and basketball, major league baseball, and professional golf. Millions of people know Mr. Goodwrench. That's because General Motors Parts advertising creates 3 to 4 billion advertising impressions for Mr. Goodwrench every year.

The Mr. Goodwrench program is designed to build a positive image of GM dealer service and, thus, improve traffic at GM dealerships. Therefore, heavy emphasis is placed on Mr. Goodwrench promotions at the dealership level — both "in-store" and in local advertising media. These programs are fully integrated with the national advertising effort for Mr. Goodwrench and enable GM dealers to tie-in with service specials of their own. Materials include newspaper ads, radio scripts, posters, banners, and other in-dealership materials.

Attractive permanent signs and other point-of-sale materials are available from General Motors Parts. Quarterly parts and service promotions are also developed by General Motors Parts for use by General Motors dealers.

Mr. Goodwrench started as an idea; an image. The advertising and the efforts of General Motors dealers and General Motors Parts have established Mr. Goodwrench as a strong force in the automotive aftermarket; a positive aid to the selling of service and parts through GM dealerships throughout the country. Research paid off.

Computer-assisted telephone interviewing permits the rapid development of marketing information on a national basis. As the telephone interview proceeds, the trained interviewer enters the data into the computer and the results are available quickly, enabling management to speed marketing and advertising decisions. Careful supervision of the interview process is important to make sure that every interviewer asks the same questions in the same manner.

can also have our print advertisements inserted into copies of real magazines, and then test them for consumer recall. We can do a headline test, showing people several possible headlines and thereby determining which headline seems to have the greatest stopping power. We can do portfolio tests — making up a booklet of several advertisements, showing them to people, and recording measures of appeal, recall, and understanding.

Media Research

The most carefully created advertisement can get maximum results only if we, the advertiser, have made the wisest media selection. Our advertisement must reach the greatest number of prospective buyers at the lowest possible cost. Every newspaper and magazine, every television and radio station, provides data on the size and demographics of the audience it reaches. We must evaluate this information in relation to our product, our market, and our budget. Of course, it is very important to know the *number* of people in the medium's audience, but we would like to know the sex, age, location, income, occupation, and marital status of that audience as well. We also want to know the image projected by the medium itself because that image comprises the environment in which our message must do its job. We shall examine all aspects of media in coming chapters.

One word in closing — we also want to monitor the advertising efforts of our competitors. Fortunately, this information is readily available from a number of syndicated services which provide the advertising schedule for all national advertisers in all well-defined product categories.

Summary

Although we are intent on delivering our advertising message to our target market, we have to remember that our prospective customers may have something to tell us, too. Our prospective customers will deliver their message to us by choosing between our product and its alternatives in the marketplace. The failure rate for new products has been estimated at four out of every five. It is probably higher. Therefore, before our product reaches the marketplace, we must obtain as much information as possible about the people who may buy it. We want to know what products they presently buy, what appeals may be effective in convincing them to try our product, and what media we should use to carry our appeals.

Marketing intelligence can be obtained from two basic sources: *primary data* and *secondary data*. We can obtain much valuable information from secondary sources — from company records or from data that have already been compiled by someone else. We must collect primary data for ourselves. We may do this through observational methods or through survey methods, which include *personal interviews, mail surveys, diaries, telephone interviews,* and *panels.* Naturally, we cannot survey the entire target market; therefore, we must select a representative *sample* of the people we want to reach.

Motivation research and *psychographic profiles* will give us even more data on our target market. From *focus groups, depth interviewing,* and *psychological tests,* we will obtain information that can help us see our prospective customers as individuals, not merely statistical abstracts.

Questions for Discussion

1. Prepare a questionnaire on travel. Your object is to discover themes for travel advertising. Administer the questionnaire to a small sample of people you consider appropriate. Describe the results of your survey. What would be your recommendation for advertising?

2. Why are population figures alone not the best index of market potential? What other information would you want? Where could you find it? Be specific.

3. If you were to be responsible for the advertising of central air-conditioning systems for private homes, what information would you need about
   a. the market;
   b. the media;
   c. the buying appeal?

4. If you were going to advertise a new dog food and wanted to test market the product in two or three cities, how would you select the cities? What information would you need? Where would you find it? Be specific.

5. For a local bank (one office), what marketing intelligence would you need to prepare an advertising plan? Where would you find the information you need? Be specific.

6. The manufacturer of a new shampoo wants to name the product. How would you go about selecting the name? How can you be sure the name would be well received by consumers?

7. Suppose you were hired as an advertising consultant to an importer of French and Italian racing bicycles. What information would you need to prepare an advertising program? Where would you get the information you need? Be specific.

____Marketing Intelligence Reference Guide____

Government Sources

Directory of Federal Statistics for States, Government Printing Office, Washington, D.C. 20402

Sources of State Information and State Industrial Directories, Chamber of Commerce of the United States, 1615 H Street, NW, Washington, D.C. 20006

Statistical Abstract of the United States, Superintendent of Documents, U.S. Government Printing Office, Washington, D.C. 20402

Publication Sources

American Newspaper Publishers Association (ANPA), The Newspaper Center, 11600 Sunrise Valley Drive, Reston, VA 22091

Advertising Age, 740 Rush Street, Chicago, IL 60611

Editor and Publisher Market Guide, 575 Lexington Avenue, New York, N.Y. 10022

Magazine Publishers Association, Inc., 575 Lexington Avenue, New York, N.Y. 10022

Radio Advertising Bureau, 485 Lexington Avenue, New York, N.Y. 10017

Sales & Marketing Management Survey of Buying Power, 633 Third Avenue, New York, N.Y. 10017

Television Bureau of Advertising, 485 Lexington Avenue, New York, N.Y. 10017

Private Information Sources

A. C. Nielsen Co., Nielsen Plaza, Northbrook, IL 60062

The Arbitron Company, 1350 Avenue of the Americas, New York, N.Y. 10019

Burke International Research Corporation, 420 Lexington Avenue, New York, N.Y. 10017

The Conference Board, 845 Third Avenue, New York, N.Y. 10022

Emhart-Babic Associates, Inc., 120 Route 9W, Englewood Cliffs, N.J. 07632

Home Testing Institute, 900 W. Shore Rd., Pt. Washington, N.Y. 11050

Starch INRA Hooper, Inc., 566 East Boston Post Road, Mamaroneck, N.Y. 10543

W. R. Simmons & Associates Research, Inc., 219 East 42nd Street, New York, N.Y. 10017

Sources and Suggestions for Further Reading

Bass, Frank M. "The Theory of Stochastic Preference and Brand Switching." *Journal of Marketing Research* (February 1974).

Bogart, Leo, and Charles Lehmann. "What Makes a Brand Name Familiar." *Journal of Marketing Research* (February 1973).

Boyd, Harper W., Jr., Ralph Westfall, and Stanley F. Stasch. *Marketing Research.* 6th ed. Homewood, Illinois: Richard D. Irwin, Inc., 1985.

Brown, Barbara, I. "How the Baby Boom Lives." *American Demographics* (November 1984).

Burger, Phillip C., and Barbara Schott. "Can Private Brand Buyers Be Identified?" *Journal of Marketing Research* (May 1972).

Cooke, Ernest F. "Why the Retail Action is East of the Mississippi." *American Demographics* (November 1984).

Dichter, Ernest. *Handbook of Consumer Motivation.* New York: McGraw-Hill, 1964.

Dunn, William. "Selling Books." *American Demographics,* vol. 7 (October 1985), no. 10.

Granger, C. W. J., and A. Billson. "Consumers' Attitudes Toward Package Size and Price." *Journal of Marketing Research* (August 1972).

Hare, William. "The Best Metros for Blacks." *American Demographics,* vol. 8 (July 1986), no. 7.

Holbert, Neil. *Advertising Research.* Monograph Series #1. Chicago: American Marketing Association, 1975.

Kraft, Frederic B., Donald H. Granbois, and John O. Summer. "Brand Evaluation and Brand Choice." *Journal of Marketing Research* (August 1973).

"Marketing to the Affluent." *Special Report, Advertising Age* (March 13, 1986).

Martineau, Pierre. *Motivation in Advertising.* New York: McGraw-Hill, 1957.

Morrison, Bruce J., and Marvin J. Darnoff. "Advertisement Complexity and Looking Time." *Journal of Marketing Research* (November 1972).

Nesbit, Marvin, and Arthur Weinstein. "How to Size Up Your Customers." *American Demographics,* vol. 8 (July 1986), no. 7.

Newman, Joseph W., and Richard A. Werbel. "Multi-variate Analysis of Brand Loyalty for Major Household Appliances." *Journal of Marketing Research* (November 1973).

"Social Trends and Moods Affecting the Purchasing of Products and Services Today." *Consumer Currents* (Spring 1984), published by Advertising to Women, Inc.

"Teenagers in the 1980s," published by Y & R Media Research (April 1984).

Wells, William D., ed. *Life Style and Psychographics.* Chicago: American Marketing Association, 1974.

6 THE ADVERTISING BUDGET: INVESTMENT OR EXPENSE?

What Is the Advertising Budget?

How Management Philosophy Affects the Advertising Budget
   The "Expense" School of Thought
   The "Investment" School of Thought
The Upper Hand on the Bottom Line
   The Controllers
   The Marketing Executives
The Advertising-Sales Relationship
   Advertising Is Postpurchase Reassurance
   Advertising Wins Dealers

Methods of Setting the Advertising Budget

The Objective, or Task, Method
Matching Competitors — the Share-of-the-Market Method
Percentage-of-Sales Method
Take Your Choice
Influence of the Product on the Appropriation
   Stage in the Product's Life Cycle
   Type of Product
   Favorable Primary Demand
Some General Guidelines for Budgeting

Time to Set the Budget

Budget Periods and Flexibility

What Belongs in the Advertising Budget?

Working Vocabulary

budget	**share-of-the-market**	**fixed sum-per-unit method**
reassurance value	**method**	**empirical method**
objective, or **task, method**	**percentage-of-sales method**	

A famous company president once said: "Advertising, to me, is really one of the mysteries of American business. . . . I can figure my taxes, estimate my depreciation, determine my sales cost, derive my return per share. Yet there are times when I spend as much as $18,000,000 a year on advertising—and have no idea what I am really getting for my money."

Rosser Reeves
Reality in Advertising

Once we have made the decision that advertising will be a component of our promotional mix, we cannot simply sit back in our chairs and begin dreaming up ideas for our campaigns. Instead, we must sharpen our pencils and go back to work, seeking the answers to a new set of questions.

1. How much advertising will we need to achieve our agreed-upon *marketing* objectives?
2. How much can we *afford* to spend on advertising and still achieve the agreed-upon *profit* objective?
3. Can we compromise: can we accept less advertising and still achieve our marketing objectives or our profit objective?
4. How much advertising should we devote to each of our company's individual products or to each group of products?
5. How much advertising should we devote to our new products and how much to our established products?

The answers to these questions will guide us in making one of the most difficult advertising decisions: the setting of our advertising budget.

What Is the Advertising Budget?

In business management, a **budget** is the dollar representation of planned activities over a specified period of time. The advertising budget is a single dollar figure that represents a company's total planned advertising investment, including any reserve for unforeseen expenses. The advertising budget is usually set for a one-year period and contains a detailed breakdown of the advertising activities that the company will spend its money on during that year. In other words, the advertising budget describes proposed advertising activities in terms of dollars.

The benefits of such long-range planning are obvious. It forces advertising and marketing executives to carefully review past and/or proposed results of the company's advertising effort, and it provides management with a standard against which they can judge current performance.

How Management Philosophy Affects the Advertising Budget

A company's top management is generally concerned only with setting budget *totals*. The question of how the total advertising budget should be divided among the company's different products is usually left to the discretion of the company's marketing executives. Those questions are considered mere details that can be cleaned up by less than top management.

In setting the total budget for advertising, top management will consider the company's advertising effort in relation to the company's profit objective.

For most companies that advertise, a fundamental goal is to increase profits. Among many business executives there exist two schools of thought on how their company's advertising budget relates to their company's profit objective. One school believes that advertising is an expense; the other believes that advertising is an investment. The attitude of a company's top management is important because, in any year, profits can be increased by reducing expenses or by increasing sales volume, or market share. As background to our discussion of how top management sets the advertising budget, we should first examine the philosophies of these two schools.

The "Expense" School of Thought   Management that belongs to the "expense" school believes that their company's advertising, if any, should be kept to a minimum. They begrudge every penny the company spends on advertising. When they must cut expenses, advertising is one of the first things to go. It is an easily reducible expense — that is, cutting back on advertising will not have an immediate impact on the company's operations. Telephone service is an expense, too, but cutting back drastically on the use of telephones will have a dramatic impact on the way the company does business.

The "Investment" School of Thought   Management that belongs to the "investment" school believes that advertising is an investment, and, like any investment made by the company, should have a predictable rate of return. In their minds, advertising is similar to an investment in bonds or in shares of stock. They feel that devoting a certain amount of money to advertising will yield a certain percentage of increased sales volume. Unfortunately, advertising does not lend itself to this sort of evaluation. As we learned in chapter 2, advertising is only one component of the marketing mix. It is not possible to determine how much of the result of a given marketing program is attributable to advertising alone, because it is difficult to isolate the effect of advertising from such factors as product quality improvements, price changes, or competitive changes. The investment school's attitude might be compared to that of a health food enthusiast who claims that wheat germ mixed with yogurt will make one healthy. Wheat germ and yogurt will *contribute* to a person's health as a component of a program including a balanced diet, adequate rest, and exercise. So, too, will advertising contribute to the success of our marketing program.

The Upper Hand on the Bottom Line

When it is time for a company to set its budget for the coming year, the question of how much money is to be budgeted for advertising may be fiercely debated by representatives of the investment and expense schools of thought. Let us examine the reasoning of members of each school of thought and their methods for setting the advertising budget.

The Controllers   Controllers, or financial vice-presidents, are not necessarily enthusiastic about allocating monies to achieve an unpredictable result. Some consider advertising an expense, and their method of setting the advertising budget may be referred to as the "leftover" technique. In simplified form, their method of arriving at an advertising budget is as follows: First, they add up what they consider to be the company's necessary expenses. These include administrative expenses, research and development costs, interest on borrowings, and taxes. Then, they subtract the total of these necessary expenses from the company's estimated gross profit for the coming year, as based on projected sales volume. This gives them a figure for the company's net profit. From the net profit, they subtract the dividend that the company's board of directors wants to pay stockholders. Whatever is left over can be budgeted for advertising. It is really a very simple method, requiring only the most ordinary arithmetical skills for which a pocket calculator may be substituted. Some controllers do not appreciate the fact that there *may be* a correlation between the advertising budget and sales volume.

The Marketing Executives   In contrast, the company's marketing vice-president believes that there is some relationship between advertising

Who advertises where and how much do they spend? *Leading National Advertisers* (LNA) Multi-Media Service reports enable an advertiser to see what the competition is doing. The reports cover advertising expenditures in the categories of consumer magazines, newspaper supplements, network television, spot television, network radio, outdoor, and cable television. The reports are published quarterly in three formats (see examples on right): class/brand ad expenditures in each medium, company/brand ad expenditures in each medium, and ad dollar summary. LNA also provides a monthly service that details brand advertising by magazine (see sample below) — the LNA Magazine Analysis Service. The LNA Magazine Analysis Service is also available on-line.

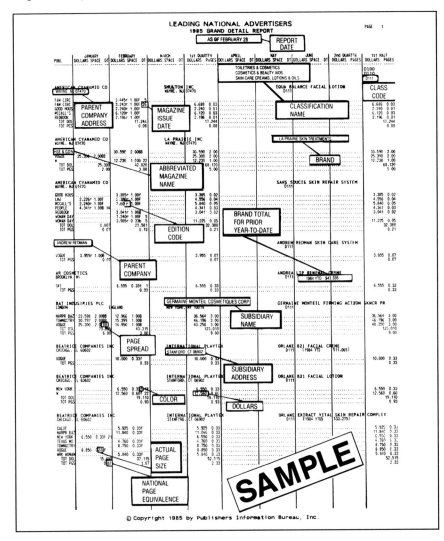

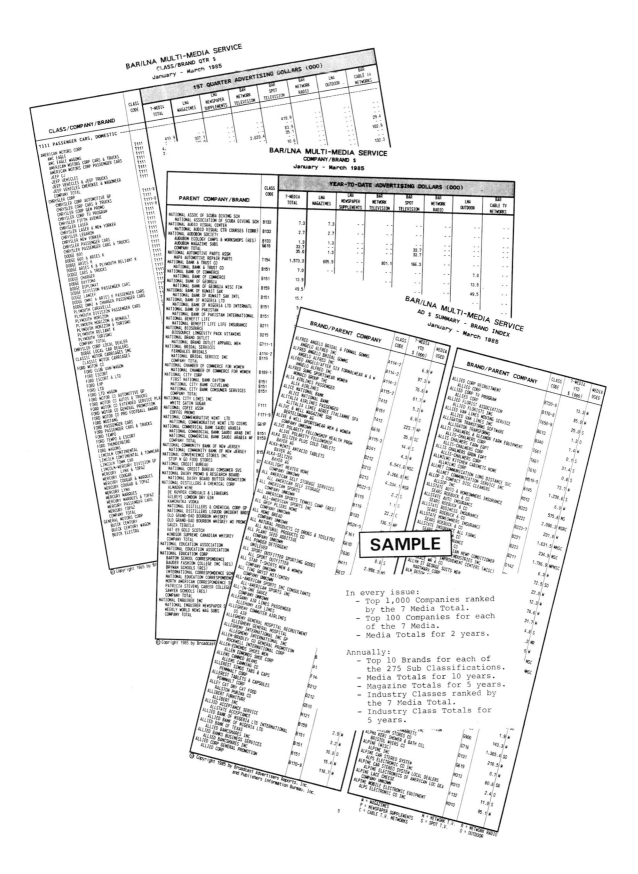

SAMPLE

In every issue:
- Top 1,000 Companies ranked by the 7 Media Total.
- Top 100 Companies for each of the 7 Media.
- Media Totals for 2 years.

Annually:
- Top 10 Brands for each of the 275 Sub Classifications.
- Media Totals for 10 years.
- Magazine Totals for 5 years.
- Industry Classes ranked by the 7 Media Total.
- Industry Class Totals for 5 years.

expenditures and sales volume. The marketing executive wants to increase the company's profit by increasing sales volume rather than by decreasing expenses. In setting the advertising budget, the marketing vice-president relies on a method that might be termed the "intuitive" technique. This method relies on the judgment of the company's marketing executives. These executives are familiar with the company's past advertising expenditures and past sales volume. They reason thus: If next year we hope to increase our sales by 10 percent, we should also increase our advertising expenditures by 10 percent. In other words, a 10 percent increase in the advertising budget should yield a 10 percent increase in sales. These marketing executives also take competitive activities into consideration. If, they reason, one of our competitors is spending 5 percent more than we are now on a sales volume no greater than our own, we had better increase our appropriation by an additional 5 percent — no, make it 10 percent — in order to offset the competitive factor.

Executives who think in this way *assume* there is a relationship between advertising expenditures and sales volume, but they really *do not know.* Some critics of this technique say it is nothing more than guessing. It is. If we did know that every *x* dollars' worth of advertising would produce *y* dollars in sales, all we would have to do to achieve unlimited sales is continue to increase our advertising budget.

Some controllers do not credit advertising with any productive role, however, and do not recognize any relationship at all between advertising expenditures and sales results. Marketing executives like those described above recognize the existence of a relationship, but have made no attempt to relate advertising expenditures to the attainment of specific objectives. Let us attempt to determine just what the relationship of advertising to sales is.

The Advertising–Sales Relationship

The value of advertising lies in its ability to persuade a sufficient number of prospects to do what it says or to buy what it sells. Much advertising is designed to assist the sales force. It makes it easier for a salesperson to sell consumers something at some future time. Advertising on radio and television, the food pages in newspapers, and the array of ads in magazines are all designed not to make a sale but to make the prospect *aware* of a product or a service, *to stimulate interest, to develop desire,* and *to secure an inquiry or "lead,"* thereby making it possible for the actual sale to be consummated at some other place and time.

Of course, today in so many buying transactions the salesperson has disappeared. Self-service is the practice. Here advertising fills a critical role. It preinforms and presells customers to such an extent that when they enter the place where the purchase will actually be made — the supermarket, for example — the necessity for personal salesmanship has entirely disappeared. Advertising, then, works six ways to help make sales:

1. Advertising makes the prospect familiar with the product.
2. Advertising reminds the prospect about the product.
3. Advertising brings news of new products.
4. Advertising adds a value not intrinsic to the product.
5. Advertising reassures and helps retain present customers.
6. Advertising increases the confidence and enthusiasm of the people engaged in the marketing process of that product.

Advertising Is Postpurchase Reassurance   Research into advertising indicates that consumers read the advertising for a product *after* they have bought it as carefully as they do *before* they buy it. This is particularly true with regard to major purchases such as an automobile or a major appliance. Having made a serious buying decision, the buyers want reassurance that they have acted wisely and bought well. They find that reassurance in the advertising for the product. There they find a reaffirmation of the values that induced the purchase in the first place. The continued appearance of advertising for that product is testimony to the wisdom of the buyers. They are, therefore, very likely to buy the same product again when the need arises.

Few businesses can operate successfully without sales to customers who are satisfied enough to repeat their purchases. This **reassurance value** is one of advertising's most important contributions to sales. The postpurchase impact of advertising explains in large measure why no major advertiser ever stops or sharply curtails advertising.

Advertising Wins Dealers   Retailers find their image enhanced by the brands they sell. It is difficult to imagine the disorientation consumers would feel if they entered a supermarket and found no familiar brands. The chances are they would do little, if any, shopping in that store. Therefore, retailers prefer to stock well-known, fast-moving, nationally advertised brands. Shelf space is at a premium. Retailers are most reluctant to make room for an unknown brand. Once again, we see the relationship between advertising and sales. A company must invest in advertising to build an effective distribution network. Without a network of dealers, sales would be unobtainable.

We have examined two procedures for arriving at the advertising budget. Today, most knowledgeable executives are aware of the relationship between advertising and sales. At the same time, they know that it is impossible to isolate the effect of advertising on their company's sales volume. As advertisers, we must approach the problem of budget allocation in a businesslike manner. We want to protect the profits that are the concern of the company controllers and presidents, and, at the same time, we want to make a sufficient investment in advertising to ensure the growth and stability of our company. We must balance need against affordability.

Methods of Setting the Advertising Budget

We can develop our advertising budget in several different ways. We can ask ourselves:

1. How much money must we spend on advertising in order to meet our marketing objectives? (The **objective,** or **task, method.**)
2. What does our nearest competitor spend on advertising? (The **share-of-the-market method.**)
3. What percentage of sales, or what percentage of the price of each unit we sell, should we set aside for advertising? (The **percentage-of-sales method.**)

The Objective, or Task, Method

In this method, we define the budget as a plan to achieve certain marketing objectives, and use advertising as a tool to achieve them. What must we

Task Method Budget Form			
Objective	Subobjectives	Strategy	Budget
Increase number of inquiries	1. From retailers 2. From consumers	Trade advertising Print advertising	$ 25,000 $100,000
Improve image	1. As a modern company 2. For a quality product	Television advertising Publicity program	$500,000 $ 60,000
Stimulate sales volume	1. For purchase of larger sizes among present users 2. For new tries	Television advertising Newspaper coupons Cooperative advertising and dealer aids	$100,000 $100,000 $ 50,000

Although the data used to fill out this form are fictitious, the task method can be used to determine the advertising budget for any company or product line. In addition to the advertising objectives listed, a company might have the hiring of more people for its sales force as an objective. In order to hire more salespeople, the company has to find and interview applicants. Advertising could be used to draw applications and to improve the image of the company in order to help its recruiters on college campuses.

spend to have a program adequate for the job? We begin by stating our objectives: What do we want our advertising to do? *Stimulate* leads for the sales force? *Force* a level of brand awareness among a specific group of consumers? *Force* distribution of our product through particular channels? Once these goals are set, we can go on to determine how many ads in which magazines or how many commercials on which radio or television stations it will take to stimulate the leads or force the distribution we seek. If the selection of the type and quantity of advertisements is the art of advertising, then budget development is the science, because clearly defined objectives make measuring the effectiveness of the advertising much more accurate.

Of course, once we have determined the final costs, management must decide if the company can afford them. If the company is not able to invest the amount of money called for in our plan, then we must determine which of our objectives can be modified or sacrificed to bring the budget within reasonable limits. In any case, the task, or objective, method precludes hasty judgments.

Advertising managers are generally in agreement that, in theory, the ad budget should be determined only after the objectives have been approved and the program for achieving these objectives has been worked out. However, most of them find that, in practice, management has strong views on how much the company can "afford" to spend on advertising, either in dollars or as a percentage of either total sales revenues or total marketing costs.[1]

Matching Competitors — the Share-of-the-Market Method

A simple way for us to establish our advertising budget is to take the budget of a company that already has a market share and match those figures or exceed them. We assume that our competitor must be doing something right

---

[1] Saul S. Sands, "Setting Advertising Objectives," *Strides in Business Policy,* National Industrial Conference Board, no. 18 (1966), p. 15.

to have achieved its market share, and that it has learned from experience what its promotional mix should be. The concept is intriguing but hardly sound management. Of course, we should consider the competition in calculating our budget, but we must keep in mind the fact that their figures are derived for *their* company, with *their* objectives — and *before* we came on the scene. Now it's a new ball game.

Percentage-of-Sales Method

Nothing could be easier than to take a specific percentage of the sales of our product and apply that sum to advertising. What percentage? The percentage can be based on the industry average or on the percentage the company applied the preceding year. The use of the industry average is an excellent guide if the *range* of percentages that compose that average is not too large.

But even if the range is small, there are other pitfalls that we must avoid. Imagine an industry in which the top spender uses 6 percent of sales for its advertising budget, while the stingiest uses 1 percent of its sales. We can take a mean percentage and spend 3.5 percent of our sales on advertising. But suppose the industry in our example is the computer industry, and the stingiest spender is International Business Machines Corporation? Even with only 1 percent of their total sales from computers budgeted for advertising, IBM will no doubt have a lot more money to spend than our 3.5 percent will allow us. We have to consider the other companies in our industry in terms of their profitability, their length of time in the industry, their market share, and their marketing objectives.

The basic strength of the percentage-of-sales method is that it recognizes that a relationship exists between advertising and sales. The basic weakness is obvious: *We are basing the budget for this year's advertising on last year's sales.* If our sales were up sharply last year owing to certain market conditions that may or may not have been within our control, we would have loads of money to spend. On the other hand, if sales were down sharply, also for reasons that may have been beyond our control, we would have less to spend, perhaps at a time when we need more. We must remember that the market is dynamic and that products change, as do customers and their tastes.

The **fixed sum-per-unit method** is a variation of the percentage-of-sales method. A specific number of dollars (or cents) for each unit produced is allocated to the advertising budget. The same criticisms may be applied to this method that were applied to the percentage-of-sales method: That is, we have not considered the individual advertising *requirements* for our particular product, and we have made our assessment based on *last year's* sales or production. The fixed sum-per-unit method (also called the *unit-of-sales* method) is not truly formulated to meet the challenges of a dynamic business world.

Take Your Choice

If all the methods we have described have weaknesses, which method is best? The reply to that question is that there is no single best method. Most companies use a percentage-of-sales method, and that method appears to work. Many companies use the fixed sum-per-unit method, and this method is particularly suitable for determining cooperative budgets. For example, if the manufacturers of cotton fabrics were to combine their efforts to stimulate the sale of cotton apparel and linens, each member might contribute *x* cents per yard or per pound or per whatever unit amount would be most convenient for all. The manufacturers of new products can also use this method by basing it on *anticipated* sales. Of course, to a degree this is merely an educated guess, and, if optimistic, the result may be more money budgeted for advertising than is needed. If pessimistic, however, the budget may be inadequate and thereby become a self-fulfilling prophecy.

One method that has been suggested for determining an optimum advertising budget is an **empirical method** based on trial and error. The idea of the method is to advertise at varying levels of expenditure, using the same medium in different test cities to see if sales results will vary with the level of advertising. After a series of such trials, the most productive level of advertising expenditure should be readily identifiable.

There are several flaws in this concept. The first is that any sales results will be entirely attributable to the advertising. The second flaw is that there are variables that can cause a difference in results between one test city and another, no matter how carefully we try to match cities in terms of demographic characteristics. Finally, although the tests use the same *type* of medium, there may be differences in the impact of *specific media* in the different test cities.

Our ultimate choice of a method will depend on our company's objectives, its financial capabilities, and its philosophy of management. But perhaps most important of all, our choice of method will depend on our company's product.

Influence of the Product on the Appropriation

Stage in the Product's Life Cycle   It takes substantially more advertising money to launch a new product than it does to keep an old one going. Most companies do not expect to make a profit during the introductory period of a product's life cycle. During that period advertising dollars should come from capital rather than from income, as should all the other costs that are incurred in getting a new product ready for market.

Type of Product   As the table on page 131 shows, there are wide variations from product to product in the percentage of sales invested in advertising. To what can we attribute the variations? An examination of the table reveals that products more capable of being differentiated seem to justify a greater advertising investment. Products that are sold primarily on the basis of price do not justify the expenditure of many advertising dollars to create a brand preference in consumers. Price is relatively unimportant for *Soaps and Detergents* but is an important factor for *Industrial Chemicals*. Note that the figures in the chart are *averages* and may themselves include wide variations.

Favorable Primary Demand   Advertising intended to stimulate *brand preference* is much more effective if the product classification is in demand. No matter how many millions of dollars we spend on advertising our brand of 78 RPM records, we shall never succeed in substantially increasing our sales because most turntables manufactured today do not play records of this type.

Advertising as a percentage of sales varies widely — from 0.2 percent for petroleum ▶ refining to 21.1 percent for phonograph records. Consumer goods traditionally show higher ratios than do industrial or business goods, but even among consumer goods there is a wide range. Keep in mind that variations may be caused by what items different firms consider to be part of the advertising budget, and data gathered from advertisers in several industries may represent an average.

Advertising-to-Sales Ratios 1983

	Advertising as % of Sales
FOOD PRODUCTS	
Food & kindred products	4.9
Meat products	2.2
Dairy products	3.5
Canned products	5.3
Flour & other grain mill products	2.3
Bakery products	1.8
Malt beverages	7.3
Distilled rectified beverages	6.6
Bottled and canned soft drinks	5.9
TOBACCO PRODUCTS	
Cigarettes	4.5
Cigars	4.3
TEXTILE MILL PRODUCTS	
Textile products	1.4
Floor covering mills	1.2
APPAREL PRODUCTS	
Apparel & finished products	3.5
MANUFACTURERS OF FURNITURE & FIXTURES	
Household furniture	1.9
Office furniture	1.3
PAPER	
Paper products	0.9
PRINTING & PUBLISHING	
Newspapers	2.3
Periodicals	3.5
Books	4.5
CHEMICALS & ALLIED PRODUCTS	
Chemicals	1.3
Industrial inorganic chemicals	9.2
Plastic materials & synthetic resins	1.1
Ethical drugs	8.4
Soap & other detergents	7.4
Paints, varnishes & lacquers	2.6
Perfumes, cosmetics, toilet preparations	9.0
PETROLEUM & COAL PRODUCTS	
Petroleum refining	0.2
Paving & roofing materials	1.5
RUBBER & MISC. PLASTICS PRODUCTS	
Rubber & misc. plastic products	1.5
Footwear, except rubber	3.0
STONE, CLAY & GLASS PRODUCTS	
Glass containers	1.3
Pottery & china	1.5

	Advertising as % of Sales
FABRICATED METALS	
Heating equipment & plumbing fixtures	2.1
MACHINERY & EQUIPMENT	
Farm & garden machinery & equipment	1.2
Metalworking equipment	2.9
Computers, mini and micro	5.0
Computers, mainframe	1.3
ELECTRIC & ELECTRONIC EQUIPMENT	
Household appliances	2.5
Radio, TV sets & home entertainment	3.5
TRANSPORTATION EQUIPMENT	
Motor vehicles & car bodies	1.6
Truck & bus bodies	.5
Motorcycles, bicycles & parts	1.9
MISC. MANUFACTURING INDUSTRIES	
Jewelry & precious metals	3.5
Musical instruments	2.5
Toys, games & sporting goods	6.7
Pens & other writing instruments	5.5
Phonograph records	21.1
COMMUNICATIONS	
Radio – TV broadcasts	3.7
CATV companies	2.0
RETAILING	
Lumber	2.3
Department stores	3.1
Variety stores	2.1
Grocery store chains	1.3
Automotive dealers & supplies	1.4
Women's ready-to-wear	2.1
Shoes	1.6
Furniture stores	6.8
Household appliances	5.4
Restaurants and eat-in places	3.2
Mail-order houses	17.1
FINANCIAL	
Savings & loan	0.5
Consumer finance	1.6
Financial service	3.1
MISC. SERVICE INDUSTRIES	
Hotels & motels	2.6
Personal & family services	5.9
Motion picture production	9.5
Educational services	4.7

Source: AD$ FORECASTS, 8th ed. Copyright © 1984 by Schonfeld & Associates, Inc., 2550 Crawford Ave., Evanston, IL 60201.

Some General Guidelines For Budgeting

The guidelines for ad expenditures, listed below, are based on research by the Strategic Planning Institute of Cambridge, Massachusetts, a nonprofit organization dedicated to the advancement of strategic business management. SPI manages the PIMS (Profit Impact of Marketing Strategy) database, which consists of over 200 corporate members that provide data. By analyzing their business experiences, the PIMS staff discovered some general "laws" that determine what marketing strategies produce profit results.

In order to provide business managers with answers to the question, "How Much to Spend on Advertising," Cahners Publishing Company analyzed data from PIMS. These are the ten guidelines they suggest:[2]

1. Higher market share typically requires higher ad expenditures.
2. Higher new product activity typically requires higher ad expenditures.
3. Faster growing markets typically require higher ad expenditures.
4. Lower plant utilization typically requires higher ad expenditures.
5. Lower unit price typically requires higher ad expenditures.
6. Products that represent a low portion of customers' purchases typically require higher ad expenditures.
7. Premium-priced products and discount-priced products typically require higher ad expenditures.
8. Higher quality products typically require higher ad expenditures.
9. Broad product lines typically require higher ad expenditures.
10. Standard products typically require higher ad expenditures.

Time to Set the Budget

Budgets are usually set for one year at a time. For large advertisers whose fiscal year coincides with the calendar year, budget preparation often starts in July. Preparation begins so far in advance of the end of the year because it may take months to work out and revise the details of all the various allocations. In addition, advertisers must be particularly careful to have their budgets completed in time to meet deadlines for media commitments. To place an advertisement in the March issue of a consumer publication, advertisers must order the space they need in December, and supply the publication with copy or artwork for the ad in early January. Therefore, budget preparation can hardly take place in a flurry of activity during the last few weeks of the year.

Budget Periods and Flexibility

Advertisers can maintain budget flexibility by monthly planning and by relating expenditures to objectives. In most instances, the changes that take place during the operational year will involve a *reduction* in budget. However, to take advantage of opportunities for which *additional* funds might be needed, a certain amount for contingencies—not earmarked for any specific purpose—would be included in the total budget.

Top management wants to know how the company's money will be spent. Therefore, we should itemize our budget by products, by markets, and

---

[2] Cahners Publishing Company (Boston: 1984).

New Car Market Shares in the United States 1985*

	Regis., 12 Mos., 1985	Percentage Share of Market
Chevrolet	1,577,349	14.48
Ford	1,364,829	12.53
Oldsmobile	1,067,881	9.81
Pontiac	785,098	7.21
Buick	851,031	7.82
Mercury	515,895	4.74
Dodge	425,755	3.91
Chrysler	371,292	3.41
Cadillac	301,228	2.77
Plymouth	324,257	2.98
Lincoln	164,295	1.51
AMC	128,318	1.18
GENERAL MOTORS	4,582,587	42.09
FORD MOTOR CO.	2,045,019	18.78
CHRYSLER CORP.	1,121,304	10.30
AMC	128,318	1.18
IMPORTS	3,011,132	27.65
MISC. DOMESTIC	248	0.00
TOTAL	10,888,608	

* *Automotive News* analysis of new-car registrations, based on R. L. Polk & Company statistical report. Oklahoma figures from manufacturers' sales records.

Reprinted with permission from *Automotive News.* Copyright © 1986.

We note from the table on page 131 ("Advertising-to-Sales Ratios") that the advertising ratio for automobiles is 1.6 percent of sales. If we look at the sales volume for the various brands, we can understand that it is possible for a firm with a larger share of the market to spend a smaller percentage than a firm with a much smaller share. For example, Chevrolet held a 14.48 percent share, while AMC held 1.18 percent. If each firm were to budget an equal percentage, Chevrolet would have far more dollars to invest in advertising. Under such circumstances, it is not illogical to assume that AMC invests a slightly larger percentage of sales in order to maintain, and hopefully improve, its position in the new car market.

by objectives. We should break down costs by individual projects so that if we must make cuts in the course of the program, executives in the organization will be able to cut projects, not merely dollars. Monthly planning is also an indication to management that the advertising program is flexible, designed to meet changes in marketing conditions, and adaptable to fast-breaking situations.

Sometimes we may have to revise our budget to bring total costs within the limits dictated by management. The amount of money available may be restricted by other, more critical, financial needs.

Once our budget has been approved, it is the job of the advertising manager to supervise expenditures so that costs remain within the amounts specified. The advertising manager's supervision of the budget would certainly

Perrier

How do you market a sparkling water from France when there are any number of well-known brands and dozens of private-label store brands? The fact is that the club soda and mineral water business has been declining about 5 percent a year, while the seltzer category (no sodium) has been growing 25 percent annually. (The still-water category is not considered competition because they are, for the most part, inexpensive and sold in areas that have problems with poor-tasting or contaminated tap water.)

Perrier has been around, literally, for ages, but came on strong in the United States about ten years ago. Source Perrier established its own subsidiary here called Great Waters of France. Perrier quickly became the 'in' drink. Drinking Perrier is chic — it makes a statement about the drinker.

Perrier could not compete with domestic sparkling waters on price, so it had to project an image of quality and prestige. It has both. A major factor in its success has been the interest in health and fitness. Perrier is salt-free. (An interesting note in the marketing of soft drinks in

PERRIER.
EARTH'S FIRST SOFT DRINK.

When the earth was new, mountains rose and valleys were
carved and there was created, in what is now called France,
a spring that is now called Perrier.

MUSIC THROUGHOUT.
CAVEMAN: Eh?

SFX: SLURPS...

SFX: KISS SOUND.
CAVEMAN: C'est magnifique!
Un miracle!

ANNCR: Sparkling, refreshing

Perrier. Created by the earth
when it was new.

Perrier, Earth's First Soft Drink.

PP45   © 1982 Great Waters of France Inc., Greenwich, Conn. 06830 recent years has been the stress advertisers place on the ingredients they don't contain rather than what they do.)

In any case, Perrier quickly built sales to around $60 million by the late 1970s. As might be expected, success brought competition—a parade of rival imports as well as all the domestic brands of club soda, seltzer, and plain bottled water. Tastes, like fashion, had also changed, and the company had to sell the product on its merits, not its value as a status symbol. In 1980, Great Waters of France commenced a new campaign for Perrier—"Earth's first soft drink,"—which extolled the quality and purity of the product—a clear, sparkling drink that is an alternative to sweet soft drinks or alcohol. In 1981, they shifted media from television to magazines because they believed that Perrier consumers are better educated, watch less television, and read more. Has the campaign succeeded? Yes. Sales of Perrier by 1984 approached the previous high of $60 million, and 1985 sales increased by 50 percent. (See color plate 17.)

BEFORE MAN
HAD HYPERTENSION,
HE HAD SALT-FREE
PERRIER.

In the good old days there was lots to be tense about. The Ice Age was coming. You might be run over by a mammoth. Your cave might cave in on you. But no one suffered from high blood pressure.

Why? First, because you could work out all your anxieties by pounding rocks, chewing animal skins and running around a lot in the fresh air.

Second, because the salt-shaker had yet to be invented.

If you were really lucky, you lived near the Perrier spring, somewhere in the south of France. Because that sparkling fresh and salt-free refreshment was just the thing after a hard day's hunt. It was earth's first soft drink.

Today, civilization has introduced such amenities as canned soup, pickles, soy sauce and high anxiety. The combination of all these might very well have led to modern hypertension and all kinds of civilized problems.

But down through the ages, Perrier has kept its innocence, freshness and happy taste. And best of all, Perrier is still naturally salt-free.

Perrier. Earth's First Soft Drink.

© 1982 Great Waters of France, Inc. Exclusive Importers

include the use of cost estimates; and controls over media schedules and contracts as well as expenditures for materials and services; a system to assure that all goods and services have been provided as specified and paid for promptly; and a method for comparing actual costs against budget estimates.

What Belongs in the Advertising Budget?

If we are going to judge the effectiveness of the advertising appropriation, we want to be certain that the budget does not include costs for activities that are not directly related to that effectiveness. In some firms, the advertising budget becomes a catchall for expenses that cannot be classified elsewhere. For example, is the cost of a pair of tickets to the World Series for a good customer an advertising expense? Hardly. Here is what properly belongs in the advertising budget:

1. Paid advertising space and time in all recognized media
2. Literature intended to perform a selling function, such as brochures, circulars, catalogs, and package inserts used for advertising, not for directions on product use
3. The salaries and operating expenses of the advertising department

PROFILE

William Bernbach

Perhaps advertising would have reached new creative heights in the 1950s and 60s even without William Bernbach, but since 1949, when he and Ned Doyle and Maxwell Dane founded the Doyle Dane Bernbach agency, advertising has never been the same. William Bernbach is credited with having started a revolution on Madison Avenue.

He believed that there was far more power in a simple message that was artfully and provocatively stated than in a loud and cluttered presentation. His belief that advertising should be uncluttered and built on simple ideas led him to create such successful advertising as the "Think small" campaign for Volkswagen and the "We try harder because we're only number two" campaign for Avis Rent-a-Car. He has also created well-known campaigns for such clients as Polaroid, Levy's Jewish Rye Bread, Mobil Oil, American Airlines, and Colombian Coffee.

A native New Yorker, William Bernbach at-tended New York University. After service in the Army during the Second World War, he became a copywriter, soon rising to become vice-president in charge of art and copy at Grey Advertising Company. When Doyle Dane Bernbach, Inc., opened its doors in 1949, it had only $500,000 in billings, but by 1985, the agency had grown to $1.729 billion in billings with a network that covered 17 countries, in which DDB had an interest in 16 other advertising agencies. Major accounts in the United States include H. J. Heinz, IBM, ITT, Philip Morris, Polaroid, Volkswagen, and Seagram.

In recognition of his creative contributions to the advertising industry, William Bernbach received numerous awards, including the Parsons School of Design Diamond Jubilee Award for "his creative contribution to the graphics communications industry." In 1977, he was inaugurated into the Advertising Hall of Fame.

GUESS WHAT ROSE EVEN HIGHER THAN MALCOLM'S BALLOON THIS YEAR?

Our press pickup. In fact, it soared. A record 10,100 clips in the first six months of this year. Far higher than Forbes and Business Week combined. Just like last year. Shouldn't your advertising be in a magazine that doesn't just report news, but makes news?

FORTUNE
REQUIRED READING
FOR THE BUSINESS CLASS.

SOURCE: Burrelle's Press Clipping Service (excludes general FORTUNE 500 clips).

100% FAT FREE.

The lean new look of Nation's Business is all business.

Every element of the streamlined editorial format is designed to help you manage your business more effectively. By describing the newest management theories and techniques. By profiling people and performance more intimately. By translating the impact of government into more precise opportunities for business.

And by doing it more quickly and more efficiently.

No fat. All lean meat. That's Nation's Business. The business magazine that works as hard as the people who read it.

Nation'sBusiness

Now you can advertise in The Wall Street Journal on the weekends.

There's only one way you can advertise in The Wall Street Journal on the weekends because there's only one "weekend edition" of The Journal. It's The Wall Street Journal Report on Television.

Employing a network of over 85 stations in 74 major markets, The Wall Street Journal Report on Television is the perfect complement to your existing Journal advertising and an ideal medium on its own. Like its printed namesake, The Wall Street Journal Report on Television offers the same authority and comprehensiveness to its advertisers.

If you'd like to see your advertising message in this formidable environment, call Art Pickens (Dow Jones) at 212-285-8212 or Bill Koblenzer (Syndicast) at 212-921-5091.

W.S.J THE WALL STREET JOURNAL REPORT
On Television

Business publications compete vigorously for a share of the budget that advertisers use to reach the lucrative business-to-business market. These ads appeared in an advertising business publication. (Also see color plate 16.)

4. Fees paid to advertising agencies, writers, artists, and for other ancillary *advertising* services
5. Mechanical costs involved in the preparation of advertising material such as photography, typography, artwork, engravings, radio transcriptions, television films, etc.

Some of the many items that may be charged against the advertising budget but do not belong there include: cartons, labels, packaging, house organs, sample portfolios for the sales force, company stationery, charitable contributions, annual reports, display signs on the factory building, premiums, showrooms, and booths at trade shows.

Summary

A company's advertising budget is a plan that defines its proposed advertising activities in dollar amounts. The budget is usually set for one year. Although advertising costs are listed as an expense on a company's balance sheet, today most executives are aware that advertising can more properly be viewed as an investment. They know that advertising will influence their company's sales, and therefore its profitability.

There are four principal methods in use for determining the amount of money to allocate to advertising. These are: the objective, or task, method, the share-of-the-market method, the percentage-of-sales method (and its corollary, the unit-of-sales method), and the empirical method. These classifications of the approaches to budget determination are useful only as a general guide, however. There will always be certain arbitrary elements factored into any budgetary decision. Marketing and advertising requirements vary greatly, for example, as a product moves through its life cycle. A new product may call for much higher levels of advertising than are needed for an established product. The degree of product differentiation probably has the greatest influence on the need for advertising dollars: a well-differentiated product being able to achieve a positive market share more easily, and with fewer dollars, than one with little to distinguish it from the competition.

If a company decides to allocate a certain percentage of its sales to advertising *(percentage-of-sales method)*, it still has to determine the exact percentage to use and what items to include in the advertising budget. This method also has a major weakness in that its future advertising needs are being based on its *past sales.* This same weakness also exists in the *unit-of-sales method,* by which an advertiser allows a certain amount of the sale price of each unit of its product for advertising.

The activities of competitors have an important influence on the need for advertising dollars. Fewer advertisers arrive at their final appropriation without being very mindful of competitors' levels of appropriation. In fact, some companies set their appropriation by merely matching or exceeding the budget of a competitor with a similar market share *(share-of-the-market method)*. However, this method does not take into account the unique strengths and weaknesses of each company.

The specific goals assigned to advertising during the budget period will also influence the size of the advertising appropriation. To *increase* market share may require more dollars than to maintain market share. The budget needed to win *new* users may be substantially greater than that needed to increase frequency of use or size of purchase among present users. The expense of introducing a new product, of shifting people's buying habits, or of providing them with the information they need to evaluate the new product, will be considerably greater than the cost of maintaining a mature product's share of the market. Determining how much money the company must spend to achieve each of its advertising goals *(the objective method)* is probably the most effective way of setting its advertising budget.

The dollar level for advertising may also be influenced by the profits we expect to generate. A high volume of sales may support a larger advertising appropriation because it generates a greater amount of revenue to finance the appropriation. Nor can the appropriation decision be separated from the long-range profit picture of the firm. A company operating with a high fixed cost may find that extra advertising will increase sales so that the fixed costs are spread over a larger number of units, thereby reducing the per-unit cost. Under such conditions, increased advertising expenditures may be well-justified. Every advertising budget will ultimately be reflected in the profit and loss statement, no matter what the nondollar goals of advertising may be.

Questions for Discussion

1. What is an advertising budget? What purpose does it serve?
2. What are some of the ways advertising contributes to the achievement of sales volume?
3. The advertising budget as a percentage of sales tends to be lower for industrial products than for consumer products. Why do you think this is so?
4. In what ways might cyclical fluctuations in business affect the advertising budget?
5. What relationships exist between marketing intelligence and the advertising budget?
6. What budget procedure would you recommend for
   a. a new prescription drug
   b. a household plant food for regional distribution
   c. a line of children's sweaters?
   Justify your recommendations.
7. What is the role of sales forecasting in the preparation of the advertising budget?
8. Why do opportunities for product differentiation make such a difference in the advertising budget?

Sources and Suggestions for Further Reading

Aaker, David A. *Advertising Management.* 2d ed. Englewood Cliffs, N.J.: Prentice-Hall, 1982.

Dirksen, Charles J., and Arthur Kroeger. *Advertising Principles and Problems.* 6th ed. Homewood, Ill.: R. D. Irwin, 1983.

Donnermuth, William P. *Promotion: Analysis, Creativity and Strategy.* Boston: Kent Publishing Co., 1984.

Dunn, S. Watson. *Advertising.* 5th ed. Chicago: Dryden Press, 1982.

Kleppner, Otto. *Otto Kleppner's Advertising Procedures.* Englewood Cliffs, N.J.: Prentice-Hall, 1983.

Sachs, William. *Advertising Management: Its Role in Marketing.* Tulsa, Oklahoma: Penn-Well Publishing Company, 1983.

Sandage, Charles Harold. *Advertising Theory and Practice.* 11th ed. Homewood, Ill.: R. D. Irwin, 1983.

Stansfield, Richard H. *Advertising Manager's Handbook.* Chicago: The Dartnell Corp., 1982.

Work Book for Estimating Your Advertising Budget. Boston: Cahners Publishing Company, 1984.

7 ADVERTISING MEDIA: AN OVERVIEW

Working Vocabulary

medium	durability	cumulative audience
nonmedia advertising	coverage	schedule
cost effectiveness	circulation	flighting
cost per thousand (CPM)	secondary circulation	blitz schedule
selectivity	reach	bunching
flexibility	duplication	insertion order
frequency	gross audience	

The salesman in the Sumerian market place of 3,000 B.C. had three advertising media: his voice, perhaps a few tricks and his merchandise display. . . . Today, the advertising agency has such a wide range of media that planning an advertising campaign for a new product requires a tremendous amount of judgment, experience, and research.

G. Allen Foster
Advertising: Ancient Market Place to Television

The media offer us *reach*—the opportunity to communicate with people who are the target market for our product. The responsibility for the effectiveness of any advertising program is shared by both the advertising message and the medium that carries it. The ability to nurture a *favorable customer attitude* toward a product is a shared responsibility. The ability to *stimulate action* on the part of the individual consumer is a shared responsibility. And the ability to develop *additional sales* of a product is also a shared responsibility. It is important, therefore, that we study the characteristics of each of our partners in the advertising process.

Looking at the Media

A **medium** (singular of "media") is a vehicle that conveys information or entertainment to the general public. People buy, subscribe to, turn on, or tune in a particular medium for the informative articles or the entertaining programs contained in that medium's format. At the same time, each medium is used as a vehicle to distribute commercial messages. The newspapers that we purchase at the newsstand for news of the world, the magazines that we subscribe to for news of sports events, the radio stations we turn on for music, and the television programs we tune in for news or entertainment—these are all vehicles for advertising.

We have omitted transit and outdoor advertising from our general description of media because, although advertising people generally refer to them as media, they are not media in a true sense. They do not have either editorial or program formats. No one turns to, buys, or subscribes to the posters in a bus or a train. No one purposefully seeks out billboards along the highway (unless they want to know how far it is to the next Howard Johnson's). However, outdoor and transit are considered media by advertising professionals and are therefore included in this chapter and in subsequent discussions of media.

The general categories of advertising media are shown in the table below.

PRINT	Newspapers		Magazines		
	Daily	*Sunday*	*Consumer*	*Business*	*Farm*
	Weekly	Sunday supplements	General interest	General	National
			Special interest	Industrial	State or regional
			Demographic	Trade	Agricultural
			editions	Professional	product
				Institutional	

BROADCAST	Radio	Television	TRANSIT	OUTDOOR
	Network	*Network*		
	Spot	*Spot*		

Not included in the table is **nonmedia advertising** — persuasive communications that, instead of being transmitted by one of the media, are distributed through the mails or by various other means — everything from stuffing the advertisements into mailboxes and under front doors to handing them out on street corners.

Media Strategy

The media strategy is part of the marketing plan. The broad media decisions are:

1. What general category of available media will serve our advertising needs best?
2. Which individual medium in each category will provide the best vehicle for our advertising?
3. What combination, or mix, of media might we use?
4. What would be the best specific schedule for the appearance of our advertisements in each of these media?

Media Selection Factors

With an appropriation for media expenses in hand, we are faced with the problem of allocating the budget among the various categories of media, and then among the specific media in each category. Our first decision — what general category of available media will serve our advertising needs best? — is influenced by several factors. Among these are (1) cost, (2) the nature of our target market, (3) our product distribution pattern, (4) our product itself, (5) the objectives of our advertising program, and (6) such special media characteristics as editorial environment, flexibility, frequency, and durability.

Cost

The most important consideration when comparing media is cost. Media charges, in fact, are usually the largest single item in advertising budgets. Our concern is *not* with absolute cost, but with **cost effectiveness** — that is, with the ability of the medium to deliver our advertising message to the largest number of prospective customers at the lowest possible price. Some of the media number their audiences in the millions, but not all of these people will be prospective customers for our product. A medium with a small audience that has a high concentration of product users is a more economical buy than another medium with a much larger audience but a much lower percentage of prospects.

One simple ratio used frequently for comparing media charges is **cost per thousand,** usually abbreviated as *CPM.* For print media, the formula for determining CPM is:

$$\text{CPM} = \frac{\text{cost of 1 black and white page} \times 1{,}000}{\text{circulation}}$$

For broadcast media, the formula is:

$$\text{CPM} = \frac{\text{cost of 1 unit of time} \times 1{,}000}{\substack{\text{number of homes reached by} \\ \text{a given program or time}}}$$

When data are available from the medium detailing the demographic characteristics of its audience, advertisers can replace total circulation or audience figures with figures for the specific market segment they want to reach. For example, if a particular magazine had a total circulation of 50,000 and charged $500 for a single page, black and white advertisement, its CPM would be $10. But, if the advertiser only wanted to reach males over 35 years of age, and a detailed analysis of the magazine's circulation showed that it reached 14,000 men in this demographic segment, the advertiser could derive a new CPM. The CPM based on this figure would be: $500 \times 1,000 \div 14,000$, or $36.

Matching Media and Market

To increase the cost effectiveness of our advertising, we must attempt to match the profile of our target market, supplied to us by our marketing intelligence system, with the demographic characteristics of a given medium's audience. If our product is cigars, for example, our marketing intelligence may tell us that our target market is men 35 to 70 years old. Therefore, we might consider placing our advertisements in a special-interest magazine that appeals to an all-male audience. But, even if we were to choose a magazine with a 100 percent male audience, part of this audience would consist of younger men (18 to 34), part of the audience would be nonsmokers, and part of the audience would be addicted to cigarettes and would rather fight than switch. We are still paying for a large amount of waste circulation. But at least by placing our advertising in a men's magazine we have held the waste to a minimum. (See color plate 18 for an all-male target market advertisement.)

Some media—such as network radio and television, general-interest consumer magazines, and newspapers—offer us the means to transmit our advertising message to a cross section of the consumer market. They appeal to people of all income levels, ages, sexes, and occupations. Other media—such as spot radio and television, special-interest magazines, and business and farm publications—offer us **selectivity:** the ability to aim our appeal at a distinct target market or a particular area of the country. As part of their effort to sell us time or space, the media themselves will supply us with a great deal of information on the demographic characteristics of their audience. More specific details can be obtained for a fee from media research organizations such as the Arbitron Company and W. R. Simmons & Associates Research.

Matching the Distribution Pattern

The previous example of an all-male target market is one of *class selectivity,* class being an abbreviation for demographic classification, such as sex, age, marital status, and occupation. We will find, however, that the subscribers to the men's magazine in which we have considered placing our advertisements are scattered throughout the country. If we only distribute our cigars on a regional basis, many of the men who are stimulated to buy our product will find that it is not available in their local stores. These men will add to the amount of waste circulation that we must pay for. We may find, therefore, that we would like to obtain a degree of *geographic selectivity* as well as class selectivity.

It is often difficult for regional or local manufacturers to find a magazine that will reach only the limited geographic area in which their product is distributed. It is difficult—but not impossible, now that more national con-

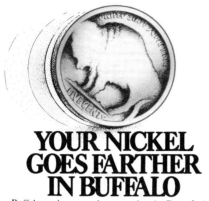

This advertisement by *The Buffalo News* is in advertising and marketing publications. It informs ad agencies and prospective advertisers about the size of the market and the way the newspaper reaches that market. This ad is one of a series that tell about the various categories reached by *The Buffalo News,* such as new car buyers, people who travel, and food shoppers.

sumer magazines offer demographic editions. But, unless the demographic edition is distributed only in areas that coincide exactly with the manufacturers' areas of product distribution, there will always be some waste. Local radio and television, newspapers, transit, and outdoor media provide exceptional opportunities for geographic selectivity. They can be used to carry our message to certain states, to certain counties, to certain cities, and even to specific neighborhoods within the cities.

Matching Medium and Product

The nature of our product will also exert an influence on our choice of medium. Perhaps our product requires demonstration. Only television offers us the ability to transmit both sound and motion. Perhaps color is an important aspect of our product's appeal. The high-quality color reproduction available in magazines is superior to that offered by television. In chapters 8 – 12, we will discuss the unique advantages and limitations of each of the categories of media.

Media Selection Factors **145**

Houston Magazine is top dog among Houston's top executives.

Houston Magazine fetches more Houston executives more efficiently than any other local publication.

Compared to Houston Business Journal, Houston Magazine has a greater paid circulation* (18,771 vs. 18,038), lower page rate ($1,160 vs. $1,350) and more efficient CPM ($61.80 vs. $74.84). Plus the great reproduction advantages of coated stock over newsprint. And the longer life of a monthly magazine over that of a weekly newspaper. If you want to collar more executives and dig up a more efficient buy, just give us a whistle.

Houston
MAGAZINE

1100 Milam 25th Floor
Houston, Texas 77002
Call Mike Marshall, (713) 658-2412

* Audit Bureau of Circulations, Dec. 31, 1982

In addition to the competitive benefits *Houston Magazine* lists in this ad — circulation size, page rate, and cost-per-thousand (CPM) — it stresses the longer life of a monthly over a weekly. What counterclaim might a weekly magazine make? What advantages should a daily claim? *Houston Magazine* describes its readers as 59.7 percent in top management, 69.7 percent college graduates, median age 46.4, and with an average household income of $100,862. Certainly a very upscale market. It claims a readership of 3.14 readers per copy.

Advertisers of consumer products of an intimate nature may not be able to use certain types of media for fear of offending portions of the public. Although media in general have become more broad-minded, some media still do not accept advertising for certain products. Television stations will not accept whiskey or cigarette advertising; neither will some publications. Even more important, the image of the product may be enhanced or distorted by certain publications or broadcast programs. Stock brokerage companies do not advertise in *Playboy* magazine, or in the entertainment section of a newspaper, or during a Saturday-morning children's television program.

Program Objectives

The objectives of the advertising program also influence media selection. A company that wants to build an "image" with an institutional campaign might use high-quality television programs to carry primarily institutional messages. It might also use general-interest magazines to carry the same messages, even if it would not find such magazines the best vehicles for its product advertising. The General Motors advertisement on page 7 is a good example of this type of promotion.

Special Media Characteristics

Editorial Environment   The editorial content of some media can be an important consideration in our analysis. Some media command great loyalty from their audiences, particularly radio and television programs that feature popular local personalities, disc jockeys, and commentators. Similarly, the authority and prestige of certain publications can lend greater impact to the advertisements that appear in them.

Flexibility and Frequency   A very broad comparison of media can be made on the basis of **flexibility** — that is, the speed with which changes can be made in the advertising schedule. If we would like to advertise our snow tires just as the first snow of winter hits, we will find this much easier to do through newspaper or local radio advertising than through a consumer magazine. Why? With a newspaper or radio station, we can schedule our ads to run on the day or even within hours of the first snowfall. With a magazine, our ads may run only within a week or a month of the first snow. Flexibility may not be important for some products, but it is critical for others.

Frequency is another time-related characteristic of any medium. **Frequency** refers to the number of times we can present our message to an audience within a fixed period of time. Radio is a high-frequency medium; we could have our commercial aired several times every hour if we could afford it. Newspapers offer us lower frequency: once a day or once a week. Magazines offer even lower frequency: weekly, monthly, or even quarter-annually.

Durability of the Message   The **durability** of the message — that is, the potential for a single delivery of a message to be seen or heard again after the initial delivery — is a characteristic of certain media. It is not critical, except where repetition would help strengthen the selling impact of our message. Clearly, the broadcast media do not offer us durability. Our message appears or is spoken and then vanishes. The viewer or listener cannot refer to it again. Daily newspapers, on the other hand, offer some durability, and weekly magazines offer even more. The greatest durability, however, is offered by monthly magazines that the reader will pick up and read several times during the life of each issue.

Retail Impact   Another factor we must consider is the importance of a given medium in the minds of the retailers and wholesalers who are responsible for the distribution of our product. Advertisers often feature their national consumer advertising schedules prominently in their trade advertising. In this way they hope to convince retailers that it is to their advantage not only to stock but to push a nationally advertised brand.

Measuring the Medium's Audience

As we compare media types according to such characteristics as class and geographic selectivity, we will also consider the size of each medium's audience. Data on audience size are available from a number of different sources

S&MM's SURVEY OF TELEVISION MARKETS

												EFFECTIVE BUYING INCOME	RETAIL SALES	

| STATE S&MM/ARBITRON TV MARKET (ADI) | Total Pop. (Thous.) | Total House-holds (Thous.) | Black Pop. (Thous.) | Spanish-Origin Pop. (Thous.) | \multicolumn{6}{c}{Population by Age Group (Thousands)} | Total EBI ($000) | Total Retail Sales ($000) | Buying Power Index |

STATE S&MM/ARBITRON TV MARKET (ADI)	Total Pop. (Thous.)	Total House-holds (Thous.)	Black Pop. (Thous.)	Spanish-Origin Pop. (Thous.)	2–11 Years	12–17 Years	18–24 Years	25–34 Years	35–49 Years	50 & Over	Total EBI ($000)	Total Retail Sales ($000)	Buying Power Index
IOWA													
CEDAR RAPIDS-WATERLOO-DUBUQUE	893.7	329.7	13.7	5.3	127.7	84.3	122.6	149.8	148.7	230.7	9,115,500	4,010,926	.3448
DAVENPORT-ROCK ISLAND-MOLINE	878.0	328.9	23.4	25.0	129.5	82.3	98.3	145.2	155.9	237.4	9,624,431	4,117,320	.3559
DES MOINES	970.5	376.3	17.4	8.7	132.0	83.0	123.2	159.7	165.8	276.1	10,377,601	5,090,139	.4005
OTTUMWA-KIRKSVILLE	78.6	29.2	.4	.4	9.9	6.0	11.9	12.2	12.2	24.2	616,412	324,747	.0261
SIOUX CITY	425.8	160.1	1.3	2.7	62.4	37.8	48.8	64.1	67.5	129.9	3,824,607	2,023,186	.1570
KANSAS													
TOPEKA	394.9	145.3	26.7	13.2	53.3	30.8	65.9	68.7	62.7	99.5	4,384,375	2,010,701	.1644
WICHITA-HUTCHINSON	1,099.3	420.0	41.7	33.9	154.4	92.7	131.2	181.4	188.0	313.7	12,916,697	6,350,131	.4901
KENTUCKY													
BOWLING GREEN	104.8	37.2	7.6	.7	14.3	8.7	17.4	17.3	18.3	25.5	860,723	577,080	.0388
LEXINGTON	886.6	314.7	54.4	6.5	132.3	81.6	118.5	155.2	158.5	212.0	7,776,636	4,139,740	.3209
LOUISVILLE	1,409.6	502.3	146.8	10.9	209.9	132.0	171.2	247.0	256.2	347.1	13,751,977	6,882,592	.5451
PADUCAH-CAPE GIRARDEAU-HARRISBURG-MARION	861.6	326.7	53.2	5.4	114.5	72.6	105.8	130.3	147.7	265.8	7,380,595	4,065,801	.3100
LOUISIANA													
ALEXANDRIA	309.9	105.3	66.1	5.2	48.8	30.0	42.3	48.7	52.6	75.5	2,480,450	1,276,391	.1038
BATON ROUGE	763.3	254.2	248.3	13.6	124.5	76.2	110.6	141.6	131.4	149.8	7,458,122	3,825,485	.2972
LAFAYETTE	571.7	194.2	143.4	11.4	95.2	61.4	74.9	92.6	98.0	126.8	5,205,219	3,079,888	.2202
LAKE CHARLES	220.0	76.0	46.2	2.9	35.5	21.8	28.0	37.2	39.9	49.2	2,125,280	1,145,417	.0863
MONROE-EL DORADO	535.1	186.8	179.8	4.9	86.2	52.3	66.7	77.3	87.5	145.1	4,015,397	2,144,666	.1715
NEW ORLEANS	1,782.0	633.6	529.8	60.0	281.6	176.8	224.6	323.1	314.7	395.6	17,536,353	9,647,279	.7134
SHREVEPORT-TEXARKANA	1,231.8	443.4	345.2	20.7	189.8	114.2	134.0	189.9	212.7	348.2	11,341,470	6,010,402	.4626
MAINE													
BANGOR	347.0	123.8	.4	1.1	48.9	32.4	41.7	57.5	61.2	94.9	2,905,762	1,713,877	.1252
PORTLAND-POLAND SPRING	871.2	321.8	2.3	4.0	119.9	80.7	99.8	147.9	154.3	243.4	8,581,853	5,392,690	.3645
PRESQUE ISLE	87.9	29.4	.7	.5	13.7	9.3	11.0	14.5	15.4	21.1	703,327	383,361	.0299
MARYLAND													
BALTIMORE	2,429.2	874.6	591.1	23.8	315.2	230.1	291.2	435.3	469.9	621.1	25,698,240	13,710,370	1.0201
HAGERSTOWN	116.6	41.7	5.1	.7	14.6	10.7	14.0	19.7	21.9	32.7	1,043,303	669,440	.0454
SALISBURY	228.9	84.0	51.9	1.8	29.5	21.1	25.5	36.1	40.9	69.2	2,017,248	1,519,826	.0934
MASSACHUSETTS													
BOSTON	5,469.5	2,017.0	207.8	111.2	687.6	501.9	675.6	967.2	987.9	1,508.8	68,793,523	37,060,628	2.6516
SPRINGFIELD	583.1	211.3	33.4	24.5	72.4	52.3	84.7	95.8	96.9	165.9	6,120,765	3,483,409	.2483
MICHIGAN													
ALPENA	41.9	15.5	.0	.1	5.9	4.4	4.4	5.7	7.7	12.6	356,698	171,059	.0142
DETROIT	4,629.8	1,674.3	908.1	78.5	682.6	446.1	559.7	825.6	848.9	1,125.8	53,052,652	25,063,702	1.9979
FLINT-SAGINAW-BAY CITY	1,267.8	445.9	122.1	30.8	199.9	131.2	158.6	210.0	230.0	294.9	12,351,331	6,308,573	.4916
GRAND RAPIDS-KALAMAZOO-BATTLE CREEK	1,630.4	580.5	98.1	31.9	245.8	154.8	213.9	279.6	286.5	393.9	17,047,873	7,886,466	.6507
LANSING	616.3	215.1	36.1	16.2	90.0	56.1	97.7	116.6	108.3	127.7	6,696,619	3,137,814	.2544
MARQUETTE	158.7	55.5	1.5	.8	21.3	13.3	25.5	25.8	24.4	43.1	1,290,705	554,377	.0515
TRAVERSE CITY-CADILLAC	417.3	153.6	2.6	2.4	59.8	40.9	42.7	65.3	72.3	122.8	3,403,260	1,961,493	.1465

(see, for example, the survey on page 148), including the media themselves, who have their figures verified by independent auditing organizations. Buyers of advertising space or time are understandably concerned with obtaining reliable figures. We need accurate information to guide us in making the second media decision—which individual medium in each general category will provide the best vehicle for our advertising?

Circulation and Coverage

Different media use different methods to measure the size of their audiences. If, for example, we are interested in telling the consumers in Boondock County about our product, this is how the different media there will describe the size of their audiences to us.

Radio and television stations will tell us about their **coverage,** that is, about the number of homes in Boondock County that can receive their stations' transmission signals clearly. One radio station may then claim that 80 percent of the homes in its coverage actually listen to its morning news program, and a television station may claim that the same percentage actually watches its Friday evening movie. Out of all the homes that can *receive* these stations' signals (their coverage), the number of homes that *actually tune in* is their **circulation.**

Newspapers and magazines will also use the term *circulation* to describe the number of copies they sell in Boondock County, either at newsstands or by subscription. The *Boondock Bugle* may have an audited circulation of 80,000 copies, and a national consumer magazine such as *Time* may have 5,000 subscribers in Boondock County and newsstand sales there of another 15,000 copies. These figures represent each publication's *primary circulation.*

Outdoor and transit media in Boondock County will also offer to sell us a certain amount of coverage. Their data on coverage will tell us what percentage of all the people living in Boondock County will pass by or be exposed to all of our outdoor or transit advertising during a 30-day period. For example, they may promise us that during the month of November 200,000 people will drive by our billboard on the outskirts of Boondock City. If the total population of Boondock County is one million, then our billboard gives us 20 percent coverage.

Refining Circulation Data

In describing their circulation, the broadcast media in Boondock County have used the term "homes" or "households." Not all members of a family or household are prospective purchasers of our product, however. Some purchases are indeed "family" purchases. The household collectively establishes

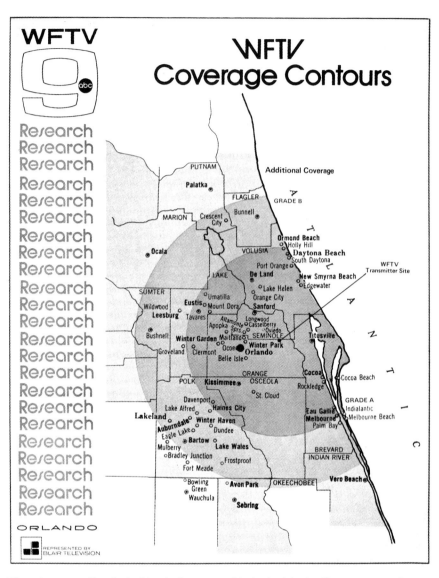

The advantage of local television is the geographical selectivity it offers — we can choose the counties or regions to which our message can be directed. Before we can even consider the number of homes that may be tuned into any station, we want to know the areas in which the station signal can be received — its coverage. Television and radio stations provide advertisers with maps such as this, showing their strongest signal areas (Grade A) and weaker signal areas (Grade B).

buying potential for many products, such as automobiles, washing machines, and color television sets; and the decision to purchase these products may be made by the entire household, though the actual purchase may be made by the family's "buying agent." But most advertisers would prefer to have demographic information on all the individuals in a home or household.

Magazines and newspapers usually describe their audiences in terms of individuals. In addition to data on their primary circulation, however, *Time* and the *Bugle* will also supply us with information on their **secondary circulation,** or pass-along readers. Secondary readers do not purchase or subscribe to a publication, but pick up and read copies in barbershops, beauty salons, doctors' waiting rooms, offices, and libraries. For some publications, pass-along readership can be two to three times greater than their primary circulation.

The Media Mix

Each of the major media has certain characteristics that we must consider before we make the third media decision: What combination, or *mix,* of media might we use? The logical media combination will be arrived at by examining our company's marketing objectives and target market, and then by matching, as far as possible, the gross audience of our media mix to our target market. We say "as far as possible" because, although the ideal combination would be one that reached only prospective customers (no waste), at a low cost, and with maximum impact, we can rarely obtain such an ideal in practice.

Although we will consider each media category in detail in chapters 8–12, at this point we should briefly examine the characteristics of each major class of media.

Magazines offer audience selectivity, durability, editorial climate, high-quality color reproduction, and, in many cases, opportunities for regional coverage.

Newspapers can deliver our message to the target market daily. They offer exceptional geographic selectivity that we can tailor to meet our specific market needs. However, newspapers are not very selective as to audience.

Television's greatest attribute is its ability to provide an active demonstration of our product. Over 94 percent of all the homes in the United States have one or more television sets. This makes television the most efficient means of reaching a large, national audience. If local coverage is an objective, we can buy television time on a station-by-station basis.

Radio's principal advantage is its ability to deliver an advertising message at a low cost per thousand. Its major weakness is its inability to provide a visual presentation of our product. Because radio audiences are so dispersed and fragmented (there are over 6,000 commercial radio stations in the United States), radio is generally considered a supplementary medium.

Outdoor and *transit* can be used on a national basis or on a local basis, depending on the market coverage desired. However, outdoor and transit are, for the most part, nonselective, providing exposure to all economic and social classes.

Reasons for a Mix

As we have said, the media strategy we pursue will be determined by our advertising objectives. If our general advertising objective were to provide leads for our sales force, then our most important criterion for setting our media strategy might be **reach** — that is, the ability to bring our message to as many people as possible. To achieve this goal, we might use a media mix of 60 percent television, 30 percent magazines, and 10 percent newspapers. A percentage of the audience of each of these three media will be people who have not been exposed to our message through either of the other two. If, on the other hand, our objective were to provide important new information, we would want *frequency* — that is, the ability to deliver our message as often as possible within a given period of time. In this case, our choice might be 100 percent television, 100 percent newspapers, or a combination of the two. Both of these media offer us high frequency and large audiences. The most important concept in evaluating a possible media mix is *balance.* Does the mix strike the best possible balance among all the media selection factors that are important to us? Does it offer us a balance between the reach we want and the frequency we want? Between the reach, frequency, and degree of demographic selectivity that we desire? And so on, until we have considered all the factors that are important to us.

Finally, the most important consideration in choosing the proper media mix is cost. Some media are more expensive than others on an absolute cost basis. For example, we might consider allocating half our budget to television and half to magazines, or half to newspapers and half to magazines. Although we are spending the same amount of money — half our budget — on each medium, that money will buy far less in television than it will in magazines, and less in magazines than it will in newspapers. Of course, we must weigh the cost against how well the media type will match the needs of our product and of our market.

A media mix may distribute our budget among various types of media, or it may concentrate our budget on one media type. In recent years there has been an observable trend toward *concentration,* particularly among large advertisers. Concentration offers us the opportunity to obtain great impact on a specific market segment. We may even be able to dominate competitive advertising in one particular medium. Advertising our brand in such a manner will create an impression of its widespread acceptance by consumers across the nation. Furthermore, that impression will carry over to dealers. "Look at the way we back you up," we can say to the retailers who carry our brand. If they are impressed, they may increase their support of our brand. We may be able to obtain preferential positioning on store shelves and to negotiate favorable rates and discounts.

In contrast, some advertisers prefer a widely varied media mix. By choosing an assortment of media, we can deliver different messages about the same product to different market segments. This is of great importance to advertisers who have more than one target market. An advertiser may use Saturday morning television to reach children and *Good Housekeeping* or *Woman's Day* magazines to reach their mothers.

Furthermore, a mix of media enables us to reach the same prospects in different "climates" or editorial environments. The difference in "climate" will help prevent early "wear-out" of our message. "Wear-out" is the time it takes for people to become bored with an ad or commercial.

With a media mix of several different types of media, we can also increase the reach of our message beyond what we can obtain through concentration, since a certain percentage of each medium's audience is not reached by any other medium. When we considered the advantages of concentration, we listed its strong impact. But that impact tends to be uneven. If we concentrate our advertising in television, for example, we reach both heavy viewers *and* light viewers. We are making substantial impact on the heavy viewers but little impact on the light viewers, thus leaving weak areas in our message exposure potential. Since light television viewers tend to be heavy magazine readers, we can level out the imbalance if we devote some of our budget to magazines. But a mix of two or more types of media will require that a larger portion of our budget be invested in the costs of preparing our advertising copy and artwork.

And then, of course, there will be fewer dollars available for time and space. Therefore, advertisers must beware media mixes that spread their budgets too thin.

Duplication

Advertisers who use a media mix are necessarily concerned with duplication. **Duplication** refers to the number of prospects who are reached by more than one of the media in a mix. Many executives who read *Fortune* magazine, for example, also read the *Wall Street Journal.* These executives are counted in the circulation figures of both publications, and the advertiser who buys space in both publications pays to reach some of the prospects twice.

In theory, every advertiser would like to have unduplicated reach among its best prospects, but in practice this may be very expensive, or impossible, to obtain. As total reach of our media mix approaches 100 percent of our target market, any new vehicle we add to it will pick up relatively few new prospects. Most of the cost of advertising in each new medium after this point will be for duplicate coverage.

Data on audience or circulation duplication can be obtained from audience studies made by research firms or by the media themselves. If we know how much overlap there is among the audiences of various vehicles, we can place our advertisements in those media that will provide us with the greatest number of exposures per audience member. This can be especially important during critical periods of an advertising campaign — the months before Christmas, for example. We can analyze many alternative vehicles until we find the best combination in terms of the size of the exclusive audience each medium contributes to the mix.

Gross Audience

The term **gross audience** refers to the total number of people exposed to any or *all* of the forms of advertising used in a single campaign. This may include the audiences for radio and television programs, outdoor and transit displays, circulation figures for various publications, and the number of people attending trade shows. Some advertisers want to know the size of the gross audiences offered by alternative campaigns so that they can choose the mix that delivers the greatest number of exposure alternatives.

The Role of the Media Planner

The media planner has responsibility for making the fourth media decision: What would be the best specific schedule for the appearance of our advertisements in each medium? In working out the fine details of the media schedule, the media planner must seek the answers to such preliminary questions as: How many times shall we deliver the same message to the same audience? During what months or on what days should our advertisements appear? At what location within the magazine or newspaper do we want to place our advertisements? Should our broadcast or newspaper advertisements appear in the morning or in the evening? Media planners use media research and market research, as well as their experience and intuition, to shape the final media plan.

This well-known media research organization will tell any advertiser who wants to know what his or her competitors are doing in 75 different markets. By matching the competition's schedules with Arbitron or Nielsen ratings (measures of popularity or viewing), knowledgeable advertisers can then punch up their own media schedules in weak areas, goad their sales forces into more aggressive action, or do whatever else they think is necessary to meet and beat their competitors.

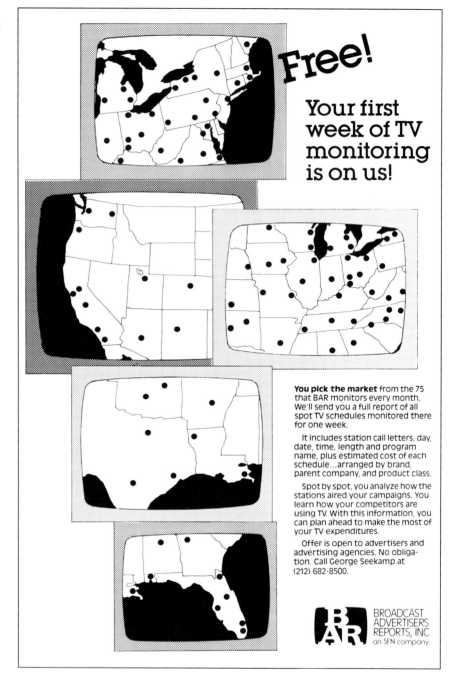
Cumulative Audience

When arranging for a series of advertisements to appear in a single medium, a media planner must take into account the vehicle's cumulative audience, or cumulative reach. The **cumulative audience** is the number of people exposed to the medium over a given period of time. For example, Mr. Smith, Mrs. Jones, and Mr. Cleary may read the November issue of a magazine in which we have placed our advertisement. If we also place our ad in the December issue of the same magazine, that issue may be read by Mr. Smith, Mrs. Jones, and Mr. Cresap. Therefore, although each issue was read by only three people, if we placed our advertisements in both issues, we reached a cumulative audience of four people: Smith, Jones, Cleary, and Cresap. In the same way each episode of a radio or television program will be seen or heard by a certain number of people who did not tune in to the previous episode. For national television shows and for some mass magazines, the cumulative reach of four or five programs may be two or three times that of any single program or issue.

Seasonal Concentration

Because consumers purchase many products only at certain times of the year, it is usually very difficult to persuade them to buy these products out of season. In order to maximize the effectiveness of the media, our advertising should be concentrated at the time when product interest is highest. Temperature and weather conditions affect the sales of many products. Swim suits, water skis, and soft drinks are sold most heavily during the warm summer months. Snow tires, antifreeze, and sleds are sold at the onset of winter. Certain food products tend to be consumed more heavily at specific times of the year. The wide variations in weather and temperature across the nation must also be taken into account.

Holidays are a seasonal variation offering special opportunities for media concentration. The Christmas season, which begins about mid-November and extends almost to December 25, is a period when many products are advertised much more heavily than usual. Toys, gift items, small appliances, and alcoholic beverages are intensively promoted at this time. (See color plate 19.) Other holidays and commemorative days are very important for some products — for example, champagne around New Year's Day; pens, watches, and cameras around graduation time. Mother's Day, Father's Day, and Easter are traditional periods when certain products sell at greater volume than usual. The knowledgeable media planner will take advantage of this kind of consumer interest when arranging media schedules for these products.

Scheduling

Having taken into account the seasonal demand for our product (if any) and the cumulative reach of the media we are using, the media planner determines a schedule for the appearance of our advertisements. This **schedule** shows the number of advertisements that are to appear in each medium, the size of the advertisements, and the dates on which they are to appear. There are many different ways to schedule any advertising program. No single type of schedule is best for all advertisers. Each company must arrange its schedule to suit its market and its advertising objectives. What may be best for one company or product may be bad for another.

For example, an advertiser may decide to buy six pages in a monthly consumer magazine. The media planner may arrange for a one-page advertisement for that firm's product to appear in every other issue of that magazine for a year. Or, the media planner may decide to have a one-page advertisement run in every issue of the magazine for three months, followed by a period of no advertising, followed by the reappearance of one-page advertisements in the next three issues. The latter schedule is a wave strategy called **flighting.** Flighting simply bunches the advertising — in print or broadcast media — to provide a concentrated impact. At the same time, flighting allows advertisers to take advantage of seasonal demand for their products.

Sometimes — particularly for the introduction of a new product or the implementation of a new marketing strategy — a media planner might use a **blitz schedule.** Taking the six pages described in the example above, a media planner might arrange a blitz schedule calling for the insertion of two double-page advertisements in three consecutive issues of a magazine.

One of the more recent innovations in print advertising is called bunching. In **bunching,** several different versions of the same advertisement are run on three to five consecutive right-hand pages of a magazine. Bunching provides concentrated impact within a single issue of a publication.

The Use of Computers in Media Selection

Several years ago many of the largest advertising agencies turned to computers in their search for a more scientific approach to media selection. Much effort (and much publicity) was devoted to the development of models that would enable a load of relevant data to be processed. The computer would then churn out the optimum media selection along with the best media schedule. Computers, alas, merely process data, and much media analysis is qualitative rather than quantitative. Computer technology can certainly be utilized to analyze quantitative data, but the qualitative aspects are subject to many widely differing interpretations. Media decisions continue to require the exercise of experience and judgment.

An insertion order from a well-known agency's New York office to a publication. The ad is a repeat of one previously run, as the line — "Repeat 1985 Ad" — indicates. The space calls for a full page in black and white. Note the admonition to the publication at the bottom. The advertiser's ad is not to be backed up by or to be facing a competitor's ad. And, the ad is not to be backed up with an ad that contains a coupon.

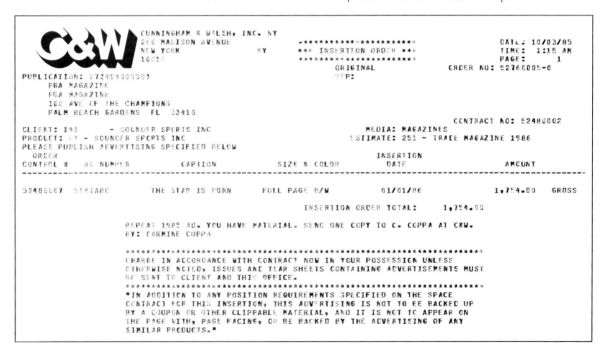

Media Buying Procedures

The actual purchase of time and space is made by the advertising agency's media department or—for the small agency that does not have a department—by the media person. Broadcast purchasing often involves negotiation of rates and schedules. Orders for space in newspapers and magazines are almost always made from the publisher's rate card, which lists the entire rate structure. Once the media buy has been decided upon, a contract will be issued by the agency on behalf of the client to cover the rate and the frequency discounts. Then, when the schedule has been worked out, the agency will issue individual **insertion orders** (see example on page 156) to specify the particular date and space, or time and position, for each advertisement or commercial.

People in Media

Print media are organized somewhat differently from other businesses with which we may be familiar. The publications deliver to the advertiser a not-quite-tangible product—the attention of people, customers and prospects.

PROFILE

John Philip Cunningham

An all-around advertising man, John Philip Cunningham could write copy, draw illustrations, conduct research, select media, and plan campaigns. From the time he graduated from Harvard in 1919 until he retired from the active management of Cunningham & Walsh, Inc. in 1961, he spent his entire life in the advertising business. His first job was as an artist and layout man at the Newell-Emmett agency in New York. Newell-Emmett became Cunningham & Walsh in 1950, at which time John Cunningham was elected executive vice-president. He was elected president of the agency in 1954 and chairman of the board in 1958. In 1985, Cunningham & Walsh was the 24th largest agency in the world, with billings of $340 million.

In 1934, when the agency was appointed to the Texaco account, John Cunningham put on a service attendant's uniform and for two weeks he pumped gasoline and made oil changes in a Texaco service station. He learned at first hand that a clean rest room and cheerful attendants are sometimes more important to motorists than the brand name of the gasoline they buy. From this experience he developed a unique concept for his agency—account executives, artists, and copywriters spent a week a year working in the field for their clients, learning at the point of sale what the consumer wanted. Other well-known accounts on which he personally worked included Johns-Manville industrial products, Sunshine Biscuits, and Chesterfield cigarettes.

John Philip Cunningham worked hard to raise the standards of creativity in the advertising industry. During the Second World War he was active in the creation of advertising campaigns for the Red Cross, the U.S.O., and the United States Treasury's war bond drive. In 1973, he was elected to the American Advertising Association's Hall of Fame—the first living advertising executive to be so honored.

In February 1985, at age 87, John Cunningham died in his sleep while vacationing on St. Croix in the Virgin Islands.

Last year Family Circle made a number of significant improvements.

This year Family Circle made significant improvements in its numbers.

We knew it would happen—and it did. The editorial and design changes we made last year (better inks, better stock, more people-oriented photographs, a more graphic presentation of features) resulted in the great SMRB numbers we just received.

Of course, a major investment in consumer advertising helped, too.

	1983	1984	Change	%
Total Women Readers	16,613,000	17,209,000	+596,000	+3.6%
Women 18-34	5,894,000	6,536,000	+642,000	+10.9%
Attended College	5,366,000	6,138,000	+772,000	+14.4%
Household Income $25,000+	7,625,000	8,397,000	+772,000	+10.1%

We now have the highest number of women readers per copy in our history.[1] Here's how some of the 1984 SMRB numbers break out for an average issue of the world's largest selling women's magazine.

It's nice to know that women noticed what we did—because we did it for them. Now let us do something for you.

FamilyCircle®
The most read women's magazine.*

Source: All figures based on 1983 and 1984 SMRB.
[1] 2.52 women readers per copy.
*1984 SMRB one year accumulated female audience estimates for women's magazines.

NYT A New York Times Company
© 1984 The Family Circle, Inc.

Family Circle is a women's magazine and provides important circulation details, such as the education, income, and age of its readers. The numbers include pass-along readership as well as primary circulation. *Family Circle* expresses its reach as based on 2.52 readers per copy. *SMRB* refers to the Simmons Market Research Bureau, Inc., an organization that issues an annual syndicated survey of media audiences.

So the medium must first sell itself, through its editorial contents, to people. That is the job of the editorial department, of the editors, writers, and artists who create and assemble the articles and illustrations that make up a publication. The circulation department is actively involved in getting as many people as possible to buy the publication, either by subscription or at the newsstand. The job of the advertising department, on the other hand, is to *sell* the publica-

As the ad says, by 1984 *USA Today* had moved to third place in circulation. To potential advertisers this national newspaper provides a demographic profile of its readers: median age 37, median household income $31,441, 62 percent men, 38 percent women. These statistics are meant to be compared with those of the U.S. population as a whole. The advertising rate for a full-page, four-color ad is $28,332. Each issue has a maximum capacity of 48 pages, with a 16-page maximum of color. How is a national newspaper printed and distributed every day? Material is transmitted by Westar III, a satellite located in stationary orbit directly above the west coast of South America. Transmission time is about three and a half minutes for a full black and white page. It is printed in strategically located plant sites all across the country.

tion as an advertising vehicle to advertisers and their agencies. All three of these departments contribute to the success of the publication. However, it is not on the income from subscriptions or newsstand sales, but on the revenue from sales of advertising space, that the publication will make its profit. Without the audience, there would be nothing to sell.

HOW DO YOU *REACH* NEW YORK?

You can reach almost *two-thirds* of all New York newspaper readers with one insertion in New York's Hometown Paper.

NEW YORK'S HOMETOWN PAPER

DAILY◉NEWS

◀ The *Daily News* has the largest circulation of any local newspaper in the United States. Its emphasis in this ad, which appeared in an advertising business publication, is *reach*. Keep in mind that New York City boasts four daily newspapers. Other factors that influence advertisers, in addition to reach or total circulation, are income levels, sex, and shopping habits.

Broadcast sales are simpler, but the principle is the same. It is the program or editorial format of the radio or television station that attracts the audience. That is the job of the producers, directors, writers, announcers, and disc jockeys — to give the station a "personality" that attracts a consistent audience. This consistent audience is "sold" by the station's advertising department to potential advertisers. There is no circulation department to promote purchase of anything — radio and television programs are free. Also, it is very interesting to note the extensive use of the print media (newspapers usually) to boost the audience for a television broadcast and the frequent use of radio to sell magazine readership. Outdoor, of course, has no editorial format. Outdoor advertising companies are known as *plants,* which sell and install, or "post," the available locations.

The largest spending categories are leisure time (fast foods, movies, etc.), auto dealers, supermarkets, banks, department stores. Overall retail use of television for 1985 increased by 12 percent. Personal and health retail services showed the largest percentage increase in television advertising, the two most prominent categories being medical and dental services, up over 40 percent, and legal services, up over 35 percent from the previous year.

Local/Retail Estimated Television Advertising Expenditures 1985 by product classification	
Automotive	$449,628,700
Apparel stores	132,245,500
Business & financial services	273,484,800
Department, discount & variety stores	353,361,800
Drug & food stores	354,298,100
Household services	165,510,600
Household stores	389,408,700
Leisure time stores & services	1,116,053,300
Local media	170,109,600
Medical & health related services	159,414,000
Personal services	71,738,000
Public utilities & fuel dealers	42,846,600
Retail & local stores, other	63,007,600
Retail services, miscellaneous	120,032,200
Political advertisements	22,369,800
TOTAL	$3,883,509,300

Source: Television Bureau of Advertising, from Broadcast Advertisers Reports data on the *top 75 markets.*

CASE HISTORY

Riunite on Ice Is Nice

Imported wines have gone from 15 percent in 1970 to 25.7 percent in 1985 of total U.S. wine consumption. We are talking about millions of cases. And although per capita consumption of wine in the United States may never reach the per capita consumption of many European countries, it was up slightly last year to 2.55 gallons per capita.

For the wine industry, Italy is to the area around San Francisco what Japan is to Detroit for the auto industry. Usually, the public thinks French when they think of imported wine. But France is actually number two, and, as of 1985, Italy is number one. Italian wines have come on strong in the past ten years. We are by now familiar with Folonari, Soave, and Fazi Battaglia (Verdicchio). But the winner is the Lambrusco-type wine — fruity and fizzy. It comes from the Po Valley in Northern Italy. A small, private importer — Villa Banfi, headquartered in sub-

urban Long Island — is responsible in a large measure for the growth of Italian wines in the United States. Their import is Riunite, a wine with an alcoholic content of 8½ percent to 9 percent, compared to 12 percent for most table wines.

Riunite found a niche by offering American consumers, accustomed to soft drinks, just what they wanted: a sweet, fruity, lightly carbonated wine that is served cold. No other wine had come close, except Yago Sant'Gria, which set a record of two million cases in 1974.

Riunite's success must be attributed to marketing savvy. The product matched the public's taste. They dropped the mystique that exists about wine drinking and marketed it as a beverage. Riunite considers its competition to be soft drinks, beer, and iced tea.

Banfi was a small importer of classic Italian wines when it first brought Riunite into the United States in 1967. The name Riunite was derived from Cantine Cooperative Riunite, which translates as United Cooperative Wineries, owned by some 1,000 farmers.

At first, and for many years, the firm did no advertising. The wine was promoted mainly at tastings organized for groups like Knights of Columbus lodges. The principals of the firm, John and Harry Mariani, and Frank Gentile, the sales manager, pushed the distributors to urge the wine retailers to stock the product. It worked. When they started to advertise, they used low-budget ads. Even the radio jingles were prepared inexpensively using, among others, the voice of Harry Mariani and the president of their advertising agency. Subsequently, their advertising became more sophisticated, but they never lost sight of their basic appeal, even when they produced award-winning commercials. (See color plate 20, too.)

Our new ski commercial is a nice way to bring the "Riunite On Ice" story home to your customers!

JINGLE: Riunite. . .

it tastes so fine. . .

Riunite pure and natural wine. . .

Riunite on ice. . .

Riunite so nice. . .

Riunite. . .

Riunite it tastes so light. . .

Riunite so refreshing. . .

and bright. . .

Riunite on ice. . .

Riunite so nice. . .

Riunite. . .Riunite!

The Media Rep

Since most newspapers and radio stations are local in scope, their sales force tends to be limited to home base. But the radio station in Council Bluffs or Wichita Falls wants to solicit advertising from the large national advertisers as well as the local retail business organizations that are its main source of revenue. Out of this need there has developed the media sales representative —an individual or a firm that represents a number of noncompetitive media. Located in major marketing centers, the representative organization or *rep,* as it is called, makes frequent and regular contact with the national advertisers and the agencies responsible for buying time and space. For national advertisers and their agencies, the rep provides a local source of information regarding media in other areas of the country. For example, by contracting one of any number of rep organizations in Atlanta, an agency in that city can obtain current information about newspapers, television, or radio in most other parts of the United States and frequently in Canada.

Summary

If advertisers had unlimited amounts of money to spend, then media decisions would present no problems. But no advertiser, not even the United States Government, has an unlimited advertising budget. Therefore, advertisers (and their agencies) must carefully select the medium or combination of media that will reach the greatest number of prospective customers with their advertising message at the lowest possible cost.

In planning a media schedule, advertisers have to consider several factors in addition to the all-important one of cost. These factors include the nature of their product's target market and its area of distribution, since each medium is aimed at particular demographic and geographic market segments; the nature of their product, since it may require active demonstration (television) or high-quality color reproduction (magazines); and the overall objectives of their advertising program. As they examine the media, advertisers will also consider the length of time people can spend in examining the advertisement *(durability),* the *frequency* with which the medium can repeat the advertisement, and the editorial contents of the medium, because the editorial environment has an important effect on the way in which the audience responds to the actual advertising message.

An advertiser can reach the same audience repeatedly because of the audience's loyalty to their favorite medium—although the advertiser knows that most audiences, particularly those for the mass media, do not buy, watch, or read a medium for the advertisements it carries. Quite the contrary, the advertising is an interruption of the viewer's enjoyment, breaking into the action of the program. Outdoor billboards, car cards, and train posters carry no editorial matter and are neither bought nor requested by their readers. Readers of magazines, for the most part, read them because they are looking for articles that will inform and entertain them. However, special-interest magazines and newspapers are often read as much for the product advertisements as for the editorial contents.

In choosing among the various media available in each media category, advertisers work with circulation figures and costs, with audience research data and market research data. For broadcast media, they measure *coverage,* the number of homes that can receive a station's broadcast signals, and *circulation,* the number of homes that actually tune in. For print media they measure circulation as the number of copies of the publication sold on the newsstand or by subscription. Publications will sometimes emphasize their pass-along readership, or *secondary circulation.* This is the number of people who read a publication without having purchased it.

Balance is the most important consideration for advertisers who place their messages in a combination, or mix, of media. Does the media mix achieve the best possible balance among all the important media selection factors? For example, if timeliness is important, radio or television lend urgency to the advertising message. So do newspapers, and the newspaper message will be longer lasting and permit more reflection on the part of the prospect. If this durability is also an important factor, the advertiser might want to consider a mix of radio and newspapers. If the product requires demonstration, television may be added to the mix. And so on. In using a media mix, however, an advertiser also pays for a certain amount of duplication. A message is reinforced by duplication, but the advertiser may want to trade some of this duplication for greater frequency or more reach.

To analyze all the various combinations of media, some advertisers and their agencies have used computers in the hope of obtaining the optimum prospect exposure. But the computer has proven more useful in performing clerical functions, storing and retrieving large quantities of data efficiently, than in performing analytic functions. In the complex process of weighing both the quantitative and the qualitative factors involved in media selection, the computer has not been able to replace the experience and intuitive judgment of the media buyer.

Questions for Discussion

1. What is the importance of *selectivity* in media planning?
2. How do *reach* and *frequency* relate to each other?
3. What benefits does the advertiser derive from *flighting?*
4. Can you find examples in which media cooperate with one another to boost audience?
5. Newspapers appear to dominate in total media expenditures. How do you account for this?
6. For what classes or types of products would editorial environment be very important?
7. For what products do you think cost might not be the most important factor in media evaluation?
8. Based upon what you learned so far, what media recommendations would you make for
   a. cold cereal
   b. men's deodorant
   c. expensive cigars

Circulation Data

Audit Bureau of Circulations, 900 N. Meacham Rd., Schaumberg, Ill. 60195

Business Publications Audit of Circulation, Inc., 360 Park Avenue South, New York, N.Y. 10011

Standard Rate & Data Service, Inc., 3004 Glenview Road, Wilmette, Ill. 60091

Traffic Audit Bureau, 708 Third Avenue, New York, N.Y. 10017

Media Associations

American Business Press, Inc., 205 E. 42nd Street, New York, N.Y. 10017

American Newspaper Publishers Association, Box 17407, Dulles International Airport, Washington, D.C. 20041

Cable Television Advertising Bureau, 767 Third Avenue, New York, N.Y. 10017

Institute of Outdoor Advertising, 342 Madison Avenue, New York, N.Y. 10173

Magazine Publishers Association, Inc., 575 Lexington Avenue, New York, N.Y. 10022

Radio Advertising Bureau, 485 Lexington Avenue, New York, N.Y. 10017

Television Bureau of Advertising, 485 Lexington Avenue, New York, N.Y. 10017

Transit Advertising Association, 22 E. 40th Street, New York, N.Y. 10016

Independent Research Organizations

Audits & Surveys, One Park Avenue, New York, N.Y. 10016

The Arbitron Company, Inc., 1350 Avenue of the Americas, New York, N.Y. 10019

Leading National Advertisers, 136 Madison Avenue, New York, N.Y. 10016

McCollum/Spielman/& Company, Inc., 235 Great Neck Rd., Great Neck, N.Y. 11021

NPD Research, Inc., 900 West Shore Rd., Port Washington, N.Y. 11050

A. C. Nielsen Company, Nielsen Plaza, Northbrook, Ill. 60062

Opinion Research Corp., P.O. Box 183, Princeton, N.J. 08540

Perception Research Services, Inc., 440 Sylvan Avenue, Englewood Cliffs, N.J. 07632

SAMI, Time & Life Building, New York, N.Y. 10020

Scarborough Research Corporation, 10 E. 40th Street, New York, N.Y. 10016

Simmons Market Research Bureau, 219 E. 42nd Street, New York, N.Y. 10017

Starch INRA Hooper, Inc., 566 East Boston Post Road, Mamaroneck, N.Y. 10543

Sources and Suggestions for Further Reading

Aaker, David A. _Advertising Management._ 2d ed. Englewood Cliffs, N.J.: Prentice-Hall, 1982.

Baker, S. _Systematic Approach to Advertising Creativity._ New York: McGraw-Hill, 1983.

Barton, Roger, Ed. _Advertising Agency Operations and Management._ New York: McGraw-Hill, 1970.

Dirksen, Charles J. and Arthur Kroeger. _Advertising Principles and Problems._ 6th ed. Homewood. Ill.: R. D. Irwin, 1983.

Donnermuth, William P. _Promotion: Analysis, Creativity and Strategy._ Boston: Kent Publishing Co., 1984.

Dunn S., Watson. _Advertising._ 5th ed. Chicago: Dryden Press, 1982.

Faison, Edmund W. J. _Advertising: A Behavioral Approach for Managers._ New York: John Wiley & Sons, 1980.

Graham, John, and Susan K. Jones. "Print Media: Strategy and Execution." _Direct Marketing_ (May 1986).

Hedges, Michael. "Radio's Lifestyles." _American Demographics,_ vol. 8, no. 2 (February 1986).

Kalish, David. "Sampling the Great Outdoors." *Marketing & Media Decisions* (June 1986).

Maver, Martin. *Madison Avenue, U.S.A.* New York: Harper & Row, 1958.

Pope, Daniel. *The Making of Modern Advertising.* New York: Basic Books, 1983.

Ray, Michael L. *Advertising and Communication Management.* Englewood Cliffs, N.J.: Prentice-Hall, 1982.

Sachs, William. *Advertising Management: Its Role in Marketing.* Tulsa, Oklahoma: Penn-Well Publishing Company, 1983.

Sandage, Charles Harold. *Advertising Theory and Practice.* 11th ed. Homewood, Ill.: R. D. Irwin, 1983.

Sonenklar, Carol. "Women and Their Magazines." *American Demographics,* vol. 8, no. 6 (June 1986).

Stansfield, Richard. *The Dartnell Advertising Manager's Handbook.* Chicago: The Dartnell Corporation, 1982.

GUIDE TO ADVERTISING MEDIA

◀ Although you can't tell it from this black and white photograph, this balloon is very colorful. Sponsored by Anheuser-Busch, it flies in balloon races. When it does, its picture appears in newspapers and on television, and millions of people get the Budweiser message. The balloon is advertising that begets publicity.

8 PRINT MEDIA: NEWSPAPERS AND CONSUMER MAGAZINES

Newspapers: Advertising Workhorse

Advantages of Newspapers as an Advertising Medium
Limitations of Newspapers
Tear Sheets and Checking Copies
Newspapers by Type
  Daily Newspapers—Morning and Evening
  Weekly Newspapers
  Sunday Newspapers
  Sunday Supplements
  Ethnic and Foreign-Language Papers
Buying Newspaper Space
  Positions and Premiums
  ROP Color
  Rate Comparisons
  Combination Buys
Special Newspapers

Consumer Magazines

Types of Consumer Magazines
Advantages of Magazines
Magazine Circulations
Magazine Space and Rates
Demographic Editions
Comparing Magazines
  Audit Bureau of Circulations

Working Vocabulary

closing date	contract rate	island half
tear sheet	short rate	square third
checking copy	ROP (run of paper)	bleed page
make-good	premium position	spread
rotosection	split run	matched color
open rate	combination rate	

While one might compare the circulation of a newspaper with coverage of a radio station, these intermedia comparisons cannot be made on a statistical basis and instead would have to be made on some subjective basis.

The basis of these latter comparisons, however, are not entirely subjective. They are founded on the idea that all media have inherent qualities that make them desirable.

Jack Z. Sissors and E. Reynold Petray
Advertising Media Planning

In 1985, advertising volume in the United States in all media totaled more than $94 billion. Of this amount, newspapers received the largest single share — $26.5 billion. In recent years, the volume of newspaper advertising has increased. In fact, the volume for 1985 was up 7.9 percent over 1984. Nevertheless, the percentage of total advertising volume committed to newspapers has declined, from 34 percent in 1955 to 26.5 percent in 1985. This decline took place in the same time period that saw advertising volume quadruple. During this 30-year period, television increased its share of advertising volume from 11 percent in 1955 to 21.9 percent in 1985. Although newspapers still represent the largest share of all advertising dollars, the major portion by far — 23 percent — is local retail, as compared to 3.5 percent national.

Newspapers: Advertising Workhorse

Advantages of Newspapers as an Advertising Medium

Newspapers provide intensive coverage of specific geographic markets. By using newspapers, advertisers can obtain the high degree of geographical selectivity they need to meet a number of marketing and advertising objectives. Newspapers provide the most cost-efficient medium for advertising when product distribution is regional. National advertisers who are slowly building a distribution network can use newspapers to introduce their products to the major metropolitan markets, one market at a time. National advertisers can also use newspapers to meet competition from local or regional products.

Newspapers have very short deadlines. Most metropolitan daily papers have a **closing date** — that is, a deadline by which they must receive advertising copy — of only 48 hours in advance of publication. In contrast, consumer magazines have closing dates three months or more in advance of publication. Thus, newspapers' comparatively short deadlines allow advertisers the freedom to alter their copy to tie in with current events, fast-breaking discoveries, or sudden changes in the weather.

Newspapers are local. Newspapers are filled with local news and local advertising. Local advertising offers the national advertiser excellent opportunities for cooperative advertising with local retailers.

Cooperative advertising is advertising placed by retailers in their local newspapers, the cost of which is *shared* by the national advertiser. The subject of vertical cooperative advertising is dealt with more fully in chapter 19.

Newspapers offer excellent opportunity for frequency. Published daily, with loyal readers comprising the bulk of their circulation, newspapers can deliver an advertising message day after day — five, six, or seven times a week.

All of these heavy newspaper users are also among the 100 leading advertisers in the United States. It is interesting to note the kinds of goods and services they represent — cigarettes, automobiles, travel, and entertainment. Note, in particular, the sizable percentage of total advertising expenditures placed in newspapers by the airlines.

Newspapers reach a well-educated audience. Eighty-seven percent of all college graduates read a newspaper every day. Eighty-three percent of high-school graduates read a newspaper. Only 64 percent of the people who have *not* completed high school read a daily paper. We also know from market surveys that regular newspaper readers have higher incomes than occasional readers. Almost 90 percent of families with annual incomes of $15,000 or more read a newspaper regularly.

Newspapers contain a wide range of editorial material aimed at a broad audience. Whatever the interests of the readers may be — finance, sports, homemaking, fashion, politics — their newspapers will contain news and editorial features that hold their attention and expose them to the advertising message. (See color plate 21.)

Newspapers offer great flexibility in the size of advertisements, from a few inches to a full page. This means that there is also considerable flexibility in the cost of the advertisement.

Limitations of Newspapers

Some of the advantages of newspapers can, however, be considered detriments by some advertisers. Newspapers do indeed have a short deadline. They also have a very short life. Not many people will read a two- or three-day-old newspaper. Of course, readers may always return to an article or review that they missed; but when they do so, there is very little chance that they will also look over the paper's advertisements again. Usually, if the reader missed the message on the first go-round, *the message will not get a second chance.*

Daily newspapers are able to produce a new issue every 24 hours only by using a high-speed rotary printing process. But, because the papers are printed rapidly on coarse wood pulp paper called newsprint, the reproduction of fine detail in photographs or drawings is impossible. Therefore, although advertisers enjoy the speed with which their advertising message is produced, the quality of reproduction leaves much to be desired.

Newspapers are demographically selective only to a limited extent. Men and women read the same newspaper. Old people and young people read the same newspaper. Rich and poor and those in between read the same newspaper.

National advertisers who commit themselves to the use of a large volume of newspaper advertising also commit themselves to the completion of a large volume of paperwork. To place an advertisement in *TV Guide* that will reach 20 million readers, agency personnel must fill out one insertion order, one invoice, and check one copy of the magazine to verify the appearance of the ad. A newspaper schedule with only a fraction of *TV Guide*'s reach requires agency personnel to make dozens of phone calls for space reservations; fill out dozens of insertion orders; arrange for the delivery of reproduction materials to dozens of cities; check dozens of tear sheets; and check, verify, and pay dozens of invoices.

Tear Sheets and Checking Copies

A few words in explanation of the process of verifying the appearance of an ad in the print media are appropriate here. A **tear sheet** is a copy of the page on which an advertisement was printed that has been cut (or torn) from the particular edition in which it appeared. A newspaper will enclose a tear sheet along with its invoice for the space cost as a verification of the appearance of the ad. A **checking copy** is a copy of the entire newspaper or magazine that contained the ad. Advertisers, or their agencies, use the checking copies to examine the editorial climate of the newspaper and, perhaps, to see what competitive products were advertised in that issue. Magazines generally follow the same practice, sending a tear sheet with their invoice to the agency's accounting department and a checking copy to the media department. Checking copies are often sent to the account executive at the agency and to the advertiser.

What happens if the newspaper or magazine made a mistake in running an ad? What if they inserted an incorrect ad or placed an ad in the wrong issue of the publication? Perhaps, as very rarely happens, an ad was poorly printed. If the error is the fault of the publication, they will rerun the ad in the first available issue. This rerun ad is commonly called a **make-good.**

National advertisers also want to verify the appearance of newspaper and magazine advertisements placed by their dealers in order to answer the following questions:

1. Are dealers featuring my products or those of my competitors?
2. Are dealers passing my price reductions on to consumers or taking them as additional profits for themselves?
3. Which products in my line are being featured most frequently?
4. Are the dealers tieing in with our national advertising?

To get the answers to these and many other questions regarding newspaper and local broadcast advertising, many national advertisers use the services of the Advertising Checking Bureau, Inc. The ACB, as it is usually called, was established in 1917 to act as a clearinghouse for newspaper publishers in the distribution of checking copies to agencies and national advertisers throughout the country. The agency sends copies of the newspaper insertion orders to ACB and ACB checks for proper date, size, key number, reproduction quality, competitive ads on the same page, and so on. ACB reads virtually every daily newspaper in the country and the more important weeklies. They provide tear-sheet service and verification of cooperative ads. For subscribers who are interested, they report on secondary brand mentions, as when an appliance is advertised as "powered by a General Electric motor." ACB also reports on the use of material provided by the national advertiser as it is used in ads placed by retailers. These reports tell the national advertiser which models or styles appear to be most popular with dealers.

Newspapers by Type

To understand the use and value of newspapers, we will find it helpful to separate them into five categories:

1. *Daily newspapers* publish morning and/or evening editions in cities or large metropolitan areas.
2. *Weekly newspapers,* or country newspapers as they are often called, are usually published in small towns, and their circulation is predominantly rural and suburban.
3. *Sunday newspapers* are the large Sunday editions of daily papers and often include a Sunday supplement.

Compare this table with that shown in the *USA Today* ad on page 159 in the preceding chapter. This ranking excludes national newspapers. The circulation figures shown are as of September 1984. The first nine newspapers are major city newspapers, three of them in New York City alone; the tenth is not a big city newspaper, but is circulated primarily in Nassau and Suffolk counties, New York, a very important MSA (Metropolitan Statistical Area).

Top 10 Newspapers	
1. New York Daily News	1,346,840
2. Los Angeles Times	1,046,965
3. New York Times	934,530
4. New York Post	930,026
5. Chicago Tribune	776,348
6. Washington Post	728,857
7. Detroit News	656,367
8. Chicago Sun-Times	649,891
9. Detroit Free Press	647,130
10. Newsday	539,065

4. *Ethnic and foreign-language newspapers* are directed to various ethnic groups in the population of the United States and are circulated nationally, or, in some cases, only in the ethnic communities of metropolitan areas.
5. *National newspapers* are distributed nationwide. There are eight: the *Christian Science Monitor* and *USA Today* are daily national consumer newspapers; the *Wall Street Journal, Journal of Commerce,* and *American Banker,* which are daily business newspapers; and *Grit, National Enquirer,* and *The Star,* which are weeklies and could properly be classified as magazines but for their newspaper-type format.

Daily Newspapers — Morning and Evening There are about 1,760 newspapers in the United States with daily editions — 446 morning, 1,284 evening, and 29 "all day" editions. Over 75 percent publish evening editions because many advertisers believe that a morning paper enjoys a shorter period of readership and fewer secondary readers than an afternoon paper. They argue that the afternoon paper, purchased by a commuter during the ride home, or delivered to the home in the afternoon, is then perused in a leisurely manner at home by all the members of the family or household. They believe that the morning paper, however, leaves the house with one of the members of the family, is taken on the train or bus, is read in transit, and is often left at the station or at work. Although there is some logic to this analysis, many readers also bring their morning paper home with them to finish their reading. Newspapers are read in 75 percent of U.S. households and by 67 percent of adults every day. The circulation of daily newspapers, morning and evening, comes to over 62.6 million. An estimate by NAB in 1983 based on a 1983 SMRB Study of Media Markets, indicates that, for the total United States, there are 2.13 readers per copy for weekdays and 2.25 readers per copy for Sunday/ weekend editions. Readership for newspapers in the top 25 ADIs is stated as 2.52 readers per copy.

Weekly Newspapers There are over 7,500 weekly newspapers in the United States, most of which circulate in small towns. Published once a week, these newspapers cannot compete with big-city dailies or broadcast media for coverage of national, or even state, news events. Their existence is justified by the publication of hometown news that is neither carried in big-city papers nor delivered over broadcast media. The local news is of interest to local readers, and these papers are an excellent medium for local retailers. At the same time, suburbanization and changing media consumption patterns have added interest for national advertisers. Grouped together, weekly newspapers provide an effective medium to reach some affluent audience and to reinforce others by duplication. When national advertisers choose to include these publications in a national advertising program, they usually arrange to place their ads through a representative organization that will accept one insertion order from the agency and will then distribute copy to the weekly papers involved. The task of ordering, checking, and billing would be so onerous without the aid of the representative organization that few agencies would bother, particularly considering the marginal coverage such papers offer.

Sunday Newspapers In the United States there are 772 newspaper editions published on Sunday with a total circulation of almost 57 million.

This coupon entitles you to thousands of free shoppers

Why? Because your food ad reaches so much extra spending power in Syracuse that it's like getting thousands of extra food shoppers free. In fact, Syracuse spends an average of $1,474* per person on food, while the average market spends only $1,150.*

Let us show you why the Syracuse Newspapers are the best way to reach this profitable audience. Send this coupon today.

*1983 S & MM Survey of Buying Power

**Syracuse.
More than you
bargain for.**

Mail to: Charles Vella,
Syracuse Newspapers,
Syracuse, NY 13221 or
call 315-470-2089.

Name

Address

City

State   Zip

**The
Syracuse
Newspapers**

Herald-Journal
Herald American
The Post-Standard

Represented Nationally by Newhouse Newspapers

Syracuse, New York, boasts three newspapers — *The Post-Standard,* a morning paper; the *Herald-Journal,* an evening paper; and the *Herald American,* a Sunday paper. An advertiser, national or local, may take into account the circulation rate and demographics of the two daily papers, or may seek to obtain a combination of rate and coverage through the use of the morning paper and the Sunday paper. The Syracuse newspapers cover a four-county trading area. Syracuse's demographics make it an excellent city for test marketing.

They usually have larger circulations than the daily editions. For example, the "all day" newspaper in San Antonio, Texas, *Express News,* has a daily circulation of 170,262. Its Sunday circulation is 205,106 — 20 percent larger. The Sunday edition is read at home by all members of the family. The Sunday edition usually provides in-depth coverage of a wide range of subjects. Advertisers may choose the section that provides the most appropriate editorial environment. The advertiser expects greater effectiveness because the reader has more time on Sunday; other members of the household have an opportunity to read; and the interest-focused sections enhance the impact of the selling message.

Most Sunday papers include a comics section, which is a syndicated section. At one time advertisers placed ads in these sections to reach children and adolescents. Today, however, advertisers use other media, notably television, to reach this market. As a result, the amount of advertising in comic sections has declined. Advertisers must remember, however, that about 70 percent of the comics section's audience are adults, not children.

Sunday Supplements   The magazine (or **rotosection**) of the Sunday papers is not truly a magazine, nor is it properly a section of the newspaper.

While some newspapers find their competition in other newspapers in the same market, the *Houston Chronicle* proposes that advertisers consider a combination with broadcast. Note the emphasis on reach and frequency in terms of a specific target market that is defined by sex, age, and household income. GRPs represents *gross rating points,* a term which will be clarified in the next chapter on broadcast media.

Standard Rate & Data Service (SRDS) carries the listing for Sunday supplements in its Consumer Magazine and Agri-Media Rates and Data book, as well as in its Newspaper Rates and Data book. The Sunday supplement has the characteristics of a consumer magazine, but it does not have the same duration. It offers advertisers the same depth of local market coverage that a newspaper offers plus excellent four-color reproduction. Sunday supplements do have long closing dates, however; some may be even longer than those of many consumer magazines.

© 1984 Toyota Motor Sales, U.S.A., Inc.

Remember that ridge you always wanted to go to but never could? That strip of sand you thought was just out of reach? The way this 1985 4Runner SR5 breaks through, you'll swear it was designed by Houdini.

Sure, 4Runner's got the highest running ground clearance of any small sport utility vehicle, but that's just the beginning.

Its all-new 24 liter engine with 116 hp is the *most powerful* ever built for a small sport utility vehicle. And its computer-controlled Electronic Fuel Injection has tricks up its sleeve others still can't figure out. It's simple.

Like every brilliant escape artist, 4Runner's exclusive EFI only uses power and fuel when needed. No wasted motion or energy here.

On the inside is rich, door-to-door carpeting, room and comfort for 5, a separate heating system for the boys

in the back room, an outstanding AM/FM/MPX sound system, reclining bucket seats and an option that makes running away even more comfortable —a 7-way adjustable driver's Sport Seat.

OH WHAT A FEELING!

TOYOTA

And, to bring the outdoors indoors, here is the only small sport utility with a removable top.

Inclinometer. Altimeter. Tachometer. You name it. The 4Runner SR5's got it. All it needs is you and your itch to run away. Where? Just use your imagination.

BUCKLE UP. IT'S A GOOD FEELING!

THE 4WD TOYOTA 4RUNNER SR5. HOW FAR YOU GO DEPENDS ON YOU.

COLOR PLATE 18

COLOR PLATE 18 This Toyota ad is classic in its way. Appearing in *Playboy*, it touches base with its target market in so many ways. The target is the young, active, outdoor man. An exciting photograph with rugged terrain, the powerful caption at the bottom, and good copy combine to help "sell" this vehicle that has all the features to warm the heart of any adventurous young man.

100% GRAIN NEUTRAL SPIRITS 94.6 PROOF. IMPORTED BY DISTILLERS SOMERSET, N.Y., N.Y. © 1985.

Share the wreath.
Give friends a sprig of imported English greenery.

Tanqueray Gin.
A singular experience.

Send a gift of Tanqueray anywhere in the U.S.A. Call 1-800-243-3787. Void where prohibited.

COLOR PLATE 19

COLOR PLATE 19 Tanqueray makes clever use of the product (about 125 bottles worth) to make a seasonal ad that is appropriate and distinctive.

COLOR PLATE 20

COLOR PLATE 20 Riunite created a very contemporary version of the testimonial, using a well-known dancer. Note, too, the mild play on the word *gold* which rhymes with—you guessed it—*cold*—which is the way Riunite D'Oro is supposed to be sipped.

Color Plate 21 The *New York Times* has been using a series of fantasy ads in advertising business publications to demonstrate the range of its editorial contents. It does it with a minimum of words and a set of clever, stylized illustrations.

Color Plate 22 *Parade* offers flexibility and reach. The advertiser can choose *Parade*'s total circulation—which reaches more than 24 million homes—or one of the 11 regional editions, or individual market buys in selected cities. *Parade* is distributed as the Sunday supplement in 132 newspapers across the country, including Hawaii and Alaska. It is the magazine with the largest circulation in the United States.

Color Plate 23 *Sports Illustrated* brings human interest to prospective readers. Of course, readers have an interest in all kinds of sports, but the writer, in just a few words, combined with a dramatic photograph, tells the readers what to expect—a feeling.

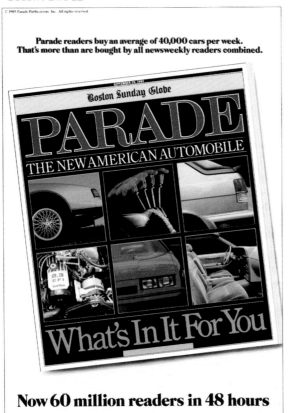

Schwepping is looking good in glasses.

COLOR PLATE 24 The play on words is memorable, and the package identification is provided in a very subtle way. This ad is in keeping with the class image Schweppes has always projected.

The entire Eastern Seaboard was just wiped out by a single cup of coffee.

It can take hundreds of hours to fill up the memory on a computer diskette. And just a second to erase it.

That's why Shade offers their high-quality diskettes in a rigid plastic carton.

For just a little more, you get a permanent storage library for ten 5¼" diskettes.

When your precious memories are in the carton, they aren't being bashed with notebooks. Or drowned with coffee. Or scorched with cigarette ashes. And they aren't being lost.

Call us at 1-800-742-3475 and we'll tell you how you can order Shade diskettes in the plastic carton. Do it today.

Before you're wiped out by a paperweight.

SHADE

COLOR PLATE 25

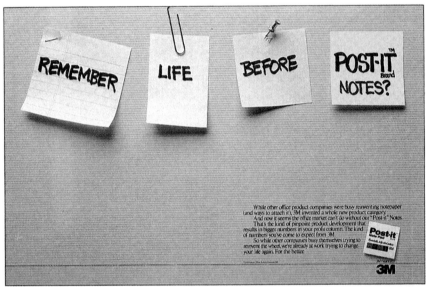

REMEMBER LIFE BEFORE POST-IT™ Brand NOTES?

While other office product companies were busy reinventing notepaper (and ways to attach it), 3M invented a whole new product category.
And now it seems the office market can't do without our "Post-it" Notes.
That's the kind of pinpoint product development that results in bigger numbers in your profit column. The kind of numbers you've come to expect from 3M.
So while other companies busy themselves trying to reinvent the wheel, we're already at work trying to change your life again. For the better.

Post-it

3M

COLOR PLATE 26

COLOR PLATE 25 Diskettes tend to be a commodity-like product—many users consider one as good as another. It is difficult to project a distinct image. This spread by Shade hits the boss where it can hurt—the loss of data. Thus, the Shade user receives not only a high-quality diskette but also a rigid plastic carton that protects it from disasters like that shown in the photograph.

COLOR PLATE 26 The success of this product is now a modern legend. If any reader were so out of touch that he or she did not know what a Post-It note could do, the witty illustration tells it all.

COLOR PLATE 27 A business ad? Absolutely. Hyatt Hotels, recognizing that increasing num- ▶ bers of women are traveling on business, directs this ad to them with a good illustration and copy that fulfills the promise of comfort—specifically, shampoos for women, skirt hangers, and hair dryers. The brief description of the locations emphasizes the comforts of convenience—convenient to the airport, convenient to downtown, a walk to government agencies. This four-color ad appeared in *Business Week*.

COLOR PLATE 28 One medium uses another to sell itself in this outdoor display by a television station.

COLOR PLATE 29 This commercial is such an obvious spoof that it is entertaining by itself. Notice how easily the Stroh's name is introduced. Notice the number of frames in which the cans appear. Entertaining to be sure, but the commercial never loses sight of its objective—to help build an image for Stroh's beer. Good identification with the young male target market.

Today about 500 newspapers include either *Parade* or *Family Weekly* magazines in their Sunday editions. The newspaper contracts for the supplement, and it is delivered in bulk. The paper then simply inserts the supplement into its Sunday edition as a self-contained section. The name of the paper is carried on the masthead of the magazine and to the reader it looks like a section of the newspaper. *Parade* is distributed through 132 of the larger big city newspapers to about 24 million homes. (See color plate 22.) *Family Weekly* distributes through some 366 smaller newspapers with a total circulation of almost 13 million. Another supplement, *Sunday,* is distributed through a network of 55 newspapers, including such large and well-known papers as the *New York Sunday News* and the *Chicago Tribune. The New York Times* and the *Los Angeles Times* publish their own independent Sunday magazines.

Ethnic and Foreign-Language Papers   The difference between ethnic and foreign-language newspapers is that foreign-language papers are directed to members of ethnic groups that do not read the English language press. New York's Chinatown, for example, boasts four Chinese-language newspapers. But, as dependence on the former native language has lessened, so has dependence on foreign-language media.

On the other hand, there are more than 200 newspapers in America that are basically reflective of — and primarily oriented toward — the distinct needs and problems of black Americans. These papers reach black consumers at a sales identification level comparable to that of papers primarily oriented to white Americans.

While in the past the bulk of the advertising in most ethnic and foreign-language newspapers has come from local retailers or regional distributors of specialty products, national advertising in these media is increasing.

Buying Newspaper Space

Newspaper space is sold in units of measurement called SAU — standard advertising units — which represent a specific number of columns and inches. The SAU can vary from one paper to another. In a standard-size newspaper (broadsheet), such as *The New York Times,* a full page is a unit 6 by 21, which means 21 inches deep by 6 columns wide — a total of 126 column inches. A half page is a unit 4 by 15.75, representing 4 columns width and 15.75 inches depth, for a total of 63 column inches. A full page in a tabloid-size newspaper is 6 columns wide by 14 inches deep for a total of 84 column inches. There are restrictions that every newspaper sets for itself with regard to specified depths or certain column widths. A newspaper with a tabloid format would not be likely to accept an ad 13 inches deep by 6 columns. They might require the advertiser to pay for the full page, which is 14 inches deep.

Newspapers issue rate cards or sheets that contain the rates, the copy size, the restrictions, and all pertinent information. The information is available in the *Standard Rate & Data Service* Newspaper edition. Newspaper advertising rates are listed on the rate card as **open rate** (rates with no discount) or **contract rates** (rates that are reduced if the buyer fulfills certain contract provisions), based on the total amount of space called for. There are also contracts calling for specified frequencies, from 7 times to 52 times in one year. The contract rates are lower rates because of the quantity of advertising space purchased and the larger the contract, either in total space or in frequency, the lower the rate.

The New York Times offers not only high circulation (over one million), but a high median household income ($44,747). Its advertising rates reflect that quality combination. The cost of a full page (126 column inches) weekdays at the open rate is $31,521.42. *The Times* is a morning broadsheet newspaper with a page size that is 13 inches by 21 inches.

For a national advertiser, advertising rates are subject to the 15 percent agency commission. Local retail advertising is offered at a lower rate, with lower rates for quantity of space and/or frequency, and not subject to agency commission.

If we, or our agency, issue a contract calling for a specified quantity of space at a contract rate and then fail to fulfill the schedule, the newspaper has the right to bill us at the rate actually earned. The difference between the contract rate and the earned rate is called the **short rate.** The procedure for determining the short rate is simple: Suppose our agency had planned a series of ten ads in a particular newspaper, each ad 50 column inches (SAU 5 by 10). The open rate might be $100 per column inch. Intending to use 500 inches (10 × 50), we contracted for the program at the 500-inch rate of $90 per inch. If, after only five insertions, we cancel our schedule, the newspaper would send us a short-rate invoice to the next rate we had earned. This might be the 250-inch contract rate of $95 per column inch, in which case, we would owe the newspaper an additional $1250. Five ads of 50 inches each = 250 inches. The difference between the contract rate and the earned rate is $5 per inch. $5 × 250 inches = $1250. If the newspaper did not have a 250-inch rate, the earned rate would revert to the open rate.

Positions and Premiums   Unless we specify where we want our advertisement to appear within a newspaper, the publisher may place it wherever it happens to fit. Newspaper insertions placed in this manner are described as **ROP,** meaning **run of paper.** Specific positions within the newspaper, on the other hand, offer the advertiser a number of advantages. In a standard-size newspaper, the top of the page generally has a better opportunity for readership than the bottom of the page. In making up the page, the publisher usually places the large ads at the top of the page and the small ads at the bottom. We may request *top-of-the-page position* and hope for the best. But to be sure of obtaining a top-of-the-page position, our insertion order should specify *top of the page paid.* The publisher will then guarantee us that our ad will appear at the top of the page and will add a standard extra charge to our bill for that **premium position.**

Top or bottom location on a page is not the only position some advertisers are willing to pay extra for. Some may want to place their ad on page 2, or in the back of the first section, or on the editorial page. For men's products, advertisers frequently specify the sports section. For women's products, the fashion page or the food page may be most desirable. Such specific positioning of the ad within the paper improves the demographic selectivity.

Many newspapers offer split-run facilities. The **split run** is a process by which alternate copies of the same newspaper are printed with different ads for the same product. We can use this technique to test the appeal of our ad, the copy, the illustration, or any of the other elements that can be varied. By tabulating the response to different ads — through reader letters, phone calls, or coupon redemptions — we can select the most effective for use in other papers, or we can adapt the most effective ad for use in other media. Of course, newspapers will charge us extra for the use of their split-run service.

ROP Color   Consumers like to see the same full-color advertising in newspapers as they see on television and in magazines. Today, more than a thousand newspapers can reproduce four-color in full-page size only; another few hundred can print ads in black plus one color, usually in full-size only. While newspapers in the West and Sunbelt states are the most frequent users of color, almost every market in the country is served by at least one paper that has, or plans to have, color capability. But the number of papers acquiring color capability is limited, because to produce color of a quality at least comparable to glossy magazines, a newspaper needs new presses, and the existing facilities are

1 col-1½ inches	2 col-3¹/₈ inches	3 col-4⅝ inches	4 col-6¼ inches	5 col-7¹³/₁₆ inches 4½ col-7 inches		6 col-9¾ inches
N 1 × 14 CLE-200 lines NCI-14"	N 2 × 14 CLE-400 lines NCI-28"	N 3 × 14 CLE-600 lines NCI-42"	* N 4 × 14 CLE-800 lines NCI-56"	N 4½ × 14 * CLE-900 lines NCI-63"		N 6 × 14 CLE-1200 lines NCI-84"
N 1 × 10.5 CLE-150 lines NCI-10.5"	N 2 × 10.5 CLE-300 lines NCI-21"	N 3 × 10.5 CLE-450 lines NCI-31.5"	* N 4 × 10.5 CLE-600 lines NCI-42"			* N 6 × 10.5 CLE-900 lines NCI-63"
N 1 × 7 CLE-100 lines NCI-7"	N 2 × 7 CLE-200 lines NCI-14"	N 3 × 7 CLE-300 lines NCI-21"	N 4 × 7 CLE-400 lines NCI-28"			N 6 × 7 CLE-600 lines NCI-42"
N 1 × 5.25 CLE-75 lines NCI-5.25"	N 2 × 5.25 CLE-150 lines NCI-10.5"	N 3 × 5.25 CLE-225 lines NCI-15.75"	* N 4 × 5.25 CLE-300 lines NCI-21"			
CLE-50 lines NCI-3.5" N 1 × 3.5	CLE-100 lines NCI-7" N 2 × 3.5	N 3 × 3.5 CLE-150 lines NCI-10.5"				
CLE-42 lines NCI-3' N 1 × 3	CLE-84 lines NCI-6" N 2 × 3					
						N 6 × 2.5 CLE-210 lines NCI-15"
CLE-28 lines NCI-2" N 1 × 2	N 2 × 2 CLE-56 lines NCI-4"					
CLE-21 lines NCI-1.5" N 1 × 1.5						
N 1 × 1 CLE-14 lines NCI-1"						

DEPTH IN INCHES (0–14)

These are the various SAUs (standard advertising units) for a *tabloid* newspaper. The full page consists of 84 column inches (6 columns by 14 inches). Note the wide range of space options available to an advertiser.

very expensive to adapt or replace. Additionally, in some areas (the New York City market, for example), the newspapers have not been under pressure to add color capacity because advertisers have the option of using color in existing vehicles — such as free-standing inserts, direct mail, spot television, and demographic editions of magazines.

In certain cities it is possible for newspapers to offer their advertisers very high-quality color reproduction with the use of HiFi rotogravure preprinted paper. HiFi color is produced by Standard Gravure Corporation of Louisville, Kentucky, and about 1,750 newspapers take advantage of the service. The advertiser or the agency provides the artwork, the list of newspapers that will carry the ad, and the insertion date. The producers of HiFi do the rest.

In the rotogravure process, the advertisement is printed on only one side of a roll of paper. After printing one side, the paper is rerolled and shipped to the local newspapers that will carry the ad. When the preprinted roll reaches the newspaper plant it is placed on the newspaper press just like a blank roll of newsprint. Current news and advertising is printed on the blank, or back, side of the roll as it runs through the newspaper press and the HiFi ad becomes an integral part of that day's edition of that newspaper.

A similar rotogravure process is used for SpectaColor, which also is produced by Standard Gravure Corporation. But SpectaColor differs from HiFi in that SpectaColor is designed for a registered cutoff. This means that each page will be cut off in exactly the same spot so that it is the same size as a full newspaper page. To do this, the SpectaColor rolls are printed with "eye marks" positioned along the edge of the roll at the top and bottom of the ad. Electronic inset equipment on the newspaper press "reads" these eye marks so that the paper is always cut off in the right spot. SpectaColor, however, is currently used only by two newspapers — the *Courier Journal* and the *Louisville Times.*

HiFi is used much more commonly, and is designed for those newspapers that do not have inset equipment on their presses to control the cutoff of the page. This means that the HiFi ad must be designed in a continuous or wallpaper pattern, so that the full advertising message will be delivered no matter where the cut occurs.

Rate Comparisons It is difficult to compare space rates for different newspapers in the same city because the circulation numbers for each are also different. If rates and circulation were the only criteria, we would create some sort of index to get a rough rule of thumb. For example, if we were to divide the circulation in thousands by the column/inch rate, we would have an index. Thus, to compare the *Boondock Times* with the *Boondock Bugle,* we develop these indexes:

$$\text{Boondock Times:} \quad \frac{557{,}632 \text{ (circ.)}}{\$187 \text{(col. in. rate)}} = \frac{557.6}{187} = 2.98$$

$$\text{Boondock Bugle:} \quad \frac{397{,}816 \text{ (circ.)}}{\$174 \text{(col. in. rate)}} = \frac{397.8}{174} = 2.28$$

The higher the index, the better. It suggests more circulation per column/inch rate.

Of course, if space rates and circulation were the only criteria, the *Times* might then have all the advertising and the *Bugle* would have to reduce its rate to be competitive. But the *Times* would *not* have all the advertising, because the advertiser cannot afford to disregard several hundred thousand consumers represented by the newspaper with the lower index. Furthermore, we know that there are important differences between newspapers besides their circulation — the demographic characteristics of the audience, for example, and the nature of the paper itself. In some instances, the demographic characteristics of the audience for one newspaper more closely fit the target market for the product and the advertiser will select that paper regardless of rate or

Circulation: 438,217   **Discount*: 38.7%**   **Inch Rate: 84.00**

1. Coastline Publishers Inc.
A. (San Clemente) Daily Sun/
Post (D)

7,119
Broadsheet
Offset
Open Rate: $6.85
Audit: ABC

2. W. Orange Publishing Corp.
A. Anaheim Independent
B. Buena Park News
C. Huntington Beach
Independent
D. Orange County News

140,174
Broadsheet
Offset
Open Rate: $26.69
Audit: VAC

3. Fullerton Publishing Co.
A. (Fullerton) Daily News
Tribune (D)
B. Anaheim Journal
C. Anaheim Hills Journal
D. Brea Advocate
E. The Fullerton Forum
F. La Habra Advocate
G. Placentia Journal
H. Yorba Linda Journal

103,203
Broadsheet
Offset
Open Rate: $22.89
Audit: ABC/VAC

4. The Tustin News
A. The Tustin News
B. Tustin/Irvine Outlook

28,261
Broadsheet
Offset
Open Rate: $12.32
Audit: VAC

**5. The Irvine World
Publishers**
A. The Irvine World News

37,931
Tabloid
Offset
Open Rate: $10.92
Audit: VAC

**6. Golden West Publishing,
Inc.**
A. Capistrano Valley News
B. Leisure World News
C. Saddleback Valley News
D. Dana Point News
E. Laguna News-Post
F. Laguna Niguel News

84,518
Tabloid
Offset
Open Rate: $39.48
Audit: VAC

**7. Orange Coast Publishing
Co.**
A. The Orange Coast Daily
Pilot (D)

37,011
Broadsheet
Offset
Open Rate: $17.92
Audit: ABC

Standard Ad Units

SAU	Cost	SAU	Cost
6xFD	9,854.04	3.7	1,764.00
6x18	8,510.88	3x5.25	1,323.00
6x14	6,975.84	2xFD	3,391.56
6x10.5	5,632.68	2x18	2,943.84
6x7	3,528.00	2x15.75	2,656.02
5xFD	8,478.90	2x14	2,432.16
5x18	7,359.60	2x13	2,304.24
5x15.75	6,640.05	2x10.5	1,764.00
5x14	6,080.40	2x7	1,176.00
5x13	5,760.60	2x5.25	882.00
5x10.5	4,410.00	2x3.5	882.00
5.7	2,940.00	2x3	882.00
4xFD	6,783.12	2x2	882.00
4x18	5,887.68	1xFD	1,695.78
4x15.75	5,312.04	1x18	1,471.92
4x14	4,864.32	1x15.75	1,328.01
4x13	4,608.48	1x14	1,216.08
4x10.5	3,528.00	1x13	1,152.12
4x7	2,352.00	1x10.5	882.00
4x5.25	1,764.00	1x7	882.00
3xFD	5,087.34	1x5.25	882.00
3x18	4,415.76	1x3.5	882.00
3x15.75	3,984.03	1x3	882.00
3x14	3,648.24	1x2	882.00
3x13	3,456.36	1x1.5	882.00
3x10.5	2,646.00	1x1	882.00

LEGEND
★ County seat
--- Incorporated area
••••••• County boundary in MSA
mmmm County boundary not in MSA
━⑱━ Interstate highway
─⑫─ US highway
River
✈ Scheduled service airport

POPULATION KEY
100,000 and above   **GRANDSVILLE**
25,000 to 100,000   BIGGERSVILLE
5,000 to 25,000   Middleton
less than 5,000   Tiny Town
Population indicated by size of letters

*Discount represents savings of USSPI network rate versus the publisher(s) open rate(s).

Special Instruction – Individual publishers' open rates are subject to change.

R.O.P. Depth Requirement – Ads ordered 13 inches or more in depth will be charged for full depth in tabloids.

– Ads ordered more than 18 inches deep will be charged for full depth in broadsheets.

Effective 7/2/84 – Rate Card No. 26

◀ U.S. Suburban Press, Inc., is a national newspaper network of 1,037 newspapers covering 45 markets. One insertion order can buy one market, the entire 45-market network, or any combination of interest to the advertiser. USSPI thus makes it convenient to penetrate suburban markets that may not be reached by metropolitan dailies. There is also a substantial discount that comes with buying a market rather than paying the publishers' open rates. USSPI is headquartered in Schaumburg, Illinois, with sales offices in principal cities across the country.

Illustrated is a typical market sheet from USSPI. For the Anaheim suburban market, we can see the publishing companies, the names of their newspapers, and the circulation, format (broadsheet or tabloid), printing process, open rate, and circulation audit for each newspaper.

circulation differences. All the factors must be considered in the light of the advertising objectives.

Combination Buys In areas where the same publisher owns one or more newspapers, an advertiser may buy space in all of them at a special **combination rate.** If the publisher owns both the morning and evening newspapers in a city, advertisers may place their ads in both papers for a combination rate that is little more than the open rate for one paper. A publisher might, on the other hand, own several newspapers in different cities

	Top 25 Magazine Advertisers 1984		
Rank	Advertiser	Expenditures ($000)	Percent of Total Advertising Expenditures
1.	R. J. Reynolds Industries	$193,816	28.6
2.	Philip Morris, Inc.	140,070	24.6
3.	Ford Motor Co.	97,101	17.4
4.	General Motors Corp.	96,064	12.6
5.	American Telephone & Telegraph	79,102	14.0
6.	International Business Machines	63,098	16.8
7.	Chrysler Corp.	61,596	19.4
8.	Procter & Gamble Co.	49,735	5.7
9.	Loews Corp.	49,255	35.7
10.	General Foods Corp.	48,578	10.8
11.	RCA Corp.	47,564	19.9
12.	CBS Inc.	47,423	26.4
13.	Beatrice Cos.	43,525	6.4
14.	U.S. Government	40,043	13.9
15.	Time Inc.	39,539	29.5
16.	Jos. E. Seagram & Sons Co.	37,918	32.7
17.	Dart & Kraft	36,233	13.5
18.	Batus Inc.	36,216	31.9
19.	American Broadcasting Cos.	33,679	48.9
20.	Volkswagen of America	33,515	32.5
21.	Bristol-Myers Co.	32,624	12.6
22.	American Brands	31,583	23.7
23.	Johnson & Johnson	31,424	10.5
24.	Grand Metropolitan p.l.c.	28,523	37.4
25.	E.I. du Pont de Nemours	27,430	30.1

Source: Reprinted with permission from the September 26, 1985, issue of *Advertising Age.* Copyright © 1985 by Crain Communications, Inc.

As might be expected, these advertisers are among the 100 leading advertisers in the United States. The mix of products includes cigarettes, automobiles, and communications. Of particular note is the U.S. government, and do note the range of percentages placed in magazines from a low of 5.7 percent to a high of 48.9 percent.

American Passage is the representative for virtually all the college newspapers in the United States. This ad, which appeared in an advertising publication, stresses the reach that college newspapers offer the advertiser and suggests that the college campus is often isolated from the community at large. According to the ad, student readership of college newspapers is close to 60 percent, much higher than student readership of the local newspaper, for example, which is just above 40 percent. As a segment, college students represent 12 million upscale men and women with a large appetite for records and cassettes, cameras, pizza, and beer. American Passage makes such advertising convenient — with one order an advertiser can place an ad in all or as many college newspapers as strategy requires.

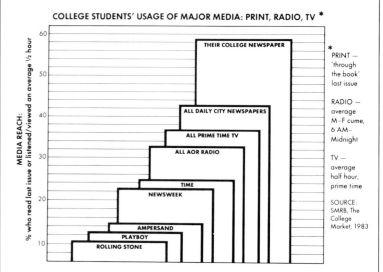

scattered throughout a geographic area. The combination rate for these papers is usually far less than the total of the individual rates for each of these papers.

Special Newspapers

Most high schools and colleges issue a weekly newspaper. Why should any national advertiser consider such media? High-school and college students represent a very selective market for phonograph records, soft drinks, beer,

Over the years, The Advertising Checking Bureau has broadened its services to include some specialized newspaper and magazine advertising research services. *Mintsystem* is an acronym for Marketing Intelligence Tracking System. It provides reports on how retailers are advertising the manufacturer's product versus the competition, at what price, at what advertising cost, and at what frequency.

cigarettes, and books. The U.S. government uses these papers for recruiting for the military. Magazines also use these newspapers to solicit subscriptions.

Union newspapers, religious newspapers, and military newspapers are usually of little or no interest to national advertisers. SRDS carries listings for such papers in its magazine edition. The shopping news, or pennysaver as it is commonly called, is not a newspaper. Generally it contains no news and little, if any, editorial content. Pennysavers are rarely used as a vehicle for national advertising.

Consumer Magazines

About 1,200 consumer magazines are published in the United States. It is very difficult to consider their value as advertising vehicles without separating them into categories based on the type of audience they appeal to. The question of clarification is made more complicated by the magazines' frequency of issue and method of distribution — some are weeklies, some are monthlies. There

Reader's Digest is offering an innovative format to help the publication compete against the strong magazines in the homemaking arena. "Foodshopper Showcase" is a section within the magazine where food advertising will be enhanced by the editorial surroundings. In addition, the format availabilities permit less than full-page ads, plus the use of full pages at half circulation of 9 million each. The advertisers may, in this way, test two different creative concepts.

are even some bimonthlies and a few quarterlies. Some magazines are distributed only by mail subscription; some are sold on the newsstand; others, at the supermarket.

In recent years, the problems of profitable publication have been exacerbated by rising costs of paper and printing and by repeated increases in postage rates. The competition of television has also changed the character of many magazines: their editorial emphasis is no longer on fiction—television provides enough of that—but, rather, on news and informative articles.

The Hispanic market is, in fact, three markets in three areas of the United States. Much of this market is not reached by English-language publications. The U.S. Hispanic Magazine Network provides advertisers the opportunity to feature products by region, to change copy by region, and, most important, to select those magazines that will meet their marketing objectives — and meet them in Spanish.

Types of Consumer Magazines

The first choice that advertisers face in selecting a consumer magazine as a vehicle for their advertising is whether to use a *mass,* or general-interest, magazine or a *class,* or special-interest, magazine. Mass circulation magazines today include *People, TV Guide,* and *Reader's Digest.* These publications contain reading matter for the entire family with editorial contents of broad general interest. Among class magazines, we find such widely diverse publications as

As promotion costs have risen over the years, advertisers have become aware that more precision in segmentation is critical in getting the most for every dollar invested in advertising. The publishing industry has risen to the challenge with demographic editions and with new publications aimed at very narrow targets. This ad describes *Goodlife,* a magazine whose readers receive it without charge, that is, direct. The criterion for being on their circulation list is residence in areas known to be very affluent. For example, the 25,000 recipients of the South Florida edition boast a median annual income of $77,360. Contrast *Goodlife's* total circulation of 345,000 with other magazines which have circulations in the millions but much less specific target audiences.

Time, Better Homes & Gardens, Sports Illustrated, and *Woman's Day.* These publications are aimed at specific demographic groups or at groups with certain fairly well-defined interests. There are probably no subject areas of interest to a sizable group of people that are not reached by a special-interest magazine. There are magazines for horse lovers, stamp collectors, do-it-yourselfers, tennis players, even model-railroad buffs. Class magazines aimed at groups with certain demographic characteristics, such as age or sex, include *Seventeen* for teenage girls, *Good Housekeeping* for homemakers, and *Retirement Living* for senior citizens.

Most consumer magazines are issued monthly. In order to keep current with changing news events, newsmagazines are issued weekly. A few publications are issued quarterly. The editorial approach of quarterly magazines is generally highly selective and of interest only to a well-defined social or demographic group. Quarterly magazines may be of more importance to an advertiser than their usually low circulation figures indicate, however. If the demographic characteristics of an advertiser's target market match those of a specific quarterly magazine's audience, advertising in that magazine will be exceptionally cost effective.

Advantages of Magazines

Most magazines offer high-fidelity color reproduction—an important factor when a product's color provides much of its appeal.

Magazines offer an exceptional range of selectivity. We have earlier lamented the fact that much of our advertising is wasted. If we advertise a detergent for dishwashing machines on an evening television program, for example, we will find the majority of the program's audience do not own a dishwasher. In contrast, magazines, through their editorial content and format, aim at certain people. The media analyst's task is to find the magazines whose audiences are closest to the target market for the advertiser's product. For a start, we might choose either women's or men's magazines. But, merely specifying women's magazines is not enough. We can select a women's magazine where the editorial emphasis is on fashion. Or we can select a women's magazine where the editorial emphasis is on home, beauty, and furnishings. Still others deal with homemaking, cleaning, cooking, and family health care.

Magazines have a long life. The television commercial is over in sixty seconds or less—if you missed it, you missed it. The newspaper might linger in the home an extra day or two after it is published. A monthly magazine has at least a month of durability, that is, it offers a month-long opportunity for the readers to receive the message. As a matter of fact, monthly magazines have a life span of more than a month. The October issue, for example, is usually in the mail or on the newsstand toward the end of September. Readers may even pick up a weekly newsmagazine weeks after it is published and read or glance through it again. This long life is an important advantage because it gives the reader time to read slowly, to return to the advertisement a second time, and to reflect on the product—a valuable factor if we are selling a complex or expensive product.

Magazines enable the advertiser to use some artistic variety. Although space is sold in standard units, design possibilities include bleeds, spreads, gatefolds, inserts, multiple pages, return cards, and pop-ups.

Many magazines offer demographic editions that enable the advertiser to buy circulation only in certain sections of the country or only for certain sections of the audience based on socioeconomic or occupational attributes. *Time* magazine offers a *Time B* demographic edition that circulates in the United States solely to business readers who are qualified by job title and industry. *Sports Illustrated* offers *SI Select,* a demographic edition of upscale readers as based on the ZIP codes of the most affluent communities in the

United States. There are also about thirty magazines that circulate only in a particular metropolitan area — from *Boston Magazine* to *Gold Coast of Florida,* from *Houston* to *Honolulu,* and many cities in between.

Magazines have a considerable secondary readership. The original subscribers or purchasers may pass the magazine to other members of their family or to friends. In professional offices, barbershops, and beauty parlors, the volume of secondary readership is tremendous.

Magazines, because they are selective in their editorial contents, tend to build a loyal body of readers who value the magazines as sources of information. A good deal of this prestige spills over to the advertising, and readers tend to believe that any advertiser in their favorite magazine is a reliable company with a quality product. An added value accrues to the advertiser from the stimulation of interest that the editorial contents arouse. An article on redecorating a nursery or playroom may prompt a reader to consider the ideas presented in the article for his or her own home and to read with more interest advertisements for decorating materials.

Magazines offer a convenient means to obtain national coverage. One insertion order to magazine X buys millions of readers all over the country. With a careful mix of magazines, advertisers can reach unduplicated segments of the market with a minimum amount of paperwork and mechanical preparation.

The only real general limitation that applies to magazines as a vehicle is their long deadlines. Advertisers are required to provide printed copy and art for their ads two months or more in advance of publication. This limits the advertisers' flexibility; they cannot make quick shifts in appeal that may be needed to meet changes in competition, market conditions, or legal restrictions. Nor can advertisers capitalize as quickly as they might like on some unique discovery or product innovation. Some advertisers consider magazines' lack of localized appeal to be a limitation, but such a limitation is highly subjective and of importance only to certain types of advertising campaigns.

Magazine Circulations

All major publications provide advertisers with audited circulation figures. Any one issue may, however, experience a substantial increase or decrease in its circulation: An issue with an unusual editorial feature may spark sales one month, while a particularly dull issue may result in poorer than average sales. Therefore, publishers always describe their rate base. The *rate base* represents the circulation that is *guaranteed* by the publisher and on which the publisher's advertising rates are determined. If the circulation exceeds the rate base, the magazine's advertisers receive the additional circulation as a bonus. If the circulation falls below the rate base, the advertisers will receive a rebate. Most publications set a conservative rate base, however, so that a bonus is more likely than a rebate. But the circulation of a publication that depends heavily on subscription varies little from month to month.

Magazine Space and Rates

Consumer magazines offer advertising space in standard size units. This means that advertisers will not have as wide a choice of advertisement size in a consumer magazine as in a newspaper. The units of space depend on the format of the magazine. A standard magazine uses an advertising page that measures 7 by 10 inches. That is not the size of the entire page, but the amount of space that is available for advertisements. Most magazines have a 3-column format

As you can see from this ad for *TV Guide,* there are more comparisons to be made than only circulation and cost-per-thousand readers. Where do people read magazines? At home? At the work place? In the doctor's waiting room? In transit on a train or bus? To choose between publications the advertiser has many *qualitative* factors to consider. *TV Guide's* circulation is over 17 million, but 2.3 readers per copy makes for 39 million readers.

that permits an advertiser to buy fractional space in several forms (see layouts on page 196) : a half-page, a two-thirds page, a one-third page, or a one-sixth page vertically, half the page horizontally, or what is called an **island half** — a space 2 columns wide by 7-1/2 inches deep. A one-third page may be ordered as a single column or as a **square third** — 2 columns wide by 4-7/8 inches deep. In some instances, the island half carries a slightly higher rate because it is usually surrounded by editorial material and therefore offers improved visibility. Other publications range from a tabloid size, such as *Rolling Stone,* to a digest size, such as *Reader's Digest.* Magazines that maintain a two-column format offer a vertical or horizontal half-page, quarter page, or eighth of a

NAME: Dede Thompson Bartlett

EDUCATION: B.A., Vassar College; M.A., New York University.

CAREER: President of the Mobil Foundation. Assistant to the Chairman of the Mobil Corporation.

FAMILY: Husband, one daughter, and son.

HOME: "Our third child," a gracious center-hall colonial.

DISTINGUISHING HABITS: Rises with the sun to admire her garden. Fixes the week's meals in marathon weekend cooking sessions. Vacations once a year in the Caribbean with ten spy novels and a case of good wine.

PARTICULAR PLEASURES: Great food, oriental rugs, polished floors, fresh flowers by the armload.

PERSONAL STYLE: Poised, vivacious.

If there were a fable to teach the rewards of a well-ordered existence, Dede Bartlett would be its heroine. She has a talent for organizing wildly divergent responsibilities. She puts them on a list—and turns her thoughts to the job at hand. Consequently, she possesses an inward serenity that imbues everything she does with elegance.

House Beautiful is essential reading for people like Dede Bartlett. It's about leading a multi-focused life, with flair. About cooking with panache, for two or for twenty. About making your garden grow, beautifully. About romantic vacations and terrific weekend getaways. About decorating—the news and the trends, the textures and the colors. Most of all, House Beautiful is about living with fashion in the home.

There's no other magazine like House Beautiful. That's why it has 6.4 million readers. Each House Beautiful woman has an unflappable sense of fashion. And each one is committed to everything House Beautiful stands for. As committed as Dede Bartlett.

HOUSE BEAUTIFUL
The magazine of home fashion.

page. Tabloid-size magazines offer space in a wider variety of shapes that are based on the number of columns in their format.

A **bleed page** advertisement is one in which the copy runs off the edges of the paper. In addition to providing more message space (it utilizes the white border that normally frames a full-page advertisement), a bleed ad offers greater impact. For a bleed page, most publications add an extra charge, usually 15 percent, to the space cost. Bleed may be permitted in some magazines in less than full-page space; it is used quite often in two-thirds page and half-page spaces.

A **spread** is an ad run on two facing pages, and the rate for a spread is simply that for two pages. In most cases a spread entitles the advertiser to a *gutter bleed* at no charge. The gutter is the border of white paper that appears in the center of the magazine between the two facing pages. The gutter bleed adds to the uniformity and impact of a spread. If any of the copy runs off the paper in any *other* direction, however, the magazine will add a bleed charge. Magazines that are bound together with staples offer advertisers a particularly desirable position known as a center spread. The *center spread* refers to the two pages that appear in the exact middle of the magazine. With a binding of this type, the magazine tends to spring open at the center, luring readers into that particular ad and thereby adding to its readership. Magazines charge a sizable premium for a center spread.

Charges for other special positions are generally stated on the magazine's rate card. The inside front cover (also called the second cover), the inside back cover (the third cover), and the outside back cover (fourth cover) all carry sizable premiums, with the fourth cover being the most expensive. Other special positions — page 1, opposite the table of contents, or next to a particular editorial feature of the magazine — also carry premium charges.

A magazine's *card rate* is always quoted for a black and white ad only. If advertisers want to use color, they must pay a standard charge usually described in the publication's rate card as *AAAA color.* The AAAA designation is applied to a group of standardized colors established some years ago by the American Association of Advertising Agencies. Standard AAAA colors are generally red, blue, yellow, green, and orange. Any color other than those standard colors will represent a **matched color** — that is, a color matched to the advertiser's specifications. A matched color is usually charged at a higher rate. If we want our ad to be printed in blue, whether AAAA or matched blue, we will pay for space cost plus one additional color — blue. A four-color ad carries a rate of its own; it is not calculated simply by adding the cost of three colors to the space cost, but is considerably more expensive. Black ink is all advertisers are entitled to for the space charge.

Just as newspapers charge advertisers an open rate for a single insertion and contract rates for two or more insertions, magazines offer one-time rates and volume rates. Advertisers planning to run a series of ads in one magazine can obtain reduced rates for *frequency contracts* — for three, six, twelve, or more,

Shown are the various units of advertising space that can be purchased in magazines.

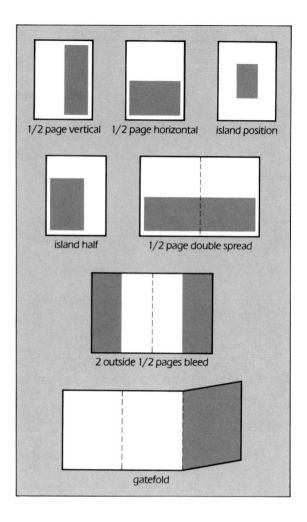

1/2 page vertical   1/2 page horizontal   island position

island half   1/2 page double spread

2 outside 1/2 pages bleed

gatefold

insertions, depending on the magazine's frequency of issue. A space contract covers a twelve-month period, just as a newspaper contract does, with similar provisions for short rate. On application to the publisher, advertisers can make use of such innovative space options as fold-out pages, inserts, reply cards, and tipped-in coupons. An *insert* represents advertising material that has been printed by the advertiser and delivered to the publisher for binding (insertion) into the magazine. When the material is to be glued to a page, it is said to be *tipped* in — that is, a thin line of adhesive is run along the edge of the advertising matter.

Advertisers (or their agencies) are required to provide a publisher with copies of their ads ready for printing in accordance with the specifications of the magazine.

Demographic Editions

As mentioned earlier, many major publications today offer demographic editions that enable advertisers to select the geographical market that they wish to reach. Demographic availability makes it possible for regional marketers, and for national marketers expanding their distribution in stages, to use important consumer magazines. Some consumer magazines can also provide split-

Top 10 Magazines 1984		
Rank	**Publication**	**Average Circulation**
1.	Reader's Digest	17,866,798
2.	TV Guide	17,115,233
3.	Modern Maturity	10,770,688
4.	National Geographic	10,392,548
5.	Better Homes & Gardens	8,058,839
6.	Family Circle	6,920,333
7.	Woman's Day	6,517,684
8.	McCall's	6,311,011
9.	Good Housekeeping	5,184,559
10.	Ladies' Home Journal	5,058,538

Source: Audit Bureau of Circulations.

run facilities. *Time* magazine offers demographic editions based on income, class, and occupation. *Sports Illustrated* offers a "market track system" that permits the advertiser to choose any one, or any combination, of fifty metro markets. *Sports Illustrated* also has a homeowners' edition that reaches 640,000 households. (See color plate 23 for a *SI* readership campaign.)

Comparing Magazines

Magazines are simple to compare in some ways and difficult to compare in other ways. In comparing two magazines reaching the same market segment — homemakers, for example — an advertiser might be considering *Family Circle* and *Woman's Day*. The first basis for comparison would be cost per thousand of circulation, or CPM, as it is commonly referred to. For such a comparison we would use the magazine's primary circulation figures. Secondary readers may be considered a bonus. To calculate the CPM we take the cost of a full-page black and white ad at the one-time rate, multiply by 1,000, and divide by circulation.

Family Circle	*Woman's Day*
circulation: 6,920,333	circulation: 6,517,684
rate for one page b&w: $63,200	rate for one page b&w: $60,970
CPM: $9.13	CPM: $9.35

CPM might be meaningful for this comparison if the advertiser had to choose between the two very similar magazines. Would an advertiser concentrate all advertising in one and skip the other when most of the circulation is unduplicated? Not likely.

Comparisons on the basis of mere CPM become much less meaningful when comparing two or more publications that have widely different circulations in both number and demographics. For example, a CPM comparison between *TV Guide* and *Business Week* would give us these figures:

TV Guide	*Business Week*
circulation: 17,115,233	circulation: 855,590
cost for one page b&w: $72,000	cost for one page b&w: $24,130
CPM: $4.21	CPM: $28.20

The two publications are obviously widely dissimilar in numbers of readers, but it is not merely numbers that must be considered. We must analyze the type of audience and the editorial climate. We would not use *TV Guide* to advertise business equipment. We would certainly not use *Business Week* to advertise diet pills or a cake mix. We realize that the editorial climate of the publication enhances the advertising. We might also take into consideration the method of circulation — what percentage through subscription, what percentage through single copy sales. Is the annual subscriber a more valuable reader than the reader who purchases the magazine at the newsstand or supermarket checkout counter? We assume the reader who buys single copies *wants* to read that magazine. On the other hand, the advertiser can build on the readership of annual subscribers with opportunities to repeat and reinforce the advertising thrust. Another important consideration in an advertiser's choice might be the distribution of the magazine's circulation. Some national publications are stronger in some cities or regions of the country. The point is that

Shown is an advertising rate card from *Houston Magazine,* one of a growing number of magazines published in large, affluent cities. The circulation of *Houston Magazine* is small (about 18,000) compared to the huge circulation of many national magazines, but its subscriber demographics make it valuable for advertisers who want to reach top business executives with an average household income in excess of $100,000 and an average home value of over $188,000. *Houston Magazine* claims readership of 3.14 adults per copy.

ADVERTISING RATES

BLACK & WHITE	1X	3X	6X	12X
Full page	$1240	$1215	$1195	$1080
2/3 page	945	890	865	760
1/2 page (vertical)	835	825	790	690
1/2 page (horizontal)	710	700	675	595
1/3 page	485	475	455	410
1/6 page	310	300	290	270

COVERS

Cover II	$1800	$1760	$1740	$1700
Cover III	1670	1615	1570	1520
Cover IV	2300	2265	2215	2010

SPECIAL POSITION

Add 15% to gross space cost.

COLOR

Any one matched color: $300 plus black & white space charge.

Any one PMS color: $400 plus black & white space charge.

Four-color Process: 1/2 page or larger: $650 additional; 1/3 page or smaller: $400 additional

INSERTS

Pre-printed inserts furnished to printer. (Back-up printing, inserting and handling charges, if any, on request.)

1 page	1605		4 pages	2835
2 pages	2230		6 pages	3835

BLEED

No additional charge.

PRODUCTION CHARGES

Advertisers will be charged a minimum set-up charge of $25.00 for production work on ads which are not camera-ready. Typesetting and engraving charges over and above the set-up charge will also be added.

MECHANICAL REQUIREMENTS

AD SIZE	WIDTH	DEPTH
Full page	7 1/4"	10"
2/3 page	4 3/4"	10"
1/2 page (vertical)	4 3/4"	7 3/8"
1/2 page (horizontal)	7 1/4"	4 15/16"
1/3 page (square)	4 3/4"	4 15/16"
1/3 page (vertical)	2 5/16"	10"
1/6 page	2 5/16"	4 15/16"

Keep all live matter 1/2" from trim edges.

ONE PAGE BLEED SIZE: 8 3/4" by 11 1/4" deep trimmed to 8 1/2" by 11".

PRINTING SPECIFICATIONS

Printed offset, sheet fed. Paper stock: 60# Lithofect Gloss; Cover: 100# Black and White Gloss. Pressed-glue, slotted binding.

Prefer 133-line screen. Maximum: 150; Minimum: 110.

Prefer one-piece offset negative, right reading, emulsion side up. Acceptable copy: velox, Scotchprints, camera-ready artwork, repro proof. Proof shown only on request. Progressive proofs required for four-color ads.

PAGE FORMAT

there are many qualitative as well as quantitative factors to be evaluated in making specific media decisions.

Audit Bureau of Circulations   People in the advertising business are familiar with the Audit Bureau of Circulations (ABC) as the authority on circulation figures for newspapers and magazines throughout the United States and Canada. ABC is one of print media's counters of circulation. It is valued by advertisers who want trustworthy numbers before investing their ad dollars. ABC's objective is to deliver the facts. To that end, ABC produces a yearly report containing a numerical breakdown of the circulation numbers of a publication. That report is supplemented by reports every six months which contain the unaudited circulation statement issued by the publisher. The ad revenues of publications are often contained in these reports.

PROFILE

Leo Burnett

In 1935, Leo Burnett and eight associates founded Leo Burnett Company. In its first year, this new advertising agency had billings of $600,000. In 1985 the agency was the 10th largest in the world with billings of $1.87 billion and an international network that encompassed 37 countries.

After graduation from the University of Michigan in 1914, Leo Burnett worked for a short period as a newspaper reporter before starting his advertising career as editor of the Cadillac Motor Company's house magazine. Later, he moved to the Homer McKee advertising agency in Indianapolis, where he spent the next ten years fulfilling both creative and executive duties. After moving to Chicago to take a job as vice-president and creative head of Erwin Wasey & Company, he decided to found his own agency in that city "because there was nobody else here in Chicago."

The Leo Burnett agency is probably best known for its famous Marlboro cigarette ads, for which it developed the symbol of the tattooed cowboy. Today, the company still serves the Green Giant Company of LeSueur, Minnesota, for whom it created the Jolly Green Giant. Some other well-known accounts on which Leo Burnett worked included Schlitz beer, Maytag washers, Pillsbury cake mixes, Kellogg's cereals, and Campbell soups.

When he retired in 1967, Leo Burnett left behind not only a worldwide agency that employs more than three thousand people but a major imprint on the creative thinking that helps shape the advertising business. He played a dominant role in the development of a creative approach that some advertising people have called "the Chicago school of advertising." It was Leo Burnett's idea to look for the inherent drama in a product and to write the advertising copy based on that drama. *Inherent drama,* he said, is "what the manufacturer had in mind . . . when he conceived the product." This drama, he believed, can be found in all good advertising. As he explained:

> . . . it gives the effect of news, even in an old product, and has about it a feeling of naturalness which gives the reader an emotional reward and makes him feel good about it.

Among the many honors that came to Leo Burnett were election to the Copywriters Hall of Fame, the special merit award of the New York Art Directors Club, and election as Marketing Man of the Year in 1966 by the American Marketing Association.

CASE HISTORY

Schwepping It Up

Schweppes has used its advertising to add value to its product. Its sophistication and humor go back many years to the time when Schweppes' consumers viewed themselves as "gentlemen." Those characteristics in its advertising have been retained and built upon in the past 30 years as the company saw the marketing opportunities that result from dissolving social barriers. Such an opportunity was available in the United States for a product that had made its mark in England.

The firm was founded by Jacob Schweppes, a Swiss jeweller, who, in 1780, began to develop a system for the manufacture of artificial mineral waters. By 1793, he had established his firm in London.

One of the most remarkable achievements has been the exploitation of the name. No one attempting to devise a name for a new brand would choose Schweppes, but the strange foreign word lent itself to imaginative advertising, from the early slogans — such as, "Thirsty? Take the necessary Schweppes" — to the word that sums up the concept after World War II — "schweppervescence." Schweppes married its name to the image of the product nearly two hundred years ago when it first started to advertise the product in London newspapers. By 1900, Schweppes' advertising had begun to use illustrations rather than only typography.

In 1931 Schweppes began using an advertising agency, and one of the results of hiring professional advertising people was a substantial increase in the ad budget. Their first programs began with ads in class magazines. The ads were backed up with displays at bars and clubs and the distribution of promotional items such as trays, barometers, golf score books and such, which carried the Schweppes brand name.

Prior to World War II, the ads in England were distinguished by pleasant, clever, literate humor. During the war, Schweppes was unable to produce the product, but continued to advertise with good humor about other "similar crises in the nation's history." When the war ended, Schweppes launched a major advertising campaign aimed at the general public.

"Schweppervescence" was dreamed up at a brainstorming session in England. That advertising approach continued to be gently humorous and very English, very civilized. It was in 1949 that David Ogilvy met Commander Whitehead and realized that the Commander would make a perfect ambassador in the United States for the product. The use of the company's chief executive as the advertising model fitted perfectly with the marketing task that Schweppes had set for itself. Commander Whitehead's job was to convince consumers that Schweppes' traditional quality and taste was in no way affected now that the product was produced in America. The first ad appeared in the *New Yorker* magazine and showed Commander Whitehead descending from a BOAC plane. The impact was very, very British. For the next twenty years, the approach changed very little. The ads showed Commander Whitehead in various situations. They enjoyed much free publicity as Commander Whitehead appeared on radio shows and numerous newspaper interviews.

One of the effective techniques was to place an ad in the local newspaper when Schweppes appointed a new bottler. The ad would show the Commander arriving at the airport to be met by his new business partner. The bottlers loved to appear in the ad with Commander Whitehead, the epitome of an English gentleman. In ten years, Schweppes sales increased by over 500 percent. Through the years, Schweppes advertising has maintained a faith in the intelligence of the consumer, which enables Schweppes to address them in a sophisticated style, and with an implicit expectation that the American consumer recognizes and is willing to pay for the best. (See color plate 24.)

The man from Schweppes is here

MEET Commander Edward White-head, Schweppesman Extraordinary from London, England, where the house of Schweppes has been a great institution since 1794.

The Commander has come to these United States to make sure that every drop of Schweppes Quinine Water bottled here has the original flavor which has long made it the essential mixer for an authentic Gin-and-Tonic.

He imports the original Schweppes elixir, and the secret of Schweppes unique carbonation is locked in his brief case. "Schweppervescence," says the Commander, *"lasts the whole drink through."* It took Schweppes almost a hundred years to bring the flavor of their Quinine Water to its present bitter-sweet perfection. But it will take you only thirty seconds to mix it with ice and gin in a highball glass. *Then,* gentle reader, you will bless the day you read these words.

P.S. You can now buy Schweppes Quinine Water at popular prices!

ABC is a nonprofit organization funded largely by publishers, who represent 90 percent of the dues-paying members. The rest of the support comes from advertisers and agency members. The organization employs 76 full-time salaried auditors who operate out of the headquarters in Schaumburg, Illinois, a suburb of Chicago. The auditors check the publication's press runs, distribution methods, and financial records.

Summary

The print media category is composed of newspapers and magazines. In terms of delivery of an advertising message, the benefits that each vehicle in this category provides are dependent upon the advertiser's product, the nature of the advertiser's target market, and the distribution of the advertiser's product. Newspapers offer advertisers immediacy — instant access to local markets in an editorial environment that is local and current. Although the quality of reproduction in newspapers is not as good as may be desired, the short closing date enables advertisers to tie in with fast-breaking news or to take advantage of weather or seasons that may have an important bearing on the sale of a particular product. Air conditioners, for example, should be advertised with the advent of summer heat.

Newspapers provide a high degree of geographical selectivity; advertisers can choose to reach only selected cities or metros. In this way, advertisers can use newspapers to keep pace with expanding distribution and to provide strong dealer support at the local level. Advertisers can also obtain some measure of demographic selectivity through the use of preferred positions within a newspaper. Generally speaking, newspaper reading peaks in middle-age groups, when people's interest in news and civic affairs runs highest. Readership is also greatest among upper socioeconomic groups in large metropolitan and suburban areas.

The cost of running an ad in a newspaper depends on its frequency of insertion, size, and position. ROP color adds to the cost, but studies have found that color advertising pays for itself by attracting additional readership. Advertisers of automobiles and foods are the heaviest users of national newspaper advertising, but the bulk of the advertising in newspapers is sponsored by local retail firms. Over the years, though total national advertising expenditures have increased, the percentage devoted to newspapers has declined.

The greatest advantage of magazines is heightened demographic selectivity. Depending on the editorial scope of the magazine, advertisers can reach both men and women, women only, men only, young women, married women, older people, health food addicts, gourmets, travel enthusiasts, sports fans, yachting enthusiasts, and so on. Each magazine delivers a market segment interested in that magazine's editorial content, and that interest spills over to the advertising. Advertisers can deliver their messages with beautiful color in a vehicle that the reader can examine slowly, digest, and reflect on. Furthermore, the issue can be referred to again and again and is often passed along to other members of the family or friends. Sometimes the secondary readership of a magazine will be two to three times the circulation that the publisher promises an advertiser as a rate base or guarantee.

The only disadvantage of magazines is their long deadline for the submission of advertising copy: usually about eight weeks prior to publication. The long closing hinders flexibility and demands long-range planning, which is difficult to revise quickly enough to meet changing market conditions.

Comparisons between magazines reaching the same market segment are difficult to make. CPM (cost per thousand) is a good starting point, but media planners are also concerned with a magazine's editorial climate, frequency of issue, and the buying habits and life-styles of its audience.

Questions for Discussion

1. Why is primary audience more important than secondary audience?
2. What kinds of magazines would you specify for reach? What kinds for frequency?
3. What are some of the ways you could utilize demographic editions of consumer magazines?
4. Can you suggest any types of products for which newspapers would be the best medium? For which magazines would be best?
5. How does the editorial climate of a magazine affect the advertising message?
6. If circulations were about equal, what factors would you consider in choosing between a morning paper and an evening paper?
7. Would the size of the publication format have a bearing on your choice of medium? For example, on what grounds would you base a choice between a tabloid newspaper and a standard newspaper, or between a digest magazine and a standard-size magazine?

Sources and Suggestions for Further Reading

Baker, S. *Systematic Approach to Advertising Creativity.* New York: McGraw-Hill, 1983.

Barban, Arnold M., Stephen M. Cristol, and Frank G. Kopec. *Essentials of Media Planning.* Chicago: Crain Books, 1976.

Bogart, Leo. *Strategy in Advertising, 2nd Edition: Matching Media and Messages to Markets and Motivations.* Chicago: Crain Books, 1984.

Donnermuth, William P. *Promotion: Analysis, Creativity and Strategy.* Boston: Kent Publishing Co., 1984.

Kastiel, Diane Lynn. "How to Read a Publication's Circulation Audit." *Business Marketing* (August 1986).

Levin, Gary. "Adding Sections to Capture Readers, Advertisers." Special Report, *Advertising Age* (July 28, 1986).

"Newspaper Ads at the Speed of Light." *Inside Print* (June 1986).

Ray, Michael L. *Advertising and Communication Management.* Englewood Cliffs, N.J.: Prentice-Hall, 1982.

Sachs, William. *Advertising Management: Its Role in Marketing.* Tulsa, Oklahoma: Penn-Well Publishing Company, 1983.

Sissors, Jack Z., and E. Reynold Petray. *Advertising Media Planning.* Chicago: Crain Books, 1976.

Sonenklar, Carol. "Women and Their Magazines." *American Demographics,* vol. 8, no. 6 (June 1986).

9 PRINT MEDIA: BUSINESS AND FARM PUBLICATIONS

Selling the Decision Makers

Farm Publications

Working Vocabulary

buying power	horizontal publications	reader service card
paid circulation	vertical publications	crop editions
controlled circulation	inserts	

Standard Rate & Data Service, Inc., lists about 3,300 publications under more than 175 different market categories in its *SRDS Business Publication Rates and Data* book. The number of business publications changes from year to year as some publications disappear and new ones spring up. Some business publications disappear because the industry or market they serve has dwindled or disappeared. New publications are introduced as new industries are created or mature industries expand. Although the percentage of the total advertising volume in the United States that is invested in business publications is far less than that devoted to television or consumer magazines, the total outlay for business advertising was well over $7.4 billion in 1984. It had more than doubled in the preceding five-year period and represents a rapidly growing area of the advertising industry.

Selling the Decision Makers

Business publications are distinguished from consumer publications by their editorial focus, and by the fact that the information in the advertisements they carry is often as important to the readers as the magazine's editorial contents. In fact, it is quite common for companies to expect their managers and technicians to read pertinent business publications on company time. Very often the company itself pays for subscriptions to certain business publications. It then circulates each issue among its employees with an attached routing slip that indicates to whom readers should pass the magazine once they have read it. Reading business publications is one way the company's decision makers keep abreast of developments in their industry.

Business publications may be divided into five categories:

1. general business publications
2. industrial publications
3. trade publications
4. professional publications
5. institutional publications

The distinctions between these types of business publications are not always clear; a magazine will often exhibit characteristics of two or three categories. But the above list will serve as a rough map to help guide us over the topography of the world of the business press.

Buying Power

Unlike advertisers in national consumer magazines, who analyze their audience in terms of demographic characteristics such as age, sex, marital status, and level of education, advertisers in business publications are interested

Top 25 Business/Industrial Advertisers 1984

Company	Ad Expenditures ($000)
1. International Business Machines	$21,308
2. American Telephone & Telegraph	20,347
3. Hewlett-Packard Co.	13,182
4. General Electric	13,076
5. E.I. du Pont de Nemours	11,980
6. General Motors Corp.	11,025
7. Texas Instruments	10,713
8. American Express Co.	10,342
9. 3M Co.	10,321
10. Motorola Inc.	8,701
11. Xerox Corp.	7,575
12. Ford Motor Co.	7,432
13. RCA Corp.	6,957
14. Honeywell	6,758
15. ITT Corp.	6,539
16. Eastman Kodak Co.	6,371
17. Digital Equipment Corp.	6,251
18. Phibro-Salomon	5,896
19. Rockwell International	5,802
20. First Boston	5,595
21. Goldman Sachs & Co.	5,441
22. Allied Corp.	5,303
23. Gould Inc.	5,171
24. GTE Corp.	5,063
25. Harris Corp.	5,048

Source: Reprinted with permission from the September 26, 1985, issue of *Advertising Age.* Copyright © 1985 by Crain Communications, Inc.

The data for this table were developed by Rome Reports, Inc., by counting ad pages in 527 business publications representing more than 90 publishing categories. Note that high on the list are computer firms, manufacturers of business systems, financial organizations, and transportation equipment companies such as General Motors and Ford. These automotive manufacturers advertise fleet cars and trucks to business organizations and also use business publications to advertise personal cars to affluent business executives.

in the buying power of their audience. **Buying power** is the amount of money, or budget, that potential customers for our product have to spend on goods and services. (See color plates 25 and 26 for ads aimed at buyers of office supplies.) In his book *Marketing Strategies,* P. Dudley Kaley points out the differences in buying power of the consumer and the industrial customer.

> In developing segmentation strategies, it is worthwhile to consider some differences between market segments for consumer products and for industrial products. In the consumer market, no one customer for toothpaste has enough buying potential to warrant consideration as a market. If there were not tens of thousands of these individuals with similar desires in the marketplace, no company would find it profitable to market such a product. At the other extreme, however, one industrial customer might have enough purchasing potential to comprise a market segment unto itself. Take, for example, fiber glass insulation. United States Steel Corporation's 64-story office building in Pittsburgh required carloads of insulation. So did the new World Trade Center in downtown New York. In such cases, each building can represent a market segment, but with a very definite time relationship—a segment opportunity that exists only once.[1]

---

[1] P. Dudley Kaley, *Marketing Strategies* (New York: The Conference Board, 1974), pp. 56–57.

The Audience for Business Publications

Business publications also differ from consumer publications in the way they build their audiences. Few specialized business publications are sold on newsstands. If we place an advertisement in one of these magazines for machinery costing hundreds of thousands of dollars, then obviously we are not interested in reaching the random or occasional reader. The stakes are high. We want to reach the people who buy, specify, and make decisions for their companies that involve very substantial amounts of money. We are interested in learning what companies each business publication's readers work for and what their job titles are within those companies. In the *SRDS Business Publication Rates and Data* book and in their own circulation documentation, business publications list the kinds and sizes of the companies they reach — by Standard Industrial Classification (SIC) number and by size of plant in number of employees. As you can see, comparing business publications is as complicated as comparing consumer magazines. We want to know how many plants the publication reaches and how many people work in each plant because we know that pass-along readership of business publications is very high.

Although many business publications build their circulations by selling subscriptions, the readers of many important business publications receive copies of the magazine free. The number of readers who buy subscriptions is known as **paid circulation;** the number of readers who receive free copies is known as **controlled circulation.** Some magazines have circulations that are part paid and part controlled. Others, usually magazines published by a trade or professional association, have circulations that are entirely controlled. (Each member of the society or association is given a subscription to the magazine as part of his or her membership rights.) In order to build its audience, a controlled-circulation publication sends subscription request forms to members of the industry it serves. Recipients of this form can obtain a free subscription to the magazine merely by filling out the form and sending it in. Publishers obtain the names of prospective subscribers from trade associations, from professional organizations, and from industry directories. Many publishers will require that the recipients, either as companies or as individuals, are *qualified* to receive that publication on the basis of product, line of business, SIC category, plant size, job title, job function, or any other combination of attributes that the publisher sets. For example, *Industrial Maintenance and Plant Operation* states that "recipients must be employed in plants with 50 or more employees, or with a minimum Dun & Bradstreet rating of $50,000." Such requirements are significant, for the publication will use them to prove the quality of its circulation to advertisers.

General Business Publications

General business publications have no specific editorial focus; like mass-circulation consumer magazines, they try to have something for everyone. The total thrust is usually all business. A quick glance at the table of contents of such general business publications as *Business Week, Dun's Review,* or *Fortune* will reveal an editorial mix of current business news plus features that include in-depth reports on companies, individuals, and industries. Some general business publications that are published by well-known business schools tend more toward analysis of trends and ideas in their editorial mix.

BARRON'S OUTSMARTS THEM ALL.

Barron's audience has the highest concentration of college graduates of any publication measured by Simmons, including Forbes, Fortune and Business Week.

Source: SMRB, 1983 Copyright, Dow Jones & Company, Inc., 1984.

A *Barron's* ad appears every week on page 8 in *Advertising Age.* The thrust of the program is to show that *Barron's* offers a better audience than competing publications. *Barron's* does not emphasize "reach" but the "quality" of its circulation — highest median employment income, highest percentage of single issue newsstand sales, and, as the ad says, "the highest concentration of college graduates."

The *Wall Street Journal* is essentially a business newspaper; that is, it contains primarily news of interest only in the world of business. Published every weekday, the *Wall Street Journal* has become important reading for over 2 million people. It is available nationally and internationally. The U.S. edition is available nationally and in four regional editions — Eastern, Midwestern, Western, and Southwestern. The international edition combines the Asian edition and the European edition, each of which is available separately.

Advertisers in these general publications may have several objectives. They may want to reach hidden influences their salesmen cannot see — top executives of companies who can affect the sale of their product. The Paper Mill Study[2] revealed, for example, that for suppliers of chemical products, only 17 of the 40 identified buying influences were on their customer lists. Suppliers of process machinery learned that of the 45 identified buying influences, only 3 were on their lists.

Advertisers frequently want to influence the financial community — either to enhance the value of their company's stock or to build their company's image in preparation for the time when it may want to go to the market for funds. Another important objective is the stimulation of executive thinking in new directions — perhaps to suggest the purchase of a company airplane, a site for the location of a new plant, the installation of a data processing system, or the purchase of a fleet of company cars. Business publications offer advertisers the opportunity to reach business executives in a business environment with a minimum of waste. Advertisers of consumer products have also turned to the use of general business publications to reach upscale men and women who buy automobiles, whiskey, cigarettes, and other personal products. (See color plate 27 for an ad targeting businesswomen.)

Industrial Publications

Industrial publications are read by people in manufacturing industries that change the shape or form of a product, convert raw materials into semifinished or finished goods, or assemble components or semifinished products into finished goods. In any particular plant, people in different job capacities will read those business publications that are related to their work.

For example, in a company that manufactures hi-fidelity amplifiers, the electronics engineers might read *Electronic Design, Electronics, Electronic Component News,* or any of the more than 20 publications covering some part of the industry. The person responsible for the maintenance and operation of the factory might read *Plant Engineering* or *Industrial Maintenance and Plant Operation.* The purchasing agent might read *New Equipment Digest, Industrial Bulletin, Purchasing Magazine, Purchasing World,* or any of the many publications serving his or her interests. The top brass might read *Electronic Business, Electronic News,* and other publications related to the hi-fidelity business in general, as well as general business publications. All of these people want to keep up with the industry, to learn quickly about new developments that may affect their work and their company's future.

The importance of industrial magazines and the advertisements they carry becomes obvious once we realize that in 1983 the cost for an industrial salesman to make one face-to-face sales call was estimated to be $205.40 (see page 213). Often, however, an industrial purchase involves the participation of several operating people, many of whom our salespeople will not know or could not call on even if they did know them. Advertising in an industrial publication enables the advertiser to reach the engineer who specifies the product, the purchasing agent who buys it, and the manager who must pass on it. Industrial products are not bought on the basis of emotional appeal. The buyers are hard-nosed people with sharp pencils who want reliability first.

---

[2] "The Paper Mill Study," Commissioned by Miller Freeman Publications (New York: American Business Press, 1975).

This technical ad is aimed at several people involved in the manufacture of coatings — the plant manager concerned with efficiency and cost reduction, the research chemist concerned with product improvements, and the purchasing agent who is expected to be alert to cost-cutting opportunities. Frequently, the decision to change from one raw material to another involves reaching many people. The supplier's sales force can often see only the purchasing agent. It is the supplier's advertising that informs and persuades the other hidden influences to switch — to replace, in this ad, half of their titanium dioxide with Min-U-Sil.

There are two types of industrial publications: horizontal publications and vertical publications. **Horizontal publications** reach several specific categories of job function across many different industries. *Industrial Maintenance and Plant Operation,* for example, reaches 107,000 people in 69,000 plants. The publisher's statement of editorial policy will give us a better understanding of its focus:

> Editorial purpose: provide recipients with news on new and improved products and methods used in maintaining and operating plant equipment, buildings, facilities, and grounds.

The table of contents for this publication, which serves design engineers, reveals the kind of editorial mix its readers demand: new information on engineered components, materials, and systems. It is issued every other week to a controlled circulation of over 157,000 in over 35,000 OEM (original equipment manufacturers) plants.

DESIGN NEWS

September 17, 1984
Volume 40/Number 18

Pg.16 Oil platform for the deep | Pg.74 PCs enter electronics age | Pg.130 Rankine cycle engine

FEATURES

Cahners Publishing • Publishers of 30 specialized business magazines in Building & Construction • Electronics & Computers • Foodservice • Manufacturing • Health Care •

VBPA DESIGN NEWS (USPS 076-070) is published twice monthly, with one directory issue in each of the months of March, May, July, September, and November, by Cahners Publishing Company, Division of Reed Holdings, Inc., 221 Columbus Avenue, Boston, MA 02116. Norman L. Cahners, Chairman. Saul Goldwertz, President and Chief Executive Officer.
ABP Ronald G. Segel, Executive Vice President and Chief Operating Officer. DESIGN NEWS is published by the Cahners Magazine Division. J. A. Sheehan, President. William Platt, Executive Vice President. Ellsworth M. Brown Jr., Group Vice President. Circulation records maintained at Cahners Publishing co. 270 St. Paul St., Denver, CO 80206. Second class postage paid at Denver, CO 80202 and additional mailing offices. Postmaster: Send address changes to DESIGN NEWS, 270 St. Paul St., Denver, CO 80206. Advertising and editorial offices: 221 Columbus Ave., Boston, MA 02116. Telephone: 617-536-7780. Subscription offices: 270 St. Paul St., Denver, CO 80206. Telephone: 303-388-4511. DESIGN NEWS is circulated to design engineers in the U.S. original equipment industry in plants with more than 20 employees and which manufacture machinery or equipment of their own design. Design engineers responsible for specifications of components, systems, materials or engineering equipment may receive DESIGN NEWS without charge. Complete qualification form and company letterhead required. Subscription to others in continental U.S. $55 per year. Canada/Mexico $60. Foreign surface mail $75 and foreign air mail $150. Single copies $4 U.S. $5 Canada, $6 Foreign. Send requests for qualification forms and/or change of address to DESIGN NEWS, 270 St. Paul St., Denver, CO 80206. 1984 by Cahners Publishing Company. Division of Reed Holdings, Inc. All rights reserved.

Reprints of DESIGN NEWS articles are available on a custom printing basis at reasonable prices in quantities of 500 or more. For a specific quotation, contact Arthur W. Lehmann, Manager, Marketing Services, 1350 E. Touhy Ave., Des Plaines, IL 60018; phone 800-323-4958.

The editorial content of this type of magazine provides information of interest to many people in many plants that all have common problems. If we are advertising a product that is used in several different industries, we would want to use a horizontal publication to get maximum reach.

On the other hand, if the product advertised is designed for a very clearly delineated industry, we would want to use a vertical publication.

A publication is described as **vertical** when it reaches various segments in the *same* industry. If our product were printing presses or printing ink, for example, we might advertise in *Graphic Arts Monthly,* which reaches over 87,000 people in the printing industry. The printing industry is composed of many segments, each producing or marketing a different product, but *all related* to printing processes and the printing business. Thus *Graphic Arts Monthly* could be used to advertise inks, presses, bindery equipment, engraving and platemaking equipment, paper, photography, and typesetting and numbering devices.

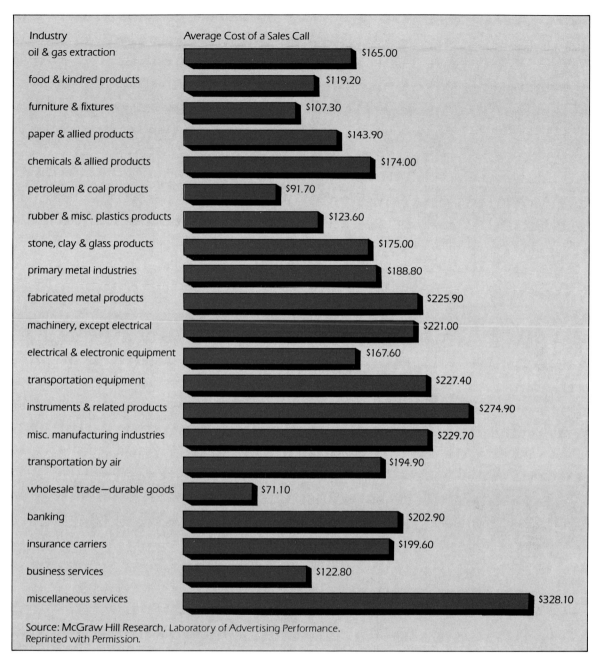

Industry	Average Cost of a Sales Call	
oil & gas extraction		$165.00
food & kindred products		$119.20
furniture & fixtures		$107.30
paper & allied products		$143.90
chemicals & allied products		$174.00
petroleum & coal products		$91.70
rubber & misc. plastics products		$123.60
stone, clay & glass products		$175.00
primary metal industries		$188.80
fabricated metal products		$225.90
machinery, except electrical		$221.00
electrical & electronic equipment		$167.60
transportation equipment		$227.40
instruments & related products		$274.90
misc. manufacturing industries		$229.70
transportation by air		$194.90
wholesale trade—durable goods		$71.10
banking		$202.90
insurance carriers		$199.60
business services		$122.80
miscellaneous services		$328.10

Source: McGraw Hill Research, Laboratory of Advertising Performance.
Reprinted with Permission.

The data for this chart were compiled by McGraw-Hill Research from responses to a questionnaire administered to 1,155 sales executives in 1984. The questionnaire asked "What was your approximate cost per sales call in 1983?" And, "Approximately how many calls does it take to close a sale?" As shown here, the cost ranged from a low of $71.10 to a high of $328.10. The number of calls ranged from 2 for Food & Kindred Products (Standard Industrial Classification 20) to 7.1 for Chemicals & Allied Products (SIC 28). Curiously, the most expensive call — for miscellaneous services — required 6.7 calls to close a sale for a total cost of $2,198.27. Of course, the point of the research is that media advertising helps make the sales calls more effective by providing the initial contact and preparing the way for the sales force. Advertising also helps keep customers sold. According to McGraw-Hill Research, the cost to reach a prospect through advertising in business publications is just 19 cents.

Core binders are the material used in making molds for casting metal products. As might be expected, to reach foundries, the product is advertised in a foundry magazine. Do note the copy — technical, yet simple and straightforward, with the benefits described without puff or useless adjectives.

NO SMOKING

Sodium Silicate Core Binders Can Help You Clear The Air

"Smoking" or "Non-Smoking" core binders? The choice is yours.

Today, there are new sodium silicate core binders that are not only low in cost but can rid foundry air of toxic gases and noxious fumes. And they are available from Foundry Supply Houses across the U.S.

What's more, these new inorganic, no-bake or warm-box silicate core binders offer improved shake-out, excellent reclamation, longer working time, better early strength, and long core storage life—all this without spewing dangerous contaminants into the air.

Water-based sodium silicate core binders ensure additional production efficiencies and advantages that include:

■ Smooth surface finish for the finished casting
■ Low-energy requirements for making cores and molds
■ Dimensional stability for the core, mold and casting
■ Suitable for automatic core production systems

■ Good green strength
■ Excellent work time-to-mold release time ratios.

New formulation sodium silicate core binders put to rest the questions of difficult shake-out and poor reclamation. Bonded sands can be reclaimed using either wet or dry methods when these advanced state-of-the-art sodium silicate core binders are specified.

Let us help you make the connection with a Foundry Supply House near you. Phone (215) 293-7305, or write to PQ's Industrial Chemical Division - Marketing Department for a list of Foundry Supply Houses which have these new core binder formulations ready for immediate delivery.

 **The PQ Corporation**
P.O. Box 840, Valley Forge, PA 19482
Combining silicate chemistry with imagination.

Scheduled for publication in 1985 issues of Foundry Management & Technology

The advertiser interested in marketing any of the products mentioned would find *Graphic Arts Monthly* and other publications in that category very efficient.

Advertisers must pay for a certain amount of waste circulation in both horizontal and vertical publications, however, because not every product is suitable for every factory or every type of manufacturing operation. Horizontal publications may indeed reach nonprospects. Vertical publications, reaching all the job functions and different levels of management in a single industry, will also include a number of readers in their circulation figures who will not be prospective customers for a given product. For example, *Graphic Arts Monthly* will reach commercial printers, converters who make packaging materials, noncommercial printers (internal operations in businesses, government, or schools), typesetters, plate makers, and binderies. However, only the commercial or noncommercial printers would be prospective customers for the manufacturers of printing presses or printing ink. The readers in other areas of the printing industry would represent waste circulation.

Trade Publications

Trade magazines contain news and advertising of interest to people employed in both the wholesale and retail distribution of specific lines of consumer goods and services. Virtually every retail field is covered by one or more trade magazines such as *Snack Food, Music Retailer, American Drycleaner,* and *Supermarketing.* Although the editorial focus of trade magazines is aimed predominately at retailers, most of them tend to reach a vertical audience. For example, a grocery magazine such as *Supermarketing* would reach independent grocers, chain supermarket managers and executives, and food wholesalers, as well as the manufacturers of many products *sold through* supermarkets or *used by* supermarkets in their operations. In addition, many regional trade publications are available. The manufacturers of hardware products can reach their regional markets through such publications as *Southern Hardware, Northern Hardware Trade,* and *New England Hardware.*

Institutional Publications

Institutional publications circulate to executives, managers, and supervisors in organizations that provide a service to the public on their premises — such as hotels, hospitals, nursing homes, schools, and resorts. These institutions represent tremendous buying power — for furniture, linens, uniforms, food, and cleaning and maintenance supplies. Publications in this category include *Hospitals, Modern Healthcare, Club Management, Hotel & Motel Management, Resort Management,* and *Ski Area Management.* The titles are indicative of their areas of editorial interest.

Professional Publications

When we think of professionals, the people that come to mind are physicians, lawyers, architects, veterinarians, accountants, and engineers. They are professionals by training, and the journals they read are written with an editorial focus that is often very specialized. The professional market is important to advertisers because these are the people who influence the purchases others make and who, in many cases, write the actual specifications. Advertisers would want to place their ads in the *American Bar Association Journal* to reach attorneys who may influence plant location or method of financing; *Engineering News-Record* to reach civil engineers who specify the machinery and materials used in highway construction; *Dental Management* to reach dentists who prescribe medication and dentures; *Medical Economics* to reach physicians who prescribe drugs; *Architectural Digest* to reach architects who specify the materials used in building construction. The medical field alone is covered by over

The two business magazine ads here are both published by the same professional organization. However, each is clearly addressed to different reader interest. The *SPE Journal* reaches *research people* in the petroleum industry — only about 15,000 readers who pay $12.50 annually for a bimonthly subscription. On the other hand, almost 53,000 *field engineers* pay $18 a year to receive the *Journal of Petroleum Technology.*

200 specialized publications ranging from *The American Journal of Cardiology* to *Urology.* As in many industrial publications, the advertising is very important to the readers. It is often through the advertising pages that professionals learn of new products and new techniques. Such interest adds impact to the advertisers' message and demands advertising that is very informative. Consider the statement by P. Dudley Kaley earlier in this chapter. An architect or engineer involved in the design and construction of the 64-story office building he mentioned specified the use of glass fiber insulation, a sale amounting to several hundred thousand dollars.

Comparing Circulations

Circulation figures are essential (though of course not the only) criteria for choosing a publication in which to advertise. Fortunately, several auditing organizations exist to verify the circulation claims of publications; these include the Audit Bureau of Circulations, the Business Publications Audit of Circulation, and the Verified Audit Circulation Company. Circulation statements shown in Standard Rate and Data Service (see page 219) are taken from one of these services, or else from a sworn statement from the publisher. Many publications will list the ABC or BPA circulation figure on their table of contents or their copyright page.

The ABC, BPA, and VAC all base their figures on semiannual statements submitted by the publishers, and verified by post office mailing receipts. The

Before they ask you about dental care programs, ask us. Last year 4,114 benefit managers did.

Last year thousands of employee benefit managers contacted the American Dental Association for information on dental benefit plans. Why?

Dental care plans are a rapidly growing employee benefit—from two million people covered in 1965 to an estimated 48 million today. Employers and union officials recognize dental plans as a worthwhile employee benefit.

Further, the American Dental Association has experience gained from longstanding cooperation with the nation's largest carriers and purchasers of dental insurance.

We can help you better understand dental care and make the right decisions for your company and your employees.

Return this coupon, and we'll send you a package of useful background information on dental prepayment.

If you are considering a dental plan for your company, or presently have coverage, we believe you will find this information important. Please send the coupon to: James Y. Marshall, Council on Dental Care Programs, American Dental Association, 211 East Chicago Avenue, Chicago, Illinois 60611.

```
For your information kit send this coupon to:

    James Y. Marshall
    Council on Dental Care Programs   [ada logo]
    American Dental Association
    211 East Chicago Avenue
    Chicago, Illinois 60611

Name
Title                     Phone
Company
Address
City            State          Zip
Number of employees
Presently have a dental plan? Yes      No
```

A most unusual ad, sponsored by the American Dental Association, appeared in *The Personnel Administrator,* a professional publication for personnel managers and other company officers concerned with the personnel function. In this ad, the ADA is seeking to build goodwill, out of which might develop more programs covering dental benefits. Here we see one group of professionals (dentists) addressing another group of professionals (personnel people) who have the ability to specify and choose for their companies dental programs that can amount to millions of dollars of business.

ABC provides its figures based on *paid* subscriptions; the BPA and VAC base their figures on *paid* and *controlled* subscriptions combined.

When two different circulation statements (ABC and BPA, BPA and VAC, or ABC and Sworn) appear in any one listing, the figures are not to be added from the two statements to arrive at the total circulation for the publication.

Rates and Spaces

Business publications vary in size and format in the same way that consumer magazines do. There are tabloids, standards, and digests. They also vary in their editorial approach, with some emphasizing, or devoted entirely to, new product information. Others may contain a mix of new product informa-

As business publications compete with other important business publications whose circulation figures are relatively close, they seek differences that will convince the advertiser. One may stress the advantage of larger circulation; another may stress the education or income level of its audience; another its importance to readers. In this ad, *Forbes* attacks its competitors on the basis of premium offers to solicit subscriptions, the duration of subscriptions, and the number of copies distributed after a reader's subscription has expired.

Can expensive premiums cure sick circulation?

Finding out who's got the healthiest circulation is as easy as ABC.

The latest ABC statements for Forbes, Business Week and Fortune contain some very interesting information indeed. For one thing, Forbes' U.S. circulation is now 116,754 more than Fortune's and almost equal* to Business Week's. For another, Forbes' average newsstand sales are higher than either Fortune's or Business Week's.

Not only that, both Fortune and Business Week had to sell more subscriptions during the period than Forbes did to maintain their rate bases—61% more for Fortune, 55% more for Business Week. In fact, Business Week failed to make its rate base in over a third of its issues. And Fortune had to sell almost twice as many short-term subscriptions as Forbes in this period.

But perhaps the most telling statistic is the one telling how many premiums were used to sell subscriptions to Fortune. We can't help but wonder just how "premium" is the quality of the subscribers (who make up almost a third of
*See box re "Post Expiration Copies."

Fortune's total of new subscriptions sold) that have to be baited with premiums such as "A Travel Alarm Clock, Telephone, Pocket Calculator, Fortune Sport Bag, Pocket Diary, Money Exchanger/Metric Converter or Lucite Desk Clock." (Forbes' premiums, when offered, were samplings of the magazine in the form of reprints.)

Last but not least is the matter of Post Expiration Copies Included In Paid Circulation (what ABC used to call "arrears"). A glance at the chart will tell you that Forbes has none, while both Fortune and Business Week include a substantial number of these unpaid-for copies in their paid circulation figures. In fact, just about any ABC statistic you care to examine shows that Forbes' circulation is healthier than either Fortune's or Business Week's.

If the success of your company is vital to you, be sure your ads are in the magazine whose circulation shows the greatest vitality—Forbes.

Publishers Statements To ABC For 6-Month Period Ended 6/30/84			
Circulation:	FORBES	FORTUNE	BUSINESS WEEK (North America)
Paid Circulation	726,736	709,903	775,223
U.S. Circulation (Analyzed Issue)	720,962	604,208	762,806
Post Expiration Copies Included in Paid Circulation	0	18,702	37,852
Subscriptions:			
Ordered by Mail	86.4%	81.5%	74.9%
Ordered for 3 Years or More	19.0%	7.9%	4.7%
Ordered at Basic Price	73.6%	46.6%	63.1%
Number Ordered for Less than 1 Year	84,146	162,763	142,647
Number Ordered with Premium	34,342	128,330	82,730
Total Sold in 6 Month Period	244,189	392,629	378,541
Average Single Copy Sales (Newsstand Sales)	33,467	32,580	23,191

Forbes
Capitalist Tool
Forbes Magazine—60 Fifth Ave., N.Y., NY 10011

tion and feature articles. Space is sold in full pages or in the same range of fractional space available in consumer magazines. Most business publications sell cover positions; some even sell the front cover positions. Contract rates and color rates are similar to those of consumer publications. Business paper advertisers make frequent use of **inserts.** An insert is an advertisement, one page or more, that is prepared and printed by the advertiser and then bound into the magazine by the publisher. The publisher charges the advertiser the black and

From Standard Rate & Data Service's *Business Publications Edition,* this is a listing for ▶ *Plant Engineering,* a horizontal publication. There are two points of interest in this listing: circulation is controlled, that is, without charge to qualified recipients, and the publication carries an audit by BPA (Business Publication Audit) and an audit by ABC (Audit Bureau of Circulations) that indicate identical circulation. The publication offers four geographic editions. Manufacturing processes differ from industry to industry, but the plant engineering function remains very much the same. It is the function involved in designing, building, equipping, and maintaining industrial plants. Eighty-five percent of the circulation goes to plants with 100 or more employees. Over 37 percent of the plants have more than 500 employees. All recipients are addressed by name and title or function — a fact considered important in evaluating business media.

113B Plant Engineering, Facilities Maintenance & Plant Operations

Plant Engineering

A Technical Publishing Publication

BPA ABP

Media Code 7 652 5500 5.00 **Mid 004543-000**

Published 24 times a year by Technical Publishing, a company of The Dun & Bradstreet Corp., 1301 S. Grove Ave., P.O. Box 1030, Barrington, IL 60010. Phone 312-381-1840.

For shipping info., see Print Media Production Data.

PUBLISHER'S EDITORIAL PROFILE

PLANT ENGINEERING is edited for those responsible for designing, building, installing, operating and maintaining the systems, equipment and services of the industrial plant. Problem-solution articles cover electrical systems, heating, ventilation, air conditioning, pumps, compressors, piping, valves, mechanical and fluid power transmission, materials handling, maintenance, construction, pollution control, safety, fire protection, employee facilities, lighting, instrumentation and controls, protective coatings, lubrication, fuels, tools and fastening, insulation, energy management, telecommunications, plant engineering management and organization, and computer and robotic systems. Special features: News Briefs; Human Side of Engineering: Suggestions and Solutions; Material Handling Roundup; New Equipment Reports; Manufacturer's Literature, Control Technology. Rec'd 2/8/83.

1. PERSONNEL

Publisher—Ciro A. Buttacavoli.
Sales Manager—Charles F. Minor III.
Vice President, Circulation—Joseph J. Zaccaria.
Production Manager—Paula Krambeer.

2. REPRESENTATIVES and/or BRANCH OFFICES

New York 10022—Gary Gadek, 875 Third Ave. Phone 212-605-9662.

Chicago, 60601—John M. Archibald, Jerry Preston, Ray Dombrowski, 303 E. Wacker Dr., Suite 218. Phone 312-938-2900.

Plymouth Meeting, PA 19462—William J. McCaw. Plymouth Plaza, Suite 201. Phone 215-825-4410.

Newton, MA 02159—James Doherty, 181 Wells Ave. Phone 617-964-3730.

Troy, MI 48084—John Dolan, 3221 W. Big Beaver Rd., Suite 212. Phone 313-649-4330.

Cleveland 44114—Jack Lange, 815 Superior Ave., Suite 1617. Phone 216-696-4492.

Pittsburgh 15220—Robert Coburn, 200 Fleet St., Suite 4045. Phone 412-921-7802.

Los Angeles 90035—Craig Dixon, 1801 S. La Cienega Blvd.P.O. Box 35910 Phone 213-559-5111.

Atlanta 30329—Gordon Crane, 35 Executive Park Dr., NE., Suite 3515. Phone 404-633-5112.

Garland, TX 75041—Bill Sutherland, 1700 Eastgate Dr., Suite 103. Phone 214-270-6461.

Houston 77074—Richard W. Sheehan, 8515 Fondren Rd., Suite 104. Phone 713-981-4090.

Japan—Haruki Hirayama, EMS, Inc., Room 801, Shinjuku Komuro-Heim, 1-22 Shinjuku 4-chome, Shinjuku-ku, Tokyo 160. Phone 03-350-5666. Cable: EMSINCPERIOD.

England—Bob Saidel Managing Dir.-Europe, 130 Jermyn St., London SWIY 4UJ. Phone 01-839-3916.

3. COMMISSION AND CASH DISCOUNT

15% to agencies on space, bleed, color and position charges, net 30 days from date of invoice. 5% discount for payment 1 year in advance. No commission allowed on back-up, tip-in and other production charges.

4. GENERAL RATE POLICY

Advertising copy subject to acceptance by Publisher. Advertising not easily distinguishable from editorial must be labeled "advertisement." On contracts not completed, earned rate will apply. Orders are accepted subject to change in rates upon notice from the publisher. Advertisers may cancel or amend schedule at time rate revision becomes effective without incurring short-rate adjustment.

ADVERTISING RATES

Rates received October 19, 1983.
NOTE: Rates are effective for all advertisers with the January 6, 1983 issue.

5. BLACK/WHITE RATES

	1 pg	2/3 pg	1/2 pg	1/3 pg	1/4 pg	1/6 pg
1 time	5180.	3790.	2960.	1995.	1620.	1115.
3 times	4955.	3620.	2830.	1890.	1545.	1070.
6 times	4825.	3520.	2760.	1845.	1510.	1035.
9 times	4690.	3425.	2670.	1790.	1460.	1010.
12 times	4550.	3330.	2595.	1740.	1420.	980.
18 times	4410.	3220.	2515.	1680.	1375.	945.
24 times	4300.	3150.	2460.	1650.	1350.	930.
36 times	4190.	3060.	2390.	1600.	1305.	905.
48 times	4150.	3030.	2365.	1580.	1295.	890.
60 times	4100.	...	...	...	...	...
72 times	4040.	...	...	...	...	...
84 times	4025.	...	...	...	...	...
96 times	4010.	...	...	...	...	...

Black and white run-of-paper rates. Earned rate based on total number of insertions within a 12-month period. A spread counts as 2 insertions.
Island half pages, extra 20%

FREQUENCY SAVINGS PLAN

Any advertiser running three 1-page advertisements (or equivalent in spreads and pages) is entitled to buy three 1/4 page ads at a 50% saving off the earned rate (3 pages plus 3 quarter pages earns 6 time rate for both). Advertisers running over 3 pages may participate in the plan per the schedule below.

No. of full pages scheduled	No. of 1/4 page ads earned at 50% saving	Frequency incentive rate earned
3-5 pages	3 1/4 pages	6x
6-11 pages	6 1/4 pages	12x
12-17 pages	12 1/4 pages	24x
18-23 pages	18 1/4 pages	36x
24 or more pages	24 1/4 pages	48x

continued

6. COLOR RATES

Standard colors, red, blue, green, and yellow, per page or fraction:
Black and 1 standard color .... 400.
Black and 2 standard colors .... 800.
Black and 3 standard colors .... 1250.
Matched 2nd color .... 450.
Matched 3 colors .... 900.
Metallic inks available.
4-color process (Web offset):

	1 ti	7 ti	13 ti	19 ti	26 ti
Per page or fraction	1250.	1200.	1150.	1100.	1050.
Per spread	2050.	1950.	1850.	1750.	1650.

4-color charges based on frequency of color insertion.
A spread counts as 2 insertions.

7. COVERS

Available.
Cover schedules can only be cancelled if 90 days' written notice is given prior to closing date for issue. If covers are cancelled before schedule is completed, a short rate premium charge of 100.00 will be applied to each cover used in addition to the earned rate.

8. INSERTS

Furnished by advertiser, ready for binding and not requiring back-up. Regular black and white rates apply.
Back-up charges:
1 page .... 605. 2 pages .... 855.
Rates for special binding or handling available.
Insert quantity or special insert information available.

9. BLEED

Per page, flat rate .... 100.
No charge for spreads that bleed into gutter only.
No bleed charge for 4-color ads.

10. SPECIAL POSITION

All special or specified positions require a position charge added to run-of-paper rate. Position charges depend on location and mechanical consideration and must be quoted individually.
Island half page—space rate plus 20%.
Facing 2/3 pages—space rate plus 10% of one 2/3 page.
Facing 1/2 pages—space rate plus 15% of one 1/2 page.
Facing 1/3 pages—space rate plus 20% of one 1/3 page.
Publisher reserves right to repeat previous ad if insertion instuctions are not received by published closing date for issue.

11. CLASSIFIED/MAIL ORDER

For complete data, refer to Business Publication Rates and Data - Classified.

12. SPLIT RUN

Available. National rate plus mechanical charges. Consult publisher. Charge is non-commissionable. Split-run availabilities parallel geographic break-down of regional editions.

13a. GEOGRAPHIC and/or DEMOGRAPHIC EDITIONS

Only full page units accepted: ROP or inserts.
Regional advertising accepted in 2nd cycle only.
Preparation and position of regional advertising will depend on mechanical requirements of each issue as it goes to press.

EASTERN

(Maine, Vermont, New Hampshire, Massachusetts, Rhode Island, Connecticut,Delaware, New York, New Jersey, Pennsylvania, Maryland, West Virginia, Virginia, Dist. of Columbia.)

Rates:	Per page	Rates:	Per page
1 time	1960.	12 times	1845.
3 times	1935.	18 times	1825.
6 times	1910.	24 times	1805.
9 times	1880.		

Circulation:
SWORN 12-31-83—30,477

MIDWEST

(Michigan, Ohio, Indiana, Illinois, Wisconsin, Minnesota, Iowa, Missouri, North Dakota, South Dakota, Nebraska, Kansas.)

Rates:	Per page	Rates:	Per page
1 time	2070.	12 times	1935.
3 times	2040.	18 times	1920.
6 times	2020.	24 times	1915.
9 times	1990.		

Circulation:
SWORN 12-31-83—31,375

SOUTHERN

(Kentucky, North Carolina, South Carolina, Tennessee, Georgia, Florida, Alabama, Mississippi, Arkansas, Louisiana, Oklahoma, Texas.)

Rates:	Per page	Rates:	Per page
1 time	1335.	12 times	1265.
3 times	1320.	18 times	1255.
6 times	1305.	24 times	1240.
9 times	1290.		

Circulation:
SWORN 12-31-83—23,062

WESTERN

(Washington, Oregon, California, Nevada, Arizona, Utah, Idaho, Montana, Wyoming, Colorado, New Nexico, Alaska, Hawaii.)

Rates:	Per page	Rates:	Per page
1 time	1130.	12 times	1070.
3 times	1100.	18 times	1055.
6 times	1090.	24 times	1030.
9 times	1075.		

Circulation:
SWORN 12-31-83—14,401
Combination rates:

Two regions in same issue, combined rate less .... 150.
Three regions, combined page rate less .... 300.
No combination discount allowed if copy changes from region to region.
National advertising frequency may be applied to earn regional advertising rates. However, a combination of national and regional insertions is not additive: national frequency is the base. Regional advertising will not earn frequency discounts for national schedules.

Color:
Standard AAAA colors, red, blue, green and yellow.
2nd color per page .... 300. 4-color .... 800.
Matched 2nd color .... 375.
Multicolor pages acceptable as inserts only.
Regional combinations: regional color rate, plus 60.00 per color for each additional region, providing same color used.
Inserts:
Preprinted inserts may be included in regional editions. Black and white rates apply. Regional inserts less than standard page size-black and white rates plus 10%.
Back-up charges. Not commissionable.

	1 page	2 pages
Eastern edition	210.	305.
Midwest edition	225.	340.
Southern edition	165.	240.
Western edition	145.	225.

Bleed:
Per page flat rate 50.00. No charge for gutter bleed Regional combination: 1st region 50.00; each additional region, 20.00.
Issue and Closing dates:
Accepted only 2nd cycle.

14. CONTRACT AND COPY REGULATIONS

See Contents page for location—items 1, 2, 3, 5, 6, 7, 8, 10, 11, 12, 13, 14, 15, 17, 18, 19, 20, 21, 22, 25, 29, 30, 31, 32, 35, 36.

15. MECH REQUIREMENTS

For complete, detailed production information, see SRDS Print Media Production Data.
Printing Process: Web Offset.
Trim size: 8 x 10-3/4.
Binding method: Perfect.
Colors available: AAAA/ABP; Matched; 4-Color Process (AAAA/MPA); Simulated Metallic.

DIMENSIONS-AD PAGE

1	7 x 10	1/3	4-1/2 x 4-7/8
2/3	4-1/2 x 10	1/3	2-1/4 x 10
1/2	7 x 4-7/8	1/4	3-3/8 x 4-7/8
1/2	3-3/8 x 10	1/6	2-1/4 x 4-7/8
(*)	4-1/2 x 7-1/2		

(*) Island half.

16. ISSUE AND CLOSING DATES

Published 24 times per year, issued every 2nd and 4th Thursday of the month. Mailed 8 days preceding issue date. Advertising forms close per schedule below. Copy to be set or plates for which proofs are required must be received by closing date. Contracts may be cancelled on 30 days written notice. Individual insertions may not be cancelled after closing date. Cancellations for regional advertising not accepted after closing date.

Cycle:	Issue	Closing	Cycle:	Issue	Closing
1	Mar. 8	Feb. 7	1	July 12	June 12
2	Mar. 22	Feb. 21	2	July 26	June 26
1	Apr. 12	Mar. 13	1	Aug. 9	July 10
2	Apr. 26	Mar. 27	2	Aug. 23	July 24
1	May 10	Apr. 10	1	Sept. 13	Aug. 14
2	May 24	Apr. 24	2	Sept. 27	Aug. 28
1	June 14	May 15	1	Oct. 11	Sept. 11
2	June 28	May 29			

17. SPECIAL SERVICES

MCC Media Data Form registered 8/9/83
Received 9/7/83.
B.P.A. Unit Data Report Nov/82.

18. CIRCULATION

Established 1947. Single copy 3.00; per year 50.00.
CAUTION: Each of the following statements give the total circulation of this publication. Do not combine.
Summary data—for detail see Publisher's Statement.

B.P.A. 6-30-83 (6 mos. aver. qualified)

Total	Non-Pd	Paid
102,506	102,506	...

Average Non-Qualified (not included above):
Total 7,951

TERRITORIAL DISTRIBUTION 5/83—102,508

N.Eng.	Mid.Atl.	E.N.Cen.	W.N.Cen.	S.Atl.	E.S.Cen.
7,198	18,934	24,366	6,840	13,308	5,755
W.S.Cen.	Mtn.St.	Pac.St.	Canada	Foreign	Other
8,516	3,182	10,113	3,788	...	508

BUSINESS ANALYSIS OF CIRCULATION

For location of SIC explanation, see contents page.
* —Total manufacturing.
† —Other SIC groups—each group less than 1% of the total
‡ —Total non-manufacturing.
TL —Total.

SIC. TL. Total. A. Manage all plant eng. &/or maintenance. B. Supervise sub-group within plant eng. and/or maintenance. C. Provide staff and consulting services for plant eng. and/or maintenance. D. Manage other operations in addition to plant eng.and/or maintenance. E. Other function.

SIC	TL	A	B	C	D	E
20—	6242	2636	1348	1074	1184	...
21—	294	87	90	81	36	...
22—	2293	1072	414	346	460	1
23—	1283	632	134	96	421	...
24—	1639	707	303	179	450	...
25—	1504	646	216	178	464	...
26—	4490	1513	1249	974	751	3
27—	1926	872	317	205	532	...
28—	11156	2543	3251	3715	1645	2
29—	1971	413	618	660	280	...
30—	3375	1349	636	674	716	...
31—	491	253	60	32	146	...
32—	3576	1227	726	830	793	...
33—	6915	2018	2266	1512	1119	...
34—	8098	3208	1260	1310	2320	...
35—	10611	3716	1789	2291	2813	2
36—	8218	2749	1646	1959	1862	2
37—	4866	1337	1354	1323	850	2
38—	2785	961	554	623	647	...
39—	1427	605	186	173	463	...
*—	83160	28544	18417	18235	17952	12
10-14—	1800	440	617	412	331	...
15-17—	2096	426	427	778	465	...
89—	9867	767	737	7834	529	...

SIC	TL	A	B	C	D	E
†—	5585	2433	1194	745	1213	...
‡—	19348	4066	2975	9769	2538	...
TL—	102508	32610	21392	28004	20490	12

A.B.C. 6-30-83 (6 mos. aver.—Gray BP Form)

Total	Non-Pd	Paid	(Subs)	(Single)	[Assoc]
102,506	102,506	...	...	...	...

Average Other Distribution (not included above):
Total 7,951

TERRITORIAL DISTRIBUTION 5/83—102,508
NOTE: Identical to B.P.A. 6-30-83 reported above.

BUSINESS ANALYSIS OF CIRCULATION
NOTE: Identical to B.P.A. 12-31-82 reported above.

(C-B1(

Advertising a Repair Method for Hospital Linens

The most critical area in the operation of a hospital laundry is the handling of surgical linen. Because these linens are in constant contact with sharp-edged equipment and instruments, they are often damaged. But, years ago, it was determined that such linen should not be repaired by sewing because the needle holes created breeding places for bacteria. Fortunately, Thermopatch Corporation developed a procedure for the heat-seal mending of linen. With this method a tiny hole or a long slit in a piece of linen could be covered completely with a fabric of the same physical characteristics as the original. Tests proved that the heat-seal repairs maintained the highest level of sterility.

The advertising objective of the Thermopatch Corporation was to bring its technique to the attention of both hospitals and commercial laundries. For those hospitals that operated their own laundries, the advertising was intended to generate sales leads. At the same time, the advertising would seek to make such mending desirable for hospitals that sent their linen to commercial laundries. The company also wanted to stimulate sales inquiries from commercial laundries of all kinds because many other linen services could use the Thermopatch process for mending.

To reach the two basic market categories (commercial laundries and hospitals) for the Thermopatch process, the company's advertising agency specified a mix of business publications that included: *Hospitals, Modern Healthcare, Executive Housekeeper,* and *American Laundry Digest.*

Hospitals magazine was selected to reach hospital administrators, the executives responsible for the business side of hospital operations. *Modern Healthcare* was chosen to reach the owners and managers of nursing homes, and *Executive Housekeeper* was chosen to reach the people responsible for linen service in hospitals, nursing homes, and hotels. To reach laundry plants and their management, the agency placed ads for Thermopatch in *American Laundry Digest.* All these publications carried Business Publications Audit (BPA) circulation, an important qualification for an advertiser seeking assured circulation values.

Calculation of CPM for two of these publications proved to be an interesting exercise. *Hospitals,* for example, with a circulation of approximately 77,000 and a black and white page rate of $1,570, had a CPM of $20. *American Laundry Digest,* on the other hand, with a circulation of only 16,000 and a page rate of $965, had a CPM of $60. On the face value of CPM, there would seem to be a considerable difference in cost between the two publications. But *Hospitals,* with its larger circulation, reaches many people who are not involved in hospital laundry operations, especially since many hospitals do not even operate their own laundry facilities. Thus, subtracting unwanted circulation left *Hospitals* with an effective reach of about 10,000 and a CPM of about $160. Therefore, the laundry magazine, with virtually 100 percent effective circulation, proved to be the better buy when all factors were considered.

Thermopatch's advertising program proved to be an outstanding success. The company received many requests for information on its heat-sealing process and continues to increase its sales of patches.

Courtesy Richard-Lewis Corporation.

---

white earned rate plus a binding charge, which is noncommissionable to the advertiser's agency. The use of inserts offers advertisers several benefits. If they use the same insert in several magazines, the cost for color printing can be kept relatively low. By printing their inserts on a paper that is different in weight and texture from the paper used in the rest of the magazine, advertisers can add impact to their message. The advertiser can also get extra mileage from copies of the insert material by using them for direct mailings or by distributing them at trade shows.

Another unique feature of many business publications is the reader service card, commonly known as a "bingo card." A **reader service card** is a postage-paid postcard that is bound into every copy of the magazine. One side of the card bears the name and address of the publication; the other side contains a series of numbers. Each of these numbers corresponds to a service key number that the publisher has placed below the copy of every advertisement in the magazine. The purpose of the reader service card is to stimulate inquiries by making it easy for readers to request more information. Rather than sending in a coupon or writing a letter, busy readers simply circle the numbers on the service card that correspond to the advertised products or services that interest them. They then fill in their names and addresses and drop the postage-free card into the mail. The publisher sorts the cards and sends each advertiser the names and addresses of those who inquired. The advertisers then send these readers more information on their product or have one of their salespeople call on the prospect. In this way, the advertisers will receive clear feedback on the effectiveness of their activity by counting the number of inquiries obtained from a specific advertisement in a specific publication.

Media Decisions for Business Advertisers

Although there are thousands of business publications from which to choose, the nature of our product limits the number which we have seriously to consider. In many cases, however, there may still be too many publications in the field for us to think of using them all. To narrow the choice, we need to make a simple media analysis by asking ourselves a few pertinent questions.

1. *Is circulation paid or nonpaid?*
   Some media analysts believe that paid circulation indicates greater interest on the part of the reader because the reader was willing to pay for the subscription. This is not necessarily true in practice. Often the reader's company has paid for the subscription.

2. *Is the editorial content of value to the type of person we want to reach?*
   Remember, we are looking not only for the individual who signs the purchase orders, but also for the many others who influence the buying decision.

3. *Is the publication a weekly or a monthly?*
   Publishers of monthly magazines argue that each issue has a longer life with more opportunity to make contact with the audience. Publishers of weekly magazines claim that their timeliness is important to keep readers abreast of the latest news of the industry. Both are correct, but media decisions should be based on editorial content, circulation, and rates — not frequency of issue. If the publication serves its audience properly, it will be read regardless of its publication schedule.

4. *How often are the readers of a publication qualified?*
   How frequently does the publication update its circulation list to prune out individuals who have left the business (moved, retired, deceased)? If they don't do it every year, the list will be out of date.

5. *What is the inquiry average?*
   Publications have data on inquiries, particularly when they employ reader service cards. Needless to say, we should maintain a record of our experience with every publication.

THE MANAGEMENT MAGAZINE FOR THE SEWN PRODUCTS INDUSTRY

BOBBIN ®

(ABC)   **ABP**

Media Code 7 155 0800 8.00   **Mid 002599-000**
Published monthly by Bobbin International Inc., P. O.
Box 1986, 1110 Shop Rd., Columbia, SC 29202. Phone
803-771-7500, 800-845-8820.

PUBLISHER'S EDITORIAL PROFILE
BOBBIN serves the Needles Trade Industry (Primarily but
not exclusively the Garment Industry) and is oriented and
geared primarily to the manufacturing-executive function.
Articles deal with the various aspects of this function.
Representative categories are: production management,
engineering, administration, personnel and labor relations,
advanced technology, interviews, supervision communications, machines, devices, equipment, production control, scheduling and product analysis, quality control.
Reprints from general magazines and book publications in
the United States. Rec'd 8/20/74.

18. CIRCULATION
Established 1959. Single copy 2.00; per year 18.00.
Summary data—for detail see Publisher's Statement.
　　A.B.C. 6-30-83 (6 mos. aver.—Blue BP Form)
Tot.Pd.　(Subs)　(Single)　(Assoc)
8,172　　8,172　　　...　　　　...
Average Other Distribution (not included above):
　Total 1,499
TERRITORIAL DISTRIBUTION 5/83—8,604
N.Eng.　Mid.Atl.　E.N.Cen.　W.N.Cen.　S.Atl.　E.S.Cen.
　491　　1,493　　　657　　　361　　1,905　　　753
W.S.Cen.　Mtn.St.　Pac.St.　Canada　Foreign　Other
　473　　　193　　　569　　　463　　1,180　　　66

Apparel Industry Magazine

▽BPA

Media Code 7 155 0600 2.00   **Mid 002594-000**
Published monthly by Shore Publishing Co., 6255
Barfield Rd., Ste. 110, Atlanta, GA 30328. Phone 404-
252-8831;. 800-241-9034.
PUBLISHER'S EDITORIAL PROFILE
APPAREL INDUSTRY MAGAZINE is edited for apparel
manufacturers (men's, women's and children's) as well as
for contractors. Editorial emphasis is on production
techniques, new equipment, fabrics, supplies, finance,
merchandising sales, design and fashion, plus other approaches beneficial to the apparel plant in boosting efficiency, decreasing costs and improving quality. Rec'd 6/
20/75.

18. CIRCULATION
Established 1946. Single copy 3.50; per year 36.00.
Summary Data—for details see Publisher's statement.

　Total　Non-Pd　Paid
18,675　18,675
Average Non-qualified (not included above):
　Total 2,105
TERRITORIAL DISTRIBUTION 6/83—18,697
N.Eng.　Mid.Atl.　E.N.Cen.　W.N.Cen.　S.Atl.　E.S.Cen.
1,114　　6,548　　1,091　　　628　　2,852　　1,229
W.S.Cen.　Mtn.St.　Pac.St.　Canada　Foreign　Other
1,011　　　372　　3,832　　　　　　　　1　　　19

THE
OIL DAILY
A Whitney Communications Co. Publication

Media Code 7 635 3600 0.00   **Mid 004472-000**
Published every business day by The Oil Daily, Inc.,
1301 Pennsylvania Ave., NW, Suite 1010, Washington,
DC 20004. Phone 202-638-5159.

PUBLISHER'S EDITORIAL PROFILE
THE OIL DAILY is a newspaper edited for managers and
operating executives in the energy industries. Full time
bureaus and correspondents in oil centers plus news and
financial wire services provide current and concise international coverage of significant developments in
various phases of the industry (exploration, drilling,
production, transportation, refining-petrochemicals and
marketing). News and regular features cover political,
legislative, financial, economic, technological and statistical information useful in day-to-day and long range
operations, planning and purchasing policies. Rec'd 11/
18/80.

18. CIRCULATION
Established 1951. Single copy 1.50; per year 327.00.
Summary data—for detail see Publisher's Statement.
　　A.B.C. 9-30-83 (6 mos. aver.—Newspaper Form)
Total　Non-Pd　(Subs)　(Single)　(Assoc)
5,597　　...　　5,597　　5,597　　...
Average Other Distribution (not included above):
　Total 1,185
TERRITORIAL DISTRIBUTION 9/83—5,654
N.Eng.　Mid.Atl.　E.N.Cen.　W.N.Cen.　S.Atl.　E.S.Cen.
　103　　　631　　　747　　　426　　　601　　　189
W.S.Cen.　Mtn.St.　Pac.St.　Canada　Foreign　Other
2,050　　　393　　　453　　　31　　　28　　　2

OIL&GAS JOURNAL
A PennWell Publishing Co. Publication

(ABC)   **ABP**

Media Code 7 635 4050 7.00   **Mid 004474-000**
Published weekly by PennWell Publishing Co., 1421 S.
Sheridan, Tulsa, OK 74112. Phone 918-835-3161,
TWX492345.

PUBLISHER'S EDITORIAL PROFILE
OIL & GAS JOURNAL is edited for operating and
management personnel of oil and gas companies worldwide. Operating people from managers to foremen are
included. News articles give weekly information and
detailed interpretation of world developments. Feature
articles deal with technology, politics, operation,
economics, finance, and industry surveys. Petroleum industry divisions covered: exploration, drilling, producing,
pipelining, transportation, gas processing, refining, pe-
trochemical, marketing and all LNG/SNG activities.

18. CIRCULATION
Established 1902. Per year 31.00.
Summary data—for detail see Publisher's Statement.
　　A.B.C. 6-30-83 (6 mos. aver.—Blue BP Form)
Tot.Pd.　(Subs)　(Single)　(Assoc)
63,351　63,338　　13　　　...
Average Other Distribution (not included above):
　Total 3,842
TERRITORIAL DISTRIBUTION 5/83—64,825
N.Eng.　Mid.Atl.　E.N.Cen.　W.N.Cen.　S.Atl.　E.S.Cen.
　914　　4,340　　3,527　　2,137　　2,665　　1,444
W.S.Cen.　Mtn.St.　Pac.St.　Canada　Foreign　Other
27,626　　5,225　　5,665　　2,189　　9,033　　　60

Journal of the American Medical Association

An American Medical Association Publication
Official publication of:
American Medical Association.

▽BPA

Media Code 7 515 1275 7.00   **Mid 003873-000**
Published weekly by American Medical Association,
535 N. Dearborn St., Chicago, IL 60610. Phone 312-
645-5000.

PUBLISHER'S EDITORIAL PROFILE
JOURNAL OF THE AMERICAN MEDICAL ASSOCIATION
reports on progress in clinical medicine pertinent
research, and landmark evolutions in other areas as they
interface with medicine. It publishes various directories,
medical news items, letters, original papers, abstracts,
questions & answers, obituaries, and practice opportunities. Rec'd 12/20/77.

18. CIRCULATION
Established 1883. Single copy 4.00; per year 52.00.
Summary data—for detail see Publisher's Statement.
　　B.P.A. 6-30-83 (6 mos. aver. qualified)
　Total　Non-Pd　Paid
318,619　71,340　247,279
Average Non-Qualified (not included above):
　Total 8,988
TERRITORIAL DISTRIBUTION 5/83—319,580
N.Eng.　Mid.Atl.　E.N.Cen.　W.N.Cen.　S.Atl.　E.S.Cen.
16,568　53,303　59,140　23,506　50,764　17,609
W.S.Cen.　Mtn.St.　Pac.St.　Canada　Foreign　Other
31,558　14,623　44,735　　864　5,182　1,728

Journal of Pediatric Ophthalmology and Strabismus

A Slack Incorporated Publication

Media Code 7 515 1100 7.00   **Mid 003921-000**
Published bimonthly by Slack, Incorporated, 6900
Grove Rd., Thorofare, NJ 08086. Phone 609-848-1000.
PUBLISHER'S EDITORIAL PROFILE
JOURNAL OF PEDIATRIC OPHTHALMOLOGY AND
STRABISMUS is a publication of interest to
Ophthalmologists. It reports through original papers,
editorial reviews and abstracts, the diagnosis, treatment,
correction and prevention of eye disorders in infants,
children and adolescents.

18. CIRCULATION
Established 1964. Single copy 5.00; per year 40.00.
　　SWORN 6-30-83 (6 mos. aver.)
　Total　Non-Pd　Paid　(Subs)　(Single)　(Assoc)
1,473　　14　1,459　1,459　　　　168
TERRITORIAL DISTRIBUTION 5/83—1,493
N.Eng.　Mid.Atl.　E.N.Cen.　W.N.Cen.　S.Atl.　E.S.Cen.
　46　　　182　　　139　　　63　　　155　　　47
W.S.Cen.　Mtn.St.　Pac.St.　Canada　Foreign　Other
　94　　　49　　　147　　　65　　　485　　　1

◄ There is much to be learned from reading the details provided in the *Business Edition* of Standard Rate & Data Service. Along with advertising rates and mechanical specifications, each publication provides its own editorial profile and circulation figures. Of course, it requires experience and the study of each publication to make media decisions, but the details of the publication shown are noteworthy. For example, there is a wide difference in the circulation of the two publications addressed to the apparel manufacturing industry. One of them has a large distribution in the Pacific states. As for the oil publications, both are addressed to management; both reach paid subscribers; one is a weekly; the other a daily. The circulation difference is very substantial.

There are many publications addressed to members of the medical profession. Some are addressed to all physicians — the *Journal of the AMA* is one, issued weekly, with some subscribers controlled and others paid. In contrast, there are numerous very narrow focus, specialized journals like the one listed — issued every other month to a small number of paid subscribers who have a professional interest in the subject.

Farm Publications

Although Standard Rate & Data Service lists farm publications as a section in its *Consumer Magazine and Agri-Media Rates and Data* book, these publications are a cross between business publications and consumer publications. To be sure, farmers and their families are consumers, buying most of the products bought by consumers everywhere. At the same time, farmers operate a business — an agricultural business. For the operation of their agricultural enterprise, they buy seeds, machinery, chemicals, and buildings. For the family-run farm, farming is more than business; it is a way of life.

The total farm population in the United States in 1983 was 5,862,000, representing 2,400,260 farms and 1,698,960 households. The number of farms has been dropping steadily for the past 50 years. The number of family farms has been declining even more rapidly. While in the year 1900 one out of three Americans lived on a farm, today it is less than one out of 30. At the same time, many of the farms that remain have become larger. According to the U.S. Census, the median income for farm families in 1981 was $17,082.

According to the 1982 Census of Agriculture, 72 percent of farms in the United States are defined as small with less than $40,000 in gross sales of farm products a year. At the other end of the scale are the large farm operators, those selling $500,000 or more of farm products a year. There were 28,000 large farms in the United States in 1982 — a little over 1 percent of all farms — but they received two-thirds of the total net farm income.

Do farmers and their families also read consumer magazines? Of course they do, and national advertisers reach farm family consumers through most of the usual consumer media. The value of farm publications lies in their unique editorial climates — climates that are just right for the advertisers of products farmers buy to run their agricultural businesses. A family farm today may consist of 4,000 acres of farm land, with over $1 million invested in farm machinery and equipment. The farm may spend over $250,000 a year on chemicals and fertilizers and over $60,000 a year on seed.

Farm publications are a very selective medium. When farmers and their families read farm publications, they are farmers first and consumers second.

For media consideration, farm publications are usually grouped into three types:

1. national publications
2. state or regional publications
3. specialized publications

As we might expect, the list contains manufacturers of chemical products — insecticides, pharmaceuticals, fertilizers — and farm machinery and vehicles.

National Farm Publications

The term "national" is somewhat misleading because the coverage of these publications is not truly national — some states are covered only sparsely by "national" farm publications. *Farm Journal* has a circulation of just over one million. *Progressive Farmer* has a circulation of 679,000, and *Successful Farming* has a circulation of 582,000.

Progressive Farmer, for example, is not circulated all over the United States. The advertiser may buy advertising in the "national" edition or in any of four regional editions (Southwest, Midsouth, Upper South, Southeast), as well as single state editions and crop-market packages to reach growers of corn, cotton, soybeans, wheat, hogs, etc., in various states.

Farm Journal offers a national edition and a wide range of demographic options. There are four regional editions — east, central, west, and south — with any combination of these editions also available. The advertiser may buy **crop editions** for corn, soybeans, wheat, sorghum, or cotton to reach those farms that comprise a very particular market segment for some herbicide or piece of machinery. There are state editions and livestock editions for beef, hogs, or dairy.

What are the interests of the readers of these publications? Consider this sample of articles from an issue of *Progressive Farmer:*

"When a practice helps me get heifers in the line sooner, it pays off. That's why I worm with TBZ."

Your heifer management program is geared to bringing them up to breeding weight in the shortest time for the least cost. But worms can hold back weight gain, delaying the time when you can put heifers into the line and onto the credit side of the ledger.

That's why worming with TBZ® makes real economic sense. Administered in handy paste, boluses, crumbles or pellets, TBZ removes the worm burden so heifers can gain weight faster, more efficiently. And because TBZ works without stressing or setting-back the animals, they'll also get more value out of your other good management techniques.

Worming with TBZ is especially important for your first calf heifers. Since they start out weighing less than mature cows, the stress of calving, milk production and re-breeding can be really tough on them.

In more than 150 pasture trials,* TBZ helped young animals grow quicker and healthier than those that weren't treated. TBZ can help get your replacement heifers working for you sooner, too. TBZ. The no-stress, no-setback wormer.

*Details on request

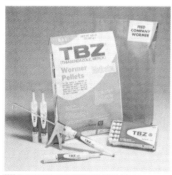

MSD AGVET

Pharmaceuticals for cattle? Yes, indeed. An important part of a farmer's business is practicing animal husbandry. Therefore, pharmaceutical manufacturers with highly specialized products use farm publications to bring important information about their products to farmers.

Baits lure worms to a deadly feast
Forage sorghums and millet—fast summer feeds
Weed shifts cause new headaches
Should you lease your next tractor?
Muskrat control for your farm pond
How to avoid a grain bin explosion

This same issue contains articles on the home vegetable patch, recipes for cookies, spring menus with pork, recipes for cooking carrots, how to make a boot cleaner, and sewing patterns for a collection of dresses and blouses.

State and Regional Publications

The opportunities for geographic selectivity are limitless because there are farm publications issued in most states and regions of the country. Typical of such publications are *Hoosier Farmer* (Indiana), *Iowa Farm Bureau Spokesman, Kansas Farm Bureau News,* and *The Grange News* (Washington and Oregon).

Specialized Farm Publications

The use of specialized farm magazines related to very specific reader interest, such as peanuts or poultry or hogs, provides the advertiser with a unique editorial climate. *Poultry Tribune, Shorthorn World, The Sunflower, Su-*

A well-known chemical company uses a farm publication to tell peanut farmers about a very special herbicide. Notice how specific the copy is and how the illustration of the peanut is used to "flag" the peanut farmer.

William A. Marsteller

William Marsteller founded Marsteller, Inc., in 1951. Over the years, it grew to be one of the largest advertising agencies in the world and its sister agency, Burson-Marsteller, which Marsteller co-founded, has grown to be the world's largest public relations agencies. The phenomenal growth of these companies is a tribute to the skill and drive of one man — William A. Marsteller.

In 1985, Marsteller, Inc., merged with a leading European agency, Havas Conseil, to form HCM (Havas Conseil Marsteller). It is the first true American-European agency, with more than $500 million in billings and 32 offices in the United States and Europe.

William Marsteller was born in Champaign, Illinois, in 1914. While majoring in journalism at the University of Illinois, he worked as a reporter for the *Champaign News Gazette* and later, from 1937 to 1941, as an insurance agent for the Massachusetts Mutual Life Insurance Company. In 1941, he obtained a position in the advertising department of a manufacturing company, Edward's Valves, leaving this company in 1945 to join Rockwell Manufacturing Company as advertising manager, a newly created position. By 1949, he was vice-president for marketing at Rockwell, and two years later he followed up a suggestion that he start his own advertising/market research agency. The new agency had two accounts — Rockwell Manufacturing and Clark Equipment.

In the field of advertising, William Marsteller believes in "total communications with all publics." He is considered a pioneer in the development of the editorial evaluation concept of media selection. He is a member of the Advertising Hall of Fame, and is the author of the books, *Creative Management* and *The Wonderful World of Words*.

---

garbeet Grower, Spudman, and *Rice Farming* attract readers who subscribe to the magazine not only for the editorial matter, but for the information contained in the advertisements. Rates vary widely. A black and white page in *Soybean Digest* costs $5,500. *Rice Farming* costs $985 a page. *Wheat Life,* published by the Washington Associations of Wheat Growers, costs $675 for a black and white page.

Summary

Management's *need to know* has been well served by the business press — with 3,300 publications serving over 175 business categories. There is, in fact, no business, industry, trade, or profession that does not have at least one publication to provide news and information to its practitioners and to serve as a highly selective vehicle for the delivery of important advertising messages. And the advertising messages are important — important enough for executives, technicians, and professionals to read them at work as part of their responsibility to keep up with developments in their fields.

The various types of business publications can be roughly divided into five categories, based on the kind of business market the publication serves. The

CASE HISTORY

Gillette Brush Plus

In late 1984, the Gillette Company's Personal Care Division launched a major shave cream innovation, Brush Plus®, an all-in-one brush-and-concentrate system, with a $13 million campaign. The Brush Plus® system consists of a soft brush and a rich concentrate that contains lubricants and softeners. The media schedule

was designed to reach a target audience of men ages 18 to 49. Television uses national sports programs, and print media include *TV Guide, Reader's Digest, Family Circle, People,* and *Newsweek.*

The product had been test marketed for nine months in Peoria, Illinois, and Tucson, Arizona. The repurchase rate was very high (80 percent) and market share built steadily each month of the test.

Throughout the development of the product, testing revealed a high degree of consumer enthusiasm and satisfaction. These positive responses indicated that the product clearly met a consumer want. Prior to the actual development, potential users were asked to rate the Brush Plus concept against a competitive product concept (which was already on the market) with a fictitious identity. Consumer response was particularly strong in the areas of purchase interest, uniqueness, and believability.

Advertising for the new product was also tested. Results showed that the appeal persuaded and motivated consumers to try the product. The test market effort used local television, couponing, and point of purchase displays in food, drug, and mass merchandise retailers. Consumers were interviewed at three different times after the start of the test market. Repurchase intentions ran very high.

categories are: (1) general business publications, (2) industrial publications, (3) trade publications, (4) professional publications, and (5) institutional publications. Some business publications span many industries with a focus on subjects of common interest and with an appeal to readers with similar job functions. These are *horizontal publications.* The readers of *vertical publications,* on the other hand, often run a gamut of job functions, but are confined within a single industry. Some business publications are distributed as consumer magazines

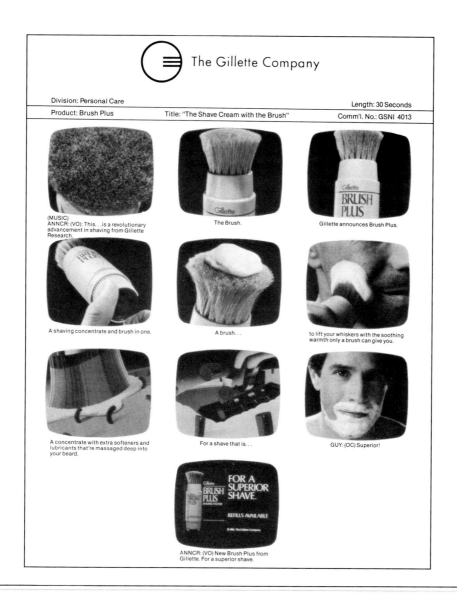

The Gillette Company

Division: Personal Care

Length: 30 Seconds

Product: Brush Plus

Title: "The Shave Cream with the Brush"

Comm'l. No.: GSNI 4013

(MUSIC)
ANNCR: (VO): This...is a revolutionary advancement in shaving from Gillette Research.

The Brush.

Gillette announces Brush Plus.

A shaving concentrate and brush in one.

A brush...

to lift your whiskers with the soothing warmth only a brush can give you.

A concentrate with extra softeners and lubricants that're massaged deep into your beard.

For a shave that is...

GUY: (OC) Superior!

ANNCR: (VO) New Brush Plus from Gillette. For a superior shave.

are—on the basis of paid subscriptions. There are, however, many which are distributed to controlled groups of people qualified to receive the publication by virtue of their job titles or functions.

Business publications come in all sizes from tabloid to digest size and their frequency of issue ranges from daily to monthly. These publications sell space to advertisers in standard size units—and offer contract and color rates—similar to those of consumer magazines.

Summary

Farm publications serve the nation's farm population in two ways — as business magazines and as consumer publications — in recognition of the dual role of the American farmer. These publications are usually divided into three categories: (1) national publications, (2) state or regional publications, and (3) specialized publications, which are devoted to particular crops or to particular breeds of livestock.

Questions for Discussion

1. Is it possible for an industrial manufacturer to discontinue all business publication advertising and put the money into the sales force? What advantages or disadvantages would result from such a decision?

2. A manufacturer of mouthwash advertises in three general magazines in the belief that these publications adequately cover the country. What reasons can you provide for adding farm magazines to this schedule?

3. If you were considering a media schedule for advertising a company jet, what publications would you recommend and why?

4. Why do advertisers use inserts more frequently in business publications than in consumer media?

5. Why would a manufacturer of consumer products advertise in business publications? Why would a manufacturer of industrial products advertise in consumer magazines? Can you find some examples of both?

6. What are some of the demographic breakdowns that are commonly used by business publications?

7. What does a publisher mean by "qualified" circulation?

Sources and Suggestions for Further Reading

Arthur D. Little, Inc. "An Evaluation of 1100 Research Studies on the Effectiveness of Industrial Advertising." New York: American Business Press, May 1971.

Bailey, Earl L., ed. *Marketing Strategies.* New York: The Conference Board, 1974.

Bertrand, Kate. "Taking Care of Media Business." *Business Marketing* (August 1986).

Bly, Robert W. "Ten Ways to Stretch Your Advertising Budget." *Business Marketing* (July 1984).

Garbett, Thomas F. "15 Creative Strategies for Corporate Advertising." *Business Marketing* (August 1984).

"Industrial Advertising Effectively Reaches Buying Influences at Low Cost." Report by U.S. Steel. New York: American Business Press, 1969.

Morrill, John D. "How Advertising Helps Sell Industrial Products." Report commissioned by Westinghouse. New York: American Business Press, 1975.

"The 100 Leading Business and Industrial Advertisers." *Business Marketing* (July 1986).

Poppe, Fred C. "Commitment to Excellence and Other Heresies." *Inside Print* (June 1986).

Sissors, Jack Z., and Jim Surmanek. *Advertising Media Planning,* 2nd ed. Chicago: Crain Books, 1984.

Yankelovich, Skelly and White, Inc. "A Study of Corporate Advertising Effectiveness." Prepared for *Time* magazine, 1978.

10 THE BROADCAST MEDIA

Radio
Where It All Came From
AM and FM Radio
AM Stereo
Radio as an Advertising Medium
Spot Radio
Network Radio
Radio Audiences
   GRPs: Gross Rating Points
Buying Radio Time

Television
The Television Audience
Network Television
Spot Television
Buying Time
   GRPs Again
Audience Ratings
   Gross Impressions
   Reach and Frequency
   Flighting
Cable Television

Working Vocabulary

spot radio	cume	package house
network radio	gross rating points	participations
drive time	package plan	adjacencies
sponsored program	run of station (ROS)	gross impressions
sustaining program	prime time	

Especially through the medium of television, advertising has brought to millions of Americans new ideas, not only about which soap to buy, but where to live, for which goals in life to aspire, what jobs to seek, and what to do with their increasing amounts of leisure time.

Sam J. Ervin, Jr.
Advertising Age

The broadcast media are the media of the twentieth century. Radio was first made available to advertisers as a commercial medium about 60 years ago, and it is only within the past 40 years that commercial television has become a national medium. In a relatively short time, these media have made a profound impact, not only on the advertising industry, but on almost every facet of our society.

Radio

Radio advertising began in August 1922, with an $8\frac{1}{2}$-minute commercial for a housing development in New York. The price for the spot was $100.

For decades, radio had served as America's principal entertainment and information channel. It had served American business as well, as an advertising medium: In 1949, business spent $425 million on radio, representing about 10 percent of all the advertising expenditures in that year. But, as the United States moved into television, radio's commercial future was in doubt. Many people expected that when the full impact of television would come on, that radio would be out. Needless to say, the obituary notices were premature. Radio did survive the tremendous growth of television. In 1955, radio advertising revenues were only $456 million — just a little bit more than they were in 1949. But by 1968, advertising billings on radio had exceeded $1 billion. For 1983, radio's advertising revenues were in excess of $5 billion. Radio overcame the threat of television because it was versatile, adaptable, and could be used by a wide range of businesses.

In 1983, there were almost 500 million radios in use in the United States, more than two per person. Seventy million new radios were sold that year. There are now about 8,260 AM and FM stations on the air, and 88 percent of the public listens to the radio sometime during any week.

In recent years, advertising expenditures in radio have been enhanced by the proliferation of stations, especially FM stations. The increase in FM broadcasting was prompted by the saturation of radios in U.S. households and by FM radio's ability to "narrowcast." Narrowcasting — in contrast to mere broadcasting — is aimed at a very specific market segment, which is selected by the programming. Classical music stations, for example, reach a relatively small (but affluent) market. In the younger days of radio, a broadcast reached a very wide audience of differing incomes, education, and interests. Today, we can target our radio programming for men, women, blacks, Hispanics, other ethnic groups, and target it as well for specific income levels.

At the same time, radio is succeeding because sponsors have improved their messages. Better commercials make radio better. New audiences and new approaches to the consumer have made radio a powerful advertising tool.

Television trades heavily in attractive people and glamorous images, but radio can talk about some unattractive physical problems. To be sure, television

```
FEMALE:     Excuse me, is this stool taken?
MALE:       Uh, no.
FEMALE:     Mind if I sit here?
MALE:       Help yourself.
FEMALE:     Thanks.
MALE:       Would you, uh, pass me the peanuts?
FEMALE:     Sure — (sound of a glass being knocked over) — oh, oh, I'm terribly
            sorry. Oh, I've ruined that tie, and it's so beautiful too. Let me wipe it up.
MALE:       (softly) That's okay.
FEMALE:     Um, that's a very interesting cologne you're wearing.
MALE:       Huh? It's beer!
FEMALE:     (Chuckle) Oh, no, I'm sorry. Let me buy you another one, please.
MALE:       No, that's all right — I'll just suck my tie.
FEMALE:     (Chuckle) Let me make it up to you. How about a Molson Golden?
MALE:       Molson Golden?
FEMALE:     Yah, imported from Canada. It's excellent. Crisp, clear, smooth — you'll
            really love it.
MALE:       Uh, yah, yah . . .
FEMALE:     You will?
MALE:       Are you trying to pick me up?
FEMALE:     (Chuckle) The thought never entered my mind.
MALE:       Well, think.
FEMALE:     (Chuckle)
ANNOUNCER:  Molson Golden beer, from North America's oldest brewery. Since 1786,
            Molson makes it golden. Imported by Martlet, Great Neck, New York.
MALE:       Well, you're not doing a very good job of this.
FEMALE:     I know, let me start over: Is this stool taken?
MALE:       (Shouts) Hold the peanuts!
```

Molson Golden's radio commercials have been a delightful series of boy-meets-girl-meets-beer skits which have contributed to the Canadian beer's marketing success in the United States. They capitalize on the listener's ability to fantasize. What do these people look like? The charismatic characters entertain the consumer and, at the same time, instill brand awareness. (Courtesy Martlet Importing Company.)

```
DAUGHTER:   Hey, Ma . . . you know I've really grown to like Friendship Cottage
            Cheese.
MOTHER:     See . . . Friendship is good anytime. And it's not just what you eat for a
            week after you eat a whole chocolate cake for lunch. In fact, Friendship is
            better than chocolate cake.
DAUGHTER:   It is? What gave you that idea?
MOTHER:     Therapy.
DAUGHTER:   (Pause) You were in therapy? Why?
MOTHER:     Well . . . I couldn't decide whether to marry your father. Or Carlos.
DAUGHTER:   (Pause) Car-los?
MOTHER:     Oh could he cha-cha. What a dreamboat. But you see, Carlos was like
            chocolate cake. For ecstasy, you pay. What a bum.
DAUGHTER:   And daddy?
MOTHER:     Oh Daaady . . . well, daaaddy is like Friendship Cottage Cheese. Always
            sweet. Always fresh. Doesn't make me break out. What a doll. I wonder
            if Carlos is in the phone book?
DAUGHTER:   Ma!
ANNOUNCER:  Friendship Cottage Cheese. When you know what good is.
```

How do you sell a product that women view as a commodity? The idea was to create an image of superiority — to show that Friendship is better — without talking about a premium price. The agency created a sophisticated conversation between mother and daughter. It gives Friendship Cottage Cheese a personality — to make people think about cottage cheese instead of merely throwing it into the grocery cart. Momma gets the idea across. Will she look up Carlos in the phone book? (Courtesy Friendship Food Products, Inc.)

commercials give us advice about dandruff, bad breath, and wet armpits, but they do it with beautiful people. Radio talks one-to-one with listeners about their unfashionable, unsightly conditions — acne, tobacco-stained teeth, etc. Radio avoids the problem of graphically portraying the malady and the cure.

During its pre-television period, radio had an excellent mixture of programs and advertisements with many effective singing commercials and the delivery of the commercial message by the star of the program. By the 1970s, radio had found its most successful operation by using pairs of performers in clever and carefully staged dialogue — Stiller and Meara, Burt and Harry, Bob and Ray, to name a few.

Today, actors speak their lines as though they were part of normal conversation, where responses and questions overlap and where sentences are not always completed. Other successful radio commercials use clever words, sound effects, and memorable music. John Cleese, of Monty Python's Flying Circus fame, contributes much of the copy to the radio spots he has performed for Kronenbourg beer and Callard and Bowser candies.

Where It All Came From

Although a number of physicists had been working on the use of electromagnetic energy, it was an Italian engineer, Guglielmo Marconi, who transmitted the first radio signal in 1895. Only 25 years later the first commercial radio station, KDKA in Pittsburgh, was opened by the Westinghouse Broadcasting Company. In 1922, several radio stations broadcast the World Series and by 1926 the National Broadcasting Company had established a network of 24 stations, which was followed by the establishment of the Columbia Broadcasting System the next year. And so the radio industry grew. Today, there are over 7,300 radio stations. Each station is licensed by the Federal Communications Commission (FCC) and assigned call letters for national identification. Stations west of the Mississippi use call letters beginning with K. Stations east of the Mississippi use call letters beginning with W. Call letters that were assigned in the early days of radio, such as KDKA, present some exceptions to this rule.

AM and FM Radio

Radio stations transmit the sound of voices or musical instruments from their broadcasting studios to your radio receiver by means of electromagnetic waves. These electromagnetic waves, like waves of water on a pond, have both height, or *amplitude,* and width. The width of the wave determines its *frequency.* The narrower the waves are, the greater the number that can pass by a fixed point in a second — or the higher their frequency; the broader the wave, the lower the frequency.

The designation AM is derived from the term *amplitude modulation.* An AM radio station broadcasts its programs by varying the height, or amplitude, of the electromagnetic waves that it radiates from its transmitting tower. Some of these waves follow the contour of the ground, and are therefore called *ground waves;* others radiate upward into the sky, and are known as *sky waves.* During the daytime, radio receivers pick up only the ground waves; the sky waves travel through the earth's atmosphere and out into space. At night, however, the sky waves bounce back to earth and can be picked up by receivers far beyond the range of the station's ground waves.

The strength of the AM signal, expressed in watts, is assigned by the FCC. The stronger the signal, the greater the distance it will travel. On the basis of strength of signal, there are three kinds of stations. First, there is the local station, with a broadcast range of about twenty-five miles. Second, there is the regional station, which may cover an entire state. Last, there is the clear-channel station with up to 50,000 watts. Stations that broadcast with that range are few and no other station is permitted to operate on the same frequency during evening hours. Generally, the lower the frequency, the farther the signal will travel. The signal of a 1,000-watt station at the lower end of the radio dial will cover a greater territory than a station with equal power (watts) at the top of the dial.

FM stands for *frequency modulation.* An FM radio station broadcasts its programs by varying the width, or frequency, of the electromagnetic waves that it radiates from its transmitting tower. FM transmission follows the line of sight, and the distance for which reception is satisfactory depends on the height of the antenna. For this reason, many FM transmitting towers are located on tall buildings or mountains. But as a rule, FM signals cannot be received over great distances.

When a group of two or more stations broadcast the same program simultaneously (as is done on radio networks), the program is transmitted from the originating station over telephone lines. The other stations in the group receive the program from the originating station over the telephone and re-broadcast it from their transmitting towers.

AM Stereo

All across the United States AM radio stations are investing in stereo transmitting equipment to enhance their broadcast fare with stereo music. They hope to halt some of the small loss they have each year to FM stations, which have broadcast stereo music for over 20 years. The problem has been that few radio manufacturers have plunged into production. It is unlikely that home listeners in big numbers will abandon their favorite FM station for the slightly lower fidelity of AM, but in the car it hardly makes any difference. The best opportunities for AM stereo exist in car radios.

As of the end of 1984, there were about 250 AM stereo broadcast stations.

Radio as an Advertising Medium

Radio is a *high-frequency* medium. If we think that we need to repeat our advertising message often, radio is the ideal medium for us. The total cost is relatively low, and there are many stations to choose from with time available to build a high-frequency plan.

Radio is a good *supporting* medium. We can use radio to support the other media in our media mix because its cost is low. And it can provide us with good reach into selected target markets.

Radio is very *selective.* It enables us to reach a wide range of geographical markets — city, metro, state, and national. It also offers us a remarkable degree of demographic selectivity. We can use drive time — the hours in the morning and afternoon when people are on their way to and from work — to reach workers who commute. Daytime radio, on the other hand, accompanies people on their shopping trips. The last advertising message they receive before they enter the supermarket or department store may be delivered to them over their car radio.

Radio offers us great *flexibility.* Fast, low-cost production can meet changing market conditions and make it possible for us to tie our advertisements in with current news events. Pepsi Cola's use of radio is an excellent example of the way one company utilizes the medium's flexibility. Several commercials are distributed to each station with instructions to use a particular commercial when the temperature reaches 90 degrees. Radio lends itself equally well to the

These are listings from the *Spot Radio* edition of Standard Rate & Data Service. Every station describes its programming, facilities, hours of operation, and network affiliation, if any. Many stations do not list their advertising rates, but make them available through their representatives.

advertiser who wants to tie in with a particular event. For example, a commercial could be delivered to the stations waiting only for the name of the winner of the Indy 500 or the Daytona race to be dropped in.

Radio offers us many opportunites for low-cost *market testing*. For example, the advertiser makes an offer over the radio — for a sample or a booklet, some reason for the listener to write or telephone. Such an offer provides a quick way to determine the interest in a product. There are no long deadlines or extended preparation time for announcements. By using *spot radio* in different markets, the advertiser can obtain a low-cost market test.

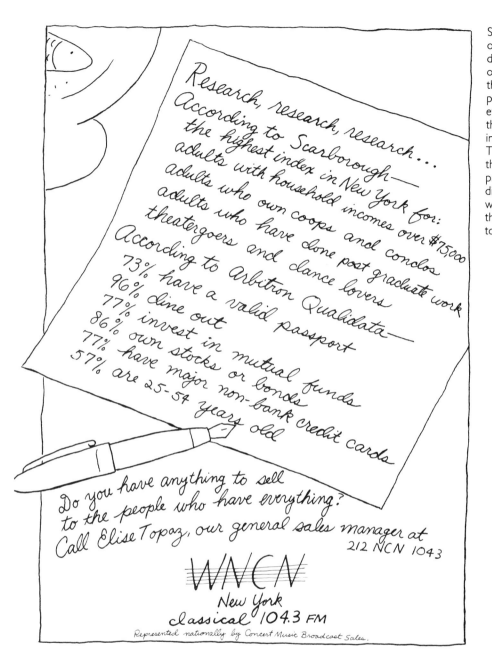

Research, research, research...

According to Scarborough — the highest index in New York for:

adults with household incomes over $75,000

adults who own coops and condos

adults who have done post graduate work

theatergoers and dance lovers

According to Arbitron Qualidata —

73% have a valid passport

96% dine out

77% invest in mutual funds

86% own stocks or bonds

77% have major non-bank credit cards

57% are 25-54 years old

Do you have anything to sell to the people who have everything? Call Elise Topaz, our general sales manager at 212 NCN 1043

WNCN

New York

classical 104.3 FM

Represented nationally by Concert Music Broadcast Sales.

Station WNCN programs only classical music and defines its audience with a set of demographic attributes that include age — 57 percent age 25 to 54. However, as you can see, the thrust for this FM station is income and educational level. The advertiser will evaluate the station or stations that provide the largest target audience for the product and will consider the nature of the programming in relation to that product.

But radio has limitations that the media analyst must weigh. In some markets there are so many competing stations that no one station can achieve dominance. In New York City, for example, there are 29 stations (AM and FM) plus 34 in the surrounding metro areas. The audiences for these stations tend to be segmented — which is great if we want to reach a particular segment, but frustrating if we want a mass audience.

Since radio appeals to only one sense, it is of limited value to us if our product needs to be seen or demonstrated. What's more, consumers often listen to their radios while reading, working, or driving. Under such conditions, it may be difficult for us to get our message across.

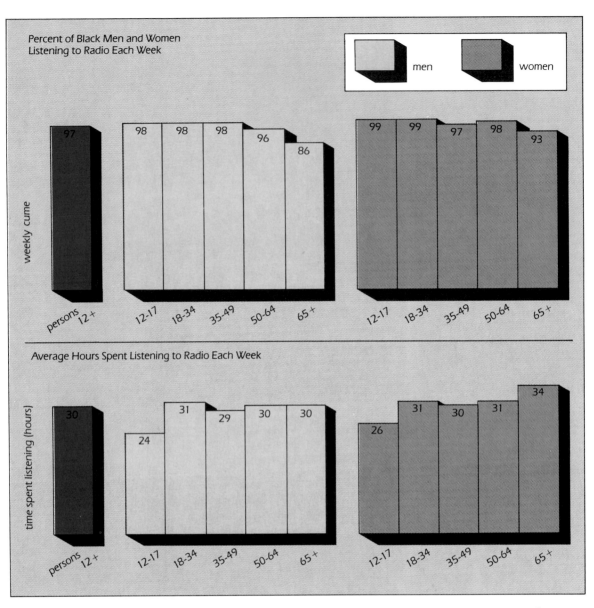

Percent of Black Men and Women Listening to Radio Each Week

men women

weekly cume

persons 12+ · 12-17 · 18-34 · 35-49 · 50-64 · 65+ — men: 97 | 98 98 98 96 86
women: 12-17 · 18-34 · 35-49 · 50-64 · 65+ — 99 99 97 98 93

Average Hours Spent Listening to Radio Each Week

time spent listening (hours)

persons 12+ · 12-17 · 18-34 · 35-49 · 50-64 · 65+ — men: 30 | 24 31 29 30 30
women: 12-17 · 18-34 · 35-49 · 50-64 · 65+ — 26 31 30 31 34

In 1984, Arbitron surveyed black listeners for all radio stations in ten metropolitan markets with significant black populations. As we can see from the diagram, radio reaches almost all black persons 12 years old and above. The highest percentage reached — 99 percent — was for black women age 12 to 34. As for total listening time — the average for the United States is 25 hours, while black listeners spent 30 hours a week with radio. Black women 65 and older listen the most. Among the other valuable information documented by the Arbitron study were the age and sex listening patterns according to dayparts — that is, according to different segments of the day. Women 65 and older tune in most weekdays 6 AM to 10 AM. Male teenagers age 12 to 17 tune in most on weekends. Black listening peaks at 7 AM weekdays and 10 AM Saturdays. More listening occurs at home than at any other place.

An Arbitron 12-market study of black television viewing in May 1984 indicated that black households range from 13 percent to 43 percent above the general population levels for households using television during daytime and early fringe (5 to 7 PM) dayparts. Black women range from 5 percent above general female population in prime time to 47 percent above female population in the 9 AM to noon daypart. (Courtesy Arbitron Ratings Company. Copyright © 1984. Reprinted with permission.)

The low costs for radio time yield very little revenue in media commissions for the advertising agency. Therefore, many agencies are reluctant to assign their best, highly paid creative personnel to work on a client's radio advertisements. Also, handling the paper work involved in spot radio buys — with thousands of stations to choose from, many with 24-hour broadcast days — is economically unfeasible for some agencies.

Spot Radio

When we say we are using **spot radio** it means that we are contracting with individual radio stations to carry our advertising message. The word *spot* distinguishes a radio advertisement broadcast on separately owned radio stations from advertising on **network radio,** which involves the simultaneous broadcast of a program over a group of stations. A *radio spot* is a short commercial, sometimes called a spot announcement. The term radio spot represents a time unit. The term spot radio represents a geographical unit.

The importance of spot radio is clear: It permits us to deliver our sales message area by area, city by city. This can be particularly useful if we do not have national distribution. We can also use spot radio to tie in local retailers in specific market areas. Spot radio is also extremely flexible, enabling us to take advantage of local conditions, fast-breaking news, or competitive activities.

Above all, spot radio is beautifully segmented: Its wide variety of programming attracts sharply defined audiences. In such major markets as New York, Chicago, and Los Angeles, there are forty or more stations available, most providing vertical programming. *Vertical programming* refers to a particular listening segment of people who prefer a certain kind of program — all news, hard rock, country, soul, Spanish (and other ethnics), good music, classical, and so on. Radio stations promote themselves every few minutes by mentioning their call letters. This allows listeners to switch around to whatever programming suits them — to an all-news station or to a station that broadcasts traffic reports every fifteen minutes.

Thus, we can gear our message to the listening habits and the living habits of our target market. The time periods 6 to 10 in the morning and 4 to 7 in the evening Monday through Friday are known as **drive time** and are to radio what *prime time* (7:30 to 11 in the evening) is to television. After the drivers get to work, we can concentrate on reaching people who are getting ready for the day's shopping. Late afternoon, when young listeners are out of school, is prime time for FM progressive rock. In agricultural areas, farmers listen early in the morning for news of livestock and grain prices.

Network Radio

A network is a group of radio stations permanently connected by telephone lines. This connection makes it possible for the advertiser's message to be broadcast simultaneously over all the stations in the network. The network may be national or regional and is usually composed of a number of company-owned stations together with independent stations that have contracted for network programming. There are four major radio networks — Columbia Broadcasting System, National Broadcasting Company, Mutual Broadcasting

WMAQ offers country music out of Chicago, Illinois, and claims to be "America's Number 1 Country Music Station." As the map on this page shows, it has a 50,000-watt daytime signal which covers eight states in mid-America, including Illinois, Indiana, Iowa, Michigan, Minnesota, Missouri, Ohio, and Wisconsin — an area of 23,839,000 people. It describes its audience as adults age 25 to 54 — over one million people. At night the station's coverage (see map on next page) is greater and extends from the East Coast almost to the Gulf Coast — and all the states in between and up into Canada, including the cities of Montreal, Toronto, Ottawa, and Winnipeg.

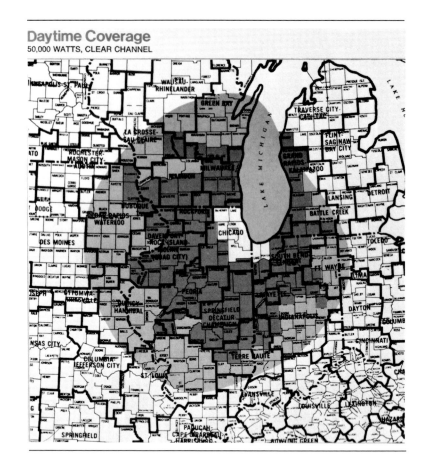

System, and American Broadcasting Company. Some regional networks are the Beck-Ross Group, the Groskin Group, and the Intermountain Network. Most of the state networks are rural and, for the most part, specialize in farm news. These are not true networks as we use the term to describe the CBS network or the NBC network. Regional networks are groups of independent stations that are assembled as a "package" by a station representative as a convenience for advertisers. These stations are not linked together electronically.

Local stations that affiliate with a network enjoy the benefit of programs generated by the network, often featuring top talent. The networks provide *sustaining* programs as well as *sponsored* ones. A **sponsored program** is one that is paid for by one or more advertisers. A **sustaining program** is one that has no advertisers; it is generally provided by a network to build an audience in the expectation that a sponsor will become interested. In return, the network has an option on part of the local station's time, generally the choicest hours. Network programming is generally adult-oriented. In 1983 network radio carried 22 percent of all radio advertising, while spot radio accounted for 78 percent.

Network radio is not as selective as spot radio, but it does offer greater reach. The CBS radio network, for example, claims an audience of 2,400,130 adults (age 18 and over) from 6 to 10 AM every weekday. From 7 PM to midnight on Saturday night, which is the least listened to time period, a spot on CBS will still reach 475,000 adults. This reach makes network radio very

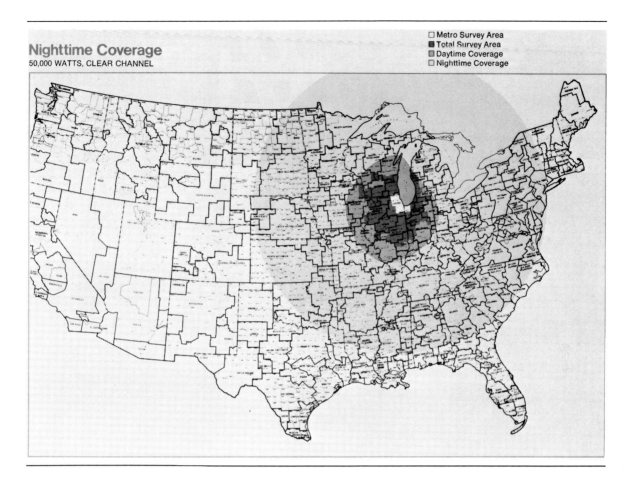

☐ Metro Survey Area
■ Total Survey Area
☐ Daytime Coverage
☐ Nighttime Coverage

attractive to national advertisers. Food, automobile, and drug manufacturers are the primary users of network radio. Food, automotive service, and travel companies are the heaviest users of spot radio.

Network radio and its programming have grown since the 1960s, when the major networks were primarily news services. There are now about 19 national radio networks programming concerts, talk shows, sports events, and dramas. Generally, radio networks send their affiliates programming that contains national commercials and free time to be sold to local advertisers. Network radio can be a very inexpensive way to cover the entire country. The new radio networks are appealing to advertisers much as magazines do, by reaching particular demographic groups. One small, highly specialized network is the Physicians Radio Network. Each listener receives a free radio which picks up only the affiliated station's FM channel in each of about 85 major markets. It broadcasts a one-hour tape of medical news, repeated endlessly. There is live coverage of medical events or scientific discoveries when important enough. The network sells eight minutes of commercial per hour to major pharmaceutical manufacturers.

Radio Audiences

In examining a description of the audience for any particular radio station, the advertiser is most interested in the station's *coverage* — the number of homes that can pick up the station clearly. *Circulation* represents the number of homes

WNEW's programming features album oriented rock (AOR) and the music attracts the listeners. It claims to be the leading station (in terms of audience size) for males 25 to 34 in the time period from 6 AM to midnight.

that *actually tune in* to that station. *Coverage* depends on the power of the station's transmitter, the location and height of its antenna, the transmission frequency, and the terrain. Although at night AM radio covers a larger area owing to the effect of sky waves, no advertiser can count on this circulation. The national advertiser can only consider it a bonus. The *circulation* of a program depends on whether it is broadcast during the day or at night, the

Top 25 Network Radio Advertisers 1984

Rank	Advertiser	Expenditures ($000)	
		1984	1984 as % of total advertising exp.
1.	American Telephone & Telegraph	$16,344	2.9
2.	Cotter & Co.	10,201	16.0
3.	Jeffrey Martin Inc.	8,946	N/A
4.	U.S. Government	8,633	3.0
5.	Sears, Roebuck & Co.	8,630	1.2
6.	Warner-Lambert Co.	8,143	1.9
7.	General Motors Corp.	6,746	0.9
8.	Purex Industries	6,715	N/A
9.	Dow Jones & Co.	6,431	N/A
10.	Anheuser-Busch Cos.	6,231	1.7
11.	Triangle Publications	5,228	N/A
12.	Nabisco Brands	4,938	1.5
13.	PepsiCo Inc.	4,746	1.1
14.	Campbell Soup Co.	4,371	3.1
15.	Chrysler Corp.	4,141	1.3
16.	Abbott Laboratories	4,017	N/A
17.	Procter & Gamble Co.	3,977	0.5
18.	Beatrice Cos.	3,345	0.5
19.	National Distillers & Chemical Corp.	3,184	N/A
20.	American Egg Board	2,959	N/A
21.	Conagra	2,871	N/A
22.	Hartz Mountain Industries	2,809	N/A
23.	Kelly Service Inc.	2,734	N/A
24.	S.C. Johnson & Sons	2,708	3.0
25.	American Honda Motor Co.	2,647	2.0

Source: Reprinted with permission from the September 26, 1985, issue of *Advertising Age.* Copyright © 1985 by Crain Communications, Inc.

Jeffrey Martin, Inc. (ranked third) is a firm in Union, New Jersey, which obviously has found network radio very productive. The firm relies heavily on network radio (41.5 percent of their budget) because its products are targeted to two groups of heavy radio listeners — insomniacs and housewives, particularly elderly women who spend time alone with the radio, day and night. Their products include Compoz, Porcillana, and products that clean tobacco-stained teeth and relieve backaches. They spent $754,000 on network radio spots just for Compoz.

nature of the program, and the nature of competitive programs (including those on television) in the same time slot.

A media analyst wants to be able to compare and evaluate alternative station mixes. One of the factors that any analyst must consider in evaluating a mix is the *cumulative audience* of each station. The **cume,** as it is usually called, is a term devised by the Nielsen service to describe the net cumulative audience of a single program or of an entire spot schedule over a four-week period. The idea is that if a person tunes in to station Y every morning, he or she will be counted only *once.* Audience accumulation measures the number of different people that are exposed to the program. Some media people describe this factor as the station's reach. *Reach* generally refers to the net unduplicated audience of

Radio is a limited medium — limited to just the one sense of hearing. But this advertisement, sponsored by the NBC radio network, is intended to provoke the imagination of advertisers and their agencies to the creative possibilities of radio. Couldn't the sound of a child drinking a soda be more effective in catching an audience's attention than a picture of a child drinking a soda? How about the crunching sound of a fresh apple when we bite into it? Or the distinctive sounds of a champagne bottle being opened, an auto starter when the car won't start, or a busy airport terminal? A little imagination is all it takes to make effective use of this medium.

a campaign. In practice, however, both cume and reach are used interchangeably to indicate the number of people covered by a station or a program.

GRPs: Gross Rating Points   In an effort to simplify comparison between stations and station combinations, media planners use a measurement system known as **gross rating points** (GRPs). A gross rating point is an index figure that represents 1 percent of the total audience of radio listeners (or television viewers) within a specified market area or geographical area. If, for example, a particular program were heard by 10 percent of all the radio listeners in San Francisco, a commercial that ran on that program would have a rating of 10 GRPs. If the program were broadcast twice a week, the GRPs for that commercial would be 20. GRPs provide us with a method for measuring the *weight* of our broadcast campaign. For example, if we were considering using a media package consisting of one commercial on three different programs, each with a 12-point rating, and one commercial on four different programs with 6-point ratings each, we can calculate its weight as:

$$3 \text{ commercials} \times 12 \text{ rating} = 36 \text{ GRPs}$$
$$4 \text{ commercials} \times 6 \text{ rating} = \underline{24 \text{ GRPs}}$$
$$\text{TOTAL} = 60 \text{ GRPs}$$

We can then compare the total GRPs offered by this package to those offered by alternate combinations. Please note that a total rating of 60 GRPs does not mean that we will reach 60 percent of the audience; GRPs measure *gross,* not *net* audience. That is, the GRP figures contain duplications: listeners who tuned in to two, three, or even all seven of the programs. The package's unduplicated audience will be indicated by its cume.

Buying Radio Time

Compared to the cost of other media, radio time is inexpensive. If we can buy time on programs that reach our target market, then spot radio is exceptionally cost efficient. A 60-second network commercial during drive time might cost from $2,200 to $3,400 and might be broadcast over as many as 200 stations, mostly adult oriented. Compare that figure with a cost of approximately $118,840 for a 30-second commercial on prime time television or about $75,000 for the cost of a four-color page in a leading consumer magazine.

Stations generally have about 18 minutes an hour available for advertising. Time is sold, for the most part, on the basis of spot announcements in units of 60, 30, 20, or 10 seconds. Stations offer quantity discounts with rates based on the total number of announcements scheduled during the year. Rates vary with the time of day, and stations designate their time periods as Class AA, Class A, Class B, and so on. The most expensive time, Class AA, might be 6 to 10 AM, Monday through Friday. That's drive time. Class C might be 7 PM to midnight. Each station determines its own classes, basing them on the listening characteristics of its audience. A classical music FM station might find its major audience from 7 to 11 PM, Monday through Friday. A farm station might find its prime time very early in the morning when its audience tunes in for weather, crop, and livestock reports.

Most stations offer **package plans** that represent a number of spots broadcast within a consecutive seven-day period on an **ROS,** or **run of station,** schedule. ROS is for radio what ROP is for newspapers: Radio station programmers may schedule the commercial at whatever time is most convenient for them. For the advertiser who wants to specify the program, stations offer special features with high audience attention, such as five-minute news reports, late headlines, stock market reports, traffic 'copter reports, or time signal announcements (IDs). The ID (station identification) consists of twelve words or six seconds. Many time slot arrangements are not listed on a station's rate card and very often radio time is negotiated.

SPOT ANNOUNCEMENTS/FIXED POSITIONS

5x	GRID I	GRID II	GRID III	GRID IV
AA	$240	$190	$170	$150
A	$220	$180	$160	$145

10x	GRID I	GRID II	GRID III	GRID IV
AA	$220	$180	$160	$145
A	$200	$170	$150	$135

15x	GRID I	GRID II	GRID III	GRID IV
AA	$210	$175	$155	$135
A	$190	$165	$145	$130

Note: "B" rates available on request.

R.O.S. 5:30 AM-12 Midnight, Monday through Sunday

Per Week 60" Announcements

15x	$205	$170	$150	$130
20x	$195	$160	$140	$125

Program Rate $1,750 per hour. 30" Announcements 80% of above Plan Rate. Feature programs and sponsored ID's available, prices on request. Call WNCN's Account Executives for appropriate grid.

Time Classifications

Class AA:	5:30AM-10AM & 3PM-7PM	Monday through Friday
	10AM-3PM & 3PM-7PM	Saturday, Sunday
Class A:	10AM-3PM & 7PM-12 Mid	Monday through Friday
	5:30AM-10AM & 7PM-12 Mid	Saturday, Sunday
Class B:	12 Midnight-5:30AM	Monday through Sunday

Commercial Policy
Musical works are not interrupted for commercials. Due to the nature of the music, program and announcement times are approximate.
Advertisers, programs and announcements are subject to station approval and may be altered to conform with station policy.
Program sponsorship includes maximum of three 60-second spots in an hour plus appropriate sponsorship ID's. 15% commission to recognized agencies on time only.
*Programs more than 1 hour in length will be pro-rated at the one time hourly rate.

As this rate card from WNCN radio shows, the cost of radio time depends on the length of the commercial (30 or 60 seconds), the time of day, and the frequency of the schedule.

Television

Although there were five television stations in the United States that regularly broadcasted programs in the late 1930s, the Federal Trade Commission did not authorize the use of television as an advertising medium until 1941. In that year there were only about 10,000 television sets in use. But the number of television households in the United States has continued to grow: By the end of 1985 there were almost 90 million homes equipped with at least one set (representing 98 percent of all households in the United States). Of these, 90 percent had color sets and 55 percent had two or more sets.

The rapid rise of the television industry and its continued success today are for the most part due to the characteristics of the medium itself. Television

What Do People Do with Their TV Sets?

In a study made by Video Storyboard Tests/Campaign Monitor in the third quarter of 1985,* these were the uses given for television sets:

1985 Use	Net Gain/Loss from 1984
Watching PBS (70%)	17%
Recording with a VCR (27%)	14%
Playing rented videocassettes (27%)	12%
Watching cable TV other than special channels (42%)	12%
Watching 24-hour movie channels (38%)	9%
Watching 24-hour music channels/MTV (30%)	6%
Watching home movies (9%)	3%
Watching local TV stations (85%)	3%
Monitor for home computers (10%)	1%
Watching network TV (93%)	−7%
Playing video games (21%)	−11%

The usage figures in parentheses show the percentage of respondents who listed it as one of the uses of their television sets. While watching public television had a high gain (17 percent), watching the networks (93 percent) was still the favorite pastime despite a decline. The 11 per- cent decline in playing video games reflects the end of the interest in this category. The growth of PBS seems to reflect the interest that viewers have in television with fewer or no commercials.

_____

* *ADWEEK,* February 24, 1986, p. 38.

delivers sight, sound, motion, and color. The television set is, for many families, the focal point of the living room. Television also demands and usually receives the full attention of its audience. Radio listeners sometimes work, drive, or study (if possible) while listening. Not so with television. In short, television offers advertisers impact, the power to stimulate people to take action.

The Television Audience

The terms used to describe the television audience are the same as those used for the radio audience. *Coverage* refers to the number of homes that *receive* the television signal. *Circulation* describes the number of homes that *actually tune in* on the signal. The ability of any station to provide coverage depends on the power of its transmitter, the height of its transmitter antenna, the kind of terrain over which the signal must pass, and the frequency of the signal. The lower the frequency, the greater the carrying power. Coverage for cable TV is limited to the number of its subscribers.

Television stations usually provide advertisers with a map indicating their signal strength in a market. The strongest signal is designated *Grade A,* generally the primary market area surrounding the station. The secondary area coverage is designated *Grade B.* These measurements (of signal strength) are useful in determining coverage. Another way to gauge coverage is to mail a

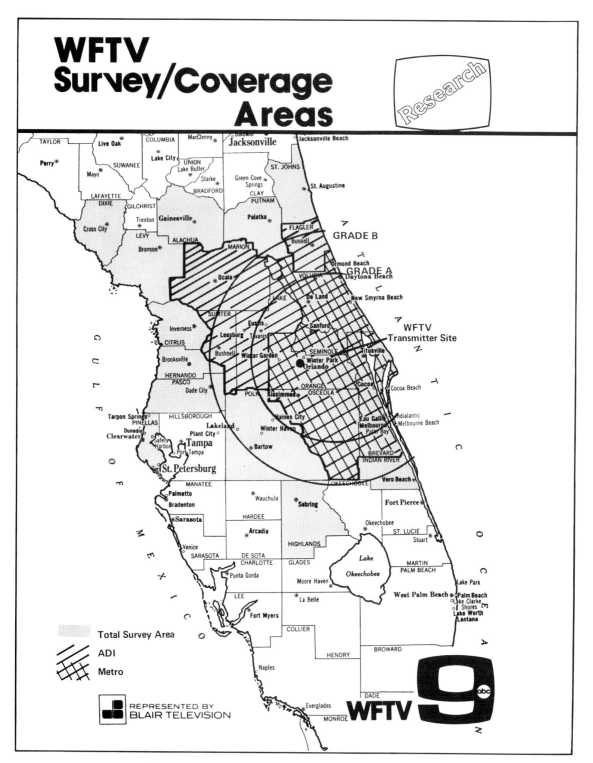

WFTV Survey/Coverage Areas

Research

Total Survey Area

ADI

Metro

REPRESENTED BY
BLAIR TELEVISION

WFTV **9** abc

The concentric circles on this coverage map for a television station in Orlando, Florida, show the broadcast range of the station. The inner circle defines the station's Grade A area, and the outer circle, Grade B. Notice that the Area of Dominant Influence (ADI) for the Orlando — Daytona Beach Market is larger than the Metro area. Notice also that the lower left-hand portion of the station's Grade B area is not included in the ADI. That area is probably included in the Tampa — St. Petersburg ADI.

questionnaire to a selected sample of homes within, and outside of, a station's A and B areas. The questionnaire asks respondents to list the stations they view regularly. From the replies, estimates are made of how many homes in each area are covered by the station's signal. *Gross rating points* are another criterion advertisers use to determine the size of the audience within a specified market area or geographic region. (See color plate 28 for an outdoor ad attracting viewers for a television station.)

The characteristics and size of the station's audience are determined by the time of day, the time of the year, the program, and the competing programs. The most popular viewing time — **prime time** — is between the hours of 7:30 and 11 PM, Monday through Sunday. The next most popular time is 4:30 to 7:30 PM, Monday through Sunday. Third most popular is 7:00 AM to 4:30 PM, Monday through Friday. Television viewing can vary considerably from winter to summer, with the greatest differences occuring during late afternoon and early evening. The smallest differences are during early morning and late night.

Although the demographics may vary somewhat, specific time slots will deliver a predictable audience. But advertisers (as well as programmers) need to keep a number of demographic factors in mind.[1] Television households view an average of $52\frac{1}{2}$ hours of television a week, but households with three or more people watch more, and households with children watch more. For the most part, women view more than men; older men and women watch more than younger adults. Younger children watch more than older children and teenagers.

Adventure appears to be the most popular type of program, followed by suspense/mystery dramas, then by feature films. Women age 18 to 34 make up the largest segment for adventure and feature films, and second largest for suspense/mystery dramas. Women age 55 and older comprise the largest audience for suspense/mystery dramas and general dramas.

Like the editorial content of a magazine, the program format of a television station to a large extent determines its audience. Individual programs may have their viewing audiences enhanced by carry-overs from the previous programs. But, unlike the reader of a magazine or newspaper, who may be exposed to all the messages in a single issue, the television viewer can watch only one program at a time. A popular program on one station may reduce the size of the audience on another station. Although the size of the potential audience is very large, each program will attract only a modest percentage of the total. When advertisers use television to reach only certain segments, they pay for considerable waste. Nevertheless, on a CPM basis, television is not expensive. The CPM for television can be calculated as follows:

$$\text{CPM} = \frac{\text{cost of 1 unit of time} \times 1,000}{\text{number of homes reached by a program or time period}}$$

As was the case in describing a radio station's audience, we are concerned here with a television program's *cumulative audience.* The value of the term may be clarified with an explanation. If a woman reading *Good Housekeeping* looks into the same issue 15 different times in a month, she is counted only once. Magazine audience accumulation is measured by total audience — the *number of people* who buy or subscribe to the magazine. In broadcast we measure the

---

[1] See the *1984 Nielsen Report on Television,* published A. C. Nielsen Company, Northbrook, IL.

number of households that tuned in to a program at least once over a four-week period. The figure may be expressed as a percentage of all television homes or as the number of homes tuned in during the four-week period. What the figure tells us is the *reach* of the program (how many homes) as well as the frequency (how often the same people are reached).

Network Television

There are three national television networks — the American Broadcasting Company, the Columbia Broadcasting System, and the National Broadcasting Company. Unlike radio programming, most television prime-time programming is network. The three networks themselves own a total of 15 stations; the remainder of the stations in the networks are affiliates. Network

All of the companies on this list are among the 100 leading national advertisers. The corporate names tell us what we would expect, given the nature of the medium — food products, household products (such as soaps and detergents), automobiles, pharmaceutical and health products, personal care products. The percentages going to network television range from a low of 14.4 for R. J. Reynolds Industries to a high of 61.3 for Kellogg.

Top 25 Network Television Advertisers 1984		
	Expenditures ($000)	
Rank Advertiser	1984	1984 as % of total advertising exp.
1. Procter & Gamble Co.	$412,747	47.3
2. American Telephone & Telegraph	253,117	44.9
3. General Motors Corp.	231,443	30.3
4. General Foods Corp.	190,223	42.3
5. American Home Products	179,024	43.5
6. Sears, Roebuck & Co.	172,446	23.1
7. Johnson & Johnson	168,639	56.2
8. Anheuser-Busch Cos.	166,416	45.7
9. Ford Motor Co.	164,253	29.4
10. McDonald's Corp.	162,462	33.8
11. Philip Morris Inc.	161,716	28.3
12. Unilever U.S.	142,982	36.1
13. Coca-Cola Co.	140,104	40.8
14. Kellogg Co.	128,080	61.3
15. Dart & Kraft	123,289	45.8
16. Bristol-Myers Co.	122,552	47.4
17. General Mills	115,608	40.8
18. Beatrice Cos.	111,591	16.4
19. Pillsbury Co.	106,983	33.6
20. R. J. Reynolds Industries	97,600	14.4
21. Chrysler Corp.	93,637	29.5
22. Ralston Purina Co.	91,837	21.4
23. PepsiCo Inc.	90,403	21.1
24. U.S. Government	87,697	30.5
25. Warner-Lambert Co.	86,976	19.8

Source: Reprinted with permission from the September 26, 1985, issue of *Advertising Age.* Copyright © 1985 by Crain Communications, Inc.

television offers its advertisers several advantages. Buying network time allows the advertiser to control the commercial so that it is delivered uniformly and efficiently to all the stations in the network. Network programs enhance the images of their advertisers. The network may not have the strongest station or affiliate in each market, but it will favor advertisers who buy the full network lineup with preference in choice of time slots and, in some cases, better rates. However, network television does have one major limitation. Unlike print media, which can expand their publications to accommodate more advertisers, network television has only a certain amount of time per hour available for advertising. If advertiser A buys the 8 PM slot, there is no other 8 PM slot for advertiser B on that network.

Programs today are either developed by the network or bought by the network from a package house. A **package house** is an independent movie-

Each firm on this list is among the leading advertisers in the United States. The percentage of the firm's total advertising expenditures invested in spot television appears to have no pattern. Wendy's devotes 43.3 percent, but McDonald's invests 19.1 percent. Toyota spends over 42 percent of its budget on spot television and Nissan almost 25 percent, but Ford spends only 7.1 percent, and General Motors invests even less, 5 percent.

Top 25 Spot Television Advertisers 1984

| | | Expenditures ($000) | |
| | | 1984 | 1984 as % of total advertising exp. |
Rank	Advertiser		
1.	Procter & Gamble Co.	$239,331	27.4
2.	PepsiCo Inc.	154,287	36.0
3.	General Mills	109,253	38.6
4.	Pillsbury Co.	99,106	31.1
5.	General Foods Corp.	96,869	21.5
6.	McDonalds's Corp.	91,454	19.1
7.	Coca-Cola Co.	64,976	18.9
8.	Anheuser-Busch Cos.	60,070	16.5
9.	Unilever U.S.	59,122	14.9
10.	Toyota Motor Sales Co.	58,377	42.3
11.	Beatrice Cos.	57,445	8.4
12.	Dart & Kraft	53,742	20.0
13.	R. J. Reynolds Industries	47,611	7.0
14.	Nestle Enterprises	47,130	25.2
15.	Philip Morris Inc.	46,589	8.2
16.	Mars Inc.	44,201	31.7
17.	Hasbro Inc.	42,953	51.3
18.	Nissan Motor Co.	40,919	24.9
19.	Kellogg Co.	40,641	19.5
20.	Warner-Lambert Co.	40,569	9.2
21.	Ford Motor Co.	39,500	7.1
22.	Wendy's International	39,354	43.3
23.	General Motors Corp.	38,520	5.0
24.	Ralston Purina Co.	35,208	8.2
25.	Sears, Roebuck & Co.	33,552	4.5

Source: Reprinted with permission from the September 26, 1985, issue of *Advertising Age.* Copyright © 1985 by Crain Communications, Inc.

producing company that creates and produces television shows — from a single special to an entire series.

Few advertisers today can afford to be the sole sponsor of a television program. Most buy **participations,** which means that the available commercial time on one program is divided up among a number of different advertisers in 30- and 60-second units. The announcements are made within the context of the program instead of between programs at station-break times. It is better to have the commercial aired *during* the program. The most popular time unit with advertisers is 30 seconds, because it enables them to spread their media budget over several different programs to reach different segments of the population. It is also possible to buy 10-, 20-, or 30-second spots on programs initiated by local stations. The ten-second spot is merely an ID (station identification). Of the time periods that precede and follow a regular network television program, usually two minutes are available for local or spot advertisers. These time slots are called **adjacencies.**

The 15-second commercial was one of the most significant developments in commercial television in recent years. It was off to a rapid start in 1985. A survey by the Television Bureau of Advertising showed that an average of 5,500 15-second commercials ran weekly during 1985.[2] It was an increase of well over 200 percent from the preceding year. Some industry experts estimate that use will double, perhaps even triple, in the coming years. Increased clutter, of course, is the most obvious concern. Nevertheless, the 15-second commercial, at half the cost of 30 seconds, attracts marketers who can't afford the network "30." Major package-goods companies see the "15" as an excellent way to build frequency for their brands. Art directors, comfortable with the "30," have found it very challenging.

Spot Television

Spot television is local station programming for sale in local markets. These stations may be affiliated with a network and carry network programming at certain times of the day, or they may be independent stations that program their own day entirely. Costs for local spots will vary from market to market, depending on the size of the audience the station delivers. As a rule, spots in New York, Chicago, and Los Angeles are more expensive because of the size of the circulation in these markets. Even within prime time and daytime programming by networks, there are segments of the day set aside for local sale. There are, in any case, numerous opportunities for an advertiser to select specific time slots to reach the target audience.

Spot television is used by both national advertisers and regional advertisers. National advertisers use spot television to supplement their national programming, and regional advertisers use it because it is not practical for them to use network television. In 1984 national advertisers spent nearly $15 billion for television commercial time, with $8.5 billion for network television and $6.3 billion for spot television — roughly 57 percent network to 43 percent spot. A network advertiser can also use spot television to add extra weight to campaigns in certain markets that may not be satisfactorily covered by the network. Or they may use it to meet unique competitive situations — perhaps to add a certain local appeal that might be needed in some markets. Or, the

---

[2] *Advertising Age,* December 30, 1985, p. 19.

advertiser may not be able to afford network television time and can use spot television to buy the top 50 markets that will reach 70 percent of the television homes in the country. Of course, the advertiser will not actually reach 70 percent of the homes; that figure represents the *potential*. It is also possible that a network program may not be as popular in some places as a local program on which spot time is available.

Buying Time

There are certain parts of the broadcast day that are programmed by the networks, which serve from 150 to 225 stations. The networks sell time to advertisers to run with specific programs. These programs are broadcast during various parts of the day, generally described as daytime, prime time, or late night.

Prime time (7:30 to 11 PM) is so called because of the large number of sets in use during this period. This time period tends to reach a family audience. Media costs for prime time are generally the highest of all three time periods. Individual program costs will vary, depending on the rating of the program. Prime time cost per 30 seconds is around $60,000.

Daytime network television (7 AM to 4:30 PM) is the least costly of network time periods. Cost per 30 seconds is in the range of $9,000—a very efficient cost for buying a largely female audience. Late night network programming generally consists of movies or talk shows. Rates for such programs —around $16,000 for 30 seconds—are much lower than for prime time programs. Although rating levels for late night programs are about the same as those for daytime, rates are higher because the audience consists of approximately equal numbers of men and women.

Sports programming, aimed at a primarily male market, often dominates network television on weekends. Beer, automobiles, and men's grooming aids are usually heavily advertised on weekend sports programs.

During prime time, network stations are permitted to sell up to $9\frac{1}{2}$ minutes of commercial time per 60-minute broadcast period. Independent stations are permitted to sell up to 12 minutes in any 60-minute period. In non-prime time, all stations are permitted up to 16 minutes of commercial time per hour. Advertisers with more than one product often buy 60 seconds and run two 30-second commercials for different products back to back. This practice, called *piggybacking*, saves money because 60 seconds is cheaper than two 30-second slots.

Sole sponsorship of a program is rare, usually limited to specials—one-shot programs related to a seasonal promotion. Advertisers who cannot afford participation in national network programs often buy spots that are available between programs in 10-, 20-, 30-, or 60-second units. The stations sell these units as *preemptible* or *nonpreemptible* time. The preemptible spot is lower in price, but can be dropped by the station if some other advertiser is willing to pay nonpreemptible rates for that time slot. Occasionally, a special event, such as a speech by the President of the United States, will preempt a commercial. When that happens, the advertiser receives a credit, a make-good, or an extension of the contract.

GRPs Again   A media planner is often given the objective of obtaining a weekly level of GRPs for the number of dollars budgeted. For example, an advertiser may believe that to keep up with competition, 80 GRPs a week are required. To meet this objective, a media planner could buy time for one spot on four programs with ratings of 20, or on ten programs with ratings of 8. Either way, the total GRPs will meet the objective. Cost and the demographic characteristics of the audience for each program will determine which schedule the media planner will buy.

Audience Ratings

Rating services (there are several) do not measure the *quality* of a television show — only the quantity of its audience. As a word, *rating* is a misnomer. Programs are rated because networks are in the entertainment business. If the stations did not provide programs that please people, if they did not respond to people's tastes, they would not remain in business very long. When the viewer tunes in a program, he or she is stating a preference for that program over all other programs aired at the same hour. Ratings are the way the preferences are added up. A program that is tuned in by the greatest number of viewers isn't necessarily the best program offered.

The *Nielsen rating* you may see reported in your newspaper is simply a statistical estimate of the number of homes tuned in to a program. A rating of 20 for a network TV program means that 20 percent of the television homes in the United States are estimated to have tuned in to that program. Since about 90 million households now have television sets, a rating of 20 means that an estimated 18 million households were tuned in. The Nielsen rating is just one of several rating methods used in the evaluation of advertising.

Another rating service is offered by the Arbitron Company. Arbitron uses a television meter to monitor set tuning and transmits the information to a computer. The service is currently available for the New York and Los Angeles markets with approximately 450 metered households in each market. Subscribers can use the information to aid them in their programming and media-buying decisions.

The Arbitron Company also offers a television market report that provides ratings of the audiences for each broadcast period. The ratings are either a percentage of the total number of television households in an area, generally a cluster of counties called an Area of Dominant Influence (ADI),[3] or a percentage of persons in a particular sex/age category in the area. An ADI rating of 10 for women 18 – 49 means that an estimated 10 percent of women 18 – 49 in the ADI were watching a particular station during an average quarter-hour of the reported time period.

A rating's value lies in its utility as a yardstick by which the advertiser may compare the relative sizes of audiences on different stations or in different time periods. It would be unfair, for example, to compare the number of households viewing a station in a large market with the number viewing a station in a small market. But a rating of 25 for each station would indicate a strong program in each market, regardless of the size of the market.

Other methods used in the evaluation of advertising will be mentioned in chapter 18.

---

[3] The Area of Dominant Influence (ADI) is a concept developed by the Arbitron Company in 1966. It is a geographic market designation that defines all the countries in which home-market stations capture the greatest amount of total viewing hours. Each county in the United States, excluding Hawaii and portions of Alaska, is allocated exclusively to one ADI.

Gross Impressions   Network advertisers who use spot television to beef up certain key markets must be able to measure the ratings of their spot program market by market. To do this, the advertisers' media analysts will examine the network ratings in each key market to see how well the local network station rates. If the network is below the level set for market (as determined by competitive GRPs), then the media analyst will have to add more GRPs with spot buys. Media planners use the term **gross impressions** to describe the entire audience delivered by a media plan in one figure. One impression equals one exposure by one media vehicle.

For example, if the advertiser buys ten commercials on a network program, and the rating for the show is 20:

$$90,000,000 \times .20 \times 10 = 180,000,000$$
gross impressions

Note however, that the gross impressions total includes duplicated exposures.

Reach and Frequency   Reach and frequency are measurements that tell advertisers and media planners about the size and viewing habits of a program's audience. *Reach* is the number who tuned in at least once during a specified period of time. *Frequency* is the number of times during that period the viewers tuned in. Reach and frequency take place at the same time, but generally in inverse proportion. If a program develops a large reach, it will have a relatively small frequency. If it has repeat viewers — that is, large frequency — chances are its reach will be relatively small. Programs that develop reach are those that change their content from week to week. A news analysis program or a special are good examples of this type of program. As the contents of the program change, so do the people who watch. There is, of course, an overlap, but in general such programs develop more reach than frequency. A regular program — a situation comedy; or the ultimate, a soap opera on five days a week, same time, same station — will develop a small audience with large frequency.

Flighting   Television and radio advertisers on a limited budget may resort to a *flighting* strategy, similar to that of magazine advertising (see pages 155–56). This is a method of scheduling in which a period of advertising is followed by a blank period, which is followed by a period of advertising, and so on. The objective of this *wave strategy,* as it is sometimes called, is to increase the impact of the messages by concentrating them in bunches over a period of time. To spread those messages out over the entire budget period would reduce their impact. For example a limited budget might permit us only 26 weeks of continuous advertising, but by advertising only every other week, we can keep our product in front of the market for a full year.

Cable Television

Cable's origin can be traced to 1948, when community antenna services were developed in areas where there was no local broadcasting station and reception from the nearest stations was either impossible or poor because of distance or topographic obstructions. Cable's slow but steady growth during the 1950s was limited to providing antenna services to these locales, but by the end of the decade, the cable industry could envision its vast potential. In the early 1960s, the number of community antenna systems and subscribers increased. By 1965, some people were predicting that cable would soon be in homes the way telephone is.

Shoppers Tune in to National Cable

The Home Shopping Network was launched nationally in 1985 and is available in about 8 million households. It is a live 24-hour-a-day direct-response service that sells everything from inexpensive clothing and costume jewelry to expensive consumer electronics. It sells anything that weighs less than 70 pounds—the limit set by United Parcel Service. The logistics of running a full-time shopping channel are complex. Hosts display the merchandise—generally obtained at closeout prices and available in limited quantities—and take phone calls on the air. More than 400 operators handle 1,200 incoming phone lines, entering sales on computer terminals linked to a sophisticated warehouse. Because of the computerized inventory, operators know instantly when an item is sold out. All orders are shipped within 48 hours.

More than just a convenience for shoppers, the network's computerized tracking system offers instant test marketing of new products. After an item is flashed on the screen, incoming phone calls determine success or failure within moments. Items that bomb are pulled off the air; successful promotions are given additional sales time.

Unfortunately, a number of forces delayed cable. Technical difficulties were encountered. Even more significant than the technical difficulties were barriers erected by the FCC. Having at first taken a hands-off approach, the FCC in 1965 claimed jurisdiction over the industry and imposed rules that essentially prohibited the importation of distant signals by cable systems situated within 35 miles of the centers of the top 100 markets. This effectively destroyed cable television's primary marketing weapon in the major metropolitan areas.

The FCC loosened its regulations in 1972. In the early 70s, cities scrambled to set up procedures for cable systems, and entrepreneurs, large and small, rushed to stake their claims to what was expected to be a gold mine. The list of entrants included such giants as Time, Inc., Westinghouse Electric Corp., RCA Corp., Warner Communications, Walt Disney Productions, American Express, General Electric, and many others. Thus, cable was an industry that shot up in 20 years. It had the potential of revolutionizing broadcasting by improving reception. It also pledged to give the broadcast networks a run for their programming money with controversial features or fresh-out-of-the-theater movies. It promised to bring a refreshing new dimension to television, answering the needs of every discriminating viewer.

Instead, cable in its early years faced an extraordinarily high number of disconnects, complaints about service, and misconceptions about programming that were far more damaging than marketers imagined. The tendency, as the medium developed, was to sell cable as a source of first-run movies, neglecting other features such as news and local sports. Viewers tuned in, but watching the same movies again and again led to frustration and dissatisfaction.

A number of companies have been romancing the public with direct mail, print, radio, cable, and broadcast ads stressing cable's special benefits—all news, all business, local sports, programming that the critical viewer wants to view. Cablevision, for example, operating in Long Island, sells an array of services. A basic hookup for $5, a "family" package, 28 channels for about $16, or any of three other packages. The company supplies up to 36 channels, costing a maximum of around $50 a month. The company has a revenue rate of about $30 a subscriber. Their disconnect rate is 1 percent a month (compared to an industry average of about 2 percent a month).

It appears that advertising-supported cable TV has evolved into two distinct media: one adhering to usual broadcast programming, and the other fulfilling cable's original promise of appealing to diverse, highly segmented audiences. Almost all of the 18 major ad-supported cable programming services are suffering losses. Cable executives say that ad-supported cable network viewing equals more than 11 percent of broadcast network viewing, but cable generates only 5 percent of broadcast ad revenue.

Cable's growth as an ad medium depends on the continued growth of gross viewing audiences, led by mass appeal networks such as Super-station WTBS, CBN, and USA Cable. Among the curious new developments is the so-called long-form commercial. The long-form commercial has attracted enough interest to justify a full 24-hour network devoted to commercials. The real curiosity is that viewers appeared to be willing to sit and watch nothing but commercials. Tested in 1983 in Peabody, Massachusetts, this network, called Cable-Shop, has already been established in several cities. Viewer reaction has been very positive. More than one-third of the cable subscribers viewed Cable-Shop regularly, with 67 percent of these viewers watching three or more "Infomercials" a month. Researchers determined that infomercials improved attitudes toward both well-known and lesser-known brands. Advertisers, though, are hesitant.

PROFILE

Jay Chiat

Jay Chiat is Chairman, CEO of Chiat/Day Inc., a 16-year-old agency billing $250 million, with headquarters in Los Angeles, and offices in San Francisco and New York.

Chiat graduated from Rutgers University, then attended the Columbia University Graduate School of Broadcasting. He graduated from the UCLA Executive Program and taught advertising for three years in the Journalism School at the University of Southern California.

He began his advertising career in Orange County, California, starting at the Leland Oliver Company as a copywriter, and rose to Creative Director of the two-man creative department. He served two years in the Air Force and another at Aerojet-General Corporation before beginning his own agency, Jay Chiat & Associates, in 1962.

Chiat has won gold and silver medals from the Los Angeles and New York Art Directors Shows. He has several Andy Awards, numerous CLIOs, a shelf full of Belding Bowls, AAF "Best in the West" Awards, CA Awards of Excellence, and has been named one of the "100 Top Creative People in the United States" in AD DAY polls. He's a past president of the Advertising Industry Emergency Fund and President of the Greater New York Cystic Fibrosis Foundation. He was voted "1977 Advertising Man of the Year" by the Western States Advertising Agencies Association and is an *ADWEEK* columnist.

Chiat/Day was named 1980 Advertising Agency of the Year by *Advertising Age*. For 1982, Chiat/Day was chosen as one of "The *ADWEEK* Eight" top creative agencies. Furthermore, Chiat/Day has won more awards per client than any other advertising agency in the world. And, in 1984, Chiat/Day won the Cannes "Grand Prix" Award.

As might be expected, almost all the companies on the list are included among the leading advertisers. The one exception is Urban General Corp. (number 25).

Top 25 Cable Advertisers 1984

		Expenditures ($000)	
Rank	Advertiser	1984	1984 as % of total advertising exp.
1.	Procter & Gamble Co.	$24,182	2.8
2.	Anheuser-Busch Cos.	15,478	4.2
3.	General Foods Corp.	13,169	2.9
4.	General Mills	11,339	4.0
5.	Time Inc.	7,192	5.4
6.	Ford Motor Co.	6,892	1.2
7.	Bristol-Myers Co.	6,242	2.4
8.	Toyota Motor Sales Co.	5,391	3.9
9.	Beatrice Cos.	5,085	0.7
10.	Thompson Medical Co.	4,456	N/A
11.	Kellogg Co.	3,594	1.7
12.	American Telephone & Telegraph	3,457	0.6
13.	Eastern Air Lines	3,395	5.6
14.	American Home Products	3,352	0.8
15.	General Motors Corp.	3,157	0.4
16.	Sears, Roebuck & Co.	3,120	0.4
17.	Warner-Lambert Co.	2,922	0.7
18.	Wm. Wrigley Jr. Co.	2,884	4.1
19.	Clorox Co.	2,813	2.6
20.	Coca-Cola Co.	2,756	0.8
21.	Chrysler Corp.	2,327	0.7
22.	Ralston Purina Co.	2,131	0.5
23.	Canon Inc.	1,948	1.9
24.	Campbell Soup Co.	1,789	1.3
25.	Urban General Corp.	1,760	N/A

Source: Reprinted with permission from the September 26, 1985, issue of *Advertising Age.* Copyright © 1985 by Crain Communications, Inc.

For its advertisers, cable television offers an environment for their product, exclusivity for their product category, and reduced clutter. It also offers the opportunity to deliver longer ad messages to its audience (which it claims is young and in high income brackets). The cost of producing or underwriting production of a 30-minute cable program ranges from about $20,000 to $30,000. Shows such as "Celebrity Chef" sponsored by Campbell Soup, and Procter & Gamble's "Great American Homemaker" and "What Every Baby Knows," are targeted toward very specific audiences. While an individual show's ratings may not be high, viewers interest in its content—both programming and advertising—usually is strong enough for sponsors to overlook the low numbers. Young parents who tune into "What Every Baby Knows" are most likely purchasers of Procter & Gamble's Luvs diapers.

To guarantee that competitor's do not take advantage of the program's environment, sponsors work out arrangements with the networks that exclude ads for competing brands. Sponsor Procter & Gamble, for example, which is given 2-1/2 of the available 5 minutes of "What Every Baby Knows," has exclusive rights to advertise diapers or laundry detergents. This precludes the addition of some logical prospective advertisers, although allows the cable company to sell many other baby products.

Alex the Dog

In a market crowded with beers, how can one beer develop consumer awareness? Detroit-based Stroh's did it in 1984 with humor so out-rageous and so unbelievable that consumers knew they were being kidded and remembered the name. Created by Stroh's agency, The Marschalk Company, Inc., the commercial "Alex the Dog" received a variety of awards. Hunter Hastings, vice-president of brand man-agement, said that the commercial helped create awareness in markets newly introduced to the brand as the company worked toward national coverage. After four months on the air in mar-kets across approximately 65 percent of the country, television viewers cited the commer-cial as one of the most memorable they'd ever seen. The curious fact is that Alex is on camera for less than 2 ½ seconds.

Imagine a group of young men (the target market) sitting around a table playing poker. The host sends his dog to the kitchen and gives a running commentary, with sound effects, on the kitchen happenings, with the great punch ending. So much of the action takes place off camera that each television viewer is required to use his or her imagination. The sequel to it, Alex II, has the host and three of his friends out camping. When the supply of Stroh's runs low, Alex is sent to town to fetch some more. And Alex hops in a car and drives off to buy more of his master's favorite brew. Outrageous and un-believable, but so memorable — and that's what counts. (See color plate 29.)

Stroh's

CLIENT: Stroh Brewery Co.
TITLE: Alex the dog

COMMERCIAL NUMBER: OUSB 3301
LENGTH: 30 seconds

POKER PLAYER: I'd sure like another Stroh's.
HOST: No, wait. Alex!

DOG: ARF

HOST: Two cold Stroh's.

DOG: ARF
HOST: Wait till you see this.

(SFX REFRIGERATOR DOOR OPENING)
He just opened the refrigerator.

(SFX BOTTLE OPENING)

He just opened one bottle.
(SFX BOTTLE OPENING)
He just opened the other.

(SFX STROH'S BEING POURED INTO GLASS)
Now he's pouring yours.

(SFX OTHER STROH'S BEING POURED)
Now he's pouring mine.
(SFX DOG DRINKING)

Alex, you better be drinking your water.

MUSIC

The commercial was aired for the first time on December 24 during NBC's telecast of an AFC wildcard National Football League playoff game. On Christmas Day, the commercial was aired during NBC's coverage of an NCAA bas-ketball game and CBS's presentation of the NFC wildcard playoff game.

By the end of 1985, cable TV reached about 35 million households or 45.7 percent of all households with a television set. In the top ten U.S. television markets, only 30 percent of the households have access to cable. Agencies continue to view cable as a second-class buy, spending only a small portion of their budget on cable. One reason is the prohibitive cost of connecting homes in major uncabled areas. Another reason derives from cable's basic premise — to transmit commercial broadcast TV service from the big city to distant or remote areas that could not receive TV signals because of their distance from the transmitter or because of topography.

Faced with competition from videocassette recorders which A. C. Nielsen Co. reports are in 40 percent of U.S. households, cable companies are offering subscribers on-demand movies and specials at a per-view fee. Predictions indicate this service will grow very slowly, but by 1990 it is expected to serve over 24 million homes.

Another cable frontier lies with hotel and motel operators who are enticing travelers by offering in-room entertainment. Lodging owners and franchisers have found that alternative TV programming is important in a competitive market. It is estimated that two-thirds of this country's 2.7 million hotel rooms offer some type of in-room entertainment. This has led to the growth of a new cable companion industry.

Summary

No matter how excellently prepared the advertising message, that message must be delivered—and to the right audience. Broadcast media have distinct characteristics that affect their ability to reach certain audiences and affect the cost advertisers must pay to reach those audiences.

Because a great number of radio stations are available in every market in the United States, radio offers advertisers a high degree of geographical selectivity. Demographic selectivity is also available, since the type of program, to a very large extent, determines the demographics of the audience. Radio is also flexible, permitting quick changes of copy in order to match competitive and seasonal conditions. The relatively low cost of radio advertising enables advertisers to bring their messages before their target markets with great frequency. Its major limitation is that it appeals to only one sense.

Television, on the other hand, appeals to both the senses of sight and sound. Television enables advertisers to show their products in action and to demonstrate their use, an ability no other medium can match. Television is *the* mass audience vehicle—ubiquitous and pervasive; it offers advertisers the ability to reach millions of viewers. Television is expensive, but only in absolute terms. On a *cost per thousand* (CPM) basis, because of its large numbers of viewers, television probably delivers more people at a lower cost than any other medium.

In measuring the audience of one of the broadcast media, advertisers consider the station's coverage (the number of people who can receive the station's signals) and its circulation (the number of people who actually tune in those signals). Unlike magazines, where advertisers can easily count the number of copies sold on the newsstand or delivered via mail subscription, the size and nature of broadcast audiences are established by a sampling procedure. Also, the individual magazine audience is a net audience. The broadcast audience, however, is a gross audience: Listeners and viewers may tune in to the same program regularly and, hence, be counted more than once.

The cost of a radio or television commercial is affected by both the length of the commercial and the time of day at which it is to be broadcast. Broadcast commercials are generally sold in units of 10, 20, 30, and 60 seconds. On radio, commercials broadcast during *drive time* (6 to 10 in the morning and 4 to 7 in the evening) are generally more expensive than those broadcast at other times during the day, because that is when radio stations reach their largest audiences. On television, commercials broadcast during *prime time* (7:30 to 11 in the evening) reach the largest audiences of the day. Advertisers use an index figure known as a *gross rating point* (GRP) to measure the percentage of a specified market area that they reach with one commercial.

Questions for Discussion

1. How can spot radio advertising be best utilized for products with seasonal variations?
2. Would you recommend radio advertising for the following? Justify your recommendations.
   a. a children's toothpaste
   b. an overseas airline
   c. a domestic airline
   d. women's high-fashion sweaters
   e. mattresses
3. For the products listed in the preceding question, would you recommend television advertising? Justify your recommendations.
4. If you were assigned to develop an advertising program for your school, what would your media plan include? Justify your recommendations.
5. What media plan would you recommend to reach a black target market?
6. Suppose you developed an excellent media plan for an advertiser, but the total cost was more than the budget allowed for. What steps could you take to solve the problem?
7. Why is flexibility so important in media planning?
8. What are the advantages in buying a network radio package instead of individual spots? Any disadvantages or limitations?
9. Watch a television station for one hour during prime time. List the commercials you viewed. Which took advantage of the characteristics of the medium? Explain your answer. Were there any products advertised that other media might promote more effectively?

Sources and Suggestions for Further Reading

Cable/Videotex: A Compendium for Direct Marketers. Edited by R. C. Morse. New York: Direct Mail/Marketing Association, Inc., 1982.

MacDonald, J. Fred. "New Luster Reflects Another 'Golden Era'." *Advertising Age,* April 14, 1986.

Ogilvy, David. *Ogilvy on Advertising.* New York: Crown Publishers, Inc., 1983.

Pearlman, Donn. "These are New Golden Days." *Advertising Age,* June 29, 1981.

"Politics Cloud Cable's Outlook." *Advertising Age,* May 31, 1984.

Sissors, Jack Z., and Jim Surmanek. *Advertising Media Planning.* 2nd ed. Chicago: Crain Books, 1984.

Steinberg, Janice. "Tuning in Strong Marketing Signals." *Advertising Age,* August 4, 1986.

11 OUT-OF-HOME ADVERTISING

Working Vocabulary

poster	embellish	full run
sheet	spectacular	half run
snipes	Traffic Audit Bureau (TAB)	end card
plant	coverage	basic bus
plant operator	100 showing	take-ones
30-sheet poster	100 GRPs	taillight spectacular
junior panel	rotary plan	total bus
3-sheet poster	space position value	station poster
paint	car card	clock spectacular

263

With outdoor, you have only seconds to reach your mobile audience. "A poster should be to the eye what a shouted demand is to the ear," said poster artist C. B. Falls. The only shout it will hear is one big idea.

Kenneth Roman and Jane Maas
How to Advertise

O f the $25.17 billion spent on advertising (total *measured* expenditures) in 1984, about 2.3 percent was invested in outdoor advertising — about the same percentage as in the preceding year. It is not an impressive comparison to the almost 60 percent spent on television advertising. However, in absolute dollars, the $596 million is not a small number, and it has been rising every year. And the figures may well be understated, because companies with small investments in outdoor advertising tend to report such expenditures under the category, "miscellaneous."

The Story of Outdoor Advertising

Outdoor advertising is the oldest form of advertising. The signs described in chapter 1, for example, date back to the days of ancient Greece and Rome. Today, however, business signs are *not* considered part of the outdoor medium. The distinction has been drawn by the industry organization, the Outdoor Advertising Association of America, in an effort to limit criticism against all outdoor advertising. The organized industry conforms with federal laws[1] that require the use of uniform panels, a specified set-back (the distance of the sign structure from the highway as measured from the center of the structure to the line of travel), and installations in appropriately zoned areas in cities.

Nevertheless, many states have limited the number of billboards that may be placed along highways, and pressure from environmentalists has caused thousands of billboards to be removed. Certainly, some of the criticism may have been provoked by the excessive number of signs, by signs in poor taste, or by physically unattractive signs in some areas. Supporters of the industry argue, however, that signs along the highway can hold a driver's interest, preventing him or her from becoming bored or hypnotized and falling asleep at the wheel.

Regardless of its merits or defects, outdoor is here to stay. It is one of the most important media options available to any national advertiser. The increase in the number of automobiles in use, the extension of our network of highways, the dispersion of population to the suburbs, and the general mobility of Americans have all spurred the growth of the outdoor medium. The more people travel, the more they are exposed to the advertising messages carried by outdoor advertising.

Outdoor Compared with Other Media

Outdoor conforms to our definition of a medium; it is addressed to people — large groups of people. There are some basic differences, however, between outdoor advertising and the media we have previously examined. Outdoor is literally out of doors — it is out of the home or place of business. There is no

---

[1] The Federal Highway Act of 1958 and the Highway Beautification Act of 1965.

editorial vehicle to carry our message. The consumer makes no expenditure for, nor exerts any effort to see, our outdoor advertising. Our message is not brought to the audience; the audience goes to the message, passing it in the course of other activities. The audience has little, if any, opportunity to dwell or to reflect on our message. However, outdoor does provide its audience with repeat opportunities to see our message — either at the same display or on an identical billboard at another location.

Billboards — an Old Friend

Curious word, "billboard." To promote attendance at theatrical performances, theater managers posted playbills outside the theaters. These "bills" were later tacked or pasted to the walls of other buildings around town. It was primitive advertising and it still exists. Fences around vacant lots and buildings with a usable wall are often plastered with posters, unless the owner puts up a sign of equally ancient origin: Post No Bills.

Today, the word **poster** is used to describe an advertising message that is *posted* on a structure built for that purpose. The original poster was one **sheet** of paper, 28 inches by 41 inches. Several "one-sheets" could be combined to make larger posters to fit different frames. Then, as presses were developed to reproduce larger sheet sizes, the meaning of the original term became obsolete, but the word *sheet* continued to be used to indicate the relative size of the poster to be placed inside a frame.

Who Uses Outdoor?

Cigarette companies are one of the largest users of outdoor advertising. What is the characteristic of cigarettes that enables them to benefit from outdoor advertising? Cigarettes are impulse goods, intensively distributed, sold everywhere, and bought by brand name — as are chewing gum, soft drinks, and beer. Outdoor is also great for automobiles and car after-market products such as gas, oil, batteries, tires, and waxes. What better time to reach your audience with a message about car care than while it is driving? Airlines use outdoor advertising along the roads that lead *out of town* to the airport. Local hotels, restaurants, and service stations use outdoor along the roads that lead *into town* in order to reach tourists.

The more the audience drives, the greater the opportunity for exposure to outdoor advertising. Although outdoor is nonselective (because people of every demographic category drive), drivers are generally considered upscale. Most high-mileage drivers (with more opportunities for exposure) are men in the higher income and educational brackets. These people are the natural targets for many products including whiskey, automobiles, and, of course, products related to highway use.

Advantages of Outdoor

Outdoor offers us *geographic selectivity*. Billboards are well-suited for spot coverage of specific markets: They permit us to vary our message to suit particular ethnic communities, areas of the country, or types of traffic. National advertisers can have the names and addresses of their local dealers added to the bottom of their posters. These dealer imprint strips are known as **snipes.** However, billboards are relatively expensive for a national advertiser, particularly when multiple markets are involved.

| | Top 25 Outdoor Advertisers 1984 | | |
| | | Expenditures ($000) | |
Rank	Advertiser	1984	1984 as % of total advertising exp.
1.	R.J. Reynolds Industries	$86,955	12.8
2.	Philip Morris Inc.	54,951	9.6
3.	Loews Corp.	28,647	20.8
4.	Jos. E. Seagram & Sons Co.	16,772	14.5
5.	Batus Inc.	12,089	10.7
6.	American Brands	11,894	8.9
7.	Hiram Walker Inc.	7,760	N/A
8.	National Distillers & Chemical Corp.	5,670	N/A
9.	Anheuser-Busch Cos.	5,514	1.5
10.	Grand Metropolitan p.l.c.	5,240	6.9
11.	McDonald's Corp.	5,129	1.1
12.	Brown-Forman Co.	5,055	N/A
13.	Rapid-American Corp.	3,714	N/A
14.	Whirlpool Corp.	3,648	N/A
15.	Coca-Cola Co.	3,620	1.1
16.	Stroh Brewery Co.	3,206	3.8
17.	General Motors Corp.	3,176	0.4
18.	Holiday Inns	3,002	N/A
19.	Distillers Co. Ltd.	2,761	N/A
20.	Bacardi Corp.	2,738	N/A
21.	Moet-Hennessy	2,372	N/A
22.	Pan American World Airways	2,274	N/A
23.	Ford Motor Co.	2,174	0.4
24.	PepsiCo Inc.	2,090	0.5
25.	Eastern Airlines	2,071	3.4

Source: Reprinted with permission from the September 26, 1985, issue of *Advertising Age.*
Copyright © 1985 by Crain Communications, Inc.

Outdoor offers us *long life.* The standard posting period for our message is 30 days, which provides us with opportunities for repetition.

Outdoor offers us *impact.* Shoppers are exposed to outdoor advertising on their way to stores or shopping centers, and this serves as an important last-minute reminder of our product. Our outdoor displays' large physical size — larger than life — and bright colors will add drama and recognition to our message. And because billboards are not usually erected in groups, our message will not have to compete for attention with other billboards in the same location.

Outdoor advertising can *complement* television advertising. Foster and Kleiser commissioned A. C. Nielsen to use their television diary survey in Los Angeles, Seattle, and New York to measure the reach and frequency of outdoor advertising over a one-month period. They found a significant correlation between television viewing and outdoor advertising exposure. The study showed that:

a. Outdoor provides 72 percent more exposure to men than women, whereas, television provides 32 percent more exposure to women than men. For products with dual audience objectives, this complementary value is significant.

b. Outdoor provides 95 percent more exposure in the upper than in the lower income group, whereas, television provides 73 percent more exposure in the lower than in the upper income group.

c. Outdoor provides 18 percent more exposure among those with college educations than those with high school educations, and 28 percent more exposure among college educated people than among grade school educated people. Television provides 45 percent more exposure among people with high school or grade school educations than people having college educations.

Breakdown of hours spent watching television by quintiles indicated that among the two quintiles that have the least television viewing time, outdoor poster passages were above average. Also the breakdown showed that in the group comprising the heaviest television viewing quintile, outdoor poster passages ran below the average.

Limitations of Outdoor

The limitations of outdoor are inherent in the medium. Since readers will be driving past billboards at highway speeds, copy must be brief—the briefer the better. Dramatic artwork is often used to get the message across. Because of this need for brevity, most advertisers use outdoor as a supplementary medium, relying on print or broadcast media to deliver longer messages.

Outdoor is nonselective. The audience is a mass audience whose members share only one characteristic: They are all riding in motor vehicles. People of every age, sex, educational and socioeconomic level make up this audience. The only type of outdoor that offers selectivity is the 3-sheet poster that is available on a neighborhood-by-neighborhood basis.

Using billboards on a national basis is relatively expensive. When expressed in CPM, the cost for outdoor is low, but the brevity of the message and the fact that the driver may not have time to comprehend it tend to make this medium more expensive than mere CPM comparisons would indicate. It is not the nature of the medium to build recall.[2]

Types of Outdoor

There are three types of outdoor advertising: *posters, painted displays,* and *spectaculars.* A **plant** refers to all of the outdoor advertising structures in a given city, town, or area operated by a single outdoor company, or **plant operator.** Plant operators own or lease the land or locations on which the structures are erected, build and maintain the structures, and operate the trucks and other equipment necessary for mounting the posters, painting the displays, or installing the spectaculars. There are about 1,100 plant operators in the United States.

---

[2] For a particularly interesting experiment, see "What One Little Showing Can Do," by Wendell C. Hewett, *Journal of Advertising Research,* 12, no. 5 (October 1972).

Posters Outdoor posters are printed on sheets of paper that, when assembled and mounted, form an outdoor sign, or, as it is often called, a *paper.* Traditionally, the most popular size had been the *24-sheet poster,* so-called because years ago, before the development of giant litho printing presses, 24 separate printed sheets were required to make a poster. When the technology improved, presses were able to accept larger sheets, and the same size could be produced with only 10 sheets, instead of 24. The terminology, however, still refers to the size of the older, smaller sheet.

The 24-sheet poster is rarely used anymore. Faster-moving traffic has stimulated the development and use of the **30-sheet poster,** which measures about 21-½ feet wide by 9-½ feet high. The 30-sheet poster usually consists of 14 actual sheets, and, if we include the white margin of paper that surrounds the copy area, its full dimensions are 25 feet by 12 feet. Many posters today use bleed sheets, which eliminate the white margin and extend the copy area to the full dimensions of the poster. Plant operators do not charge extra for posters that bleed since they fit on the same frame as posters with the white paper border. Thirty-sheet posters provide greater visibility and improved legibility and thereby greater readership.

The **junior panel** is a poster consisting of 6 actual sheets (compared to 14 actual sheets in the full-size, 30-sheet poster). It is used where space is not available for the full-size posters.

Three-sheet posters are mounted on the walls of buildings, particularly in shopping areas. The overall dimensions for the copy area are 42 inches by 84 inches. The basic purpose of the 3-sheet poster is to remind pedestrians of a product as close as possible to the point of purchase.

The 30-sheet poster (top) consists of 14 actual sheets of paper and, within the same frame that contained the old 24-sheet poster, provides a larger image that improves the visibility of the message. The 30-sheet bleed poster (bottom) may consist of up to 20 actual sheets of paper. It utilizes every available inch of space within the frame, eliminating the white margin around the copy area. Total exposed area, including bleed, is 22 feet, 8 inches by 10 feet, 5 inches.

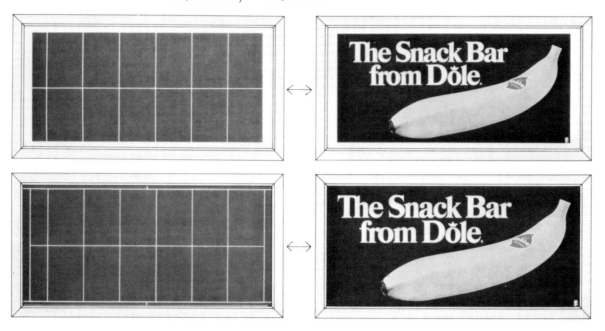

Poster panels may be regular or illuminated. Where there is a high volume of night traffic, outdoor advertisers may obtain several additional hours of use by lighting their posters until midnight or even all night. The hours of illumination will be determined by the volume of nighttime traffic in the area and by the legal restrictions of the city or municipality.

Painted Bulletins   Painted bulletins may be either painted walls or large bulletin board structures composed of panels that are individually painted. The latter are generally larger than posters; the most common size is 14 by 48 feet. The copy is reproduced by painting directly on the surface. When painting is the method of reproduction, the bulletin is called a **paint.** The most inexpensive *paint* is an advertisement painted directly on the wall of a building. It is the most inexpensive because it requires no structure. The size of the advertisement depends on the size of the wall available. The cost will vary with the location.

Painted bulletins are sold on contract. Contracts can run from one to three years and generally provide for two repaintings. Changes of copy are permitted at repaint time. A painted bulletin is usually illuminated and is often **embellished** with extensions or cut-outs that protrude from the top or sides of the bulletin's frame.

This painted bulletin for a local restaurant is cleverly embellished by having the claw and the tail of the lobster protrude beyond the frame.

Spectaculars   A **spectacular** is an outdoor advertising display built with structural steel and designed for a particular advertiser on a long-term contract. The advertising copy is presented in a "spectacular" fashion with lights, flashers (the lights go off and on), or a chaser border (the lights go on in sequence around the border, giving the impression of movement), as well as any combination of flashing or moving electrical devices. These displays are very expensive to erect and are usually used in areas that attract both pedestrian and vehicular traffic during the day and after dark. The cost of a spectacular can run as high as $500,000. The big spectaculars at Times Square in New York City are probably the most widely known in the country. Other well-known spectaculars are located on Michigan Avenue in Chicago and Public Square in Cleveland.

Less elaborate spectaculars are known as semispectaculars. They utilize flashers and mechanical devices to draw the public's attention, but are smaller in size and less expensive to build.

Measuring the Audience

Advertisers can obtain circulation figures for a plant or for each of the individual locations within a plant from several different sources. The most important of these is the **Traffic Audit Bureau, Inc. (TAB).** The Traffic Bureau does not merely audit circulation figures supplied by plant operators, but actually gathers some circulation data on its own.

All traffic circulation figures are obtained either from official traffic counts or from manual counts. Usually state highway commissions oversee programs of continuous traffic count sampling. These counts are generally obtained by mechanical counting instruments that are moved from location to location throughout the state, and the results are made available to advertisers. The resulting counts are adjusted to reflect a yearly estimate of average daily traffic, taking into account seasonal factors, weekly variations, and other variables. The traffic count is converted into potential viewers by counting 1.75 persons per car. The hours of exposure may be from 6 AM to midnight (18 hours for an illuminated display) or from 6 AM to 6 PM (12 hours for nonilluminated display). Actually, traffic volume consists of three modes of transportation: automobiles, pedestrians, and mass-transit vehicles. For the most part, outdoor circulation figures report only the number of people in automobiles.

A number of studies have indicated that outdoor offers high levels of both reach and frequency. For all practical purposes, outdoor reach is the same thing as coverage, because both measure exposure to the medium. Outdoor **coverage** is the number and percent of people who pass, and are exposed to, a given showing of billboards during a 30-day period. *Circulation* represents the gross potential audience and does not assume exposure.

Buying Outdoor

How Paper Is Sold   Plant operators set up their panels in high-traffic areas of individual markets. Advertisers will "buy" a group of these panels in order to obtain exposure for their message in that market. The basic unit of sale is still often referred to as a **100 showing,** although in 1973 the Outdoor Advertising Association of America, Inc., adopted the term *100 gross rating points daily,* or **100 GRPs.** The new designation was adopted so that plant

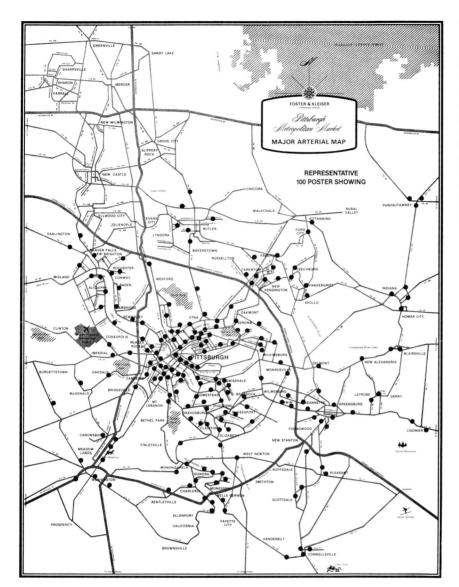

This map shows the coverage of a 100 showing in the Pittsburgh market. Coverage such as this literally blankets the area, with panels appearing on roads leading into the city from neighboring towns and on every major traffic artery running through the city. In one day, a showing of this size will generate an amount of exposure opportunities equal to the market's total population.

operators and advertisers could describe the weight of exposure opportunities offered by their panels in the same units that are used by other media.

In outdoor advertising, one rating point is equal to 1 percent of a specified market population. If we buy a 100-GRP showing, that does not mean that our message will appear on 100 billboards in our target market. Instead, it means that our message will appear on as many panels as is needed to provide a *daily* exposure equal to 100 percent of the market population. For example, in a market with a population of one million, a 100-GRP showing would deliver a circulation of one million each day. A panel distribution that provided 50 GRPs in this market would deliver a circulation of 500,000. Actually, a 100-GRP showing does not mean the billboard is passed by 100 percent of the market's mobile population, but by a percentage somewhere between 90 and 100 percent, which is quite acceptable.

Rates for paper are based on the number of GRPs bought for a 30-day period. Rates will differ from plant to plant, depending on the size of the market, the number of panels needed, and the costs incurred by the plant operator. Since the number of panels needed to obtain a 100-GRP showing will vary from city to city, the cost of the showing will vary accordingly. A 100-showing in the Chicago market by Foster & Kleiser consists of 328 panels, which will provide a daily effective circulation equal to the population of the market. Of the 328 panels, 284 panels are illuminated to provide 18 hours of exposure per day. The cost per month is $135,360. A 100-showing in the Sarasota, Florida, market consists of ten panels and the monthly rate is $2,930. In a small town, a showing might consist of only two panels — one where the highway enters the town, and the other where the highway exits.

A GUIDE TO ASSIST IN THE SELECTION OF STANDARDIZED OUTDOOR ADVERTISING

30-SHEET POSTER SHOWING	THE ROTATING BULLETIN	THE PERMANENT BULLETIN
MARKET DISTRIBUTION		
Quantity of posters distributed throughout the entire market on primary arterials.	Limited number of locations as compared to poster showings. Rotaries are located on highest traveled arterials, important intersections and freeways.	Limited number of locations. Generally on freeways or key selected areas. Purchased for unique individual coverage.
COVERAGE		
Simultaneous coverage of entire market.	Each unit covers one arterial for 60 days. One unit can cover six different traffic flow patterns in one year by rotation to a new location every 60 days.	Limited to one specific traffic flow pattern.
CIRCULATION		
The combination of poster panels in a showing result in a large total circulation.	Large average per unit circulation varies with each location in rotate schedule.	May be high or low, depending upon the specific location.
REACH		
Rapid, broad market reach. Ability to reach large percentage of the total markets population.	Slower build up of wide market reach, however, rotation to a new location every 60 days helps increase rate of market wide reach.	Slow build up of wide market reach. Reach is limited by covering only one traffic flow pattern per location.
FREQUENCY		
Exceptionally high, varies in proportion with the number of panels in the poster showing.	Relative heavy frequency for its lower market reach, due to its interception of limited traffic patterns. Slow build up of reach and frequency for individuals not normally involved in that specific flow. Rotation helps overall frequency and reach.	Extremely high when measured against its low reach percentage. Very slow to develop reach and frequency for remaining market population.
COPY CHANGE		
Normal change of copy every 30 days.	Normally three copy changes per year.	Normally two or three copy changes per year.
COST EFFICIENCY		
Lowest of all major media in C.P.M. and in G.R.P. cost.	Low C.P.M. with overall G.R.P. cost relatively low.	Since permanent bulletins are priced by location, cost efficiencies vary widely, however, C.P.M. and G.R.P. costs are still comparatively low.
FLEXIBILITY		
Large number of locations allow poster coverage of demographic, political or geographic portions of the market. Various intensities of showings can be directed toward specific areas.	Rotation every 60 days, coupled with a large number of locations in a plant allows flexibility in areas of coverage.	Permanence preclude flexibility other than initial selection of location.
AWARENESS		
Average awareness of 5,000 designs tested over a ten year period was 42%. A figure nearly double the next highest medium in awareness.	With sufficient display time and creativity, high awareness levels can be developed through impact of presentation.	Unless permanent bulletins are of a spectacular nature, overall awareness is limited by market reach. Given time, creativity and support, results can be excellent.

A comparison of outdoor advertising forms.

11 | OUT-OF-HOME ADVERTISING

Advertisers can compare the rates offered by different plant operators on the same basis that they use for other media: CPM, or cost per thousand. Plant operators offer discounts for longer contracts much the same as those offered by the owners and operators of other media.

The Rotary Plan   The **rotary plan** is a simple concept. An advertiser may buy just one bulletin for example, for a full-year contract. After two months in one location, the bulletin is moved to a second location for the next two months. By the end of the year, that same bulletin has appeared in six different locations in the market selected by the advertiser. For variety, the advertiser could buy two bulletins and have both of them rotated every month — or the advertiser could substitute a new bulletin design every month.

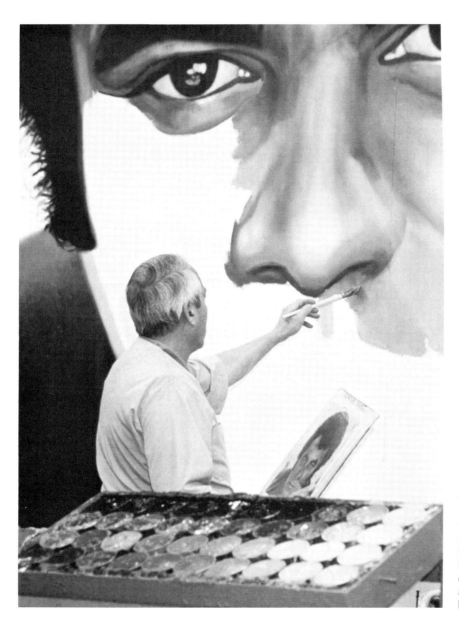

Working from the original photograph, this artist is painting a bulletin in the studios of a plant operator. The finished bulletin will be prepared in sections and transported by truck to the location where it will be installed. The final size of the bulletin can be estimated by comparing the size of the artist to the size of the face he is painting.

Buying Paint   Painted bulletins are bought by a different arrangement. There are far fewer paint locations in a market than poster locations, and each is selected *because* of its location, not on the basis of showings or GRPs. There are about 36,000 painted displays in the United States. Paint is more expensive than paper and the usual buy is for a one-year period. The copy is expected to last a year. If it deteriorates, the plant operator bears the responsibility of repainting it. If the advertiser wants to change the copy, the change will be made by the operator, but at the expense of the advertiser.

OHMS   Until the end of 1977, much outdoor advertising and billing service was provided through the National Outdoor Advertising Bureau (NOAB). NOAB had been owned by 20 advertising agencies for whom it made outdoor advertising "buys." In 1978, OHMS (Out of Home Media Service) replaced NOAB. OHMS is not owned by advertising agencies, but is a privately held employee-owned organization. The usual advertising agency commission for outdoor media is 16-$\frac{2}{3}$ percent. OHMS charges an agency a 2 percent fee for its buying services.

Space Position Value   Most cities have only one plant; some of the larger cities have several. When buying a showing, advertisers must consider the distribution and the coverage of the panel locations, particularly as they apply to the advertisers' products. Suntan lotions, such as Coppertone, would benefit most by being advertised at the seashore or in resort areas. Not that people do not sun themselves in North Dakota or Wyoming, but the cost of reaching prospects would be far higher in those areas than in Florida where more people sun themselves during the longer sunny seasons. Similarly, airlines (heavy users of outdoor) would want to be sure that their outdoor advertising messages are placed along roads leading to airports. For a product with regional distribution, the advertiser would want to be certain that coverage is heavy in, or leading to, those areas where the product is available. Any other locations would be wasteful. Other considerations affecting the relative value of a given location include the number of illuminated panels, the traffic flows, and the visibility of the panels.

The latter factor, the visibility of the panels, is of considerable importance in determining the value of the showing. **Space position value** (SPV) is an index of a poster panel's visibility based on the length of the approach, the speed of travel, the angle of the panel to its circulation, and its space relationship to adjacent panels. The longer the approach, the longer the panel is visible. The slower the traffic, the easier it is to see and read the message. The closer the approach is to head-on the better the visibility. A panel standing alone has the best chance of being seen. A cluster of panels reduces the chances of any single panel to make an impression. The Traffic Audit Bureau assesses all of these factors and arrives at an individual rating for each location.

Transit Advertising

Transit Media

Transit media include interior displays in mass-transit vehicles, exterior displays on mass-transit vehicles, and terminal and station-platform displays. These media offer the advertiser a number of advantages similar to those of outdoor. Transit can provide mass coverage of a metropolitan area. For the

COLOR PLATE 30 With a bright illustration of a tiger, this telephone booth display suggests, without words, that a trip to the Denver Zoo would be fun. Would a photograph do as well? Not likely.

COLOR PLATE 31 This billboard for Palm Springs has a unifying presentation—a good photograph coupled with clever wording that offers an easily grasped benefit—a pleasant vacation.

COLOR PLATE 30

COLOR PLATE 31

You'll love the service. Palm Springs.

Knauf Butt Strips Pass

Only Knauf Butt Strips are kiss-cut. They're fast to start and easy to apply. Even when you're wearing thick gloves.

Goes on faster.

Just fold back the tab, peel and seal. It's that easy. No fumbling, no fooling. Kiss-Cut Butt Strips give you a fast start. And an even faster finish. The contractors we surveyed reported they cut installation time up to 38%.

And best of all, Kiss-Cut Butt Strips are available in the full range of Knauf fiber glass pipe insulation.

Stays on tighter.

We put the same super-stick acrylic adhesive on our Butt Strips as we do our SSL. We put it on extra thick. And we run it all the way to the edge.

No need for staples. Or messy mastics. In one easy step, you get a tighter seal. One that will not fail.

the White Glove Test.

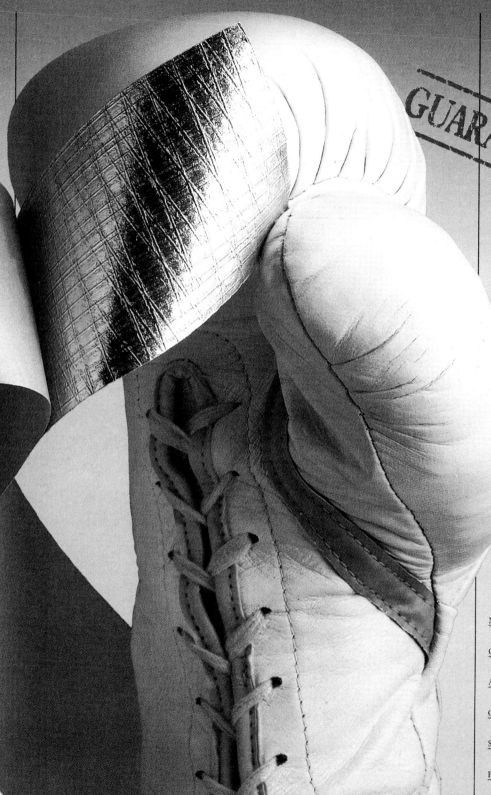

COLOR PLATES 32 AND 33 The two-page ad (see preceding pages) and the mailer demonstrate what creativity can do to present fiber glass pipe insulation. What does the man-on-the-job want? Speed and convenience. How can the advertiser demonstrate such abstract concepts? A stop-watch? How trite. But, if the contractor could peel the strips and apply them with boxing gloves, it would be a powerful demonstration. The mailer says "Peeling is Believing," and it is opened by peeling just the way the insulation strip peels.

COLOR PLATE 33

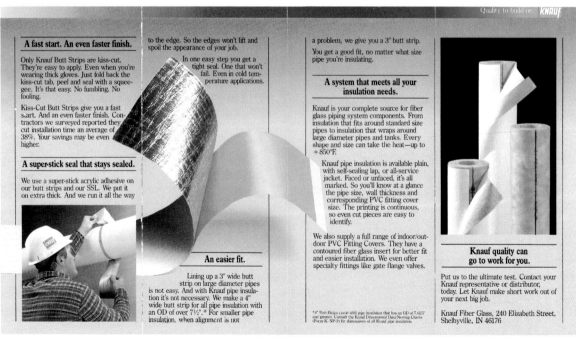

COLOR PLATE 34

COLOR PLATE 34 Canada Dry is the family name for a well-known line of soft drinks from Canada Dry Corporation, a subsidiary of R. J. Reynolds Industries, Inc., a firm well-known for tobacco products. Other divisions of Reynolds—such as Del Monte and Heublein—continue to advertise in their own names.

Kouros.

Les dieux vivants ont leur parfum.

KOUROS
EAU DE TOILETTE

Parfums
YVESSAINTLAURENT

COLOR PLATE 35

COLOR PLATE 35 We expect a perfume to have a French name. The problem is to create an image for a masculine scent. YSL combines it with a photo of a muscular young man, a package identification, and one line of copy, in French, of course (*The living gods have their perfume*).

COLOR PLATE 36

COLOR PLATE 36 In 1984, the Campbell Soup Company honored the 80th birthday of the Campbell Kids by making more use of them in its advertising and as corporate symbols to develop the company's image as the "well-being company." The Kids appeared on television for the first time in at least five years in a new animated TV spot aimed at children. In the spot, which was created by the Campbell agency, Backer and Spielvogel, the Kids convince a lethargic youngster who doesn't eat properly that he will have more energy and vitality with a proper diet including soup.

In 1904 Grace Drayton, an accomplished artist and illustrator from Philadelphia, created the Campbell Kids. In those days, a chubby child was considered to be a healthy child. And, as a symbol of a soup company that sought to establish its product as wholesome and nourishing, the children were used to personify the image of robust, happy youngsters, with dimpled knees and elbows, and round, rosy cheeks. But times change and so have the Campbell Kids. Over the years, their eyes, noses, and chins and various parts of their anatomies have been subtly changed to reflect a contemporary appearance. They may never be skinny, but they now have fewer bulges, and a generally lean, more athletic look, which is very appropriate since the company was a sponsor of the U.S. Olympic skating team. Today, their message is good nutrition and healthful exercise. The Kids are synonymous with Campbell Soup in the public mind. A 1956 poll showed them to be the fourth best animated ad symbol in the nation that year, after Aunt Jemima, the Bird's Eye Kids, and Elsie, the Borden Cow. The Kids lost some popularity in the sixties because they were considered old-fashioned. But, they became popular again in the seventies when being old-fashioned became a virtue and people began to collect Campbell Kids memorabilia. They are still very cuddly and, of course, right after they finish skating, they still eat soup.

INTRODUCING LIPTON® INTERNATIONAL SOUP CLASSICS. THE SAD PART IS THE YEARS YOU'VE HAD TO LIVE WITHOUT THEM.

But the good part is, now you can enjoy them as often as you want. And once you sample one of Lipton's new International Soup Classics, often may not even be enough.

Five incredibly delicious recipes from around the world. California Cream of Broccoli, Cream of Mushroom A La Reine, Cream of Asparagus Parisienne, Lobster Bisque and New England Clam Chowder.

Try some soon. After all, you'll want to make up for all that lost time.

Each box of soup contains two single-serving envelopes.

COLOR PLATE 37 How do you make dry, packaged soup mix into an elegant dinner contribution? With a beautiful table setting. Even the package suggests elegance. Note how the ad focuses attention on the soup and the package at the same time.

most part, it reaches adults on their way to and returning from work. Demographically, transit reaches more women than men but is evenly split between white-collar and blue-collar workers.

Advantages of Transit

Transit is primarily an urban medium with little or no reach in rural or small-town areas. But in metropolitan areas, its reach is great. Because the travel patterns of the audience are repeated 5 days a week, 52 weeks a year, there is an excellent opportunity for repeat delivery of the message. Transit is a *high-frequency* medium. Transit is very useful to local advertisers who want to reach consumers in their shopping areas. Transit advertising may be, for some consumers, the last advertising message they receive before they make a purchase in the marketplace.

Transit is also selective. Advertisers can select the train or bus routes that expose their messages to demographically defined groups. Some advertisers may want to reach the mass market of an entire transit system, and they can do that, too. Others can select the ethnic markets or certain up-scale markets that are most appropriate for their products.

Limitations

Like outdoor, transit media have a limited amount of message space available, but this is not as critical as it is in outdoor because the audience has more time to absorb the message. The reader often has ample time to read all the copy; in fact, exposure time for transit advertisements averages 20 to 30 minutes. Transit is, nevertheless, not intended for long or complex selling messages. Competition for attention is high. Transit is not intrusive. It must compete with other displays, other reading material, people, and scenery outside the vehicle. Also, people who travel the same route day after day tend to become less attentive to the transit advertising on that route.

The Transit Advertising Business

Commuter trains, subways, and bus lines are the means of transportation between suburban areas and urban centers. The advertising in and on these transit lines is operated by about 70 companies organized into 380 designated markets. The transit advertising operator places and maintains transit advertisements on the vehicles or lines for which the advertiser contracts. The printed advertisements themselves are supplied and paid for by the advertiser. The operators pay the standard 15 percent agency commission.

Although many national advertisers have used transit advertising consistently for many years, the bulk of transit advertising is used by local advertisers. For national advertisers, transit particularly lends itself to the advertising of low-priced convenience goods that are widely distributed. Transit is a supplementary component in many advertisers' media mix, used to add extra weight to urban markets. Local advertisers can use transit advantageously by taking space only on those transit lines that serve their trading areas.

Buying Transit: Forms and Rates

Car Cards   A **car card** is a standard size piece of lightweight cardboard that is printed on one side and mounted in a retaining frame on the interior walls of a train or bus. Car-card space is sold on the basis of a *run* or *service*. A **full**

run would indicate one card in every vehicle or every train car of the transit system. A **half run** means one card in half of the line's vehicles. A *double run* indicates two cards in every vehicle. Some markets, generally the larger ones, also offer a *quarter run,* but the half run is the service most frequently bought. In the New York City subway system, a full run consists of two cards in every car, because the size of the cars makes it possible that many riders would not be exposed to only one card.

Rates are usually based on monthly service, with reduced rates for contracts of three, six, or twelve months. The cards are supplied by the advertiser and installed by the operator. Cards are usually changed once a month, but the frequency of change is up to the advertiser; some leave the cards unchanged for longer periods. The advertiser usually provides more cards than are needed so the operator can replace those that have become soiled, that fall down, or are defaced. In large cities, a full run on buses can cost more than $2,000 a month. CPM runs about 14 cents in large metropolitan markets.

Car cards are 11 inches high by 28 inches wide. But greater visibility can be obtained with oversized cards 42 inches wide or 56 inches wide. All cards are 11 inches high, which is standard for both buses and train cars. Premium positions, available at extra cost, include *square-end* (an **end card** is located at the end of an aisle) cards 22 inches by 21 inches, *top-end* cards 16 inches by 44 inches, and *over-door* positions. A relatively new idea in transit advertising is the **basic bus,** which consists of *all* the advertising space on the inside of a specified number of regularly scheduled buses.

This is a 1984 rate card from TDI Winston Network. The rates shown are for their "A" package, as they designate it, which consists of 21-inch by 33-inch car cards in end positions in New York and Philadelphia, and 21-inch by 22-inch car cards in end positions in Chicago, Washington, D.C., San Francisco, and Atlanta. The firm also offers a "C" package that covers New York only, requires a minimum of two months, and includes only 21-inch by 33-inch car cards. Monthly circulation for the "C" package is 17,749,000. Rates do not include production of the cards, which are supplied by the advertiser. Advertisers are entitled to a change of copy once in any contract month without charge.

Commuters can be reached with car cards in commuter railroads five days a week, as they travel from their homes in the suburbs to their jobs in the city and then back. Statistics indicate that they are well-educated (48 percent are college graduates), affluent, and three out of four are in professional or managerial positions. Nearly one-third are female—an indication of the growing number of women in business.

	New York*	Phila.	Chicago	Wash.	San Francisco	Atlanta
Monthly Rate for Twelve Consecutive Months						
Full Run	$32,602	$3,222	$9,976	$4,955	$5,262	$1,650
¾ Run	26,090	2,532	7,846	—	4,549	836
Half Run	18,629	1,841	5,956	2,478	3,266	418
*Minimum buy two (2) months						
Number of Cards Displayed						
Full Run	3,692	356	756	200	360	75
¾ Run	3,077	297	567	—	270	—
Half Run	2,051	198	378	100	180	—
Number of Vehicles						
Full Run	2,629	356	756	200	360	75
¾ Run	2,190	297	567	—	270	—
Half Run	1,460	198	378	100	180	—
Monthly Circulation						
	22,568,000	2,791,000	6,185,000	7,184,000	8,100,000	3,375,000

11 | OUT-OF-HOME ADVERTISING

POSTERS at Stations and Terminals of TDI

	New York*	Phila.*	Chicago	Wash.	San Francisco	Atlanta	Cleveland
Monthly Rates for 12 Consecutive Months							
1-Sheet Posters							
Full	$16,173	$3,508	$6,387	—	—	—	—
3/Qtrs.	12,615	2,738	5,045	—	—	—	—
Half	9,218	2,037	3,660	—	—	—	—
2 or 3-Sheet Posters*							
Full	$21,238	$5,011	$9,153	$7,332	$3,136	$3,150	$1,470
3/Qtrs.	16,566	3,910	7,211	—	2,593	—	—
Half	12,315	2,908	5,233	—	1,889	—	735

*3 Sheet Posters available in New York and Philadelphia only

Number of Locations							
Terminal	18	5	5	0	0	0	0
Station	275	90	130	48	37	21	17
Total	293	95	135	48	37	21	17
Number of Posters							
Full	700	180	240	94	60	42	34
3/Qtrs.	525	135	180	—	45	—	—
Half	350	90	120	—	30	—	16
Monthly Circulation							
	56,466,000	4,985,000	13,780,000	14,300,000	11,450,000	3,375,000	1,400,000

SAN FRANCISCO BART SYSTEM
SIX SHEET POSTERS available at:
Full showing of 60 Posters = $6,683.00 per month.
Half showing of 30 Posters = $3,899.00 per month.
ILLUMINATED PIER UNITS (8' × 8'):
Package of 5 units = $3,160 per month.

ATLANTA MARTA SYSTEM
ILLUMINATED PIER UNITS (8' × 8'):
$850.00 per unit per month.

Affluent commuters, of which 45.3 percent are between 18 and 34 years old, can be reached with posters at the stations and terminals served by suburban transit. For New York, this 1984 TDI rate card covers terminals of the Long Island, New Haven, New York Central, Northeast Corridor, Erie-Lackawanna, and Raritan Valley lines; the North Jersey coast line, the PATH, and Staten Island Rapid Transit and ferry systems; plus the Port Authority Bus Terminal and George Washington Bridge Bus Terminal. In Chicago, it covers all stations and terminals of the Burlington Northern, Illinois Central, Rock Island, and the Chicago & North Western railroads.

These car cards had a two-fold objective: to encourage use of buses on holidays and to stimulate attendance at Chicago's cultural and educational institutions. A very efficient use of transit media, since the target market is people who ride public transportation.

Take-Ones   **Take-ones** are perforated postcards or leaflets that are attached to a pad and fastened to the bottom or corner of a car card. The postcards or leaflets are easily detached by the viewers, who are invited to send for information or to take home the leaflet and read it more carefully in private. There is an additional charge of about 10 percent for the use of take-ones.

Exterior, or Traveling, Displays   Exterior displays are carried on both sides of the bus as well as front and rear. Sizes vary, but the most common is 21 inches high by 44 inches wide. Other display sizes include the *king size* (30 inches by 144 inches), the *queen size* (30 inches by 88 inches), and the **taillight spectacular** (21 inches by 72 inches). Exterior king-size posters are sold in *showings.* A *100 showing* represents multiple coverage on every base route in the market. Contracts for showings are made by the month, with discounts for consecutive showing periods of up to 12 months.

Other variations available to advertisers include a rooftop backlighted display, called a *busorama,* that is 22 inches high by 144 inches wide. One

An end card is used in transit advertising. It is much larger than the ordinary car card and, since it appears at the ends of the aisles in railroad cars or buses, enjoys much greater visibility.

An exterior bus display is a form of transit advertising. In this case, it is being used to promote a cream liqueur.

Häagen-Dazs Cream Liqueur

PROFILE

Lois Wyse

Lois Wyse is president of Wyse Advertising, the agency she cofounded in Cleveland, Ohio, in 1951. A former newspaper reporter and magazine writer, Lois Wyse was born in Cleveland and attended Case Western Reserve University. She lives in New York City, where Wyse Advertising opened an office in 1967.

Wyse Advertising is a full-service agency that provides account and creative services, media planning and execution, marketing services, sales promotion, and merchandising material, including direct mail and brochures. It has particular expertise in package goods and retail services and is well known for its work with consumer products. Clients of Wyse Advertising include Maidenform, the Sherwin-Williams Corporation, Stouffer Corporation, Celanese, and the J. M. Smucker Company.

Lois Wyse has long been associated with the agency's advertising for the Smucker Company. For this client, she wrote the line: "With a name like Smucker's, it has to be good."

Lois Wyse is a director of the Higbee Company, a Cleveland-based department store, and a director of the Consolidated Natural Gas Company Pittsburgh. She has published more than 40 books, including poetry, fiction, nonfiction, and children's books. She has received many major advertising awards, including the Clio, and she writes a monthly column for *Good Housekeeping* magazine.

A clock spectacular (above) is a very effective eye-catcher in subway and railroad stations, bus depots, and airline terminals, where people are anxious to know the correct time. As they check the time, they are exposed to the sales message in the display.

An illuminated diorama particularly lends itself to advertising by auto rental companies, real estate developers, and hotels. They are usually placed in airline and railroad terminals to provide information to arriving visitors. This diorama targets business commuters in a train station.

Bus shelters offer eye-level impact that is visible to both motorists and pedestrians, with great opportunities for creativity. They provide 24-hour point-of-purchase power in locations near shopping malls, office buildings, corporate parks, and other high-traffic locations. Their bright illumination provides 24-hour service.

busorama is available on each side of the bus. Some operators also sell the **total bus** — that is, all the exterior advertising on the bus. The advertiser using the basic bus *and* the total bus buys the *total, total bus.*

Shelter Displays

Transit systems also offer the opportunity to display advertising in the terminals, stations, and shelters where commuters board. **Station posters** are displayed in and on stations of subways, bus lines, and commuter railroads. They are generally available in a 1-sheet size (30 inches wide by 46 inches high), a 2-sheet size (60 inches wide by 46 inches high), or a 3-sheet size (42 inches wide by 84 inches high — the same size as a 3-sheet poster used in outdoor advertising).

Transit advertising operators also offer *floor displays, diorama displays,* and *clock spectaculars* in train, bus, and airline terminals. A **clock spectacular** consists of a large electric clock set in a display framework that may include a moving message. Most of the other displays are custom designed and include many of the same components as outdoor spectaculars. Other transit media available include displays on the roofs and rear decks of taxicabs, but these displays are used mostly by local advertisers.

Phone-booth advertising provides the eye-level visual impact of a backlighted transparency, 2 feet wide by 4 feet high. It can be used to target an audience in specific local areas of a desired population density, such as a theater district or shopping district. (See color plate 30 for another example.)

Summary

Outdoor advertising represents about 1 percent of the total advertising expenditures in the United States. It is not a major outlet for national advertisers, but it is of value as a helpful supplementary medium for certain types of products. Most outdoor advertising consists of printed paper mounted on panels. The most common size is the 30-sheet poster. Other forms of outdoor include large painted bulletins, one-of-a-kind spectaculars, and smaller paper posters known as 3-sheet posters. Outdoor delivers a brief message to motorists who pass the display one or more times a day. As a medium, it is for the most part nonselective and conveys only a brief advertising message.

Outdoor displays are bought on the basis of showings—a designation representing a specific number of locations offered by a plant operator in a particular city or market. A 100 showing indicates that a message will appear on as many panels as needed in a given market to provide a daily exposure equal to 100 percent of that market's population. Painted bulletins are bought on an individual basis.

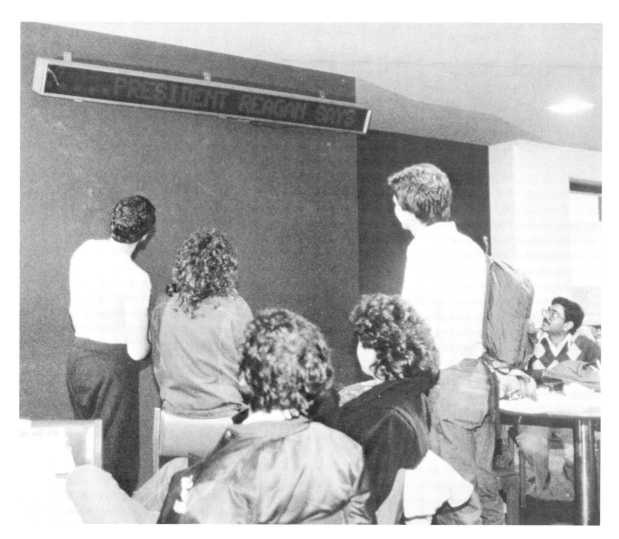

Now on-site at more than 140 major colleges and universities in 33 states, Electronic News Network's "moving message" display boards are strategically located in student unions and other indoor high-traffic areas. Twenty-four hours a day, seven days a week, an eight-minute cycle of timely news, campus activity information, and advertisements is clearly presented on these stylish 66-inch by 9-inch electronic units. Computers at the company's Dallas headquarters transmit the data via telephone lines to participating schools.

Two of the eight minutes consist of local, regional, and national advertising messages interspersed between sharply edited world and national news, collegiate and professional sports scores, entertainment segments, and updates on local campus events. By employing state-of-the-art computer-graphic technologies, ENN enables an advertiser to tailor his message to one school, a select group of campuses, or the entire network. Corporate or advertising campaign slogans for a wide variety of products and services work exceedingly well in this editorial environment, as do longer-length commercial spots.

An advertising message at just one college location appears at least 2,160 times per month during campus prime-time from 7 AM to 7 PM, Monday through Saturday. However, since ENN operates all day long during the course of the entire week, the total number of monthly spots an advertiser receives is far in excess of that figure.

ENN advertising rates are based on school enrollment figures coupled with verified pedestrian traffic counts at display board sites. For example, a 20-character message at Providence College runs $40 per month while the same message is $160 at considerably larger Oklahoma State University. The cost for every thousand persons reached is approximately 50 cents.

Summary

Palm Springs

When winter visitors arrive in Palm Springs, they expect the sun to be shining. It usually is. Selling the sun is an all-year task with specific strategies for fall, spring, and summer. A resort does not live on one season alone. The marketing of this famous desert oasis is as complex and challenging as the most sophisticated package goods product, with market differences, trade influences, timing considerations, positioning strategies, and competitive influences.

Palm Springs, California, is one of America's leading vacation and convention areas. It has 160 hotels, 40 golf courses, and boasts of 350 days of sunshine a year. During the peak vacation season — January, February, March — it attracts many visitors. Their objective is and has been to attract visitors during the shoulders of Palm Springs season, the off-peak periods. They have been using outdoor advertising for that purpose for over ten years.

Their strategy is simple — during the fall and spring periods each year, they use four different outdoor designs on a 60-day rotation program over a six-month period. Each design features a specific sales point — such as family vacations, proximity, climate, and cost. They communicate these messages with simple, colorful displays that provide excellent visibility and impact. The outdoor message is then adapted for their print media campaign, which is limited to upscale publications that can be purchased on a local or regional basis, covering the same area for the most part as the outdoor program.

Thomas D. Hanlon, Executive Director, Palm Springs Convention and Visitors Bureau, says, "For us, outdoor advertising is a basic medium because its enormous circulation, its distribution of our messages to key targets, and its cost effectiveness cannot be duplicated."

Based on "transient occupancy tax" figures, it has worked well. Regardless of economic conditions, the number of visitors has risen every year, in one recent year by 20 percent. (See color plate 31 for another Palm Springs billboard.)

Make a big splash with the kids. Palm Springs.

Outdoor is suited to impulse goods, intensively distributed and bought by consumers by brand name. Because the audience is most often exposed to the displays while passing by them in an automobile, outdoor is also a very appropriate medium for advertising products related to automobiles.

Transit advertising is an urban medium of limited value for some national advertisers, of excellent supplementary value for others, and of great usefulness to local advertisers. Transit is nonselective with a basically urban reach that delivers adult men and women, white-collar as well as blue-collar.

Questions for Discussion

1. What is the difference between an outdoor poster and a painted bulletin?
2. Why would an advertiser use transit advertising?
3. Briefly describe three different kinds of transit advertising.
4. What is the meaning of a showing?
5. What are the benefits of outdoor advertising? What are its limitations?
6. For what products would you recommend outdoor advertising? Justify your answer.

Sources and Suggestions for Further Reading

Baker, S. *Systematic Approach to Advertising Creativity.* New York: McGraw-Hill, 1983.

Barban, Arnold M., Stephen M. Cristol, and Frank G. Kopec. *Essentials of Media Planning.* Chicago: Crain Books, 1976.

Bogart, Leo. *Strategy in Advertising: Matching Media and Messages to Markets and Motivations,* 2nd ed. Chicago: Crain Books, 1984.

Davidson, Casey. "Bus Riders Read Between Ads." *ADWEEK,* July 28, 1986.

Donnermuth, William P. *Promotion: Analysis, Creativity and Strategy.* Boston: Kent Publishing Company, 1984.

Edel, Richard. "Outdoor Boards Are Growing in Stature." *Advertising Age,* August 11, 1986.

Houck, John W. *Outdoor Advertising.* Notre Dame, Indiana: University of Notre Dame, 1969.

"Out-of-Home Advertising," Special Report. *Advertising Age,* May 12, 1986.

Ray, Michael L. *Advertising and Communication Management.* Englewood Cliffs, N.J.: Prentice-Hall, 1982.

Sachs, William. *Advertising Management: Its Role In Marketing.* Tulsa, Oklahoma: PennWell Publishing Company, 1983.

Sissors, Jack Z., and E. Reynold Petray. *Advertising Media Planning.* Chicago: Crain Books, 1976.

12 NONMEDIA ADVERTISING

Direct Advertising

Point-of-Purchase Promotion (POP)

Working Vocabulary

package inserts	self-mailer	remembrance advertising
direct mail	solo mailing	premiums
list house	piggyback mailing	external house organ
list broker	co-op mailing	point-of-purchase (POP)
statement stuffer	bulk mail	
break-out	specialties	

Industrial (business/professional) direct mail in the marketing plan belongs between the mass advertising effort and the sales effort. Advertising opens the mind. Direct mail opens the door. Salespeople close the sale.

Norman J. Suslock
Direct Mail: The Return-on-Investment Advertising Medium

In using any of the media we have discussed so far, advertisers surrender much of their control over their advertising message. They have to accept the fact that the medium controls the informational environment in which their message will appear. They have to accept the characteristics of the medium's audience. They have to accept the medium's schedule for delivery of their message. They even have to accept the medium's restrictions on the size and format of their message. But now we are going to discuss a form of advertising that is controlled almost exclusively by the advertiser.

Direct Advertising

Direct advertising is advertising that uses no medium. Direct advertising is a printed message that is delivered directly to prospective customers by the advertiser. The advertiser selects the prospect and the advertiser determines the timing of delivery. How is it done? Circulars distributed on a street corner to passersby. Circulars stuffed under doors or placed in the mail boxes of prospects. Circulars distributed by salespeople. Circulars packed with the product **(package inserts).** And, of course, through a wide range of circulars, catalogues, brochures, leaflets, and other printed material sent by way of the post office to prospects selected by the advertiser — **direct mail.** (See color plate 33 for an example of a creative mailer.)

Not all of the many kinds of direct advertising are suitable for a national advertiser: It is inconceivable that any major national advertiser would have printed advertising handed out on street corners or delivered door to door.[1] The cost would be prohibitive. Such methods are most frequently used by local retailers, generally with limited trading areas. However, package inserts, literature distributed by and through retail outlets, and direct-mail advertising are used extensively by national advertisers. Direct-mail expenditures in 1984 amounted to $54 billion.

Direct-Mail Advertising

Available since the establishment of the postal service in 1775, direct-mail advertising is the most used, and so the most important, form of direct promotion. Direct-mail advertising should not be confused with mail-order selling, which is a form of retailing. The goods offered for sale by mail-order retailers are *distributed* by mail; direct-mail advertising is the promotion of goods that are distributed through other channels.

---

[1] Although that is exactly the way samples are often distributed — on a street corner or stuffed in a letter box or hung on a doorknob.

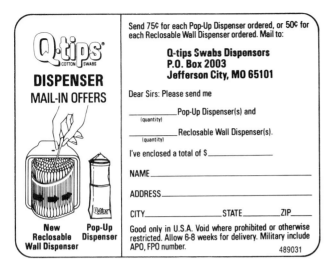

Package inserts may range from multiple page folders to a simple slip of paper printed on one side, such as this insert for Q-TIPS® Cotton Swabs. Package inserts may be used to provide more information about the use and benefits of the product than can be accommodated on the product's package, or, as in this example, they may be used to promote a premium offer.

Advantages of Direct Mail

Direct mail can be used to fulfill a number of advertising functions, including the following:

1. to determine consumer interest in a product before it is marketed
2. to create leads for salesperson follow-up
3. to sell merchandise, or encourage a trial or a request for more information
4. to reinforce product awareness
5. to develop a personal relationship between sender and customer
6. to translate mass advertising into individual customer benefits
7. to test advertising headlines
8. to test selling themes
9. to generate business through recommendation
10. to automate reorder of merchandise or material
11. to remind customers of maintenance requirements on equipment they have purchased

Direct mail is *flexible.* We can mail out our circulars at any time we choose. And we can assemble a mailing quickly to take advantage of unexpected situations. The *frequency* is also of our own choosing. We can send out mailings once a month or once a day. We are independent of publication dates. And direct mail is *selective,* both demographically and geographically. We can send out mailings to a specific city, county, or state — to a hundred names or to a hundred thousand.

Selectivity means a minimum of waste. If we were advertising a product that was of value only to home owners, even if we advertised in a homemaking magazine we would still reach a large amount of waste circulation. We would not want to reach readers of the magazine who are apartment house dwellers, for example. In contrast, we can direct our mailing almost *exclusively* to home owners with little or no waste. Direct mail is a way of localizing, individualizing, and personalizing contact with a customer or prospect in a form that is

Get tuned up for a full-blown celebration.

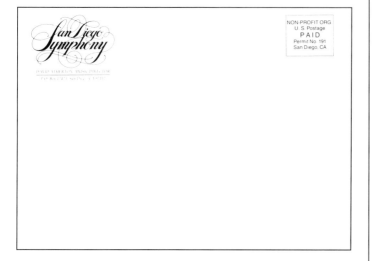

Nonprofit organizations use direct mail extensively for their fund-raising activities. This mailing piece is typical of those for musical organizations — in return for price of admission the donor receives an evening of music, food, and drink — usually set around some theme. Note the clever play on words in the caption and the light-hearted cartoon which suggests an evening of fun.

convenient and comfortable and which provides a simple way for the reader to respond.

Direct mail is *personal*, yet still within our definition of advertising. It is personal to the extent that it is received personally. A prospective customer opens a mailed letter or circular at his or her convenience. Direct mail is not an interruption the way an advertisement in a newspaper or a magazine is when it breaks into an article that a reader is trying to focus on. Nor does a direct-mail piece represent the kind of intrusion demonstrated by a television or radio commercial. The direct-mail advertising message is private and personal.

Advertising through the mail can generate leads for our sales force, and it can prepare the way for the salespeople's personal visits as a form of preselling. Advertising through the mail is also used as a follow-up to the salesperson's call; this follow-up enables advertisers to keep in touch with prospective customers, to supply additional information, and to build and maintain goodwill.

We can also use direct mail to appeal to prospects not reached by other media. How do we reach the homemaker who does not read any magazine at all? We can use television, of course, but even if we have made our media selection carefully, there will still be waste. We can also use direct mail to reach difficult-to-see business executives who might exert an important influence in the decision to purchase certain business and industrial goods. Direct mail is not a substitute for media advertising, however, but a supplementary means of promotion that we can use to reach business buyers as well as consumers. We can also use direct mail to reach the retailers who will sell our product to consumers. In fact, direct mail is, for many manufacturers, by far the most important means they have to reach middlemen, purchasing agents, and other professional people.

Direct mail can also be used as a research tool. Because the audience is carefully selected, direct mail can be used to test different appeals, illustrations, or product innovations. Information gathered in this way can then be used to make our media advertising more effective. Direct mail is measured every step of the way. Copy, art, formats and lists can be tested inexpensively to find the most effective concept *before* any large budget is committed. To test a mass advertising medium takes a sizable dollar investment. Even then, the results are tentative at best.

Limitations

With all its important advantages, why is direct mail only in third place among advertising techniques? The answer is cost. Even with no waste at all, direct mail is expensive. Costs include: the preparation and printing of the mailing piece and the envelope (if one is used); the cost of the mailing list, if it is rented or purchased; the cost of labor for stuffing and addressing envelopes; and the cost of the postage. At present, bulk-rate postage — the lowest rate for an advertiser — is 12.5 cents each. The postage cost of a thousand circulars is $125. For a million pieces, the postage alone would cost $125,000. In contrast, a full-page, four-color advertisement in *TV Guide* costs $61,000 and reaches an audience of 20,433,000. Consequently, if we want to use direct mail, our target market must be very clearly defined and the expense must be justified by results that cannot be obtained by other means.

In order to reduce the high cost of direct-mail advertising, groups of national advertisers occasionally band together to produce a single mailing. These mailings may contain coupons or inserts from five to ten different manufacturers — noncompetitive to be sure — of household or food products. By sharing the cost of postage, envelopes, lists, and labor, these advertisers can reduce their individual expenses substantially.

One of the most important advantages of direct mail — its personal reception — has its reverse side as well. It is true that a direct-mail piece is personal and private, and that it commands the full attention of the reader — *if*

Five companies pooled their effort in this mailer insert. The same sheet is used as an insert loosely inserted in a newspaper. The companies in this way are also able to obtain great economies in printing costs.

the reader reads it. But many Americans derogatorily refer to direct mailings as "junk mail" and either ignore the message or throw the mail away unopened. If the mailed piece cannot make an immediately favorable impact, it is lost. The absence of an editorial climate — described as an advantage a few pages ago — can also work against the advertiser, since the mailed message receives no editorial assistance. Overcoming these disadvantages presents a tremendous challenge to the writers and designers of direct-mail advertising.

Circulation

A magazine is mailed to its list of subscribers and is bought at the newsstand by people who find its editorial contents to their liking. The CPM is relatively low and the advertiser can tolerate the waste that is bound to occur. But direct mail is expensive unless it is successful, and it can only be successful if the audience is right, the timing is right, and the message is right. The most important of these considerations is the audience, because even the best designed message and the most carefully planned timing will be fruitless if the message is directed to the wrong people.

The perfect audience would consist only of people who are interested in, and can afford to buy, the product being promoted. That means we must know the demographic attributes of the target audience as well as their correct names, their correct addresses, and (for a business mailing) their correct job titles. Our list of names must be up to date.

It is possible to categorize lists by credit rating; age; sex; city, neighborhood, suburban, or rural area; customer or noncustomer status; and active customer or inactive customer status. Of course, not all lists need to be broken down in this way, but many should be if the advertiser is to obtain the greatest amount of selectivity possible from this very selective medium.

Mailing Lists

One of the most productive mailing lists for most advertisers is their own customer list. All the needed information is available, and the customers are already familiar with the product and the company. Advertisers can also compile mailing lists of people or companies who respond to advertisements offering further product information. Lists of likely prospects are also often obtained at trade shows, either from registers of people who visited the advertiser's booth seeking specific information or from lists of registrants compiled by the management of the exhibition. Either way, such lists are current and contain names of people who are interested, if not in the advertiser's specific product, at least in the industry.

Mailing lists can be compiled, with some effort of course, from the White Pages of telephone directories, from Yellow Pages, and from trade directories. County tract maps can be used to develop lists for mailings not addressed to individuals but to the occupants of specific street addresses. Public records are another good source of lists. Records of births, deaths, marriages, home purchases, and auto registrations can be used to obtain names. New parents, for instance, are logical prospects for baby paraphernalia and insurance.

Buying Mailing Lists Advertisers who do not have the time or the resources to compile their own mailing lists may buy or rent them. The cost of the list will vary according to its quality, completeness, and degree of selectivity, and according to the difficulty of obtaining the information it contains. A list of corporate presidents will be more expensive than a list of motorcycle owners. Lists may be bought from compilers known as **list houses,** which generally offer business lists. Business names are bought in this way more often than consumer names are.

Business publications are another excellent source of names and addresses. Many trade, industrial, and professional publications allow advertisers to use their circulation lists for direct mailings. Generally, the publications do not deliver the list to the advertiser; the advertiser is required to send its mailing pieces to the publisher, who then addresses and mails them for a specified charge per thousand names. Such charges range from $40 to $100 per thousand.

A very useful source is the **list broker,** who acts as rental agent for list owners. For example, a magazine might rent its subscriber list to a manufacturer, another (noncompetitive) magazine, or a book club or record club. A subscriber to *National Geographic* is a likely prospect for a book club or a travel service. Noncompetitive publications might exchange lists, so that each could solicit new subscriptions.

Retailers are an excellent list source — their charge-account customers make excellent targets for manufacturers of certain products sold through their stores. In fact, a **statement stuffer** is one of the most frequently used pieces for co-op mailings. It is an advertising leaflet mailed by the retailer to its charge-account customers along with their monthly statements. The retailers enjoy the extra business stimulated by the leaflet, the cost of which was borne by the manufacturers of the products advertised. The retailers' only expenses are for the envelopes and the postage, which would have been incurred anyway. It is a cooperative effort in which everyone gains.

Keeping the Lists Up to Date   Mailing lists are highly perishable items. Women marry and change their names; firms merge; people change jobs; people move, die, disappear. The rate of change is usually in excess of 20 percent each year. To put it another way, a magazine with a subscription circulation of only one million is required to make more than 200,000 changes to its list every year. What can advertisers do to avoid waste if they use rented or purchased lists? Nothing. Publications find that merely keeping up with changes in their subscription lists requires a good-sized staff. In many cases, the work is farmed out to organizations that specialize in maintaining mailing lists.

The post office helps keep mailing lists current by returning undelivered or undeliverable mail to the sender for a small charge. It's an excellent way to keep lists up to date. Many companies that use direct mail to reach their business customers will ask their salespeople to check the names and addresses of the people who live in their individual territories.

Another problem that arises from the use of mailing lists is duplication. If an advertiser rents lists for the same, or similar, target segments from two different sources, the chances are good that some names will appear on both lists. Such duplication is not only wasteful, but might even be responsible for negative reactions from the prospects. It is not unusual for advertisers using rented lists to include a statement of apology in the event of duplication. It is often impossible to cross-check lists.

The use of computers and ZIP codes has been of great help to the users of direct mail. You may recall from our discussion of the demographic editions of magazines in chapter 8 that *Time* and *Sports Illustrated* both offer demographic

QUANT	LIST	S.I.C.
1,740	Professional, Scientific Inst. Mfrs.	38XX
2,430	Misc. Mfr. Industries	39XX

By No. of Employees

Range	Cos.	Ind.
N.A.	2,030	3,500
Under 10	0	0
10 to 19	4	10
20 to 49	16,570	42,290
50 to 99	8,890	27,140
100 to 499	10,250	35,920
500 to 999	1,470	5,480
Over 1,000	1,100	4,150
Total	40,310	118,470

Executives *For State Counts See Page 23*

QUANT	LIST	S.I.C.
39,540	General Manager	
34,800	Purchasing Manager	
30,570	Engineering Manager	
34,640	Production Manager	
2,100	Metal Coating & Allied	3479+
4,760		
30		
450		
8,200		
500		
37,200		
2,100		

QUANT	LIST	S.I.C.
2,840	Big Business Cos.	
18,160	Executives of	
100	Anthracite Coal	1100
2,750	Bituminous & Lignite Coal	1200
500	Metal	1000
15,940	Oil & Gas Extraction	1300
3,200	Quarries & Mines (Non-Metallic)	1400
10,700	Mining & Constr. Mach. Whls.	5082+
250	Mining Machinery Mfrs.	3532
2,700	Minority Groups Dirs.	
5,700	Minority-Owned Bus. Firms	
13,800	Mirror & Picture Frame Stores	5271+
11,400	Mobile Home Dealers	5271+
600	Mobile Home Mfrs.	2451
13,500	Mobile Home & Trailer Parks	6515
5,550	Model & Hobby Suppl. Stores	5945B+

QUANT	LIST	S.I.C.
17,900	Music Stores	5733+
	Musical	
3,930	Instruction & Fine Arts Schools	8299F
8,120	Instrument Dealers	5733A+
400	Instrument Mfrs.	3931
2,600	Instrument Repair Serv.	7699X+
400	Instrument Whls.	5099D+
250	Mutual Funds	

N

QUANT	LIST	S.I.C.
240	Nails, Spikes & Wire Mfrs., Steel	3315
220	Nameplate Makers	3993E
2,000	National Assn. of Business Economists	
3,580	Natural Gas & Crude Oil Operations	1311

COMPUTER LIST OF BUSINESS BY STANDARD INDUSTRIAL CLASSIFICATION (S.I.C.)

LIST	S.I.C. No.	Page No.
Accounting Services	8931	65
Advertising Agencies	7311	61
AGRICULTURE, FORESTRY & FISHERIES	0270-0900	46
Air Conditioning, Etc. Contractors	1711C	47
Air Conditioning Wholesalers	5075	54
Aircraft—Eqpt. Mfrs.	3721-9	52
Amusement Services	7700	62
Apparel Mfrs.	2300	48
Appliance Stores (Household)	5722	58
Architectural Services	8911	65
Associations	8611	64
Attorneys	8111	64
Automobile Sales & Service—		
Accessory & Equip.— Wholesalers	5013	53
Battery & Ignition Repair	7538	62
Tire, Battery & Accessory Stores	5531	57
Gasoline Service Stations	5541	57
Glass Replacement & Repair	7539C	62
New & Used Car Dealers	5511 & 21	57
Paint Shops	7535	62
Radiator Repair	7539F	62
Repair Garages	7538	62
Top & Body Repair	7531	62
Used Car Dealers	5521	57
Automotive—Eqpt.—Mfrs.	3711-5	52
Automotive Services	7500-7542	62
Bakery Prods., Mfrs.	2051-2	48
Bakeries, Retail	5460	57
Banks	6020	60
Barber Shops	7241	60
Bars & Taverns	5823	58
Beauty Shops	7231	60
Beer & Alcoholic Beverage Wholesalers	5180	53
Beverage Inds.—Mfrs.	2080	48
Bituminous Coal Mining	1200	46
Department Stores	5311	56
Dies & Tools Mfrs.	3544	51
Drive-In Theatres	7833	63
Drugs, Chemicals, etc.— Wholesalers	5122	55
Drug & Proprietary Stores	5912	59
Dry Goods & Gen'l Mdse. Stores	5311	56
Dyeing & Finishing Textiles— Mfrs.	2261-9	48
Educational Institutions (Schools)	8210-33	64
Electrical Goods— Wholesalers	5060	54
Electrical Machinery Mfrs.	3600	51
Electrical Work Contractors	1731	47
Electronics	3670	51
Employment Agencies	7360	61
Engineering Services	8911	65
Excavation & Foundation Contractors	1794	47
Exterminators	7342	61
Fabric Mills Mfrs.	2211-41	48
Family Clothing Stores	5651	57
Farm Equipment Retail Dealers	5083	54
Farm & Garden Supply Stores	5261	56
Farm Products, Raw Materials, Whol.	5159	55
Farms, Commercial	0270	46
FINANCE & REAL ESTATE— SERVICES	6000-6553	60
Fish & Sea Foods Wholesalers	5146	55
Floor Covering Stores	5713	58
Floor Laying Contractors	1752	47
Florists	5992	59
Food Products Manufacturers	2010	48
Jewelry Stores	5944	59
Knitting Mills—Mfrs.	2251-9	48
Labor Organizations	8631	64
Laundries	7211-5	60
Lawyers	8111	64
Leather & Leather Products Mfrs.	3100	50
Libraries	8231	64
Liquor Stores	5921	59
Loan Companies	6145	60
Lumber & Building Material Dealers	5210	56
Lumber & Bldg. Matls.— Wholesale	5030	53
Lumber & Wood Products Mfrs.	2400	48
Machinery & Commercial Equip. Whol.	5081	54
Machinery, Except Electrical Mfrs.	3500	51
Machinery—Electrical—Equipt. Mfrs.	3600	51
Machine Shops	3599	51
MANUFACTURING INDUSTRIES	1900-3999	48
Meat Products—Mfrs.	2011-17	48
Meat Wholesalers	5147	55
Medical Equipment Wholesalers	5086	54
Medical Services	8000-91	63
Medical Laboratories	8071	63
Men's & Boys' Apparel—Mfrs.	2311-29	48
Men's & Boys' Stores	5611-3	57
Metal Products (Primary) Mfrs.	3300	50
Metal Prods. (Fabricated)		
Photography Studios	7221	60
Plastic Products Mfrs.	3079	50
Plumbing, Heating, Air Cond. etc., Contr.	1711	47
Plumbing & Heating Equip't Whol.	5074	54
Poultry and Poultry Prods.— Whol.	5144	55
Primary Metal Industries	3300	50
Printing & Publishing	2700	49
Public Elem. & Secondary Schools	8210-23	64
Quarries	1400	46
Radio Stations	4832	53
Radio & Television Stores	5732	58
Ready Mixed Concrete	3273	50
Real Estate Agencies	6531	60
Restaurants	5810	58
RETAIL TRADE	5200-5999	56
Roofing & Sheet Metal Contractors	1761	47
Rubber & Plastic Products Mfrs.	3000	50
Savings & Loan Institutions	6120	60
Sawmills & Planning Mills	2421	49
Schools & School Districts	8200-33	64
Scrap & Waste Mat'ls— Wholesalers	5093	54
Security Dealers	6211	60
SERVICES	7000-8999	60
Sheet Metal & Roofing Contractors	1761	47
Ships & Boats—Mfrs.	3731-2	52
Shoe Stores, Mens & Family	5661	57
Signs & Ad. Display Mfrs.	3993	52
Social Service Organizations	8300	64

Sample pages from the 70-page catalog of lists available from Ed Burnett Consultants Inc., New York, an organization that compiles lists and manages list rentals for other firms. Burnett provides the names on ungummed and unperforated labels that can be affixed only by machine. The lists may also be purchased at additional cost on gummed, perforated labels, on pressure-sensitive labels, on sheets, on index cards, and on magnetic tape. Base prices range from $15 to $60 per thousand names, depending on the use and the quantity of names.

editions based on ZIP codes. We can reach the most affluent communities in our market by buying lists of addresses with the ZIP codes for those areas. In the same way, we can specify the ZIP codes of ethnic neighborhoods. Computers permit the use of any number of break-outs. A **break-out** is any of the various categories into which the names on our list can be separated by the computer. From our total list of names, we could break out men or women or doctors or home owners and so forth. If we wanted to sell automobiles, for instance, we could break out the names of all automobile owners with three-year-old cars.

Forms of Direct Mail

Almost any type of material can be sent through the mail. But, in fact, the most frequently used form of direct-mail promotion is the letter. Letters are simple, direct, and inexpensive to produce, even in small quantities. Today, advertisers can use word-processing systems to customize thousands of copies of a form letter by programming the systems to make small changes in the body of the letter automatically.

Obtaining variety is not a problem for advertisers who use printed direct-mail pieces. They can have their messages printed in one to four colors, on paper of different weights, finishes, and sizes, and in many different sizes and styles of type. If the direct-mail piece is so designed that it does not require an envelope, the address of the prospect being printed or typed directly on the piece itself, it is known as a **self-mailer.**

A self-mailer is simply a postcard, circular, or brochure that has been designed to be mailed without the use of an envelope. The addressee's name and address are written, printed, or pasted on the mailing piece itself. In addition to saving the cost of an envelope, postage is reduced and the labor cost for stuffing the piece into an envelope is eliminated.

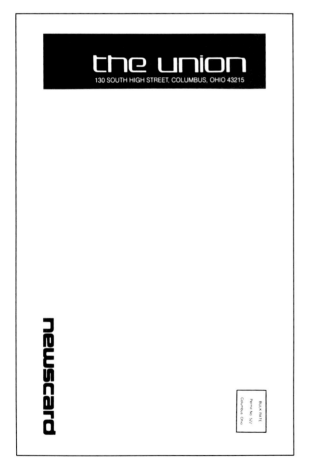

Consumers throughout the United States and Canada are cashing in on savings from billions of coupons and other promotional offers provided regularly through the unique Val-Pak direct-mail network.

Founded in 1968, Val-Pak Marketing ranks today as the largest network of cooperative direct-mail distributors in the nation. Each year, the company produces and mails nearly 100 million envelopes containing a staggering two billion promotional offers. It offers advertisers complete, one-stop service, from design and layout assistance to printing and mailing.

The Val-Pak concept is offered to local, regional, and national advertisers through the company's network of independent dealers in more than 280 major U.S. and Canadian markets. Participating clients can reach cost-conscious consumers at a fraction of normal postage and printing costs.

Sharing the cost of mailing is only one advantage of co-op mailings. The coupons, from noncompeting advertisers, are more convenient for the consumer to use — no clipping, snipping, or ripping, as the ad says. The result is consumer preference and better redemption.

Designers of direct-mail pieces can also use such special printing production techniques as die cuts and pop-ups. If a three-dimensional paper biplane appears when prospects open a direct-mail piece (a pop-up), or if prospects see the outline of a company's product or trademark cut into the cover of a brochure (die cut), won't they be intrigued enough to read the advertising message? Since the success or failure of the piece depends on that all-important initial impact, such special effects can be well worth their extra cost. For this reason, direct-mail advertisers often include gadgets (small gifts such as coins or key rings) and free samples in their direct-mail pieces.

Direct-Mail Delivery Systems

A direct-mail advertiser will often have a choice of whether to use *solo mailing, piggyback mailing,* or *co-op mailing.* A **solo mailing** is any piece delivered individually. It can be sent in an envelope or, like a catalog, be a self-mailer. It can be mailed first class or, like the overwhelming majority of direct mail, third class.

Solo mailings carry the burden of their own postage — 22 cents per piece first class, $125 per thousand third class. **Piggyback (shared cost) mailings** are inserts or stuffers that ride along free with another mailing, such as a bill or merchandise shipment. To escape paying postage, and to fit within the carrier envelope, the piece is generally restricted in size and weight.

Obviously, a solo mailing needs to pull a significantly higher percentage of return to cover the cost of postage. On the other hand, the insert fights for attention with other material sharing the total cost. The insert, of course, is limited to those advertisers making general mailings to their own lists. However, many such mailers, such as banks and credit card companies, have opened up their mailings to outside firms — and will insert a piece for a fee, usually $30 to $50 per thousand. With advantages and disadvantages to both types of mailings, the choice is almost always dictated by availability and the arithmetic of the offer. But nothing beats a successful solo mailing for making money.

Another innovation is the **co-op mailing,** with as many as ten different advertisements sent out in a single envelope. Co-op mailings rely on shared cost. There are many different co-op programs available — ranging from broad-scale occupant mailings sent to various zip codes according to census-tract information, to highly specialized co-ops for new mothers, college students, executives, and others. Perhaps the largest users of co-op mailings are giant mass advertisers, who utilize this medium to distribute "cents off" coupons. These mailings enable them to get their message across to the socioeconomic groups that represent the best prospects for specific products. Interestingly, for this reason, the giant food and grocery product companies like Proctor & Gamble, General Foods, General Mills, American Home Products — not otherwise thought of as direct-mail or mail-order people — are actually among the very largest direct-mail advertisers.

Postal Regulations

Mail in the United States is divided into four classes. *First-class* mail includes letters, written postcards, air mail under eight ounces, sealed matter, and all matter containing written material. *Second-class* rates apply only to publications and do not pertain to areas of direct mail. *Third class* represents the bulk of direct-mail advertising material. The savings over first class are substantial.

To qualify as third-class mail, the mailing piece must be printed; however, printed pieces and retail-store statements may be sent at the third-class rates, provided 20 or more identical pieces are presented at a time to the post office. The **bulk-mail** user pays the post office an annual fee of $30, exclusive of postage. For that annual fee, the advertiser is permitted to enjoy the bulk rate. The mailing pieces must be separately addressed, and the advertiser must send not less than 200 pieces at a time. Postage is paid by the pound, but it will not be less than the 12.5 cent minimum. The words BULK RATE must be printed on the envelope or address side adjacent to the permit imprint or the meter stamp. All mail must be sorted and bundled by ZIP codes.

If consumers are expected to respond to a direct mailing, advertisers must provide them with the means to mail in their reply. They may require the prospect to affix postage to an enclosed reply card or envelope. They may provide a stamped card or envelope. Or, they may use a printed business reply card or envelope. When the prospect is asked to apply the postage, the response tends to be drastically reduced. Providing a stamped return card or envelope, on the other hand, can be very wasteful, for the advertiser pays postage on a certain amount of material that will never be returned — usually the largest portion of the mailing. Printed business reply cards or envelopes are usually the best method of handling reply mail. A permit to use business reply mail can be obtained without cost. Responders use specially printed cards or envelopes to mail in their replies, and the advertiser pays only for each reply that is received. No prepayment is required.

Mail-Order Selling

In mail-order selling, now usually called direct response, the mailing piece is expected to close the sale. How do you recognize it? It's the stuffer you receive with your statement from a department store, bank, or credit card. Often it's an "occupant" envelope from a local service firm. It's an offer from a record club, or a magazine. It's an invitation to take a test drive from a local auto dealer. One thing is certain: The mailing is usually successful. That is, it generates more money than it costs. The fact is that only a small percentage of positive responses are required for the mailing to be successful. The stuffer that comes with the gasoline company's statement requires 2/10 of a percent to be profitable. That's two orders per thousand. Truly extraordinary mailings will pull a response as high as 20 percent. Two to ten percent is usually a good response. Actually, the response is not much different from any mass media advertising. How often does the consumer rush out to buy the detergent she sees advertised on television? In fact, the commercials on television may be annoying to the viewer who resents the interruption of her favorite program for four commercials in a row. Though direct mail has the highest CPM of any advertising medium, its selectivity makes the *effective cost* lower. From this perspective, so-called "junk" mail has real value for the advertiser because it is less intrusive and more efficient.

Advertising Specialties

Advertising **specialties** include an endless variety of useful items that are given to target prospects without charge. Usually the advertiser's name, address, and telephone number, and perhaps a short sales message or slogan, are imprinted on the item. The advertiser's goal is to give the recipients something that will remind them of the advertiser's company and/or product every time they use it, pick it up, or look at it. It is often called **remembrance advertising.** The ultimate goal, of course, is to stimulate sales.

The greatest advantage of the advertising specialty is its long life: The prospect is exposed to the advertiser's name or message again and again. In fact, the most widely distributed advertising specialty is the calendar, which the prospect may see as often as 365 days a year. Other specialties include pencils, pens, books of matches, key rings, memo pads, cigarette lighters, letter openers, shopping bags, and ashtrays. There are literally thousands of items to choose from. Specialty advertising, like direct mail, is highly selective, but it is costly and is a supplementary tool at best. For specialty advertising to be of value, advertisers must have carefully defined objectives, carefully defined targets, a suitable theme, and, if possible, an advertising specialty that bears a logical relationship to their product.

These ads, culled from the pages of *Advertising Age,* may serve to suggest the wide range of advertising specialties that are available to an advertiser. Ties, coffee mugs, belt buckles, key rings, luggage tags, print-ons for T-shirts, slide-charts, tote bags — the list of possibilities is almost endless. Would advertisers want to see a few hundred thousand people wearing a T-shirt with their brand's name boldly displayed? Yes indeed, particularly if the people who wear the shirts paid for that privilege.

Show 'em, tell 'em, you'll sell 'em

Visualizers demonstrate product workings at low cost. This one also gives slide-chart competitive comparisons on 27 key specs.

Be a man of vision. Let us "visualize" for you. Write us.

PERRYGRAF

Division of Nashua Corporation

THE
Slide-Chart People

19365 Business Center Drive
Northridge, Calif. 91324
(213) 993-1000

Would Your Company Logo Make a Great Looking Promotional Tie?

. . . or would it be more appropriate reproduced as blazer buttons, crests, scarves, umbrellas, polo shirts, trousers or jackets?
Call or write today for our new brochure illustrating these possibilities.

ALLYN NECKWEAR, Inc.
108 Dogwood Court
Stamford, CT 06903
(203) 322-5160 Alan Cadan

The major disadvantage of most specialties is the limited amount of space available for a message. In some cases there is just enough room for the advertiser's name and address. Also, the cost of the specialty and the cost of distribution tend to limit the size of the target market that can be reached economically. Certain specialty items, such as calendars, are so popular with advertisers that, as the year ends, prospective customers often receive many more than they can use.

Premiums

A **premium** is an article of merchandise that is offered in addition to, or in combination with, the advertiser's product. The purpose of the premium is to attract (and sell) people who do not usually buy the advertiser's product or who do not buy it very often. Premiums are different from specialties in that they carry no sales message or identification of the advertiser. Unlike the specialties, which are given away without cost or obligation, premiums may be obtained only under conditions specified by the advertiser. The strength of the premium lies in its value as a useful gift. The value would be reduced or destroyed by imprinting an advertising message on it. Therefore, premiums are not really advertising tools but rather sales promotion devices that require the support of advertising for their success.

External House Organs

Many companies publish on a regular basis a company magazine that is distributed to customers, prospects, distributors, and dealers without charge. This **external house organ** will feature articles of interest to members of the industry. Although they carry no advertising, these publications do help to build goodwill and to enhance the prestige of the company.

The external house organ is included in the advertising budget of some companies or in the public relations budget (where it belongs) of others. External house organs do not qualify as an advertising medium, but rather as a piece of direct mail that does not contain a selling message. The entire magazine (and some are quite expensively produced) is simply one large advertisement for the company.

Point-of-Purchase Promotion (POP)

Point-of-purchase (POP) advertising is promotional material located in, at, or on retail stores and is designed, produced, and supplied by national advertisers. Point-of-purchase advertising has become increasingly important in the past 25 years because of the growth of self-service retailing. Point-of-purchase advertising cannot be used in place of print and broadcast advertising but must be used to reinforce the advertising messages placed in those media. The sales messages placed in newspapers, magazines, radio, television, outdoor, and transit must make the initial impact, bringing brand awareness to the consumer, stimulating interest, and conveying information. Then, at the point of purchase — inside the retail store — the advertiser has one final opportunity to influence consumers who are actually making a buying decision in the marketplace.

Forms of POP

Point-of-purchase materials can be divided into two broad categories—interior and exterior. Gasoline retailers make extensive use of exterior signs, displays, and banners. Other retailers use interior point-of-purchase materials in store windows, on counters, and on shelves; they can hang displays from the ceiling or mount them on the floor. Much of this point-of-purchase material is of a temporary nature, such as cardboard display cards for the counter; paper shelf strips; paper streamers to be suspended from the ceiling or hung in the window; wall posters; and shipping cartons designed to do double duty as display cases. Other displays, much more permanent, include exterior store signs, interior clock displays, racks and merchandisers that store self-service goods, and decals for doors or windows.

Attributes of POP

The strength of point-of-purchase advertising is its impact on the consumer at the time and in the place where he or she is physically and psychologically ready to buy. No other form of promotion or advertising enjoys such combination of time and place. It is a unique attribute of POP. Another important attribute of POP is its ability to please two different groups of people: the retailer who will use it and the consumer who will see it. But retailers must be convinced that the POP material they are offered will en-

Point-of-purchase displays offer advertisers the opportunity to present their products to the consumer at the time he or she is about to make a purchase. The free-standing Coke® display and merchandiser not only helps stimulate sale of the product, but other products that "go with Coke."

hance the appearance of their stores, or be effective in selling, or both. Otherwise, they will not use it, install it, or accept it no matter how much care, effort, and cost the advertisers have put into it. In designing their POP material, advertisers must consider the kind of retail outlets it is intended for and the space requirements of these outlets. Still, all retailers have their own ideas about what fits and what works in their stores. To all of these difficulties, add the fact that hundreds of different POP items are supplied to retailers by hundreds of manufacturers in every field.

Who Benefits from POP?

Everyone benefits from good POP. POP reinforces the manufacturer's advertising in all other media. It is the advertiser's final chance to tie together all the selling efforts that have been made before the consumer entered the store. In order to use manufacturers' POP materials, a retailer must stock their products. What greater benefit could the manufacturers desire?

PROFILE

John Caples

Often called "the father of direct response advertising," John Caples is a man about whom David Ogilvy said: "He knows more about the *realities* of advertising than anybody else." Caples' knowledge comes from more than 53 years of experience in the advertising business. As a mail-order copywriter, he learned at the very start of his career that every direct-response advertisement must pay its own way. It cannot rely on the cumulative effect of an entire advertising program. As he has said himself: "If you run an ad in a Sunday newspaper, you know by Wednesday whether it is a success or a failure." Every word has to work.

Many of the advertisements written by John Caples are classics in their field, including one which begins with what is probably the most often quoted headline in the history of advertising: "They laughed when I sat down at the piano, but when I started to play!—" John Caples wrote that advertisement in 1925 when he was a cub copywriter in the Ruthrauff & Ryan advertising agency. Three years later he joined Batten, Barton, Durstine, & Osborn (BBDO), where he became a vice-president in 1941. While at BBDO he has become well known for his development of copy-testing methods for such clients as Du Pont, United States Steel, General Electric, and United Fruit. He has also found time to write four very influential books on advertising, including *Tested Advertising Methods* and *Making Ads Pay*.

After more than half a century of writing effective advertisements, John Caples is still hard at work. Why?

I think the reason is because I enjoy my work. I have had fun. In my school days, I liked writing and I liked science. Direct marketing advertising has enabled me to combine the best of both worlds—writing and scientific methods of testing what kinds of ads are successful and what kind are failures.

I have probably written more failures than successes. But every failure has taught me a lesson.

CASE HISTORY

Volvo of America Corporation

Volvo demonstrates its continuing interest in its customers by staying in touch with them well beyond the original new car sale. They do it with a carefully planned direct-mail program that builds customer loyalty to Volvo and the Volvo dealers. The program is based on the assumption that people will find it helpful to be reminded in a timely fashion about the maintenance that is required on their car. Maintenance work is a source of revenue for the dealer, as is sales of parts. The cost of the program is shared by Volvo and its participating dealers. It covers new car owners through five years.

The program starts with a welcome letter which describes the future contacts. Personalized maintenance reminders are mailed prior to the anniversary of purchase every 6 months through 48 months of ownership. The maintenance reminders contain computerized details regarding the specific maintenance needed. The reminders are mailed in the name of the original dealer. The program includes *Via Volvo,* an owners' magazine which provides the customer with interesting, lifestyle editorial contents, plus information on new Volvo models.

At 52 months, owners are personally invited to request an estimate for a trade-in. At 58 months, owners are invited to receive an estimate for the cost to recondition their present car or the cost for trading model for model. When the five-year program is completed, a special parts and service program starts and follows the owners for the next four years with personalized discount coupons covering required replacements.

The program budget is $1 million a year. Dealers have been pleased and their participation is close to 100 percent. Over 20,000 favorable responses were received from Volvo owners the first year, with 13,000 response cards requesting additional information about a particular Volvo product. Customer response has been very good, with 19 percent of the business coming from Volvo owners who had not been having their car serviced at a Volvo dealer.

As for small retailers, they cannot possibly design, produce, or even buy the kinds of POP material they receive, often without charge, from manufacturers. For more elaborate and expensive POP, such as merchandise racks, retailers may be required to pay an amount that is substantially less than their actual cost. This token payment is a subtle request for support. If the retailers pay for a POP display, they are more likely to use it. Sometimes the price of the display may not be specified in dollars, but in units of reorder. The point-of-purchase material thus becomes an inducement to buy. But competition among manufacturers for good display locations in stores limits their ability to pass along to retailers high charges for POP material. There are preferred spaces in every store — in the windows, at the cash register, near the wrapping desk in a department store, at the aisle ends in a supermarket, at the check-out counter or behind the counter in a restaurant or bar.

But retailers benefit greatly from the increased sales that POP materials can stimulate. Good displays convert customers who are "just looking" into

customers who buy. Some displays also serve as a source of product information for retail sales people. Point-of-purchase is of benefit to consumers, too. It frequently supplies them with information they need to make a buying decision. And, it does indeed speed up the shopping process, converting street traffic into store traffic.

Distribution of POP

Unlike other advertising methods, it is difficult to get point-of-purchase materials into the hands of the retailers. Often, manufacturers merely ship the display to the retailer at the most appropriate time and hope that the retailer will be pleased and install it promptly. Some manufacturers have field personnel deliver and install their POP material. For more complicated installations, the manufacturer may contract with a local firm to do the installation work.

Last Word on POP

Point-of-purchase is, by its nature, not truly advertising, but in many instances it is listed within the advertising budget. It should, however, be classified as a sales promotion activity or tool, not an advertising activity. We have discussed the subject of POP here because in many companies it is the job of the advertising manager to plan, select, and buy POP material. Needless to say, advertising managers must coordinate their activities with those of the sales promotion managers to make effective use of this promotional device.

Summary

The national advertiser has, in addition to the big guns of broadcast and print advertising, an arsenal of small arms for the assault on the consumer and on the dealers who serve that consumer. Direct advertising and, more important, direct-mail advertising, the most selective of all advertising procedures, offer a rifle approach after the scatter-fire of the big media barrage. Unless we aim for important targets or unless our percentage of "hits" is high, however, direct-mail advertising can be very expensive. Direct mail is a particularly effective way to reach key prospects in industry and business who are difficult, expensive, or impossible to reach through print media except with great waste. Direct mail demands not only the careful compilation of lists of targets, but the constant maintenance of that list. Mailing lists may also be purchased or rented from list houses or list brokers.

The advertiser may also choose to use specialty advertising and point-of-purchase advertising. The former is usually used to remind the business customer, the latter to remind the general consumer. The great asset of POP is that it reaches the consumer at a very important time and place — in the retail store at the time of purchase decision.

Questions for Discussion

1. What is the difference between direct advertising and direct-mail advertising? Between mail-order operations and direct-mail advertising?
2. What are the strengths and limitations of direct-mail advertising?
3. What purposes can be served by package inserts?
4. Name some sources for building a mailing list.
5. What is co-op mailing?
6. What are some uses of specialty advertising?
7. How does an advertising specialty differ from a premium?
8. Why is point-of-purchase valuable to the manufacturer of consumer products? What are some of the problems that may be encountered?

Sources and Recommendations for Further Reading

Direct Mail Advertising & Selling for Retailers. New York: National Retail Merchants Association, 1978.

Fishman, Arnold. "The Apparel Mail Order Marketplace." *Direct Marketing,* June 1986.

Fitch, Ed. "Agencies Teach Clients Some New Steps." *Advertising Age,* October 11, 1984.

Gelfand, M. Howard. "Seeking Creativity Among the Teaser Envelopes." *Advertising Age,* April 16, 1984.

Graham, John W., and Susan K. Jones. "Print Media: Strategy and Execution." *Direct Marketing,* May 1986.

Herpel, George, L., and Steve Slack. *Specialty Advertising: New Dimensions in Creative Marketing.* Irving, Tex.: Specialty Advertising Association International, 1983.

Kalish, David. "Hitting Consumers Where They Shop." *ADWEEK,* May 5, 1986.

Mintz, Steven. "Catalogues Get down to Business-to-Business. *Sales & Marketing Management,* November 15, 1982.

Ornstien, Edwin J. *Mail Order Marketing.* London: Gower Press Limited, 1970.

Paganetti, JoAnn. "Sales Sprout from the Seeds of Segmentation." *Advertising Age,* January 17, 1983.

Powell, Jim. "The Lucrative Trade of Crafting Junk Mail." *New York Times,* June 20, 1982.

Stone, Bob. *Successful Direct Marketing Methods.* 2nd edition. Chicago: Crain Books, 1979.

This emblem makes all the difference in the world.

The emblem is the mark of a leader. It is found only on a special group of cars and trucks in the world: those of General Motors.

From our beginnings, General Motors has been a worldwide leader. We pioneered now taken-for-granted basics like electric self-starters and automatic transmissions. We led the way in safety with shatter-proof windshields, energy-absorbing steering columns, side-guard door beams and crash testing. And have been responsible for many other industry "firsts."

FEEL THE DIFFERENCE GENERAL MOTORS MAKES

Today, General Motors is still leading with developments in laser technology, magnetic research and computer applications. And what we learn in the lab, we quickly put on the road.

General Motors vehicles are as advanced as the moment. Choose one. You'll feel the difference the GM emblem represents. Then keep that great GM feeling with genuine GM parts and service. It's a good feeling to have the world behind you. The world of General Motors.

 CHEVROLET
 PONTIAC
 OLDSMOBILE
 BUICK
 CADILLAC
 OPEL
 HOLDEN
 GMC TRUCK
 BEDFORD

CREATIVE ASPECTS

◀It's true. The GM emblem is recognized all over the world. And that's the effectiveness of advertising.

13 PRODUCT IDENTIFICATION: BRANDING AND PACKAGING

Working Vocabulary

trade name	store brand	collective mark
family name	distributor brand	certification mark
trademark	Lanham Act	service mark
brand name	Principal Register	logotype
national brand	Supplemental Register	slogan
private brand	trade character	

The old adage "Build a better mousetrap and the world will beat a path to your door" assumes that no one else has an improved mousetrap and that your potential customers know your improved version is available. In the real world, even a superior product may not succeed if its manufacturer fails to use every means possible to distinguish it from its competitors.

"The Nielsen Researcher"

Since trading among civilized peoples began, artisans and craftsmen have placed their name, mark, or brand on the products they have created. The object of these marks was to identify the manufacturer — who would be held responsible for a poor product, of course — but basically it was to assure buyers that they were in fact getting what they bargained for. A trademark or brand name is used today in very much the same way: to facilitate selection of a particular product that has been distinguished or presold through advertising or some other means of promotion.

Trademarks and Brand Names

Identifying the Product

If a company is to benefit from its advertising investment, consumers must be able to identify that company's products and to specify them when purchasing. We have earlier recognized that each product has a different set of attributes — either inherent in the product, or existing only in the minds of consumers. For consumers, the ability to identify the product of their choice and to receive that product consistently adds to their satisfaction. As consumers, we have, in most cases, singled out a product that provides us with the most satisfying combination of taste, smell, design, and *image.*

There are, you will agree, relatively few products today that are not clearly identified by a brand name. The most notable examples are agricultural products. We do not buy such products as corn, potatoes, or apples by specifying the grower. We do indeed recognize the difference between Long Island potatoes and Idaho potatoes, but that is a basic difference for which Nature is responsible, not the farm or the farmer who grew them. A similar comparison can be

In July 1984, Sears, Roebuck and Company unveiled a new logo in an identification program that extends to millions of catalogs, products, credit cards, vehicles, signs, and paper goods all across the United States. The new logo — replacing the familiar Sears name in a rectangle used for more than 20 years — features the Sears name in custom-designed capital letters. The company believes the new logo reflects the contemporary personality of Sears as the "Store of the Future" — following dramatic merchandising changes in the more than 600 Sears stores. The new logo is only the third in the company's 98-year history, succeeding a circular design from the 1950s and the rectangular design introduced in 1963.

made between Florida's Indian River oranges and California's Sunkist oranges. Indian River and Sunkist represent cooperative efforts by growers to identify a *type* of agricultural product. They are not brand names for the produce of individual growers. When the oranges are processed, they become Tropicana, Minute Maid, or Snow Crop brand orange juice. Only when agricultural products are processed are the producers or processors required to identify themselves. Wheat is wheat, but Hecker's Flour is not Pillsbury's. Grapes may be grapes, but Gallo wine is not Taylor wine. When we want to buy a pound of potatoes, we ask for a pound of potatoes, but when we want a bag of potato chips, we specify Pringle's or Lay's.

Trade Names

Many companies, particularly those that manufacture different products, adopt a **trade name.** Such a name might be compared to the "stage" names that movie stars or musicians might adopt because the stage names are more easily remembered by the public than their real names. In a similar fashion, companies adopt their trade names or commercial names. Consider the many famous names in American industry that are not the names of products, but of the companies producing the products: Kimberly-Clark, Bristol-Myers, General Foods, Union Carbide, Minnesota Mining and Manufacturing. Do you know the names of some of the well-known products of these companies? Sometimes a company will change its corporate name to match its more famous trade name. For years, the National Biscuit Company was best known for its Nabisco brand of cookies, crackers, and baked goods. The company ultimately changed its name to Nabisco, Inc.

Companies that produce an extensive line of products use their trade name as a **family name** to help build strong identification among their entire "family" of products. (See color plate 34.) The value of the family or trade name becomes more apparent as the company adds new products to its line and wants consumers to have as much confidence in the new product as in the old. This is particularly valuable for product lines related to health care, such as pharmaceuticals.

Identifying the Brand

In marketing, the words *trademark* and *brand name* are sometimes used interchangeably, but they do not always refer to the same thing. A **trademark** is a pictorial device, number, letter, or other symbol used to identify a product or product family, and under law it may perform no function other than identification. A **brand name** is used to identify a specific product and is a variety of trademark. For example, the word NABISCO set inside an oval surmounted by a cross is the trademark for the Nabisco corporation's line of food products. NILLA ® wafers is the brand name of one of those products; when the word NILLA is printed in the distinctive style of type featured on the package, it is also that product's trademark. Manufacturers may thus identify their products with both a trademark and a brand name — or the trademark and brand name may be identical.

The use of brand names and trademarks is not confined to manufacturers. They are also used extensively by retailers and wholesalers. A manufacturer's brands are usually called **national brands;** a middleman's brands are called **private brands, store brands,** or **distributor brands.** Kenmore products from Sears and Lucerne products from Safeway are well-known store brands.

These logos are so familiar to us that we recognize them instantly. Note how simple they are. They can be reduced to a very small size in ads or brochures and still retain their distinctive identity. They can be enlarged for outdoor displays without appearing gross. Do you recognize the second one from the top? Shell of course.

Although each product bears its own distinctive registered brand name — OREO®, RITZ®, TRISCUIT® — all of the products in this illustration are tied together and enhanced by the use of the Nabisco symbol. Consumers recognize the Nabisco trademark as identifying a good, reliable product. This makes it easier for Nabisco to introduce new products to its line — not necessarily new brands of cookies and crackers, but also products such as its cheese spreads and pitted dates.

Legalities

The **Lanham Act of 1946**[1] defines a trademark as any word, name, symbol, device, or any combination of these elements used by a company to identify its goods and distinguish them from those manufactured or sold by others. Brand names and trademarks are considered synonymous in law. The American Marketing Association considers a brand name a name that can be stated or spoken orally and a trademark a word or symbol that can be visualized.[2]

Brands are registered with the United States Patent and Trademark Office. In fact, about 20,000 trademarks are registered each year. Although recognized by common law, the brand enjoys added protection when it is registered.

Exclusions The registration of a brand name of trademark is good for 20 years and may be renewed every 20 years indefinitely. If abandoned, the brand name or trademark becomes public domain. The Lanham Act specifically *excludes* registration of four types of names and marks:

1. names and marks that so resemble existing ones for the same generic product as to be likely to confuse or mislead the consumer[3]

---

[1] The Lanham Trade-Mark Act of 1946, 15 U.S.C.A. 1051 *et seq.*
[2] "Report of the Brand Names Committee," *Journal of Marketing* (October 1948), pp. 205–206.
[3] Section 2 of the Lanham Act states the exclusion in no uncertain terms: ". . . consists of or comprises a mark which so resembles a mark registered in the Patent Office or a mark or trade name previously used in the United States by another and not abandoned, is to be likely, when applied to the goods of the applicant, to cause confusion, or mistake or to deceive purchasers."

2. any word or symbol that is merely descriptive, geographically descriptive, or deceptive and misleading
3. surnames that are the same as brands already in use
4. anything contrary to good taste or anything contrary to public policy, which means anything disparaging to people, beliefs, or institutions; flags, coats of arms, or insignia of the United States or any state, municipality, or foreign country; or the name, portrait, or signature of any living person without written permission

Registering the Trademark   A brand must be used in interstate commerce before it can be registered. To meet that requirement, the name can be used on the product's package or in its national advertising. A trademark is not like a patent; it confers no ownership. Trademark rights are recognized as common-law rights, based on priority of use, continuous use, and diligence in proper use and defense. Registration of a trademark is a validation, an official recognition of what is already in use.

Primary registration of a trademark is accomplished by registering it in the **Principal Register,** which is considered evidence of exclusive ownership of that trademark for products sold in the United States. The registration may be challenged by a person or company claiming prior use of the trademark. After five years on the Register without challenge, permanent legal right is recognized.

There is also a **Supplemental Register** used for the registration of names and symbols that cannot be registered in the Principal Register because they are descriptive words, surnames, or geographical names. Such words must be in use for at least one year prior to registration. The law recognizes that such words take on a secondary meaning after they have been used for five years or more to identify and distinguish products from a particular source. The Supplemental Register was created by the Lanham Act.

Trademark law offers the advertiser three methods of indicating (on the package or on the item itself) that a trademark or brand has been registered:

1. Registered in U.S. Patent Office
2. Reg. U.S. Pat. Off.
3. ®

® is the most convenient and practical way to indicate registration. Of course, companies must take care not to represent their trademarks as registered before they actually are; the courts may interpret such an act as a false claim. Before a trademark has been legally registered, companies usually use the notation "trademark" or "TM." Copies of material supporting the claim to first use in commerce must be presented to support the registration.

Objectives in Trademarks

National advertisers want their trademarks to be easily and quickly identifiable through the senses of sight and sound. When manufacturers identify one of their products most closely by its brand name, they will stress that word or phrase in their advertisements. Where visual identification is most important, the advertiser will use symbols, designs, pictures, or shapes because they are easily memorized. This means of identification is very important because many people read poorly and some may not even be able to read at all.

For advertisers, there are several benefits to be gained from clear identification of their products. Strong brand recognition protects them from unfair competition by distinguishing their products from products of lesser quality. Strong brand recognition offers manufacturers improved control over the channels of distribution and deflects attempts by retailers to substitute private or house brands. Strong brand recognition helps add a psychic appeal to their advertising. Strong brand recognition helps establish sales preference and may, if possible, give their products the character of specialty goods.

Brand names also help make life simpler for consumers. When making repeat purchases, consumers can avoid the brands that did not satisfy or insist upon the brands that did. And, when consumers are unfamiliar with a certain category of products, they can reduce the chance of making an unsatisfactory purchase by specifying a recognizable brand name. To the consumer, the brand name is an indicator of product quality. The name transmits an image of the product.

Choosing a Trademark or Brand Name

A trademark cannot be deceptive and cannot be confusingly similar to an existing trademark. Del Monte, for example, is a well-known and respected brand name. So for a canner of fruits and vegetables to use a name such as "Bel Monti," for example, would be so obviously deceptive as to be indefensible in a court of law. Descriptive words such as *good, large, rich, thick,* and *better* are also not permitted. Where do manufacturers find brand names for their products, then?

Historical Names   Prince Albert, Martha Washington, George Washington, Lincoln, John Hancock, and Napoleon are just a few of the many famous names that now identify a wide range of products. Can you name these products?

The Personal Name of the Company's Founder   Ford, Westinghouse, Coty, Taylor, Heinz, Lipton, and hundreds of thousands of lesser-known personal names are used to identify both manufactured products and retail stores alike.

Fictitious Names   Jack Frost, Betty Crocker, and Skippy.

Foreign Words   Ma Griffe, Tueros, Le Mans, Progresso, Lowenbrau, Goya, Chun King, Kikkoman, and Sabra add a touch of glamour or a hint of different flavor or exotic aroma. (See color plates 35 and 72 for ads promoting products with foreign names.)

Coined Words and Dictionary Words   Whirlpool, Arrow, Carnation, Acme, Premium, and Crest are all dictionary words given a new meaning by the advertiser. Supermarkets and department stores are filled with products that are branded with coined words such as Hotpoint, Frigidaire, Kodak, RIT, Kimbies, O-Cedar, Listerine, and Chux, to name only a few.

Initials and Letters   Names like Preparation H, 4711, STP, Formula 9, and ZBT have become increasingly popular, perhaps because they suggest some secret ingredient or formula.

Places and Institutions, Real or Fictional   Maxwell House, Pepperidge Farm, Parker House, Vermont Maid, French Market, Carolina Rice, and

Maryland Club benefit from the reputation that grows up around a hotel, inn, or region of the country for a particular food specialty. The name French Market coffee suggests that it is the same blend that is served in the old French quarter of New Orleans; Vermont Maid suggests the famous maple syrup from Vermont. The names of many products have been chosen to benefit from such implications.

Attributes of a Trademark or Brand

Distinctive   Because the main purpose of the brand or trademark is to identify or distinguish the product, the name or mark chosen should be as distinctive as possible. The marketplace is filled with such overworked names as Royal, Prince, Standard, Crown, and General, as well as such overused symbols as circles, crosses, diamonds, and triangles. A distinctive name or symbol is not only more easily remembered, but it offers better graphic opportunities for print and television advertising.

Suggestive   A well-chosen name may have a suggestive quality that ties in with the advertising theme of the product or with a particular product attribute. Jell-O (gelatin dessert), Chux (disposable diapers), Instapure (water filters), and Beautyrest (mattresses) are a few well-known brands whose names contributed to the marketing success of the product.

Appropriate   Many products are surrounded by a certain mystique in the minds of American consumers, and the brand names chosen for these products should take these preconceptions into account. Many people think cigars should have Spanish names. Most do. They think perfumes should have French-sounding names. Most do. Vodka needs a Russian-sounding name such as Smirnoff or Popov. Imagine a tequila called Smirnoff or a vodka called Jose Cuervo! Names that conform to the consumer's expectations contribute to the image of the product.

Easy to Remember   The name or the trademark must not only be easy to remember but easy to read, easy to spell, and easy to pronounce. Consumers will not want to embarrass themselves in front of a salesperson by mispronouncing a name. Some companies take great care to make sure that consumers do not mispronounce their products' names. Baume Bengue is a classic case in which a company simply changed the spelling of the brand name to Ben–Gay to preclude any misunderstanding. In its advertising, Dewar's Scotch reminds us to pronounce its brand name *do–ers.* One company began marketing a brand of cheese called Pollio, apparently named after the founder of the company. Consumers thought the name was pronounced *polio!* It was not long before the company precluded any problems by spelling the brand name *Polly-O* and using a parrot for a symbol. The point is: if any unpleasant association can be attached to a brand name, don't use it.

Often, consumers themselves will refer to a product by a shortened name or nickname, and advertisers usually find it expedient to adopt the abbreviated version and to register it. Consider: *Luckies* for Lucky Strike, *Pepsi* for Pepsi-Cola, *Coke* for Coca-Cola, *Bud* for Budweiser, and *Chevy* for Chevrolet. On the other hand, though a driver may refer affectionately to his or her car as a "Caddy," the advertiser has chosen to maintain the name Cadillac on the grounds that it lends more dignity to the product.

Family Names

One of the most important branding decisions an advertiser has to make is whether to use an individual brand name for each product in a product line or to group all the products together under a single *family name*. General Motors uses a different name for each of its automobile lines. So do Chrysler and Ford. But Lever Brothers and Procter & Gamble give each of their products an individual brand name.

Many companies market their products under family names. The family name lends itself to institutional advertising. The good will built by the reputation of each product spreads to all the others in the family line. The H. J. Heinz Company, for example, merely names its products Heinz soups, Heinz beans, Heinz ketchup, Heinz pickles, and so forth. Estee Lauder markets an extensive line of fine cosmetics, all clearly identified as Estee Lauder lipshine, Estee Lauder body lotion, and Estee Lauder fragrance spray. The use of family names also simplifies the launching of a new product because the problem of selecting a name for the new product is eliminated. Of course, when products are completely unrelated, they do not benefit from a common identity and may even, in some cases, be handicapped. Procter & Gamble, for example, names each of its products individually: Ivory soap (bath soap), Ivory Snow (laundry soap), and Downy (fabric softener). Although most consumers do not know the corporate name behind these products, they do know that Procter & Gamble stands for soap products. Therefore, it might be difficult for Procter & Gamble to market other types of products under its company name. People might not find Procter & Gamble cake mix or Procter & Gamble peanut butter very appetizing. Duncan Hines or JIF would be much more appealing.

What's in a Name

Every now and then manufacturers give one of their products a name similar to a nationally known brand name. Such imitation may be merely flattery or it may be intended to cause confusion in the mind of the consumer. In either case, it is illegal and constitutes a patent infringement. It doesn't matter if your name really *is* Pillsbury; you cannot market flour or a line of cake mixes under that name. Manufacturers go to great trouble and expense to build a trademark or brand name — and to protect it.

One of the problems that plagues advertisers is the public's tendency to use a brand name to refer to *a type of product*. A classic example is *cellophane,* which was developed by Du Pont Corporation and registered as a brand name. But Du Pont failed to prevent widespread misuse of the word *cellophane* as a name for all brands of transparent tape, and, consequently, it become generic. Now Du Pont and other companies with valuable brand names are careful to defend them. They are quick to point out to consumers that Kleenex is a brand of tissues, that Frigidaire is a brand of refrigerator, that Dacron is a brand of polyester, that Band–Aid is a brand of adhesive bandage, and that Scotch Tape is a brand of cellophane tape.

To protect their trademarks, some manufacturers add a descriptive word or phrase after their trademark or brand. It's not just Q-Tips, it's "Q-Tips ® cotton swabs." If the public develops an abbreviation for a brand name, such as Coke for Coca-Cola, most manufacturers will register the abbreviated form as a separate and additional brand name. They also try to educate company personnel, product users, and the news media regarding the proper use of their brand names or trademarks. The most important step a company can take to protect its trademark is to police the market vigorously, taking legal action where necessary.

Trade Characters

Trade characters are real or fictional people or animals that can be as important as brand names and trademarks in identifying products or product families. Consumers will associate a good trade character with a particular manufacturer or product, and, whenever they see that character, they will also think of that manufacturer or that product. Where possible, advertisers have taken advantage of the popularity of an existing "character" to augment recognition of their product. Mickey Mouse watches? Of course. And Mickey is joined by characters created specifically for the product — Betty Crocker, Mr. Clean, the Jolly Green Giant, the Red Baron, the White Rock Girl, the Pillsbury doughboy, Mr. Peanut, and hundreds of others.

In the mind of the consumer, a trade character may stand for a particular attribute of a product or may provide a general image that enhances the prod-

The Jolly Green Giant and Chiquita Banana are familiar trade characters.

uct. The Jolly Green Giant, representing canned and frozen vegetables and other frozen foods, adds a whimsical touch to the company's advertising as well as a nostalgic reminder of childhood and the long-forgotten story of Jack and the Beanstalk. Mr. Clean, representing a household cleaner, is portrayed as a clean, pleasant, friendly person who is willing to help the homemaker with the thankless task of housecleaning. Not a woman and not an ordinary man, Mr. Clean is dressed in a sailor's clothes because sailors are accustomed to scrubbing decks (floors) and polishing the brass (household appliances). The earring that Mr. Clean wears tells consumers that he is a genie—a fantasy character who does their bidding. Mr. Clean is a good trade character and the public has accepted both the image and the product. (See color plate 36 for an example of how trade characters change with the times.)

Other Advertising Marks

A **collective mark** is a trademark or service mark used by members of a cooperative, an association, or some other collective group. Collective marks also include marks used to indicate membership in a union. The Cotton Council's mark is an example of a collective mark.

A **certification mark** is a mark used to certify a product's origin, mode of manufacture, quality, or accuracy; it may also indicate that the product was made by members of a particular organization or association. One such mark is the Wool Bureau's pure-wool mark below.

A **service mark** is used in the sale and advertising of services and includes symbols, names, titles, designations, slogans, characters, and other distinctive features. Such marks include the Travelers Insurance Company's red umbrella mark (shown below).

A **logotype** is a representation of the brand name or trade name in an advertisement. The word is also used to designate the company name that appears at the bottom of its print advertisements. It is referred to as the *logo.*

Licensing

Unless you've been sleeping in a time capsule, you'll recognize such licensed properties as Mickey Mouse, Snoopy, Gloria Vanderbilt, Garfield, and Care Bears. In the coming few years you will meet Mirthworms, Stompers, SweetSea, Krindles, Shag E. Dawg, and Runny Nose. The licensing field is

PURE WOOL

When groups of producers plan an advertising program to stimulate primary demand for a type of product, the use of a distinctive emblem (such as the "Pure Wool" label, left) fosters recognition by the public.

In addition, the development of an identifying symbol or word allows cooperative advertising of services (such as the Travelers' umbrella, below, which links individual insurance agents all over the country).

crowded in most categories, including toys and children's items, designers and entertainment. The toy category tends to be in the forefront of changes in the developing and licensing of properties. More than half of all toys sold in recent years were licensed in some way. Licensing is entrenched as a marketing tool. Competition has forced marketers to develop sophisticated plans for advertising to sell complete license programs rather than one-shot products.

Licensing is not new. In 1904, Brown Shoe Company purchased rights to use the name of Buster Brown, a popular turn-of-the-century comic strip character, to promote its line of children's shoes at the St. Louis World's Fair. In the 1930s, classics such as Mickey Mouse, Donald Duck and other Disney properties lent their names to a range of products.

In the 1950s and 1960s, licensing started to emerge as a stronger marketing tool, but it wasn't until the 1970s that it boomed. The boom started with Strawberry Shortcake. By 1977, licensing was a $4 billion industry in the United States. By 1990, it is expected that retail sales for licensed merchandise will reach $75 billion.

Packaging

Carefully planned packaging, like carefully planned products, can benefit the manufacturer, the dealer, and the consumer. The package is often considered by consumers as a component of product quality and in this sense a change in packaging becomes a meaningful product improvement.[4]

Essentials of Package Design

Packages are forms of advertising at the point of sale. They have become an integral part of most products and may be, for many, one of their most important attributes. The pump-spray container in which a deodorant or hair spray is packaged is — in view of the potential dangers of pressurized sprays — an added quality feature. Other products offer shatterproof containers; built-in spouts for better pouring; tab-lock tops for easier closing; cutting edges; and "mix-in," "bake-in," or "cook-in" features. In many instances, the package is what keeps the product sold; that is, it helps to keep the consumer brand loyal. When consumers encounter a leaking container or a box that is difficult to open and even more difficult to reclose, the blame falls on the product, not the package. These consumers are not likely to develop loyalty to the brand despite the fact that they may have been satisfied with the product itself. A case in point is the safety cap on aspirin and cold tablet containers that many people find difficult to open. Because of consumer dissatisfaction with this type of package, a number of firms now provide bottles with ordinary caps as well as the safety caps. Consider, too, the tremendous advertising effort behind the flip-top cigarette box. Since good packaging is so important, advertisers must keep in mind the characteristics that consumers look for in a package:

1. *Product protection*
   Consumers want the package to protect the product against spoilage, leakage, evaporation, and breakage.

---

[4] Albert W. Frey and Jean Halterman. *Advertising,* 4th ed. (New York: Ronald Press, 1970), p. 23.

The evolution of the distinctive bottle for Coca-Cola is shown in the photographs above. The bottle itself became an important identification of the product. The ad on the far right was one of the first to introduce the new bottle to America.

Coca-Cola Co., in replacing what has been an old friend to the American public, may have created an even stronger position for its brands. The mistake, if it was a mistake, could prove to be one of the best things that could have happened. The new Coke provides the company with a sweeter line extension. If the firm had merely introduced the new Coke as a line extension, the bottlers might have balked. They would have asked "Who needs two different Cokes?" Astounded at the American consumers' passion for the old Coke, Coca-Cola made a fast move to bring it back under the name Coca-Cola Classic. The company admitted they made a mistake — not in introducing the new Coke but in dropping the old. Within hours of the announcement that "old Coke" would be coming back as Coca-Cola Classic, a national phone survey of consumers indicated that 68 percent of the respondents said they felt good that Coca-Cola would distribute both the original Coke as well as the new Coke.

The moral of the story is the consumer is still the boss.

2. *Convenience*

Consumers want the package to be easy to open and easy to reclose. They want it to be easy to hold and easy to pour. They want it to fit in their pantries or in their medicine cabinets, in their refrigerators or under their sinks. Odd shapes, designed to be cute or appealing, end up unused because they cannot be easily stored. The package should also be disposable. And, perhaps most important, all the contents should be removable. Nothing makes consumers feel cheated more than not being able to remove part of the contents of a jar, bottle, or tube. They want that last drop.

3. *Identification*

Consumers do not want to search for hours to find their favorite brands on the shelf. The package must join with the brand name, the trademark, and the trade character in identifying the product. Consumers want to be able to distinguish their preferred brands from among the competing brands without difficulty. And they want to be able to identify the product easily again once it is in their medicine cabinets or pantries. No mistakes wanted.

The type style and the design of a product's label must keep up with the changing tastes and styles of consumers. It is one thing to purposefully give a package or a label an old-fashioned look — if it is part of the product's image, the consumer will understand. But, to maintain a label or package design that is out of fashion can lead customers to question the modernity of the product. Campbell's soup is an old and trusted friend in a new dress. Why didn't Campbell's retain the old package the way Coca-Cola retained the shape of its bottle for 64 years? Because the shape of the bottle is distinctive in itself, the can is not. It is the label on the can that distinguishes it from other canned products.

4. Information

Consumers want product information. They want a fair and accurate representation of the product and of the results they can expect from the product. Consumers want all the necessary directions for opening, closing, mixing, cooking, and pouring. They have certain preconceptions about the type of packaging appropriate for a product, and manufacturers cannot violate these preconceptions. In Europe, condiments are commonly packaged in collapsible tubes. Such packaging can only be utilized for toothpastes and other personal care products in the United States. Jams and jellies cannot be packaged in cans. Baking powder is always in round cans.

Dealer Requirements

Retailers want the packages of the goods they stock to have many of the same characteristics that their customers want. Retailers want the package to protect the product against leakage and spoilage, to be sure. But, in addition, they want the package to be pilfer-proof. They want packages that can easily be coded and that will avoid looking shelf-worn. Dealers want to be sure that the packages will fit on their shelves or in their refrigerators or in their freezer showcases. Good packaging should also make it easier for retailers to sell more efficiently.

To the packaging characteristics demanded by consumers and retailers, manufacturers will add a few requirements of their own. The package should be economical to produce. Since the cost of the package is included in the price the retailers and the consumers pay, manufacturers do not want the package to add unduly to that price. Manufacturers want the package to have sales appeal. The package should be attractive; the style, the design, and the colors should be as eye-catching, as appropriate, and as functional as possible. Also, the product identification should be highly visible on all sides so that if store clerks do not place the package correctly on the shelf, the customer will still be able to spot it.

Briefly, then, the package should be easily identifiable and related, if possible, to the packages of all the other products in the family. It should fit well on retailers' shelves, be easy to price mark, and protect the product thoroughly. The package should conform to all the rules of the FTC, the FDA, the USDA, and all other state, federal, or local regulations that pertain. For drug products these regulations often present packaging problems. A small jar of tablets will often have barely enough room for all the necessary dosage, formula, and precautionary information that is required. These problems have often been solved with great imagination. In some cases, it has been necessary to package the labeled bottle into a paperboard carton and to enclose a printed insert as well.

The principal federal agencies that regulate packaging are:

1. the Federal Trade Commission (FTC), which regulates deceptive packaging and labeling as it relates to unfair trade practices
2. the Environmental Protection Agency (EPA), which regulates packaging and use of insecticides, pesticides, and rodenticides
3. the Consumer Product Safety Commission (CPSC), which regulates household products, flammable fabrics, and children's toys
4. the Department of Agriculture (USDA), which regulates fresh and processed meats and poultry

5. the Department of the Treasury, which regulates alcohol, tobacco, firearms, explosives, and imported goods
6. the Department of Health, Education & Welfare (HEW)
7. the Food & Drug Administration (FDA), which regulates foods, drugs, cosmetics, and medical devices

Pretesting the Package Design

Good packaging research has to profile how a package works on each of the key areas that lead to sale. *Shelf visibility* — does it break through clutter? *Label layout* — will it be read? What, if anything, is ignored? And *shopper perceptions* — is it perceived as being good value for the money, safe to use, good tasting, made by a reputable company, convenient? And, are these perceptions compatible with the long-term marketing objectives for the brand?

It's implicit that every packaging design meets two primary criteria. It must have *shelf impact,* and it must convey the *brand's personality* and uniqueness.[5] A designer can attack these areas in many ways. He has three primary tools to work with — *shape, color,* and *graphics.* His ability to integrate these variables often determines the success or failure of the brand.

Stopping power is achieved through effective use of color, shape, and graphics. High involvement with the label is generally a result of a unique package shape and/or label layout. Shoppers' perceptions of the product are influenced by the total entity.

One technique for pretesting a package design is computerized eye-tracking. If you refer back to page 102, you will see the ad for Perception Research Services. The technology provides marketers a firsthand look at the shopper's discrimination process. The eye tracker pinpoints where a person is looking, how the shelves are scanned, which items are considered and, most importantly, which are overlooked. Since the behavior pattern is recorded on TV as it occurs, the shopper moves at his or her own speed. This uncovers those categories that are "high involvement" and those that tend to foster quick, impulsive product selection. From such research, marketers can add to the shelf visibility and impact of their packages.

Packaging Is Advertising

Is packaging a component of advertising? Or is it really a component of the product? The answer to both these questions is yes. The package, as we have already discovered, is an integral part of the product. But the package also plays an extremely important role in the promotion of the product. The package has evolved from merely a cover to protect the product to a means of making an active contribution to the marketing of that product. Advertisements for the product will strongly feature the package, and the picture of the product conjured up in the minds of consumers is, in many instances, really that of its package. In fact, when different brands of the same type of product all look, feel, taste, smell, and sound alike, the differences in the packaging of each

---

[5] The story is told about Albert D. Lasker dealing with the early days of marketing sanitary napkins. When Kotex was first put on the market, it was selling very poorly. Women didn't like having to ask the druggist for the product. Lasker's agency, Lord & Thomas, conceived the idea of wrapping the packages in plain paper and leaving them on the druggist's counter. Women could walk into the store and walk away with a wrapped package without embarrassment. Sales soared.

No, it is not a label recently designed to look old-fashioned. It *is* an old-fashioned label, and so is the product. But this label is still in use today on a product that is bought and used by consumers who don't go in for "new-fangled" products.

brand becomes the basis for consumer preference. (See color plate 37 for an ad highlighting a product package.)

Here are some of the promotional functions that a product's package can fulfill:

Packaging Is POP   The package can be a product's most important form of point-of-purchase advertising. In many areas of marketing, the package is also expected to do the work that was formerly performed by the salespeople in a store. The package can provide consumers with a demonstration and an explanation of the product.

Packaging Can Increase the Unit of Sale   Light bulbs are sold in four-bulb packages, soft drinks in six-packs, chewing gum in "family packs." All of these packages were designed to increase the size of the sale. Two or more different products in the same product family can also be packaged and sold together; or, a sample supply of one product can be packaged with another product in the same family.

Packaging Can Stimulate Gift Sales   A special package design can appeal to consumers who are shopping for a gift for a holiday or special occasion. However, the package must also be designed so that units that remain unsold after the "special occasion" can be kept on the shelves.

Packaging Can Convey Quality   In this respect the color of a package and the style of the type used to print information on it are critical. Consumers may believe that a detergent that comes packaged in a red box will be "too strong" for their needs. The same detergent packaged in a yellow box might impress them as too weak, while the same detergent in a blue or a green box might be just right. The design of a package can also convey a modern, home-style, country-style, or old-fashioned image to consumers. But even packages that want to have that "old-fashioned look" have to be modernized from time to time so that they are in keeping with contemporary ideas of what looks old-fashioned.

Slogans

A **slogan** is a phrase or a sentence that describes either the benefit derived from a product or one of the product's most important attributes. The slogan may be a relatively permanent addition to the advertiser's promotion or a temporary expression that captures the essence of a campaign theme. Permanent or temporary, the slogan is a carefully polished group of words intended to be repeated by consumers verbatim and to be remembered by them with a favorable reaction.

No slogan attains wide popularity at once. Promotion over a period of time is required to establish the slogan. Although some slogans may seem to have been around for ages, they were developed diligently over many years at the cost of many dollars. To be successful, a slogan should be built on one idea. A slogan should be brief (about four words), well-balanced, and easy to say. Consider some well-known slogans and see if they satisfy all the criteria:

WE TRY HARDER

IT FLOATS

WHEN IT RAINS IT POURS

THINGS GO BETTER WITH COKE

PROFILE

Roger Ferriter

In creating the name, package, and display unit for L'eggs panty hose, Roger Ferriter combined form and function so perfectly that the product ensemble became a packaging classic almost overnight. In fact, when the product was first test marketed in 1970, the results were 1,500 times greater than the manufacturer expected. From that beginning, L'eggs went on to become the best-selling brand of panty hose in the world — from a standing start to annual sales of almost $400 million in less than five years. One of the most influential publications in the advertising field, *Advertising Age,* described the name L'eggs as "the fastest 'trigger' on a package in the twentieth century."

What sort of man conceives such unique and effective packaging designs? Roger Ferriter studied illustration as an undergraduate student at Rhode Island School of Design, became interested in typography while serving in the Marine Corps, and studied photography and printmaking as a graduate student at Yale University. With this well-rounded background, he was able to land a job as an art director with the Young & Rubicam agency in New York soon after graduating from Yale. He was a corporate vice-president and creative director for Metromedia, Inc. in 1972, when he decided to go into business for himself, first in partnership with

another famous designer, Herb Lubalin, and later as the president of his own corporation, Roger Ferriter, Inc. He has designed packages, trademarks, and magazine logos and formats for such clients as Westinghouse, *Barron's,* and the World Trade Center.

In discussing the development of the L'eggs' packaging, Mr. Ferriter has confessed that he was hampered by the lack of some very fundamental information. His solution to the problem was characteristically inventive:

> No one could tell me what size to make the egg. Solution: the L'eggs' egg is exactly the size of my left fist. I could 'squonsch' up the panty hose in that fist — measured it, and made the egg that size.

When asked what were the most important skills college students should acquire if they plan to enter advertising, Mr. Ferriter replied:

> It is hard to give priorities, but here is a list based on my experience: (1) drawing, (2) painting, (3) photography, (4) two- and three-dimensional space division, (5) fundamentals in typography, production, math, and ENGLISH!

Finally, Mr. Ferriter says: "After you secure your first job, change jobs as soon as you are not in a learning experience — whether it's six months or six years."

Today, slogans are not used as frequently as they once were. The reason may be the growth of television: It is no longer necessary to create some mnemonic phrase when a live demonstration of the product will promote the product far better. Some very old slogans are still around, but have more nostalgic value than selling power.

Summary

The promotional effort is critically mixed with the product itself. An item to be sold consists not merely of the physical product, but also of the product's brand name and its package. For the consumer, the *brand name* or *trademark* is

Heineken

Though imported beers account for only 3.2 percent of the market, their sales growth has outpaced the rest of the industry, led in no small way by the brands imported by Van Munching & Co. In 1946, Van Munching & Co. was incorporated as exclusive U.S. importer for Amsterdam-based Heineken. Sales of the green bottles have climbed steadily — reaching 34.5 million cases in 1985. Heineken represents about 37 percent of imported beer sales, well ahead of its nearest competitor, Molson.

Until the early 1970s, imported beers were consumed by a small group of urban sophisticates. By the mid-1970s, imported beers had developed a broader-based cachet. A new group of consumers, with sophisticated taste and the income to support it, took to Heineken's class image and taste. Imports do not represent the "undershirt image."

Heineken's TV commercials are unique — the focus is on the product's taste as "the very best beer in the world" and the star is the bottle itself.

Meanwhile, Van Munching has entered the growing Canadian beer category with Grizzly, aimed at the 18-to-25-year-old market. As such, its campaign is markedly different from the urbane style of Heineken. Instead, the Grizzly radio spots are humorous and run mostly on young adult stations.

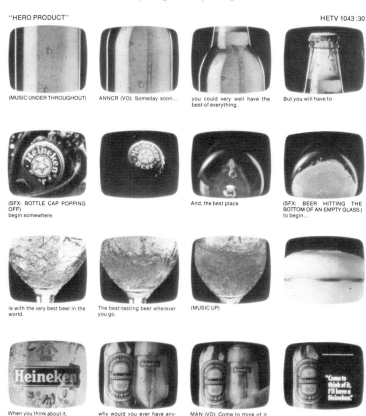

"HERO PRODUCT" HETV 1043 :30

(MUSIC UNDER THROUGHOUT)

ANNCR (VO): Someday soon...

you could very well have the best of everything.

But you will have to

(SFX: BOTTLE CAP POPPING OFF) begin somewhere.

And, the best place

(SFX: BEER HITTING THE BOTTOM OF AN EMPTY GLASS.) to begin...

is with the very best beer in the world.

The best-tasting beer wherever you go.

(MUSIC UP)

When you think about it,

why would you ever have anything else?

MAN (VO): Come to think of it, I'll have a Heineken.

virtually indispensable in identifying the company's products and in distinguishing them from competing goods. A great deal of thought must go into the creation of a brand name or a trademark: It must enhance the product's image and it must lend itself to use both graphically and orally in advertising and promotion. Legal regulations protect the brand name or trademark against infringement or against adoption as a generic term.

Packaging benefits the consumer and the dealer; it provides protection for the product, eye-catching appeal, convenience, easy identification, and information on the proper use of the product. The package may enhance sales by representing point-of-purchase impact, by stimulating trial usage, and by increasing multiple-unit purchases.

The overall packaging characteristics are determined for the most part by the size, construction, shape, material, closure, and design. The size of the package is determined by the physical characteristics of the product, the custom of the trade, the price of the product to the consumer, and the quantity that the consumer might purchase at one time. Sizes too large to fit the retailer's normal display facilities will meet resistance. Small sizes are subject to shoplifting — a serious problem today in retailing. However, it may be wise to package new products in containers that hold small amounts to stimulate trial purchases. Large sizes stimulate sales among heavy-users; large sizes are more economical and may convert light-users to heavy-users. The increase in the number of women working outside the home tends to stimulate sales of multiple packs, as they often prefer to shop less frequently.

Questions for Discussion

1. What are the benefits of using different brand names for products of different quality within the same product family? Are there any disadvantages?
2. What are the qualities the advertiser wants in a package?
3. What are the characteristics of a good trademark or brand name?
4. Can you think of several well-known products for which the original brand name has become generic?
5. What is a service mark? Under what conditions is it used?
6. What is the purpose of a label? How does the label or package benefit the consumer?

Sources and Suggestions for Further Reading

Abrams, Bill. "Exploiting Proven Brand Names Can Cut Risk of New Products." *Wall Street Journal* (January 22, 1981).
Diamond, Sidney A. "Brand Names, Trademarks." *Advertising Age* (August 17, 1981).
"Display Effectiveness: An Evaluation." *The Nielsen Researcher* (November 2, 1983).
Kalish, David. "Packages as Ads." *ADWEEK*, May 5, 1986.
Mamis, Robert A. "Name-Calling." *INC* (July 1984).
Moran, Dennis J. "How a Name Can Label Your Product." *Advertising Age* (November 10, 1980).
"Putting Teeth in the Trademark Laws." *Business Week* (October 8, 1984).
Seaman, Debbie. "Repositioning on Old-World Imagination." *Adweek* (October 8, 1984).

14 CREATIVE STRATEGIES

Working Vocabulary

appeal
creative strategy
purchasing decision
competitive strategy
frame of reference
membership reference groups
aspiration reference groups

disassociative reference groups
diffusion process
artificially new
marginally new
genuinely new
innovators
early adopters

early majority
late majority
laggards
rate of adoption
psychographics
VALS
positioning
brainstorming

We like to put expensive food on our tables, not always because it tastes better than cheap food, but because it tells our guests that we like them, or, just as often, because it tells them that we are well fixed financially.

S. I. Hayakawa
Language in Action

We have already made several important decisions — to advertise in the first place, to set up a budget or allocation of money, and to select a media plan after a careful analysis of all the pros and cons of the various media available to us. We have branded our product and registered the trademark we so carefully conceived. Now we are ready to create the actual advertisements that we will have printed in newspapers and magazines, posted on billboards and on the sides of buses, and broadcast on radio and television. We sharpen our pencils or turn to our typewriters; we are ready to begin — but what are we going to say? What words are we going to use? What pictures are we going to show?

Developing the Appeal

We can begin our search for the right words and pictures for our ads by reviewing our advertising goals. Each of our advertisements must contribute to the achievement of one or more of these goals. If our goal is to increase the quantity of purchase, what reasons can we give the members of our target market for buying more of our product? If our goal is to take customers from competing brands, what reasons can we give consumers for switching from their present brand to ours? If we want to stimulate a portion of our target market to act or to change an old attitude and adopt a new one that will lead to action in the future, we must supply them with a reason for doing so. This reason is our **appeal.** The appeal (or appeals) we choose and the combination of words and images that we use to convey it to our target market form our **creative strategy.**

The Purchasing Decision

In chapter 3, we noted that advertising's principal task is to make more sales than would have been made without advertising. For this reason, most creative strategies are designed to influence consumers' **purchasing decisions.** Because it is important to understand how consumers arrive at a purchasing decision, let's take a moment now to examine the process in detail:

1. *Awareness of a need*
   At this point a consumer's awareness may very well be unfocused. Perhaps the oven is not as clean as it should be or the bathtub has some stains on it that do not seem to come off. The consumer wants to remedy these problems, but does not know how.
2. *Awareness of a product — generic*
   The consumer learns about a *kind of product* from advertising, from general reading, or from a friend — no matter what the means, the consumer now knows that a product type exists that may remedy his or her problems. The consumer *may* then begin an active

search for the product by asking about it in a store or by carefully watching for an advertisement for such a product. Here, our advertising has one major function: to *teach* the consumer about the product. This teaching role is critical because the consumer's decision to purchase the product will depend on his or her knowledge and perception of the product. The consumer's *perception* of any product is purely subjective and based on the way the consumer sees the product satisfying a very personal need. The consumer does not want a remedy that relieves the discomfort of colds, but one that is perceived as having the power to relieve "my cold," "my headache," and "my running nose."

3. *Awareness of a specific brand*

   With or without an active search, the consumer becomes aware that a specific brand (or brands) exists that may meet his or her needs. When there are several brands of the same type of product on the market, our advertising must take a competitive approach. We want to show the consumer not only that the generic product cleans the oven or removes the stains from the bathtub, but that *our brand* does it better, faster, or cheaper.

4. *Making a purchasing decision*

   Two things can happen here. First, the consumer may not believe any of the ads, may be unwilling to spend the money for the product, or may be too lethargic to change existing buying habits. Result: no purchase behavior. Or, second, after consideration, the consumer may decide that one specific brand (we hope that it is *our brand*) will suit his or her requirements best. The consumer buys that brand and actually *tries* it. The consumer has, at long last, made a purchasing decision.

5. *Adopting a brand loyalty*

   If *our brand* has lived up to expectations, the consumer will repeat this purchase behavior and become one of our favorite people— brand-loyal customers. At this point, our advertising should reinforce the consumer's decision to stay with us. If *our brand* has not satisfied the consumer, however, the consumer will try another brand and keep switching until a satisfactory one is found.

By reaching prospective customers with appropriate messages at each stage in the purchasing decision, our creative strategy can persuade them to try *our brand*. In general, there are three basic types of creative strategies: the first emphasizes *product features* and *customer benefits;* the second emphasizes the product's or company's *image;* and the third attempts to *position* the product in the minds of our target market. The type of strategy that is best for us will depend on our advertising goals and our choice of appeal. We may, in fact, want to use a combination of any two, or even all three, of these approaches.

What Does the Product Offer?

Our search for the most effective creative strategy should begin with what we know best—our product. Our product has a number of physical attributes —such as taste, color, aroma, and texture—that can form the basis of our appeal. Very simply, then, we can list our product's features in one column and,

The Ajax power formula, with its 3 special bleaching and grease-cutting ingredients...

gives you immediate scrubbing action as it powers out the toughest greasy food stains.

There, a bright, sparkling clean sink. It's easy. And fast. Faster than Comet. Ajax turns your sponge into a scrub brush.

© 1978. Colgate-Palmolive Company.

What does the homemaker want from a kitchen cleanser? Power! Notice how the advertiser has used *power* as a verb: Ajax "powers out" the stains and does it "faster than Comet." The consumers accept the claim without requiring to know the particulars. It is enough for them to know that Ajax can power out stains faster than Comet because it has "three special bleaching and grease-cutting ingredients." This ad is purely competitive. The advertiser wants to enlarge its market share by taking customers from competing products. Note, too, that the advertiser's family name appears in *small* type in the lower left-hand corner of the ad. No one would want to think that Colgate toothpaste had *power* or that Palmolive soap had *power.*

next to each, the translation of that feature into a potential benefit for the prospective buyer. Then, we do the same, as far as we can determine, for our competitors. What do they have that we don't? What do we have that they don't?

If our product were chocolate chip cookies, for example, we might want to point out in our advertisements that the chips in our brand are made from a much richer chocolate than that used in any other brand. Perhaps our cookies are 50 percent larger than those of competing brands, or perhaps they are packaged in a special container that keeps them fresher longer than those of any other brand. For other types of products, we may want to call the consumer's attention to a unique feature of our brand, perhaps a patented device or an innovation not available from competitors.

We must take care, however, to translate the special features of our product into benefits for the consumer. A mere physical description of our product will not convince many people to buy it. Prospective purchasers are more interested in the results or benefits they will obtain from using our product. A jar of cold cream is not just a batch of chemicals; it is a smoother skin. A television set is not merely an elaborate assembly of electronic components; it is entertainment. In every case, we are selling something of interest to the buyer: fast relief; strong cleaning action; reliable service; or social success.

What if we were planning to promote a product for which there is no competition? No such thing. When the first electric slicing knife came to market, the competition was an ordinary slicing knife. At the time the first electric blanket came to market, people slept with plain wool blankets or down comforters. Many still do. If, in fact, our competition is the customary way something is done, then that type of competition demands a different strategy.

How the Product's Life Cycle Affects Creative Strategy

As we have already learned, every product has a life cycle. In developing our creative strategy, we must take into consideration the position of our product in this cycle. In the introductory stage of the cycle, our appeal should be directed toward the stimulation of primary demand. At this point the goal of our advertising should be to teach consumers about the product. We have to give them a reason to try our brand by explaining the uses, features, and benefits of all products of this type, regardless of brand. In the growth phase, after the market accepts our product, we can shift our emphasis to a **competitive strategy** — one emphasing the benefits of our brand over those of competing brands. As our product reaches the mature phase, the total market for the product becomes saturated, and our promotional effort must be directed toward maintaining our market share. In the mature phase, we are concerned with the fight for shelf space in retail outlets and with the prevention of the substitution of private brands for our own. At this stage our advertising should be designed to keep our brand name constantly before the public and to give brand-loyal consumers a reason to continue using our product.

Uncovering the Product's Subjective Appeal

When we examine the actual words and pictures that compose many successful advertisements, we often find that they tell us very little about the product's physical attributes. Consider the ads for Coca-Cola. Do they ever tell us that Coke is better than Pepsi because it contains 37 percent more kola nuts? Or consider the old ads for Winston cigarettes: "I like the box," says the man in the ad. Is that a reason for us to buy that brand of cigarette? Drink Stolichnaya, "the only vodka imported from Russia" (see ad on page 336). Did they tell you it tastes better than American vodka? Or that it is more mellow than Polish vodka? Not at all. What are they trying to communicate? (See color plate 38 for another liquor ad using a foreign image.)

Ads for imported products are usually very careful to tell readers how to pronounce the product's name. No one wants to look foolish by fumbling over the pronunciation. The ad is meant to project an image of the product. There is very little copy. What image would best represent *Russian* to American consumers? A red flag with the hammer and sickle? A symbol with bad connotations. The Kremlin walls? Not instantly recognizable. A borzoi hound? A symbol that has already been used by similar products. The advertiser has exercised considerable ingenuity in concocting an appropriate image. The bottle encased in a block of ice reminds us of the cold of the Russian climate (and the manner in which the vodka should be served), and the hammer with the Russian inscription reminds us of the traditional hammer and sickle symbol of Soviet Russia.

In our definition of a product in chapter 2, we pointed out that, in addition to its physical attributes, every product has a number of psychic attributes. In many cases, a product's psychic attributes are the major sources of consumer satisfaction. In order to develop the most effective creative strategy, we, as advertisers, have to understand what the customer wants and expects from our product. Motivation research can supply us with information that can help us understand the minds and psyches of the consumers in our target market. A cloud of meanings, some positive, some negative, surrounds every product. Once we learn to recognize the positive psychic attributes of our product, we can use them to form the basis of our appeal.

Most consumers find it hard to explain exactly why they buy a particular product. Either they don't really know why they made the purchase or they are reluctant to explain their motives to others. Cadillac's greatest sales asset is its symbolic association with achievement and financial success. But very few

Eldorado
BY CADILLAC

Unique in features. World-class in engineering. Cadillac in luxury.

This magnificent new Eldorado offers you an unprecedented combination of features found on no other U.S. car. Including "the big five": front-wheel drive ... four-wheel independent suspension ... electronic fuel injection ... four-wheel disc brakes ... electronic level control. All standard. Even side-window defoggers. But you may choose it simply because it's so beautiful. It's at your Cadillac dealer's now. At least once in a lifetime, drive a great car like this.

Cadillac owners would tell you that they bought the car for that reason. There is nothing wrong with a T-shirt and blue jeans. Yet, if you went to a doctor's office where the doctor and nurses were wearing faded jeans and T-shirts, you might have second thoughts about their professional skill. Most people consider this outfit as casual dress or as student dress. Worn by a professional in a professional setting, it represents arrested mental development. Such is the kind of meaning we attach to clothes. A dark suit and a white shirt with a tie convey a mature, responsible, serious image. A picture of the Eiffel Tower evokes France. The sound of Bouzouki music calls up images of Greece. We all recognize certain symbolic gestures that convey their meanings without words. A handshake, a pat on the back, and a wink all say something to us.

In similar fashion, special symbolism is attached to many products. Coffee represents friendliness and hospitality. Cigarette smoking has traditionally represented masculinity, virility, energy, and accomplishment. The advertisers of Marlboro cigarettes base their appeal on these psychic attributes of their product. The tattooed man in the original Marlboro ads and the cowboys and horses in the more recent ones say to the prospect: "This is a man's cigarette." To convey the appeal, the advertisements do not rely on words alone — often there is no printed message at all — but on nonverbal symbols. Recognizing the masculine symbolism attached to cigarettes, other advertisers saw that when a woman smokes, she is taking some prerogatives that were traditionally regarded as masculine and is demonstrating self-assertion, independence, and sophistication. The advertisers of Virginia Slims cigarettes made these aspects of cigarette smoking the basis of their appeal and emphasized those qualities in their advertisements.

Consumer Perceptions

We must always remember that advertising is communication with people — persuasive communication. We want to persuade consumers to do something after they have received our message. In order to get across the most effective message, we should know as much as possible about its receiver. Let's take a moment to examine the communication process.

First, we encode a message — putting it into the words, phrases, and illustrations that we believe convey our message best. The message is then transmitted to consumers by one of the mass media available. When consumers receive our message, they decode it into their own words, according to their *frames of reference.* The decoding is also affected by the receivers' *perceptions of the sender.* This is why many companies consider institutional advertising such an important part of their advertising efforts. By improving the image of a company as a whole, advertisers can improve the reception of the sales messages for that company's products.

We said earlier that consumers interpret the advertising message according to their *frames of reference.* What is a consumer's **frame of reference?** It is the cultural and social forces that have acted, and are always acting, on that individual. The cultural and social groups to which the consumer belongs affect the way he or she does things, sees things, uses things, and judges things. They help to determine what products consumers will buy and what newspapers and magazines they will read.

Reference Groups

A person is a member of many different groups at the same time. Of all the face-to-face groups, the family is usually the most important influence on an individual's choice of many products. Even if the individual acquires the symbols of another class, latent family influences will remain to affect his or her perceptions. **Membership reference groups,** to which a person automatically belongs because of sex, race, income, age, and marital status, also influence the way that person interprets an advertising message. **Aspiration reference groups** are those groups to which a person does not in fact belong, but which he or she wants to join. People will use the behavior and the purchasing decisions of their aspiration reference groups as models for their own actions. **Disassociative reference groups** are those groups to which a person *does not belong and does not want to belong.* No one wants to be fat or old or bald or grey.

You can drive the length of
Inverlocharig, Scotland, in less
time than it takes to blink.
But as local folk have known
for centuries, "Ye canna do it at rush hour."
The good things in life stay that way.

DEWAR'S
White Label
never varies.

COLOR PLATE 38

COLOR PLATE 38 Here's image advertising at its best—not selling whiskey, but selling tradition, Scotland, mystique. It would have been awkward to float a bottle in the sky, so the artist used a label, but not too modern looking because we are selling tradition.

COLOR PLATE 39 Ask any woman why she would want a luxurious fur coat. To keep warm ▶ of course. Of course. The furs mentioned in this dramatic ad are among the most expensive on the market. A fur coat is not only beautiful high fashion; it shows that a woman has arrived. It *is* pure luxury. It does keep her warm, too.

LIVE AN ADVENTURE OF PURE LUXURY

Revillon. Since 1723 creating a legend of rare, natural beauty. Since 1723 offering an adventure of pure luxury. Nearly three centuries of French fashion and the finest workmanship.

The tradition of Revillon and thrill of beauty continues in the 1985 collection. Fox, chinchilla, beaver and mink from the furriers who brought fashion to furs. Available in the United States exclusively at Saks Fifth Avenue. Revillon. From a bold legend, the thrill of beauty.

Revillon
Exclusively at Saks Fifth Avenue

**Tastes as good as Budweiser.
At a better price.**

© 1984 Miller Brewing Co., Milwaukee, WI

COLOR PLATE 40

COLOR PLATE 40 Two simple sentences position this beer at once. Note the strong package identification and the glass that someone has obviously just emptied, and, the reader assumes, found to his liking. Good creative strategy.

Bonne Maman. The French way of breakfast.

The fruits of the famed Dordogne Valley shimmer radiant and jewel-like inside our old-style French canning jars. That's why, in France where half the people still eat homemade jams, jellies and marmalades, we're the number-one selling preserve. Bonne Maman. Once you taste it, you'll buy it for good. Bonne Maman.

COLOR PLATE 41

COLOR PLATE 41 A creative concept is needed to market a new imported jam or jelly in a field crowded with many national and store brands. An image was called for, and this sample ad provides more than the good taste of a fruit preserve . . . it provides a touch of the French countryside for the sophisticated people who will buy it. Everything works together—the illustration that looks like a beautiful still life (no mere photograph here), the easily pronounced French name, the rustic look of the dishes, the checkered lid of the jar that kindles an image of a little French restaurant.

COLOR PLATE 42 The series of ads was so clever that interested readers must have followed them right to the final ad. The very subtlety of the campaign would appeal to the kind of sophisticated, well-traveled people who are the target market. This ad ties the copy and the photographs together so well into a plausible story that, as it were, everyone goes along with the gag.

COLOR PLATE 43 When copy is called for, Nike adds a ▶ written message that builds on the dramatic photo . . . crumpled, sweaty garments on a locker-room floor, not pretty, fashion-show art. And the word "sweats" conveys that although the clothing is fashionable when you want it fashionable, it is also basic clothing "to play sports in." The dig for "Woolite" suggests sturdiness, not delicacy. These sweats are meant to be washed in a washing machine. Not a wasted word. Note too how Nike has managed to describe its line of products—in the photo and in the text—shoes, socks, running shorts, warm-up jerseys, sweat suits.

COLOR PLATE 42

"Leave poor Harry alone."

"Now the bunch of you listen to me and listen good!!!

As a single parent who, a few years ago, took her twin 14 year old daughters and 11 year old son on a 3 week tour of your beautiful North and South Islands (and we hope to do it again soon), I want you to know that I have just about had enough of the way you are badgering poor Harry Bright about returning to work just to give you some silly old advertising slogans or pictures of New Zealand.

You want Harry, God bless him, to describe the indescribable... your majestic glaciers, your seemingly endless valleys of green, oh! so many, many shades of green, dotted with... how many fluffy white grazing sheep? How does one describe peace and tranquility?

(This sort of badgering of Harry has to stop!)

You want Harry to capture in photographs the feel of salt spray in his face as he stands at the rails of the ferry while crossing from Wellington to Picton or the fragrance of the most sensuous dew-covered giant roses in the morning sunlight...not our Harry. No sir!

Was it Harry who said "When in the presence of greatness, silence is the highest form of respect"?

Harry knows New Zealand's unique beauty isn't just that found in fertile land or blue water. It's found in the heart

(New Zealand. It's even harder to capture on film than my kids!)

of each New Zealander. Love, warmth, trust, caring, sincerity, wholesomeness, respect and more.

When we had engine problems there suddenly appeared a New Zealand gentleman to help. When we lost our way a farm family put us back on track. Oh, I could go on but this will have to suffice. New Zealand is the only country to which we have travelled where my children and I have felt completely at home and completely safe.

(Harry wasn't putting out your ad, because he was probably putting on our tire!)

So to the bunch of you at the New Zealand tourist office I say leave poor Harry Bright alone. He is probably helping women such as myself fix the engine in their campers or giving directions or...wait a second...as I look through my tattered travel notes I see the name of the strong, handsome New Zealand gentleman who stopped on the road to Christchurch to help me change my right front tire was Harry... it looks like BRIGH? I can't seem to make out that last letter... naw, it couldn't have been?????"

(P.S. If you really need some pictures, and if it would save Harry's job, you can have some of the color New Zealand photos we took (not all of them are blurred!)

WE HAVEN'T FORGOTTEN WHY THEY'RE CALLED SWEATS.

Call us narrow-minded, but at Nike we like to think that sportswear should be just what it implies. Clothing you play sports in.

A perfect example is the old standby, gray fleece sweats. The kind that get heavier the more you work out. The kind that get better the longer you own them. The kind you wash in a washing machine.

And not in Woolite.*

That attitude isn't exclusive to our sweats. Everything we make, from running shorts and warm-ups to singlets and jerseys, is designed first for performance.

The very same philosophy we've used in our shoes for over ten years.

Of course, we can spot a trend as fast as the next guy. And as long as clothes like this are popular among the fashion conscious, we'll make them in colors like turquoise and plum. We might even add some stylish piping here or a few extra pockets there.

But when the trend is gone and forgotten, you'll still be able to wear them to sweat in.

And we'll still be making them in our favorite shade of gray.

COLOR PLATE 44

COLOR PLATE 44 Short copy that says it all. The airline that flies the Chicago Cubs deserves to be the reader's airline as well. How clever, too, to show some of the many cities served by United by writing the names on a baseball.

COLOR PLATE 45 In the world of cars, Rolls-Royce probably stands by itself as a classic—a symbol of quality, a symbol of luxury, a symbol of affluence. If this automobile is recognized as such a symbol all over the world, why is it necessary to go into the nitty-gritty of the making of the grille? Because it reinforces the image of quality—hand-craftsmanship by a real person who is proud of his work. It is not only the words, but the meaning that is implied. The idea is that the quality of the Rolls-Royce means durability to a person who demands the best.

COLOR PLATE 45

This is a Coach® Belt.

Coach® Bags and Belts are made in New York City and sold in selected stores throughout the country. For catalogue write:
Coach Leatherware, 516 West 34th Street, New York 10001.

Calvin Klein Jeans

Coach Leatherware has done a superb job of image building through ads such as this one. Notice that there is no description of the attributes of the product, such as the type of leather that is used to make the belt or the way the belt is stitched together. The entire approach of this ad suggests a product whose quality speaks for itself. The advertiser has built identification for its entire line of leather products by using the same ad format for its bags and belts.

An illustration and three words of copy are all that is needed to convey the appeal of this product. For many consumers, the designer's name and the model's style of dress represent values of their aspiration reference group. They will interpret the message, in effect, as: "Calvin Klein jeans, that's what they're all wearing."

Reference groups are important to advertisers because members of any one group tend to be highly resistant to appeals that conflict with that group's beliefs. People are, of course, positively influenced by what others buy, particularly when those "others" belong to a membership or aspiration reference group. "Keeping up with the Joneses" still applies. The reference group can influence the purchase of a product or the choice of a brand. The reference group is the anonymous "they"—as in "that's what *they're* wearing" or "that's what *they're* buying." And the more expensive the purchase, the greater the influence of the reference group. (See color plate 39 for an ad addressing a high-income reference group.)

The Diffusion Process

The **diffusion process** is the process by which the acceptance of a new product, new service, or new idea spreads to the target market within a certain period of time. The process involves four elements:

1. the innovation itself
2. the channels of communication
3. the social system in which the innovation takes place
4. the period of time the innovation requires to penetrate the target market

The "newness" of a product may be defined by its physical features and the manner in which it satisfies the user that it is different from the old product or the old way of doing things. Some products are **artificially new,** that is, the product merely appears to be new because of some cosmetic change. Designing a new package for an old product is an example of this type of change. Other products may be **marginally new,** that is, they may contain an added ingredient or have a modified design. Still others may be **genuinely new;** they may be entirely different from older products of the same type or from older ways of doing something. A soup that can be heated in the plastic pouch in which it is packaged is genuinely new. It is a new way of doing something. A laundry detergent that contains a bluing agent is only marginally new. All of these definitions are obviously subjective and based on the consumer's perception of newness.

As advertisers, our main concern is the speed with which the product achieves sales penetration. If we knew how consumers would react to our product, if we could anticipate what features or what advertising approach would speed or retard its acceptance, then we would not have any advertising or marketing problems. Although there are no magic formulas for success, the diffusion process does demonstrate that certain of a product's characteristics appear to influence the consumer's acceptance of that product. Such characteristics include: the degree to which the new product is consistent with present practices; the complexity of the product; the cost of trying a new product (the amount of money required to try a new package of chewing gum, for example, as compared with that required for a new microwave oven); and finally the extent of social visibility of the product (a tangible product is more easily communicated than an intangible service or a product used very privately). A tennis racket is more easily diffused than a new checking account service.

From Innovators to Laggards   Consumers themselves can be divided into categories based on their willingness to try a new product. Most books on consumer behavior describe product adopters as innovators, early adopters, early majority, late majority, and laggards. The distribution of each type of purchase behavior in the population usually follows a pattern represented by the typical bell curve. A few people, the **innovators,** are willing to take risks and try a new product as soon as it reaches the market. **Early adopters,** a somewhat larger group, discover the product after the innovators and serve as role models for the early majority. The **early majority** is slow to adopt the product, waiting for the innovators and early adopters to do so first. The **late majority** needs considerable peer pressure to stimulate them to adopt a new product; and a few individuals, the **laggards,** are very conservative and tend to remain rooted in past practice.

The **rate of adoption** measures how long it takes for a new product to be adopted. The rate of adoption is contingent upon the factors previously described—the price, the social visibility, the complexity of the product, and the means that are used to communicate news of the innovation (mass media, personal selling) to the target market.

Attitudes, Customs, and Habits

Most consumers' habits, customs, and attitudes are derived from their culture and from the social groups to which they belong; they are largely the result of social conditioning. We know that much behavior is habitual. Some people automatically reach for the salt or the mustard or the ketchup. Some people buy the same product or shop in the same store out of habit. And these habits are hard for the individual—and for the advertiser—to break.

Sometimes consumer behavior is affected by customs. Turkey is served at Thanksgiving and Christmas. Why not on the Fourth of July, too? Custom. There's no logical reason for it, and it might be extremely difficult (perhaps impossible) and extremely expensive to alter a custom through advertising. Cranberry growers tried to induce people to eat cranberry sauce throughout the year, but how often do Americans eat cranberry sauce? Mostly with their turkey dinners at Christmas and Thanksgiving. However, a successful advertising campaign to change a custom of this kind can greatly expand the market for a product.

People's purchasing behavior is also influenced by certain attitudes, that is, by states of judgment that exist before new information is received. Fortunately, attitudes can be changed, but we had better know what attitudes affect the use of our product before we roll out our advertising program.

In this same context, advertisers must also be aware of some taboos that exist. In general, explicit references to sex are not in good taste. Children smoking and satires of religious or certain social groups are all taboo.

Application of Psychographics to Advertising

Psychographics represent a description of a market based on the life-style, attitudes, self-images, and interests of the consumers that comprise that market. We can use psychographics to help us develop more effective appeals and creative strategies than would be possible if we relied solely on more traditional forms of research. But keep in mind that psychographics are not a substitute for demographics; and *neither* is a substitute for creativity. Psychographics are simply another tool. How, then, shall we use it?

Psychographic life-style data can provide us with a more lifelike picture of our target consumer. The more we know about the *kind of person,* the more we can fine tune our appeal, aiming it directly at just that portion of our target market that includes our best prospects. Demographic information alone is not enough. All working women are not alike. All older people are not alike. It is a myth that individual demographic groups are relatively homogeneous entities. But with the addition of psychographic information we can refine our target. And from life-style data (gathered from marketing research) we can get ideas for the proper settings for our advertisements, the physical appearance of the characters shown, the nature of the art work, the kind of music to use, and the most appealing colors. We can also learn how much fantasy consumers will accept in our advertisements.

The creative people in an advertising agency learn from psychographic data what tone to give to the advertising. They learn whether the most effective message will be serious, humorous, authoritative, traditional, or contemporary. One very interesting application of psychographics is described by a research expert in a major advertising agency. Seeking to develop a new approach for a beer client, the agency obtained a psychographic profile of the

When she gave in to practicality,
she didn't give up her individuality.

The first baby moved her to the suburbs. The second one moved her out of her beloved sports car. But not into something square. In fact, into something rather well-rounded. The wide stance AMC Pacer Wagon.

Because a woman who knows anything about cars knows that wide is wonderful. The Pacer Wagon's extra width makes it extra efficient. So you get large size room and comfort in a sensibly sized car. And something even more important, extra stability, to make it ride and handle like a much larger car.

And she doesn't mind that the Pacer Wagon's unique wide design makes it look a little different. That's the way a woman with her own style likes to look.

The exclusive AMC BUYER PROTECTION PLAN®: AMC will fix, or replace free, any part except tires for 12 months or 12,000 miles, whether the part is defective, or just plain wears out under normal use and service.

AMC ◢ **Pacer**
The room and ride Americans want. The size America needs.

THE AMC PACER WAGON IS A PRODUCT OF AMERICAN MOTORS CORP. ALSO AVAILABLE IN 2-DOOR HATCHBACK.
®BUYER PROTECTION PLAN is reg. U.S. Pat. and Tm. Off.

This ad makes an interesting contrast to the Cadillac ad on page 337. This ad is addressed to women and clearly indicates the reference group — young, married, suburban, two children. The target consumer is a sensible, no-nonsense kind of woman who wants practicality with her style, and that is what the advertiser tells her that the Pacer offers. The lady in the Cadillac ad does not expect to drive in her evening gown.

client's target consumer.[1] The demographic data showed the target market as middle-income, male, young, blue-collar, with a high school education. He was the heavy beer drinker — part of the 20 percent of all beer drinkers who consume 80 percent of all the beer sold in the United States. The agency discovered that this consumer believed:

---

[1] Joseph Plummer, "Applications of Life-Style Research to the Creation of Advertising Campaigns," in *Life-Style and Psychographics,* William D. Wells, ed. (Chicago: American Marketing Association, 1974), pp. 159–169.

Lite

AMERICA'S BEST KNOWN BEER DRINKERS TALK ABOUT Lite BEER...

Title: "Martin/Steinbrenner"

Comm'l. No.: MOTH0530

George: You know a lot of people think Billy and I argue all the time. Actually, we agree on just about everything. Right, Bill?
Billy: You betcha, George.

George: We even drink the same beer.
Billy: Lite Beer from Miller. Lite's got a third less calories than their regular beer and it's less filling.

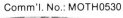

George: And the best thing is it tastes so great.
Billy: No George. The best thing, it's less filling.

George: No, Bill it tastes great.
Billy: Less filling, George!

George: Billy it tastes great.
Billy: Less filling! George!

George: Billy!
Billy: Yeh, George?
George: You're fired.

Billy: Oh, not again!

ANNCR: Lite Beer from Miller. Everything you always wanted in a beer.

And less.

Since the target market for beer is primarily male, Miller Brewing Company uses two famous sports personalities in this commercial to capture the attention of the male audience. Billy Martin or George Steinbrenner delivering a straight commercial message by himself might not provide the authenticity (and the interest) that their dialogue provides. Their argument over whether Lite Beer is better because it tastes good or because it has fewer calories emphasizes the product's double appeal.

beer a man's drink
he liked a physical, male-oriented world
he loved sports
he did not object to danger

The resulting campaign was built around the
imagery of the sea to dramatize the adventure
of one of the last frontiers. The focus of
the campaign was on the "life style" of the
men of the sea — men who lived their lives
with gusto and who enjoyed a "gusto brew." [2]

Another excellent study made by the same agency (Leo Burnett) will serve as an example of the use of psychographics for an entirely different product: heavy-duty hand soap. The heavy-users of this product were downscale — that is, their income and educational levels were low and they were for the most part older people. This is a very static market segment. One of the advertising objectives for the marketers of this soap was to attract new users.

Life-style findings indicated that this new target consumer was a home-maker in the most traditional sense of the word — comfortable in her role as a housewife and mother, confident, and conservative. She was very concerned about cleanliness. She wanted her home to be clean, really clean. How could she be persuaded to use a heavy-duty hand soap? You guessed it — the advertisers suggested that she use it on her children. This soap would get their hands clean, really clean, for the first time. The campaign was built around children and placed the mother in the authoritative role suggested by her psychographic profile. As Mr. Plummer stated, "It is accomplishing both the objective of obtaining new users and the objective of increasing usage among current users." [3]

Life-style data can also be a valuable guide for media selection. We can examine the characteristics of a medium's audience and compare them with the characteristics of the people who do *not* compose the audience for that medium. We can, for example, compare readers with nonreaders, viewers with nonviewers, for each specific medium. We might assume that what turns a viewer on or off a particular program might well be related to his or her life-style. Such a consideration can be an important factor in our media evaluation as well as our creative approach.

VALS

Knowledge of the values and life styles of the consumer population is essential to advertisers and to any organization with something to market. In 1946, the Stanford Research Institute was formed with the purpose of providing such information for business and government clients all over the world. SRI developed the **VALS** program. *VALS* is an acronym for values and life styles — a way of looking at people on the basis of their attitudes, needs, wants, and beliefs, as well as their demographics. The approach draws on many sources of data to develop a comprehensive framework for characterising the ways of life of Americans. The system is currently being applied in all areas of marketing, as well as sociology, politics, law, education, and medicine.

---

[2] Ibid., p. 165.
[3] Ibid., p. 167.

Members of the VALS program — over 150 organizations which pay up to $30,000 a year for access to its data — use the findings in different ways. The membership list includes television stations, advertising agencies, major marketers, tourist associations, banks, and publishers. The applications include marketing research, product design and packaging, and advertising, as well as strategic planning and human resource management.

A basic tool of the VALS program is the VALS typology. This typology is divided into four major categories, with a total of nine lifestyles. These are:

Need-Driven
    Survivor lifestyle
    Sustainer lifestyle

Outer-Directed
    Belonger lifestyle
    Emulator lifestyle
    Achiever lifestyle

Inner-Directed
    I-Am-Me lifestyle
    Experiential lifestyle
    Societally Conscious lifestyle

Combined Outer- and Inner-Directed
    Integrated lifestyles

These lifestyle categories are not fixed and immutable. Many people grow from one level to another as children, as adolescents, and as adults. Some very few may start at the bottom and reach the top within a lifetime, but far more common is movement of a level or two.

The concept of a person's lifestyle may be likened to the bullfighting term *querencia*. Every bull, it seems, has his favorite turf or home area in the bullring. When prodded or lured, he will sally forth into other areas of the ring, but in response to his *querencia*, or homing instinct, he will return to the piece of ground where he is most comfortable. So it is with people. The individual, at a given time, may move up or down or across to another pattern of life, perhaps in some limited life domain, such as work or marriage. Yet the tendency is to gravitate back to the place that is best understood and least threatening — the home lifestyle.

The Need-Drivens　The Need-Drivens are people so limited in resources (especially financial resources) that their lives are driven by need rather than by choice. Much evidence shows that they are the furthest removed from the cultural mainstream, are the least aware of the events of our times, and are most inclined to be depressed and withdrawn. Values of the Need-Driven center around survival, safety, and security. Such people tend to be distrustful, dependent, unplanning. Many live unhappy lives focused on the immediate specifics of today, with little sensitivity to the wants of others and little vision of what could be.

We divide the Need-Driven category into two lifestyles: *Survivor* and *Sustainer.*

Survivors.　Survivors are the most disadvantaged in American society by reason of their extreme poverty, low education, old age, and limited access to the channels of upward mobility. They are people oriented to tradition but marked by despair and unhappiness. Many, now infirm, once lived lifestyles associated with higher levels of the VALS hierarchy. Other generation-after-generation Survivors are ensnared in the so-called "culture of poverty."

Sustainers.   Sustainers are a group struggling at the edge of poverty. They are better off and younger than Survivors, and many have not given up hope. Their values are very different from those of Survivors in that Sustainers have advanced from the depression and hopelessness typical of Survivors to express anger at the system they see as repressing them, and they have developed a street-wise determination to get ahead. Many operate in the underground economy.

The Outer-Directed   This large and diverse category is named to reflect the central characteristic of the people within it: The Outer-Directeds conduct their lives in response to signals — real or fancied — from others. "Out there" is what is most important. Consumption, activities, attitudes — all are guided by what the outer-directed individual thinks others will think. Psychologically, Outer-Direction is a major step forward from the Need-Driven state in that the perspective on life has broadened to include other people, a host of institutions, shared goals, and an array of personal values and options far more complex and diverse than those available to the Need-Driven. In general, the Outer-Directeds are the happiest of Americans, being well attuned to the cultural mainstream — indeed, creating much of it.

The VALS typology defines three principal types of outer-directed people: *Belongers, Emulators,* and *Achievers.*

Belongers.   Belongers constitute the large, solid, comfortable, middle-class group of Americans who are the main stabilizers of society and the preservers and defenders of the moral status quo. Belongers tend to be conservative, conventional, nostalgic, sentimental, puritanical, conforming. The key drive is to fit in — to belong — and not to stand out. Their world is well posted and well lit, and the road is straight and narrow.

Family, church, and tradition loom large. Belongers are people who know what is right, and they adhere to the rules. They are not much interested in sophistication or intellectual affairs. All the evidence suggests that Belongers lead contented, happy lives and are relatively little vexed by the stresses and mercurial events that swirl around them.

In terms of psychological maturity, Belongers are ahead of the Need-Drivens in having a much wider range of associations (both personal and institutional), a longer-term focus for planning their lives, and a less opportunistic pattern of behavior. These are people well integrated with their surroundings.

Emulators.   Emulators live in a wholly different world from that of Belongers. Emulators are trying to burst into the upper levels of the system — to make it big. The object of their emulation is the Achiever lifestyle. They are ambitious, upwardly mobile, status-conscious, macho, competitive. Many see themselves as coming from the other side of the tracks and hence are intensely distrustful, are angry with the way things are, and have little faith that "the system" will give them a fair shake. Emulators tend not to be open in their feelings for fear of alienating those in authority, on whom they depend to get ahead. The Emulator group contains a higher fraction of minorities (24 percent) than any VALS group other than the Need-Drivens.

Psychologically, Emulators are a step ahead of Belongers in that they ask more of themselves and the system and have assumed greater personal responsibility for getting ahead, instead of drifting with events in the style of many Belongers. On the other hand, Emulators seem often to have unrealistic goals. In truth, many are not on the track to make them Achievers, but they appear not to realize this.

Achievers.   Achievers include the leaders in business, the professions, and government. Competent, self-reliant, efficient, Achievers tend to be materialistic, hardworking, oriented to fame and success, and comfort loving. These are the affluent people who have created the economic system in response to the American dream. As such, they are the defenders of the economic status quo. Achievers are among the best adjusted of Americans, being well satisfied with their place in the system. Only 5 percent of Achievers come from minority backgrounds.

Achievers are psychologically more advanced than Emulators in having a wider spectrum of values, in being more open and trusting, and in clearly having brought their ambitions into better alignment with reality. Achievers are supporters of technology and are open to progress, but they resist radical change. After all, they are on top and too radical a change might shake them off!

The Inner-Directed   People called Inner-Directed contrast with the Outer-Directed in that they conduct their lives primarily in accord with inner values — the needs and desires private to the individual — rather than in accord with values oriented to externals. What is most important to such people is what is "in here" rather than what is "out there." Concern with inner growth thus is a cardinal characteristic. Inner-directed people tend to be self-expressive, individualistic, person-centered, impassioned, diverse, complex.

It is important to recognize that, in American society today, one can hardly be profoundly Inner-Directed without having internalized Outer-Directedness through extensive and deep exposure as a child, adolescent, or adult. One implication is that inner-directed people tend not to come from need-driven or inner-directed families. Some measure of satiation with the pleasures of external things seems to be required before a person can believe in or enjoy the less visible, incorporeal pleasures of Inner-Direction. This means that the pleasures of the outer world do not disappear, but that inner needs become more imperative than outer needs. From the psychological standpoint then, Inner-Direction in today's Western culture represents an advance over Outer-Direction in that it adds new values to old, thus increasing the range of potential responses and the number of channels available for self-expression. For children raised in strongly inner-directed families, however, the psychological advance would involve the shift from Inner-Direction to Outer-Direction. This would be true, for example, of people raised according to the tenets of the great inner-directed Eastern cultures.

VALS has identified three stages of Inner-Directedness: *I-Am-Me, Experiential,* and *Societally Conscious.*

I-Am-Me.   I-Am-Me is a short-lived stage of transition from Outer- to Inner-Direction. Values from both stages are much in evidence. Typically, the I-Am-Me person is young and fiercely individualistic, to the point of being narcissistic and exhibitionistic. People at this stage are full of confusions and emotions they do not understand; hence, they often define themselves better by their actions than by their statements. I-Am-Me's tend to be dramatic and impulsive. Much of their Inner-Direction shows up in great inventiveness, a willingness to try anything once, and an often secret inner exploration that will later crystallize into lifelong pursuits.

Experiential. As the I-Am-Me's mature psychologically, they become the Experientials. At this stage of Inner-Direction, the focus has widened from the intense egocentrism of the I-Am-Me to include other people and many social and human issues. Experientials are people who most want direct experience and vigorous involvement. Life is a light show at one moment and an intense, often mystic, inner experience the next. They are attracted to the exotic (such as Oriental religions), to the strange (such as parapsychology), and to the natural (such as "organic" gardening and home baking). The most inner-directed of any VALS group, these people also are probably the most artistic and the most passionately involved with others. Although intense, this is a thoroughly enjoyable stage of life, full of vigorous activity (although less than at the I-Am-Me stage), and marked by a growing concern with intellectual and spiritual matters.

Societally Conscious. The Societally Conscious have extended their Inner-Direction beyond the self and others to the society as a whole — in fact, sometimes to the globe or even, philosophically, to the cosmos. A profound sense of societal responsibility leads these people to support such causes as conservation, environmentalism, and consumerism. They tend to be activistic, impassioned, and knowledgeable about the world around them. Many are attracted to simple living and the natural; some have taken up lives of voluntary simplicity. Many do volunteer work. The Societally Conscious seek to live frugal lives that conserve, protect, and heal. Inner growth remains a crucial part of life. Consequently, many Societally Conscious people assume a high degree of self-reliance, which extends to holistic health and a sense that they are in touch with inner forces that guide them.

Combined Outer- and Inner-Directed: The Integrateds At the pinnacle of the VALS typology is a small group called the Integrateds. These rare people have put it all together. They meld the power of Outer-Direction with the sensitivity of Inner-Direction. They are fully mature in a psychological sense — able to see many sides of an issue, able to lead if necessary, and willing to take a secondary role if that is appropriate. They usually possess a deep sense of the fittingness of things. They tend to be self-assured, self-actualizing, self-expressive, keenly aware of issues and sentiments, and often possessed of a world perspective.

Market Research Participants interested in the market research aspects of VALS have access to the large data base collected annually by Simmons Market Research Bureau (SMRB). Some 3,500 tables of data are available covering demographics, media usage, consumption of about 700 products, sport and hobby activities, and the like. VALS participants who are also members of Simmons have access, in addition, to data on several thousand product brands and media specifics.

Researchers use these data to segment markets, estimate market size, position products and services, and so forth. The automobile provides a familiar example of this kind of application. VALS data show that Achievers buy more large and luxury cars; Belongers tend toward "family-sized" cars; the Societally Conscious purchase more gas-savers; muscle cars are bought by

Emulators and Experientials; the Need-Drivens purchase used cars. Further, big differences exist in how many cars the various lifestyle households are likely to own, their assessment of features desired in a car, how they use cars, and the country of origin. The Inner-Directeds, for example, are far more likely to buy a foreign-made car than are the patriotic, America-first Belongers.

Product Development, Packaging, and Design The kind of thinking that goes into matching an advertisement with the consumer can also be applied in product development or modification, packaging, and design. Basically, the target audience is first defined in terms of attitudes, demographics, activities, needs, hopes, and the like. The critical dimensions relevant to the product are identified, and a multidimensional consumer profile is prepared. The problem then is to match this profile as exactly as possible in the design and development of the product or package.

Advertising Advertising agencies are among the most acute and imaginative users of VALS. Insights drawn from lifestyle research are used not only to select optimum media schedules, but also to select themes and ambiences best suited to target consumers.

Attuning the advertisement perfectly to the consumer is a high art that requires the creative leap from the closely defined target to the compelling expressive appeal. Successful leaps are often beautifully simple and very effective. Few campaigns have used theme symbology more adroitly than the Merrill Lynch series. The bull symbol, of course, is appropriate for an investment firm. But, originally, the symbol was a thundering herd of bulls. With the insight that the key image of investors is that of the Achiever came the image of "a breed apart" to replace the Belonger symbol of the herd. To follow up on the basic symbolism, a series of breed-apart bull commercials were designed to reflect different financial predicaments; the bull sheltered in a cave from financial storms; the bull pawing through the snow for grass in hard times; the bull in good times crossing a babbling river to reach the rich pastures on the other side; the bull threading a maze, stalking through a china shop, uncovering a needle in a haystack, and many others. These themes aligned the corporate image with the rugged individualism and "can do" spirit of Achievers.

Positioning the Product

One of the creative strategies advertisers have developed is positioning. **Positioning** refers to the "position" our product occupies in a prospect's mind in relation to the competition — its quality, value, shape, price, and function as compared with those of competing products. To develop a positioning strategy, however, we must take into account more than just the strengths and weaknesses of our own product and those of the competition. We must remember that in today's world our advertising message is competing for the consumer's attention with the messages of tens of thousands of products. We are struggling to reach consumers who are bombarded with advertising messages from every direction.

In order to cope with a tremendous volume of information, people reduce everything to indexes, or the simplest descriptions. When we ask our friends, for example, how they are doing in school, they don't tell us what their grades were on every test and paper they completed for every course they have taken since their first semester. They give us their "cume." The "cume" provides us with a simple means of comparing their positions in school with those of other students. A 3.7 is great. A 2.7 is not great, but it's better than a 2.0. This process is called ranking. And that is what consumers do with all advertising information. How is restaurant A? *It's okay, better than restaurant B, but not as good as restaurant C.* What the consumer has done in response to our question is to position restaurant A in our mind. That position is based not merely on what the chef has done with the veal marsala, but on the total impression of that restaurant—the food, the service, the decor, the price, and the atmosphere.

As consumers, we rank products and brands in our minds. If advertisers are to increase preference (and sales) for their brands, they must convince a certain percentage of consumers that their brands deserve to be moved to a higher level in the ranking game. When advertisers introduce totally new products, they create a new game; and it is sometimes difficult for these new products to get started because consumers do not know where to place them. Consider the many new products that had to be related (positioned) to old products in order to gain acceptance: horseless carriage, food processor, talking picture, pressure cooker. . . .

Competing for Space in the Consumer's Brain   There is, however, another phenomenon of consumer psychology that will affect our positioning strategy. The consumer's mind is like a data bank in a computer with a "position," or location, for bits of information it has decided to retain. A computer accepts whatever information is fed into it. It stores everything in its memory. But the consumer's mind has a filter that screens out and rejects much information. It accepts new information that is compatible with its prior knowledge or experience and refuses to accept information that seriously conflicts with its prior knowledge.

For example, when we talk about computers, the first name that most people think of is International Business Machines Corporation: IBM. When we read an advertisement or see a television commercial that tells us that RCA stands for computers, we reject it. We know that RCA means records or television sets. IBM means computers. The computer position in our minds is occupied by IBM. For a competing computer company to obtain a favorable position in our mind, it must relate its name and its product to International Business Machine's position.

Trends in Positioning   Consider the advertising campaigns for beer. In the 1950s and 1960s, advertising copywriters came up with such slogans as "cold-brewed Ballantine," "real-draft Piels," "just the kiss of the hops," and "the beer that made Milwaukee famous." But in the late 1970s, a new trend developed and the emphasis in beer advertising was on positioning, as "Michelob—first class" and "of all imported beers, only one could be number one" demonstrate. (See color plate 40.)

In 1957, Lever Brothers introduced Dove soap—not as another soap to get you clean, but as a complexion bar for dry skin. The oval shape was more feminine than the traditional rectangular soap. Dove came in a box, like a cosmetic, not in the paper wrapper of an ordinary soap. Dove's advertising promised that it would "cream your skin while you wash." In this way, Dove positioned itself as a unique brand. (Color plate 41 shows an ad introducing a new brand of preserves into a crowded market.)

Media Considerations

Our advertising goals, the phase of the product life cycle, and the nature of the market all affect our creative efforts. A final consideration in the selection of a creative strategy is the suitability of the various media to our purpose. For example, if we want to build primary demand, seeking to influence early adopters by imparting detailed product information, which medium will best serve our needs? Will the 30 seconds available on television be long enough to do a teaching job? Do early adopters watch television?

In the early stages of the product life cycle, reach will be more important than frequency. Therefore, we may want to establish a reach objective that enables us to deliver our new product story to the largest possible percentage of the target market. The creative approach to reach will be different from the creative approach to frequency. If we mean to communicate with as many people as possible, our message must contain as much information as we can squeeze in. Each prospect will seek a different benefit. We would therefore prefer to use *more* magazines or *more* television programs, as we want more people to be aware of our product. We want *reach*.

A product need not be new for media considerations to affect the creative approach. Consider the sale of baby food: no matter how popular or successful the product, purchasers will only use it for about two years. Therefore, our media strategy should emphasize reach, not frequency, since there will always be an influx of new prospects into the target market.

If our product is not new and we plan to position it head-on against the market leader, our media strategy will change; and our creative approach will again be affected. If we mean to be competitive, we will stress our strengths against those of other brands. We can do this best by hammering away at our target market. This time, we want frequency, not reach. We may find — depending on our product and its distribution — that television offers us the greatest opportunity for frequency. On the other hand, certain products may require more selectivity than television offers. In this case, magazines with sharply defined audiences are most suitable. A heavy schedule — one that will give us as much frequency as possible — in a few carefully chosen magazines may be best.

Brainstorming

We have all heard the word brainstorming[4] before and chances are we have all done it without realizing it. **Brainstorming** is the most familiar and widely used technique for prodding creativity, and advertisers employ it in their search for the proper appeal and creative strategy. There are probably as many different definitions of brainstorming as there are advertising agencies and advertising departments, but the basic concept behind this technique is as follows:

A group of people with knowledge of a product and of the market for that product get together to search for creative ways to bring that product to that

---

[4] The concept originated with Alex F. Osborn, the "O" in BBDO, still one of the country's leading advertising agencies.

PROFILE

Jerry Della Femina

Jerry Della Femina works at a desk that was once a dining room table that he salvaged from a trash pile. The room also contains a battered, old-fashioned typewriter, an ancient Zenith radio, and a poster for a movie from the 1930s. He describes the room's decor as "early poverty," but Della Femina, Travisano and Partners gained $25 million in billings in 1985. World billings for this agency, described as one of the "hot shops" in the Big Apple, were $245 million in 1985.

In a field populated by MBAs, Jerry Della Femina has achieved a phenomenal success without the benefit of a college education. He started by writing sample ads and sending them to Daniel & Charles, a New York advertising agency. After sending in five ads, he was hired as a junior copywriter at a salary of $100 a week. He subsequently worked for several other well-known agencies—always provocative, developing and flexing his creative muscle. He left the Ted Bates agency in 1967 to found his own

shop, taking with him the creative group he had assembled at Ted Bates to work on the Panasonic account. Among the team's first clients was Squire for Men, a maker of hair pieces for whom Jerry Della Femina created the line: "Are you still combing your memories?" Typically, he made a lot of noise on Madison Avenue in 1970 with his caustic book about the advertising business, *From Those Wonderful Folks Who Gave You Pearl Harbor.*

When the *New York Times Magazine* wanted to do a profile on an advertising agency to spotlight the phenomenon of modern advertising agency growth, it sent its reporters to Della Femina, Travisano and Partners. Apparently the story appealed to Schieffelin & Company, because it prompted them to visit Della Femina and to leave behind a little Blue Nun. The successful advertising that Jerry Della Femina created for Blue Nun wine contributed greatly to the creative reputation of his agency.

market. Of course, any individual could come up with some great ideas if he or she could think about the problem for a long time. But we are in a hurry, so our group of people—it may be only two or three, it may be more—begins to discuss ways to advertise the product. In ordinary conversation or discussion, the group's thoughts would tend to get sidetracked into tangential discussions of initial ideas. But in brainstorming, no critical evaluation of any of the ideas expressed at the meeting is allowed, and no negative responses are permitted either. The prime consideration is the generation of ideas, no matter how unusual or impractical they may at first seem. Only after the group has exhausted all its thoughts on the subject are the ideas evaluated and the actual advertising plans determined.

As you can see, brainstorming is primarily a technique to encourage people to get their ideas—all their ideas—out in the open. Of course, the people in the brainstorming group must have done their homework; they must have studied all the available data—demographic, psychographic, motivational research, and media research. As one famous advertising man, David Ogilvy, has revealed in a discussion of a Hathaway shirt campaign:

> I happened to have some research which showed that a wonderful factor to have in the illustration of any advertisement was 'story appeal'. So I thought of 22 different story-appeal elements to put in the photograph of the Hathaway shirts. The twenty-second of them was the eyepatch. It turned out to be a good idea. *But I would not have gone looking for it if I didn't know the research.*[5]

Summary

In order to achieve our advertising goals, we must first make consumers aware of our product and then persuade them to try it, either now or in the near future. Naturally, we must give them a good reason for doing the things we desire. This reason is our *appeal,* and our appeal and the words and images that convey it to the target market are our *creative strategy.* In general, there are three types of creative strategies: one focuses on product features and customer benefits, one on product or company image, and one on positioning the product.

Before we can begin to write copy, design a television commercial, or lay out an advertisement, we want to know as much as possible about the people who will see or hear our message. What preconceptions do they bring with them? We will, of course, have as much demographic data as we can gather. We have to know the age, income, education, sex, and marital status of our target market. We cannot even start the creative process without such information.

In recent years, many advertising people have come to believe, however, that demographic data are not sufficient. They understand that a particular segment delineated by a set of demographic statistics is not a homogeneous group of people. Psychological research — *psychographic data* — is also a valuable aid in determining the true reasons why people buy certain products. When we know their purchasing motives, we can emphasize those motives in the advertising for our brand.

We have also learned that consumers with identical demographic characteristics may have entirely different life-styles. An understanding of various life-styles can help us position our product in the consumers' minds — that is, to position the *image* of our brand in comparison to those of competing brands. If we cannot differentiate our brand from its competitors in the eyes of our most likely prospects, our advertising investment may be very unrewarding. If, however, we come armed with all the data we can assemble about our product, about its position in its life cycle, and about our target market, we can begin the creative process. Brainstorming, or the exchange of ideas among interested and knowledgeable people, is not restricted to the creation of advertising. It has come to be associated with many creative efforts, but no matter what the context, the creative process rests on a foundation of information and demands time and effort.

---

[5] Kenneth Roman and Jane Maas, *How to Advertise* (New York: St. Martin's Press, 1976), p. xi.

CASE HISTORY

New Zealand

This series of ads featured an imaginary New Zealand-based ad manager for the tourist office, named Harry Bright. In a series of all-type black and white ads, very unusual for travel ads, Mr. Bright was portrayed as never sending ads to North America because he was too busy enjoying the scenic wonders of New Zealand. Finally, the tourist office invited readers to send in their own ads extolling the joys of New Zealand. The prize was a two-week holiday for two in New Zealand. The ad generated almost 10,000 entries. For 1984, tourism from the United States to New Zealand increased by over 21 percent with much of the increase attribut-

---

[Regrettably we still don't have a New Zealand advertisement for January. But this time, we do have a rather fetching excuse.]

A bit odd this, but our seasons are flip-flop from you Yanks.' Your Christmas/New Year Holiday is our Summer Holiday and, quite frankly, to a New Zealander it seems a much better time to be running off to the beaches than running an ad.

So Harry Bright, our Advertising Manager down in Wellington, who was supposed to ship up the full colour New Zealand advertisement to us—slipped up.

Most likely because he slipped off to the beach at Golden Bay or Cape Kidnappers.

Pity though.

We've been planning since September last to run our advertisement in magazines like this, but Harry simply hasn't found time from all his seashore sunning, flower festivals, rugby rooting and glacier galavanting to really get cracking on it.

Oh well, what's done is done.

It's 1984. A chance to atone for last year's misdeeds. Hope springs eternal. Keep the faith. All that sort of thing.

And now that the New Year's arrived, could be Harry's New Zealand advertisement isn't far behind.

Things are starting to look up.

(Maybe it's Harry, away down in Wellington, finally noticing our plight up here in the States.)

New Zealand. So much to advertise. So many perfectly splendid reasons not to.

---

able to the campaign. It certainly was unique.

The media was limited to *The New Yorker, Sunset,* and *Travel and Leisure*—three publications that provided the reach to an upscale market. Research based on visitor analysis had indicated that the target market was older (65+), affluent ($50,000+), well-travelled (been to Europe several times), managerial/professional, and resident of the West. California alone accounts for 30 percent of the American visitors. Marschalk San Francisco is one of the leading travel advertising agencies in the United States and one of the most creative in the West. (See color plate 42 for another ad in the series.)

[This is becoming a bit awkward, but our full-page colour advertisement on New Zealand simply isn't ready.]

Here we go again.

Harry Bright had promised, as you recall, to have it run on this page, but it's still in his office in Wellington, only half finished.

Harry's our New Zealand Advertising Manager, you know, and the spring blooms up in Featherston were just too much to miss this week. So he up and took the whole family camping.

Our own dear Miss Barber is on the job steadfastly, however. So while all of us are awaiting Harry's advertisement, perhaps she might mail off to you a colourful packet fairly bulging with gorgeous pictures of New Zealand scenery plus a fold-out map showing all our towns, points of interest and national parks with dandy camping sites.

Just write Miss Christine Barber, New Zealand Tourist Office, 10960 Wilshire Boulevard, Suite #1530 T, Los Angeles, California 90024.

Name _____ Address _____

Next month looks more promising for our full-colour New Zealand advertisement. But the cricket finals are coming up and well…you know Harry.

(New Zealand. So much to advertise. So many perfectly splendid reasons not to.)

Questions for Discussion

1. What are the steps in a consumer's purchasing decision?
2. What is the role of advertising in each step of the purchasing decision?
3. What is meant by positioning the product?
4. What is meant by a consumer's frame of reference? What effect does it have on the advertising message?
5. Why are reference groups important to the consumer?
6. How does the position of a product in its life cycle affect the creative strategy?
7. How does the product life cycle affect media strategy?
8. What is motivation research? Can you suggest the motivation for the purchase of toothpaste? For cranberry juice? For a Mercedes?
9. What benefits can the advertiser obtain from a psychographic profile of the target market?

Sources and Recommendations for Further Reading

Atlas, James. "Beyond Demographics — How Madison Avenue Knows Who You Are and What You Want." *The Atlantic* (October 1984).

Bartos, Rena. *The Moving Target.* New York: The Free Press, 1982.

Brock, Fran. "Superpremiums Pin Hopes on VALS Segmenting." *Ad Week* (November 12, 1984).

Capelli, Elizabeth A. "Detroit Goes Psycho!" *Automotive Industries* (September 1984).

Kain, Edward L. "Surprising Singles." *American Demographics,* August 1984.

Koza, John R. "Who Is Playing What." *Public Gaming Magazine* (May 1984).

Meyer, Philip. "The ABCs of Psychographics." *American Demographics,* November 1983.

Mitchell, Arnold. *The Nine American Lifestyles.* New York: Macmillan, 1983.

Reynolds, Fred D., Melvin R. Crask, and William D. Wells. "The Modern Feminine Life-Style." *Journal of Marketing,* vol. 41, no. 3 (July 1977).

"Social Trends and Moods Affecting the Purchasing of Products and Services Today." *Consumer Currents.* Advertising to Women, Inc., Spring 1984.

Spain, Daphne, and Suzanne M. Bianchi. "How Women Have Changed." *American Demographics,* May 1983.

"Timex and VALS Engineer a Psychographic Products Launch." *Ad Forum* (September 1984).

Townsend, Bickley. "Psychographic Glitter and Gold." *American Demographics,* November 1985.

Walsh, Doris. "In the Kitchen with Ketchum Advertising." *American Demographics* (November 1984).

Wells, William D., ed. *Life-Style and Psychographics.* Chicago: American Marketing Association, 1974.

Ziff, Ruth. *Closing the Consumer-Advertising Gap Through Psychographics.* Combined Proceedings Series, no. 34. American Marketing Association, spring and fall conferences, 1972.

15 COPY FOR ADVERTISING

Working Vocabulary

puff	story headline	fact sheet
pride foods	blind headline	AIDA

357

Copy must foster action — the mental action and the physical action which lead to the purchase of our wares. Therefore, copy must suggest action. But our manner of telling our story can include the suggestion of action.

Aesop Glim
How Advertising Is Written — And Why

Years ago, before radio and television became important advertising media and before improved graphic arts technology made exciting new printing techniques available, advertisers had to rely on the written word to carry their advertising messages. Today, however, advertisers know that words are only one form of the language of advertising. They have discovered ways of conveying their ideas through form, color, and design. Nevertheless, in the majority of advertisements in both print and broadcast media, the written word (we include both printed copy and copy delivered orally on radio or television) remains the most important means of conveying the sales message to the target market.

We do not mean that written advertising copy alone is responsible for the success of any advertising program. Much of a program's success depends on the plans that are carefully formulated before the first word is written. Moreover, the success of the advertising program is contingent upon other variables, many of which are beyond the control of the marketing organization. Advertising may have the ability to draw the customer into the retail outlet, but if that outlet does not enhance the image of the product or if it fails to provide the after-sale service required in some cases, even the best-written advertising will be wasted. The phrases that proved successful last year may be inadequate in the face of changing economic conditions (such as inflation) or changing social conditions (such as smaller families).

The Function of Copy

Advertising is used to help sell products. The purpose of copy is to provide information that will stimulate the prospects to buy our product. The illustration and/or the headline will have captured their attention, generating enough interest to start the prospect reading. But it is the copy, the written or spoken words, that will influence and persuade — or fall flat. It is the copy that makes the claims, points out the advantages, explains, emphasizes, teaches, proves — in short, gives the prospect reasons, implicit as well as explicit, for buying our product. And, for buying it *soon*.

Fact Finding

If our copy is going to do all the wonderful things we want it to do, we had better be sure that what we say is the truth. Believability is the key word. We can all think of an advertisement or two that, every time we see it or hear it, we think "baloney." To achieve believability for our ads, we had better do our homework. Study the product. Surely there is something about our product that is unique, different — wanted. White-O may be a powerful bleach. It may wash out the stains ordinary detergents can't handle. Speedyrin is aspirin with antacids added. It acts as fast as ordinary aspirin to relieve pain without stomach upset. From these facts, we can build the sentences of our copy.

Where does the information come from? Copywriters study research reports from secondary sources — psychographic studies and market reports that are available from research organizations. In addition, copywriters search out firsthand sources for information. They talk to people on the streets and ask them questions about the product. They try the product themselves: they bake it, cook it, eat it, drink it, or use it in their homes. They talk to retailers about the product. They visit supermarkets and observe the shoppers. They visit department stores and watch the customers buying or trying the product. They read the magazines, such as *Reader's Digest* and *Good Housekeeping,* in which the product may be advertised. They listen to several different radio stations. They pay attention to what people — prospective customers for the products they must write about — say and do. Their copy must talk the language of the prospect; it must be written in terms the audience will understand.

Lemon.

This Volkswagen missed the boat.

The chrome strip on the glove compartment is blemished and must be replaced. Chances are you wouldn't have noticed it; Inspector Kurt Kroner did.

There are 3,389 men at our Wolfsburg factory with only one job: to inspect Volkswagens at each stage of production. (3000 Volkswagens are produced daily; there are more inspectors than cars.)

Every shock absorber is tested (spot checking won't do), every windshield is scanned. VWs have been rejected for surface scratches barely visible to the eye.

Final inspection is really something! VW inspectors run each car off the line onto the Funktionsprüfstand (car test stand), tote up 189 check points, gun ahead to the automatic brake stand, and say "no" to one VW out of fifty.

This preoccupation with detail means the VW lasts longer and requires less maintenance, by and large, than other cars. (It also means a used VW depreciates less than any other car.)

We pluck the lemons; you get the plums.

This ad is a classic. Since auto manufacturers would ordinarily never use the word *lemon* to describe their product, the use of the word in the headline is arresting. "What do they mean by lemon?" consumers ask themselves — and then read the body copy to find out. This gives the advertiser an opportunity to tell them how carefully Volkswagen inspected every vehicle.

What are some of the things that a copywriter will want to know?

1. *What is the product made of?*
   What colors, flavors, or shapes are available?
   How is it packaged?
   Is the product well made?
2. *What is the product used for?*
   What problems does it solve?
   What problems does it prevent?
   What emotional needs does it satisfy?
3. *How often is the product used?*
   How often is it bought?
   Who buys it?
   Where is it used?
4. *What is the product like?*
   Is it like another product on the market?
   Does it have masculine or feminine qualities?
   Is it modern, old-fashioned, futuristic?
   Is it for pleasure or for serious purpose?
5. *Who uses the product?*
   Men or women or both?
   Is age a factor?
   Is income a factor?
   Is education or occupation a factor?

You cannot know too much. Examine the competing products. Learn how important the price is to consumers. Find out where they usually purchase the product, and how important the dealer is. Most products provide satisfaction to the user in more than one way. An electric blanket may keep us warm on cold nights. But, so will a wool blanket. The electric blanket, however, is lighter. The electric blanket permits us to control the degree of warmth. The electric blanket is attractive. The electric blanket is washable. All of these attributes are benefits. It is the copywriter's task to sort them out and determine which one is the primary reason for the purchase.

How does our product compare with those of the competition? Sometimes one of their strong points is our weakness. We should know about it and evaluate its importance to the prospect. A medicine bottle with a child-proof closure may be important for people with kids around the house. For an all-adult household, it's not a selling feature — it's an inconvenience.

Style

People do not open a magazine or newspaper to read advertisements. They do not flip the switch on their television sets to watch the commercials. People do read and watch things that interest and stimulate them. The purpose of advertising is to persuade, and the test of good advertising copy is not its grammar, but its effectiveness.

The style of the copy is determined by the writer. There is a big difference between literary style and copywriting style, and it is important to note this distinction. In literary writing the author's personality comes through. We expect it. Dickens, Hemingway, Cheever, Kerouac — we recognize their individual styles immediately. But in writing advertising copy, the copywriter's personality must remain in the background. It is the personality of the product that must come through.

Style is the result of careful word selection. We know that verbs and nouns have more power than adjectives and adverbs. Compare the statement: "she cleaned the room fast" with "she breezed through the cleaning." One places the emphasis on the adverb *fast,* the other on the verb *breezed;* one suggests speed, the other speed *and* ease. Nouns and verbs give impact to a statement. Note also that *breeze through* is an idiomatic expression. That's the way we talk to one another. Why should our copywriting style be stilted or formal? Remember, the purpose of our advertisement is to *communicate* with people — perhaps several million of them. The best way to do this is to use simple, easy-to-understand words.

AN IRISH MIST SETTLED OVER THE EVENING.

The hills roll forever. The lakes radiate light. The dew kisses each morning. The mist settles every evening. You can taste it all, and more.

Irish Mist is the legendary, centuries old drink made from all this and sweetened with just a wisp of heather honey. Irish Mist can be enjoyed anytime, or place, or way: on the rocks; neat; or mixed with anything you like.

It's a pleasing land. It's a pleasing drink.

IRISH MIST. THE LEGENDARY SPIRIT.

Imported Irish Mist & Liqueur. 80 Proof. © 1978 Heublein, Inc., Hartford, Conn., U.S.A.

The words in this advertisement have been carefully chosen to convey a romantic mood. Such phrases as "the dew kisses each morning," a "centuries old drink," and "a wisp of heather honey" that appear in the body copy reinforce, and are reinforced by, the illustration: a romantic background of misty hills and a castle at twilight.

Words can also be used to appeal to the senses. Cigars have an aroma. Wine has a bouquet. Garbage has an odor. Perfume has a seductive fragrance. Look at the many ways we can convey an olfactory sensation with words. And in our copy we should use words that involve as many senses as possible. The words we use can evoke images in the mind of the reader or listener: the *blast* of a fog horn, the *wail* of the police car siren, the *salty smell* of the sea, the *clean look* of new snow. Colors, too, have meanings of their own. Sometimes we are *blue;* sometimes we are *bright, sunny,* or *yellow;* and sometimes we are *green* with envy. Purple connotes majesty, royalty. Blue, authority or masculinity. White is for doctors and nurses.

Writing Rules

The first rule in writing copy is that there are no rules. If there were rules, writing would be no more than following a prescription. There is no prescription for writing effective copy, but there are a few points to consider as the words begin to flow.

Is It Readable? We have pointed out that advertising is often an intrusion. Having interrupted our prospects' entertainment with our advertisement, we must be sure that they can understand what we are saying quickly and easily. Think of some of your textbooks. You don't *read* them, you study them: you may have to struggle to get the meaning. But the readers or viewers of our advertisements won't do that. They will turn the page or mentally tune us out. They don't have to *study* our advertising. Therefore, it must be easily readable, listenable, or viewable.

Is It Believable? Much advertising is pure puff. We all know that the word **puff** means a short blast of air. In advertising, the term has come to mean exaggerated commendation. The generous use of such words as *the finest, the best, the most popular,* and *natural goodness* puff out the advertiser's claims. To a certain degree such words may succeed in attracting the reader's attention or in conveying a sense of the quality of a product. But if our advertisements contain too much puff, consumers will begin to question even the most valid claims. Do you believe, for example, that an instant soup has "home-style stock that brings out all the natural flavors of the meat and vegetable ingredients"? Or that a lipstick is "drenched with moisturizers"? Or that a dishwashing liquid has "the power to lift away grease, and keep it away"? Our copy must be believable.

Does It Have Interest? Does the copy touch the main interest of the prospects who will buy the product? People do not buy cake mixes because a cake made from a mix is more nutritious than a ready made cake. And no advertisements for a cake mix will ever say so. Nor will the advertisements ever tell prospects that they can save money by using a cake mix. Homemakers use cake mixes because they want to demonstrate their cooking skills and to fish for compliments. A person may scrub the bathroom until it sparkles, but other members of the family will hardly ever remark on the sparkle of the bathtub or of the toilet bowl. They *will,* however, remark on how much they like the cake or cookies. No wonder such products are called **pride foods.** The point is, our copy must touch the reader's real interest — health, pride, safety, sex, economy, or any of the other drives that motivate people to try a product and to repeat their purchase behavior.

Ideas for Individual Media

Writing for Magazines

Stimulated by competition from television, magazines have increased in number and in circulation. As we noted in our discussion of media, magazines are, for the most part, selective. People pay to read them. They are also long-lived; they lie around the house for a week or a month. They are read at leisure, at the readers' own pace, and at a time of their choosing. The very specialized appeal of each magazine requires copywriters to tailor their copy carefully to fit the editorial environment.

Leaf through a few of today's magazines and see what their contents are all about. They are filled with information — "how to," "what to," and "why you should" articles. These magazines are *communicating* with their readers; they are printing the types of articles that provoke responses from their audiences. If they were not, they would not grow. What does this mean for advertisers? It means that their advertisements must be as good as the magazine's editorial content. It means that their advertisements must be interesting, informative, and helpful. It means that advertisers cannot rely on tired, meaningless cliches.

THE AMERICAN EXPRESS® CARD BUYS YOU THE QUEEN.

The QE2.* A city at sea. She's got 4 restaurants, 6 bars, 4 pools, ballrooms, nightclubs, a spa, a driving range and more. So for once in your life, live. And charge your QE2 cruise— or almost any cruise you choose —with the American Express® Card. Just tell your travel agent to "put it on the Card." Don't set sail without it.®

CUNARD

©American Express Travel Related Services Company, Inc. 1984   *Registered in Great Britain

A clever play on words addressed to a sophisticated magazine audience *(The New Yorker)*. The copy "sells" The Queen and much more without wasted words. And the final sentence ties in beautifully with the well-known theme of the American Express card —"Don't leave home without it."

Expressions such as *new and improved; engineered better; fast, fast, fast; tradition of excellence;* and *created with care* have all been overworked. So has the use of words ending in *ity,* such as *quality, reliability, dependability,* and *uniformity.*

Writing for magazines is easier than writing for radio or television. We can use more complicated words and phrases, if need be, because the reader will have time to dwell on them in order to grasp the full meaning. We start with one important idea. We say it, simply. That one memorable phrase or sentence is the headline. (See color plates 43–45 for some examples of magazine ads featuring strong copy.)

The Importance of the Headline   The headline of an advertisement is like a flag used to signal a train. It catches the attention of the engineer. The headline is expected to do two things: *select* from the total readership of the magazine those readers interested in the subject of the advertisement; then *promise* them a reward for reading the rest of the copy. There are two kinds of rewards:

When we finally found our dog Skipper, we also found out something about Gaines·burgers.® He loves it.

Our dog Skipper had been missing for three days when the Harrisons found him.

I hadn't slept at all. I'd been so worried that he hadn't eaten. He's so

fussy, he won't eat anything that doesn't come out of a can.

Well, there he was at the Harrisons'. The fussiest dog in the world, devouring a bowl of Gaines·burgers like he'd been eating it all his life.

Then Mrs. Harrison explained that not only is Gaines·burgers' dog food nutritionally balanced, but it's moist and meaty like canned dog food, too. And it was obvious from Skipper's clean bowl that it must taste terrific.

Anyway, Skipper doesn't stray too

far away from home anymore. He doesn't want to get that far away from his Gaines·burgers.

The canned dog food without the can.

Gaines

This **story headline** should arrest the attention of every dog lover. Was the dog lost? How did they find him again? What did they find out about Gaines-burgers? Read the copy and all your questions will be answered. The benefit: *he loves it.*

1. The reader will gain, save, or accomplish something through the use of our product. It will increase his or her mental, physical, financial, social, emotional, or psychic satisfaction, well-being, or security.
2. The reader will avoid, reduce, or eliminate risks, worries, losses, mistakes, embarrassment, unnecessary work, or some other undesirable condition. The product will decrease fear of poverty, illness, accident, discomfort, boredom, and the loss of business advancement or social prestige.

If possible, the headline will also tell the reader how quickly, easily, or inexpensively the promise will be fulfilled. Your purpose here should be to give readers who refuse to read your body copy a memorable message in the headline alone. Remember, only a small percentage of the audience will read most of your copy. And, besides, an advertisement with a blind headline can be a great waste. A **blind headline** is one that does not reveal to readers a benefit

The most effective moisturizer in the world.

Water.

If you know how to use it.

Your dry skin is thirsty. Literally. Thirsty for water. So all you need to do is soak in a tub for an hour, right? Wrong. Because although your skin soaks up needed moisture in the tub or shower, it's lost too easily from evaporation once you get out.

But we can make water work for you. Neutrogena® Body Oil was specifically formulated to maximize the moisturizing effects of your bath or shower. It's a pure, light sesame-oil-formula which is applied *after* you bathe, while your skin is still wet, to hold in the moisture.

Does it feel greasy? No, because sesame oil is so light that it seems to disappear on your skin, although it really forms an invisible moisture-holding film. But it won't stain your clothes, either.

Put the world's most effective moisturizer to work for your dry skin. Keep it there with our help.

Neutrogena®Body Oil
Use it every day.

Neutrogena Corp., 1978.

A blind headline, that is, the headline does not tell the reader what type of product is being advertised or what the brand name is. But the headline is very rational and promises a benefit to the consumer. Notice the effective use of questions and answers in the body copy, including the anticipated question: "Does it feel greasy?" Note, too, the frequent use of the words *you* and *your skin*. The advertiser is not talking to women in general, but to "you."

of product use. It requires the reader to read the body copy in order to receive the sales message. Compare these two headlines, for example:

"Revere Ware. They last so long we made their beauty timeless."

"A great Italian meal you can make in 15 minutes. It'll taste like it took hours."

Consider the words of the Revere headline, "they last so long." What do these words convey? What does "beauty timeless" convey? Puff. Compare these phrases with the wording of the second headline. Even if consumers never read a word of the body copy, they see benefits — good taste, speed, and pride ("It'll taste like it took hours")— in the headline alone. The second headline promises a benefit even if you never read another word. And, if you did glance at the

The legend continues...

Introducing the world's most sophisticated Diesel passenger car. The new Mercedes-Benz 300D.

The new, 5-passenger Mercedes-Benz 300D – the state of the Diesel passenger car art.

 Here is a most ingenious alternative to the conventional automobile. A truly remarkable new Mercedes-Benz. With a contemporary new look. With ample room for five people, an astonishing 5-cylinder engine and an unusually complete array of luxurious appointments and safety systems. The new 300D. The most sophisticated Diesel passenger car the world has ever seen.

For years, you've heard about exotic and promising alternatives to the conventional automobile engine. To date, only one alternative has kept its promise: the Diesel engine – for over 60 years, the most efficient combustion power plant in use.

Now Mercedes-Benz has synthesized its proven, 5-cylinder Diesel engine with new, technologically advanced body design, suspension, steering and safety systems to produce the most ingenious alternative to the conventional automobile.

A matter of taste

Though only a trim 190.9 inches from bumper to bumper, the new 300D is an honest 5-passenger sedan. The secret of its spaciousness lies in new Mercedes-Benz technology that puts the room in the car in the car – without adding bulk or sacrificing safety.

Enter a new 300D and you're surrounded by a complete array of security and convenience features. All are standard equipment. Such things as cruise control, bi-level climate control, electric windows, AM/FM radio, central locking system, 3-speed windshield wipers.

The new 300D is not an exercise in opulence. But it does exhibit meticulous taste. And as your senses will tell you, there's quite a difference between the two ideas.

Sports car handling

The new 300D is one of the most sparkling road cars Mercedes-Benz has ever engineered. Its sophisticated power train, suspension and steering are those of a sports car. And that is why the new 300D handles like one.

The new 300D's unique, 5-cylinder engine is the most powerful, the smoothest Diesel yet engineered into a passenger car. But you pay no penalty for this performance bonus. The EPA estimates that the new 300D should deliver up to 28 mpg on the highway, 23 mpg in town. (Your mileage will depend on how and where you drive and the condition and equipment of your car.)

The state of the art

For over 40 years, Mercedes-Benz has pioneered many of the major advances in Diesel passenger car engineering. The new 300D is the culmination of that experience. It is the state of the Diesel passenger car art.

Test drive the new 300D. Experience the most ingenious alternative to the conventional automobile. The most sophisticated Diesel passenger car in the world.

Mercedes-Benz
Engineered like no other car in the world.

©Mercedes-Benz, 1977

A long news headline that will leave a message even if the reader does not read all the body copy. The long copy is required to explain and justify the headline's claim of product superiority. The copy reinforces and amplifies the promise of sophistication with information on the car's Diesel engine, advanced body design, and suspension, steering, and safety systems. This is strong *reason why* copy.

bottom of each advertisement, just below the illustration, you would find that the Revere ad said:

"A heritage of excellence from Paul Revere."

While the Chef Boy-ar-dee ad told its readers:

"Nothing to add."

Okay? Good headlines make you want to read more. Fortunately for the Revere ad, the product's name was in the headline. That's the best we can say about it.

Long Copy or Short Copy   Body copy is the meat of an advertisement — our opportunity to say what must be said. Your readers have the time to read all the copy you can write; the trick is to get them started. Many times we write short copy because we believe people won't read long copy. Sometimes we write long copy because it looks impressive. Neither approach is correct. Write your first sentence so that it fulfills the promise offered in the headline. Write that sentence very carefully and write it so that you are sure the reader will want to read on to the second sentence. Write the second sentence the same way. Continue until you have said all that you promised in the headline, until you have made the reader want to own your product. That's how long the copy should be. More important than the length of the copy are the *kinds* of words that you use. Remember to use verbs and nouns, few adjectives and adverbs, and short, simple, easy-to-understand words that are just right for the *readers of your advertisement in that particular magazine.*

To sum up, our body copy must *explain* the product's benefits, must *support* the claims we make, must *provide* the reasons needed to convince our readers to spend their money for our product. The appeal we make may be objective or emotional. We know that most products are bought in response to an emotional appeal; we have to touch the right emotional button. Finally, we want the readers to do something; we want them to *accept* the idea, to *visit* their dealers, to *insist* upon our brand by name, to *send for* samples, or to *mail* in a coupon.

Of course, in much advertising our call to action is implicit, not explicit. No one needs to be told where to buy cigarettes, nor do people usually send in for samples or write for additional information. We are instead — particularly with a strong representation of the package — indirectly asking readers to remember our brand, to keep it in mind next time they go shopping, or, if they are already buying our product, to remain loyal.

Writing the Newspaper Advertisement

The daily newspaper is the *news medium.* It is current and it is fresh. It changes every day. It is *now.* Like a radio station's musical format, a newspaper's editorial environment has a strong influence on the nature of the advertising it carries. A newspaper is filled with news, facts, data, and information. Most newspapers feature local gossip, giving it the heaviest proportion of their news space. Many other sections of the paper consist merely of tabular listings of data, such as the stock market reports and the television program guide. The function of the newspaper is to *inform* us. We do not turn to it for entertainment as we do with radio or television. It is not written just for us the way our favorite magazine is. We buy it and read it when we want to know.

Perennial Tulips

Five Glorious Years Without Replanting

After years of testing, we now offer a strain of Tulips that is truly perennial. They have large, bowl-shaped flowers, grow to about two feet, and actually *increase* their offering of full-sized blooms for several years after planting. There is no gimmick. These recent hybrids are simply more vigorous and long-lived than any upright Tulip we've ever seen. Our top-sized bulbs will self-propagate readily in formal beds and are superb in mixed borders where their sturdy blooms start the spring show. Culture is easy: just give the bulbs a rich, well-drained site with plenty of sun, then follow the instructions that come with every shipment. So, if you normally plant new Tulips each fall, you can now figure your annual cost, and labor, at one fifth of your first cost.

Colors are somewhat limited and, for introductory purposes, we have selected three combinations that show off these remarkable Tulips at their best, whether mixed or separate. Each includes 24 bulbs, which will make a handsome display while allowing you to snitch a few for the house. The first includes a dozen each of **Red and Yellow**. Both are clear, rich hues and together they produce electricity. Order **#84421**, 24 bulbs for $16.00. The second combination offers a dozen pure **White** with the same number of a clear, little-girl **Pink**. The effect is romantic, to say the least. Order **#84422**, 24 bulbs for $19.00. Finally, we've mixed twelve each of the **Red and White**, with predictably delightful results. Order **#84423**, 24 bulbs for $19.00. Please add shipping charges of 10% east of the Mississippi, 15% west. For your convenience, phone orders to MasterCard and Visa accounts are welcome weekdays until 8 p.m. and Saturdays until 5 at our toll-free number (800) 243-2853. (Ct. residents please call 567-0801 and add sales tax.) Orders are charged upon receipt and bulbs, with complete planting instructions, will be shipped for fall planting.

In addition to a stunning Tulip display, purchasers will enjoy unlimited access to our staff horticulturist by phone or mail, free admission to our display gardens in Litchfield, and a subscription to our catalogues, known collectively as The Garden Book. Makes for a well-rounded purchase.

Sincerely,
Amos Pettingill

White Flower Farm

P l a n t s m e n

Litchfield 9057, Connecticut 06759-0050

Short copy. Every word describes some appeal in order to reach as wide an audience as possible.

This ad appeared as a one-sixth page ad (half column) in *The New Yorker* magazine. With very little space to work with, the copywriter wrote a provocative headline that stimulates the reader's curiosity and two tight sentences of body copy to explain the headline.

Long copy. When the audience and medium have been carefully selected, the longest copy will be read. This is a mail-order ad and the results of this ad are easily measured. The copy flows smoothly, in a conversational tone. The "Sincerely, Amos Pettingill" at the bottom rounds it off on a personal note.

How Does a News Environment Affect Advertising?   Readers of newspapers seek out the ads. Studies show that (for women) display ads are the second most intensively read portion of the newspaper. Newspaper readers are accustomed to act fast—to call the employment agency, to visit the store, to phone for information. They are generally in a decisive mood. They are ready to act.

Learning to Write Copy for Newspaper Ads   The trick in newspaper advertising is to be specific. Study the classified ads. Realtors really know how to squeeze the strongest, most specific appeal into the fewest words. "Good schools. Convenient shopping. View. Low taxes." They know what the prospects want. Newspaper advertising is a *now* medium—it can take advantage of new developments, new processes, and new technologies. Tie your copy in with current news events. A small-space ad with a high-impact headline and copy that concentrates on one strong selling idea can be very successful. We must remember that since newspapers are not selective, our headline has to be. "Now, prompt relief from hemorrhoids with Preparation H" flags its market instantly.

Copy for Radio

Each radio commercial, usually one minute in length, is a sales message. Our commercial is an interruption of the listener's entertainment, so we may want to embellish our selling idea with music or sound effects or deliver it in a skit or a jingle. But it is important always to keep in mind the advertising objectives that our commercial must meet. These objectives may be to build the product image, to introduce the product, to stimulate usage, or to position the product against competition. We do not want the entertainment value of our commercial to obscure the sales message we must deliver.

As we have already learned, radio is our most highly segmented medium. People who like rock or contemporary music like a complementary pace in the talk and news on that station. People who like "top tunes" like the announcers that go with them, and so on. When writing copy for a radio commercial, we must take into account the particular context in which our message will appear and write for the type of audience a given station attracts. One of the most popular ways to get a message across is to provide a product information sheet for local announcers or disc jockeys and let them ad-lib the commercial with the **fact sheet** as a guide. Since listeners like and trust the personalities that they listen to regularly, our message gains believability when these announcers read it.

Often, however, radio commercials are recorded announcements. These commercials are read from prepared scripts by professional announcers or actors and sometimes include special sound effects and music. These prerecorded commercials may take several different formats:

The skit.   A short "play" will hold the attention of the listeners and often entertain them while delivering the message. The clever skits for *Time* magazine and the skits for Blue Nun wine that featured Stiller and Meara are examples of this type of commercial.

The problem and solution.   The dead battery that won't start the car, the raspy cough that won't go away, the aches of arthritis—all are problems that might be remedied by our product.

```
VOICE A:   So that's the office.
VOICE B:   Great.
VOICE A:   Oh, if you ever need copies made, give them to that woman over there
           with the black pointy hat and the wart on her nose.
VOICE B:   Who's she?
VOICE A:   She's Griselda the office W-I-T-C-H.
VOICE B:   What?
VOICE A:   She takes big documents into that secret room over there, and they come
           out smaller, like file size.
VOICE B:   Must be a Minolta 300RE copier in there.
VOICE A:   No, it's magic. She can also take small documents into the room, and
           when she comes out, they're larger.
VOICE B:   And clean and crisp?
VOICE A:   Right.
VOICE B:   That's the Minolta 300RE.
VOICE A:   Uh-uh.
VOICE B:   Yes, it reduces, enlarges and delivers top quality copies. Look — let me
           show you what . . .
VOICE A:   No! Don't go in there!
VOICE B:   Ah-hah!
VOICE A:   What is it?
VOICE B:   The Minolta 300RE.
VOICE A:   Gee, then she's not a witch.
GRISELDA:  What are you doing in here, my pretties?
ANNOUNCER: The Minolta 300RE. Not magic, just new. Reduces, enlarges, and great
           copies, too.
VOICE B:   Gee Fred, I'm sorry if I got you into trouble.
VOICE A:   Croak.
VOICE B:   I said I'm sorry. You want another fly?
```

The task of selling a small office copier on radio is difficult. The stations are cluttered
with singing commercials, shouting announcers, and just talk. For Minolta, the agency and
the writers opted for an obviously incredible little drama. Two men in an office, one
says there's a witch in the place who turns out crisp copies, enlarged or reduced. As
might be expected, they follow Griselda, the office witch, into the copying room where
they discover it isn't witchcraft, but a Minolta 300RE. However, unexpectedly, Griselda
catches them in her room and turns one of them into a frog. And, the twist at the end is
funny and clever. (Courtesy Minolta Corporation.)

The testimonial.   The basketball star or movie star who uses the product and
delivers the message. We can also have average consumers endorse the product
as they are being interviewed by an announcer.

The slice of life.   An apparently unrehearsed dialogue between friends, mother
and child, or retailer and customer must be delivered in an everyday context
with background sounds that evoke a realistic setting. The situation may be
funny or serious. If we use dialogue, however, it must sound like the speech of
real people, but it must not wander so aimlessly that we lose the sales message.

A fantasy story.   This can be somewhat humorous. We can use a talking
animal, an elf, or a person from the pages of history.

A singing commercial.   When well done, a singing or musical commercial is
memorable and "sweetens" the selling message.

   None of these formats is exclusive; they may be combined in an endless
variety of ways. The most important thing to remember in creating a prerecorded commercial is that we have to rely on sounds — the human voice and
musical instruments — to convey the message *and* the mood. We have to think

ANNOUNCER: If you want top management to see your advertising, you have to place it in the magazine top management reads.

MAN 1: 'Scuse me . . . are you the new ad manager here?

MAN 2: Yeah, and I'm busy.

MAN 1: Well, I just came by to tell you my wife loves the new corporate ad you did.

MAN 2: So, the little woman likes it, huh?

MAN 1: She's not all that little. She's . . .

MAN 2: Hey, they can't all be skinny models, y'know.

MAN 1: Oh, I didn't mean . . .

MAN 2: So, uh, where'd the little dumpling see it?

MAN 1: The little dumpl . . . in *Business Week.*

MAN 2: Your wife reads *Business Week?*

MAN 1: Well, as chairman of the board here . . .

MAN 2: Whuh. Your wife's the chairdumpling?

MAN 1: Person.

MAN 2: Uh, person.

MAN 1: She really depends on *Business Week.* Ask her about corporate strategies, international money management, labor, the economy, and you know what she says?

MAN 2: Your . . . uh . . . chairwife?

MAN 1: She says, "Of course I'm sure. I read it in *Business Week.*"

MAN 2: Oh, *Business Week.* Yeah.

MAN 1: Boy, you can't argue with that.

MAN 2: No, don't argue . . .

MAN 1: Look, I'd better be running along. She doesn't like it when I extend these coffee breaks.

MAN 2: Yeah, well . . . give my kindest regards to . . . to . . . her excellency.

MAN 1: Well, aren't you nice?

MAN 2: Yeah, thanks.

MAN 1: And I'm sure the little dumpling will feel the same way.

MAN 2: See, when I said "dumpling," I thought that you were . . .

MAN 1: You'll find work somewhere . . .

MAN 2: Oh, no . . .

ANNOUNCER: If you're in business, you should be reading *Business Week.* If you advertise to business, you should be selling in *Business Week:* The voice of authority.

The *Business Week* radio campaign was created to reinforce the image of authority that the magazine represents. Note how the announcer concludes the commercial with "The voice of authority." The spot is truly funny as the new ad manager makes a fool of himself. The message is "Read *Business Week* and you won't be so dumb and get yourself fired." The commercial has been aired in Boston, Chicago, Detroit, Los Angeles, San Francisco, and, of course, New York.

"Dumpling" is a very clever and creative commercial and has received high praise from professional ad people, a tough audience. (Courtesy *Business Week.*)

of sounds that are appropriate to our message and that the listener can easily identify. Sounds can evoke pictures in the audience's mind. The roar of the wind, the grinding of an automobile starter, the rattle of dishes and trays in a restaurant, the crackle of flames — all are clearly identifiable sounds that can be used to set a background for our words. A simple but effective use of background sounds can be heard in a commercial for Rioja wines of Spain. A Spanish-accented voice delivers the commercial message while a flamenco guitar plays in the background. The sound of the guitar conjures up images of Spain more effectively than any words, and possibly any pictures, could.

In general, be specific — remember this is the spoken word. There will be no opportunity for the listeners to refer to the copy later as they might on a printed page. Involve the imagination of the listening audience. Conjure up images with your words and with the sound effects that you use. The opening words are critical — you have ten seconds to catch the prospects' attention. If you can't, the rest of the commercial is wasted. Try for something that will stick in their memory, such as the well-known American Express card message — "Don't leave home without it." Repetition is also important. If written carefully, you can say the same thing two, three, and even four times in that one minute. Every word must say something to, and be understood by, the audience.

The Place of Music

The McDonald's jingle, "It's a good time for the great taste of McDonald's," is one of a long line of memorable jingles. The words summarize the appeal: "good time" has a double meaning — "now" and "fun" — and "great taste" is what the product is all about. The lyrics were written by Margie Gaynor, copy supervisor, and the music by Jack Smith, vice-chairman creative services, both executives at Leo Burnett USA. The music debuted in June 1984 and has remained so memorable because of the large number of variations that have been developed. The jingle was used one way for spots targeted to children, another way for teens, another for blacks, another for Hispanics, and so on. And within the groups, variations promoted specific products such as Big Macs or Chicken McNuggets. In a similar fashion, a wide range of talent has been utilized to sing the jingle — country and western singers and jazz singers. The agency estimates that it has produced as many as 1,000 variations on the musical melody.

In contrast, Miller's "Made the American Way" depends on words to carry the message. The idea was to use values that people shared and understood — like the meaning of a handshake. The music is the Oak Ridge Boys' ballad "American Made" which appeared briefly on the charts a few years ago. It proved easily arrangeable, and more than a dozen versions of the basic melody have been produced for TV spots as well as rock and jazz-oriented radio formats.

For many commercials, most often on radio, music provides a recognition factor which conveys the product at once to the listener. For example, if a person driving a car is preoccupied by traffic and misses the advertising message, the music gets through and reminds him or her of the product.

And, if we want to describe a musical ad with staying power, it's the Chiquita Banana jingle. That jingle was first aired in 1945, and it is a classic. It clearly identifies the product and the brand. When first introduced, it was aired 376 times a day. Recordings of the jingle even appeared in juke boxes of the forties. The U.S. Government borrowed the tune for a song about conserving water and tin cans during World War II. A final note — bananas *can* be kept in the refrigerator.

Writing for Television

What an opportunity television offers — sight, sound, color, motion! Yet, with all these opportunities to be truly creative, so many of the commercials are wearying — four, five, six in a row, with people talking to each other or to us in

MALDEN: You are about to witness a crime . . .

MAN: I'm gonna dive.

I'm going to do the double reverse half-gainer with a pike.

WOMAN: O.K.
MAN: No, I'm all right.
WOMAN: Go ahead then.

MAN: O.K. Take a picture of this. This may be the last one.

MAN: Ready. Get a good one.

MALDEN: They're on vacation . . .

WOMAN: I'm watching.

MALDEN: They've saved all year . . .

WOMAN: I'm watching.

MALDEN: just for this.

WOMAN: Oooooh!

MALDEN: If cash is stolen, it's gone for good.

So carry these—American Express ® Travelers Cheques. If lost or stolen you can get these back.

Don't leave home without them. ®

Date 1/21/85

This television commercial does its job of delivering a message. The recognizable voice of Karl Malden captures the attention of the audience at the beginning of the commercial with the statement: "You are about to witness a crime." The scene is now set for the story that unfolds, and the story relates the benefit offered by the product.

stilted, artificial language. The friendly auto mechanic in his spotless uniform, the nurse or doctor type telling us about cold remedies or chapped hands; the list is endless. What's wrong?

If we want to communicate the benefit, or benefits, of our product to our prospects, the first step is to demonstrate it. Television is demonstration. All we need to do is show prospective customers what the product's main value to them is. Unfortunately, the best attributes of some products can't be demonstrated (the taste of beer or the pain-relieving qualities of headache remedies and cold tablets). That's where the need for creative writing comes in. Analogies, skits, testimonials, and slice-of-life situations can help us prove our claim. What about humor? The use of humor can sometimes be effective, but, unless

PROFILE

John O'Toole

After graduating from journalism school (Northwestern University) and completing a stint in the Marines, John O'Toole decided he would rather write advertising copy than newspaper stories. So, in 1953 he joined Batten, Barton, Durstine, & Osborn, Inc., in New York as a copywriter, moving the next year to the Chicago office of Foote, Cone & Belding Communications, Inc. There, under the tutelage of the legendary adman, Fairfax Mastick Cone, John O'Toole polished and perfected his writing skill. Apparently he learned his craft well, because he was quickly promoted from copywriter to copy supervisor and then to associate copy director. From Chicago, O'Toole was sent to Foote, Cone & Belding's Los Angeles office as creative director and later asked to return to Chicago as senior vice-president and director of the company. Ultimately, he moved to the New York headquarters of Foote, Cone & Belding as president of this prospering international agency, with world-wide billings of $1.901 billion in 1985. John O'Toole is now chairman of the agency.

Outside the agency, John O'Toole is active in many civic and professional organizations. He is a member of the board of directors of the American Association of Advertising Agencies and of the board of directors of the Advertising Council. He is a trustee of the Greenwich Academy and the American Ballet Theatre. John O'Toole also finds time in his active life to write poetry. He has published a book of poetry, and a number of his poems have appeared in various magazines.

In a recent interview, portions of which were quoted in advertisements for *The Wall Street Journal,* John O'Toole offered these thoughts on today's consumers and the copywriters who write for them:

> If I want to write to individual consumers, then I must know how they think, and live, and buy. So I believe it's essential to go beyond the statistics of public opinion, to look at what's happening in the real world. For example, you might see today as a time of reassuring quiet after the turbulence of the sixties. But that's only the surface. There's a new spirit of individualism; people seeking to satisfy their own goals, serve their ambitions, feed their individual appetites, find life styles to suit their needs. Small wonder there's such distrust of advertising that treats people as a homogeneous mass. Today's great advertising speaks to individual needs—to the strong drive to be yourself.

the humor has a relationship to the subject, it will entertain the viewer and leave no message.

A television commercial conveys both sight and sound. In writing advertising copy for television, then, the copywriter must write the words of the message with the accompanying pictures, or video, in mind. A good example of the effective use of both sight and sound is a television commercial for American Tourister Luggage showing one of that company's suitcases in a cage with a gorilla. As the gorilla throws the suitcase against the walls and jumps on it, an announcer's voice describes the sturdiness of the luggage. The words are reinforced by the video. The commercial is simple, believable, and interesting. And it makes its point in 30 seconds. Another effective television commercial shows a man driving a Volkswagen in the dark along a snow-covered road. The VW stops; a man gets out, opens a garage, and gets ready to climb into a huge tractor that will plow the snow from the roads. The announcer simply asks us: "How does the man who drives the snowplow *get* to the snowplow?" Again, a simple, believable, interesting commercial.

Most copywriting courses stress the **AIDA** of television copy, which is an acronym for *Attention, Interest, Desire, Action.* To these qualities, we must add the word *quick* because we have to do it all in 30 seconds. Because time is at such a premium, every word must pull its weight; every scene must contribute.

In a way, a television commercial is like a play. There has to be a plot with a beginning, a middle, and an end. Each part of the story must relate to and follow what precedes it. The writer builds interest and sustains that interest until the conclusion of the play. It must have pace and the audience must be able to relate to it. Unlike a play which the audience attends voluntarily, however, the opening sequence of the television commercial must instantly capture the attention of the audience. The audience must be prepared for the situation. We have caught their **A**ttention and built their **I**nterest. The action that follows presents the benefits of the product that *relate to the situation* and thus builds **D**esire and, it is hoped, **A**ction in the form of subsequent purchase behavior.

Writing Copy for Direct Mail

Think of direct-mail advertising as a rifle aimed at the target market, in contrast to the shotguns of other advertising techniques. If we only have one shot, we had better be sure we have loaded our rifle with an effective bullet. With direct mail, we want to stimulate direct, measurable action, more so than with any other medium. To get results, we must be prepared to prove every claim.

The first line of our letter is like the headline of an ad. It has to insure that the rest of the letter will be read. The copy of the direct-mail piece must be sincere. The personal way in which direct mail reaches prospects makes them very sensitive to phony appeals. They receive countless letters and circulars inviting them to join a select group, urging them to take quick action because the supply is limited, or warning them that the offer will be withdrawn soon. You cannot make the message sound sincere unless you are.

The one advantage direct mail has over other forms of advertising is the virtually unrestricted creativity permitted in the design of the shape or form of the direct-mail piece. The copy is still the most important factor in the message, but variations in form add interest and enhance the impact of any direct-mail piece you create.

CASE HISTORY

Holly Farms

In 1984, Americans ate, in assorted forms, an average of about 54 pounds of chicken each — twice the consumption of 1964. The country has been steadily switching from beef to poultry. Chicken can be bought anywhere. Any supermarket. Any deli or any corner grocery. A whole chicken. Parts. Frozen. Fresh. Deboned. All of which has meant the rise of some well-known chicken growers that control their product from newly-laid eggs to freshly-wrapped packages. One such farm is Holly Farms, a part of the Federal Company in Wilkesboro, North Carolina. Holly Farms Poultry Industries, Inc., was formed in 1961 through a merger of 16 businesses separately engaged in the various stages of producing broilers — breeding, hatching, growing, processing, rendering, and marketing. Holly Farms is one of the largest mar-

keters of fresh chicken in the United States, with over 8.8 percent of the total market. The company markets its products in 44 states. Shipments to retail chains represented 18 percent of the branded chicken market.

To build a strong identity, Holly Farms chose Dinah Shore as spokesperson. It was a good choice — Dinah Shore is a well-known personality and the author of two cookbooks. She appeared as herself in a series of television commercials introduced in 1983. In a typical spot illustrated here, the director gives her lines that she rejects, saying his lines are too complicated. With that she offers her own straightforward line "What about taste?" Dinah Shore is informal, personable, and believable. Awareness doubled in key markets and share of market jumped.

HOLLY FARMS
"WHAT ABOUT TASTE" :30

DIRECTOR (VO): Here are your lines: "I'm Dinah Shore."
DINAH: I can remember that.

DIRECTOR (VO): And then you say "Holly Farms chicken has a guaranteed freshness date."
DINAH: Got it.

DIRECTOR (VO): "And Holly Farms has more plump, tender meat per pound than most any other chicken..."

DINAH: OK. Now when do you get to the part about the taste?
DIRECTOR (VO): Oh, there's no taste in the script, Dinah.
DINAH: I know that.

But I'm talking about the taste of the chicken 'cause I cooked it and it's very good. It's from my cookbook...that's important...really.

DIRECTOR (VO): Yeah, but you have to say "More good cooks cook Holly Farms than any other chicken."

DINAH: I do? That's too complicated... More good cooks?...

no...America is cooking with Holly Farms!
DIRECTOR (VO): That's perfect!

DINAH (VO): Do you like it?
DIRECTOR (VO): Yeah!
DINAH (VO): I could go home and practice your version...

15 | COPY FOR ADVERTISING

Writing Copy for Outdoor

Outdoor is basically a graphic artist's medium. At best, the copywriter can hope only to convey one major idea on the billboard. The target audience merely glances at the poster and cannot stop to read it carefully. The reader must grasp the entire message at once. Eliminate all unnecessary words and details. If the message cannot be read and understood in ten seconds, do it over. The copy must be simple, direct, compact. The ideal poster is one that uses symbols so universal that everyone recognizes them. The symbol must evoke a response that will remain in the viewer's memory. The major difficulty is in pruning. The more you know about the product and the target market, the more difficult it is to restrain yourself. A good outdoor poster will involve the audience. Remember the Volkswagen poster that showed a VW driving off the left side of the sheet with the caption: "Everyone's getting the bug"? What a friendly feeling the reader got when even the company admitted that its car had been nicknamed the "bug."

The Last Word

All advertising copy is the result of a collaboration between the copywriter, the artist, and the market researcher. Within the short time permitted for its creation, the copy must be crafted to fit the requirements of the medium and the client company. That so much imaginative and effective copy has been written and is being written is a credit to the advertising copywriter.

Summary

Advertising copy is not literary copy. Quite the contrary. The writer of advertising copy is self-effacing; his or her art must be transparent. The objective is to sell a product. To do this effectively, the writer must know all the facts about the product—its strengths and its weaknesses, if any. The writer must also know the facts about competitive products. Armed with facts, and only then, is the writer ready to match the attributes of the product with the real wants of the target customer. What do customers want in the product? What appeal will make them buy it?

Advertisers must always remember that they are uninvited guests—interrupting viewing and listening, interfering with reading. The reader has bought the publication for news and information. The reader has turned on the radio or television for entertainment, but will watch and listen to our sales message if we say something of interest using words and symbols that are understood and believed. Therein lies the art of copywriting. The headline must stimulate attention and interest. The body copy must develop desire and action. And the writer must do these things within the framework of the media.

Each medium has attributes that, if used properly, enhance the message; when improperly used, advertising money is wasted. Magazines are a selective medium, appealing to readers seeking information on specific subjects. Newspapers create an atmosphere of speed and immediacy. Radio adds to our message the quality and warmth of a human voice and personality. Television puts it all together—the voice, the color, the action—but must do it all within a time frame of 30 seconds.

What does a copywriter need? Knowledge of the product, knowledge of the target market, knowledge of the media, and above all, an understanding of the use of words to convey images and information.

Questions for Discussion

1. What kinds of factual material are needed to formulate copy ideas?
2. What is the main difference between print and television copy? Between print and radio copy?
3. List ten words that have several different meanings. List five pairs of words that have similar meanings.
4. Draw up a set of guidelines for copywriters to follow when writing headlines.
5. Find five samples of magazine ads for which you consider the headlines poor or weak. Rewrite the headlines and justify your changes.
6. List a dozen words that can be used to evoke images.
7. Write three headlines for a breakfast cereal, each using a different appeal to the senses.
8. Choose a product with which you are familiar. Make up two lists, one that indicates what the product offers, the other what the customer wants. Do your lists match?

Sources and Suggestions for Further Reading

Ahrend, Herb. "Making Business Direct Marketing Copy Work Harder." *The Communicator,* September-October 1984.

Baldwin, Huntley. *Creating Effective TV Commercials.* Chicago: Crain Books, 1984.

Bayan, Richard. *Words That Sell.* Westbury, N.Y.: Asher-Gallant Press, 1984.

Book, Albert C., and Norman D. Cary. *The Radio and Television Commercial.* Chicago: Crain Books, 1984

Burton, Philip W. *Advertising Copywriting.* New York: McGraw-Hill, 1983.

Glim, Aesop. *How Advertising Is Written — And Why.* New York: Dover Publications, 1961.

Hafer, W. Keith, and Gordon White. *Advertising Writing.* St. Paul, Minn.: West Publishing Co., 1982.

Hayakawa, S. I. *Language in Action.* New York: Harcourt Brace Jovanovich, 1941.

Hotchkiss, George Burton. *Advertising Copy.* 3d ed. New York: Harper & Brothers, 1949.

Lewis, Herschell Gordon. "Why Don't You Say What You Mean?" *Direct Marketing,* May 1986.

Milton, Shirly F., and Arthur A. Winters. *The Creative Connection: Advertising Copy and Idea Visualization.* New York: Fairchild, 1981.

Norins, Hanley. *The Compleat Copywriter.* New York: McGraw-Hill, 1966.

Ris, Thomas F. *Promotional & Advertising Copywriter's Handbook.* Blue Ridge Summit, Pa.: Tab Books, 1971.

Schwab, Victor D. *How to Write A Good Advertisement.* New York: Harper & Brothers, 1962.

16 ADVERTISING ART

Working Vocabulary

visualization	gaze motion	stock art
layout	reverse	storyboard
thumbnail	tempera	production house
rough	wash	take
tissues	tight	dailies
comprehensive	loose	work print
optical center	line drawing	answer print
copy block	scratchboard	mini-cams

Most good ads are conceived as a totality — a combination of words, shapes, illustrations, and perhaps color — all planned to produce a certain effect, usually the selling of a product or an idea. Radio advertising is the only medium that does not appeal to our sense of sight. We call the presentation of our advertising message in its visual form the **visualization.** The person who designs our ad will give the words of the copywriter visual form to enhance their effect and then combine the words with a form of illustration to *add* to the message, to *underscore* the message, or often, especially in the case of outdoor, to *be* the message.

The Illustration

The centerpiece of most printed advertisements is an illustration. Later in this chapter we will discuss the various methods of producing a suitable illustration, but, for the moment, we should consider its function in our advertisements. The illustration, or illustrations, may serve one or more purposes. It may:

1. attract attention
2. emphasize a fact about the product or its use
3. transmit an idea of the product in use
4. create an atmosphere
5. reinforce the image of the package
6. clarify the headline or copy
7. stimulate the audience's desire for the product

Like the headline, the illustration also serves as a "flag" to attract the attention of our target market. For example, we know from research that women show *high interest* in illustrations of:

1. fashions and wearing apparel
2. "pride" foods such as pie and cake mixes
3. cosmetics and beauty products
4. pharmaceuticals that improve the appearance
5. certain types of home furnishings, such as living-room furniture, silverware, rugs, and dishes, that are highly visible and that reflect good taste.
6. children
7. appliances such as freezers, refrigerators, and toasters

Of *medium interest* are basic foods, ordinary home furnishings, household supplies, travel, books, and records.

Illustrations that are of *high interest* to a male audience include:

1. machinery
2. automobiles
3. boats
4. whiskey and beer
5. electronic products
6. cigarettes
7. entertainment
8. wearing apparel

Readers of both sexes are attracted to illustrations of puppies, kittens, horses, beautiful scenery, food, vacations, and exotic locations.

By carefully selecting an illustration that will most appeal to the members of our target market, then, we can increase the readership and the effectiveness of our advertisements.

Layout

A **layout** is the arrangement of elements in a printed advertisement — the headline, the illustration, the body copy, the subsidiary illustrations, the border, and the logotype. The layout represents a pattern, formed by these elements, that is intended to attract the reader, enhance the sales message, create an impression, make the message easy to read, direct the eye of the reader, and stimulate action. If all this sounds like a tall order, it really isn't. Every layout does all these things — some do them well, some do not.

Creating the Layout

Artists seek ideas for the layout of an advertisement in much the same way that copywriters seek ideas for the headline and body copy. They begin by immersing themselves in facts about the product and the advertiser. In addition, the artists must learn what the advertiser expects to accomplish, what the constraints are, and, of course, what medium will be used.

The first tentative designs that the artist makes are usually very small — only a fraction of the actual size. Because of their size, these sketches are called **thumbnails.** They include rough approximations of all the elements that must be incorporated into the finished ad. Thumbnails are generally not shown to anyone outside the agency, and certainly not to the advertiser. The purpose of these small sketches is to work up quickly a number of possible designs for the layout. That's why they are small. Once the ideas begin to crystallize, the artist will make full-size sketches of the best designs.

The full-size sketches are called **roughs,** because they are very unfinished, or **tissues,** because they are usually drawn on textured white tracing paper, called tissue. Roughs may be done in pencil or felt-tip pen and, again, are intended for internal agency use only. The artist will include just enough detail to show the other people involved (the copywriter, the art supervisor, the creative director, and the account executive) the style of the ad, the arrangement of the elements, and the type of illustration. Sometimes the artist will turn out as few as two or three, sometimes as many as a dozen roughs, to find the best possible combination of the various elements. After eliminating the unsatisfactory designs, the artist may do two more roughs — a little more

The artist's rough of an idea for a Hathaway shirt ad. The baby deer symbolizes softness; the trees, the power of nature. Together, these two images transmit a message of ruggedness and warmth. The eye patch identifies the shirt as a Hathaway.

A more careful rendering of the layout for the Hathaway shirt ad. This version, usually described as a *comp* (short for *comprehensive*), contains a more refined suggestion of the size and style of type to be used for the headline. This time the artist visualized the building in the background as a mansion.

detailed than the previous ones. When everyone at the agency approves one of these designs, the artist prepares a **comprehensive.** The *comp,* as it is called, is prepared with great care. The style and size of headline type is precisely indicated, the illustration is carefully delineated; every element of the ad is shown in place. Frequently, the headline is actually set in type and pasted onto the artist's drawing. If the illustration is a photograph, an actual print of that photograph may be added to the comp. The agency wants the comp to look as much like the finished advertisement as possible, because this is the layout that is shown to the advertiser for final approval.

Principles of Design

The number of possible arrangements of the elements in any advertisement is almost limitless — in theory, at least. Although advertising design is purposeful, it utilizes the same structural principles found in fine art. These principles include *balance, movement, unity,* and *focus.*

Balance The advertising designer achieves balance in the layout by placing the elements so that they complement each other in terms of size and weight. Balance may be formal and symmetrical or informal and asymmetrical.

Hathaway's Lochlana.
A tough, rugged shirt that's still blissfully soft.

Hathaway's Lochlana is so soft, your skin will think you've invested in cashmere. The imported fabric is of incredibly smooth texture. The purest combed cotton and just the "tops"—the softest part—of wool are spun together in every strand.

Two of the finest mills in the world developed special dyes to achieve Lochlana's exclusive patterns. The colors are woven into the cloth, not printed on it. The tartans snap. The solids project a rich, uniform glow.

And of course, every Hathaway Lochlana shirt is crafted with the same thorough attention to detail we lavish on our dress shirts.

Unfortunately, there is one problem. Like fine wines, only so much Lochlana is created each year. What's more, men who refuse to settle for less do hoard the shirts. We recommend haste, while your haberdasher still has your favorite color.

The Hathaway ad as it finally appeared. The illustration shows a winter scene with bare trees but no building. The bare trees reinforce the image of winter, whereas the evergreen trees shown in the preceding sketches would have contributed a note of ambiguity. The bare trees also form a contrasting background for the colorful plaid shirt. Notice that the copy has been arranged into three equal blocks of type, probably to improve readability.

Some products, by their nature, demand a very formal balance. One consideration in determining the balance of an advertisement is what is known as the **optical center.** The optical center is a point about three-fifths of the distance up from the bottom of an advertisement. The eye seems to be naturally attracted to this point and, where possible, the designer gives it a pivotal position in the advertisement.

All the elements of this ad are centered in a very formal balance. The model is in the middle of a square photograph that is framed with a thin black line; the unequal lines of copy centered above the photograph provide a contrast to the square photograph and add interest to the copy. The ad projects a conservative image that is very English in the minds of the American audience to whom it is addressed. To reinforce the image, the designer included an English constable.

The English look is the Burberry look.

Lord Lichfield is wearing a classic raglan raincoat, the Piccadilly. It comes in a variety of cloths, and in the Shearford version with a detachable lining. It is priced from $95. Available from the finest shops and stores throughout the United States. For further details contact: Burberrys Limited,* Sales Office, Suite 1710, 1290 Avenue of the Americas, New York NY 10019. Tel. (212) 582 3870.

*A New York Corporation Burberry and Burberrys are registered trade marks of Burberrys Limited.

Burberrys
OF LONDON

Movement   It is important to lead the reader through the ad so that our message is delivered in its most effective sequence. An ad is given motion by the juxtaposition of the elements, using, as far as possible, the illustration or illustrations. The direction in which a model is looking or the direction in which an arm, hand, or finger is pointing gives motion to the ad. The shape of the **copy block,** the break in the headline when it runs to more than one line — these, too, can be utilized to provide the **gaze motion** that subtly directs the reader's eyes.

Unity   We often speak of the unity of a painting — which means that all the elements work well together. We have all seen ads at one time or another that looked as if the advertiser had merely thrown all the different elements together to fit whatever space was available. Unfortunately, a jumbled ad conveys a jumbled impression of its message to prospective customers. Without being able to say why, they find the ad confusing, and they either will not read it at all or, reading it, will not be convinced by its appeal.

Jeep Wagoneer,
rugged, versatile,
accomplished,
...like its owner.

Jeep Wagoneer, built for a very special individual.
An outdoorsman who demands quality and performance from his vehicle no matter what the weather or
road conditions. He relies on Wagoneer for everyday
transportation or to take him to the special off-road
retreats so important to his lifestyle. And since he
insists on quality in every aspect of his life, he appre-
ciates Jeep Wagoneer's reputation for consistent
performance; its roomy comfort and conveniences
like automatic transmission, Quadra-Trac® automatic 4-wheel drive, power front disc brakes,
powerful 360 V-8 engine—all standard, of course.
Jeep Wagoneer—like its owner—rugged,
versatile, accomplished.

Jeep
we wrote the book
on 4-wheel drive

Jeep Corporation, a subsidiary of American Motors Corporation

This ad is an excellent example of informal balance, well suited to the image of a rugged, four-wheel drive vehicle such as the Jeep. Notice how the elements enhance the message — the weather-beaten house, the rough terrain, the sea, the hills in the distance. Yet, the vehicle itself is level — stable, dependable, sturdy. Even the type has been carefully arranged to enhance the rugged image; the left side of the type block is uneven, but the right side is straight to contrast with the irregular outline of the house and trees.

Focus   Just as copywriters emphasize a product's most important selling idea in their copy, designers must create a focus in each of their layouts that will emphasize one or more of the design's elements. Designers can develop *focus* by using any of a number of simple tricks. They can place a round or oval illustration among a group of square ones. They can **reverse** a line of type (that is, have the type printed white against a dark background) on a page of black type. They can add a spot of color to highlight one of the elements or they can use a generous amount of white space to emphasize the body copy. They can set a few words in a bold type or specify an oversize illustration. There are countless ways to create a focus for the ad.

Constraints

Keep in mind that we are not after "art for art's sake." Our art has a purpose and with it go numerous constraints. The copy must fit the available space. The advertiser's name and package must be included. We may have full

The designer of this full-page ad has used the two pens as pointers to bring our eyes down to the word "Parker." This gaze motion is reinforced by the eyes on the face of the twenty-dollar bill peeking through the window of the gift envelope and also by the angle of the box of golf balls. The juxtaposition of the various components in this ad, as in any well-designed ad, makes for the kind of unity that is pleasing to the eye. At the same time, the elements have been arranged to facilitate the reading of the sales message, which is, after all, the purpose of the ad.

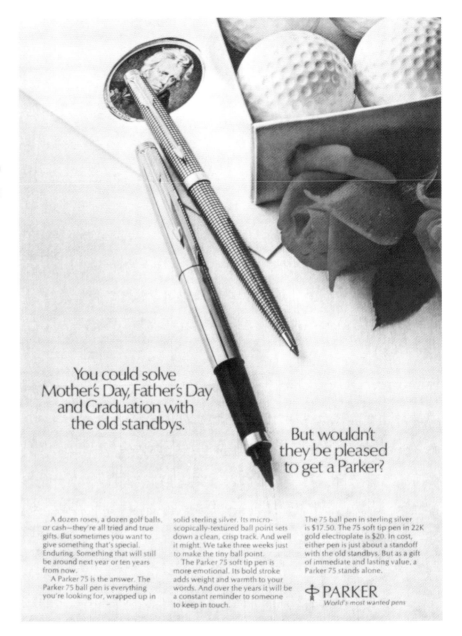

You could solve
Mother's Day, Father's Day
and Graduation with
the old standbys.

But wouldn't
they be pleased
to get a Parker?

A dozen roses, a dozen golf balls, or cash—they're all tried and true gifts. But sometimes you want to give something that's special. Enduring. Something that will still be around next year or ten years from now.
A Parker 75 is the answer. The Parker 75 ball pen is everything you're looking for, wrapped up in

solid sterling silver. Its microscopically-textured ball point sets down a clean, crisp track. And well it might. We take three weeks just to make the tiny ball point.
The Parker 75 soft tip pen is more emotional. Its bold stroke adds weight and warmth to your words. And over the years it will be a constant reminder to someone to keep in touch.

The 75 ball pen in sterling silver is $17.50. The 75 soft tip pen in 22K gold electroplate is $20. In cost, either pen is just about a standoff with the old standbys. But as a gift of immediate and lasting value, a Parker 75 stands alone.

◇ PARKER
World's most wanted pens

color to enhance our message — but more often we will have only black and white. Nor do we always have a full page. We have, then, the natural limits of our message, as well as the limits imposed by our advertising budget and by the characteristics of the medium. We can do things in a slick magazine that will simply not turn out well on the coarse, rough texture of a newspaper.

Getting Attention

Unless the ad catches the attention of the reader, it will not be read. Remember, we have said before that an ad is often an intrusion into the reader's concentration on the contents of the publication. How we catch the reader's

Everything about this ad says "lively." To convey this feeling, the copywriter told the reader to "peel one open." The artist gave the ad movement, with material moving in three directions. The bottle is in one plane, the headline another, and the glass, beaded with moisture, is vertical. The headline offers no benefit; the emphasis is on brand and product name.

attention is an art, and some methods of emphasizing one or more elements of an ad will be discussed in chapter 17. The attention-getting tricks we use, however—the size of the headline, the layout, the format of the ad itself—must call the reader's attention to the whole ad, not just to one of its elements.

Make the Message Easy to Read

The eye moves in a natural way. We read from left to right, from top to bottom. Effective placement of the elements of an ad can facilitate the reader's movement through it, leading the eye from top to bottom, idea by idea, to the ad's conclusion. Our choice of typeface, type size, and arrangement can make the text easy to read and enhance the psychic value of the message. Heavy type is masculine. Light type is feminine. Long blocks of copy are not comfortable to the reader. We have to break the copy into shorter units. Wide blocks of copy are also hard to read, and so we must split them into columns or hold them to a maximum of three inches. The use of generous amounts of white space adds air, openness, and delicacy.

We also want the reader to do something—*order* the product, *send* for the catalog, *visit* one of our dealers, *write* for a sample. That incentive can be strengthened by the position of a coupon in the layout: in the middle, at the top, or at the bottom right corner (the customary place). Where the coupon goes, or whether or not we use a coupon, depends on what we want to achieve and how we will measure that achievement.

Color

In addition to adding emphasis, colors have the ability to communicate an idea or an emotion.

1. Blue represents the law, authority, the sea. It is cool. It is masculine.
2. Green represents country, earth, fruitfulness, richness, and "go."
3. Red represents fire, passion, excitement, and "stop."
4. White represents cleanliness, hospitals, doctors, and nurses.
5. Purple represents royalty.
6. Yellow represents sunlight, heat, caution, cheerfulness.

Mass markets prefer brighter, simpler colors. Sophisticated markets prefer "different" colors. Size is often enhanced by color—yellow packages seem larger, while dark packages appear heavier. (See color plate 46 for an ad using gold to enhance an image.)

Small Space Ads

Not every ad is a four-color bleed page. There are many small but hard-working ads; ads that are often no more than three inches deep and two inches wide. Your newspaper is filled with them. The same principles that apply to the design of a large ad apply to the design of a small one—but with the added necessity of greater imagination. The designer of a small newspaper ad usually does not have the option of color to add emphasis; instead, the designer may have to use an unusual typeface or confine the message to the single most important fact.

Small space ads challenge the copywriter and designer. In this ad for paperweights, copy is held to a minimum. The odd shapes of the items and the use of white type on a black background distinguish the ad on a crowded page.

Computer-Assisted Design

Art directors have not discarded their markers or pencils yet. They need them for thumbnail sketches and concepts, but they can take advantage of computer assistance to speed their work. For example, with an Apple Macintosh personal computer and a digitizing pad with stylus the designer can create pictures. The MacPaint software displays on the screen the picture area with (icons) symbols representing painting aids on the left and various "fill" patterns running along the bottom. Any picture or type can be transferred from one picture to another or repeated. The design can be flipped horizontally or vertically. A "goodies" menu at the top of the screen includes various other options such as working in greatly magnified detail or mirroring the design. The system can be used to customize any typeface. The designer can type in text or headlines in different fonts, sizes, and weights, in italic or outlined; or create shadow lettering, condensed or expanded type. When printed, the image created on the screen becomes the ad or package design. When changes are required, the designer does not have to start from scratch but brings the layout up on the screen for revision.

Subjects for Illustration

Since it is the physical representation of what the customer will buy, the product is always the most obvious choice for illustration. The illustration of the product, however, can take any one of several different formats:

1. product alone
2. product in a setting
3. product in use
4. benefit from the product
5. explanation of product use
6. dramatization of the need for the product
7. detail of the product
8. comparison of the product with its competition
9. display of test evidence concerning the product

The nature of what is being advertised helps to determine the content of the illustration. A glass of whiskey will look like a glass of brown liquid no matter what brand it is, so whiskey advertisers also include a small photograph

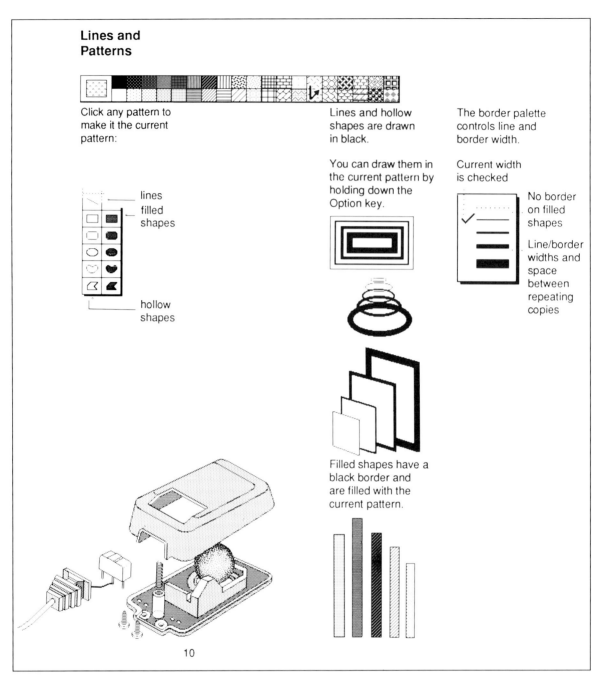

Lines and Patterns

Click any pattern to make it the current pattern:

lines

filled shapes

hollow shapes

Lines and hollow shapes are drawn in black.

You can draw them in the current pattern by holding down the Option key.

Filled shapes have a black border and are filled with the current pattern.

The border palette controls line and border width.

Current width is checked

No border on filled shapes

Line/border widths and space between repeating copies

10

This is a page from the MacPaint direction booklet. The user can choose type sizes and styles, stretch or condense words, repeat illustrations as well as words, erase or move items, and add patterns or textures.

of the bottle and its label in their ads. An illustration of a cake mix package alone, however, is hardly adequate. Consumers want to see what the finished cake will look like. On the other hand, showing personal-care products outside their packages would be in poor taste and probably offensive.

Showing the product in a carefully selected setting can enhance its prestige or can suggest a quality of its appeal. Notice how often Lincolns or

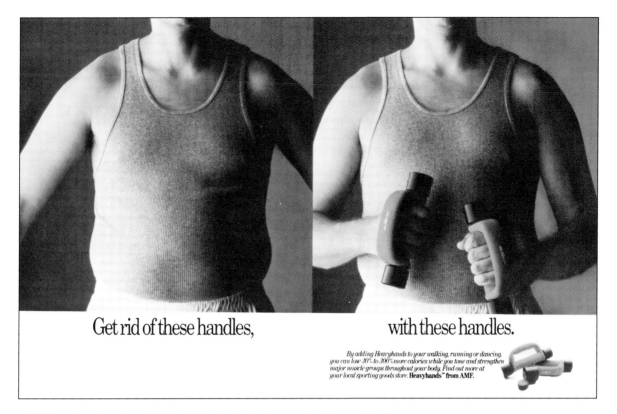

Get rid of these handles,   with these handles.

*By adding Heavyhands to your walking, running or dancing,
you can lose 30% to 300% more calories while you tone and strengthen
major muscle groups throughout your body. Find out more at
your local sporting goods store.* **Heavyhands™ from AMF.**

AMF Heavyhands are hand-held weights that help the exerciser lose weight faster.
Heavyhands appeal to all age groups and both sexes. Instead of explaining how to use
Heavyhands, the illustrations highlight the primary benefit, with the use of a split visual.

Cadillacs are depicted parked in front of a mansion or some other elegant building. Note, too, the frequent use of a purple or blue background in these ads. Royalty and masculinity are suggested in this way. Compact cars, in contrast, are generally illustrated in motion — either going uphill or driving across rugged terrain. The illustration is meant to suggest that this compact car has the power and stamina for great driving.

If there were one basic rule to guide the advertiser in the use of illustration, it would be that the illustration must be *believable.* An illustration showing a housewife who looks like a fashion model or like a Hollywood starlet does not ring true. We all know Hollywood actresses do not wax floors or clean kitchen sinks. A mechanic in a business suit, a banker with a beard, or a doctor in blue jeans — all these models would be unbelievable because they are contrary to our expectations. "Cheesecake" photos of models in bikinis say nothing to women, and, although they might catch the attention of male readers, do not enhance the impression of the product's quality or the prestige of the company.

Kinds of Art Work

Once we have decided *what* we are going to illustrate, our next step is to decide *how* we are going to create the art for that illustration. The choice depends on the cost, the subject, time, and the production requirements of the medium. There are two basic categories of illustration: photography and art. Some ads may use only photography, some only art, and many will use a combination of the two.

Photography   Photographs will lend an air of authenticity to our illustration. The people in a photograph are real. The scenery is real. The reader can relate to the photograph. High-quality photographs are not cheap, but, depending on what is wanted, they may be the most economical way to show a product or its use. (See color plate 47.)

One of the limitations of photography is that it is sometimes unable to translate the most attractive features of a three-dimensional product into two dimensions. Sometimes a successful photo of this type requires "interesting" techniques. For example, Campbell Soup Company had a problem in photographing one of its vegetable soups. The soup is indeed full of vegetables, but, when it is poured into a bowl, the vegetables settle to the bottom and all the camera catches is the liquid soup. To overcome this problem a clever photographer hit on the idea of putting marbles on the bottom of the bowl. Then, when the soup was poured into the bowl, the vegetables, resting on the base of marbles, protruded through the soup's surface. Clever? Yes, indeed, but the Federal Trade Commission found the photograph and the ad misleading.

The use of photographs for illustration presents other, not insurmountable, problems—but problems nonetheless. Foods look real and tempting, when photographed in color. But, the cake and the pudding must be prepared just right, and the props that go with the cake and the pudding must look just right. Because such careful preparations must be made, major photography studios have completely equipped kitchens. Even when the greatest care is taken, however, the beads of moisture on the cold bottle may not glisten as we would wish, or the color of the product can be off a shade. Expert retouching is usually required to add what the camera could not pick up.

Finding the "right" models is also a problem: their age and appearance must be appropriate for the product and for the medium. A housewife must look like the kind of woman to whom prospective customers can relate. The photographer and models often must work on location to take advantage of settings that add to the image being projected. Nothing can be substituted for the Trevi Fountain in Rome, the Tower of London, or other sites that are readily recognized.

Drawings or Paintings   Some subjects simply cannot be photographed. Fictitious or historical people or scenes, mythological animals, pain relievers racing through the bloodstream, or the inside of a healthy hair follicle do not lend themselves to photography. Other subjects — construction details of appliances and machines, for example — are better illustrated by drawings. For such illustrations, an artist can use one of many different techniques. (See color plate 48 for an ad illustrated with a color drawing.)

Tempera (opaque watercolor) drawings are frequently used where bright colors or heightened realism is the desired effect. When the illustration will be used in black and white, a wash drawing can be used instead of a tempera drawing. A **wash** drawing is made from either India ink or black watercolor that has been mixed with water to provide a "wash." By using more or less water, an artist can obtain various shades: from intense black to the palest of greys to the pure white of the paper. Most of the illustrations used in retail newspaper advertising are wash drawings. Illustrations of furniture or ma-

**Hathaway's Lochlana.
A tough, rugged shirt that's still blissfully soft.**

Hathaway's Lochlana is so soft, your skin will think you've invested in cashmere. The imported fabric is of incredibly smooth texture. The purest combed cotton and just the "tops"—the softest part—of wool are spun together in every strand.

Two of the finest mills in the world developed special dyes to achieve Lochlana's exclusive patterns. The colors are woven into the cloth, not printed on it. The tartans snap. The solids project a rich, uniform glow.

And of course, every Hathaway Lochlana shirt is crafted with the same thorough attention to detail we lavish on our dress shirts.

Unfortunately, there is one problem. Like fine wines, only so much Lochlana is created each year. What's more, men who refuse to settle for less do hoard the shirts. We recommend haste, while your haberdasher still has your favorite color.

Turn back to page 383 and compare the finished advertisement with this unretouched photograph. The camera did not catch the rump of the deer or enough trees to fill the width required by the ad. An expert photo retoucher patched in more trees (see if you can spot them on the finished ad) and air-brushed the hind quarters of the deer. What the camera misses, retouchers can add and improve upon.

chinery are drawn with great precision and detail — very **tight.** High-fashion illustrations are drawn in a much more imprecise (informal or **loose**) way, intended to provide the reader with only a *suggestion* of the style of the clothing. Retailers may not want customers coming to the store for the particular dress or coat in the ad; obscuring details helps sell the general style and induces the customer to visit the store.

We can obtain simpler and less expensive pen-and-ink drawings — called **line drawings** — that show the product's features in outline only. Often a combination of wash and line can be used with great effect to provide both the crispness and precision of the pen line and the touch of grey color tone that adds style. Other textures and effects can be obtained with pencil, charcoal, or scratchboard. **Scratchboard** gets its name from the procedure in which a

Subjects for Illustration

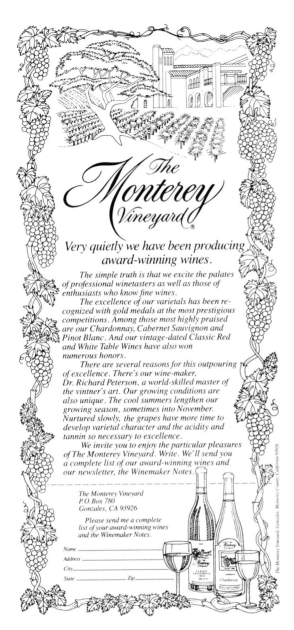

A tight drawing in which every detail is shown very realistically, and with great precision.

A loose drawing with a minimum of detail, not very realistic. Details are merely suggested with a line or a tone.

clay-coated cardboard is covered with black India ink, and a drawing is then scratched into the board with a stylus or knife. This results in a drawing composed of extremely fine lines. The effect is similar to, but much finer than, that of an old woodcut.

Stock Art Very often we will need a photo or a drawing for an illustration, but we do not have enough money (or time) to have an original photograph taken or an original drawing made. In this case, we may be able to obtain what we need from a company that maintains files of photographs or drawings illustrating a variety of subjects. There are, for example, several well-known

Imagine how expensive it would be to hire a photographer to fly down to the Gulf
Coast, rent a boat, and sail to an offshore oil rig to shoot photographs. Instead of
venturing out to sea for a needed photograph, an art director can select a stock
photograph for prices that range from $400 to $1,500 for one-time use in a black-and-
white consumer ad (half that price for a trade-paper ad). Shown is a sample page from
the catalogue of Leo de Wys, Inc., New York, a well-known supplier of stock photography. As you can see, a wide range of subjects is available.

Subjects for Illustration   **395**

sources for stock photographs. For only a fraction of what it would cost to have a photograph taken, we can buy a photograph of a doctor, a hospital scene, a family, a sexy model, a beach party, a puppy, or a lion. The list is virtually endless. We can buy a bird's-eye view of Manhattan, the wheat fields of Kansas, or the Florida swamps. We can buy the photographs in black and white or in color.

If we prefer drawings, we can buy very tight drawings of heads, people, things — or loose drawings in line or wash. We can buy ready made emblems, designs, outlines, symbols, motifs, and cartoons, as well as drawings of George Washington, Abe Lincoln, or Santa Claus to tie in with holiday seasons. All this art is ready to use and very inexpensive. Of course, it is possible that another advertiser may use the same illustration in the same publication, but the likelihood of such an occurrence is so small that, when there are budget constraints, stock art or photography should definitely be considered.

The Television Commercial

Designing a television commercial is considerably different from designing a print ad. A commercial consists not only of sound but of a continuous series of scenes. The artist must coordinate the sound or narrative with the photography or animation sequences. The design of the commercial is mapped out by means of a **storyboard** — a set of shapes resembling a television screen on which artists sketch the number and content of the scenes they envision as conveying the sales message. The number of sequences can vary from six to as many as thirty-six.

The storyboard is designed in much the same way as a print ad. Usually the agency's copywriter provides the art director with an initial draft of the copy for the sound portion of the commercial, together with suggestions for how the visual action might be shown. The art director then prepares a rough storyboard that shows the pictures that might accompany the copy. There is generally a close working relationship between these two people. The art director may have an idea for copy while the copywriter may dream up some clever visual ideas. Once the basic sequence for the words and action has been decided upon, the client is shown a copy of the rough storyboard. If the client approves, a comprehensive storyboard that is almost a scene by scene breakdown of the commercial is prepared. This storyboard indicates precisely which words go with which pictures. The commercial is now ready for production.

How a Television Commercial Is Produced

From the moment that the comprehensive storyboard is produced, all work on the production of the commercial is directed toward a deadline — the first air date. It becomes the job of the agency's traffic department to supervise the flow of production from the time the storyboard is assigned a job number to the time the film print of the completed commercial arrives at the television station for broadcast. Most networks require prints of all commercials expected to appear on a particular program at least four weeks ahead of the program's air date.

One of the first steps in the actual production of the commercial is the preparation of a budget. To arrive at firm figures for the cost of production, the producer of the commercial will submit the storyboard to companies (called

Rochelle Udell

Though only 40 years old, Rochelle Udell's resume includes work for some of the most famous names in design, publishing, and advertising. She has been art director for *Gentlemen's Quarterly, Harper's Bazaar, Self,* and *Vogue.* She has worked for and with Calvin Klein. At her present job at Della Femina, Travisano and Partners, she has been responsible for some of television's most exciting advertising.

Ms. Udell was born in the Bronx and grew up in Brooklyn. She graduated from Brooklyn College with a bachelor's degree in art and education, then went on to Pratt School of Design where she earned a master's degree in painting. She taught art in the late sixties in a Brooklyn high school. While teaching, she took a night course where the instructor, a well-known designer, was so impressed with her that he offered her a position as his assistant. This was the start. She left teaching and began work on *New York Magazine,* which was just in its infancy. In 1972, then only 27 years old, she joined *Vogue* as art director, where she worked for five years. She left to work with Calvin Klein, but returned to Conde Nast in 1980. In 1981 Klein launched his own in-house agency, CRK, headed by Ms. Udell. She left a year later to rejoin Conde Nast as creative director responsible for the redesign of *Self.* She joined Della Femina, Travisano and Partners in March 1985, as senior vice-president/executive creative director.

Ms. Udell has also designed a number of books, including Lee Bailey's *Country Weekends, City Food,* and *Country Flowers,* and Raquel Welch's *Total Beauty Book.*

production houses) for an estimate. The producer is an experienced person who is familiar with the capabilities of the various production houses. After the estimates have been received, the producer, representing the agency, will contract with one of the production houses for production of the commercial. The contract specifies costs, number of prints, and scheduled delivery dates.

A conference is then held, attended by the various agency people involved — the copywriter, the art director, the account executive, and some of the staff of the production house. Details concerning the types of actors, sound effects, and music to be used are then worked out. Every detail is considered. The actors must project an image appropriate to the message the commercial is supposed to transmit. For that reason, many agencies maintain their own casting departments for the audition and selection of actors.[1]

The production house prepares any sets or costumes that will be needed for the commercials. Rehearsals are scheduled; lighting and camera angles are worked out just as they would be for a feature-length movie. The audio portion

---

[1] All talent is paid for actual time spent in taping, filming, or recording the commercial. In addition, contracts with talent unions provide for the payment of specific schedules of fees to all talent when the commercial is actually broadcast. These fees are known as *residuals.* The principal unions involved in regulating talent payments are the Screen Actors Guild (SAG) and the American Federation of Television and Radio Artists (AFTRA).

Terms Used in Radio and Television Commercial Production

Ad-lib: to extemporize lines that are not written into the script.

Animatic: a television commercial produced from semifinished art work, generally used only for test purposes.

Announcer: the member of the radio or television staff who delivers the commercial message live or the talent who delivers the commercial message either recorded (on a television commercial as a voice-over) or on camera.

Back-to-back: two commercials or programs that are shown directly after each other.

BCU, TCU, ECU: an extremely narrow angle picture: big close-up; tight close-up; extreme close-up.

Beauty shot: a close-up of a product advertised in a commercial.

Bridge: music or sound effect linking two scenes in a TV or radio program.

Clapstick: hinged boards that are attached to the top of a slate or blackboard.

Close-up: a shot of an individual with the camera moved in close so that only the head and shoulders fill the screen. An extreme close-up may include only the head or even just the eyes.

Crawl: graphics, usually mounted on a drum, that move slowly up the screen.

Cross-fade: in television, the fading out of one picture and the simultaneous fading in of another; in radio, the fading out of dialogue, sound, or music while simultaneously fading in other dialogue or music or sound effects.

Cucalorus: projecting a silhouette against a background by putting a shape before a strong light source.

Cut-to: a fast switch from the picture in one camera to the picture in another camera without a dissolve or a wipe.

Dissolve (DS): a combination of fade-in and fade-out. A new scene appears while the preceding scene vanishes. It is a transitional device used to indicate the lapse of time.

Dubbing: the process of mixing different sound tracks into one composite track.

Fade in: to gradually increase the intensity of a video picture from dark to full brightness.

Fade out: to gradually decrease the intensity of a scene from full brightness to dark.

Follow shot: following an action with a stationary camera.

of the commercial may be recorded simultaneously with the video or some of the sound may be recorded before the actual filming of the commercial begins. Then the takes are made. Each **take** is a filming of an individual scene. The next day, the **dailies** — the takes that have been developed and printed — are ready for approval. The best take of each scene is chosen as the **work print.** The sound track is synchronized to the work prints and the laboratory work begins. Special effects, titles, and dissolves are added. The final film is called the **answer print.** Color and sound levels are checked and corrected once more on the answer print, and then, when final approvals have been received, the print is ready for release.

The production process we have described in the preceding paragraphs can take months to complete. It is possible, of course, to rush the process. A simple commercial can be made in only a few days, but its cost will be greatly

Knee shot: a shot of three-quarters of the actor's body. The bottom of the frame is just above the actor's knee.

Lap dissolve: cross-fading of one scene over another so that both pictures are momentarily visible.

Live fade: a diminution of transmitted sound created in the studio rather than in the control room.

Live tag: a short, live message added to a recorded announcement.

MS: medium shot, somewhere between a CU (close-up) and a LS (long shot).

Outtake: a scene that was shot but not used in the finished commercial.

Package clean-up: small type is not usually readable in a commercial, so it is removed from the product package to make it less cluttered. The viewer is thus able to concentrate on the name of the product.

Pan: to move the camera left or right without moving the base.

Segue: the musical transition that ties one theme to another.

Shoot: the filming session.

Sneak: to bring in sound or music at low volume so as not to distract the listener.

SFX: sound effects.

Split screen: a special effect utilizing two or more cameras so that two or more scenes are visible simultaneously on separate parts of the screen. An example would be two people talking on the phone.

Take: the filming of a scene. It begins with the slap of the clapsticks and ends when the director calls "cut."

Talent: actors, announcers, musicians, or performers.

Voice-over (VO): the actor's or announcer's voice is heard but the person is not seen.

Wipe: an optical effect in which a line or an object appear to move across the screen revealing a new picture. The wipe may stop midway and become a split screen.

Wipe-over: optical effect in which one scene moves into another geometrically.

Wrap: the end of a shoot.

---

inflated by this accelerated schedule. Typical cost of a three-day production shoot for a 30-second commercial for a nationally advertised brand, using three actors, a well-known director, indoor shots, and no special effects is $100,000.[2]

Filmed, Videotaped, and Live Commercials

Film Film is still widely used for television commercial production. Production companies in every major city in the United States have elaborate facilities for photographing virtually any kind of commercial. The major film studios in California have giant sound stages available with an extensive variety

---

[2] *Advertising Age,* February 17, 1986, p. 42.

CASE HISTORY

Mitsubishi Motor Sales of America, Inc.

In January of 1982, Cunningham & Walsh, because of its successful management of the Mitsubishi Motors Corporation account, was assigned the account for Mitsubishi sales in the United States.

The introduction of a new car and a new car company in 1982 in an already crowded Japanese/American import market was a formidable challenge for any company. It was complicated even further by a number of critical factors working against a successful introduction: a poor economic climate; record high unemployment; the highest interest and financing rates in memory; a growing anti-Japanese sentiment in much of the United States (people were blaming unemployment on the success of Japanese products); and an American import quota on Japanese cars. The import quota meant that Mitsubishi Motor Sales of America would have to spend an extremely high per-unit promotion cost on each vehicle in order to be heard.

Mitsubishi's first decision, and the basis for much of their success, was to appoint dealers who would market the new line of Mitsubishi products exclusively. This meant that Mitsubishi dealers had to make a substantial capital investment, and thus were committed to helping MMSA successfully introduce their products in America.

Cunningham & Walsh and the client marketing people had to target the consumer very carefully. They had to find the specific economic and social groups that had an open mind about the product and the wherewithal to invest between $10,000 and $15,000.

They realized that MMSA cars would compete primarily in a segment that had already demonstrated specific interest in Japanese autos. They launched an extensive market research program and evaluated the marketing position that each Japanese importer was utilizing. They positioned the products in the areas where they believed a gap existed.

They realized that performance and quality and Japanese manufacturing would be "hot buttons" to motivate customers to seek out the product. They investigated values and lifestyles (VALS) and determined that the "achiever" group—which represents 25 percent of the population but 45 percent of the income—was the right target audience.

They decided to introduce Mitsubishi as a manufacturer of high quality cars and trucks that are a cut above other Japanese imports. VALS provided them with enough information about the "achievers" so that they could tailor their communications to reach them. Television and print campaigns were then combined to efficiently promote the full line as well as individual vehicles.

The campaign was highly introductory in tone and added a "high-tech" overlay to the basic claim of performance. The theme line selected was "Mitsubishi takes you where you want to go."

The introductory advertising results were extremely impressive. Showroom traffic exceeded all objectives and Mitsubishi achieved the highest sales ever recorded by any automotive import in its first year of sales.

---

of sets. Many studios also have facilities for animation, and there are excellent production houses in Europe where scenes requiring a foreign locale may be made at substantial savings. Paris and Rome are popular locations for perfume and fashion commercials.

MITSUBISHI MOTOR SALES OF AMERICA, INC.

1985 Launch
"Mirage Desert"
:30

Leader Code: TDMM 3511

MUSICAL EFFECT THROUGHOUT
SFX: MIRAGE APPROACHING

AVO: Sleek aerodynamic styling.

SFX

Phenomenal handling.

SFX

Advanced electronics.

SFX

Unexpected comfort.

And an ingeniously smooth
powerplant.

There's even a full-blown

turbocharged model.

Until now, an economy car with
all this. . .

was only a mirage.

It still is.
The new Mitsubishi Mirage.

MUSIC: UP AND OUT.

PRODUCED BY CUNNINGHAM & WALSH

© 1984 MMSA

TRI ADS NORTH HOLLYWOOD, CALIF. 91601

In order to achieve the proper setting, certain scenes or an entire commercial may have to be shot on location. This requires transporting the actors and the production crew to the desert or seashore location where the scenes will be photographed. To show an automobile driving down a deserted beach may require hiring a huge helicopter to transport the car to that location. Location shooting adds excitement and interest to a commercial, but it also adds considerably to its cost.

Few, if any, commercials today are filmed in black and white. The cost of crew and talent is the same whether black and white or color film is used, so black and white commercials offer little savings in production costs. For most national commercials, 35mm film is used. However, 16mm reduction prints are usually made from the 35mm film because some television stations require them. At the television station, the 35mm film is transferred to videotape, and the station holds the 16mm print in reserve for emergency use. Although the original print of a commercial can be shot with 16mm film, it does not offer the same variety of special effects that are possible with 35mm film. Also, when 35mm film is reduced to 16mm, the images remain sharp and clear; when 16mm is enlarged to 35mm, however, it tends to lose some clarity of detail.

All in all, film is exceptionally versatile. Many optical effects are possible: dissolves, wipes, split screens, cross-fades, and lap dissolves — the list is almost endless. (For definitions of the preceding terms, see the glossary on pages 398–99.) One creative advantage of film is that the producer can have several takes made of each scene, shooting from several different angles, and then choose the best take later, in the editing room.

Tape   Television stations use videotape extensively today to record sports events, news stories, and studio shows. Originally, almost all commercials were recorded on videotape because it was fast and inexpensive. Also, in the early days of television, when many commercials were live, broadcasters turned to videotape to eliminate such errors as an actor's fluffing a line, mispronouncing the name of a product, or being unable to open a package. Videotape was convenient and could be used over and over again. The main drawback to the use of videotape at that time was the huge size of the necessary cameras and recording equipment. Now, however, videotape recording equipment can be placed in mobile cruisers, and the new **mini-cams,** handheld video cameras with portable recorders, can be used by news teams everywhere.

Today, tape has several advantages over film. Film must be developed and printed before it can be edited, while tape can be played back immediately. A commercial can be taped in hours, and corrections and improvements to the original shooting can be made immediately. To correct or to add new scenes to a filmed commercial, the entire crew and talent must be reassembled several days after shooting the original film.

Film, on the other hand, can be used in the production of any commercial; videotape cannot. The limitations of videotape — no reverse, no fast action, no slow motion, no animation — make it impossible to create many of the special effects used in film. Film can also be edited frame by frame — a procedure that is invaluable for commercials with children and animals, who may not always give us the performances we require.

Live   As we have said, live commercials were common in the early days of television. The problems that occurred — dogs that would not eat the advertiser's dog food or pantry doors that stuck — led to the use of film and videotape. Today, most live commercials are delivered by the hosts of personality shows on local and national television. The commercials are either read from prepared scripts or ad-libbed from product fact sheets. The scripts for these

AS CONTEMPORARY AS IT IS CADILLAC.

Here is a 1986 luxury car built for the 1990s.

With state-of-the-art technology that contributes to your driving comfort. Aerodynamic styling for reduced wind noise. Plus an independent four-wheel suspension and a transverse-mounted, front-wheel-drive V8 engine, a Cadillac exclusive.

It doesn't get any more contemporary than this.

It's De Ville for 1986.

It doesn't get any more Cadillac than this, either.

With a new limousine-style back window. Plus Cadillac comfort touches such as Electronic Climate Control and the increasingly rare luxury of room for six. And a 4-year/50,000-mile limited warranty.

In some cases a deductible applies. See your dealer for details.

1986 DE VILLE
BEST OF ALL...IT'S A CADILLAC.

GM
LET'S GET IT TOGETHER...BUCKLE UP.

COLOR PLATE 46

COLOR PLATE 46 In America the Cadillac is the symbol of achievement. Not infrequently, an enthusiastic salesperson will stress the quality of a product by describing it as "the Cadillac of _____." In this ad Cadillac reinforces its contemporary styling by posing the automobile against some very clean-looking architecture. The copy describes how the technology as well as the design is contemporary. The gold color adds to the image projected.

COLOR PLATE 47 Nike advertising uses creative photography to communicate. Copy is ▶ not required in this two-page bleed spread because the image is intended to engage the mind as well as the eye. The same motif has been used with athletes in various forms of activity. Note the stark background with strong shadows, the runner's body glistening with sweat, and the clever use of a cloth label in the upper left corner as the only identification of the product aside from the modest name visible on the garments. This ad is part of an award-winning series for Nike.

Return to innocence: J.G. HOOK's gentled cotton chambray skirt and a delightful pleated shirt with embroidered puritan collar. Above all, the nicest hand-knit cotton vest we've seen. *At fine stores nationwide.*

Send for "The J. G. Hook Woman," an informative brochure

485 Seventh Avenue · New York · 10018

J. G. HOOK

COLOR PLATE 48

COLOR PLATE 48 The style of the illustration—a crisp watercolor painting—serves to complement the style of the garment. The ad has a simple "American" look as distinguished from a "Continental" look.

COLOR PLATES 49 ▲ AND 50 ▶ Jockey is a well-known maker of quality men's underwear. When this firm introduced a line of Jockey underwear for women, how did it give the ads a feminine touch (beyond showing a female model)? It used type and color. The words "For Her" are set in a distinctive, feminine script. The body copy in the men's ad is set in a sans serif typeface. It looks crisp, masculine. The women's ad is set in a Roman face, delicate, with serifs. The dominant color in the men's ad is blue; in the women's ad it's pink. Naturally. Do note the way the artist has taken advantage of the tone values of the photographs. In the men's ad, with a dark background, the type is reversed, appearing as white against the blue. In the women's ad, the type surprints black over the light tone of the photograph. The manner in which the model breaks into the name JOCKEY helps tie the model and the name together. An example of good design.

COLOR PLATE 51

COLOR PLATE 52

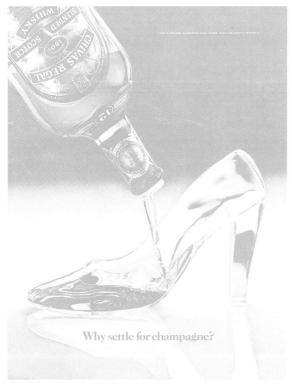

COLOR PLATE 53

COLOR PLATE 54

COLOR PLATES 51, 52, 53, 54 ▲ AND 55 ▶ A four-color ad for a very well-known product. From the color photograph, the photoengraver prepares color separations for the four colors used—yellow, red, blue, and black, which give the illustration rich, brilliant color. This ad was prepared by Doyle Dane Bernbach, Inc., for General Wine & Spirits Company.

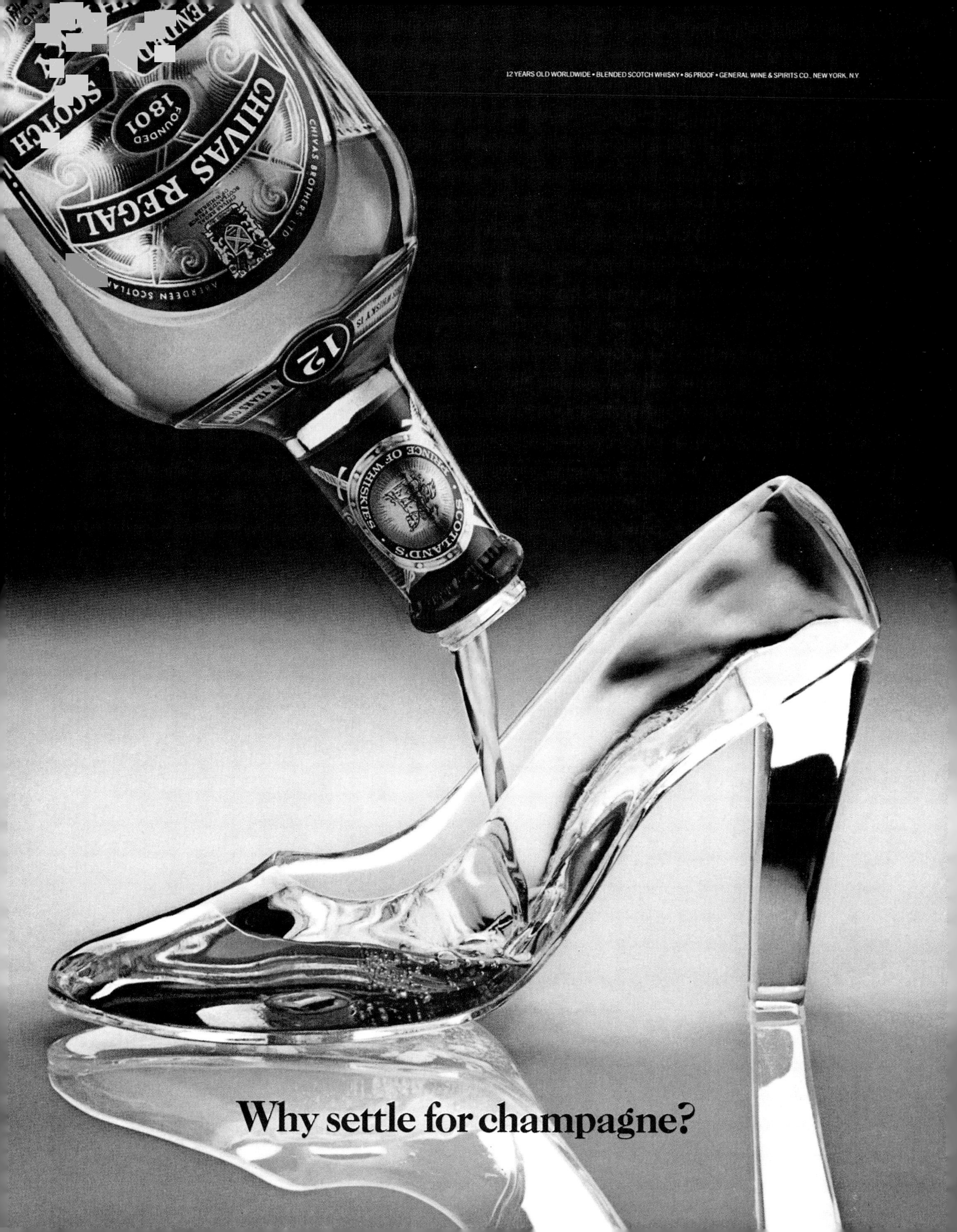

12 YEARS OLD WORLDWIDE • BLENDED SCOTCH WHISKY • 86 PROOF • GENERAL WINE & SPIRITS CO., NEW YORK, N.Y.
CHIVAS REGAL
SCOTCH
FOUNDED
1801
CHIVAS BROTHERS LTD
ABERDEEN SCOTLAND
12
SCOTLAND'S
PRINCE OF WHISKIES
Why settle for champagne?

Sony turns eensy into eensy-weensy.

This is an actual-size photo of the eensiest, teensiest, weensiest cassette player ever made—the new Sony Super Walkman." The only thing that isn't teeny-weeny is the sound.

THE WORLD'S SMALLEST CASSETTE PLAYER PRESENTS THE SMALLER THE BETTER SWEEPSTAKES.

Test listen to the remarkable new Super Walkman at your participating Sony dealer, and you could win to the tune of $25,000.

Just bring the game card accompanying this ad and enter the Smaller the Better Sweepstakes. (If the game card's re-

THE SMALLER THE BETTER SWEEPSTAKES GRAND PRIZE A SMALL FORTUNE $25,000

2 FIRST PRIZES A VACATION FOR 2 ON A SMALL CARIBBEAN ISLAND

10 SECOND PRIZES $500 WORTH OF SONY EQUIPMENT

100 THIRD PRIZES A SMALL COLLECTION OF SONY CASSETTES

moved, you can get an entry form at your participating Sony dealer. Or you can send a self-addressed stamped envelope to P.O. Box 823, Paramus, N.J. 07652.*)

When you get there, you'll find our Sweepstakes display, complete with a Super Walkman personal stereo. What you hear on its prerecorded tape will tell you whether you've won,

and how to get a second chance if you didn't.

For more details, see your Sony dealer. There's no purchase necessary. The offer expires December 31, 1983 (it's void where prohibited by law).

So do yourself a small favor. Test listen to the new Super Walkman and enter the Smaller the Better Sweepstakes today.

SONY.
THE ONE AND ONLY

COLOR PLATE 56

COLOR PLATE 56 It is usual to show the small size of a product by placing a ruler in the photo or some object whose size is easily recognized. In this photo, the tweezer is used to demonstrate the size and light weight of the Walkman.

commercials must be kept simple and must not rely on any gimmicks or on product demonstrations.

Restrictions

Television, considered a family medium, imposes a number of restrictions on advertisers. We may not show anyone drinking beer — pouring, yes; the empty glass, yes; but quaffing, no. Nor can we show undergarments on a live model. Undergarments, such as girdles and brassieres, may only be illustrated on a form or worn by the model over street clothes. We may not put white jackets on models and pretend they are doctors.

Summary

Creating the art for advertising demands not only aesthetic sensibilities, but a knowledge of psychology in general and an understanding of consumer behavior in particular. The advertising designer must understand the purpose of the illustration or illustrations and the interests of the target market toward which the commercial message is aimed. The illustration often plays a major role in print advertising, and the designer must be aware that each market segment may have a different perception. Choosing the right illustration will enhance the impact of the ad. The layout itself, which is the arrangement of the elements, helps make the message easier to read and will often guide the eyes of the reader. The layout artist will begin by making several small sketches, called *thumbnails,* seeking to find the most effective arrangements for the elements.

Once the artist has settled upon the most effective arrangements, carefully detailed sketches, called *comprehensives,* are made to exact size. The idea is to make the layout resemble as closely as possible an actual ad in order to submit it for approval. The design itself will have the characteristics of any work of art: balance, unity, movement, and focus. However, advertising is not art for art's sake but a vehicle intended to convey a persuasive message. The ultimate objective of that message is to stimulate the reader to some form of action — to order the product, to visit a dealer, to send for more information, to accept an idea. As the artist works, there are choices to be made — of the typeface and the kind of illustration. Should the product be shown alone or in use? Should the illustration be a photograph or a drawing? Each method of representation adds a different effect. The choice of model and background can strengthen the message. Even the color used in an ad is an important element, communicating a mood or feeling. Good professional art — photography or illustration — is expensive. Some artists will try to use *stock art* where possible, buying photographs or drawings that are carried in stock by a number of firms. The cost of such stock art is far less than that of custom-prepared material.

The preparation of a television commercial is much more difficult and expensive than the preparation of a print ad. The designer works with sketches, called *storyboards,* which depict the sequence of scenes. Once the ideas and dialogue have been approved, the storyboard will be submitted to a *production house* — a firm that will produce the actual commercial. The production house, under the supervision of the agency, will arrange for the actors, the props, the music, and the filming. The entire process is complicated and expensive. The cost can be well over $1,000 a second for a 30-second commercial. Today few commercials are presented live; most are prepared on movie film or videotape.

Questions for Discussion

1. Why is knowledge of the market essential to the visualization of an advertisement?

2. Why is it important for some advertisers to show their products in use? Why is it important for some advertisers to show their product's package?

3. Find examples of advertisements that demonstrate:
   a. gaze motion
   b. formal balance
   c. focus

4. Find several examples of advertisements that use the connotative value of color.

5. Describe two sets of circumstances in which an advertiser could justify the additional cost of color for an advertisement.

6. What are the advantages of photographs as illustrations in an advertisement? When would drawings be recommended?

7. What is the value of "white space" in an advertisement?

Sources and Suggestions for Further Reading

Book, Albert C., and Norman D. Cary. *The Radio and Television Commercial.* Chicago: Crain Books, 1984.

Nelson, Roy Paul. *The Design of Advertising.* Dubuque, Iowa: Wm. C. Brown Co., Publishers, 1977.

Wainwright, Charles Anthony. *Television Commercials.* New York: Hastings House, Publishers, 1965.

Wales, Hugh G., Dwight L. Gentry, and Max Wales. *Advertising Copy, Layout, and Typography.* New York: Ronald Press Company, 1958.

17 REPRODUCTION PROCESSES

Working Vocabulary

points	spec	doctor blade
body copy	mechanical	screen process
serif	sheet-fed	squeegee
pica	web-fed	halftone
flush	letterpress	screen
justify	offset	four-color process
leading	gravure	coated stock

Advertisers make a mistake when they try to create distinction by using exotic type faces. The classic faces are always the best. And type size should be large enough for easy reading.

Howard G. "Scotty" Sawyer
Business-to-Business Advertising

After the copy has been written and the layout has been carefully worked out to everyone's satisfaction, the job is far from over. Once all the approvals have been secured for the copy, the illustration, and the layout, the material is returned to the art department. There, the type for the headline and body copy must be specified by a member of the art staff who is a type specialist, familiar with the characteristics of the many typefaces available and with the purpose of the advertisement. Final art work for the illustration must also be prepared, together with instructions for its reproduction. The layout, illustration, and copy are then turned over to a commercial printer or to the printer for the medium in which the advertisement will appear. The printer, following the directions from the advertiser or the agency, will then set the type, prepare the art work for reproduction, and do the printing.

Advertisers should familiarize themselves with the mechanics of print production, since a poor-quality reproduction of an advertisement will blunt or destroy its effectiveness. Advertisers should consider the requirements, possibilities, and limitations of the preparation and printing processes right from the inception of their advertisements. They should know, for example, that small wash drawings or detailed photographs won't fare well on a newspaper's coarsely textured paper. Nor will delicate typefaces. It is appropriate, therefore, to examine the characteristics of type and of the various printing processes.

Typography

Typefaces differ in several ways — in style, in weight, in depth, and in width. We have to consider all the characteristics of the typeface or typefaces we use in our ad because these characteristics can make a contribution to (or detract from) the ad's effectiveness.

Measuring Type

Type is measured by the height, not of the letter itself, but of the body on which the individual letters sit. If you examine a printed line, you will notice how each letter varies — the *l* is tall; the *i* is short; the *p* extends below the *i*. But each of these letters sits on a body the same height. We specify type by a measurement called **points.**

Common type sizes are 6, 8, 10, 12, 14, 18, 24, 30, 36, 42, 48, 60, and 72 point. Not every face is available in the complete range of sizes. Some typefaces are only suitable for headlines and are, therefore, only available in the larger sizes. The text of an ad, called **body copy,** is usually set in 8-, 10-, or 12-point type, depending on the face. (For example, this book is set in 10-point Bembo; captions are set in 9-point Gill Sans Light.) Even in the same point size, some faces are larger than others — the space on the type body being occupied by

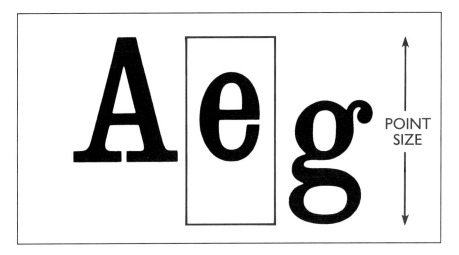

POINT SIZE

When type was set by hand, letter by letter, the size of type was measured in points. The piece of metal on which the letter was mounted was the *body.* Thus, every type character's *body* was uniform in size — 72 points, one inch tall; 36 points, one-half inch tall — but each character had its own individual configuration and varied according to the typeface. If you examine a printed line, you will notice how each letter varies — the *l* is tall; the *i* is short; the *p* extends below the line; the *m* usually takes twice as much width as the *n* and far more than the *i.*

Actual type size — 144 points in this illustration — is measured from one end of the body to the other. It must include the capital letters and the letters' ascenders and descenders. Some typefaces may appear larger than others, even though they are equal in point size. The reason the letter *A* in the illustration does not occupy the total area available on the body is that there must be room for the descenders. Thus, the lower case *g* on this body must have room below the feet of the capital *A.* A typeface with particularly long descenders has a lighter, more open look. A typeface with short descenders may require leading to achieve an open feeling and, sometimes, to improve legibility.

long ascenders or long descenders. Newspapers are generally set in 8-point type. Headlines may be set in 18-point type and up, depending on the length of the headline, the space available, and the kind of effect we want the headline to make.

Typefaces

Roman   Typefaces fall into several families that bear a resemblance to each other, as families should. The most extensively used typeface is called *roman.* The family name derives from the inscriptions carved on ancient Roman monuments. The roman family is distinguished by two characteristics: (1) the letters are composed of thick and thin lines; and (2) they contain short bars, called **serifs,** at the ends of the main strokes of each letter. The main feature of this family is legibility. Newspapers, magazines, and books are usually printed in some variety of roman type. The legibility derives from the thick and thin strokes, the serifs, and the ascenders and descenders — the *d* that ascends above the *e,* and the *j* that descends below it. Our eyes can distinguish these letters quickly.

Since the days of ancient Rome, type designers have incorporated an endless variety of modifications into the roman family. The variations are still recognizable as members of the family, but they are more like cousins than brothers and sisters. For the most part, these modifications have affected the

abcdefghijklmnopqrstuvwxyz
ABCDEFGHIJKLMNOPQRSTUVWXYZ
1234567890.,;:"'&!?$

abcdefghijklmnopqrstuvwxyz
ABCDEFGHIJKLMNOPQRSTUVWXYZ
1234567890.,;:"'&!?$

abcdefghijklmnopqrstuvwxyz
ABCDEFGHIJKLMNOPQRSTUVWXYZ
1234567890.,;:"'&!?$

abcdefghijklmnopqrstuvwxyz
ABCDEFGHIJKLMNOPQRSTUVWXYZ
1234567890.,;:"'&!?$

Although Giambattista Bodoni designed the original of these faces in the late 18th and early 19th centuries, they are classified as modern. They are characterized by strongly contrasting thick and thin strokes, as if designed with an engraver's stylus, and by flat, unbracketed serifs, which help to give the type a crisp, modern look. Shown here are Book, Regular, Bold, and Ultra.

thick and thin parts of the letters. If the thick part is very thick as in *Ultra Bodoni,* it gives the face weight and a very contemporary look — strong, bold, modern. If there is little contrast, as in *Caledonia,* we get a clean look — modern, but not too modern. Compare these members of the roman family with *Goudy,* in which the thin line is much heavier than in Bodoni or Caledonia, and the face has an old-fashioned character about it.

Sans Serif   Designers interested in "modernizing" typefaces developed a range of faces that eliminated the serif as well as the thick and thin characteristics. The style is called *sans serif* or *gothic.* The letters are mechanical in feeling, rather than hand formed as in most roman alphabets. They appear to have been designed by an engineer or an architect. The characters of the sans serif family are crisp, clean, geometric, and modern. Over the years, countless variations of this family have been created — some of the styles very tall and thin such as *Alternate Gothic;* some delicate and graceful, such as *Vogue;* some bold and powerful, such as *Tempo Black.* Sans serif faces lend themselves well to headlines and subheads but, in blocks of body copy, they are more difficult to read. Such faces are rarely used for the editorial matter of any newspaper or magazine.

Egyptian   Striving for something different, type designers developed a family of hybrids known as *Egyptian,* perhaps because someone had seen a similarly styled inscription used on an ancient tomb. Be that as it may, the

abcdefghijklmnopqrstuvwxyz
ABCDEFGHIJKLMNOPQRSTUVWXYZ
1234567890.,;:"&!?$

abcdefghijklmnopqrstuvwxyz
ABCDEFGHIJKLMNOPQRSTUVWXYZ
1234567890.,;:"&!?$

abcdefghijklmnopqrstuvwxyz
ABCDEFGHIJKLMNOPQRSTUVWXYZ
1234567890.,;:"&!?$

abcdefghijklmnopqrstuvwxyz
ABCDEFGHIJKLMNOPQRSTUVWXYZ
1234567890.,;:"&!?$

abcdefghijklmnopqrstuvwxyz
ABCDEFGHIJKLMNOPQRSTUVWXYZ
1234567890.,;:"&!?$

Futura, a sans serif type designed by Paul Renner in the late 1920s, was inspired by Bauhaus functionalism. Shown here are several weights: Light, Medium, Demi Bold, and Bold. The italic of a sans serif is a slanted roman, and is technically an oblique.

designer used the uniform thickness and geometric character of sans serif letters, and then added a square serif. The result is a series of typefaces called *Cairo, Memphis,* and *Karnak.* They, too, are more difficult to read than roman, but find application in circulars, brochures, and occasionally in ads.

Miscellany   Also available is an incredible assortment of typefaces that fall into none of the preceding categories. They range from *Old Gothic* to various kinds of simulated handwriting (such as *Commercial Script* or *Mistral*) to brush lettering styles (such as *Flash* or *Dom*), with dozens in between. Such faces can be used for particular effects or distinction.

Italics and Bold Type   *Italics* are *not* a separate type family but versions of regular faces that have been slanted to the right. We can use the slanted line formed by italics to add emphasis to a word or a phrase in the body copy, just as has been done throughout this textbook. In a headline, italics lend a feeling of motion or action to the word or words. Almost every typeface in the roman and

a. abcdefghijklmnopqrstuvwxyz
ABCDEFGHIJKLMNOPQRSTUVWXYZ
1234567890.,;:"&!?$

b. *abcdefghijklmnopqrstuvwxyz*
ABCDEFGHIJKLMNOPQRSTUVWXYZ
1234567890.,;:''&!?$

c. abcdefghijklmnopqrstuvwxyz
ABCDEFGHIJKLMNOPQRSTUVWXYZ
1234567890.,;:'&!?$

Goudy Old Style, roman (top) and italic (center), was designed by F. W. Goudy. It was based, he said, on Renaissance lettering. Italic was once a form of type rivaling the roman. Italic is based on humanistic handwriting and should properly be called "cursive." Note the diamond-shaped period.

Caledonia (bottom) is one of the most popular text faces used today. It was designed by W. A. Dwiggins in 1938.

sans serif families is available in italic. (Compare the typefaces in *a* and *b* of the illustration above.)

In line with the same idea—to add variety, distinction, or emphasis—many typefaces are available in different weights; that is, the *thickness* of the characters can be increased. For example, *Bodoni* is available as *Bodoni Regular, Bodoni Bold,* and *Bodoni Italic. Futura* is also available as *Future Light* and as *Futura Bold.* Naturally, the variety can be overdone, giving the body copy and the ad itself a cluttered, spotty look. When used sparingly, however, bold type can punch up a word or phrase.

Selecting the Typeface

As you may imagine, with such a wide range of type styles to choose from, a graphic designer could spend days deciding which faces to use for an ad. But, in actual practice, selection is very often influenced by a number of considerations, the most important of which are the nature of the product and the nature of the appeal. A cosmetic or fashion product would call for a typeface with a light, delicate, feminine style. A powerful detergent—although usually a product bought by women—would profit from a strong, masculine typeface to suggest the power and the utility of the product. (See color plates 49 and 50 for examples of the way type can convey masculine or feminine images.)

The medium, too, affects the choice of type style. The smooth surfaces of the slick paper used for magazines will hold the delicate serifs of slender faces. Not so with the rough texture of newsprint. The size of the ad and the amount of copy that must fit in that space will also influence the choice of type style. If we want to print a lot of copy in a small space, we must specify a face that is tight, compact, and extremely readable even in a small size.

See how the powerful type in these headlines works to help give impact to a half-page. Note the brief, easy-to-read text and the strong package identification that is so important in self-service marketing. Also note the period that ends each phrase — it adds impact by making the thought definitive.

Fashion also influences the choice of typeface. Look through a current magazine and you will see that three or four styles of type are used for most of the ads. Compare those ads with ones that are ten or twenty years old, and you will immediately see how the fashion has changed. Some type styles will look out of date — not old-fashioned, but simply out of date.

The characteristics that govern a choice of typeface are readability, appropriateness, and distinction, in that order. As was true of the layout, the reader should not be aware of the typeface as such.

Achieving Emphasis   As we have already stated, most typefaces are available in various weights and most are available in italics. However, the techniques available are virtually endless when the artist wants to add emphasis: underlining, capitals, small capitals, boxes, reverse, even color can be used to snap out a word, phrase, or sentence. The purpose is to add interest, emphasis, and variety. But remember, although two or more typefaces may be used in the same ad, the faces must be compatible. One paragraph in roman and the next in sans serif may add variety but would be generally unattractive. To alternate a paragraph of light and bold in the *same face* would be more attractive, adding variety without calling attention to the type itself.

Typography   **411**

Achieving Readability   Some typefaces are more legible than others. Obviously, the larger the typeface, the more legible it will be. We are constrained, however, by the size of the space available to us and by the amount of copy that must be accommodated by that space. But readability is affected not only by the size and style of type but by the length of the line to which it is set. Most newspaper columns are less than 2 inches wide; most magazine columns are about 2-1/4 inches wide. For advertising copy, a line length of not more than 3 inches is most readable. Width of line is frequently stated in picas. A **pica** is 1/6 inch, so that a line length of 18 picas or less is recommended.

The lines of copy may be set to a uniform width, so that the text block is even — **flush** — on both the left and right edges, *flush left and right* as it is usually described; or the copy may be set *flush left, staggered right,* even on the left edge but not on the right; or *flush right,* even on the right edge but with an uneven left margin; or staggered left *and* right. Generally it is best to have long blocks of copy set flush left and right. When we wish to have all the lines of copy of equal length, we must **justify** them. The typographer *justifies* the lines by adding a little extra space between words (word spacing) or by adding a bit of space between the individual letters of a word (letter spacing). Look at the columns of type in any newspaper and notice how the lines were justified. This makes them neater and easier to read. Short blocks may be staggered on the right. Very short blocks may be staggered on both sides for a more informal effect.

Spacing is another technique used to improve readability. We can add openness to a block of text by increasing the amount of word spacing or even by increasing the amount of letter spacing. We may also add extra space *between* the lines of copy by increasing the amount of **leading** — a term derived from the former practice of using pieces of lead to separate lines of type. Typefaces with very long ascenders and descenders generally have an open, airy look and may require little or no leading. We can improve the readability of dense blocks of condensed or heavy type, however, by adding more leading.

A block of copy in print carries a visual weight that is a product of the size of the block, the size of the type, and the openness of the type. If you squint your eyes when you look at a block of copy, you will see not the individual letters but a grey shape. The tone color of that grey area may range from light grey to dark grey, depending, as we said, on the face itself and its leading. Leading lightens the tone value. Compare two pages of typewritten material, for example, one single-spaced and the other double-spaced. The double-spaced page will have a lighter grey tone, although both pages were typed with the same black ribbon.

Reverse copy blocks (white type on a black or colored background) demand extra caution. The serifs of many roman faces tend to disappear when they are reversed, as do the thin strokes of the letters. In general, a large block of reverse type is difficult to read. Caution must also be exercised when the text is to be printed over a photograph, an illustration, or a patterned background. The light and dark areas of the background can seriously impair the legibility of the type.

Specifying Type

In ordering type, the instructions to the typographer specify the typeface, the size, and the width of the copy block or line. If a copy of the layout is included, the dimensions of the line or block may not be necessary. How can you tell if the typewritten copy will fit the ad space? The headline usually presents no problem. Examine any type specimen sheet or type "spec" book. A specimen sheet is a page, generally provided by a commercial typographer, which shows several lines of copy repeated in different sizes and styles of type. From such a page, the person who is to **spec** the type can judge how well the copy will fit when set in one of the various sizes shown. A specimen book is a compilation of type pages, usually provided by a commercial typographer. We can determine if the headline copy will fit by simply counting the letters in the headline and counting an equal number of the letters shown in the specimen.

Calculating the space required for the body copy often presents a problem, but there is a simple procedure to follow:

1. Determine the number of characters in the copy by counting the number of characters in the typewritten line and then multiplying that number by the number of lines. Each space counts as one character. Disregard any short lines that may appear at the end of a paragraph.
2. Measure (in picas) the width of the copy block in the layout. Use a pica rule or measure in inches and count six picas to the inch.
3. Select the typeface desired.
4. In the type specimen book usually provided by the typographer, find the number of characters per pica for every size (6-point, 8-point, 10-point, etc.) in the typeface you are considering.
5. Since the width of the copy block in picas is known, calculate the number of characters that will fit in the size you wish to specify. Simple multiplication will then determine how many lines in the typeface will be needed. If the copy runs too long for the space allotted in the layout, it may be set in a smaller type size or in a more condensed typeface that will provide more characters per pica. If the copy runs too short, it may either be leaded to fill the depth or specified in the next larger size.

Typesetting Methods

Hand Composition Hand composition, the oldest typesetting method, required the typographer to assemble individual letters into words, letter-by-letter. It was a tedious process. Next, the typographer had to print proofs of the type. An artist would then cut the proofs and paste them into position on a board to create a **mechanical** of the ad or printed piece.

Linotype Composition Composition was a slow process for a daily newspaper until the invention of the *linotype process,* which cast metal type, line-by-line, as the typographer sat at a keyboard not unlike a typewriter keyboard. The individual lines of type, fully justified (that is, lined up on the right as well as the left) were assembled for printing. It was a much faster process. When the paper had been printed, the metal type would be melted down for recasting.

Computer Composition Linotype has been replaced by *computer composition,* which is familiar to many people as a more complex form of word processing. From "programs" of typefaces, the typographer sits at a computer keyboard and sees the type on the screen as it will appear in its print proof form. Adjustments in width and line spacing are made at the terminal. Individual words can be reversed (that is, made white letters on a black background).

A reverse option in the computer typesetting process automatically permits white characters on a black background. It eliminates the need to make photostats and speeds productivity.

In addition to typefaces, photocomposition techniques offer an extensive range of rules and symbols, commonly referred to as "dingbats."

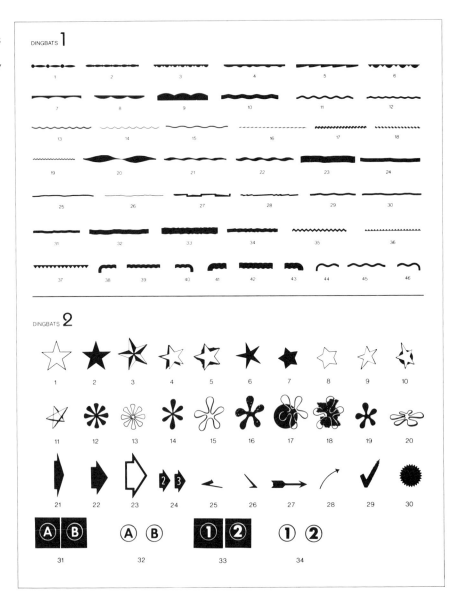

MACHINE BOLD	**Neil Bold**
MANDARIN	Neil Bold Open
Mandate	News Gothic
Palatino Semibold OUTLINE	**News Gothic Bold**
UMBRA	News Gothic Condensed
Melior Semibold	News Gothic Extra Condensed
Melior Semibold Italic	**Novel Gothic**
Melior Bold	**STENCIL**
Melior Bold Condensed	Stymie Light
Melior Bold Outline	Stymie Medium
MOORE COMPUTER	Stymie Bold
Murray Hill Bold	**Stymie Extrabold**
Pistilli Roman Open NO 2	***Stymie Extrabold* ITALIC**
PRISMA	**Stymie Black**
PROFIL	*Park Avenue*
Stymie Black ITALIC OUTLINE W FLAIR	PEIGNOT LIGHT
Bauhaus Medium	PEIGNOT DEMI BOLD
Bauhaus Demi	**PEIGNOT BOLD**

A small sample of the range of photolettering available to the graphic designer. Photo-lettering is reproduced by the word and is used for headlines, logotypes, package design or labels — wherever a distinctive appearance is desired. Just like computer type, many photolettering faces are available in families, so the artist can mix light with bold, or bold with italic, or regular with condensed, yet remain consistent in overall impression. Too wide a type mixture is distracting for the reader.

Entire pages can be prepared in this way, at high speed. There are no heavy pieces of metal to handle. In many cases, it may not even be necessary to cut the proofs apart because all the words, headline, and text are in position. With the computer technology and telephone transmission lines, editors and writers in offices around the country can transmit their stories from the field office to the publication office where the material is set in type at once. Full pages of news material for magazines and newspapers can be set simultaneously for printing in different areas of the country.

It is also possible for the computer process to modify the type, slanting the words, curving the lines, contracting or elongating words or lines.

Printing Processes

The printing process used for advertisements appearing in newspapers and magazines is specified by the individual publication. When preparing advertising material for other media, the advertiser chooses the printing process — a choice governed by considerations of cost, quality, speed, and the effect desired.

The job shop, as the small neighborhood printer is called, may use systems ranging from small, slow presses into which the paper is fed by hand, to large automatic presses into which the paper is fed automatically, the plate is inked automatically, and the printed sheets delivered automatically. When paper is fed to the press in cut sections, it is **sheet-fed.** When fed from a continuous roll, it is **web-fed.** Web-fed processes are so sophisticated today that the paper may be printed in four colors in sequence, different sections of the press applying a different color. At the delivery end, a knife automatically cuts the paper to the desired size.

Letterpress

Letterpress is by far the oldest printing process. It is quite simple. The surface that prints is raised. A roller with ink is literally rolled over the surface, the ink coating only the raised areas. Paper is then pressed against the surface, and the matter to be printed is transferred to the paper. The process has long been used by artists for printing woodcuts. Gutenberg used a letterpress method to print his famous Bible. Letterpress is rarely used for commercial printing. Magazines and newspapers too have turned to offset lithography and gravure.

Lithography

The lithographic process is a printing technique that has been used by artists for many years. The basic concept of the lithographic process is simple. The artist draws upon a soft, flat stone with a grease pencil. He or she then applies water to the surface of the stone with a roller. The water, which will not adhere to the drawing because the greasy lines reject it, is absorbed by the nonprinting areas of the stone. Then, with another roller, the artist applies greasy ink to the stone. The ink adheres only to the greasy design because the water in the nonprinting areas rejects the ink. Paper then picks up the image from the inked surface.

In adapting this simple process to commercial applications, the lithographer uses a grained plate made of aluminum or zinc. The image is applied to the plate photographically. Thereafter the process is the same as the one the artist uses: water dampens the areas that do not contain the photographic image; the greasy ink adheres only to the photo image areas; and the printing proceeds. The entire process is automatic, and is called direct lithography. The plate can be curved to accommodate web-fed paper. However, the process has advanced a step further, to offset lithography, usually simply called **offset.** The grained plate, instead of printing directly on the paper, prints on a rubber roller — the offset roller — which, in turn, prints on the paper. The advantage is that the rubber roller accommodates rough or textured paper. The result is a cleaner impression on a wider range of paper.

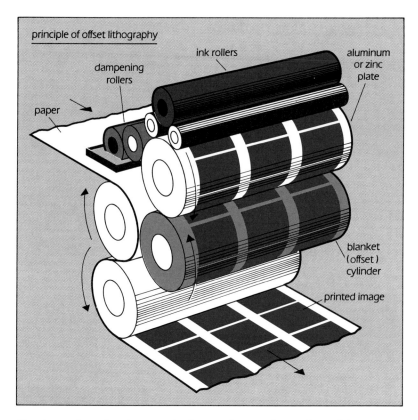

The dampening rollers in a trough of water dampen the portions of the metal plate that are not to print. Using a greasy ink, the ink rollers apply the ink to the plate. The ink adheres only to the portions that are to print. From the plate, the image is transferred to the offset cylinder (blanket cylinder), which transfers it to the paper.

Today, small offset presses are widely used. They utilize very inexpensive plates made of aluminum or paper that are discarded after use. For large press work, the plates are cleaned and reused. Most of the magazines and newspapers presently published in the United States are printed by this offset process. It is by far the most widely used method for the preparation of brochures, circulars, and other direct advertising material.

Gravure

Gravure is a printing process used primarily for magazines. This process reverses the letterpress technique: With gravure, the surface that prints is *below* the level of the plate. The image of the material to be printed is transferred to a printing plate by a photographic process. This image is then etched into the plate with acid. The tiny grooves created by the etching are filled with ink that is deposited by a roller. The surface of the plate is then wiped clean by a **doctor blade,** leaving ink only in the tiny etched grooves. When the paper comes into contact with the plate it literally sucks up the ink in the grooves of the plate and thereby obtains the image of the copy. The greatest advantage of gravure is the superb reproduction quality it offers. The special gravure paper that absorbs the

As the cylindrical plate rotates in its trough of ink, the surface is flooded with ink. A squeegee, called the doctor blade, automatically wipes the surface of the plate clean, leaving the ink only in the below-the-surface grooves. As the paper passes over the plate, the ink is drawn up by capillarity into the surface of the special gravure paper.

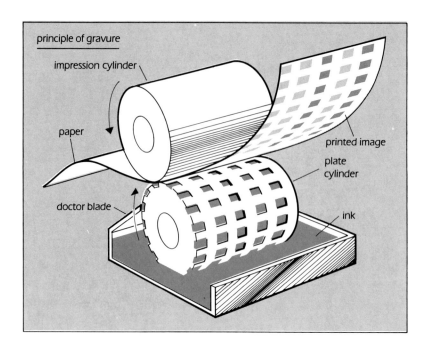

ink tends to give to the illustration a soft quality that most closely resembles the continuous tone of a photograph. Gravure is the process used to print the roto section of Sunday newspapers; it is also being used by growing numbers of magazines.

Screen

Screen printing is used to reproduce advertising material needed only in limited quantities, such as car cards, posters, and point-of-purchase materials. The **screen process** is the simplest of all the printing techniques we have discussed. A screen, made of silk or other fine cloth or metal or some other porous material, is covered with a nonporous plastic film. The plastic film is then cut away from the areas that are to be printed. Ink is then flooded onto the screen, penetrating the fabric only where the plastic film has been removed. The printer uses a **squeegee,** a tool with a rubber or sponge blade, to force the ink through the screen and onto the surface to be printed.

The principal advantages of this printing process are: its ability to print on a variety of materials, including glass, wood, plastic, and heavy cardboard; and the intense, brilliant colors that result from the very heavy deposit of ink, which resembles paint in density and consistency. Also, because the process is so simple, it can be used to print quantities of 50 or 100 pieces, for which an offset run would be too costly. The process is coarse; it does not lend itself to delicate illustrations.

Halftones

You will recall that the cost for placing an ad in a publication includes printing in black ink, and black ink only — not grey, or any other shade between black and white. But, when we examine a photograph or a wash drawing, we can see that its character is derived from the infinite variations in

17 | REPRODUCTION PROCESSES

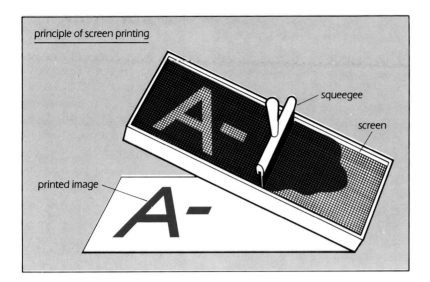

principle of screen printing

squeegee

screen

printed image

A-

The plastic film that covers the screen prevents the ink from passing through the screen to the paper, except for those portions where the plastic has been cut away. A separate screen is necessary for each color, and the colors will be printed one by one. After the heavy deposit of ink has been laid down, the paper must be allowed to dry. Screen printing, because of its value in short runs, is the most common method for making street name signs and road signs on and over the highway.

the middle tones — the areas that are neither solid black, nor white, but **half-tones.** The printing process requires that translation of those varieties of grey into black and white.

In order to reproduce all of the delicate tones that give an illustration its character, it is first necessary to make a film negative of it. The halftone art work is photographed with a **screen,** formed of fine black lines on a piece of glass or plastic, placed behind the lens of the camera and in front of the film. These lines are placed at right angles to each other, forming boxes, or dots, of clear space. When the illustration is photographed in this manner with a high-contrast film, the grey areas of the original are broken into black boxes or dots. The lines on the screen prevent the light from affecting the film, and each dot is separate and discrete. Areas of dark grey in the original art work will have a heavy concentration of dots, while the light grey areas will have fewer dots. The density of the dots in any area of the negative will vary with the tone quality of the corresponding area on the original photograph or drawing. We have literally broken up the illustration into black dots. If we could not do this photographically, we might still be using woodcuts to reproduce illustrations. Woodcuts utilize a similar process, except that the dots are cut by hand.

Screens used for making halftone negatives may have from 65 to 150 lines to the inch, and the choice of which screen to use depends on the printing process. Because of the coarse quality of newsprint, newspapers generally require a 65 screen, that is, a screen with 65 lines per inch. Magazines that use the offset process require 110 or 120 screens, depending on the kind of paper that they use. The smoother the paper, the finer the screen we can use. For publications that use the gravure process, we need provide only the art work, since they prepare their own printing materials.

Plates and Duplicates

For magazines and newspapers that use the offset or gravure printing processes, the plates are prepared by the publications from material furnished by the advertiser. For offset, the advertiser provides a film negative. The publication specifies the screen to be used and any other pertinent technical

New photographic techniques make possible a variety of screen methods, instead of the usual dot form. Note how the areas that appear grey are formed by the varying intensity of the screen patterns, yet they are simply black lines.

details. When, as is often the case, the same ad is inserted into several publications at the same time, it is necessary to provide duplicates to each publication. For publications that use offset, we can have the plate-maker prepare positive prints from the original negative. These are high-quality prints, ready to be photographed, which the publication will easily convert to its own use.

65-line screen

85-line screen

110-line screen

133-line screen

The difference in the quality of detail obtained by the different halftone screens is made clear in these side-by-side examples. For printing on newspaper stock, a 65-line screen is needed. Any finer screen would fill in and look fuzzy on such coarse-textured paper. Notice how the details of the illustration become clearer as the screen becomes finer.

Nancy Axthelm

Nancy Axthelm grew up in Rockville Centre, New York, and pursued a liberal arts college education in Boston. Her father had been at Grey Advertising before he passed away and, at the suggestion of her mother, Nancy tried for and landed a summer job at Grey during her college years. Under the tutelage of Florence Goldin, who had been named "Advertising Woman of the Year" many times, she worked as a speech writer and stylist every summer, Christmas vacations, and as many long weekends as she could, until graduation. She was then hired full-time in the fashion office. As she describes it, "The very first time I was exposed to a commercial filming I was hooked. It has always been extremely intriguing and interesting to me to help move an idea from conception to final film. As a producer you get exposed to the many necessary people and all the areas of film and tape production as well as advertising and marketing." Within two years Ms. Axthelm was named a producer and has remained at Grey ever since. She is presently a vice-president, production group head for a department of 27 producers and 12 assistants. She has worked on virtually every account at Grey including Procter & Gamble, General Foods, Timex, Revlon, and AMC/Renault. She has received many prestigious awards for her work and in 1984 was named to *ADWEEK*'s 1984 Creative All-Star Team as Television Producer.

How did they shoot that? Anyone who has seen this great commercial on television must wonder how they ever got what looks like hundreds of red Renault Alliance cars streaming down a main thoroughfare in 30 seconds. The idea, from Grey Advertising, was to demonstrate that Alliance was the best-selling new car in 1983. It was one tough job. It was most important that it take place in New York and on a broad, high-class street — Park Avenue, of course. American Motors was prepared to ship in all the cars from Detroit for the shoot, but it wasn't necessary. The agency rented just 36 cars from area dealers. Under the production supervision of Nancy Axthelm, a vice-president of Grey and production group head for a department of 27 producers and 12 assistants, the agency plotted four blocks of Park Avenue and planned how the automobiles would be scheduled for their run. Grey flew in a precision stunt driver from Los Angeles to help choreograph the cars. R. Greenberg Associates was the production company that made it all possible. The city of New York cooperated. Scaffolding was erected with a locked down motion-picture camera. An armed guard stood watch over the scaffolding and the cars that were parked in the street the night before. The side streets, as well as four blocks of Park Avenue, were closed off for 10-minute shooting intervals between 10 AM and 3 PM for three shooting days. Only 36 cars were used, but the shots were optically combined by the production studio to make it appear as though hundreds were passing through. All the cars had to be driven at exactly the same speed to avoid "bumping" into each other when the takes were combined. Every car had two-way walkie-talkies and coordination had to be split-second between cameraman, director, and drivers. The cost to produce this eye-catching commercial was in line with many typical auto commercials.

Color Reproduction

To reproduce illustrations in full color, we use a technique called **four-color process.** To the three basic colors — red, yellow, and blue — black is added, and with these four colors, advertisers can reproduce all the mouth-watering realism of their food products or the scenic beauty of an outdoor back-

ground. Mixing red and yellow ink will give us orange. Red and blue provide purple, and blue and yellow provide green. (See color plates 51–55.)

Printing a full-color advertisement is very different from printing a mere black-and-white ad. A separate screened negative is made for each color by using a filter that blocks out all the colors but the one we want to photograph. The screen for each color is also tilted 15° so that the individual dots or squares

CASE HISTORY

The Sony Walkman

Sony Corporation is a well-established manufacturer of electronics equipment in Japan. Its products include television sets, radios, high-fidelity components, tape recorders, cassette players, and tapes, in an extensive range of types and sizes. They are marketed all over the world. Among such famous names as Panasonic, Hitachi, and Yakamura, all of which represent fine quality electronics products made in Japan, Sony represents the top of the product category. The Sony Walkman represents literally a classic marketing case in which a company did everything right, combining in one piece of electronics equipment the two desirable qualities that the public wanted—high-fidelity audio quality and portability. The Sony marketing staff put everything together: product design, consumer testing, package design, brand name, and promotion. The Sony Walkman has become one of the greatest marketing successes in recent years. First introduced in mid-1979, millions of the little machines have already been sold all over the world.

In October 1978, an organizational change at Sony transferred the tape recorder division to the radio division. The tape recorder division had been producing radio cassette recorders. At that point, the tape recorder division conceived the idea to make a portable stereo recorder. Sony was already producing two compact recorders, one of which was a dictating machine for business use. Someone connected one of these recorders to a pair of large headphones. Everyone was delighted with the quality of the sound. It was the beginning of the Walkman. Then an-

other fortuitous accident—one of the Sony executives dropped in on the tape recorder division and saw the prototype. He thought the headphones were too large. He knew that the research laboratory was experimenting with new, lightweight headphones, and recommended that the two be combined.

When he learned about the new product, Mr. Akio Morita, Sony's Chairman, sensed the tremendous potential and set up a launch team composed of ten people from different Sony divisions. The team approach was needed to launch the product within six months. It usually takes one or two years. Cost structures and pricing were evaluated. Package designs were created. Consumer tests were conducted.

Naming the product was more of a problem. The name Stereo Walkie came up, but it turned out that a competitor had already registered the name "Walky" for one of its radios, so Sony could not use "Walkie." Everyone liked the concept of "Walk." They settled on "Walkman" because it was a typical Japanese-made-English word that would appeal to Japanese consumers. They planned to use different names in different markets. Mr. Morita thought the use of different names was wasteful and decided to use "Walkman" everywhere. An international warranty system was introduced so that the customer could receive after-sales servicing in just about any country in the world. In fact, the name caught on so quickly that it has become almost a generic term rather than a brand name. (See color plate 56.)

---

of color do not fall on top of each other when the ad is printed but print side by side, overlapping slightly. The reader's eyes blend the pattern of color dots into a uniform color. If the screen were not tilted for each separate plate, the black dot, which is printed last, would obliterate all the other dots. The colors are usually printed in the following sequence: yellow, red, blue, and black.

Filters are needed to separate the original illustration or color photograph into its three primary color components. A green filter blocks out blue and yellow and creates the red portion of the plate. An orange filter blocks out all the red and yellow tones, permitting only the blue tones to come through. A purple filter is used for the yellow plate.

In printing a four-color illustration, the printers must make sure that each color falls precisely into its place in the order described above. A slight variation in paper or plate can spoil the effect. Color printing is far more costly than is black and white.

Paper

A few words suffice to describe the advertiser's requirements for paper. Publications offer very little choice in paper: newsprint for newspapers, magazine finish for most magazines. The slick paper used for magazines has a clay coating that permits the use of fine screens with substantially better reproduction quality. Magazine covers are made of a heavier paper known as **coated stock.** Only with direct mail are our opportunities for using paper of different weights, colors, textures, and sizes virtually unlimited.

Summary

Advertisers must be familiar with the various methods of reproducing print advertisements because even the best-written copy, the most effectively designed layout, and the most attractive illustration can be rendered ineffective through carelessness in the final assembly and printing of the ad. In preparing the final copy of an advertisement for publication, a *typeface* must be selected for the *body copy* and the headline and final prints of the illustrations must be obtained. The art department of the advertising agency or the printer will then assemble these elements, using the designer's comprehensive as a guide.

The typefaces that we chose for the body copy and the headline should enhance the total effect of our ad without being obtrusive. These are three major families of typefaces—Roman, Sans Serif, and Egyptian—as well as many different miscellaneous faces. Each of the available typefaces has a different degree of readability and weight, and each has different psychological connotations of masculinity, femininity, quality, or fashion attached to it. In selecting a typeface, the advertiser is constrained by limitations of available space, the process to be used in printing the ad, and the kind of paper that it is to be printed on.

An understanding of the major printing processes—offset, rotogravure, and silk screen—will help advertisers arrange for the most effective reproduction of their ads. Illustrations that contain a wide range of tone values, for example, can be reproduced best by the rotogravure or offset process. Two other factors that affect the reproduction of an illustration are the fineness of the screen used to make the halftone negative of the artwork, and the finish of the paper on which the illustration will be printed. The finer the screen and the smoother the finish on the paper, the higher the quality of reproduction.

Questions for Discussion

1. What are some of the factors that help determine the choice of typeface?
2. What factors determine the legibility of type?
3. Explain the offset process. What is its major advantage?

4. Find an example of what you consider an appropriate type selection in an advertisement. Find another that you consider inappropriate. Justify your choices.
5. Find a sample of each of the three families of typefaces.
6. Find an example of a two-color ad and, then, of a four-color ad. What kind of illustration was used in each?

Sources and Suggestions for Further Reading

Baldwin, Huntley. *Creating Effective TV Commercials.* Chicago: Crain Books, 1984.

Bockus, H. William, Jr. *Advertising Graphics.* 2d ed. New York: Macmillan, 1974.

Brunner, Felix. *Handbook of Graphic Reproduction Processes.* New York: Hastings House, 1962.

Cardamone, Tom. *Advertising Agency & Studio Skills.* Rev. ed. New York: Watson-Guptill, 1970.

Croy, Peter. *Graphic Design and Reproduction Techniques.* Rev. ed. New York: Hastings House, 1972.

Gottschall, Edward M., and Arthur Hawkins. *Advertising Directions.* New York: Art Directions Book Co., 1959.

Nelson, Roy Paul. *The Design of Advertising.* 3d ed. Dubuque, Iowa: Wm. C. Brown, 1977.

Stanley, Thomas Blaine. *The Technique of Advertising Production.* 2d ed. Englewood Cliffs, N.J.: Prentice-Hall, 1954.

"Son, that's where the Statue of Liberty used to be."

Let's make sure this never happens. With our help, this 99-year-old lady can live forever. Please send what you can to: The Statue of Liberty/Ellis Island Foundation, P.O. Box 1992, Dept. F, New York, NY 10008.

This advertisement created as a public service by Saatchi & Saatchi Compton Inc.

THE WORLDS OF ADVERTISING

◄ This ad was one of the more than 200 contributed by advertising agencies all over the United States to promote the renovation of the Statue of Liberty. Like the others, it is a "soft-sell" meant to appeal to our best instincts. Notice what creative people can do with a simple headline and just two sentences of copy. For other excellent examples, see color plates 63 and 64.

18 THE ADVERTISING CAMPAIGN

Working Vocabulary

campaign
tactical objective
regional campaign
SMSA
product promotion campaign

corporate advertising
horizontal cooperative advertising
sales promotion
forcing methods

push strategy
pull strategy
loss leader
split run
test marketing

An advertising executive usually thinks of advertising in terms of an advertising campaign, a series of advertisements supporting a common objective and which may include such different media as television, radio, and magazines. This advertising campaign must be coordinated with other promotional and marketing efforts and will involve a host of decisions and decision makers.

David A. Aaker and John G. Myers
Advertising Management

As advertisers, we hope that our advertising investment will yield dividends in the form of brand-loyal customers. We want to create a continuing habit. One of the worst mistakes that advertisers make is spreading their advertising efforts thin. Most products have several good selling points, but it is very difficult to get the target market to grasp two or more equally valid facts simultaneously. If someone were to throw two or three balls to you at the same time, chances are you wouldn't catch any of them. But you could easily have caught one.

It is the advertiser's job, then, to make it easy for the target market to catch the ball — to understand one important point or benefit provided by the product. Therein lies the campaign concept: the choice of appeal, the selection of media, and the creation of the advertising layout must all be focused to achieve concentration and dominance.

Some chapters ago we talked about advertising as if it were a battle we were waging. The campaign concept perpetuates the analogy: we plan a strategy; we position our product; we concentrate our forces; we aim at a target market. Fortunately, that's as far as the analogy goes. In the advertising war, no one wins except the consumer. The battle for market share and for brand loyalty goes on and on. We *launch* a new product; *concentrate* our attack in certain markets; we *dominate* a field; we *capture* and *hold* a share of the market; we *defeat* competitive efforts. It really is a continuing battle.

Planning the Campaign

A **campaign** is an advertising effort that is planned for, and conducted over, a specific period of time. The time period may be as long as a year or as short as four weeks. A campaign to sell antifreeze may run its course in only a few weeks of intensive promotion — from the beginning of October to the end of November, depending on the area of the country. There are three criteria that distinguish a campaign from a mere series of unrelated advertisements:

1. *Visual similarity*
   In *print,* the ads would have a similar format — the same kind of photo, the same type style, the same color arrangement. In *television,* the commercials would involve the same kind of demonstration or the same actor, actress, or fictional character.
2. *Verbal similarity*
   The same words, the same slogan, the same jingle are used. *"Things go better with Coke."* On radio, the listener would hear the same voice or voices and the same music.

HOLDER: You've already read the news that 7UP has no caffeine. . .

But have you read today's news?

7UP also has no artificial color. (SFX: CAN OPENING)

These are artificially colored.

7UP has no artificial flavor.

These have artificial flavor.

So naturally 7UP has a clean, refreshing, unspoiled taste!

Just look at the contents! (LAUGH)

LYRICS: Don't you feel good about 7UP?

7UP delivers memorability with this bright, sparkling commercial as one in its campaign series created in 1983 that focuses on the good taste of this soft drink. The speaker delivers the strong competitive message in a very pleasant way, and just look at the last two frames.

3. *Similarity of approach*

The use of a consistent approach to the market is difficult to describe, but is exemplified by General Motors' advertising for its Chevrolet automobiles. For many years, GM's approach has been to portray the Chevrolet as the type of car all Americans want. Explicitly or implicitly, Chevrolet's advertising has told consumers: "Chevrolet is as American as apple pie."

In its broadest sense, the advertising campaign is the culmination, not only of our advertising program, but of all the components of our marketing program. Now, having defined our target market, set our advertising budget, agreed upon our appeal and creative strategy, packaged and branded our product, and analyzed the available media, we are faced with the difficult task of bringing all these elements together in a single campaign coordinated with all our other marketing efforts. The following is a brief summary of the factors that will influence an advertising campaign:

1. our company's financial resources
2. our company's position in the market
3. our product and its present stage in its life cycle
4. the extent to which our product can be differentiated from others of its type
5. the potential market in numbers and types of customers
6. seasonal variations in demand
7. media availability and costs
8. the channels of distribution and the extent of dealer cooperation possible
9. the competition — their number, strength, and apparent marketing strategies

Campaign Objectives

Important decisions that concern the duration of the campaign and the selection of media schedules are contingent upon the explicit purposes of our advertising effort. We must, therefore, very carefully define the objectives of our campaign. A careful statement of campaign objectives serves two purposes:

1. In choosing between two or more potential campaigns, we can turn to the objectives and use them as decision criteria, rather than relying on aesthetic judgment.
2. At the conclusion of the campaign, we can use our objectives to evaluate the effectiveness of our effort.

When asked to state the objective in any advertising program, an advertiser may be prompted to reply that it is to increase sales, or to maximize profits. Of course, we hope to maximize profits, but this objective does not satisfy our second criterion for a campaign objective. It would be difficult to evaluate the results of an an advertising campaign on this basis. Sometimes, in fact, the advertising effort may require the reduction of profits for the short term in order to develop an improved long-range position.

To increase sales is an enticing advertising objective, but such an objective is not always measurable. Advertising is only one of many factors affecting sales, and it is very difficult to isolate its contribution. A growing market may stimulate an increase in sales volume even though the advertiser's share of the total market may be declining. Again, the contribution of advertising often only emerges over the long run. Since there is often a time lag before our advertising begins to work, the effect of an advertising campaign may not be evidenced until well after the campaign's end. It may require two years or more to change the attitudes of some prospects.

The ultimate objective of most advertising programs is usually the maximization of profits through sales. Such an objective may be very desirable, but it is not very operational. If, then, we cannot use immediate sales and profits to form the bases for evaluating the results of a campaign, what else can we use?

Tactical Objectives

Although we should never lose sight of our ultimate objective — profits through sales — we may have to set tactical objectives. **Tactical objectives** are short-range goals that will lead to our ultimate objective. Such tactical objectives may include:

1. to extend the selling season
2. to promote new uses for a product
3. to increase the unit of sale
4. to stimulate primary demand for a product type
5. to build a family concept for a group of products
6. to develop brand preference
7. to motivate dealers to stock or push a product
8. to develop a new image for the company

We may, for example, believe that our sales will be increased in the long run if consumers recognize our company as one that produces only high-quality products. But their perception of the quality of our product must make them willing to buy it more readily; that is, we must be careful not to give them the impression that our product is too expensive for their budgets. Or, if our objective is to develop brand preference for our product, we may attempt to reposition it in the minds of consumers. Our creative strategy — positioning — is derived, then, from our objective. If we want to position the Ford Granada as an automobile superior to a comparable Chevrolet model, we can show the Granada in certain settings and with certain kinds of people that seem to put it in the same class as well-known luxury cars. By relating the Granada to a Mercedes, for example, we hope consumers will think of the Granada as being "as good as," or "almost as good as," a Mercedes.

The Influence of the Product Life Cycle

The duration and intensity of our campaign will be very markedly affected by our product's stage in its life cycle. A completely new product, for which no exact competitor exists, will require a different campaign than will an old, well-established product that is fighting to retain its market share. In fact, every product has competition, even if it is only the old way of doing something. But, a new product demands a campaign that will inform and educate. An older product demands a retentive, or reminder, campaign. Campaigns for such established cigarette brands as Marlboro are good examples of reminder campaigns. With only the slogan "Come to Marlboro Country," the advertiser reminds smokers — both present users and prospective switchers — of the Marlboro brand. We must, however, acknowledge that a product that has reached the mature, reminder stage of its life cycle did so through other types of campaigns. Again, we can turn to cigarette advertising to find good examples of introductory and competitive campaigns. Advertisements in the recent "tar derby," for instance, bombarded consumers with lengthy copy that was filled with information on the tar content or type of filter of each new brand or variant of an established brand.

Duration of the Campaign

A campaign for consumer products will usually last one year — the customary time period for setting advertising appropriations. The campaign may be of shorter duration, especially if it is based on the selling season of the product, the 13-week segments that are a feature of broadcast media schedules, or the frequency discounts offered by other media. Men's colognes, for example, have two short selling seasons — about two weeks before Father's Day and about four weeks preceding Christmas. This is not to say that such products are not bought all through the year, but their sales volume will peak during a short period and that's when their advertising will be most effective. We mentioned earlier that antifreeze has a short selling season. There is little point in advertising antifreeze after the first freeze of winter or during the summer. Certainly drivers do replace their antifreeze during other periods of the year, but the season for the vast majority of sales is very short.

Monthly publications, as we know, offer contracts based on a one-year period, with lower rates based on a specified number of insertions — three, six, or twelve — during the contract year. As the frequency goes up, the rate per ad goes down. Weekly magazines offer contracts for 13, 26, and 52 insertions. Thus, the media lend themselves to schedules based on specific divisions of the year. It is possible for an advertiser to use two campaigns of six months each in a contract year.

The Importance of Repetition

By placing a single ad in one newspaper, a retail store might draw all the customers it wants for the particular product advertised. But, for that store to develop patronage — that is, a core of regular customers — it must place advertising over many months to build its reputation. In fact, the success of any single ad is more than likely the result of past advertising, perhaps placed over a period of several years, that has built the image of that store.

This same concept — the cumulative effect of advertising — also applies to national advertising. One or two ads are not ordinarily enough to do a selling job. We are not aiming for a single sale. We want our customers to repeat their purchase behavior. Otherwise, our advertising investment will never pay off. We know that our advertising is an interruption of the customers' other interests. We also know that they are being inundated with information on many other products. Repetition keeps our impression alive. The effect of repetition does not depend on the placement of large advertisements or color ads, or the use of dramatic copy or illustrations. It does require the steady investment of advertising dollars over a period of time.

Of course, the process of repetition cannot go on forever. After a while it is necessary to create a new impression. But a unified theme will provide psychological continuity for our advertising. We can make a fresh impact with a new illustration, a new appeal, or a new headline. We may even be able to obtain new impact from the same appeal or the same advertisement by placing it in a different context. For example, after consumers have passed the same transit poster twice a day for several weeks, it becomes part of the scenery. But by placing the same ad in a newspaper or magazine, we can make a fresh impression. We want to avoid *wear-out.* You may recall that one way to avoid it in outdoor advertising was to rotate billboards.

Types of Campaigns

Campaigns can be roughly divided into three basic categories, based on the advertiser's objectives. These categories arc:

1. regional
2. product promotion
3. corporate, or institutional

Regional

A company planning to distribute its product nationwide may find it expedient to launch a **regional campaign.** The regional campaign, launched in a few neighboring states, will serve several purposes. First, it will save money. Although conserving money may not be the most important consideration for a large and prosperous company, it can be critical for a newly established one. By concentrating promotional efforts in a region close to its headquarters, a company can minimize its advertising costs and sales-force expenses. Management can also retain greater control over a localized promotional effort. Many large companies use a regional campaign to test the strength of their advertising appeal. They can get a feel for the market before investing the large sums of money that a national "roll-out" requires.

In discussing a regional campaign it is appropriate to examine a term that marketers use to describe different geographic areas. When marketers want to promote a product in a specific city, for example, they are aware that, for marketing considerations, they are concerned with areas *around* the city as well. We often use the terms *Greater New York,* which includes a portion of nearby New Jersey and Connecticut, and *Greater Chicago,* which includes Gary, Indiana. To help marketers define markets with a set of common terms, in July 1983, the Bureau of the Census developed a new classification for urban areas, eliminating the term SMSA which had been in use since 1949. Typically, an **SMSA** (Standard Metropolitan Statistical Area) was comprised of a large central city and its surrounding area and contained at least 50,000 people. The broad definition thus served a small city with a population of 50,000 and a city like New York or Los Angeles with a population in the millions. To remedy this awkwardness, the Bureau created three new categories — MSA (Metropolitan Statistical Area), PMSA (Primary Metropolitan Statistical Area), and CMSA (Consolidated Metropolitan Statistical Area). An MSA contains either a city of at least 50,000 or an urbanized area of 50,000 with a total population of at least 100,000 and social and economic homogeneity. A PMSA consists of at least 1 million people and includes a large urbanized county or a cluster of counties that have strong economic and social ties as well as ties to neighboring communities. A CMSA represents several overlapping and interlocking PMSAs. They comprise the 23 largest metropolitan areas and include Los Angeles, Chicago, and New York.

Product Promotion

We can also separate campaigns into those promoting a product and those that are institutional in nature. **A product promotion campaign** is intended to sell the product — to make it more desirable than competitive products. The

We have said that a unity of presentation is characteristic of a campaign. Here are some samples from a campaign created by Foote, Cone & Belding, Chicago, for Sunkist Soft Drinks, Inc. As the agency says in its strategy statement: "The Sunkist advertising program has been designed to generate widespread awareness and broadscale trial by building a distinctive and durable identity for the brand." Note the repeated use of the words "good vibrations," and illustrations of the same models to provide a relationship between all the elements of the campaign.

A full-page, four-color ad that appeared in *TV Guide* in 1978. Note the strong product identification and the large cents-off coupon to induce trial by reducing risk.

A car card for bus and rapid-transit rail lines (below).

18 | THE ADVERTISING CAMPAIGN

Thirty-second television commercials (above left) produced in 1984 continued the "good vibrations" theme and addressed the target market — young active people. Note the opportunities to show the product in both bottle and can.

A premium was used in 1979 to stimulate sales with these in-store promotion ads — a "take-one" shelf display card (left) and a hang-tag to fit over bottles (above).

Types of Campaigns

campaign revolves around the benefits and satisfactions the purchasers will gain with the product; one of these will be the campaign theme. The theme becomes the point of each individual advertisement, provides the continuity that enables prospects to focus on the message, and thereby enhances the message's reception. For products that are totally new, the campaign has educational value. The advertising may have to change attitudes and habits of long standing. And that takes time. For a long-established product, where differentiation is often trivial, the campaign may be based on something as minor as the product's package. (See color plates 57 and 58 for an example of a product campaign.)

Corporate, or Institutional, Advertising

Advertising that promotes the company rather than its products or services is called institutional or **corporate advertising.** (See color plate 59.) The objective of an institutional campaign may be to favorably influence consumer attitudes by stressing company size, leadership, age, integrity, personnel, or facilities. At the same time, such advertising will influence members of the company's other publics — suppliers, stockholders, governments, and its own employees. The benefits expected from an institutional campaign (in addition to sales, of course) might be:

1. to promote more, or less, government regulation of an industry
2. to help open the door for company salespeople
3. to increase goodwill among suppliers
4. to enhance the reputation of all the company's products
5. to facilitate the recruitment of new personnel
6. to facilitate the sale of company securities

Horizontal Cooperative Advertising

A group of competing companies will often sponsor a common advertising effort to promote the generic product — milk or fruits, for example. The cooperative group will attempt to stimulate *primary demand* for the products of the entire industry or to place a business or social problem before the public at large. In the first instance, the ad campaign will try to generate a widening interest in a *type of product* or service. In the second, the campaign will help the companies (generally combined as a trade association) influence the government's and the public's opinions on a current issue or a piece of impending legislation. The purposes of such a campaign are to educate, inform, describe, cajole, explain, or justify. Advertising by a trade association, usually referred to as **horizontal cooperative advertising,** is not meant to be a substitute for each company's own advertising program.

Typical objectives of horizontal cooperative advertising might include:

1. providing the public with a clearer picture of the products or services provided by the industry
2. explaining the position of the industry on a particular subject
3. influencing legislation and government regulation of the industry
4. promoting in a general way goodwill for the industry

Coordination with Other Promotional Efforts

Personal Selling

The advertising campaign must be coordinated with the efforts of the *field sales force*. Wholesalers and retailers must be persuaded to stock and push the product; otherwise, much of the advertising expenditure will be wasted. Distribution must be expanded. There is no sense in stimulating interest in and desire for a product among consumers if they are unable to find a dealer who stocks it. Trade advertising is usually needed to tell dealers about our upcoming campaigns. Such advertising helps establish a favorable climate even before our salespeople call. Our sales force must also know what appeal is featured in the advertising so that they do not in any way contradict that message.

Sales Promotion

The campaign must be coordinated with the company's sales promotion efforts. By **sales promotion** we mean the company's efforts to stimulate sales by methods other than media advertising or face-to-face selling. Sales promotion involves **forcing methods** intended to get fast action at the retail level. A manufacturer's effort to stimulate sales through retailers is often described as a **push strategy.**

Manufacturers have no desire to reduce their prices. They do not wish to start price wars. They are also well aware that price is often considered an index of quality by consumers. A reduction in price might make consumers nervous about the quality of the product. Instead, the manufacturers will make special arrangements with retailers to promote a given product with coupons, cents-off specials, premiums, and deals. The retailers, because of the protential for extra profits or because of some other beneficial arrangement with the manufacturer, will feature (push) the product. Coupons and cents-off specials are two ways of reducing the price to entice first-time triers. If brand-loyal users take advantage of coupons to save money, that is the price the manufacturer has to pay to win *new* prospects. A premium, as we discussed in chapter 12, is a gift the consumer receives for making the purchase. It may, in fact, be self-liquidating, but it is nonetheless a promotion device.

In contrast to the push strategy, manufacturers may use a pull strategy. A **pull strategy** directs advertising to consumers, rather than to dealers, in order to attract (pull) customers into retail outlets. By stimulating demand for a product in this way, advertisers hope to convince retailers to stock it. Some manufacturers will emphasize push or pull strategies at different times for different objectives. Other manufacturers will launch a coordinated campaign, perhaps as the fastest way to get new products on the market or perhaps as a tactical maneuver to fight regional competitors.

Our advertising campaign must also be coordinated with any *point-of-purchase promotion efforts*. Where possible, a program to get preferential shelf space or to encourage the installation of POP displays must be timed so that the advertising enhances the display while the display reinforces the advertising message. Once more, trade advertising can play an important role in transmitting important information to the dealer network.

Deals are just what the word implies: they are an inducement for the dealer to stock the product. We may make a combination deal — for every two cartons of product X we will deliver one carton of product Y at half-price. Sometimes the deal may be the kind that dealers can't refuse — for instance, a reduced price that they may either pass along to consumers as a *loss leader* or retain for themselves as added profit. A **loss leader** is an item of merchandise that a retailer offers at a reduced price, often below cost (hence the term), in order to attract customers to the store. The idea is that customers, coming in to buy the leader, will buy other items at regular prices. Supermarket "specials" are typical loss leaders. Whatever the deal, retailers are stimulated to buy and stock the product.

Publicity

The final area that must be coordinated in the company's advertising campaign is public relations. *Public relations* is a communication technique and a component of the promotional mix. We distinguished between advertising and publicity in chapter 1 of this book. Indeed, publicity and advertising may appear in the same media. Each has the same long-range goal. Our concern in this regard is to make sure that our publicity is consistent with our advertising message.

Media Selection

The campaign concept must also be applied to media selection. If our advertising objective is defined on the basis of a particular market segment, then our media planning must concentrate on reaching this target. Mass media are not capable of very sharp focus; it may, therefore, be of considerable value to us to concentrate our advertising in media that reach only certain demographic or psychographic segments of the public. In other words, the target market that we wish to reach will dictate our choice of media.

One issue that will arise during the planning of a campaign is scheduling — whether to use ten full-page insertions in one publication, for example, or five full-page insertions in each of two, or ten half-page insertions in each of two. Advertising readership is influenced by the size of the ad. According to a report by Cahners Research, the readership increases as the size of the advertisement increases. Cahners Research analyzed 2,353 business advertisements that were sorted by size and indexed against the overall average. A full-page ad had an index score of 124. A two-page ad had a score of 213. Half-page ads scored 91 and quarter-page ads scored 55.[1] Readership must be weighed against frequency as the advertiser decides whether a series of half-pages is better than a smaller number of full pages.

Measuring Results

In chapter 14, we pointed out that a consumer's decision about whether or not to purchase a product is the result of a distinct learning process. During this process, the consumer becomes aware of a brand, develops an attitude toward

---

[1] *Cahners Advertising Research Report No. 110.1* (Boston: Cahners Publishing Co., n.d.).

it, and then decides to make a trial purchase. We also know that we cannot precisely measure which sales are the result of a particular advertising campaign, because it is impossible to separate these sales from those motivated by other factors in our marketing program. Unlike a change in the quantity of sales, however, a change in the number of people who are *aware* of a brand's existence can be attributed to advertising. Such a change in awareness will usually occur *immediately after exposure* to advertising, while trial purchases may take place at a much later date.

Have Consumers Changed Their Behavior?

To measure the effect of our advertising, therefore, we have to consider the behavior that the advertising is expected to induce, influence, or reinforce. What behavioral action may be desired? We might want to encourage trial purchases by new customers, for example, or to reinforce brand loyalty among existing customers. We might want to increase the frequency of purchase or to encourage consumers to visit a retailer. Our problem is identifying methods to measure these actions.

When the objective is, for example, to encourage a new application of the product, we would find it impossible to measure the number of people who used the product in the new way as a result of advertising. But, if the task assigned to advertising is to communicate the idea of a new use, we could measure the extent of this *knowledge.*

It is difficult to determine to what extent brand loyalty is a result of our advertising effort. Brand purchases by loyal customers tend to be habitual and not likely to be influenced over the short term by advertising. A more appropriate analysis of what motivates brand loyalty might be obtained by measuring the consumer's *attitude* toward our product. In assessing the response of adult customers toward peanut butter, for example, we might find a mildly negative attitude. Perhaps adults consider peanut butter a food for children. From a position of zero, representing absolute neutrality, we might assign to peanut butter a *valence,* or measure of attractiveness, that could be quantified as minus one (-1). Thus, the attitude being studied has both valence ($-$) and strength (1). If, after an advertising campaign that stressed the nutritional value of peanut butter, we measured consumer's attitudes again and discovered a value of plus one ($+1$), we might conclude that advertising contributed to a change in attitude.

Methods of Evaluation

Measuring Individual Ads   What we learn from measuring the effectiveness of an advertising campaign can help make our next campaign better. Having spent large sums of money to launch the campaign, we want to know if the advertising did what it was supposed to do. As the campaign progresses, we have opportunities to evaluate individual ads. Starch Readership Reports, for example, is a syndicated research service that provides reports on the advertisements in about 100 business and consumer publications from *Air Transport World* to *Woman's Day.*

Starch Ratings   The purpose of Starch Reports is to show to what extent respondents have seen and read advertisements in each issue studied. More than 100,000 people are personally interviewed each year on their reading of over 75,000 advertisements. Approximately 1,000 individual issues are studied annually. Interviews are conducted during the early life of a publication, following a suitable waiting period after its appearance, to give readers an opportunity to read or look through the issue.

Interviewers ask the respondents about the ads they have seen, and also record basic demographic data on sex, age, occupation, marital status, race, income, family size, so that sampling can be checked and cross tabulations of readership can be made.

Comparison is the main value of Starch readership data. The advertiser and agency can compare current ads against those of competitors, against previous campaigns, and against Starch Adnorm tables. Properly used, Starch data help advertisers and agencies to identify the types of ad layouts that attract and retain the highest readership and those that result in average or poor readership.

Advertisement readership scores such as those provided by Starch are only relative measures of advertising performance. The level of such scores can vary significantly from issue to issue, and from publication to publication. In addition, no readership service measures or pretends to measure how many of those who received a copy of the publication actually read it. Therefore, though Starch readership studies are useful for comparing *advertisements,* they cannot and should not be used to compare *publications.*

Gallup & Robinson Ratings   Gallup & Robinson (G-R) uses a different technique to probe the respondent's recall of sales messages in a particular issue of a magazine. Three levels of rating are provided: the PNR score, which gives the percentage of readers who proved they remembered the ad by describing it; a measure of the amount of the advertisement's sales message that readers can recall; and finally, the *Favorable Buying Attitude* score, which measures the message's persuasive power.

The Starch reports and the Gallup & Robinson reports are not custom services; they are syndicated. Advertisers receive the information by subscribing to the reports. Such data would be inordinately expensive to obtain independently.

Another simple method for determining the effect of individual ads or for comparing different appeals is the **split run.** Two different ads are inserted in the same issue of a publication so that some copies of the publication will contain the first ad while others will carry the second. The use of a coupon or of some other form of direct request will provide us with the data needed to judge the comparative effectiveness of the two ads. The split run merely eliminates the effect of other marketing variables when comparing two different appeals, two different headlines, or two different illustrations. However, the split-run evaluation procedure is more suitable for pretesting copy than for measuring the effectiveness of a campaign.

Nielsen Ratings   Television advertisers spend billions of dollars to reach and sell their products to millions of American families. It is important to know how many households—numbers and types of people—are being reached by each program and the advertisers who use it as a vehicle for their message. Such information helps advertisers predict performance and guides their agencies in buying television schedules and in evaluating the efficiency of their buys. It also serves as a programming and sales tool for the stations. The foundation of Nielsen television audience estimates are statistically reliable samples.

A Starch Readership Report on advertisements includes a copy of the magazine that has been rated. Attached to the rated ad are labels that show "Ad-As-A-Whole," which indicates the percentage who: "Noted" the ad in the issue (who remembered having previously seen the ad in the issue being studied); "Associated" it with a specific advertiser or product; and "Read Most" (read more than 50 percent) of the word matter in the ad. The other labels indicate the percent of readers interviewed who saw the specific illustration or read the particular copy to which the label was affixed.

The national Nielsen sample is, in reality, two separate samples of television households: the Nielsen Television Index (NTI) sample, which is used to obtain household tuning information; and the National Audience Composition (NAC) sample, which is used to obtain information regarding who is viewing a particular program. Some 1,200 households are used for NTI and approximately 3,200 are utilized for NAC. Additional unused households are available for future use.

Although the end uses of the samples are slightly different, they are chosen via the same process: a multi-stage area probability sample. An *area probability sample* is one in which the sampling frame consists of small areas and each area is selected with a probability equal to the proportion of the total housing units in the area. For example, if the Chicago area accounts for 5 percent of the total housing units in the United States, then approximately 5 percent of the Nielsen sample will be in the Chicago area. The NTI/NAC sample consists of four stages: the selection of counties within the country; the selection of Census Enumeration Districts (EDs) or Block Groups (BGs) within the counties; the selection of blocks within the EDs/BGs; and the selection of housing units within the blocks.

Using computer tapes of the latest U.S. Census counts of all housing units in the country, Nielsen's Statistical Research Department designates the sample areas. Then, trained surveyors visit these areas to identify and list each sample housing unit in the area. Sample housing units are selected from the lists and the locations are given to the Nielsen representatives whose job it is to secure cooperation from the selected households for the installation of the Nielsen Audimeter.

Every year the sample must be updated with new housing units to keep pace with population shifts and growth. In addition, after a period of five years for NTI and three years for NAC (long enough to provide continuity of trend information) the households are systematically replaced. The end result of the Nielsen multi-state area probability sampling techniques is a geographically dispersed national sample of housing units.

Installed out of sight in a closet, basement, or cabinet, the Audimeter home unit silently measures all television set usage within a household. Small and unobtrusive, the Audimeter stores in its electronic memory exactly when each set is turned on and off, how long it stays on the channel tuned, and all channel switchings. Even backyard and patio usage of battery portables can be recorded. The Audimeter home unit is designed to operate with accuracy even in the event of temporary power outages.

Each Audimeter home unit is connected to a special phone line used only by A. C. Nielsen Company. At least twice a day, a central office computer dials up each home unit and retrieves the stored information. The entire process is automatic and requires no work on the part of the sample household. Backup computers serve as protection against electrical failure.

While the Audimeter tells whether a household has a set on and what station it's tuned to, another method is necessary to determine who in the household is watching—by age and sex. Using the NAC sample already discussed, diaries are placed in households spread across the country. These diaries, called Audilogs, permit the members of the household to write in which programs were viewed by which members during a one-week period, including how long a family member watched each program.

With the exception of the very largest markets, local ratings are conducted three times a year in four-week periods known as "sweeps." Sometimes, for any number of reasons, a client can't wait for his local market report to be issued or, perhaps, a special program he is interested in is aired outside the report period. For situations like these, Nielsen offers a *telephone coincidental service* that provides household ratings and shares (demographics optional) within a few days. The sample households are selected by computer to assure a geographic dispersion throughout the DMA, and the interviews are conducted by phone.

Arbitron Ratings   Arbitron surveys 209 television markets across the country, four times a year for four weeks, in November, February, May, and July. In addition, in October, January, and March, larger markets are surveyed again. Arbitron uses computers to select the households to be surveyed. Households agreeing to participate receive a diary in which to record their viewing choices for a week, receiving a small premium in return. The age, sex, and geographic location of the members of the household are also recorded. In New York, Los Angeles, Chicago, San Francisco, Dallas – Ft. Worth, Detroit, Miami, Boston, Houston, and Washington, Arbitron measures television audiences with its Television Meter Service, providing overnight television audience estimates. The meters record when the set is turned on and the channel selected. Arbitron measures station audiences by local areas. Counties are assigned to an ADI (Area of Dominant Influence) based on measurable patterns of television viewing. Ratings measure quantity, not quality.

Test Marketing   Before launching a multimillion-dollar advertising program, the advertiser wants to be as sure as possible that the product is "right" and that the advertising approach is "right." One of the most common techniques is **test marketing** — advertising and selling the product on a geographically limited basis. If the city or cities for the test are properly chosen, the results of the test program should enable the advertiser to judge the reception of the product and the effectiveness of the advertising approach nationwide. A good test market will be (depending on the product) one that is demographically representative of the rest of the country. The degrees of media availability and of media isolation (Will there be "spill-in" from media beyond the market being tested? Will there be "spill-out" in that the media reach areas in which the product is not available?), and the facilities for control and verification, also influence the choice of the test market. Every agency and every research organization has its preferred test-market cities.

Test marketing in different cities or regions of the country may provide an excellent measure of a product's potential, but such advertising does not provide enough information to evaluate a sustained effort. Intervening variables,

These are some of the most popular test markets, but the list is hardly complete. Every marketer and every advertising agency has its favorite cities. There are also many research firms that provide a complete service to marketers for test marketing, which includes arrangements with retailers (the "sell-in") that assure distribution and the evaluation of results.

Popular Test Markets

Albany-Schenectady-Troy	Nashville
Albuquerque	Peoria
Amarillo	Phoenix
Charlotte	Portland, ME
Dallas – Forth Worth	Sacramento-Stockton
Des Moines	San Diego
Erie, PA	Seattle-Tacoma
Fargo, ND	South Bend
Fort Wayne	Syracuse
Green Bay, WI	Tucson
Lexington, KY	Tulsa
Lubbock, TX	Wichita

such as weather, market characteristics, position in the medium, and so on, may affect our results.

How to Evaluate the Overall Campaign   The effectiveness of entire ad campaigns can be judged according to the following criteria:

1. sales increases
2. trial purchases
3. awareness
4. attitude
5. knowledge

In these advertisements, which appeared in a leading marketing publication, newspaper publishers in Albany, New York, and in Portland, Maine, tell test marketers how the demographics of their cities match those of the nation as a whole. Albany, in particular, appears at the top of many lists of potential test cities. Note how the Portland ad covers all the qualities the marketer wants in a test market city.

Sales and trial purchases. Coupon response and direct sales enable us to measure the effectiveness of an ad campaign. Count the coupons, add up the sales, and there are your results. Most consumer ads are not, however, intended to provoke direct response. The advertiser can often get clues on trial purchases from organizations that maintain consumer panels. A panel is actually a permanent sample, and the diaries of panel members provide valuable information about trial use. The question is: how many new trials do we require before we deem the campaign a success?

Awareness, attitude, and knowledge. Through the use of appropriate sampling procedures and questionnaires, the advertiser can question the target market to obtain some measure of their awareness of the product, their attitude toward it,

PROFILE

George Gallup

In the minds of most Americans, the name Gallup is usually associated with the word "poll." For many of us, the Gallup Poll has become virtually synonymous with opinion research, and Dr. George Gallup has provided information on our attitudes on various subjects of interest to political leaders and ordinary citizens alike. However, it was in the field of advertising research that Dr. Gallup first started nearly 55 years ago. And it is in that field that he and one of the organizations he founded, Gallup & Robinson, Inc., continue to make many important contributions that are used to guide advertisers and agencies in their search for the "right" appeal.

George Gallup's career in the research field began in 1922 when he took a summer job for the D'Arcy advertising agency as an interviewer. During that summer, he worked on a study to determine what articles and advertisements people read in the St. Louis newspapers. Believing that the methods used to conduct this survey could be greatly improved, he began to study research techniques when he returned to the University of Iowa in the fall, making them the subject of his Ph.D. thesis in 1928. In 1932, he was hired by Young & Rubicam advertising agency to help set up their copy-research department. The president of the agency, Ray-

mond Rubicam, told Gallup that his only assignment would be to learn how Young & Rubicam could make the advertising it created more effective. George Gallup spent the next 15 years learning how advertising does its work, and he has this to say about the importance of setting measurable goals for an advertising campaign:

> Almost every campaign, to begin with, has specific objectives. The whole process of advertising is designing a strategy that will create a sale. You can find out if the strategy is working. Are you changing people's minds about this particular fact about the product? You can measure that. Every advertiser, even if he spends only a few thousand dollars, should demand some kind of evidence of the effectiveness of his advertising.

In 1947, George Gallup moved into the field of public-opinion polling that has made him famous. But in the advertising field he is best known for the development of methods to measure quantitative (recall) and qualitative (idea communication, persuasion) reactions to individual magazine ads and television commercials. He was elected to the Advertising Hall of Fame of the American Advertising Federation in 1978. Dr. Gallup passed away in 1984.

CASE HISTORY

ITT Life Insurance Corporation

For many years, the mainstay of the life insurance industry was a product commonly known as "whole life." Whole life combines term insurance with a savings account feature. It does not represent a great investment because its yield generally represents about 4-1/2 percent. As consumers became more knowledgeable about their spending, insurance companies had to offer products that provided a better return on investment. Now many insurance companies are competing to replace other companies' whole life policies with less costly forms of life insurance. In 1984, ITT Life introduced the Signature Series Interest Sensitive Plans to offer the best possible benefits at the lowest possible cost. In order to introduce the Signature Series, ITT Life chose to lure customers away from whole life with a $100 challenge. If ITT Life could not beat the coverage and return of any whole life policy, they would pay the owner of that policy $100. A print advertising campaign was created to reach the top prospects — men aged 35 to 54. Publications included *Money, Sports Afield, Popular Mechanics, Science Digest,* and *Sports Illustrated.* The campaign utilized nontraditional executions in what has always been a low-interest, straight category. It explained a complicated subject in plain English to show how ITT Life offered the consumer a better deal for his money. The Signature Series proved to be right-on strategy. The advertising provided support for ITT Life agents all over the country, while creating leads at the same time with the toll-free phone number.

and their knowledge of its use or purpose. Some of the recall (Gallup & Robinson) and recognition (Starch) tests used to evaluate individual ads may also provide a basis for judging a campaign. Recall tests tell us not only whether or not the respondent has seen or read the ads; they also measure the depth of the ads' impressions on the reader and, to some extent, the *meaning* the ads convey. The tests do not, however, indicate whether or not the respondent will buy the product; nor do they indicate whether or not the respondent believed the message even if he or she happened to remember it. If we are prepared to accept the limitations inherent in these recall and recognition evaluations, they can nevertheless be instructive. Provided with a measurement taken before the campaign and a measurement taken afterward, the advertiser can gauge the campaign's effectiveness either in reinforcing or producing *shifts* in consumer awareness, attitude, and knowledge or in maintaining existing attitudes.

Summary

An advertising *campaign* is the culmination of our advertising effort. In a sense, it is a battle that the advertiser fights to capture the minds of a portion of the target market. The advertiser plans the campaign's advertising to provide a powerful selling message and then repeats that message in various forms that have visual or verbal similarity or a common approach.

In planning the campaign, an advertiser's most important task is setting measurable objectives. These objectives will help determine the creative strategy and will also be used at the end of the campaign as a means of evaluating its effectiveness. Advertisers must also take care to coordinate the campaign with the company's personal selling, sales promotion, and public relations efforts.

Advertising takes time to do its job because its function is to change or reinforce the buying behavior of the consumer. We are well aware of how difficult it is to break habits such as smoking or biting one's fingernails. Buying behavior, for the most part, is also a habit. Once consumers find a brand that satisfies most of their needs, they are not inclined to switch. Just as it takes time to build up a habit, time (and repeated advertising) is required to change that habit and substitute another for it.

Advertisers can rarely determine the effectiveness of a campaign by measuring the change in product sales that has occurred, because too many variables can affect this result. They must measure, instead, the prospect's awareness of, and attitude toward, the product. Any shift in awareness and attitude can be attributed to the advertising campaign. Syndicated research services such as Starch Readership Reports will measure the readership levels and persuasive power of individual ads. Advertisers may also use *test marketing* to help determine the effectiveness of a campaign. By testing a campaign only in certain regions or cities, an advertiser can gather information that will improve the campaign before it is rolled out nationwide. But the results of test marketing will also be influenced by variables beyond the advertiser's control, such as the weather. In order to obtain the most accurate evaluation of their campaigns, some advertisers measure sales increases and trial purchases, as well as awareness, attitude, and knowledge changes.

Questions for Discussion

1. What factors influence the length of an advertising campaign?
2. Why would an advertiser run more than one campaign at a time for the same product?
3. What are some measurable objectives an advertiser might set for an advertising campaign?
4. What are some objectives that an advertiser might set for an institutional campaign?

5. Why might advertising have an impact only a year or more after it has appeared?
6. What is the relationship between the product's life cycle and the kind of campaign planned?
7. If you were the advertising manager for a new toothpaste, what kind of advertising campaign would you recommend?
8. What is the role of trade advertising in implementing an advertising campaign?
9. What are the problems in attempting to use sales as a measure of the effectiveness of an advertising campaign?

Sources and Suggestions for Further Reading

"Advertising and Sales Relationships." *The Nielsen Researcher,* no. 1 (1980).

Boyd, Harper W., Jr., Ralph Westfall, and Stanley F. Stasch. *Marketing Research.* 6th ed. Homewood, IL: Richard D. Irwin, 1984.

Exter, Thomas. "Looking for Brand Loyalty." *American Demographics,* April 1986.

Holbert, Neil. *Advertising Research.* Monograph Series #1. Chicago, IL: American Marketing Association, 1975.

"Multiple-Page Units: Too Much of a Good Thing?" *Inside Print,* June 1986.

Petty, Priscilla Hayes. "Behind Brands at P&G." *Harvard Business Review,* November-December 1985.

Sachs, William. *Advertising Management: Its Role in Marketing.* Tulsa, OK: The Penn-Well Publishing Company, 1983.

Saporito, Bill. "Has-Been Brands Go Back to Work." *Fortune,* April 28, 1986.

Schultz, Don E., Dennis P. Martin, and William P. Brown. *Strategic Advertising Campaigns.* 2nd ed. Chicago, IL: Crain Books, 1982.

Schumer, Fern. " The New Magicians of Market Research." *Fortune,* July 25, 1983.

Shields, Mitchell J. "Screening the Nation for the Four-Star audience." *Advertising Age,* February 21, 1983.

Walsh, Doris L. "Rating the Test Markets." *American Demographics,* May 1984.

19 RETAIL ADVERTISING

Working Vocabulary

scrambled merchandising	**big ticket items**	**slug in**
traffic	**omnibus ad**	**canned advertising**
want slip	**tonnage ad**	**Robinson-Patman Act**
distress merchandise	**vertical cooperative advertising**	

Retailing describes the process of selling products or services directly to consumers, usually through a physical establishment: a retail store. There are many different kinds of retail stores. Although a group of such stores may join forces to form a national or regional chain with a common name and common brands of merchandise, their business is still local — or retail — in nature. In general, we can separate retailers into three basic types:

Design by Jacqueline de Ribes. Artistry created by a woman of singular elegance and sophistication. An artistry that reflects her understanding of grace, of polish, of fine beauty. Here, from her Spring collection, the lilac and malachite silk evening gown. Its diagonal drift creating a softness of line gently inventive. Its color, freshly evocative of the season to come! Designer Import Collections.

Saks Fifth Avenue is a leading fashion store — class store — that bases its appeal on updated classic fashion merchandise. Price does not dominate. The style of the ad and the focus on a single item combine to attract an affluent, fashion-conscious customer.

1. *The class store*

   This store stocks and sells the finest quality merchandise, appealing to upscale customers. The authority of the store in matters of style is very great, with prices to match this prestige. The store does some regular-price advertising and some institutional advertising. The percentage of its sales that this store devotes to advertising, however, is small.

2. *The promotional store*

   The reputation of this store is built on aggressive promotion and reduced prices. Services are few and regular patronage is not considered important. Advertising is highly promotional — that is, the emphasis is on price or sales or special purchases. The percentage of its sales that this store devotes to advertising is large.

3. *The in-between store*

   For the most part, this type of store does regular-price advertising, storewide promotions, and occasional clearances and special sales. It also does some institutional advertising. The percentage of its sales that this type of store devotes to advertising is moderate.

Alexander's is a promotional store for which price is the dominant advertising appeal. The use of photographs to strengthen the sense of real merchandise at a very boldly featured price is typical of a promotional store. The objective of such ads is to sell very specific merchandise.

Planning Retail Advertising

As we learned in chapter 3, there are three distinguishing characteristics of retail advertising: (1) it is intended to reach only a limited area; (2) it emphasizes price; and (3) its appeal is for an immediate response. Retail managers are very much concerned with their stores' advertising for these reasons:

1. Advertising costs are probably the fourth largest retail cost after the cost of goods, salaries, and rent.
2. Advertising is a discretionary investment. It is the retailer's one cost that is most susceptible to change.
3. Advertising affects every other facet of store operations — buying, pricing, new store locations, personnel policies, and, most of all, sales activities.
4. There is increased competition between retailers as the result of *scrambled merchandising* and a population that is dispersed and mobile. **Scrambled merchandising** refers to the sale of products that are not traditionally found in a certain kind of retail outlet. Drugstores may, for example, stock hardware and garden supplies; ready-to-wear clothing stores may carry colognes or luggage.
5. We have increasingly become a service-oriented society. Buying decisions often hinge on intangibles — attitudes and images — which the store can project through advertising.

Retail Advertising Objectives

Product promotion advertising is basically intended either to stimulate the immediate sale of merchandise at regular prices or to clear out certain merchandise at sharply reduced prices. In most cases, retailers want to create store **traffic** — that is, they want to get customers to visit their store to see and buy the advertised merchandise. The retailers assume that, once in the store, customers will see and buy other merchandise that was not advertised. Just as national advertisers hope to create brand-loyal customers, retailers want their customers to get into the habit of buying in their stores; they want their regular customers to buy more, and at the same time they want to acquire new customers. Retailers expect that the greater volume of sales thus generated will result in a greater profit.

A retailer can also use institutional advertising to build a store's prestige and enhance its reputation for merchandise. The object is to create a personality for the store. The retailer builds goodwill among prospects by telling regular and prospective customers about the store policies, facilities, services, and philosophy.

Just as national advertisers have advertising objectives, retailers have objectives for their own advertising. To be sure, retailers also use advertising to obtain more profit through sales, but let us briefly list some of the broad objectives a retailer might set and see if they are dissimilar to those of a national advertiser:

1. to attract new customers
2. to sell more merchandise to present customers
3. to sell specific kinds or brands of merchandise
4. to create a store image
5. to create store loyalty

Shamask is still setting precedents — with an unprecedented new softness. Still uniquely cut, now in luxurious wool jersey, damask prints and more. Meet him at 11 today, and see his newest treasures modeled informally from 12 to 4 at Prestonwood. Informal modeling with a special representative, 12 to 4 tomorrow at NorthPark; 11 to 3 Monday, Downtown.

Ronaldus Shamask in person with his complete collection for fall.

Neiman-Marcus

Nationally known Neiman-Marcus, headquartered in Dallas, now has branches in many upscale areas of the country. Neiman-Marcus caters to anyone who wants some of the world's finest merchandise. As a "women's specialty store," it concentrates on women's apparel. However, it also offers excellent gifts, antiques, precious jewelry, epicurean items, and men's clothing. It does not carry appliances, hardgoods, automotive parts, or furniture. Its customers are mature (42–55), well-educated, and in an upper-income bracket. Its customers (or the customers' spouses) are likely to be professionals, managers, or white-collar workers. Neiman-Marcus uses national advertising to position the store as a fashion leader. Its local advertising — magazine, newspaper, and broadcast — also serves to position the store, as well as to generate traffic and sales. Its direct mail programs include a magazine, a Christmas Book, and thank-you notes which its salespeople personally write to customers. (See color plate 60.)

To attract new customers, retailers might try to extend their stores' geographical trading area by introducing new departments and new merchandise. To sell more merchandise to present customers and to build store loyalty, they might want to inform those customers of new departments, new brands, new services, and new policies that will benefit them.

What to Advertise   National manufacturers usually have no problem deciding what to advertise. They may make only one product, or they may want to advertise the one product most likely to produce profitable sales from their advertising investment. Retailers, however — particularly the large supermarket or department store — stock and sell hundreds of items. They have three options when considering what to advertise. They can:

1. Advertise the most popular products of the fastest-selling lines. These products would sell well even without advertising.
2. Advertise the seasonal specialties. This builds traffic, and attracts customers who will buy other, unadvertised, items. Supermarkets frequently advertise products as loss leaders to build traffic.
3. Advertise to clear out slow-moving merchandise or to clear out stock at the end of the season.

LIZ CLAIBORNE TWO-PIECE DRESSING WITH SATINY STRIPES AND LOTS OF DOTS

Liz has done it again, designed that special look for you. In the year of the print, what could be better than an abundance of dots? Satiny striping adds extra appeal. Shoulder pads and an all-around pleated skirt create a statement-making silhouette. White/black dots. Polyester. 4 to 14. 140.00

1 0 0 Y E A R S
CHAS A STEVENS
Celebrate Stevenstyle

This retail ad builds a store image by featuring the name of the famous designer fashions it carries.

The choice must be made on a short-term basis, and most stores will plan for all three. Obviously, retailers hope that clearance advertising will not be necessary. Well-kept records on what products have sold well and when they were sold are the retailer's most valuable guide to advertising. Retailers can base their sales forecasts and budgets on performance records for previous years, and still remain flexible enough to capitalize on changing tastes or styles or on unexpected merchandise "buys." If all this sounds as if it requires careful planning, you are right. It does indeed.

Marketing Information for Retailers

What Does the Retailer Want to Know? The retailer's need for information is much the same as the national advertiser's. Although small retailers are able to get to know many of their customers personally, they usually do not have the resources to conduct any additional market research. Large retailers, with more customers but also with more resources at their disposal, can conduct full-scale market research programs. What type of marketing intelligence would a retailer particularly want to have?

1. What are the attitudes of customers toward the store and toward its merchandise?
2. What local tastes and preferences are most significant?
3. Which family members shop at the store?
4. How many customers does the store lose and gain each year? What are the reasons for the turnover?
5. What are the demographics of the store's market?
6. What are the most important departments or product lines?
7. What are the most important selling days of the week?
8. Which media reach the largest possible number of the store's customers and prospects?
9. How large should the store's advertising allocation be?

Secondary Data Much of the information a retailer needs is available from secondary sources — that is, from data that was collected for some other purpose. For example, the store's own internal records are an excellent secondary source of information. Such records will show on what day, week, or month sales for various categories of merchandise peaked, and which colors, styles, and products sold best. From records of previous advertising programs, the retailer might learn which medium is the most effective for advertising certain merchandise. Charge account billings will provide records of where customers live, how often they shop, and what they buy. The store may also keep records of competitors' advertising activities; if not, such information can be readily obtained from other sources.

Newspapers, radio and television stations, and transit media operators will provide retailers with demographic data on their medium's circulation and, often, with data on competitive advertising activities. The United States Department of Commerce is an excellent source of information. Trade publications, too, are a valuable source of sales data. *Women's Wear Daily* supplies information on women's and children's ready-to-wear clothes; *Drug Topics* supplies information on pharmaceutical store sales; *Sporting Goods Dealer* has information on sporting goods; and many other excellent retailing publications provide general as well as specific data that will be useful to a retailer in planning advertising. Two particularly good sources for retail advertising information deserve special mention. One is the *Newspaper Advertising Planbook,* which is issued to retailers by the Newspaper Advertising Bureau, Inc., and is a step-by-step guide for any retailer. The other is *Advertising Small Business,* which is published by the Bank of America and which contains helpful information on all the media available to retailers.

Data on the percentage of sales allocated to advertising by various kinds of retail stores are available from many different sources. These figures are, of course, averages; some retailers will allocate a percentage of sales to advertising that may be higher or lower than the average, depending on their competitive situations and their stores' profit objectives.

Primary Data   After the retailer has exhausted the available secondary data, there may remain questions that can only be answered by collecting primary data, especially on such topics as customer attitudes, customer preferences, customer shopping habits. Such information is gathered by surveys, interviews, and observation. A mail or telephone survey of a sample of customers or noncustomers may be made from time to time to determine how people perceive the store image. Personal interviews, although more expensive and time consuming, may be used to gather information to guide the retailer in its advertising and merchandising operations. Skilled observers, sometimes with the aid of hidden cameras or one-way mirrors, can provide clues to shopping behavior. How do shoppers move through the store? How do they handle the merchandise? Or the retailer may want to conduct an experiment. Will toilet water sell in the lingerie department? Will barbecue-sauce sales increase if the display is next to the meat counter? Most retailers use **want slips** — forms used by store employees to record requested merchandise not in stock. An analysis of such requests may provide the retailer with clues to trends and changing tastes.

Budgeting Methods

The two methods that retailers most commonly use to determine their advertising budgets are the percentage-of-sales method and the task method. We examined both of these methods in chapter 6.

Percentage of Sales   This system is the method most widely used by retailers because it is based on past experience. This is not to say it is the preferred method, but it does work well. The percentage-of-sales method is particularly helpful when a store has to divide funds among departments. Store management has every opportunity to learn the percentages commonly used in their field of retailing. Information for various retail categories is available in published reports. The percentages listed for advertising are averages, of course, and each store is expected to adjust that average as its marketing circumstances require. Among the different categories of retailers, variations in advertising budget are very wide. Low-budget retailers include bakeries, building-materials suppliers, food stores, service stations, taverns, children's-wear shops, and automobile dealers. Big spenders include department stores, movie theaters, sporting-goods stores, large dry cleaners, large floor-coverings dealers, florists, furniture stores, jewelers, toy dealers, and photography studios. But, as we pointed out in chapter 6, the percentage-of-sales method has one important weakness: it is not based on present market conditions but on past performance. Times change, customers change, competitors change . . . entire markets change, and no retailer can afford to overlook today's opportunities.

Task Method   This method for setting the retailer's advertising budget is based on a set of objectives. The retailer then allocates resources to attain those objectives. It is a forward-looking method that forces management to think carefully about what it wants its advertising to do. It is a method well suited to retailers, because retail management can determine very quickly the extent to which each objective is being attained: an ad in a Sunday paper will either achieve or fail to achieve its objectives within the next week. To be sure, a store will benefit in the long run from the cumulative effect of its advertising, but a retail ad for specific merchandise, unlike ads placed by national advertisers, demands direct action: *Visit the store. Order by phone. Do it today.*

Advertising-to-Sales Ratio   Large retailers may vary the amount of advertising devoted to different departments of the store because each department has different characteristics that affect the store's overall profitability. In this case, each department's advertising budget may be allocated on an advertising-to-sales ratio. Some merchandise classifications may be given as little as 1 percent of their projected sales volume, while others may receive as much as 5 percent. The furniture department of a large store, for example, produces many dollars of sales volume but very little traffic. Such a department may be profitable with a smaller advertising-to-sales ratio than the hosiery department, for instance, which produces a much smaller volume of sales dollars each month, but generates much more store traffic. Such a department may receive a higher advertising-to-sales ratio than its volume would justify because of the traffic it stimulates.

Large retailers segregate their advertising expenditures from their public relations and sales promotion expenditures. The legitimate expenses of advertising include the cost of media (space and time), advertising production costs, and the payroll of the advertising department. Small stores tend to lump everything together in one catchall account. There is always some confusion, too, about whether or not charitable donations (such as placing a message in a local high-school yearbook or in the program of a local garden club, or sponsoring a local Little League team) should be listed under the heading of advertising. Such expenditures properly belong in the public relations account.

Factors That Influence the Budget Decision

Regardless of which method is used to determine the budget, there are certain other considerations that strongly influence the retailer's advertising allocation.

1. *The place of advertising in the store's basic promotion policy*
   A center-city store that attracts pedestrian traffic must rely heavily on its window and in-store displays. Such a store might require less advertising to stimulate traffic. In a similar fashion, a store that is flanked by retailers that advertise heavily, as is often the case in shopping malls, will benefit from the traffic those stores draw.
2. *The extent of manufacturer advertising*
   If most of a retailer's merchandise is heavily advertised by the manufacturer, customers will come to the store presold. Retailers

How does a hair salon distinguish itself from many other hair salons offering essentially the same services? Since the clientele was small, there was little money for media or production. Rather than show the salon's great haircuts, the agency chose to show other people's bad ones. They selected characters from history to made ads that were clever and memorable. The ads were placed in Twin Cities publications such as *Arts Magazine* and *Guthrie Theatre Magazine* to reach a sophisticated audience. Business has risen markedly since the ads first appeared. The ads are so popular, in fact, that salons in other areas of the country have started to pirate them.

need only establish their stores as places to buy the branded, nationally advertised merchandise. The manufacturer carries the burden of advertising.

3. *The nature of the market*

If the market is suburban and mobile, or if it is transient as in a resort area or a college town, retailers' advertising requirements are greater than usual because they are trying to attract new customers.

4. *Available media*

The fewer the number of newspapers and broadcast media available in a retailer's trading area, the smaller the advertising investment that is required. When, as in large cities, there are two or three newspapers and 15 radio and television stations to choose among, and none of them is dominant, the retailer must spend more to obtain effective market coverage.

5. *The nature of the merchandise*

Cantaloupes, fish, or fashion merchandise cannot be held over too long. To a certain extent, the perishability of the merchandise determines the need for advertising. Having a large quantity of high-fashion merchandise in stock at the end of the season is as serious as a power failure in the frozen-foods section of a supermarket. Advertising can be far less expensive than price reductions for **distress merchandise.** For example, at the end of the selling season for bathing suits, the retailer has several choices: hold the leftover merchandise until next season; drastically mark down the merchandise; or advertise a seasonal clearance sale. Styles may change. The colors may not be suitable in the following season. And the bathing suits held in stock tie up money. Instead, a modest markdown combined with clearance-sale ads helps move the distress merchandise and may attract new customers to the store.

6. *The nature of the store*

The age, the size, and the location of the store also affect the advertising allocation. A large and growing store with many departments has to reach a varied group of people in order to insure that all departments remain profitable. Advertising is needed to generate traffic, to bring in the crowds. For an established neighborhood delicatessen, advertising is of little benefit.

Media for Retailers

The greatest portion of retail advertising goes into *newspapers.* Retail advertising is concentrated in newspapers because they are geographically selective — they cover the retailers' trading areas. Newspapers are also a "now" medium: They evoke a quick response from shoppers who read the ads before they go shopping, and they offer high frequency. Unfortunately, small retailers cannot take advantage of newspapers in large cities unless they are offering a specialty — that is, some product or assortment that is not available everywhere and for which the customer will go out of his or her way. (Bridal apparel is a good example.)

For the most part, *magazines* are not a retailer's medium. Only chain stores, such as Sears, Montgomery Ward, or Woolworth's, can take advantage of advertising opportunities in consumer magazines. Even the demographic editions generally deliver circulation to an area far too wide for a local department store. A few consumer magazines do, however, offer metropolitan editions that are geographically very selective and are, therefore, of use to certain department and specialty stores.

Broadcast media have not been extensively used by retailers. Thirty seconds of radio or television commercial time are insufficient to present a wide variety of merchandise. And, because television is demographically not very selective, it is not very cost effective for retailers. Although highly segmented, radio offers retailers even less opportunity to supply consumers with the information they need to make a wise buying decision, and it provides no opportunity to display merchandise.

Retail advertising information for the Syracuse newspapers is contained in a rate card, a portion of which is shown here. Note the sizable rate drop from the open rate to the 14,300-inch rate, and the combinations available — morning and evening, morning and Sunday. These are retail rates, and there is no agency commission.

THE SYRACUSE NEWSPAPERS

Clinton Square
P.O. Box 4915
Syracuse, N.Y. 13221-4915
(315) 470-2085
Telecopier (315) 470-2050

Herald-Journal	Herald American	The Post-Standard
(Evening)	(Sunday)	(Morning)

Rate Card #53   Issued October 1, 1985
Effective to contract holders November 1, 1985

Member Bureau of Advertising, A.N.P.A.
Subscriber to Media Records
Subscriber to Advertising Checking Bureau
Newhouse Newspapers

1. PERSONNEL

President - Stephen Rogers
Editor & Publisher - Stephen A. Rogers
Advertising Director - Robert T. Hennessey, Jr.
Retail Advertising - William W. Browning, Jr.
Classified Advertising - Carl Sweeney
National Coordinator - David Junod

2. REPRESENTATIVES

NEWHOUSE NEWSPAPERS

485 Lexington Avenue
NY, NY 10017
(212) 697-8020

6520 Powers Ferry Rd
NW, Suite 170
Atlanta, GA 30339
(404) 955-2335

9100 Wilshire Blvd
Suite 710
Beverly Hills, CA 90212
(213) 205-7647

221 North LaSalle St.
Chicago, IL 60601
(312) 641-6242

30300 Telegraph Rd Suite 131
Birmingham, MI 48010
(313) 540-5606

703 Market St.
Suite 913
San Francisco, CA 94103
(415) 362-3367

AMERICAN PUBLISHERS LTD
41 Britain St., Suite 303
Toronto, Ontario
Canada M5A 1R7
(416) 363-1388

THE LEONARD COMPANY
P.O. Box 6757
Hollywood, FL 33081
(305) 961-5664

Lenha, Hawaii
379 Olohana St. #203
Waikiki, Honolulu, Hawaii 96815
(808) 941-9011

SOUTH GEORGIA OFFICE
P.O. Box 7624
401-D Northridge Ave.
Tifton, GA 31793
(912) 386-0917

3. COMMISSION AND CASH DISCOUNT

Not Available

4. POLICY

A. The publisher reserves the right to cancel the conditions indicated herein upon 30 days' written notice to holders of contracts.
B. All advertising subject to approval of publisher.
C. No allowances will be made if errors do not materially affect the value of advertisement or for non-appearance of key numbers not incorporated in the original printing material.
D. Not responsible for advertising material over 30 days.
E. Advertising which simulates editorial content must be labeled "advertisement."
F. Contracts must be completed within one year from date of first insertion.
G. Political, Public Opinion, and Amusement advertising is accepted with cash in advance.
H. Publisher makes every effort to avoid back-to-back coupons but cannot guarantee same.

I Guaranteed Position: All restrictions, including without limitation, positioning, separations, facings, editorial adjacencies or other stipulations are at the sole discretion of the publisher.

5. BLACK & WHITE RATES

A. RETAIL BULK SPACE CONTRACT RATES

SAU Inches	M/E Combo*	Sun*	Sun/ Morn*	Morn*	Eve*
Open Rate	52.26	52.76	64.21	33.35	38.83
25	37.09	37.32	46.54	22.14	27.62
40	35.59	35.83	45.04	20.40	26.14
50	34.34	34.84	43.80	18.17	25.63
100	33.85	34.58	43.30	17.92	25.38
250	33.35	34.10	42.80	17.66	24.63
500	32.59	33.60	41.56	17.17	24.39
1,200	31.31	32.29	39.69	16.51	23.92
2,400	30.82	31.81	38.96	15.78	23.66
4,800	30.57	31.31	38.71	15.29	23.42
9,600	29.80	30.78	37.61	14.41	22.96
12,000	29.32	30.29	37.13	13.92	22.48
14,300	28.83	29.80	36.65	13.44	21.99

*Constitutes one unit of purchase.

Full pages camera ready 12.5% discount

Rates over 14,300 inches on request

CONTRACT REGULATIONS: Advertising purchased in combination may start either morning, evening, or Sunday. The combination must be completed within the next 6 days. Contract completion will be determined by the amount of space placed in each unit purchased and accumulated during the contract period. Advertisers will be billed monthly at applicable contract rate for entire contract year. At end of contract year, advertiser will be refunded if a lower rate is earned or rebilled at the higher applicable rate if contract is not fulfilled.

B. PREPRINTS

DAILY INSERT RATES

Rates per thousand inserts

Tabloid pgs or equivalent	48 times	33-47 times	26-32 times	19-25 times	13-18 times	6-12 times	1-5 times
2 to 8 pgs	35.70	37.80	38.64	39.27	39.90	41.16	42.00
12 pgs	36.55	38.70	39.56	40.21	40.85	42.14	43.00
16 pgs	38.25	40.50	41.40	42.08	42.75	44.10	45.00
20 pgs	39.95	42.30	43.24	43.95	44.65	46.06	47.00
24 pgs	41.65	44.10	45.08	45.82	46.55	48.02	49.00

Single Sheet Inserts 8½"x11" / 5½"x8½" Min. Wgt. 67 lb. stock. $30.00 per thousand. Printing charges on request

Rates over 24 tabloid pages on request

RESERVATION DEADLINE: 14 Days prior to insertion
MATERIAL DEADLINE: 7 Days prior to insertion

SUNDAY INSERT RATES

Rates per thousand inserts

Tabloid pgs or equivalent	48 times	33-47 times	26-32 times	19-25 times	13-18 times	6-12 times	1-5 times
2 to 8 pgs	37.60	39.95	42.30	43.24	44.65	46.06	47.00
12 pgs	38.40	40.80	43.20	44.16	45.60	47.00	48.00
16 pgs	40.00	42.50	45.00	46.00	47.50	49.00	50.00
20 pgs	41.60	44.20	46.80	47.84	49.40	50.96	52.00
24 pgs	43.20	45.90	48.60	49.68	51.30	52.92	54.00

RESERVATION DEADLINE: 21 Days prior to insertion
MATERIAL DEADLINE: 10 Days prior to insertion

However, radio has proven to be an effective medium for some retailers who can take advantage of its selectivity and low cost. Discount electronics stores, discount furniture outlets, and auto dealers use radio extensively. Restaurants and theaters, too, have been able to use radio to reach very specific markets at relatively low cost.

Transit, although offering some degree of geographic selectivity, does not offer adequate space for most retailers' messages. Its inflexibility effectively limits its value to institutional advertising. *Outdoor* is limited for the same reasons.

Direct mail is one of the most suitable forms of advertising for all retailers, small as well as large. Small retailers can control the circulation of their direct mailing, confining it to their specific trading area in order to reach only valid prospects. If a retailer maintains a mailing list of regular customers, direct-mail

The Syracuse Newspapers Total Market Coverage Program now provides you the means to reach virtually every household in Onondaga County and Total Market Coverage of important zip codes in Madison and Oswego Counties. Rates apply only to free-standing pre-printed inserts distributed in the daily Post-Standard and Herald-Journal combination or the Sunday Herald American and to non-subscriber households in the Total Market Coverage Program.

CONTRACT REGULATIONS: For purposes of frequency discounts, inserts appearing in the combination of the Herald-Journal and The Post-Standard will be counted as one.

* Daily and Sunday inserts may be combined to achieve frequency discounts.
* To qualify for frequency discounts, inserts must run within one year from the date of first insertion. A contract is required in order to immediately qualify for discounts.
* Advertising purchased in combination may start either morning or evening. The combination must be completed within the next 6 days. Contract completion will be determined by the frequency of inserts accumulated during the contract period. At the expiration of this contract, if the Advertiser has used sufficient frequency to earn a rate lower than that contracted for, Publisher will reimburse Advertiser the difference between the amount paid and the rate earned as determined from rate cards in effect during contract period.
* Full and part run inserts eligible for frequency discounts.

MECHANICAL REQUIREMENTS: Material supplied should be shipped to us to arrive wire-banded on skids (non-returnable) in turns of 50, 100, 150, etc. Material supplied should not exceed a maximum of 13½'' wide x 11½'' long or a minimum of 5½'' wide x 6'' long (width is the folded edge.) Material exceeding these sizes may be refused.
Should inserts be smaller in size than 10'' x 12'', it is suggested they be boxed in cardboard containers before being placed on skids. Skids should be wire-banded with a protective pallet over the top to protect inserts from being mutilated by pressure applied on the wrapping band.

SHIPPING INSTRUCTIONS: At least 14 days prior to material deadline of the inserts, shipping instructions should be in our hands telling us the shipment's point of origin, shipment number and the trucker so in the event of a breakdown, a tracer can be put on the shipment. All shipments should be addressed to The Syracuse Newspapers, Clinton Square, Syracuse, New York 13221. Receiving hours 9 am to 4:30 pm Monday to Friday.

PRINT ORDER: Full run circulation varies with day of the week and season of the year. Sales representative will estimate print order requirements based on most current data.

On inserts over 50,000 total pieces add 2% for spoilage; under 50,000 add 5% for spoilage to arrive at total print order.

6. GROUP COMBINATION RATES - Not Available

7. COLOR RATES & DATA

COLOR RATES

BLACK &	M/E	Sun	Sun/M	Morn	Eve
1 Color	$ 785	$ 560	$ 830	$480	$ 545
2 Colors	1,060	865	1,215	655	840
3 Colors	1,285	1,040	1,470	800	1,000

(Plus Black & White space charge)

DOUBLE TRUCK

BLACK &	M/E	Sun	Sun/M	Morn	Eve
1 Color	$1,015	$ 710	$1,050	$ 605	$ 680
2 Colors	1,595	1,250	1,670	840	1,215
3 Colors	1,995	1,500	2,080	1,100	1,465

(Plus Black & White space charge)

MINIMUM SIZES

Spot color .... 43 inches
2 colors or more .... Full page

COLOR DISCOUNTS

TIMES	FULL PAGE	LESS THAN FULL PAGE
13	15 %	2½%
26	20 %	5 %
39	25 %	7½%
52	33⅓%	10 %

Note: Discount based on full page or less than full page cannot be combined for greater discount.

8. SPECIAL ROP UNITS -Not Available

9. SPLIT RUN

$100.00 each paper. True A/B split accepted only on days when mechanical requirements permit. Minimum 10 inches.

10. SPECIAL SERVICES

Market Research Department: Current market and audience research information is available to our advertisers at no cost. (315) 470-2089

Manufacturers' co-operative advertising accrual and recovery assistance is available to our advertisers at no cost. (315) 470-2092

Shopping center advertising co-ordinator is available to assist shopping center Promotion Directors and individual merchants. (315) 470-2072

11. SPECIAL DAYS/PAGES/FEATURES

	HERALD AMERICAN		
SUN	TV-Cable Guide Comics	Parade Stars	Real Estate (Travel & Entertainment)

	THE POST-STANDARD	HERALD-JOURNAL
MON	Business Extra Sports Extra	Money Matters
TUE		Best Food Day
WED	Best Food Day	Fashion/Accent† HJ Zone†
THU	Neighbors‡/Accent†	Preview
FRI	Weekend	Sports Weekend
SAT	Sports Extra	

†Madison, Oswego, and Cayuga Counties only.
‡ Onondaga County only.

12. ROP DEPTH REQUIREMENTS

All ads must measure as many inches deep as they are columns wide. Example: 3 cols. x 3'' minimum. Exception: minimum depth for 1 column ads - ¾ inch.
Standard broad sheet size: all copy over 18½ inches deep centered and charged at full column depth.
Tabloid size: all copy over 11 inches deep centered and charged at full column depth.

13. CONTRACT AND COPY REGULATIONS

See Contents page of SRDS for location of regulations-items 1, 2, 4, 7, 9, 10, 11, 12, 13, 16, 18, 19, 20, 21, 23, 26, 30, 31, 32, 33, 34, 35.
No guarantee on competitive clearance for pre-printed inserts or ROP ads in either daily or Sunday papers.

advertising can be the most effective way to reach prospects. Stores that maintain their own charge accounts have a ready-made mailing list, and the postage required to mail the customer's monthly statement can often serve to deliver an advertising message as well. Many manufacturers will supply statement stuffers without charge or at only a fraction of their actual cost.

Advertising Schedules

Unlike national advertisers, who have to chose between reach and frequency (or arrive at some compromise between the two), retailers can focus on frequency. Retailers do not schedule their ads in the context of a campaign. Flexibility is always the retailers' main consideration. They give most of their attention to deciding which seasons of the year to advertise which products and

Quality. Our Magnificent Obsession.

This is as close as we can come to showing you Lands' End Quality in black and white. In our free catalog—and please send for one—living color does it more justice.

Finally, though, you'll need to feel the fabric itself in this Pinpoint Oxford shirt to understand the outer limits of Quality we insist on in Lands' End products, and why we're capitalizing the word in this advertisement.

In this shirt, Lands' End Quality is revealed in the material itself, in the construction of the shirt, and in the generous proportions of the finished garment.

The material is woven in Japan of the exceptionally fine cotton yarn it is possible to spin there. As to the make of the shirt, it is characterized by the fact that even the side seams are single-needle stitched, the collar and cuffs are double-track stitched as they should be,

and the collar is non-fused, the only way to give it the natural roll that makes buttondowns what they are.

Finally, we grace the shirt with a box pleat and locker loop, extra long tails, and a 7 button placket—plus generous proportions, the kind you deserve.

All this Quality with a capital Q and our Lands' End Pinpoint is yours for just $29.50, whereas $45 might not buy a comparable shirt in your favorite men's shop.

We're obsessed with Quality at Lands' End. It's a matter of first principle: Principle 1:

We do everything we can to make our products better. We improve material, and add back features and construction details that others have taken out over the years. We never reduce the quality of a product to make it cheaper.

Clip the coupon, won't you? Better still, give us a call (800-356-4444) any hour of the next 24. Ask for a free catalog and get to know Quality in our definition of the word in everything we make or offer. All of it GUARANTEED. PERIOD.

Please send free catalog.
Lands' End   Dept. G-30
Dodgeville, WI 53595

Name _____
Address _____
City _____
State _____ Zip _____

Or call Toll-free:
800-356-4444

then, within the seasons, which day(s) of the week to run their advertisements. This is why newspapers are a prime medium for retailers, because they permit a high level of frequency and flexibility. Retailers know from experience that Wednesdays, Thursdays, and Fridays are the best advertising days. Mondays, Tuesdays, and Saturdays are light. Of course, small retailers can purchase better positions for their ads by placing them on the light days.

Retailers must also anticipate peak seasons. Consumers start thinking about their needs days, often weeks, in advance of the actual time of purchase; this is particularly true for customers seeking high-fashion apparel. Naturally, retailers want every ad to draw customers for the advertised merchandise. At

COLOR PLATE 57

COLOR PLATE 58

COLOR PLATE 59

COLOR PLATES 57 AND 58 Visine used a consistent message—
"Wake up to Visine. Visine gets the red out."—in both its print
advertising and its network television campaign. "Venetian
Blinds" appeared continuously through 1984. Note the strong
package identification, so important in a competitive category where consumers can become confused by different
products.

COLOR PLATE 59 The Association of American Railroads
campaign is a corporate advertising campaign that promotes
the freight railroad industry as an entity, not the separate
railroads that comprise the industry. The campaign addresses
such subjects as computer technology in the railroad industry
and the advantages of rail as a mode of freight transportation.
The AAR publication schedule includes *Business Week, Forbes,*
the *Wall Street Journal,* the *New York Times,* the *Christian Science Monitor, Barron's, Traffic Management, Distribution,* and
Handling & Shipping Management.

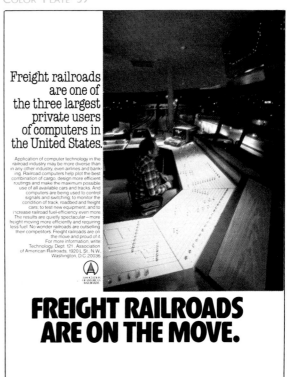

COLOR PLATE 60

COLOR PLATE 60 This is the cover of the Autumn 1985 issue of the Neiman-Marcus publication, *NM*, which began circulation in 1980 to Neiman-Marcus charge customers. It is not a catalog. It is, as we might expect from this famous store, a beautifully illustrated, full-color fashion magazine, which presents the most up-to-the-minute information from the fashion centers of Europe and New York.

PRINCE BORROWS A
SIMPLE IDEA TO KEEP PLAYERS DRY.

When you play tennis, you sweat. That's why Prince borrowed a simple idea from today's leading diaper makers and took it one step further.

Prince combined technology and fashion to introduce Prince Polypro tennis shirts and shorts with a durable "stay-dry" lining. The lightweight polypropylene liner transports perspiration to the outer shell, then keeps it away from the body. So players can work up a sweat without having sticky clothes clinging to their every move. They stay drier, cooler and more comfortable.

There's a whole line of technologically minded Prince Polypro and Prince tennis wear. From shirts and shorts to

warm-up suits and sweaters. All made to the highest standards of quality Prince standards.

Plus, all Prince tennis wear is cut to give players more room to reach for the passing shot or wind up for an overhead smash. No matter how vigorously they cover the court, their clothes won't get in their way.

We're going to spend a lot of advertising dollars on Prince Polypro and the full line of Prince tennis wear. All you have to spend to find out more is some time. Call 1-800-257-9480. In New Jersey call 1-609-896-2500. Because now there's tennis wear that really does something for a player's game. And for your sales.

INTRODUCING PRINCE POLYPRO TENNIS WEAR.
DESIGNED TO KEEP YOU DRY.

COLOR PLATE 61

Fisher-Price will make you smile in 1984.

The focus is on Fisher-Price in 1984, with a total program that will bring smiles to you and your customers:

- **Our most exciting product line in years:** Nearly 60 new items, including a real camera designed especially for children. An array of classic concepts, promotional lead items, and price points that will ensure a strong year-round business as well as a dynamic Christmas season.
- **An even more aggressive advertising program:** Last year we increased advertising by 34%. In 1984 we're adding another 25%. Year-round advertising that will feature not just new but a long list of continuing toys.
- **The strongest franchise in the toy business.**
  —Consumers say so: In a recent Gallup poll among mothers, Fisher-Price was selected as the favorite infant/preschool toy manufacturer by an 8 to 1 margin over the nearest competitor.
  —Retailers say so: In an independent national survey of discount store managers, Fisher-Price was named the top toy brand across all types of discounters.
- **A continuation of our aggressive 1983 trade policies.** Terms and co-op advertising that will increase your profits and make it easier to feature Fisher-Price, a proven traffic builder.

So this year, smile and say "Fisher-Price." Your customers will too.

© 1984 Fisher-Price Toys, East Aurora, New York 14052. Division of The Quaker Oats Company

COLOR PLATE 62

COLOR PLATE 61 Prince moved from tennis rackets to tennis wear—shirts, shorts, warm-up suits, and sweaters. It uses a trade paper ad like this to provide the facts to the trade and to suggest that retailers tie in to a line that will be well advertised.

COLOR PLATE 62 What does a retailer want from a manufacturer? New products. Good products. A well-advertised line. Favorable trade policies. In this two-page ad, Fisher-Price says it all. Note the emphasis on year-round business.

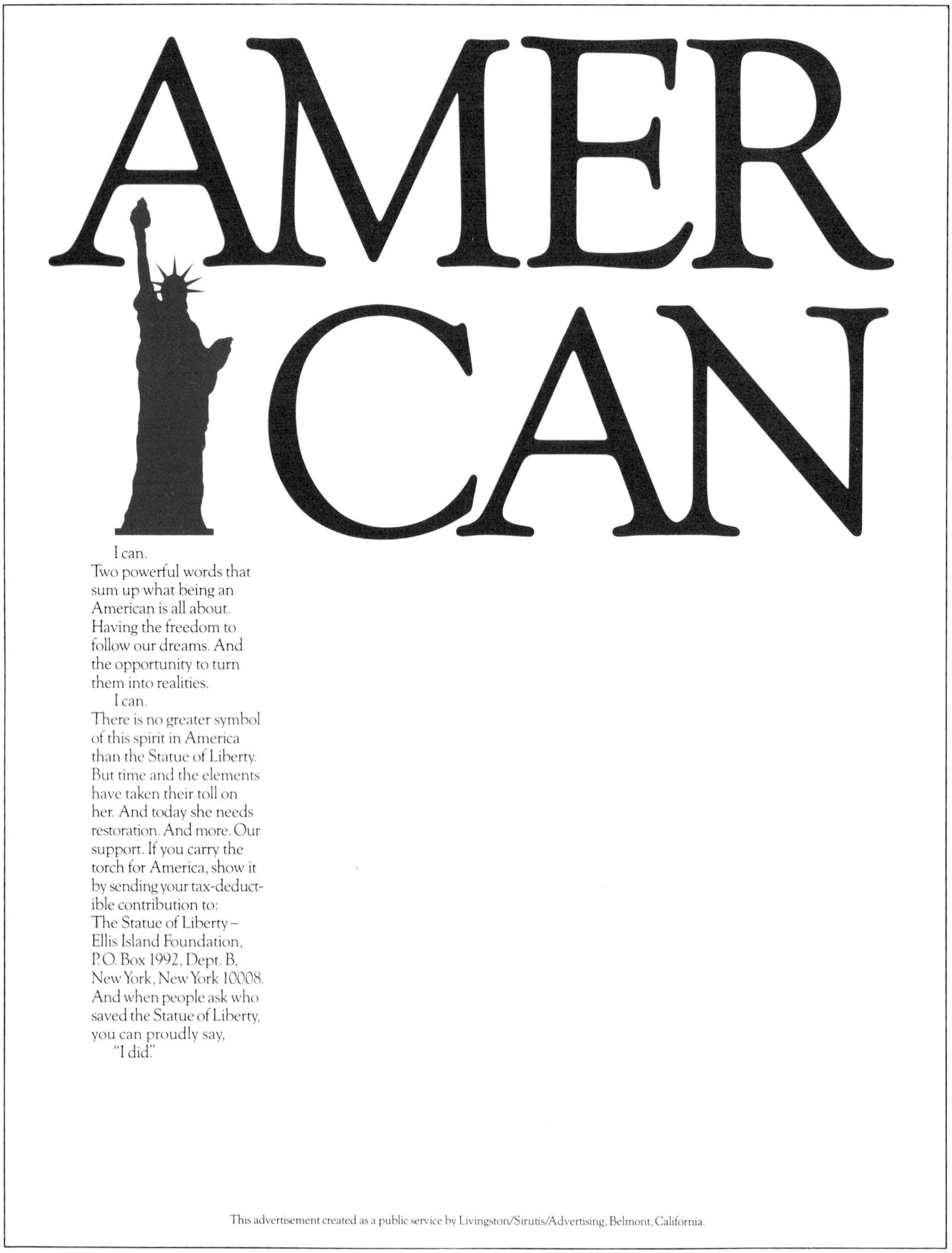

AMER
ICAN

I can.

Two powerful words that sum up what being an American is all about. Having the freedom to follow our dreams. And the opportunity to turn them into realities.

I can.

There is no greater symbol of this spirit in America than the Statue of Liberty. But time and the elements have taken their toll on her. And today she needs restoration. And more. Our support. If you carry the torch for America, show it by sending your tax-deductible contribution to: The Statue of Liberty – Ellis Island Foundation, P.O. Box 1992, Dept. B, New York, New York 10008. And when people ask who saved the Statue of Liberty, you can proudly say, "I did."

This advertisement created as a public service by Livingston/Sirutis/Advertising, Belmont, California.

COLOR PLATE 63

COLOR PLATES 63 ▲ AND 64 ▶ These two ads are merely a sampling of the work of the 218 ad agencies that put their creative talents to the job of "selling" the Statue of Liberty as a public service. It is interesting to note the ways we can create a strong message with various illustrations and layouts. *Time* donated 18 pages in its national edition for this worthy project.

☐ Enclosed please find my contribution to the restoration of the Statue of Liberty and Ellis Island. I understand both these irreplaceable American symbols are urgently in need of everyone's support.

☐ No. I'm not interested in liberty at this time.

Name_____

Address_____

City_____ State_____ Zip_____

The Statue of Liberty/Ellis Island Foundation, P.O. Box 1992, Dept. C, New York, NY 10008.

This message created as a public service by Quinn & Johnson/BBDO, Boston, Massachusetts 02116.
Photograph by Jake Rajs.

We're a nation exporting food. We've got to

In the United States we often fail to express a constructive discontent. We fail to take a public stand to protect our national strengths.

The risks of not taking a stand to protect the crucial industry of agriculture are substantial, and there are ample indications we should be concerned.

While there is broad agreement that the approaches of the past have had a disastrous impact on our world leadership in food production, there is an equally widespread disagreement on what shape a new program should take.

Debate on such a critical issue is constructive and necessary. But protection of special interests to the detriment of the national interest

while our farmers go hungry. change that.

has proven to be counterproductive—everyone suffers including ultimately the special interests themselves.

The essential point is that we express our discontent where policies endanger U.S. agriculture, and our approval where they protect it. IMC is committed to support new policies aimed at restoring the worldwide competitive strength of this uniquely valuable resource.

We intend to work closely with those who share our commitment.

International Minerals & Chemical Corporation
421 E. Hawley Street
Mundelein, IL 60060
(312) 566-2600

◀ COLOR PLATE 65 A provocative headline that is in the nature of an "advertorial," seeking to sell understanding of a point of view. The expected photo might have been a farmer or a wheat field. This ad gets more impact by an unusual illustration that is, of course, directly related to the farm problem presented.

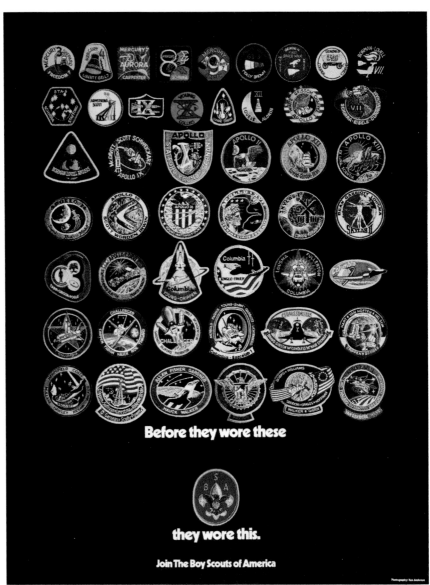

COLOR PLATE 66

COLOR PLATE 66 This ad is part of a recruitment campaign for the Boy Scouts. It is an effort to sell an idea—that most of NASA's astronauts are former Boy Scouts. Isn't that a wonderful recommendation for joining the Boys Scouts? The illustrations are individual space mission patches.

MACY'S 4TH OF JULY FIREWORKS
ON · THE · EAST · RIVER

Wednesday, July 4th, 9:15pm.
Celebrate America's 208th birth-
day with Macy's! Call our special
Fireworks Hotline: (212)
560-4495.
Tune to WNBC 66AM for
Macy's exclusive musical pro-
gram: The American Spirit. Or
take in the view from your living
room with WPIX Independant
Network News, 9pm to 10.
Take public transportation.
Call The Transit Hotline for your
best route: (212) 330-1234.
Macy's specially thanks The
City of NY and The Mayor's Office
of Special Projects and Events,
The US Coast Guard, The Port
Authority of NY and NJ, WPIX TV,
WNBC Radio and Hospital
Audiences, Inc.

macy's
SHOP SUNDAY 12 TO 6

An institutional ad for a famous store that helps New York City celebrate important seasonal festivities. Notice that this full-page ad does not even mention merchandise for sale. The fireworks display was televised to reach an even larger audience, and its musical program, "The American Spirit," added to the goodwill generated by the store. The only event greater is Macy's traditional Thanksgiving Day parade. Institutional ads, though, are unusual for a retailer.

the same time, however, retailers must try to build a store image in the minds of customers. The store must be seen by the public as a *source* for future purchases. A common fault of small retailers is their failure to build continuity, and only continuity builds an image.

Building the Schedule

A retailer's media schedule for the year ahead is usually based on the store's sales plan, that is, the sales projected by each department on a monthly basis. Each department breaks down its total allocation of advertising dollars into month-by-month appropriations, which are based on the department manager's or buyer's knowledge of consumer purchasing patterns.

Children's wear, for example, sells best in late August when parents make back-to-school purchases. There is, however, little value in promoting such merchandise in July. As a rule, retailers do not attempt to modify seasonal sales curves but are content to follow sales patterns of prior years. Even within the month and within the week there are better sale days, and a retailer's ad schedule will go heavy on the better days and light on the off days.

Big ticket items (such as appliances and home furnishings) are usually featured on Sundays because they represent major buying decisions that require the deliberation of the entire family. Women's fashions are generally scheduled for Sundays, Mondays, or Fridays. Traffic-generating merchandise such as domestics (towels, sheets, tablecloths, etc.) and housewares are advertised on Wednesdays or Fridays. An **omnibus ad** — a storewide ad that features items from many different departments — produces traffic. A **tonnage ad** — an ad that features one item stocked in large quantities at a very special price — produces both sales volume and traffic. A store will usually develop some scheduling expertise based on its own peculiar merchandise and determine a media mix that produces traffic, volume, and profits.

Finally, in addition to distributing their advertising allocation among departments and products, retailers must schedule extra advertising for special events, holidays, and seasonal promotions.

Retail Copy

Retailers know that they can catch the attention and interest of consumers more easily than national advertisers can because consumers often seek out retail advertising regularly and intentionally. These consumers may be interested in buying specific merchandise, they may be looking for a special sale, or they may merely want to keep informed on which new products are being offered. Therefore, retailers' advertising copy should stress news — new prices, new products, new assortments, new store hours.

Since selling peaks are brief, most retailers expect their ads to provoke customer response within a few days. It is not the job of retail ads to develop confidence in specific brands. National advertisers, on the other hand, must sell their brand, which, they hope, will satisfy the needs of consumers best. No other manufacturer can offer the same brand. But the retailer's assortment of goods is wider than that of most manufacturers, and many other retailers in the same area may offer consumers the same brands. This makes writing retail advertising copy difficult; the writer must generate interest not only in the products for sale but also in a particular retail store as *the* place to buy that product.

To do all this, retail-advertising copy usually promotes merchandise by stressing product features. Good retail copy is informative and factual. Retailers must emphasize product features in order to stimulate interest in their products. And, because they do not have to strain to command attention and interest from consumers, retailers can devote more of their advertising time and space to describing a product's uses and features than national advertisers can.

Price is also a prominent feature in a retail ad. Although manufacturers avoid price comparisons, preferring to compete on the basis of product differentiation, retailers are not reluctant to emphasize price. When a number of retailers have similar merchandise assortments, locations, and services, price is the natural basis for comparison.

Most retailers (see the ad on page 467 for an exception) cannot afford the luxury of institutional advertising. They prefer to let their regular product offerings demonstrate their values, variety, and pricing rather than devote dollars to building an image. Unlike the manufacturer, retailers do not produce merchandise; they merely sell it. There is, therefore, no reason to promote their plants, research, or industry reputation.

The Retail Advertising Department

A small store, as a rule, does not maintain an advertising department. Generally, small-store owners wear several hats, one of which is that of advertising manager. However, they can usually call upon local media for professional help. Radio or television stations will help prepare their commercials. Local newspapers will help retailers write, design, and produce their print ads.

Large stores, on the other hand, maintain an advertising department staffed with writers and artists and headed by an executive of the store who may also be responsible for supervising window and interior displays. Large stores will rarely make use of the artwork supplied by manufacturers as part of cooperative programs. Nor do large stores require the assistance of media in preparing their ads.

As a general practice, retailers tend not to use advertising agencies for two reasons. First, the low retail advertising rate allowed by most media does not include a 15 percent agency commission. Any retailer using the services of an advertising agency would, therefore, be required to pay a fee over and above the space costs. The last-minute deadlines that frequently mark retail advertising are the second deterrent. When a stock of merchandise sells out, when merchandise has not arrived on time, or when a special purchase is suddenly available, a retail store's own advertising department and staff can be swiftly coordinated to take the necessary action. However, a larger retailer may employ an agency to create advertisements for media in which the store's own advertising department lacks expertise. In such circumstances, a retailer might use an agency for television or radio advertising, advertising in national magazines, or newspaper advertising of an institutional character.

Vertical Cooperative Advertising

Vertical cooperative advertising is advertising for which the manufacturer and the retailer share the cost. The retailer places an ad in the local newspaper featuring one of the manufacturer's branded products over the signature of the store. The ad is usually prepared by the manufacturer and provided in the form of a repro proof. Retailers who use these ads need only have their store logos **slugged in.** The procedure is most commonly used for ads featuring specialty goods, such as ready-to-wear clothing, shoes, appliances, and cosmetics. It is also a common practice for advertising food products. Cooperative advertising is, on the other hand, rarely used for products that are distributed intensively through retailers of every type and size — products such as cigarettes, chewing gum, and soft drinks. *Co-op* is ideally suited for manufacturers who have given a few select retailers in each market the right to distribute their products.

Many national advertisers offer retailers completely prepared advertisements for their merchandise. The ads, as you can see from this example, are ready for insertion in a local newspaper; the retailer need only add the price and the store name and address in the space provided. Quite often, the space charge for the ad will be paid for in part by the manufacturer as part of a vertical cooperative advertising effort.

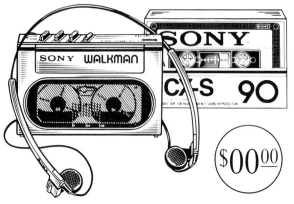

THE SMALLEST CASSETTE PLAYER IN THE WORLD

YOU'VE GOT TO HEAR IT TO BELIEVE IT!

Quite a statement. And quite exciting, too, once you come down and pick one up for yourself. The Super Walkman® WM-10 slips into your pocket and yet offers all the performance of full-size cassette players. The ultra-flat pancake motor uses the same brushless, slotless design as on Sony's home high fidelity cassette decks. You'll enjoy the benefits of Dolby® noise reduction and a metal-normal switch so you can play back any tape. Just wait 'til you try on the extremely light MDR acoustic turbo headphones with extended frequency response. There's also the WM-F10 with a built-in FM radio. With either model, the sound will have you smiling from ear to ear! And, of course, along with all this performance, you'll be getting all the quality you expect when the name is Sony.

THE ONE AND ONLY SOUND OF **SONY**.

DEALER NAME

There are advantages to co-op for both manufacturers and retailers. The manufacturers enjoy such benefits as:

1. Advertising that features their brands over the names of local retailers. Such advertising is a strong selling point when manufacturers want to add other retailers to their distribution networks.

Joyce Beber

Joyce Beber is president of Beber, Silverstein & Partners, the largest privately owned, female-controlled advertising agency in the United States. Elaine Silverstein is the other half of the team. Since their start in 1972, in a little two-room office with little capital but a burning desire for success, the agency has enjoyed remarkable growth. With billings of $65 million, Beber, Silverstein is the largest agency in Florida and has a reputation as one of the most creative agencies in Miami.

Headquartered in Miami, the firm has offices in New York and Washington. Although headed by two women, the firm's 103 employees are divided more or less evenly between men and women, with more men in the creative and account departments and more women in media. Among the agency's hundreds of awards are Clios for Norwegian Caribbean Line, the *Miami Herald*, NOW, and the National Education Association. Other well-known clients include Helmsley Hotels, the Empire State Building, Sophia Perfume, and State of Florida Tourism.

Ms. Beber, born in New York City, majored in English at Purdue University. She worked briefly in the advertising division of the *San Francisco Examiner*, then as editor of a science fiction magazine, before moving to Florida.

2. The knowledge that retailers who take advantage of cooperative advertising programs will stock and display the merchandise that is being advertised.
3. The increased volume of advertising for a particular brand of merchandise. The very availability of cooperative dollars is a stimulus to retailers to do more advertising than they would normally do. In addition, co-op often stimulates other retailers to advertise the manufacturers' brands in order to meet competition.
4. An enhanced image for their products through association with prestigious retail stores.
5. The reduction of advertising costs, since co-op is placed at the retail advertising rate, which is not only lower than the national rate but also enjoys the benefits of the retailer's volume-space contracts with local newspapers.

The retailer's benefits include:

1. A cost saving, since the manufacturer pays for a portion of the cooperative ad's space or time. The retailer is also spared the expense of copy preparation, since the manufacturer supplies top-quality advertising material.
2. An advertising link with an important nationally advertised brand that can enhance the image of a retail store.

The only drawback for retailers, and it is minor, is that manufacturers' ads tend to look **canned**, that is, they may look far too professional for small retailers in small towns.

CASE HISTORY

Victory Shirt Company

Mary Sprague, president of Victory Shirt Company in New York, has carved out a unique niche for her shirt and accessories company. She started her company in 1974, originally as a manufacturer and retailer of men's shirts. At that time, she narrowed her line to 100 percent cotton shirts with hand-turned collars and fine tailoring. In 1977, she introduced a line of women's shirts featuring the same high-quality tailoring; Mrs. Sprague herself, looking slim and well-groomed, began appearing regularly in the advertisements. The advertisements were part of an overall marketing strategy in which Victory was positioned as "the shirt experts" catering to business and professional men and women at very competitive prices. Readers of her ads see her looking out of a display ad, wearing one of her own shirts and ties, accompanied by straightforward copy: "My shirts work for the working woman." The campaign has been so successful that her face and name are remembered more often than the name of the company itself.

Victory's cachet was a kind of personal touch.

It's not unusual for a customer to talk to Mary behind the counter during a purchase. A customer may buy a Calvin Klein shirt or a Liz Claiborne skirt, but neither Calvin nor Liz will be selling it. At Victory, the woman behind the counter can be Mary Sprague herself. The strategy has worked. She now puts her own name on the inside label of her women's shirts: "Mary Sprague for Victory."

When the ad program started, they ran small space ads in the news section of the *New York Times* to reach a larger audience of business people. Sales were good and they enjoyed a larger contingent of repeat customers. In 1982, they added a new medium — *New York Magazine.* It provided two benefits — a new audience of young professional-type people, and an opportunity to establish a dominant position on the magazine page. It has worked. As of this writing, Victory has three stores in New York and two in Washington, D.C. The media mix now includes both the *New York Times* and *New York Magazine* plus the *Washington Post* and *The Washingtonian.*

Mary's reputation is at stake.

Every time a man or woman puts on a VICTORY shirt, my reputation is on the line.

I'm Mary G. Sprague.

I don't just sell VICTORY shirts, I make them. With the finest imported cottons. Each one of them has a hand-turned collar, split-yoke back, removable collar stays, seven-button front and placket sleeves. Ready for you in a full range of sizes. Each one is sold to you at great savings because we manufacture it ourselves.

If one of my customers is less than satisfied, he or she knows where to find me.

My goal is simple. I want to give you the best possible shirt at the lowest possible price.

VICTORY™
The Shirt Experts.

Midtown: 345 Madison Avenue (at 44th St.), New York, NY 10017. (212) 687-6375.
Wall Street: 10 Maiden Lane (off B'way), New York, NY 10038. (212) 349-7111.
Downtown: 96 Orchard Street (off Delancey), New York, NY 10002. (212) 677-2020.

Most cooperative dollars go into newspaper advertising, although cooperative advertising programs are also available for other media. The basis for sharing costs varies with the deal offered by the manufacturer. The manufacturer may pay from 25 to 100 percent of the costs, but the most common split is 50–50 with the manufacturer setting a limit on the total amount to be spent, based on the store's dollar volume of purchases. Thus, a manufacturer may agree to allow retailers up to 5 percent of their volume of purchases for cooperative advertising. A retailer who bought $10,000 worth of the manufacturer's goods, for example, would receive a $500 advertising allowance. The retailer would then have to spend $1,000 for advertising to be reimbursed $500 by the manufacturer. As a rule, the retailer is required to provide *tear sheets* as proof of insertion.

To facilitate the processing of tear sheets and notarized affidavits covering radio commercials, many manufacturers use the services of the Advertising Checking Bureau. As we learned in chapter 8, the ACB verifies rates, appearances, editions, and any improper use of brand names.

Whatever the arrangement, the manufacturer must be careful that there is no violation of the **Robinson-Patman Act,** which forbids discrimination among competing retailers. Any co-op advertising deal offered to one retailer must be available under the same terms to all retailers.

Summary

Retailing describes the process of selling products or services directly to consumers, usually through a physical establishment. Retailing is local in nature, although in the case of national or regional chain organizations, a group of stores may be tied together by a common name or by common merchandise. Retailers are major advertisers. The pages of our local newspapers are filled with advertising for department stores, home-furnishings stores, food stores, building-materials and automobile dealers, and movie theaters.

The retailer's need for marketing intelligence is similar to that of the national advertiser. Like the national advertiser, the retailer can draw on both secondary and primary sources for marketing data. Store records, charge-account billings, and trade publications are important sources for secondary data. Questionnaires, telephone surveys, personal interviews, and want slips can be used to gather primary data.

The retailer's methods of setting the advertising budget are also similar to those used by national advertisers. The percentage-of-sales method is perhaps the most widely used among retailers. Large retailers, however, may want to assign an advertising-to-sales ratio to each department of the store. A department that generates a high volume of store traffic but a low volume of sales can be assigned a higher advertising-to-sales ratio than a department that has a high volume of sales but draws little traffic.

Retail advertising is one segment of the advertising business in which an ad's effectiveness is often measured on the same day it is seen or heard by the public. The focus of retail advertising is on direct action, and most retailers maintain careful records of sales directly attributable to a given ad. Large retail organizations, such as department stores, discount stores, and chain stores, can afford to maintain complete advertising departments to produce all their advertising copy and artwork. Small retailers must depend on the creative abilities of the stores' owners or the advertising departments of the local media. The advertising department for a large retailer is usually part of the sales promotion division, which is also responsible for window displays and floor displays, market research, and public relations.

Vertical cooperative advertising, in which the manufacturer of a nationally advertised brand pays for a portion of the cost of the retailer's ad in a local medium, is an important component of many retail advertising programs, an arrangement advantageous to both retailer and manufacturer.

Questions for Discussion

1. How does retail advertising differ from national advertising?
2. What is the purpose and the nature of the advertising plan?
3. Why are newspapers the primary advertising medium for retailers?
4. What kind of market research could a retailer undertake to make its advertising more effective?
5. Find a national ad and a retail ad for the same brand. What differences do you note?
6. What are the benefits that the manufacturer derives from a vertical cooperative advertising program?
7. Explain the importance of price in retail advertising and its frequent absence from a manufacturer's national advertising.
8. Find some samples of "canned" cooperative ads in your local newspaper.
9. What differences do you see between the media scheduling of the retailer and the media scheduling of the national advertiser?
10. What are the media considerations that affect a retailer's advertising? What are the desirable characteristics of the various media from a retailer's point of view?

Sources and Suggestions for Further Reading

Barmash, Isadore. "A Lean A&P Flexes Muscles." *The New York Times,* June 7, 1986.

Berman, Barry, and Joel R Evans. *Retail Management.* 3rd ed. New York: Macmillan, 1986.

Cooke, Ernest F. "Why the Retail Action Is East of the Mississippi." *American Demographics,* November 1984.

"Cooperative Advertising—New Fields to Conquer." *Sales & Marketing Management,* May 16, 1983.

"Everyone Wants A Share." *Sales & Marketing Management,* May 14, 1984.

Gentile, Richard J. *Retail Advertising.* New York: Chain Store Publishing Corp., 1976.

Gilbert, Betsy. "Safeway Strives to Fill Everyone's Needs." *Advertising Age,* April 28, 1986.

Haight, William. *Retail Advertising.* Morristown, N.J.: General Learning Press, 1976.

Johnson, Kenneth M. "Rural Retailing Reborn." *American Demographics,* September 1982.

Reed, Cecelia. "Expanding Customer Base on Shopping List." *Advertising Age,* August 9, 1984.

Schultz, Don E. "Why Marketers Like the Sales Promotion Gambit." *Advertising Age,* November 7, 1983.

"This Business Is Anything But Threadbare." *Business Week,* August 18, 1986.

20 INDUSTRIAL AND TRADE ADVERTISING

Working Vocabulary

trade advertising	process materials	telephone/address directory
industrial advertising	MRO	product directory
raw materials	make or buy	literature directory
major equipment	new buy	trade show
component parts	short channel	

Advertising is, actually, a simple phenomenon in terms of economics. It is merely a substitute for a personal sales force — *an extension, if you will, of the merchant who cries aloud his wares. It puts rapidly in print (or on radio and television) what would otherwise have to be handled by word of mouth. It does this at lower cost.*

Rosser Reeves
Reality in Advertising

In chapter 9 we examined business publications as part of our general consideration of media. At that time we were concerned with the characteristics of the print media directed to men and women in business and with the decisions that face advertisers in evaluating these publications. Now, armed with far more knowledge about media, budgets, copy, art, and ad campaigns, we can take a closer look at business advertising and its place in our advertising program.

Business advertising is simply advertising that is addressed to people in their *business capacities.* Considered as a whole, a business is a consumer in the truest sense of the word. A steel mill buys raw materials and consumes them in the production of steel. A retail store buys office supplies and packaging materials and consumes such supplies in the course of day-to-day business. And, much more importantly for national advertisers, a retail store buys manufacturers' products that it then resells to the general public. As you can see, businesses buy products and services for the purpose of doing business and rarely for the pleasure or satisfaction of an individual, and it is this distinction in purpose that differentiates business advertising from consumer advertising.

Our examples above of a steel mill and a retail store also illustrate the difference between the two major categories of business advertising: an advertisement aimed at selling goods or services to the steel mill to use in the production of steel would be an example of *industrial advertising;* an ad aimed at selling goods or services to retailers (or other dealers) for resale to consumers would be an example of **trade advertising.** But these two categories of business advertising are much more complex than this simple illustration suggests. Let us examine both in detail, beginning with industrial advertising.

Industrial Advertising

Industrial advertising is defined as the promotion of goods and services used in the manufacture and marketing of other products and services. Based on this definition, we can include farm advertising and professional advertising in this category. Farmers buy seed, fertilizer, and machinery used in the production of their goods. Doctors, lawyers, and other professionals buy equipment, services, and office supplies needed in the production of their services. Our definition would apply to both of these types of advertising.

Our purpose in this chapter, however, is to examine the advertising of machinery, chemicals, and components used by manufacturing and large service industries. It is on these products that most industrial advertising dollars are spent. There are six major categories of industrial goods: raw materials, major equipment, minor equipment, component parts, process materials, and operating supplies. Each category demands different advertising considerations.

476

Classifications of Industrial Goods

Raw Materials   The designation **raw materials** describes basic commodities that have undergone no manufacture or only such processing as is necessary to store or transport them. Transactions for the purchase and sale of raw materials are generally conducted at high levels of company management. There is no product differentiation, most raw materials being marketed to recognized standards. The little advertising that is done for raw materials is institutional, or designed to stimulate primary demand.

Major Equipment   Large machines that are charged to a capital account fall under the classification **major equipment.** The purchase decision is often extended over a long period of time, not because of price negotiation, but

An equipment ad addressed to a very narrow market — dry cleaners. Note the technical language needed to indicate the benefits of what would be a capital investment for the operator of a dry cleaning plant.

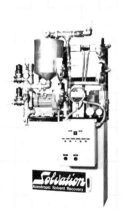

because of the many approvals needed for the expenditure of such large amounts of money. The purchase decision for such equipment generally involves multiple influences, many of whom are unknown to the marketer. One of the most important objectives of industrial advertising is to reach all the decision makers who affect a major equipment transaction.

Minor Equipment Purchases of small machines and accessories usually involve routine buying action and, therefore, require fewer approvals than do purchases of major equipment. In fact, manufacturers of minor equip-

Minor equipment, although less expensive than major equipment, nevertheless requires a thorough explanation of its benefits.

20 | INDUSTRIAL AND TRADE ADVERTISING

ment usually market their products through middlemen. Advertising plays an important communication role in the marketing of minor equipment.

Component Parts   Finished goods, usually made to custom specifications, are referred to as **component parts.** The purchaser is interested primarily in uniformity and reliability, and, for those reasons, will often use more than one source for component parts. The identity of the manufacturer of a component part may not only be visible in the finished product but may even be an important selling point for that product. Advertising can make a number

An ad for components. This ad appeared in full color in an electronics publication addressed to design engineers. Note the technical language as the copy describes both the wide range of IF components offered as well as some very specific benefits.

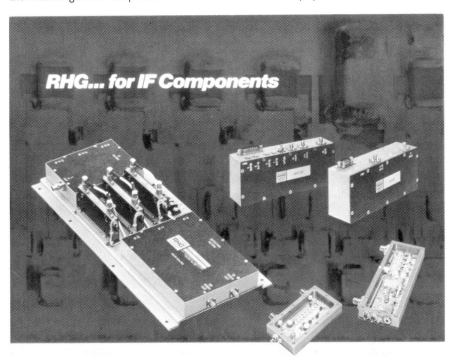

RHG... for IF Components

Leading the Industry in Innovative IF Processing Designs

For over twenty years, receiver design engineers have been specifying RHG IF components. We are constantly refining our technology and production capability to offer the industry's most complete line of state-of-the-art catalog IF processing devices. In addition, we can draw upon a design file of over 7,500 special models to solve almost any receiver design problem.

RHG for...

Logarithmic IF Amplifiers - RHG continues to lead the industry in log amp innovations. You can depend on RHG.

for unsurpassed linearity, stability, pulse fidelity and rise time. Our newest models feature octave bandwidths to 1 GHz and rise times less than 3 nsec.

Linear Amplifiers - Catalog models available from 10-1000 MHz, can provide IF and/or video outputs and variable gain via external bias. Many models are available with closed loop AGC, IAGC, blanking, gain and phase tracking, and other special features to meet radar, communications and ESM requirements.

Constant Phase Limiting IF Amplifiers - Miniature and subminiature hybrid thin film designs are available for all standard IF's. The constant transmission phase shift over a 70 dB dynamic range is applicable to monopulse systems, EW, DF, and radar phase comparison applications.

Phase Detector Subsystems - RHG provides dual and three channel models at all standard IF's.

Limiter Discriminators - FM discriminators at all standard IF's for both CW and pulse applications. The new delay line series offers unmatched linearity and bandwidth combinations.

AFC Processors - Models cover all standard IF's and multioctave RF's to provide AFC signals for solid-state LO's.

AGC Driver Assemblies - Designs are available to provide AGC drive voltages for IF amplifiers and preamps. Standard models provide simultaneous control of 3 IF amps plus 3 IF preamps from video or IF signal inputs.

For further information on the latest in MIC Microwave and IF/RF products, call or write today.

RHG ELECTRONICS LABORATORY INC.
161 East Industry Court ■ Deer Park, New York 11729 ■ (516) 242-1100 ■ TWX 510-227-6083

CIRCLE 2 ON READER SERVICE CARD

of valuable contributions to the marketing of component parts. For example, component producers can advertise over the heads of the manufacturers who use their parts, to emphasize their value to the ultimate user of the finished product.

Process Materials   These are similar to component parts, except that **process materials** are purchased on standard — not custom — specifications and, therefore, more emphasis is placed on price and service. Process materials are not identified in the final product, so there is little value in advertising them directly to the ultimate customers.

The specifications to which process materials, components, and raw materials are manufactured and sold are indicated by such abbreviations as NF, USP, ASME, and ASTM. The designations USP (United States Pharmacopeia) and NF (National Formulary), represent standards and specifications used to evalu-

This ad for a process material stresses the convenient form in which the product is available, an appeal that is emphasized by the photograph of the scoop full of flakes. The details of the benefits provided by Vultac 7 are all spelled out in the copy. If this information were not available, the form of the material would be meaningless.

ate the quality of pharmaceutical ingredients. ASME designations, used to describe rated pressure capacities for boilers and other pressure vessels, have been set by the American Society of Mechanical Engineers. Particular specifications for construction components and materials are designated ASTM. For example, ASTM—A36 indicates structural steel with a specified yield point and tensile strength.

Operating Supplies   These goods are usually designated as **MRO,** which stands for maintenance, repair, and operating supplies. Although consumed during the manufacturing process, such supplies do not become part of the finished product. Of the six categories of industrial goods, operating supplies most closely resemble consumer goods. Companies buy MRO supplies in small quantities from middlemen and often buy several different brands of the same product.

An ad for operating supplies requires a clear explanation of the product's advantages. This advertiser says it simply. It saves money by eliminating cleaning. It reduces fumes. It is compatible with other products. And last, it is available in four different forms.

The Industrial-Buying Process

Just as we have examined the purchasing behavior of the buyers of consumer goods, we must also examine the industrial-buying process; the differences are far deeper than mere terminology. In order to devise the most appropriate advertising strategy for our product, we must examine not merely the behavior of a single purchasing agent, but the entire buying process within a company — which is influenced by many different people. The buying process will vary — not only from organization to organization, but also within each organization from time to time — depending on the product and prevalent economic conditions. The following steps, however, are typical of the industrial-buying process:

1. A department discovers that it needs a product or service to overcome a problem.
2. The department head fills out a requisition form describing the specifications that the product or service should meet to solve the problem. The requisition is sent to the company's purchasing department.
3. The purchasing agent searches for qualified sources of supply.
4. The purchasing agent solicits offers from qualified suppliers. The offers are analyzed.
5. Comparisons are made between **make or buy** — that is, the company chooses whether to buy the components it needs from its suppliers or to produce them itself.
6. If the decision is made to buy, a source or sources are selected, and the order is placed.
7. After delivery and use, a follow-up is made with the department that originated the request, in order to evaluate its level of satisfaction or dissatisfaction with the product or service.

Many variables will affect this process — variables that are entirely different from those that may affect a general consumer's purchasing behavior. For instance, there are considerations of make or buy for many industrial products, particularly component parts and process materials. Companies will always make the components they need if they can do so more cheaply than they can buy them from outside sources or if the component is so vital to their operations that they cannot allow another company to control production. In a **new buy** — a purchase from a supplier the company has never done business with before — the supplier's credentials may be more critical than the product or the price. Reciprocity, too, is an important variable in industrial buying. Paint company A buys fleet automobiles for its sales force from auto company B. Other things being equal, auto company B will reciprocate by ordering paint from paint company A. That's just good business.

The Importance of Advertising

The place of promotion in the marketing mix of industrial products varies. Sometimes advertising serves little or no purpose, and a company may delegate all of its promotional effort to its sales force or, as is frequently the case, to agents or brokers. Our first category of industrial goods, raw materials — and other products with commoditylike characteristics — can rarely be differentiated. Their purchase is negotiated under long-term contracts by top levels of management. Obviously, if the product supplied by one company

THE BIG PLUS IN SURGE SUPPRESSORS.
Only Wire Tree Plus From Networx Protects Both Modems and Computers.

Complete protection of a modem-equipped microcomputer system—in one surge suppressor? Only one product does it. Wire Tree Plus™ from NETWORX™. The only filtered power source with RJ 11 modular jacks—the exclusive feature that saves your customer the expense of buying modem protection separately. That's the difference that makes Wire Tree Plus a fast mover—in a category that enjoys the industry's highest mark-ups.

Conventional surge suppressors leave phone/modem lines vulnerable to power surges and voltage spikes. Transients that prey on memory, data integrity—even modem and computer hardware. And prompt nearly 70% of all service calls. Without Wire Tree Plus protection, your customer risks exorbitant repair and downtime costs.

To protect computers and peripherals, Wire Tree Plus features five outlets controlled by two recessed, illuminated switches. A sixth is continuously on line to protect volatile memory. Together with the RJ 11 modular jacks, all

six act fast to eliminate surges, spikes, RFI, EMI and noise interference. Protecting hardware and memory in modems, computers, peripherals. And with its five-year warranty, Wire Tree Plus gives your customer complete security. Peace of mind motivation that makes Wire Tree Plus an easy add-on to a system sale or a perfect gift item all by itself.

Other pluses include a built-in circuit breaker, a safety minded cable organizer and a universal mounting bracket.

Features that make Wire Tree Plus the most versatile work station accessory you can offer. An exclusive problem-solver in the industry's fastest growing, most profitable category.

Don't wait. Sell Wire Tree Plus—the surge suppressor with a difference. To take advantage of dramatic new-dealer discounts, call toll free, 1-800-522-2222. Get started with the Starter-Pak, a P.O.P. display featuring Wire Tree Plus and the entire high-profit NETWORX line.

NETWORX™
Computer Station Accessories
Networx, 203 Harrison Place, Brooklyn, NY 11237-1587
A North American Philips Company

Showcase the entire Networx line in 1.29 cubic feet with the Starter Pak P.O.P. display.

This business-to-business trade paper ad appeared in full color addressed to computer systems dealers. Note the point of view — this quality product will help the dealer's customer because of its features and yield a profit to the dealer. Note also the illustration of the POP display unit offered by the manufacturer.

cannot be distinguished from that of any other company and if the market is limited to a relatively small number of customers, advertising can be of little use. But, for all the other industrial product categories, we set about formulating our advertising objectives and strategies in much the same manner as we do for consumer products.

The cost of an average industrial sales call was a mere $9.02 in 1942. In 1983, the cost of the average industrial sales call was $205.41, a figure 15.4 percent higher than in 1981.[1] Although the cost of advertising in industrial magazines has also risen in the past decades, the average cost of getting a person to see an ad in such a publication was just 18 cents in 1983. This cost was based on a one-page, two-color ad.

---

[1] *Laboratory of Advertising Performance.* Bulletin no. 7020.6 (New York: McGraw-Hill, 1983).

The mandate for industrial advertising is obvious:

1. Substitute advertising for as many sales calls as possible.
2. Use advertising to make the sales force's efforts more productive.

Setting Advertising Objectives

If the marketers of industrial goods want to take advantage of advertising to increase their sales and profits, they must set specific objectives for their advertising programs. As we shall see, many of these objectives are similar to those of national advertisers of consumer products. Others, however, are vastly different, but are easily understandable when we reexamine the industrial-buying process. Consider these typical general objectives for the marketers of industrial goods:

1. *Identifying the company that stands behind the product*
   Once again we see the value of institutional advertising. If the reputation of a company is important in the marketing of a consumer product, it is doubly important for an industrial product. The reliability of a company is an essential consideration when an industrial buyer is looking for new sources of supply. As a matter of fact, reliability is more important than price.
2. *Gaining the attention of the financial community*
   This is rarely a primary objective, but it is certainly an important consideration for companies whose shares are traded on the open market.
3. *Creating loyalty and demand*
   Nothing new about these objectives except that, since industrial orders are large, every single customer becomes correspondingly more important. When a consumer is dissatisfied with a product and switches brands, one 59¢ brand wins a customer and a different brand loses one. But when a purchasing agent changes brands, the value of the sales lost may be many thousands of dollars.
4. *Introducing a new product to buying influences*
   Here's where advertising can perform a vital function. Industrial advertising may be the only way to reach busy, important executives who affect a company's buying decisions — executives our salespeople never see, can't find, or do not have the time to cover.
5. *Securing sales leads*
   This is a new objective. Consumer advertising generally requires indirect action on the part of the target market — *visit your dealer.* Now we want our advertising to provide us with the names of potential customers so that *we* can arrange for *our* sales force to call on *them.* Remember, many industrial products are sold through a **short channel,** that is, they are sold directly by the manufacturer to the consumer.
6. *Attracting good personnel*
   Many companies, particularly those in high-technology industries, must keep abreast of new developments in their fields in order to keep growing. To do this they rely on the knowledge and skills of highly trained personnel. Many companies are always wooing

engineers and scientists away from competitors or from industries in other fields.

7. *Maintaining an effective distribution network*
Operating supplies, small equipment, and process materials are commonly sold through distributors. Advertising can play an important role in keeping distributors informed about, and sold on, the products and the company behind them.

These are by no means all the objectives that a company might set for its advertising effort. Every company will develop its own set of objectives based on its production capability, the stage in its product's life cycle (yes, industrial products have a life cycle, too), and the buying motives peculiar to that product or market. In any case, any general objective must be measurable and specifically related to the problems and opportunities of a particular product line and/or market segment. The strategy, the media mix, and the advertising appeal chosen are judgments dependent on the company's sales forecast, financial strength, and production capabilities. We have already mentioned the possibility of component manufacturers advertising over the heads of their industrial customers to reach those customers' customers. General business publications can often be used to reach both the hidden buying influences high up the corporate ladder *and* the financial community simultaneously. Direct mail can reach executives that we consider key buying influences but whom we cannot reach through other media.

Industrial Copy Appeals

We mentioned at the beginning of this chapter that businesses buy products for the purpose of doing business. For this reason, we cannot resort to the psychic and emotional appeals that characterize some consumer advertising. The men and women in our target market are going to take a hard look at the cost and quality of our products. The future profitability of their businesses may be directly affected by their purchasing decisions. What do we tell business prospects about our product then? What do they want to know in order to reach a decision?

1. Will the product increase their company's production?
2. Will it decrease their manufacturing costs?
3. Will it improve the salability of their products?
4. Will it help increase profits for their company?
5. Will it eliminate or minimize production bottlenecks?
6. Will it reduce downtime?
7. Will it minimize scrap or rejects?
8. Will it improve the durability of their product(s)?
9. Will it simplify maintenance and repair?

This list is far from all-inclusive, nor is it in order of importance. Of course, every industrial buyer wants to contribute to his or her company's profits; that's the role of the purchasing agent and all other personnel who influence the buying decisions. Although every one of these advertising appeals contributes to profit *indirectly,* increasing profits is listed as one appeal (no. 4) because in certain cases, the advertised product may contribute to profits *directly.*

These two IBM ads are worlds apart in focus. One ad is addressed to the professional who will want this IBM 7350 display system for a range of geological analysis by scientists. Note the absence of price information. If this piece of business equipment provides improved analysis and increased productivity, price is not a major consideration. The IBM PCjr, on the other hand, is aimed at a broad consumer market with many different applications for personal use as well as business. Price is apparently an important attribute. So, too, are some of the physical characteristics provided in detail which are entirely omitted from the ad for the 7350. Note, too, that the 7350 inquiries are to be directed to the IBM office in Houston, whereas for the PCjr, the prospect is invited to visit an authorized IBM Personal Computer dealer or IBM Product Center.

To be effective, industrial copy should be as specific as possible. It should be related to the needs of the prospect, and, as far as possible, it should anticipate questions that industrial buyers will ask about the company and its product. This will make the sales force's job easier, freeing them to perform their main function — to sell the product.

Schedules and Campaigns

In the planning stage, an industrial advertising campaign is not very different from a consumer campaign. In fact, the industrial campaign is much easier to plan than a consumer campaign because our media choices are very restricted. We do not have to evaluate the effectiveness of broadcast as compared to print media because we *know* we'll use print media — and we know with a fair certainty what *kind* of media. Comparisons are usually made between various *industrial publications* only, and once we have clearly stated our objectives, we can select among competing publications on the basis of CPM or whatever other media selection factors are important to us. From time to time, a business advertiser such as IBM or Xerox will place an ad in a consumer magazine or run a commercial on a television program directed to a nonbusiness audience. This advertising is almost always institutional. Many of the people watching a television program may work for companies that are considering purchasing Xerox copiers or IBM office equipment, but the main purpose of institutional advertising is to enhance the company's image, not to sell products.

Industrial advertisers do not have to make the critical media choice between reach and frequency. Frequency should be the rule. Since they do not know when a need will arise or how and when a purchasing decision will be made, they want to be certain that all the *buying influences* — all the people who can affect the decision to purchase their products — receive their messages. Months or even years of internal discussion and consideration may pass before a buying decision is finally made. A study by Cahners Publishing Company revealed that 33.8 percent of industrial buyers see salespeople regularly, 42.8 percent see salespeople seldom, *and 23.4 percent never see salespeople at all.*[2] Obviously, two-thirds of the key decision makers in that industry (railroad equipment) rely on information sources other than salespeople. Do these decision-makers read business magazines? The answer is an emphatic *yes.* To the question: "On the average, how much time do you spend weekly reading industrial and professional magazines?" the average recipient answered: "Two hours and 22 minutes a week."[3]

---

[2] *Cahners Advertising Research Report No. 2000.1* (Boston: Cahners Publishing Co., n.d.).
[3] *Cahners Advertising Research Report No. 420. 1* (Boston: Cahners Publishing Co., n.d.).

Make money hand over fist.

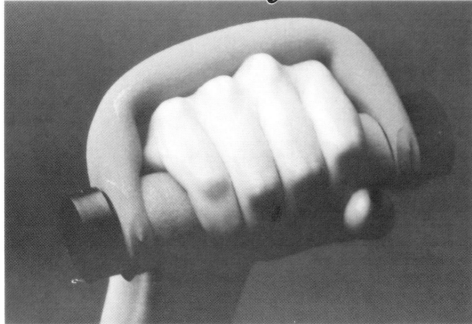

In 1983, AMF Heavyhands was the number one selling product in the booming fitness category. Sales were so strong that some retailers faced out-of-stock situations early during the peak holiday season. In 1984, AMF wanted to avoid a repeat of 1983 and encouraged sporting goods buyers to order sufficient stock well in advance. In this typical ad, AMF appealed to the basic motivator of the retailer — profitable sales. The headline is a clever play on words and ties in well with the product. It was backed by a strong image of the product — the unique design and red color (the ad appeared in two colors, red and black) are instantly recognizable. And AMF reminded the buyers of the stock-out that had occurred the preceding year. The ads appeared in the industry's trade publications — *Sporting Goods Business, The Sporting Goods Dealer,* and *Sports Merchandiser.*

Seasonal influence on the sale of industrial products is moderate, not at all like the peaks and sharp dips that characterize the sales of consumer products. For this reason, much industrial advertising is spread out over the year. Unlike consumer advertising, industrial ads suffer less from wearout. A successful, effective industrial ad can be repeated three or four times a year, or even more often, depending on the publication. Studies have been made that indicate that there is a minimum of *cumulative recollection.* When an industrial ad is repeated, it is usually seen and read by as many new readers as by readers who recall having seen it before. The McGraw-Hill Laboratory of Advertising Performance has documented a number of such cases.

Business publications, by virtue of the relatively lower cost of their ad space, also permit an aggressive advertiser to achieve a measure of dominance not possible in the consumer field. Multi-page inserts are used much more frequently in business publications than in consumer publications. For example, Jones and Lamson Machine Company, a well-known machinery manufacturer, usually schedules six 12-page inserts a year in two business publications.

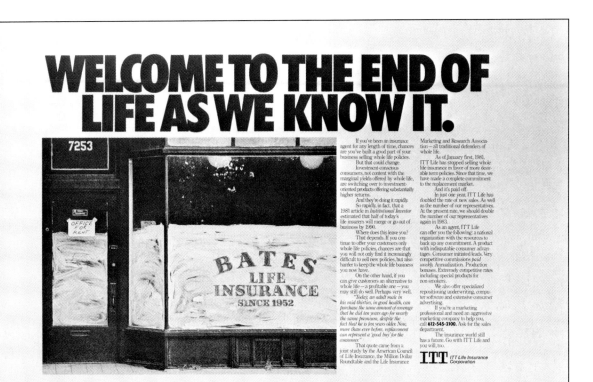

In the chapter 18 case history we described the efforts of ITT Life to stimulate acceptance for a new concept of life insurance. At the same time, the company faced the problem of recruiting agents to sell its product. The primary target audiences were field marketing directors and general agents. These are people who head groups of agents. The objective of the advertising was to generate qualified leads. The company also used its advertising as a forum to position its product within the insurance industry. The recruiting ads appeared in the industry's trade magazines — *Life Insurance Selling, Best's Review, The Financial Planner,* and *Broker World.*

Hilton Hotels used a 40-page insert in *Successful Meetings* magazine to tell business people about its worldwide meeting and convention facilities. The prize probably goes to Babcock & Wilcox, however, who used a 75-page insert to celebrate their 75th anniversary.

Trade Advertising

To return to some of the military analogies we have used before — we are approaching the part of our campaign that deals with logistics. For the military, logistics is concerned with the problems of obtaining and transporting supplies and personnel to the front lines. In a similar fashion, advertisers are concerned with the problems of moving their products successfully through the various channels of distribution to the front line — the retail outlet. We have used media and creative strategies to guide us in our choices of a media mix and an appeal. If our powerful print ads, our dynamic, exciting television commercials, coupons, and samples have been successful, we will have brought our target market to the point of sale. Our concern now is what happens when the consumers go to buy the product at the retail outlet.

Why Advertise to Dealers?

What happens if we don't reach the middlemen—the wholesalers and retailers—with our message? They stand between us and the customers we want. They are the people who can stock our product or run out of it. They are the people who can give it prominent shelf space or bury it behind other products. They are the people who can switch brands or push ours. Without the active cooperation of wholesalers and retailers, even the greatest consumer promotion can fall flat.

If the dealer doesn't have it, the consumer can't buy it. The consumer who asks for it in a store that doesn't carry it will most likely walk out with a substitute. It's a rare product that has no substitute. The trade must be told what the consumer is being told. Some advertisers believe that's what their sales force is supposed to do. And, it's true, the sales force should be able to do the best job of transmitting the product story to the trade. *If* they can get to all of the dealers in time. But no manufacturer has enough salespeople to call often enough on all the present and potential outlets.

Doesn't consumer advertising reach dealers too? Yes, it does, and very well, too. But, it reaches them as consumers, not as dealers. It reaches them when they are wearing their consumer hats, not their business hats. Consumer advertising tells them about the product while they are eating their dinners, watching a baseball game, or listening to music. Our consumer advertising wants to talk business when dealers are trying to forget business. How do we do it, then?

Trade advertising in business publications provides full coverage and frequency and does so very economically. Most successful manufacturers use business publications as their primary contact with the trade. The best part is that business readers do not find the ads an intrusion. Business magazines are their news sources. That's where they learn what's happening in their industry and about merchandising trends. The trade magazine is their marketplace.

Retailers Buy for Resale

The difference between trade advertising and industrial advertising should now be patently clear. Retailers buy products for resale. Yes, we know they also buy equipment and operating supplies, and we can use the same trade media to sell them these industrial goods. But, our main goal in trade advertising is to sell dealers our product so that they will sell it to their customers. (See color plates 61 and 62.)

What Do Retailers Want to Know?   What can we tell them in our trade advertising that will achieve our objectives and theirs?

1. *Product description and consumer appeals*
   In the area of product description, there is little difference between the advertisements aimed at dealers and the advertisements aimed at general consumers. Only the emphasis changes. Dealers want to know our product's major sales points, so we stress the product's uses, the colors and sizes available, the guarantee, the trade-in value, and the service.
2. *The company behind the product*
   If there is something about our company or the way the product is made or designed that could be vital to the sale, we have to tell our dealers about it. They would like to know about the manufac-

TRAVELERS CHEQUE CUSTOMERS ARE YOUR BEST CUSTOMERS.

WHY SELL THEM ANYTHING BUT THE TRAVELERS CHEQUE THEY THINK IS BEST.*

According to our research, bank customers who buy travelers cheques use more of a bank's key revenue producing services.* More of them have NOW accounts. Time deposits. And long-term CD's. And they have a better demographic profile. In short, travelers cheque customers are the kind of customers you want to get. And keep.

The study also shows that 60% of bank customers who used travelers cheques want American Express® the next time they buy travelers cheques.*

How many want our nearest competitor? Just 6%.

So when it comes to travelers cheques, there is a difference. And that should make a difference to you.

Because selling travelers cheques is just like selling anything else. As everyone in business knows, it pays to give your customers what they want.

And the travelers cheques more travelers cheque users want the next time they buy them is American Express.

If you're interested in the travelers cheque that your best customers think is best, just call

THE DIFFERENCE IS AMERICAN EXPRESS

*R. H. Bruskin Omnitel Study of Bank Customers. Aug., 1984. © American Express Travel Related Services Company, Inc. 1985. REPRINTED WITH PERMISSION

turer's design awards, research and development department, testing facilities, warehousing, and distribution systems. We cannot expect the sales force to pass on all of this information.

3. *Proof of consumer acceptance*
Nothing succeeds like success. If our product is a winner, we want dealers to know that. If some dealers have had tremendous success with our product, the others will want to know how they did it.

IN THE SPRING
A.R.M.® RETAIL SALES
DOUBLE!*

Don't get caught short on the shelf!

Starting March 15 . . .
The most advertising
EVER for any allergy product!

Buy now . . .
The best A.R.M. Deal **EVER!**

Menley & James Laboratories, Philadelphia. Pa. 19101
a SmithKline company

*A.C. Nielsen

A trade paper ad for a pharmaceutical manufacturer that appeared just before the beginning of the hay fever season. Notice that the ad mentions that the manufacturer will run "the most advertising EVER for any allergy product." Often, trade paper ads of this kind will provide details on the consumer advertising for the product — the number of magazine insertions, the number of commercials scheduled — to convince retailers that consumers will soon be crowding their stores to buy the product.

We can show them the window displays and the retail ads that our leading dealers have used. We can show them sales figures and offer them testimonials and data from market preference studies.

4. *Pricing and financing*
Everyone is in this for the money, so we might as well tell retailers exactly how much they can expect to make. That's what

the dealers most want to know. Markup, price maintenance, delivery, and inventory are all important considerations when the dealers come to the bottom line.

5. *Consumer advertising strategies*

Are we backing up the dealer with a well-planned campaign aimed at the consumer? Our consumer advertising, regional and national, literally pulls the product through the dealer. It can increase the amount of traffic in the dealer's store, too. We will want to tell our dealers as much as we can about our consumer advertising program: what the strategy behind it is and when and in what media the ads will run. We can show them how to tie in with the national campaign through our co-op program; we can mention all the advertising materials we supply, such as mats, logos, canned commercials, and radio scripts.

6. *Point-of-purchase materials and sales aids*

A good product demands good point-of-purchase displays and other sales-promotion materials. Good promotion materials boost sales, and if we want our dealers to promote our products, we have to *promote our promotional materials* to them. We should tell them about our training films, contests, statement stuffers, display units, point-of-purchase merchandisers, give-aways, and premiums.

Trade Campaigns

There are trade magazines that reach every trade worth reaching. Most are national; a few are regional; all are highly selective with a minimum of waste. Schedules in trade publications usually run in advance of consumer advertising programs. This permits retailers to order and shelve the merchandise and to prepare their own tie-in advertising. Some trade advertising precedes consumer advertising by as much as six months. As for seasonal influences, trade advertising more closely resembles consumer advertising, with which it is closely tied. There are peaks and valleys representing the high seasons and the slack periods. Unlike industrial ads, trade ads are not often repeated. Trade advertising is generally news advertising. We cannot repeat the ad we used two months ago. By then the deal will have expired; the season may be finished.

One More Look at Co-Op

The dollars spent for cooperative advertising must be included in the manufacturer's advertising budget. As far as the media are concerned, the retailer is the advertiser. It is the retailer's contract with the newspaper that establishes the rate. The retailer bills the manufacturer according to the terms of the co-op contract. Co-op advertising may be an important consideration for many retailers. Our trade advertising should, therefore, point out to retailers the extent of our co-op effort.

This is intended as a reminder that we must budget co-op advertising because it is part of our total advertising appropriation. To establish some idea of costs, the manufacturer prepares a contract for co-op advertising. Some manufacturers offer a fixed allowance, a predetermined dollar amount to be used for a grand opening or for a designated seasonal promotion such as Mother's Day or Easter. Or, the allowance may be an open one, in which case the manufacturer will pay for half the cost of any and all advertising that the retailer employs as long as it is for the manufacturer's product. Some allowances are based on earnings accumulated by the dealer. The amount is proportional to the volume of business the retailer places with the manufacturer. The allowance will be a percentage of dollar purchases — 5 percent is the most common figure. The percentage may be raised for brief periods to allow retailers to punch up their advertising to coincide with peak seasonal demand and with the manufacturer's own national advertising program. Under such terms, a retailer's $1,000 order generates a credit of $50 in a co-op account. The manufacturer then pays out this money to the retailer when the retailer advertises the manufacturer's product. Sometimes the credit is applied as a fixed amount per unit, such as 50¢ a carton or $50 a car, as is common in the automotive field.

Directories

There are more than 4,000 directories published in the United States, many of which sell advertising space in the pages of their listings. These directories are published by directory publishers, magazines, trade associations, chambers of commerce, and government agencies at all levels. Most directories are published to serve business — trade, industrial, and professional. For many buyers of industrial products, the industrial directory is a valuable tool for locating sources of supply. Chief among industrial directories is the *Thomas Register,* which is a general industrial directory. In addition, there are numerous directories known as vertical directories that are designed to serve the needs of a single industry.

The use of an industrial directory by a national industrial advertiser does not replace the need to advertise in an industrial publication. Directories work hand in hand with the advertiser's other promotional activities. The company's advertisements in industrial and business publications are designed to provoke interest in the advertiser's product, while the directory, in effect, completes the selling cycle by providing would-be purchasers with information about the product and where to buy it *when the need arises.* The directory is meant to be used, not read.

To document the use of directories, Cahners Publishing distributed some 41,000 questionnaires and received 12,403 usable returns. Specifically, respondents were asked, "In your role as a purchasing influence, where do you look for information on new products, technical help, new sources of supply and supplies capability?" Sixty-seven percent (8,392) of the respondents indicated that they use directories for at least one function.

One of the most widely used directories is the *U.S. Industrial Directory.* This directory is issued in sets of four: a telephone/address directory, a product directory, a literature directory, and a catalog file. The **telephone/address directory** is just that — an alphabetical listing of industrial suppliers of virtually every category of product. The **product directory** carries listings by product category so that a prospective buyer is able to learn which companies make a particular product. The **literature directory** carries listings, again by product category, of the literature that each supplier has available on request. The catalog file contains a copy of the advertiser's own printed material — a circular, a catalogue, even a sample, if feasible — which, together with the literature of other advertisers, is bound into one volume.

The circulation of the *U.S. Industrial Directory* is 38,364 manufacturing plants. Advertising costs range from $2,575 for a full page to $180 for a one-inch display card, with ten other sizes in between. The publisher claims 8.7 users per set.

Yellow Pages

The most commonly used consumer directory is the Yellow Pages issued by the telephone companies. The Yellow Pages provides national advertisers with an opportunity to make a tie-in with their local dealers at a time when the consumer is interested in buying. Every household and business receives a Yellow Pages directory either as separate books or bound together with the White Pages.

NYPSA is an acronym for National Yellow Pages Service Association, an association of more than 180 telephone directory publishers and 135 authorized selling representatives, who represent more than 6,000 directories across the United States, Canada, and other foreign countries.

The NYPSA Advertising Bureau provides agencies and advertisers with a responsive central source for market information, promotional materials, rates and data publications, and assistance useful in the analysis of National Yellow Pages advertising. NYPSA makes it easy to buy advertising in all of the represented yellow pages telephone directories with just a single contact.

National Yellow Pages Service Association is a sales organization that enables advertisers to make one contract for as many as 5,000 different Yellow Pages sections. It has been found that 82 percent of the adult (over 20 years of age) consumer population refers to the Yellow Pages an average of 116 times a year. Industrial buyers refer to the Yellow Pages 67 times a year. Ryder Truck Rental claims, for example, that it gets 80 percent of its consumer business from national Yellow Pages advertising. The company rents and leases 50,000 trucks out of 500 company-owned locations and 2,500 authorized dealers in the United States and Canada. The company uses national advertising to develop long-term leasing business with business firms, but uses the Yellow Pages to reach the occasional renter.

The National Yellow Pages Service Association issues a monthly publication of up-to-date computerized information on closing and publication dates, length of issue, population of covered area, advertising rates, and additional technical information.

Trade Shows

A **trade show** is an exhibition of the products and services of a particular market or industry, and attendance is usually restricted to members of the "trade." In the United States, nearly 6,000 trade shows, exhibits, and conventions are held each year. Visitors flock to consumer and industrial exhibits to see demonstrations of new products and to learn of innovations within their industry.

The Advantages

For some manufacturers the value of a trade show is excellent. It exposes the firm and its products to many potential customers in a very short time. It enables sales, advertising, and technical people to meet prospective buyers face to face. It is one of the few occasions when the buyers come to the sellers. The advantages of the trade show are many. It can:

1. reinforce the company image
2. provide an opportunity to demonstrate a product that cannot easily be demonstrated by the sales force
3. provide an opportunity to supply in-depth information to a live prospect
4. help build a mailing list
5. generate sales leads for further follow-up
6. provide an opportunity to study industry interest

There are, however, a few disadvantages to exhibiting at a trade show. Attendance at the exhibit takes salesmen out of the field. Many times the most frequent visitor to the exhibit booth is not a new prospect but an old customer. And, exhibiting at a trade show is expensive. Although trade shows are not properly an advertising expense, many companies often include them in their advertising budgets.

But Is It Worth the Cost?

When exhibiting at a trade show is considered an advertising expense, the advertising manager should monitor these expenses closely. The fee for rental of exhibit space, the expense of flying sales personnel to the exhibit location and paying for their hotel rooms and meals, the cost of setting up the exhibit, the expense of transporting the product or equipment being displayed, and the cost of the executive time needed to supervise the entire procedure — all add up to a very sizable dollar investment. Would that money be better spent in buying more advertising pages?

PROFILE

Harrison King McCann

Harrison King McCann, who founded what was to become one of the world's largest agency networks, was born in 1880 in Westbrook, New Hampshire. He worked his way through Bowdoin College in Brunswick, Maine, as a bellboy, a hotel clerk, and a salesman for Poland Springs bottled water. After graduation he moved to New York City and joined the four-man Amsterdam Advertising Agency. There he was involved in every facet of the business from writing copy to keeping the books. He then accepted a job with the New York Telephone Company, where he spent eight years, rising to advertising manager.

In 1911, McCann was offered the position of advertising manager at the Standard Oil Company, only a few months before the famous antitrust decision forced the company to reorganize. McCann then proposed that he form an agency to handle advertising for the new Standard Oil Companies, and he incorporated the agency in the same year. In 1912, the H. K. McCann Company opened for business with a capital of slightly over $5,000. Its professional philosophy was expressed in a simple, three-word slogan: "Truth Well Told." The agency's first client (now Exxon/Esso) is still served by McCann-Erickson offices around the world.

In 1930, the H. K. McCann Company merged with the Erickson Company, a successful New York agency established by Alfred W. Erickson in 1902. The new McCann-Erickson then became the fifth largest agency in worldwide billings.

H. K. McCann served as president of the agency from 1930 to 1948, as chairman for the next ten years, and as honorary chairman of the board until his death in 1962. A man of great personal warmth and integrity, his success has been attributed to his foresight in business, combined with an understanding of advertising and, above all, to a particular gift for dealing with people.

In 1945, McCann, who had helped to launch the American Association of Advertising Agencies and the Audit Bureau of Circulation earlier in his career, was inducted into the Advertising Hall of Fame. He was a director of the National Outdoor Advertising Bureau and also devoted time and effort to many civic causes.

Today, McCann-Erickson creates and places more than $2 billion worth of advertising through 111 offices in 65 countries. McCann's U.S. agencies are located in New York, Atlanta, Dallas, Detroit, Houston, Los Angeles, Louisville, San Francisco, and Seattle.

The spirit of McCann-Erickson in the United States has its foundation in great advertising campaigns like "Coke is it!" — L'Oreal "Because I'm Worth It" — "Wouldn't You Really Rather Have a Buick?" — "SONY. The One and Only" — "Shearson/American Express. Minds Over Money" and "Exxon. Quality you can count on."

The agency is the largest component of The Interpublic Group of Companies, a publicly owned business whose shares are listed on the New York Stock Exchange under the symbol IntpGp.

CASE HISTORY

U.S. WEST

After the breakup of AT&T, seven regional holding companies were struggling to establish an identity on Wall Street. Tracking research showed that while raw awareness of the companies as a group was improving in the brokerage community, there was a problem with institutional investors. This critical segment was less enthusiastic about the companies, less informed, and particularly unaware of the strengths of U.S. WEST and its region compared to the other companies.

U.S. WEST's management wanted to aggressively increase the percentage of its stock held by institutions (only 22 percent at the time of divestiture).

The advertising objective was to clearly distinguish U.S. WEST from the seven sisters. This distinctive positioning was necessary because U.S. WEST needed a patient financial marketplace that would allow the company to evolve away from dividend policies associated with a utility, and toward expectations associated with a more growth-oriented telecommunications company.

The mission of corporate advertising at U.S. WEST is tightly defined. It functions as the leading edge of their investor relations program. The nation's leading business magazines deliver an extremely high percentage of the target audience, and do so in an editorial environment that fits the message.

U.S. WEST's 1984 corporate advertising strategy called for a continuation of the main themes established in the introductory campaign:

Separate U.S. WEST from the pack and position the company as philosophically different and better prepared to take advantage of divestiture.

Promote the strengths of the region.

Stress the company's pro-competition stance and its support for a deregulated telecommunications environment.

The "Spirit of The West" theme was definitely retained and extended. The agency and client agreed that building a corporate brand identity is a distance event.

The agency recommended a continuation of the campaign that had established U.S. WEST's presence in the financial community during the divestiture period.

However, there were some important tactical changes. Media units went to full color on both pages of the spreads. Copy length was short-

---

To make participation in a trade show productive, the advertising manager must determine what the desired objectives of the exhibit should be and then weigh them against alternative expenditures. What can exhibiting at a trade show do that print advertising cannot do at least as well?

1. *Introduce a new product*
   Demonstrating a product is often the most effective way to sell it. At a trade show, a prospect can not only see a demonstration of the product, but touch, try, smell, or taste it. For test marketing, a trade show provides instant feedback.
2. *Bring together key dealers*
   Company salespeople are always calling on dealers. But bringing

We're not AT&T anymore. We're the 73,000 men and women who work for the companies of U S WEST: We're Mountain Bell, Northwestern Bell, Pacific Northwest Bell and a growing number of unregulated companies, continuing a legacy of strength and a tradition of character.

We have reduced bureaucracy so that each of us has a very real stake in making our company grow and prosper. We serve more customers now than ever before, yet through re-organization, advanced technology and our own hard work, we have reduced our total work force by a third since 1981.

Start thinking of us as a growth company. If you haven't already, you will soon. We are not a utility. And we are not acting like one.
For a 32 page report, call 1-800-828-2400 or write U S WEST Report, 7800 East Orchard Road, Englewood, Colorado 80111.

USWEST

Mountain Bell, Northwestern Bell, Pacific Northwest Bell. And a growing number of unregulated companies.

---

ened. Since advertising no longer needed to be a source of detail about the company, copy could now be more single-minded. The headlines and visuals were crafted to forge a philosophical bond with the business and financial leaders who read *Fortune, Forbes,* and *Business Week.*

The "Spirit of The West" works to clarify the company's attitudes toward competition, deregulation, and the need for entrepreneurial business expansion.

U.S. WEST's institutional ownership rose to 40 percent, the highest of the seven AT&T spin-offs. In the first quarter of 1984, it was one of the five most traded stocks by institutions among all those traded on the New York Stock Exchange.

---

most or all of the key dealers together permits the company to build morale and to transmit new-product or policy information to them with unsurpassed opportunities for feedback.

3. *Enhance the company's image*
   The advertising that the company places in trade, industrial, or professional journals does indeed build an image, but it is a distant image. No amount of carefully designed and well-written advertising copy can take the place of a handshake from key personnel or a few explanations delivered with a friendly smile.

4. *Improve the distribution network*
   The trade show is one place where the dealers and distributors *come to the company.* Dealers or distributors who are willing to fly a

thousand or more miles at their own expense to attend a trade show are active and aggressive business people—the kind we want to add to our network.

5. *Help build a mailing list*

It is customary to ask visitors for their name and affiliation at a trade show, so that advertisers can build lists of interested people on the spot to whom they can send catalogues or whom they can have salespeople contact. In fact, it is not even necessary to ask. Most visitors are required to wear a badge with their name and company printed on it.

Summary

Business advertising is the promotion of products and services bought by business organizations for the purpose of doing business. In general, advertising appeals aimed at business people are rational, not emotional, and are related to saving or making money for their companies.

Advertising plays a very important role in industrial marketing; it can make the efforts of the manufacturer's sales force more productive. As the cost of an industrial sales call has risen, industrial advertising has become more valuable in stimulating sales leads, building brand loyalty, and developing a company image. The industrial buying process differs sharply from consumer buying behavior. A more careful search, more evaluation, and the required approval of more people distinguish industrial buying from consumer buying. The need to reach and convince more people, particularly hidden buying influences, becomes apparent as the price of the "buy" goes up. In industrial markets the loss of a customer can have grave financial repercussions.

Retailers and wholesalers are also business buyers, but unlike the industrial buyer they buy for resale. The manufacturer's consumer advertising campaign can be rendered ineffective without the active support of the dealers and distributors through whom the product is sold. Trade advertising is used to carry the message. Every trade has one or more magazines that reach dealers in that business with a minimum of cost and waste. Advertising to the trade keeps retailers informed about the manufacturer's product and sales policies, provides information on future consumer campaigns, and elicits the support and co-operation of dealers in co-op advertising, in the use of point-of-purchase displays, and in the assignment of shelf space. A trade advertising program is a vital component of the national advertiser's campaign to build profits through sales.

Questions for Discussion

1. What are some of the appeals the industrial advertiser might use?
2. What makes industrial advertising more difficult to prepare than consumer advertising?
3. How can industrial advertising substitute for a salesman?
4. How does advertising for major machinery differ from advertising for operating supplies?
5. Why would an industrial advertiser advertise in a consumer publication?

6. How does industrial buying behavior differ from the consumer's buying behavior?
7. What are some objectives we could set for our industrial advertising?
8. How does trade advertising differ from industrial advertising?
9. Name some appeals we could use in trade-paper advertising.
10. Why is trade advertising important?
11. What are the values of a trade show?

Sources and Suggestions for Further Reading

Arthur D. Little, Inc. "An Evaluation of 1100 Research Studies on the Effectiveness of Industrial Advertising." New York: American Business Press, May 1971.

Bertrand, Kate. "Taking Care of Media Business." *Business Marketing,* August 1986.

Bly, Robert W. "What Business/Industrial Copywriters Can Learn from the Mail Order Folks." *Business Marketing,* February 1984.

Faria, A. J., and Dickinson, J. R. "What Kinds of Companies Use Trade Shows Most —And Why." *Business Marketing,* June 1986.

Hammet, Jim. "Hot on the Track of the Sales Lead." *Advertising Age,* June 14, 1982.

Hutt, Michael D., and Thomas W. Speh. *Industrial Marketing Management.* 2nd ed. Chicago: The Dryden Press, 1985.

"Industrial Advertising Effectively Reaches Buying Influences at Low Cost." Report by U.S. Steel, New York American Business Press, 1969.

Kern, Richard. "At Long Last! Changes in the SIC System." *Sales & Marketing Management,* April 28, 1986.

Kreisman, Richard. "Getting Ready for Show Time." *INC.,* August 1986.

Kriegel, Robert A. "Positioning Demystified." *Business Marketing,* May 1986.

Lane, Joseph J. "Data Sheets that Sell." *Sales & Marketing Management,* May 14, 1984.

McNutt, George. *Business/Industrial Marketing and Communications.* Chicago: Crain Books, 1978.

Messner, Frederick B. *Industrial Advertising.* New York: McGraw-Hill, 1963.

Murray, Bernard T., Jr., "Financial Direct Marketing: A New Approach." *Direct Marketing,* July 1986.

"The 100 Leading Business and Industrial Advertisers." *Business Marketing,* July 1986.

The Range and Depth of Buying Influences in a Typical Plant. New York: American Business Press, 1975.

Sawyer, Howard G. (Scotty). *Business-to-Business Advertising.* Chicago: Crain Books, 1978.

Swandby, Richard K., and Jonathan Cox. "Trade Show Trends: Business Up and Growing." *Business Marketing,* May 1984.

21 ADVERTISING AND SOCIETY

Criticisms of Advertising

Policing Advertising

Working Vocabulary

Federal Trade Commission Act
Wheeler-Lea Act
cease-and-desist order
puffery
tombstone ad

bait-and-switch ad
corrective advertising
Food and Drug Administration
Federal Communications Commission

National Advertising Review Board (NARB)
National Advertising Division (NAD)

The statement that "without advertising the U.S. economy would be better off" is widely rejected. Most people seem to feel that advertising is good for the economy.

Rena Bartos and Theodore F. Dunn
Advertising and Consumers New Perspectives

As we learned in chapter 1, throughout recorded history sellers have found it advantageous to send messages to prospective buyers and to send these messages in the most economical manner possible. History also shows that consumers search for information that can be acquired at the lowest possible cost to themselves. Supplying information to prospective buyers by means of mass media would appear to satisfy both buyers and sellers.

Criticisms of Advertising

Nevertheless, much criticism has been directed at the advertising business. Critics claim that advertising:

1. adds to the cost of products
2. causes people to buy products they do not need
3. reduces competition and thereby fosters monopolies

The purpose of this chapter is to examine these criticisms — social and economic — to see if they are valid.

Advertising Adds to the Cost of Goods

If advertising did add to the cost of the goods and services consumers buy, it would have no economic justification. From the standpoint of the manufacturer, advertising is used because it is considered to be the most *cost-effective* marketing technique. If manufacturers knew of a marketing tool that offered them lower costs or greater returns than advertising, it would be foolish for them to continue to invest heavily in advertising. In fact, manufacturers in many industries invest most of their promotional effort in their sales forces and do very little, if any, consumer or business advertising.

For the manufacturers of most mass-marketed goods, however, advertising is really only a substitute for salespeople who call in person on individual prospects. Advertising cannot completely replace a sales force; while an advertisement must be designed to communicate with large numbers of prospective customers, each member of a sales force can tailor his or her message to reach each prospect individually. Salespeople also receive instant feedback from the customers they call on — another advantage over advertising. Advertising, on the other hand, can greatly reduce the size (and cost) of the sales force required to promote a product by performing many tasks that would otherwise have to be performed by salespeople. Could a chewing gum company, for example, afford to employ salespeople to sell its product door to door the way the Fuller Brush Company does? Of course not; the gum company relies on advertising to perform this selling function, and advertising does so at a much lower cost.

Economies of Scale   Like everything that goes into the production, distribution, and sale of a product or service, advertising is a cost. There is no question that the consumer ultimately pays for it. But the reason for advertis-

504

ing's existence, as we have shown, is that it performs its essential selling function more efficiently and at a lower cost than any other method. If all manufacturers had to rely on salespeople to promote their products, the cost of retaining a large sales force would be passed on to consumers too. And these costs would be substantially higher than those of mass-media advertising. If manufacturers were not allowed to do any advertising at all (nor allowed to substitute another form of promotion for advertising), the cost of their goods might be reduced by a fraction of a cent, perhaps by even more for certain types of products. But the reduced number of sales brought about by this ban on advertising would force manufacturers to cut back on the amount of goods they produce. And the limited scale of production would, in turn, cause the price of these products to rise.

You can get some idea of the increased costs that would result from this turn of events if you compare the price of a custom-tailored garment with that of any nationally advertised brand. Can you believe that the national advertiser, buying thousands of yards of fabric, and employing high-speed cutting and sewing machines, cannot offer consumers lower prices than the custom tailor who buys fabric three yards at a time and cuts each piece by hand? And, in addition to lower prices, the national advertiser can offer consumers a much wider range of styles and colors than can the custom tailor.

In its role as a substitute and aid to a manufacturer's sales force, advertising helps develop the volume of sales that the manufacturer needs in order to take advantage of the economies of mass production. Thus, advertising helps make more goods and services available to more people. Instead of raising the cost, advertising keeps it lower. Advertising raises our standard of living by keeping the wheels of industry turning.

Advertising Keeps the Price of Media Low   While on the subject of cost, critics of advertising might want to consider the fact that it is the advertising in our newspapers and magazines that makes it possible for readers to buy them at a price that is less than their cost of production. The entertainment enjoyed by millions of people on radio and television is delivered to them every day without charge. This is only possible because advertising revenues pay for the cost of producing and broadcasting television and radio programs. Even the programs on commercial-free public television are paid for in large part by grants from national advertisers. The most common reply made by critics of advertising to this point is a criticism of television. Terrible programs, they say; too much violence; too many commercials. However, advertisers are not ultimately responsible for deciding which types of programs will be broadcast and which will not. Advertisers (as sponsors of programs), networks (as producers of programs), and individual stations (as purveyors of programs) are extremely responsive to consumer tastes and desires. When consumers decide they do not like a program, that program goes off the air — and quickly. A program that is viewed by millions of households must be providing them with entertainment they enjoy. And it provides that entertainment for free. If millions of people want to watch situation comedies, advertisers will spend their money to sponsor comedy programs. If millions of people want to watch westerns, advertisers will sponsor westerns. If grand opera and Shakespearean plays were demanded by millions of viewers, advertisers would sponsor these programs.

Advertising Fosters Diversity   The argument that advertisers only sponsor programs demanded by millions of viewers is based on the assumption that the advertisers' only objective is to reach millions of people with their

Does our government care about the health of its citizens? Indeed it does and so do the managers of American businesses. Thus, this ad is addressed to business people and appeals to their business sense as well as their basic human concern. This ad appeared in *Business Week*.

Is your business suffering from
HIGH BLOOD PRESSURE?

High blood pressure can make your business suffer . . . in lost productivity and profits.

Almost 1/3 of all workers in this country have high blood pressure. About 29 million workdays, representing $2 billion in earnings, are lost each year because of high blood pressure related diseases, such as heart attack and stroke.

You can help save lives and your company's money with a High Blood Pressure Control Program in your company.

Look, you pay for their Christmas party, their vacations, their bonuses . . . how about their life expectancy? You'll find a program like this is far better for your people and your profits.

To find out more, write to: Work Place Coordinator, National High Blood Pressure Education Program, 120/80 National Institutes of Health, Bethesda, MD 20205

High Blood Pressure Control Programs
BETTER FOR BUSINESS

The National High Blood Pressure Education Program
The National Heart, Lung, and Blood Institute, National Institutes of Health,
Public Health Service, U.S. Department of Health and Human Services.

messages. As we have learned, however, advertisers would much rather have their commercials reach a small audience that contains a large number of prospective purchasers of their products than reach a large audience that contains relatively few prospects. For this reason, advertisers do indeed sponsor many programs that would not be seen on television if the size of the audience

COME AND SEE THE BURIED TREASURE.

Nearly 2000 years ago, a prosperous, sophisticated city was buried under 12 feet of volcanic ash.

In less than two days, the homes and temples of 20,000 people literally disappeared. A civilization was frozen in time.

Now the glory that was Pompeii has come to New York. The stunning paintings, the gold and silver jewelry, the marble and bronze sculptures are alive again.

You can walk through an elegantly frescoed room, pause under a garden portico as if 20 centuries ago were yesterday.

Vesuvius destroyed Pompeii. And saved it at the same time.

For information, call (212) 999-7777. This exhibition is made possible by grants from the National Endowment for the Humanities and Xerox Corporation.

POMPEII AD 79
American Museum of Natural History
April 22 through July 31

XEROX

they attract were the sole criterion for media selection. Documentaries, travel narratives, special-events news programs, and new or classic films, plays, and operas are continually being sponsored by advertisers who are interested in reaching the specialized audiences that these programs attract. This is a trend that will become more and more important in the future as advertisers segment

Criticisms of Advertising

507

their target markets with greater precision. The broadcast media will take on more of the attributes of the print media, with programming that, like the wide array of consumer magazines, offers something for everyone.

Advertising Makes People Buy Things They Don't Need

The "things" that advertising is usually accused of "forcing" people to buy are either inferior products or products that people do not require or cannot afford. To the first part of this charge, advertisers can reply that the ultimate test of the quality of any product takes place in the marketplace. While advertising may stimulate consumers to try a new product or a new brand, it cannot hypnotize them into continuing to buy a product that does not satisfy. This is merely common sense: you would not continue to buy a soft drink that had an unpleasant metallic aftertaste, or a light bulb that burned out in a month, or a detergent that never seemed to get your clothes clean. And advertising is not only incapable of selling a poor product; it often cannot sell a good product that the public does not want. The marketing graveyard is filled with products no one bought despite the blandishments of powerful advertising. The Edsel and Corfam (a synthetic leather) spring to mind at once in this regard. Ford Motor

Although drinking alcoholic beverages, like smoking cigarettes, may be increasingly linked to perceived hazards, liquor has a far deeper role in American society — at the family table and in our living rooms as a form of communion. Alcohol serves as a celebration of life. For many reform groups, the culprit is the liquor industry which they accuse of marketing its products to problem drinkers and the impressionable young. The industry's reply — and that of its individual marketers — is temperance.

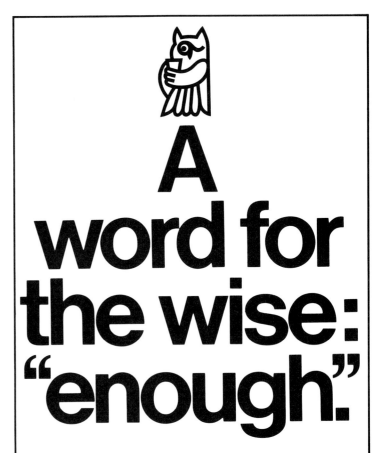

Don't drink too much of a good thing.
The Distilled Spirits Council of the United States.
1300 Pennsylvania Building, Washington, D.C. 20004

Company and Du Pont, respectively, spent millions of dollars advertising these products, and yet they were failures in the marketplace.

To the second part of the above charge — that advertising makes people buy things that they don't really need or cannot afford — advertisers must again point out that advertising cannot hypnotize people into acting against their own best interests. The question of whether or not a consumer can afford to buy certain products is one that must be decided by each consumer individually. This is not to deny that advertising is a persuasive form of communication that may create wants, but wants are also created by people themselves, their aspirations, their friends, their families, and their educational and vocational backgrounds. As the economists have always told us, human wants are insatiable.

HOW TO HELP A LITTLE GIRL MAKE IT ALL THE WAY TO 7.

It wasn't long ago that if little Kamala Rama drank the water in her village she would have taken her life in her hands.

Today, thanks to Save the Children, she can have clean water to wash with, and fresh water for her mother to cook with.

And she can do something else that was once unheard of in her village for a little girl.

She can go to school. Even go past the fifth grade.

When you first sponsor a child through Save the Children, you have no idea how much just $16 a month can do.

By combining your funds with other sponsors', we're helping families, even entire communities, do so much. The result is that children are now getting things they didn't always have:

Better food. Clean drinking water. Decent housing. Medical care. A chance to go to school.

In fact, for over 50 years, Save the Children has been working little life-saving miracles here in America and around the world.

And the wonderful feeling of sponsoring a child comes to only 52¢ a day. The cost of a cup of coffee.

What's more, you'll get a photo of the child you sponsor, a personal history, progress reports and a chance to correspond, if you'd like.

Please, won't you help. Send in the coupon today.

There are still so many children who need the chance Kamala Rama got.

The chance to make it to 7.

Gary Shaye

Advertising makes an invaluable contribution to important humanitarian causes. Do note the many ads in newspapers and magazines that solicit our contributions to causes like this. The reach and selectivity of media are combined to make these ads effective. This ad appeared in the *New York Times* book review section.

In general, when critics accuse advertisers of making people buy things that they don't need, much depends on how the word *need* is defined. All that people really require is enough to eat and drink; plain, serviceable clothing; and a place to sleep at the end of the day. They don't really *need* stereo components, washing machines, rock albums, paperback novels, motion pictures, toothpaste, deodorant, perfume, ballpoint pens, or jewelry. But all of these things make our lives easier or more pleasant to live.

Advertising Reduces Competition

Giants and Giant Killers Some critics of advertising contend that advertising fosters monopoly. In support of this claim they point to the rising costs of launching a national advertising campaign — costs that the critics claim are prohibitive to all but the established giants of each industry. In certain industries, such as soap, automobile, and cigarette manufacturing, it does indeed seem that advertising costs would tend to restrict the entry of new firms into these fields. In fact, however, the inroads made by foreign companies into several of these markets (most notably that for automobiles) speak well for the opportunities open to competing firms to wrest a market share from the well-entrenched giants. Similar opportunities exist for small domestic companies that can exploit a regional market and build a market share for themselves, even in the face of competition from larger, more established corporations. This has happened recently in the market for breakfast cereals, where manufacturers of "natural" whole-grain cereals have managed to achieve respectable market shares, and in the market for tea, where the manufacturers of herbal teas have managed to obtain market shares in spite of competition from such giants as Lipton. Such successes can be attributed in large part to the power of advertising.

In general, we can return to the point we made earlier: if manufacturers did not use advertising to promote their goods, they would have to depend on other, more expensive, methods of promotion. They would have to hire hundreds of additional salespeople to do the selling jobs now done by advertising. The cost of launching a nationwide advertising campaign may be formidable, but the cost of supporting larger, nationwide sales forces for mass-marketed goods would be greater still.

Advertising Inhibits Price Competition Critics who claim that advertising fosters monopolistic practices also point to the tendency of advertisers in certain industries to promote their products on the basis of such attributes as package or brand name, rather than on the basis of price. This, they claim, enables these advertisers to keep their prices high while focusing consumer attention on trivial differences among the various brands. A number of studies have found, however, that although the manufacturers of certain brands choose not to compete on the basis of price, there is a considerable amount of price competition in the marketing of these products on the retail level. Discount drugstores, mass merchandisers, and chain supermarkets consistently offer consumers nationally advertised brands at prices lower than those maintained by traditional drugstores, grocery stores, and department stores. One reason for the rapid growth of these new discount retail outlets is that today consumers are often equipped with extensive knowledge of product types and brand differences. Consumers have gained this knowledge from reading, watching, and listening to the advertising for these products. This, in turn, has made it possible for mass merchandisers to employ fewer salespeople to aid

FLORIDA DEPARTMENT OF CITRUS
PROCESSED ORANGE JUICE
"BIRTHDAY PARTY"

COMM'L NO.: FCOJ 3343   LENGTH: 30 SECONDS

LITTLE GIRL: 16 glasses of Florida orange juice, please.

SONG: Orange You Smart,

(SFX: TAP TAP) for drinking orange juice,

with that clean and sunny taste. (SFX: BUM BUM)

Orange You Smart for drinking orange juice,

pure refreshment anyplace.

Hey, Orange You Smart for drinking to your body's content.

the taste that only nature could invent. ANNCR: 100% pure from Florida.

SONG: Hey, Birthday Girl,

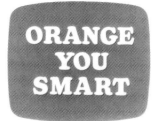

Orange You Smart!

(SFX: TAP TAP)

Changes have had an impact on the Florida orange business. The processing industry has been taken over to a large extent by major corporations — among them, Coca Cola Company, Beatrice Foods, and Procter & Gamble. These companies are interested in promoting their brand names rather than oranges and grapefruits from Florida.
The industry, which has long maintained very strict standards regarding fruit sizes, maturity, and grades, is now undertaking a strong Florida citrus identification program. To fund the marketing effort for Florida orange juice, growers are assessed a charge per box.

Criticisms of Advertising   **511**

consumers in making purchase decisions. And this savings in labor costs is passed on to the consumer in the form of lower prices.

But, if manufacturers keep their prices high enough, won't consumers still be paying more than they ought to, even if they make their purchases at discount stores? No, not if the mass merchandisers offer a wide range of private brands to choose from. If the manufacturers of nationally advertised brands keep their prices too high, the makers of private-label goods will be able to make substantial profits even though they sell their products at greatly reduced prices.

If advertising does not do all the bad things its critics say it does, what *does* it do?

Advertising Is Information

It has often been said that building a better mousetrap is not enough. We have to tell many people why it is better. Advertising teaches people about new products and, in doing so, hastens their adoption. Also, by describing new and different products, advertising broadens the range of choices available to the consumer. Advertisers who are interested in serving human wants, then, must have the opportunity to tell prospective customers news about what they are offering. Whether it is the choice of a tube of toothpaste or the choice of a president of the United States, the principle is the same. The freedom to choose depends on the freedom to provide information.

Information Encourages Innovation   The competitive pressure of advertising has led to increasingly higher standards of quality that new products have had to meet in order to gain a share of the market.

The television set, now in over 94 percent of American homes, is an excellent example of the way technology combined with advertising has given the public more for its money. The original television sets, black and white only, featured a seven-inch or ten-inch screen that looks like a toy today. A giant color set today costs very little more than that black and white set did 30 years ago. Furthermore, in addition to receiving color transmission from more channels, we receive broadcasts from overseas via satellite, or we can connect to cable and receive first-run movies, major sporting events, and important documentary films. Many more programs are now available — in many cases, 24 hours a day.

By sustaining this pressure for better products and lower prices, advertising contributes directly to better values for the consuming public. When a company is confident of its ability to bring its product improvements quickly to the attention of the public, it is more willing to invest dollars in the research needed to bring that improvement from the laboratory to the marketplace.

Information Satisfies Wants   Some critics say that advertising is not interested in providing information as much as in persuading customers to buy something. It is true that advertising is the art of *persuasive* communication; it is a business technique that has to pay its way. But note that we said it is communication — that is, an exchange of information. Manufacturers make products that people want. No manufacturer today can afford to make the product first and then hope that advertising will induce people to buy it. It simply does not work that way. Manufacturers cannot succeed with advertising unless they listen to consumers, understand their wants, and then attempt to satisfy them. If advertisers do not do this, consumers will not pay attention to the manufacturers' advertising or buy their products.

Once manufacturers have done everything they can, through market testing and research, to make their product a good one, then, as we learned in chapter 14, one of the best ways to persuade consumers to try it is to describe what the product is and what it does. Print advertising is particularly suited to the dissemination of product information. A quick glance at any consumer magazine will reveal a number of ads that consist almost entirely of copy that describes the product — its uses and benefits — in detail.

A purist may claim that only price and ingredients should be classified as information. Consumers do not, of course, base their buying decisions, as industrial buyers do, on purely functional choice. There are psychic values in a product that provide satisfaction for the purchaser. Consumers want more than transportation in an automobile: they want style and status and pizzazz. Such psychic value carries no visible price tag. To separate the information portion of advertising from the psychic portion is impossible because they are so much a part of each other.

Advertising Is Ideas   Advertising also provides information in the world of ideas. Industry, consumer groups, and political parties advertise to encourage interest in current issues. Advertising is used to help build understanding among the various constituencies and ethnic groups around the country. Advertising is also a strong force for assimilation and democratization. It encourages freedom of choice. The Advertising Council, founded in 1942 to help support our war effort, places millions of dollars' worth of advertising every year to encourage charitable contributions, to promote traffic safety, to help stop forest fires, to find jobs for the unemployed, to win understanding for the handicapped, and to sell government bonds. (See color plates 63–66.)

Policing Advertising

The efforts by the federal government to regulate advertising go back a hundred years to the passage of laws to combat postal fraud. Early demands for reform were stimulated by the blatant fakers who thrived in the patent medicine field in the late nineteenth century. Congress passed the first major federal law for the protection of consumers — the Pure Food and Drug Act — in 1906, and, at the same time, newspapers and magazines began to establish standards for the advertisements that they would accept. In 1910, the Curtis Publishing Company, which published the *Saturday Evening Post,* issued the Curtis Advertising Code in order to "protect both our advertisers and our readers from all copy that is fraudulent and deceptive." In 1911, the advertising industry itself was providing support for the adoption of state laws against deceptive advertising. Advertisers urged passage of a model statute, drawn up by the advertising magazine *Printer's Ink,* which made deceptive or misleading advertising a misdemeanor. In revised form, the model statute has been adopted by 37 states. Thus, historically, policies governing the regulation of advertising have proceeded from three sources: the government, the media, and the advertising industry itself.

The Government Regulates Advertising

The FTC   The **Federal Trade Commission Act** of 1914 represented an entirely new approach to the government's regulation of business. The federal responsibility to guard against monopolistic practices was being extended (the Clayton Antitrust Act was passed in 1914, too) by making "unfair methods of competition" unlawful. It was hoped that the FTC would identify unfair business practices and that the business community would avoid them. The FTC's authority over advertising was eventually derived from Section 5 of the original act which stated:

> The Commission is hereby empowered and directed to prevent persons, partnerships, or corporations, except banks and common carriers subject to the Acts to regulate commerce, from using unfair methods of competition in commerce.

In 1938, the Federal Trade Commission Act was amended by the **Wheeler-Lea Act,** which expanded the responsibility of the FTC to cover "unfair and deceptive acts in commerce." Under this provision, the FTC was given authority to act against a firm guilty of deceptive practices that might harm consumers, even though those practices might not have an effect on competition. Section 12 of the Wheeler-Lea Act then declared that "the dissemination or the causing to be disseminated of any false advertisement . . . shall be an unfair or deceptive act or practice in commerce with the meaning of Section 5." In addition, the FTC was given power to monitor deceptive business acts and practices related to contests, guarantees, and trade names.

Enforcement of the Federal Trade Commission Act and the provisions of the Wheeler-Lea Act is vested in five commissioners appointed by the President of the United States, with the advice and consent of the Senate, for seven-year terms. The president designates one of the commissioners as chairman. Not more than three commissioners may be members of the same political party. Their terms are staggered to assure continuity of experience, and, according to congressional intent, to keep the commission nonpartisan. The chairman has responsibility for the personnel aspects of the commission's operations. The full commission, however, must act on all matters involving development and implementation of FTC law enforcement policies.

The FTC has authority to stop business practices that restrict competition or that deceive or otherwise injure consumers, as long as these practices: (1) fall within the legal scope of the commission's statutes; (2) affect interstate commerce; and (3) involve a significant public interest. After an administrative hearing on a case, the FTC may issue a **cease-and-desist order,** which defines the offense and forbids such action in the future, or it may apply to the federal courts to issue an injunction against the offender.

In addition, the FTC defines practices that violate the law, so that businessmen may know their legal obligations and consumers may recognize those practices against which legal recourse is possible. The commission does this through Trade Regulation Rules and Industry Guides issued periodically as "dos and don'ts" to business and industry, and through business advice—called Advisory Opinions—given to individuals and corporations requesting it.

The ever-present question concerning the enforcement of laws in the advertising business is: What is truth? Outright deceptions are usually easily recognized, but even well-intentioned advertisers will engage in puffery. **Puffery** is generally defined as exaggerated praise and is not actionable under common law. We often use puffery in our everyday speech. "That was a great movie," we might say. Do we mean to say that it was one of the best movies of all time or merely that we enjoyed the movie? In a similar vein an advertiser might say that a pen "writes smoother." Smoother than what? This is just puffery. Read any print ad, listen to any radio commercial, watch any television commercial, and you will find examples of puffery. It is often very difficult to draw a line between what is meant only as puffery and what is meant to be deceptive. In one area of advertising, however, the use of puffery is very strictly regulated. The Securities and Exchange Commission (SEC) has strict regulations against puffery in the advertising of securities. The **tombstone ads** in the financial sections of newspapers are closely watched by the SEC to insure that the ads confine themselves to basic statistical information about any forthcoming stock issue. No discussion of a stock's merits is permitted.

Years ago the priority of the FTC was action against fictitious price ads, misuse of words like "guarantee," and bait-and-switch ads. In a **bait-and-switch ad,** an advertiser would advertise one product at a very low price as bait

---

This announcement is neither an offer to sell nor a solicitation of offers to buy any of these securities. The offering is made only by the Prospectus and the related Prospectus Supplement.

NEW ISSUE   September 30, 1985

$500,000,000

General Motors Acceptance Corporation

10% Notes Due October 1, 1990

Price 99.75%
plus accrued interest, if any, from October 10, 1985

Copies of the Prospectus and the related Prospectus Supplement may be obtained in any State in which this announcement is circulated only from such of the undersigned as may legally offer these securities in such State.

The First Boston Corporation

Merrill Lynch Capital Markets	Morgan Stanley & Co. Incorporated
Salomon Brothers Inc	Shearson Lehman Brothers Inc.
Bear, Stearns & Co. Daiwa Securities America Inc.	Deutsche Bank Capital Corporation
Drexel Burnham Lambert Incorporated E. F. Hutton & Company Inc.	Kidder, Peabody & Co. Incorporated
The Nikko Securities Co. International, Inc. Nomura Securities International, Inc.	PaineWebber Incorporated
Prudential-Bache Securities	Swiss Bank Corporation International Securities Inc.
UBS Securities Inc.	Yamaichi International (America), Inc.

California Clause

Copies of the Prospectus and the related Prospectus Supplement may be obtained in any State in which this announcement is circulated only from such of the undersigned as may legally offer these securities in such State. These Securities are redeemable prior to maturity as set forth in the Prospectus and the related Prospectus Supplement.

Tombstone ads can be found in the financial sections of daily newspapers as well as in a number of general business publications. The format for these ads is fairly standard, and the disclaimer copy, "this announcement is neither an offer to sell nor a solicitation of offers to buy," is mandated. The designation *tombstone* was probably suggested by an advertising designer who likened the ads to a tombstone that contains nothing more than the name of the person and the dates of birth and death.

to lure consumers to visit a certain store. When the consumers arrived at the store, however, they would be told that the advertised product had been sold out and store personnel would then attempt to convince them to switch to a more expensive product. Today, the FTC's objectives are much broader. Of particular interest is its "advertising substantiation" program. Under this program, many advertisers in widely varied fields have been required to prove the claims made in their advertising.

Recently, the FTC, when deciding its cases, has been attempting to restore conditions to what they were before the deceptive or misleading action took place. Some recent cease-and-desist orders included requirements for the offender to correct earlier misstatements.

A few examples of **corrective advertising** will serve to make the FTC's power in this area of advertising abundantly clear. In September 1978, an FTC administrative law judge ordered that $24 million in future Anacin ads state: "Anacin is not a tension reliever." Although American Home Products, the manufacturer, had stopped making the claim by December 1973, evidence showed that consumers believed tension relief to be an important attribute of Anacin. The judge said the image was likely to persist for "some time" in the absence of a corrective message. The $24 million represented the FTC's estimate of the average annual Anacin advertising budget from 1968 to 1973. The manufacturer was also barred from claiming in future ads that its Arthritis Pain Formula had "special" or "unusual" ingredients, because such ingredients are also available in other products.

When you see a commercial for Listerine, you will also see the corrective disclaimer: "Listerine will not help prevent colds or sore throats or lessen their severity." The colds/sore throat issue was the subject of years of litigation between the FTC and Warner-Lambert, the manufacturer. Warner-Lambert lost and was required to use that disclaimer in its next $10 million worth of advertising. What's more, the FTC contracted with a market research organization to do consumer surveys that would gauge the impact of the corrective ads on consumers.

Additional legislation has augmented the capacity and scope of the FTC in the years since the passage of the Wheeler-Lea Act. The Wool Products Labeling Act of 1939, administered and enforced by the FTC, was passed to protect manufacturers and consumers from the deliberate mislabeling of wool products. The Textile Fiber Products Identification Act, 1958, requires that clothing, rugs, and household textiles carry a generic or chemical description of the fiber content of these products. The Fair Packaging and Labeling Act, 1962, regulates packaging and labeling of the food, drug, and cosmetic products under the jurisdiction of the Department of Health, Education and Welfare and of all other consumer products under the authority of the FTC.

Other Regulatory Agencies   Paralleling the work of the FTC, the **Food and Drug Administration** polices the labeling of foods, drugs, and cosmetics. In 1938, the passage by Congress of the Federal Food, Drug, and Cosmetic Act divided regulation between the FTC and the FDA. The FTC is responsible for advertising in promotional media and the Food and Drug Administration has power over claims that appear on the label or package. Additional legislation in 1962 gave the FDA virtually unlimited authority over prescription drugs. While the FDA's jurisdiction is confined to the *label,* its role is broader than the word implies. If it finds that any claim in an ad is not supported by the information on the label, the FDA can proceed with a mislabeling action. The agency's interest in ads is deeper than it may seem from the enabling legislation. However, the FDA has not been merely a policeman. It has cooperated with the food industry in the development of standardized nutritional labeling systems for foods.

Closely allied to the FTC and FDA in much regulatory activity is the fraud staff of the U.S. Postal Service. Since 1872, post office fraud laws have provided criminal and civil remedies against the use of the mail to defraud. Because fraud, from a legal standpoint, involves "intent to deceive," postal service cases ordinarily involve misrepresentation that goes beyond the "false advertising" handled by the FTC. Most problems have been in the food and drug fields. The most serious cases of postal fraud are turned over to the Department of Justice, but the majority are handled administratively in civil procedure hearings similar to those of the FTC.

In the area of broadcasting, the **Federal Communications Commission** (FCC) enforces rules regarding the types of products that may be advertised on broadcast media, the number and frequency of commercials allowed within a certain period of time, and what broadcast programs and commercials may or may not state or show. Under the Communications Act of 1934, the FCC was empowered to operate our communications system in "the public interest, convenience, and necessity." Through its control over licensing, the commission wields indirect control over broadcast advertising. Specific problem areas with which the FCC has dealt include misleading demonstrations, commercials considered in poor taste, and overlong commercials.

In addition to the FTC, FDA, the U.S. Postal Service, and the FCC, there are many other federal agencies with specialized roles related to advertising Among these agencies are the following:

1. The Department of Agriculture, under the Packers and Stockyards Act, plays a role similar to that of the FDA in regulating the labeling of meat products.
2. The Environment Protection Agency (EPA) does for pesticide labels what the FDA does for food labels.
3. The Consumer Product Safety Agency asks advertisers to avoid any themes that may promote unsafe use of products.
4. The Federal Deposit Insurance Corporation and the Federal Home Bank Board both exercise close supervision over the advertising practices of banks and of savings and loan associations.
5. Under the Truth in Lending Law, the Federal Reserve Board regulates installment credit ads by banks.
6. The Treasury Department's alcohol bureau enforces a rigid advertising code on the advertising of alcoholic beverages that precludes many of the advertising techniques used by other products. These regulations specifically ban any attempt to impute therapeutic benefits to alcoholic beverages. They also ban any brand names that might imply that a product was produced in another country. For example, American manufacturers of vodka may not name their products *St. Petersburg Vodka* or *Leningrad Vodka*. To avoid such problems, American vodka producers have been content to use Russian-sounding names with labels adorned with what may look like the imperial crest of the czars.
7. The Civil Aeronautics Board monitors the advertising of airlines and travel agents.

Advertising Polices Itself

The degree of restraint and the quality of information in most advertising today reflects the integrity of advertisers themselves as much as the requirements of law. For the most part, the advertising industry polices itself. Advertising agencies and trade associations circulate standards set for advertising copy and appeals in order to alert their employees and members to bad advertising practices. In this way, much poor advertising is rejected or rewritten long before it might have been seen by the public at large. The Direct Mail/Marketing Association, for example, offers the following advice to advertising media to help them avoid inadvertently contributing to misleading or fraudulent mail-order advertising:

> If the offer is vague, do not approve it. If you have read the copy through twice and you still do not know what you are getting, ask the advertiser for clarification of the copy. Do not accept an offer unless it is clearly spelled out.
>
> Make yourself the surrogate viewer or reader or listener. Are the copy and/or pictures outlandish? Are the claims so strong as to be unbelievable? Be particularly wary of ads that claim to cure physical ills such as arthritis, psoriasis, or gout.[1]

As we have seen, the advertising industry began to formulate self-regulatory policy as early as 1911 by urging the adoption of the *Printer's Ink* model statute. Like the marketplace itself, self-regulation of advertising tends to be segmented, with different associations and agencies working to eliminate abuses in certain product categories or in certain media. With the creation of the **National Advertising Review Board (NARB)** in 1971, however, the entire advertising industry pledged to police deception and bad taste in advertising wherever it occurs. The NARB responds to complaints by the public and does its own monitoring as well.

The NARB consists of 50 members: 40 advertising professionals and 10 members of the public. Complaints about national advertising, whether from consumers, competitors, or from local Better Business Bureaus, are first referred to the **National Advertising Division (NAD)** of the Council of Better Business Bureaus. A staff of advertising professionals at NAD investigates the complaints and determines whether the offending advertising should be modified or discontinued. If the advertiser will not comply with the NAD's request to cease or modify advertising that is considered misleading or offensive, the matter is turned over to the NARB for review by a panel consisting of five members who act as judges in the case. This panel may then either find the advertising not misleading and dismiss the case, or it may accept the NAD recommendation that the advertising be discontinued or modified. If the advertiser refuses to comply with an NARB request to discontinue its advertising, the NARB may then turn the matter over to the appropriate government agency for further action.

The NARB–NAD procedure, which generally expedites complaint actions, alleviates the workload of the FTC, while allowing advertisers to avoid the adverse publicity that usually comes from FTC action.

---

[1] *1979 Fact Book* (New York: The Direct Mail/Marketing Association, Inc.), pp. 143–145.

In 1984, the NAD heard 105 cases. Of those challenges, 31 percent resulted from NAD's monitoring, 45 percent were generated by competitors' complaints, local Better Business Bureaus contributed another 10 percent, and 9 percent resulted from direct consumer complaints to NAD. Food and beverage advertising remains the most controversial ad arena, accounting for about 25 percent of the total complaints. For example, in December 1984, NAD maintained that the campaign for Panhandl'rs, a new scouring pad, was too specific in its claims. The product ads headlined "S.O.S. and Brillo you're all washed up." The ads, print and television, went on to claim that "New *steel-less* wool Panhandl'rs with super grease-cutting detergent clean and shine like steel wool, but last five times longer. Without rusting, splintering, or scratching!" After examining data provided by the company, NAD agreed that claims for cleaning and shining performance held up under scrutiny. However, NAD requested information to support the statement that Panhandl'rs does not scratch surfaces. In response, the firm indicated that the claim had been withdrawn from further use.

PROFILE

Fallon McElligott Rice

In 1982, the fledgling Minneapolis agency, Fallon McElligott Rice, walked away with three Andy awards at the New York Advertising Club Show — the only non-New York agency to do that well.

In that same year, the agency won five Clio awards plus medals for other shows. There is no other agency outside of New York that has won such spectacular peer recognition. The creative force behind all the great advertising is Tom McElligott. As the son of a minister, he has nothing in common with the stereotypical huckster of the advertising business. Now 41, vice president and creative director of the agency, McElligott is a graduate of the University of Minnesota. He began his advertising career in 1970 as a copy chief for Dayton's Department store in Minneapolis. After two years, he joined the Knox Reeves agency as copy chief. In 1974, McElligott moved to Bozell & Jacobs, where he worked for eight years as a senior vice president/creative director. In late 1981, McElligott, Patrick Fallon and Nancy Rice started their own agency — Fallon McElligott Rice.

Their billings have climbed to over $30 million and among their clients are such major accounts as U.S. West, ITT Life Insurance, Control Data Corporation and AMF. They have created the ads for the American Association of Advertising Agencies.

While most agencies go after awards as a by-product of their campaign planning, FMR considered award-winning a part of their business plan. Their plan called for them to be the most creative agency in the region in the first year and to establish a national reputation in the second. They've done just that. A cynic might suggest that ads created to win awards may not be good for selling the client's product. They point out that ITT Life experienced a 200 percent increase in sales and added over 4,000 new agents. Armour Gold'n Plump Poultry gained 23 percentage points in market share. The agency's credo: "We believe there is no such thing as a 'me-too' product, only 'me-too' advertising." They were named by *Advertising Age* as Agency of the Year for 1983.

CASE HISTORY

American Association of Advertising Agencies

Research indicated that a majority of the American people don't like advertising. In 1983, the AAAA decided to initiate a campaign to improve the image of advertising. Nothing could be done about ads that were in bad taste, but they could and did provide information to dispel the misconceptions about the *purpose* of advertising. Ads were created by Fallon McElligott Rice of Minneapolis, Minnesota. Each ad was specifically designed to reply to consumers questions. The ads had a no-nonsense approach planned to avoid the slick Madison Avenue

WITHOUT ADVERTISING EVEN THE BEST IDEAS TAKE AGES TO CATCH ON.

Every now and then, a new product becomes popular by word of mouth alone. But that process usually takes many months. Sometimes years. By then, the company that makes the new product may be in serious trouble — if they're around at all.

Advertising is the surest way to get an idea to the public. By advertising a new product or service, more people are able to try it more quickly than if it were allowed to "catch on" by itself.

Good ideas become popular right away and bad ideas...well, who needs a square wheel, anyway?

ADVERTISING.
ANOTHER WORD FOR FREEDOM OF CHOICE.
American Association of Advertising Agencies

image held by many consumers about advertising and advertisers.

There was no media schedule. The ads were run without charge by newspapers and magazines. Because they were in print (rather than on radio or television) the ads could be read, re-read, clipped, and saved. Magazines that have run the ads or promised to run the ads include business publications, farm publications, and such important consumer magazines as *Good Housekeeping, Glamour, Money, Sports Illustrated, Time,* and *U.S. News & World Report.*

LIE #1: ADVERTISING MAKES YOU BUY THINGS YOU DON'T WANT.

Advertising is often accused of inducing people to buy things against their will.

But when was the last time you returned home from the local shopping mall with a bag full of things you had absolutely no use for? The truth is, nothing short of a pointed gun can get *anybody* to spend money on something he or she doesn't want.

No matter how effective an ad is, you and millions of other American consumers make your own decisions. If you don't believe it, ask someone who knows firsthand about the limits of advertising. Like your local Edsel dealer.

LIE #2: ADVERTISING MAKES THINGS COST MORE.
Since advertising costs money, it's natural to assume it costs *you* money. But the truth is that advertising often brings prices down.

Consider the electronic calculator, for example. In the late 1960's, advertising created a mass market for calculators. That meant more of them needed to be produced, which brought the price of producing each calculator down. Competition spurred by advertising brought the price down still further.

As a result, the same product that used to cost hundreds of dollars now costs as little as five dollars.

LIE #3: ADVERTISING HELPS BAD PRODUCTS SELL.

Some people worry that good advertising sometimes covers up for bad products.

But nothing can make you like a bad product. So, while advertising can help convince you to try something once, it can't make you buy it twice. If you don't like what you've bought, you won't buy it again. And if enough people feel the same way, the product dies on the shelf.

In other words, the only thing advertising can do for a bad product is help you find out it's a bad product. And you take it from there.

LIE #4: ADVERTISING IS A WASTE OF MONEY.
Some people wonder why we don't just put all the money spent on advertising directly into our national economy.

The answer is, we already do.

Advertising helps products sell, which holds down prices, which helps sales even more. It creates jobs. It informs you about all the products available and helps you compare them. And it stimulates the competition that produces new and better products at reasonable prices.

If all that doesn't convince you that advertising is important to our economy, you might as well stop reading.

Because on top of everything else, advertising has paid for a large part of the newspaper you're now holding.

And that's the truth.

ADVERTISING.
ANOTHER WORD FOR FREEDOM OF CHOICE.
American Association of Advertising Agencies

Advertisers are also very careful and responsive to any touch of scandal regarding their advertising or the celebrities they frequently use. Within hours of hearing the news of Vanessa Williams' appearance in *Penthouse,* American Greetings started withdrawing its ads for an upcoming series. In 1973, Procter & Gamble quickly changed the illustration when the model shown in its Ivory Snow ads turned out to be Marilyn Chambers, who had appeared in a porno movie.

A few years ago people from the American Cancer Society met with reporters from major newspapers and asked: How could colon cancer, an unsavory and usually taboo topic, get more coverage in the press?

Not easy, said the reporters. Only if it happened to a well-known person. As might be expected, when President Reagan's colon cancer was announced in July 1985, public awareness became high. For any company with an anticancer product—from bran cereal to home tests for hidden rectal bleeding—it was a good time to advertise. However, most advertisers were reluctant to take advantage of someone's misfortune by trying to sell a product.

Policing by the Media

While the NARB has been assuming a leadership role, broadcasting stations, newspapers, and magazines impose their own standards on top of the general ones. Self-regulation includes many problems of taste that are hard to define and for which legislation cannot be provided. These problem areas include, for instance: the portrayal of racial, sexual, or ethnic stereotypes in ads; the endorsement of certain products by athletes or other public figures; and the promotion of good ecological and safety habits. The demonstration of good ecological habits would include showing the proper disposal of empty containers, wrappers, bottles, jars, and packages (closed or capped). Homemakers are required to be shown neatly dressed in attire appropriate to that activity. No one is supposed to be seen drinking beer or soda from the bottle. Athletes are not supposed to drink alcohol.

Advertising Unmentionables

Advertising requires a flow of information on consumer needs and the availability and benefits of products and services. The existence of unmentionability means that one of the marketer's most effective techniques is unusable. What are unmentionables? Unmentionables are products or services that for reasons of delicacy, decency, or morality tend to elicit anger or outrage when openly presented. Some products, though purchased by large numbers of consumers, have evoked enough negative response to cause their advertising to be banned by some media. Cigarettes and hard liquor on television are the two most obvious examples. Another group of products are generally acceptable to society, but the advertiser is severely limited in discussion or presentation. The users themselves have raised objections prompted by embarrassment or distaste. Unmentionables of this kind include a range of personal hygiene products from adult diapers, contraceptives, hemorrhoidal medications, pregnancy tests, to sanitary napkins. For products of this kind, the restrictions have come primarily from television stations, because of the nonselective nature of the audience, which includes men, women, and children of all ages. Of course, time tends to erode objections and we now see television commercials for baby diapers, underarm deodorants, and sanitary napkins. An interesting example was the testing for tampons of the use of the colloquialism "period" on television in March 1985. ABC accepted the commercial as did NBC. They considered the copy to be tasteful, low-key, and informative. CBS believed "period" was too slangy, but would have accepted "menstrual cycle" as a substitute. There was no adverse reaction from women. The status of another "unmentionable"—contraceptives—is different, because it is so imbued with religious overtones that it has to contend with a political problem. There is little likelihood that such advertising will ever be permitted on television.

Summary

No one will ever claim that advertising is above criticism. To be sure, some advertising is in questionable taste. On balance, however, advertising's social and economic contributions far outweigh its lapses. Most serious criticism of advertising centers on three claims: advertising increases the cost of products; advertising induces people to buy products they don't need; and advertising fosters monopolies.

To the first point, advertisers can reply that they in fact help to reduce manufacturing costs by making possible the large markets which permit the use of large-scale product facilities and techniques. Compared to other methods of promotion, such as personal selling, advertising actually reduces distribution costs and, therefore, the price of goods.

To the second point—the claim that advertising makes people buy products they don't need—advertisers can point to thousands of examples of high-quality, useful products that no amount of advertising was able to convince people to buy. Every year, in fact, many highly advertised products disappear from the marketplace because consumers simply do not want them.

Critics of advertising also claim that advertising fosters monopolistic business practices by inflating the cost of promoting products nationwide to levels beyond the means of most small companies, thus reducing price competition. Again, advertisers can point out that although the cost of launching a national advertising campaign is high, such campaigns are more cost effective than any other form of promotion now available. Advertising has also made possible the growth of mass-merchandising stores, which do their part in promoting price competition. Since consumers can make their buying decisions based on product information that they have obtained from advertising, these stores can reduce their costs by employing fewer salespeople.

Historically, advertising has been regulated by three sectors of society: government; the advertising industry itself; and the media. The federal government regulates advertising primarily through the offices of the Federal Trade Commission. Since 1971, the advertising industry has regulated itself through the National Advertising Review Board, while the various media have regulated the advertising that they carry by instituting media associations and individual advertising copy-review systems.

Questions for Discussion

1. From the point of view of the seller, advertising has two functions—to persuade and to inform. What is the distinction? Which is more important?
2. What would be the economic effect of banning all advertising?
3. What would the social effects be?

4. What is the difference between puffery and misleading advertising?
5. In what ways does advertising affect American tastes and culture?
6. What are the government agencies that watch over and regulate advertising?
7. Do you believe children should be permitted to view television commercials? Why or why not?
8. Do you believe that advertising for certain products should be banned? Why?
9. Which of the regulatory agencies should have the most influence over advertising? Why?

Sources and Suggestions for Further Reading

Adams, G. "New Mail Order Law Tightens the Screws on Deceptive Advertising." *Marketing News,* October 26, 1984.

Alwitt, Linda F., and Mitchell, Andrew A., eds. *Psychological Processes and Advertising Effects.* Hillsdale, New Jersey: Laurence Erlbaum Associates, 1985.

Bernstein, Sid. "The Miracle of Advertising." *Advertising Age,* June 25, 1984.

DeMott, J. S. "Pitchmen on the Potomac." *Time,* March 7, 1983.

Foltz, Kim. "Wizards of Marketing." *Newsweek,* July 22, 1985.

Freeman, Larry. "Pay Heed to Active Older Folks: Census." *Advertising Age,* September 24, 1984.

Lewis, Herschell Gordon. "Why Don't You Say What You Mean?" *Direct Marketing,* May 1986.

Mitchell, Arnold. *The Nine American Lifestyles.* New York: Macmillan, 1983.

Posch, R. J., Jr. "Boundaries of Risk: Advertiser and Agency Responsibility." *Direct Marketing,* July 1984.

Sharkey, Betsy. "The Father of VALS Looks Ahead." *ADWEEK,* December 1984.

22 ADVERTISING IN THE FUTURE

Working Vocabulary _____

  microfiche   **hotelvision**

For the society of the future will offer not a restricted standardized flow of goods, but the greatest variety of unstandardized goods and services any society has ever seen. We are moving not toward a further extension of material standardization, but toward its dialectical negation.

Alvin Toffler
Future Shock

Advertisers are concerned with the future: with changing consumer tastes and with shifting population groups. They spend large amounts of time and money in the analysis of current trends, trying to predict how consumers will behave a month, a year, or ten years from the present. But where does the future of advertising itself lie? There appear to be two segments of today's advertising industry that offer the greatest promise of future growth: advertising to markets overseas, and the advertising of services.

International Advertising

Although exports account for less than 10 percent of America's gross national product, overseas earnings make very important contributions to the profits of many American firms. Coca-Cola earns 55 percent of its profits abroad, for example, while Gillette earns 51 percent and Revlon 36 percent — to name only a few.

The world market often offers growth opportunities to American companies whose products have reached the mature stage of their life cycle or whose new products face strongly entrenched competition in the domestic market. Thus, in recent years the volume of overseas advertising by American companies has been increasing. This fact is dramatically illustrated by the fact that Young & Rubicam, the largest advertising agency in the United States, had total billings of $3.575 billion in 1985, of which 36.4 percent ($1.303 billion) were from non-U.S. billings. The agency network covers 23 countries and 32 agencies worldwide.

The Problems of Advertising Overseas

At one time, agency facilities were a problem, but during the past decade giant multinational agencies have come into being. Today, every major agency in the United States has overseas branch offices or affiliates that are able to serve the advertising needs of the international marketer. Many foreign-based agencies, too — such as Daiko Advertising, Eurocom, Publicis Conseil, and one of the largest advertising agencies in the world, Dentsu Inc. — offer advertisers international facilities.

American companies have discovered, however, sometimes to their great regret, that international advertising differs significantly from domestic advertising. Although consumers in foreign markets may purchase many products for the same reasons that Americans buy them, advertisers cannot merely translate their domestic advertising into the language of another country. Many factors can prevent a successful American advertising campaign from enjoying an equivalent success in a foreign market.

The major problem areas of international advertising now include:

1. differing market structures between countries
2. cultural differences
3. variations in the media available to advertisers

The Market Structure   Each country has a different market structure. In the advanced industrialized nations of the world, these differences may not be extreme, but in less developed nations, channels of distribution may be highly fragmented or even nonexistent in some areas of a country. In general, small stores and businesses abound overseas, each serving a limited geographic area. In the United States, for example, the supermarket dominates the distribution of food products, while in France supermarkets are the channel for little more than 25 percent of all retail food volume.

Cultural Differences   Family structure, customs, and religious beliefs vary in ways that inevitably affect a company's advertising program. Advertisers in Japan, for example, find that they cannot make direct comparisons between products. Japanese consumers feel that even subtle comparisons run counter to their country's tradition of respect. Therefore, many advertisements in Japan use a light approach to deliver their messages. Cultural traditions and language differences may affect an advertiser's use of symbols and brand names. Although many symbols carry similar connotations throughout the world, advertisers should commission market studies to determine how their products' symbols will be perceived in each country. In many cases, it may be necessary to adapt or change a brand name that does not translate well into another language.

Cultural traditions and religious beliefs can also strongly influence foreign consumers' attitudes toward an entire product class. As Dr. Ernest Dichter has pointed out:

> In Puritanical cultures it is customary to think of cleanliness as being next to godliness. The body and its functions are covered up as much as possible.
>
> But, in Catholic and Latin countries, to fool too much with one's body, to overindulge in bathing or toiletries, has the opposite meaning. It is *that* type of behavior which is considered immoral and improper.[1]

The Range of Media Available   In the United States, the requirements of the marketing plan, the product, the cost, and other criteria all will influence media needs. In other countries, however, media planning is further complicated by the fact that the full range of media available in the United States either may not be available in a particular area of the world or may exist only in a greatly modified form.

Broadcast.   Commercial television is not available in some foreign countries. Television networks may be state-controlled and not available for use by advertisers. Even in those countries that do have commercial television, its programming may be extremely different from its counterpart in the United States. In some countries, for example, commercials are not run at intervals

---

[1] Ernest Dichter, "The World Customer," *Harvard Business Review* (July–August 1962), pp. 112–122.

within individual television programs, but are shown as a block at the beginning or end of each program. The single television network in Swaziland, in southern Africa, broadcasts only from 6:00 to 10:30 PM each day. In Japan, 70 percent of all television commercials are only 15 seconds long, making it impossible for advertisers to run heavy, fact-oriented messages. Instead, most Japanese television commercials rely either on a humorous approach or on an image strategy. For instance, a typical commercial for Kleenex tissues in Japan shows a cherubic child pulling tissues from a box in slow motion and sending them airborne. The image conveyed to viewers is one of a delicate bird floating in a light breeze — suggesting the qualities of the product that Kleenex wants to promote.

This is a storyboard for a tea commercial that was broadcast on British television. Would this kind of whimsical commercial appeal to American audiences? In America, tea is sold to compete with coffee as a "pick-me-up" beverage. Since most Englishmen prefer tea to coffee, it is not necessary to convince them to switch beverages; Ty-Phoo need only remind the audience of its brand name.

Humor is an ingredient common to the television commercials of many countries. Here are a few examples:

1. A Frenchman, interrupted during the delivery of a commercial for fly spray when a fly lands on the demonstration table, smashes the fly with the butt of the spray can, saying, "It's not expensive and it works."
2. An Australian commercial for toilet paper opens with a wide angle view of a gingerbreadlike outhouse. The announcer informs the viewers that this particular toilet paper has played a trusted "roll" in Australian history.

In Western Europe, international commercial radio is important. Because radio stations there are allowed to have a transmitting power of up to 275,000 watts (the U.S. limit is 50,000 watts), at least four radio stations in Europe reach audiences in several different nations. The leading station is Radio Luxembourg, which broadcasts in five languages. It counts over 40 million listeners throughout Western Europe—from England to southern France and into East and West Germany, Austria, and Switzerland. In Latin America, commercial radio is especially valuable in reaching illiterate audiences in remote areas.

Print. As is true in the United States, magazines in other countries provide advertisers with varying degrees of selectivity. In India, more than half of that country's total advertising volume is channeled through the print media; in Europe print is the dominant medium, with as much as 75 percent of total volume going into magazines. French advertisers rely heavily on two-page spreads with relatively little copy but striking illustrations. (Fashion advertisements in France are illustrated by famous photographers who sign their ads.) In Germany, the emphasis is 180 degrees in the opposite direction—advertisements contain loads of copy but fewer illustrations.

In addition to using local publications, international advertisers can use such American-based magazines as *Reader's Digest* and *Time,* both of which provide international editions. Newspapers are a universal medium and, like one or two American papers, some European newspapers have nationwide, rather than merely local, circulations. Nevertheless, in many other countries around the world, newspapers reach a much smaller proportion of the total population than they do in the United States. This circumstance is particularly prevalent in countries where literacy and income levels are low.

While the lack of a full range of media in many countries frequently limits the amount of advertising a firm can do, in countries where wages are lower than they are in the United States, marketers can compensate by hiring much larger sales forces.

The Need for Continuity

We have pointed out that a specific campaign in one country will survive the move to another only if the advertisers are careful to adapt it to the characteristics of the available media and of the new target market. But advertisers have also found that it is important to establish a strong worldwide product identity. As far as possible, advertisers should have the same brand names and the same packages available in all countries, as well as a similar look to all their ads. The advantages of establishing a strong international product identity have been proven by the experiences of the European Economic Community. Many migrant laborers—Turks, Greeks, Italians, Spaniards, and North Africans—have moved to Germany, France, and other countries of northern Europe where jobs are plentiful and the pay better than in their native countries. Eventually, most of these migrant workers return to their homelands, bringing back with them new consumer habits. Smart advertisers make it possible for such people to find their newly discovered brands in the retail stores of their native lands. In addition, the many millions of tourists visiting foreign countries are a market segment that makes the necessity for brand-name and packaging continuity all the more important.

Young people are another important market segment that has increased the need for advertising continuity. Throughout the world, young people tend

The Sony Walkman apparently sells in Japan without the need to change the name into Japanese symbols. It is interesting to note that the control functions on the face of the product itself are in English. It must be difficult to translate "the one and only" into other languages.

شاحنات جنرال موتورز
اماكن ممتعة للعمل تبعث على البهجة والسرور

قد يصعب التصديق بأن هذا التصميم الداخلي الانيق هو
لشاحنة مصممة للاعمال الثقيلة. ولكن لا عجب في ذلك،
فهذه الشاحنة، وبالتحديد شاحنة سابربن، هي من صنع
جنرال موتورز. ومعروف عالميا ان جنرال موتورز
التزمت دوما بانتاج شاحنات مريحة وذات اداء رفيع.
وباستخدام احدث اساليب التكنولوجيا المتوفرة لانتاجها فان
شاحنات جنرال موتورز تقوم بذلك خير قيام.

بالاضافة الى السعة التامة، فان التجهيزات المتوفرة مثل
جهاز تكييف الهواء، وجهاز راديو الستيريو، والمعدات
الاختبارية كهربائيا او هيدروليكيا جميعها تضفي
جوا من السعادة والسرور الى مكان العمل. تتسع شاحنات

اشعر بالفرق
الذي تقدمه
جنرال موتورز

جنرال موتورز الى الاحمال الكبيرة، ولها جدران مزدوجة
السماكة في الاماكن الهامة. كما ويتوفر في كثير من طرزها
محركات قوية بثمان اسطوانات على شكل ٧ مقرونة باجهزة
للدفع بالعجلتين او بالاربع عجلات.

تشمل شاحنات جنرال موتورز شاحنات جي. ام. سي.
وشاحنات شيفروليه. يدعم كلاهما شبكة متكاملة من الوكلاء
الذين يستخدمون الصيانة والقطع الاصلية من جنرال
موتورز لكي تحافظ انت على ذلك الشعور العظيم الناتج
عن اقتناء منتجات جنرال موتورز.

شاحنات جنرال موتورز الجديدة. لن تجدوا مكانا او طريقة
للعمل افضل منها.

CHEVROLET   PONTIAC   OLDSMOBILE   BUICK   CADILLAC   OPEL   HOLDEN   GMC TRUCK   BEDFORD

COLOR PLATE 67

COLOR PLATE 67 With work gloves and a hard hat, the designer of this ad identifies the vehicle as a truck. The caption (in Arabic) confirms it with a benefit: *Truck from General Motors. Very nice place to work.* The background seen through the window? A desert of course.

(Man sieht es auf dem Foto nicht.
Aber er verbraucht nur 10.9 l Normalbenzin auf 100 km.)

Der Buick Skylark Limited gehört zu einer völlig neuen Automobilgeneration: den Euro-Amerikanern von GM.
Besondere Kennzeichen: querliegender 2.8 l V6-Motor mit 85 kW (115 PS), extrem laufruhig und doch voller Temperament. Erstaunlich: der geringe Normalbenzinverbrauch von nur 10.9 l auf 100 km*. Frontantrieb, Servolenkung, Servobremssystem, Automatic-Getriebe. Gewohnt amerikanisch: die komplette und luxuriöse Ausstattung, vom Radio bis zum elektrisch verstellbaren Sitz. Gewohnt europäisch: das kompakte Außenmaß bei großzügig bemessenem Innenraum. Erstaunlich der Preis: 19 980.– DM (unverbindliche Preisempfehlung inklusive 13% MwSt., zuzüglich Fracht ab Bremerhaven).
*Verbrauch Liter/100 km, nach DIN 700 30, Teil I Neufassung: im Stadtverkehr: 13.8; bei 120 km/h: 10.87; bei 90 km/h: 8.74.

Buick, Chevrolet, Oldsmobile, Pontiac. Die Euro-Amerikaner von GM.

COLOR PLATE 68 Can General Motors sell American cars in Europe? Of course. In Germany, an American car offers much the same status that a Mercedes or a BMW offers in this country. This ad reinforces the high-status image of the Buick Skylark—modest type for the headline; small, compact body copy; and a very simple illustration. All these elements suggest prestige.

$1100. Qantas bribes vacationers with Tahiti, New Zealand and Australia.

Thumbs down on Qantas. I know why Qantas offers you the lush tropics of Gauguin. The majestic fjords of New Zealand. The underwater extravaganza of the Great Barrier Reef.

This great circle around the South Pacific is a ploy.

What Qantas really wants is to entice you to Australia. To Sydney. And to us–the maligned and abused koalas.

Qantas wants to crowd us out.

If you agree that giving vacationers all this for just $1100 is nothing short of cruelty to animals, unite with us.

Together we will stand firm against Qantas.

Koalas Against Qantas. (The Australian Airline.)

Round trip Circle 8 APEX fare from Los Angeles or San Francisco for travel between April 1 and August 31. Slightly lower from Honolulu. Ticketing, reservations and payment must be completed at least 21 days in advance. Some restrictions apply. Fares subject to change without notice.

For more information, see your travel agent or write Qantas, Dept. NH, P.O. Box 476, San Francisco, CA 94101.

COLOR PLATE 69

COLOR PLATE 69   What would suggest Australia at a glance? A kangaroo. A koala. A kangaroo is not cute. A koala is cute and looks even cuter with an aviator helmet and a white silk scarf. Thus, the "stopper" of a photo is combined with an obvious benefit in the headline and tongue-in-cheek copy to create a soft sell appropriate for the sophisticated traveler who will visit Australia and other exotic places down under.

BERMUDA
NOW

The Nix family on their third trip to Bermuda.

Yellow and red floats on a translucent blue-green sea. Bermuda. Now.

The putt, putt, putt of an unhurrying moped. The welcoming warmth of our luxury hotels and intimate guest houses. Lazy days and dance 'til dawn nights.

There is no island...no place...no experience quite like Bermuda.

Maybe that's why nobody comes to Bermuda just once.

Contact your Travel Agent, or for a free Bermuda brochure, write: Bermuda Department of Tourism, P.O. Box 7705, Woodside, NY 11377, or call 800-223-6106 (NY: 800-223-6107).

Name_____
Address_____
City_____State_____Zip_____

COLOR PLATE 70 Bermuda's Department of Tourism clearly incorporates the target market into the scenery. If any picture is worth a thousand words, this one surely is. Look at the clean, pink sand, the transparent water, charming pastel bungalow, all enjoyed by an American family. The most important copy line tells us that this family is there for the third visit.

COLOR PLATE 72 Frangelico has carried the psychic image of an imported liqueur to a new height. The ad serves two purposes. When you serve this liqueur to your guests you appear as a sophisticated person of obvious good taste. When Frangelico is offered to you, your recognition of it identifies you as a smart, sophisticated person who knows the good life. That's a tasty background, too.

Close your eyes.

Imagine yourself someplace away.

Far away.

Are you there yet?

Good.

Now you're ready for
the delicate Italian liqueur
made from the hazelnut.

Now you're ready for

Our formula has **not** changed.

In some states, the business "climate" fluctuates as wildly as the political weather. Red tape magically turns into red carpet. One year, high taxes break businessmen's backs; the next year the survivors are offered tax breaks. Politicians who once turned cold shoulders now blow hot air. Are you suspicious? You should be. Newfound pro-business attitudes have a history of not lasting past the next election. In South Dakota, Republicans and Democrats have come and gone, but our state government has always been a friend to business. Our pro-business attitude is here today—and here tomorrow. In fact, the prestigious study of business climates by Alexander Grant and Company of Chicago ranks South Dakota first in America— almost twenty percentage points ahead of the second-best state. So we are not about to change what works. If your state's business climate is leaving a bad taste in your mouth, try South Dakota's traditional formula for success. South Dakota tastes great—and it's more filling for your bank account.

South Dakota

John Simpson, Office of the Governor, State Capitol, Pierre, South Dakota 57501, 1(800)843-8000

COLOR PLATE 73

COLOR PLATE 73 This ad for South Dakota appeared in an issue of *Crain's Chicago Business*, a regional business publication. It was prepared under the direction of the Department of State Development. The timely copy capitalized on the interest in the soft drink industry at the time. The state is talking about its stable, pro-business climate at a time when change is the order of the day. The object, of course, is to have business organizations establish facilities in South Dakota.

to dress alike, eat similar foods, and enjoy similar diversions: dancing, music, books, and films. The youth market has spurred the spread of fast-food outlets all over Europe and Asia. There are about 100 McDonald's hamburger restaurants in Japan alone.

The Advertising Climate in Other Lands

Following the pattern of the United States and Canada, the consumer movement in Europe has been gaining momentum. It has, however, made little headway in Latin America and Africa, where countries are preoccupied with laying the foundations for modern, technologically advanced societies. Paralleling consumer activities, government agencies have stepped in to regulate advertising practices in many countries. Taxes on advertising have already

Kodak film is
over, using m
advertising ap
country — bec
photographs.
is as beautiful
detail." No m
the Kodak nar
This ad was pi
Lintas, Hambu
that is partially
SSCB.

Ningún desayuno es nutritivo hasta que alguien lo come.

Para que cada mañana su familia empiece bien el día, el desayuno tiene que ser lo más atractivo posible. Y ahí es cuando los Corn Flakes de Kellogg's caen de maravilla. Se sirven con leche y azúcar. Acompañados con jugo o fruta, pan y mermelada . . . proporcionan un delicioso desayuno para su familia.

Corn Flakes de Kellogg's. Un cereal sabroso que puede disfrutarse a cualquier hora del día.

Kellogg's®

Lo mejor para usted cada mañana.

How are Kellogg's ready-to-eat cereals sold in Latin America? In much the same way they are sold in the United States: by saying that cereal is part of a nutritious breakfast for the entire family. Notice the familiar Kellogg package and logo, and that the name of the product remains the same.

been passed in some countries and are under consideration in others. Government actions have also been taken against misleading advertising in the marketing of pharmaceuticals. Canada has published "Truth in Advertising" guidelines which are used as models by other countries.

The major concern of most governments is cigarette advertising; it has been banned in many countries and in the coming years will be banned in still more. Canada, England, Ireland, Italy, Denmark, Norway, Sweden, Finland, and Switzerland have already banned cigarette advertising from all or some media. Another category of promotion that is receiving government attention in many countries is advertising directed to children.

Governments do not ignore the benefits of advertising, however; many governments use the advertising process to promote ideas and products deemed important to public health and safety. In Sweden and England, the transition from left to right side of the road driving was promoted through advertising. In

France, the promotion of milk consumption and the conservation of energy were the subjects of concerted ad campaigns.

The Challenge

The challenge of world markets is certainly a provocative one for American companies. For one thing, American goods must often compete against foreign goods of a very high quality. The United States has not had a monopoly on product development. In the area of consumer products, for example, Europeans were first with a wide range of innovations — stainless-blades, enzyme detergents, cordless electric shavers, instant coffee, yogurt with fresh fruit, dried soups, soft margarine, throwaway ballpoint pens, and throwaway cigarette lighters. With the exception of automatic transmissions, most automotive innovations have come from Europe. (See color plates 67 and 68 for ads selling American cars in foreign markets.)

The weakening of the dollar, while making American goods less expensive in foreign markets, has made foreign companies more dependent than ever on their home markets because the value of the goods that they sell to the United States has declined. German and Japanese companies have been particularly hard hit by the devaluation of the dollar, and they have been scouring the world for new marketing opportunities. In many markets, then, American firms will face tough competition from large, foreign multinationals.

In general, for American companies to win a share of overseas markets, they must:

1. Adapt the product to the market.
2. Know the impact of cultural, social, and religious differences in each market.
3. Expand into new markets one at a time, rather than try to expand into several new markets at once.
4. Build a managerial staff composed of talented men and women native to each country.
5. Recognize that different levels of literacy among countries, as well as within a country, will affect media selection.
6. Develop a strong product identity through branding, packaging, and advertising, recognizing, however, that these promotional elements may have to be adapted to suit each individual country.
7. Recognize the differences between one nation's distribution practices and another's.
8. Recognize the differences between the range and impact of one nation's media and another's.

The Service Economy

One of the most dramatic changes in our economy in recent decades has been the share of income spent for services. In 1984 Americans spent approximately 48 percent of their incomes for products that could not be touched, smelled, or tasted — and in some instances could not even be seen or heard. About half of the labor force works in service industries, and more than one-third of all commercial enterprises are service establishments.[2]

---

[2] Mentzer & Schwartz, *Marketing Today. 4th ed.* (San Diego: Harcourt Brace Jovanovich, 1985), p. 314.

The long period of prosperity that the United States has enjoyed since the end of the Second World War has meant increased disposable income, increased leisure time, and a general rise in the standard of living for most American consumers. As the desire for goods becomes fulfilled and as many products lose their images as status symbols, consumers turn to services. Witness the growth in education, travel, and sporting events and such sporting activities as tennis and skiing.

The rate of growth has not been uniform, however. As personal disposable income has increased and as life-styles have changed, the demand for some services has grown faster than for others. There are services now that will walk your dog, drive your car to Florida or California, work out your loan payments, find you a job (or a husband or wife), rent you a garden tractor, clean your swimming pool, mow your lawn, and care for your house plants.

The attributes of services are entirely different from those of products — services are intangible, personal, unstandardized, and perishable. Consumers in the target market cannot see, hear, smell, taste, or touch a service *before* they buy it. This presents unique problems to the marketers of services.

A brief examination of some of the services available will provide clues to the nature of the advertising they require:

> *Housing* — including hotels and motels
> *Household services* — utilities, repairs, cleaning, landscaping
> *Recreation* — entertainment and amusements, sporting events, the rental and repair of sports equipment
> *Travel* — (See color plates 69 and 70.)
> Personal care — laundry, dry cleaning, beauty care
> *Medical/health care* — medical, dental, hospitalization, nursing
> *Education*
> *Business services* — legal, accounting, management consulting, and marketing consulting
> *Insurance and financial* — investment counseling, credit and loan services, property and personal insurance
> *Transportation* — airlines, bus companies, and automobile rental and repair companies
> *Communication* — telephone and specialized communication services (See color plate 71.)

Characteristics of Services

Consider the problems involved in advertising services.

Services Are Intangible   In most cases it is impossible for the target prospect to try the service before buying it. There are no product ingredients or packages to describe or illustrate. The thrust of the advertising effort must be the benefit or satisfaction the user will derive from the service.

Services Are Personal   For the most part, we cannot separate a service from the person who performs that service. The doctor's service is inseparable from the doctor. And the same is true of the barber, the dentist, and the manicurist. There is only one channel of distribution. What is the purpose of advertising if the number of customers is limited to what an individual can personally handle?

The boom in direct marketing continues. Each year, more and more companies have diversified into product-related marketing. In the face of increasing costs of media and sales effort, and with the development of sophisticated marketing analysis, direct marketing will continue to grow. The American Express catalog is targeted to more than 14 million American Express Card members in the United States. The company has had remarkable success in selling brand name quality merchandise that covers products for business as well as home and personal use. The array of merchandise includes furs, luggage, jewelry, home furnishings, and state-of-the-art electronic products.

Services Are Not Standardized   It is impossible to develop any uniformity among sellers of the same service; it is not even possible for a single seller to provide the same quality of service each time. The repair service performed by one mechanic is not always of comparable quality. The service at a hotel may vary with each visit. This week's concert given by a popular singer may be better (or worse) than last week's. Can we promise a benefit in advertising a service, if we are not sure we can deliver it?

Services Are Perishable   By *perishable* we mean that services cannot be stored or held in inventory. When a barber's chair is empty, it represents business that cannot be recovered. A ski resort without guests represents business that is lost forever. And this problem is exacerbated by widely fluctuating consumer demands. A haircutting salon may be overwhelmed with patrons on Friday and Saturday, but be empty on Monday and Tuesday. A movie theater that is empty Monday through Thursday may have to turn away customers on Friday and Saturday. Advertising can do much to help level demand; it can shift demand to slack periods or stimulate new demand for idle facilities. The telephone company, for example, has been using advertising for years to encourage people to make calls during off-peak hours and on weekends, when some telephone equipment is idle.

Hon, the mortgage payment's due. Did you deposit your check today?

Mom, I need new ballet slippers.

They need me.

When we got married, we said my income was for extras. We didn't want to be dependent on it when we had children. Well, we have a daughter now—and it's a *good* thing I went back to work when she went to school.

With the cost of day-to-day living, we couldn't possibly afford our house, let alone put money aside for her education on only one income. If anything happened to me, my family would have to make a lot of difficult adjustments—especially Jenny. That's why I have my *own* piece of the Rock—Prudential insurance—to help make sure they can live as comfortably as we do now. They need me.

The more they need you, the more you need Prudential.

Life Health Auto Home

Insurance is a service business, and, although the product is intangible, insurance companies must keep abreast of demographic changes just as the manufacturers of clothing, automobiles, and frozen foods must. In this ad, Prudential Insurance Company acknowledges the growing number of working women in the United States by suggesting insurance for mothers working outside the home.

Advertising Services

We can see the difficulties inherent in creating meaningful advertising programs for services. In order to overcome these difficulties, our advertising will have to perform three critical tasks:

1. Portray clearly the benefits to be obtained from the service.
2. Differentiate as far as possible our service(s) from those of competitors.
3. Build an image for the provider of the service as a friendly, efficient, and courteous company.

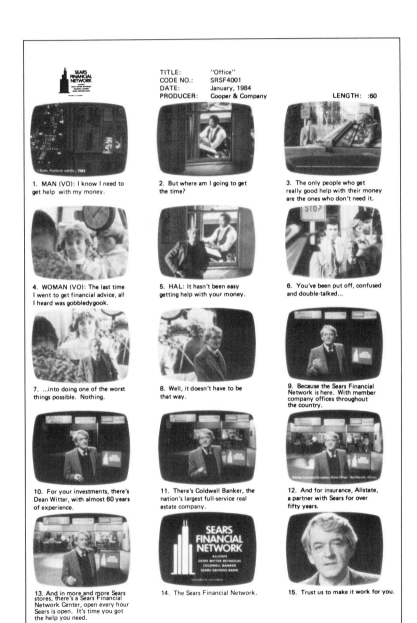

TITLE: "Office"
CODE NO.: SRSF4001
DATE: January, 1984
PRODUCER: Cooper & Company
LENGTH: :60

1. MAN (VO): I know I need to get help with my money.

2. But where am I going to get the time?

3. The only people who get really good help with their money are the ones who don't need it.

4. WOMAN (VO): The last time I went to get financial advice, all I heard was gobbledygook.

5. HAL: It hasn't been easy getting help with your money.

6. You've been put off, confused and double-talked...

7. ...into doing one of the worst things possible. Nothing.

8. Well, it doesn't have to be that way.

9. Because the Sears Financial Network is here. With member company offices throughout the country.

10. For your investments, there's Dean Witter, with almost 60 years of experience.

11. There's Coldwell Banker, the nation's largest full-service real estate company.

12. And for insurance, Allstate, a partner with Sears for over fifty years.

13. And in more and more Sears stores, there's a Sears Financial Network Center, open every hour Sears is open. It's time you got the help you need.

14. The Sears Financial Network.

15. Trust us to make it work for you.

The second year of the Sears Financial Network advertising campaign featured straight-talk from Hal Holbrook about how to get help with your money. The campaign was created to increase awareness of Sears Financial Network and its four member companies, and to increase awareness of the growing number of Sears Financial Network centers in selected Sears stores. The advertising appeared on network and spot television, as well as in consumer magazines throughout 1984.

Service firms have to segment their markets with more precision than do the advertisers of goods. They have to place greater emphasis on institutional advertising to develop their companies' "personalities," and they have to reconsider their advertising media. Some media do not provide an editorial climate suitable for the discussion of certain services. Since many services are local, the advertiser may be more concerned with newspapers or radio or spot television. Nor is the service organization as concerned with *reach* as is a company with a tangible product. They have to be more selective. They cannot afford to advertise in the hope that the necessary business will come to them at some future date. Services do not keep. Advertising can make abstract benefits concrete and appealing to consumers. The friendly image of a bank, for example, will tell consumers that it is receptive to inquiry for loans and that it avoids banker's jargon.

Advertising an intangible product, such as a banking service, is very difficult because there is nothing to show. In this 30-second commercial, the Foote, Cone & Belding agency uses a mnemonic device to represent the benefits of a financial product. The nest egg symbolizes the security and long-term growth of an Individual Retirement Account. As it gets larger in size, the customer in turn becomes more pleased with his investment decision. The techniques in this spot include rotoscoping to make the egg appear larger in each frame, and music in combination with sound effects to reinforce the announcer. Notice how the advertiser's logo is used as a backdrop for much of the commercial.

Advertising can raise the social and economic status of services and persuade customers that these services are, in fact, worth the money. A consumer will spend 50 cents for a cup of coffee and $9,000 for a new car, but may resent having to spend $40 to have a refrigerator repaired — even after the appliance has provided years of faithful service. With the help of advertising, service industries will expand and become more consumer-oriented. Advertising will then be able to do the job it does best — stimulate demand and motivate action.

Recently, restrictions against advertising by such professionals as dentists, doctors, and lawyers have been removed. These professionals may now advertise certain services and the fees they charge for these services. Because the market for the services of a particular doctor, lawyer, or dentist is a local one, advertising for such services appears predominantly in newspaper, transit, and radio media.

Exercise you can put your heart into
...your doctor wants you to keep up the good work

Today there are an estimated 10 million joggers, 15 million serious swimmers, 25 million regular cyclists and 29 million tennis players in the U. S. That's good.

A recent Gallup Poll found that the number of Americans who say they use some form of exercise *daily* has nearly doubled in the last sixteen years. From 24% to 47% today. That's even better. Because the evidence keeps piling up that regular physical activity may be of significant benefit in the prevention of coronary heart disease, America's #1 killer.

A case in point is the results from a recent study of San Francisco longshoremen. Those whose jobs required heavy physical activity had 46% fewer deaths due to coronary disease than longshoremen with less physically demanding jobs.

Now, just a word of caution from your doctor who is your partner in keeping you healthy. You are not a longshoreman, so don't overdo it. Your doctor can work out an exercise program with you, shaped to your capabilities and interests.

American Medical Association, 535 North Dearborn Street, Chicago, Illinois 60610.

Your Doctor's Your Partner
Help your doctor help you

Doctors, dentists, and lawyers are now permitted to advertise, and some of them do. Advertising by professionals may serve the public by encouraging people to seek reasonably priced medical, legal, or accounting services. This advertisement is sponsored by a national professional organization, the American Medical Association.

Government Advertises Services Too

Federal government advertising expenditures in 1984 amounted to $287.8 million—making the federal government the twenty-sixth largest advertiser in the country. We can expect government expenditures (both state and federal) for social goods, such as environmental protection, health services, public housing, and transportation, to continue to increase. We can also expect increased government advertising as government agencies will use advertising techniques to market the social goods that they produce. The government already uses advertising to recruit for the Army and Navy and to "sell" Amtrak and the Postal Service. Other governmental advertising programs include efforts to promote safe driving, to counter alcoholism and drug abuse, and to stop pollution. The United States Travel Services advertises abroad to lure Europeans to visit America. (See color plate 73 for a state advertisement.)

Changing Media

Advertising media will be affected by changes in consumer activities. We have already mentioned, for instance, that the increase in working women will mean that the audiences for daytime television programs will be smaller than in

States from coast to coast spend more than $60 million a year to advertise gambling. The biggest spender is New York state, which used its $12.3 million budget to promote its twice-a-week Lotto, daily numbers, and instant games. The major portion of the ad budget goes into television, with smaller amounts for radio and transit. The State Department of Revenue runs the Colorado lottery. The game is marketed under the slogan, "For a more beautiful Colorado." Thirty-five cents of each $1 ticket goes to a conservation trust fund for parks and recreation. The Illinois State Lottery spends $7 million a year to promote its PayDay game. It uses television, print, and outdoor with the major thrust being television.

Advertising Spending on Lotteries	
State	**1983 – 1984 Budget**
Arizona	$3,800,000
Colorado	3,800,000
Connecticut	2,500,000
Delaware	450,000
District of Columbia	2,000,000
Illinois	7,000,000
Maine	522,000
Maryland	3,200,000
Massachusetts	5,900,000
Michigan	6,500,000
New Hampshire	280,000
New Jersey	2,500,000
New York	12,300,000
Ohio	4,000,000
Pennsylvania	7,500,000
Vermont	182,000

Source: Reprinted with permission from the June 29, 1984, issue of *Advertising Age.* Copyright © 1984 by Crain Communications, Inc.

▲ Campbell's Soup offers a line of products that reflects its awareness of the special nutritional requirements of the growing numbers of older citizens. This four-color, one-third page appeared in *Modern Maturity*.

◄ The old carnival-coming-to-town has been replaced by the shopping mall event created by Shopping Center Network. There are 1,700 enclosed shopping malls, which want special events to attract more shoppers for their merchants. There are major national advertisers, who want an opportunity for the public to see, touch, taste, and smell their products. It is a feat that cannot be accomplished in a 15- or 30-second television commercial. Shopping Center Network can target the market the national client wants to reach. If the client wants affluence, the event is held in a mall that has a Lord & Taylor or a Neiman-Marcus. If they want to reach a blue-collar audience, they go for the malls with a J. C. Penney's. If they want an older audience, there are 26 markets where the average age is 57. There are Latin malls, black malls, and Yuppie malls.

There are two types of shows national advertisers can buy into — the average tour travels to 26 malls over eight months. Other than tie-ins, no local businesses are accepted. One type of show is the multi-client theme show in which 20 to 30 major companies band together, each with its own booth and displays, in a merchandising promotion that takes up most of an enclosed mall. Each advertiser pays from $1,000 to $1,500 a mall — a cost that includes everything except manning the exhibit. The other type of mall promotion is the single sponsor show where the event is built around one brand.

None of the shows competes with the traditional media. Mall events often generate newspaper, radio, and television editorial coverage of their own in the areas where exhibits are scheduled.

the past. But the media will be affected not only by demographic and social changes but by changes in technology.

It is difficult to believe that television became a *national* advertising medium little more than 30 years ago. And color television came to full flower only about 15 years ago. Consider the new developments in communications that are awaiting their cue. We already have video cassettes, microfilm, satellites, and facsimile reproduction. Satellite technology will permit what E. B. Weiss has called "narrowcasting."[3] The word *narrowcasting* refers to the manner in which radio is segmented into numerous groups of listeners, each with its favorite type of music and program format. Weiss recognized that, in a much more limited manner, television is also moving in that direction. Video cassettes, cable tv, and satellite broadcasts have already given the public many more program choices than were available only a few years ago.

Newspapers of the future may be available on television — perhaps featuring editions broadcast from abroad and transmitted to your home via satellite. The age of the international newspaper may usher in a wave of international advertising and offer consumers throughout the world access to a truly global market. Or, imagine a newspaper delivered to your home as a sheet of microfilm about six inches long and four inches wide (called a **microfiche**), containing as many as 465 pages of printed material. This microfiche could be popped into a home reader for enlargement or examined on the way to work in a battery-powered portable reader. Even catalogue and direct-mail pieces could be sent out to consumers as microfiche.

What will happen to television advertising in the years to come? Recently, cable television has become more and more popular and, if it continues its growth, more people will be watching commercial-free television in the future. Video cassettes are very popular. If a large market develops for rented video cassettes, then advertisers might place their commercials in these cassettes the way they now place ads in magazines. A soap-opera cassette might include commercials by food advertisers or by advertisers of household cleansers. A tennis cassette might include commercials for racquets, balls, warm-up suits, and resorts. The possibilities are almost endless. Most hotels and motels today offer **hotelvision,** that is, a closed-circuit television system that transmits movies and other special programs only to the rooms of the lodging's guests. Hotelvision may provide advertisers of the future with a new medium. Local retailers and services in particular may welcome the opportunity to advertise to travelers.

City and Regional Magazines

In 1970, Standard Rate and Data Service carried listings for 23 publications in the city and regional category. At the end of 1984 there were 147 such listings. Circulations have grown steadily and large monthlies such as *Chicago, Los Angeles, Philadelphia,* and *The Washingtonian* carry more than 150 pages of advertising a month. The editorial mix consists of restaurant reviews and life-style and service features that cater to the interests of upscale readers. These upscale readers are not old-line aristocrats or old-line business tycoons. Rather, they are new, young, mobile men and women, some of whom have recently

---

[3] E. B. Weiss, "Advertising Nears a Big Speed-Up in Communications Innovation," *Advertising Age* (March 19, 1979), pp. 51–52.

moved into a new city and others who may have lived in the area but are new to the downtown affluent life style.

Foreign-Language Press

The 1980 census found that more than 10 percent of Americans age five and over speak a language other than English at home. About 43 percent of all Americans who speak a language other than English are Hispanic: 77 percent of Mexican-Americans, 86 percent of Puerto Ricans, and 92 percent of Cuban-Americans said they spoke a language other than English at home. About 20

Hideharu Tamaru

When Hideharu Tamaru was appointed president of Tokyo's giant Dentsu Incorporated (formerly Dentsu Advertising Ltd.) in June 1977, one of his first official duties was presiding over the 76th celebration of the company's founding. Dentsu is not only one of the world's largest advertising agencies but one of the oldest. Despite the staid impression these facts may convey, under Hideharu Tamaru's guidance Dentsu is a progressive and forward-looking company. Of his role as president, he remarks: "I am confident that my function as president is to set up a bridge to the twenty-first century."

Hideharu Tamaru was not always so concerned with the future or with mass communications, however. Exhibiting a flair for literature and history, he began as a high school teacher after graduating from Tokyo University in 1938. Ten years later, he was offered his first job in the field of advertising by the president of Dentsu himself, Hideo Yoshida, who also became Tamaru's self-appointed mentor. Yoshida repeatedly assigned Tamaru difficult tasks that a less determined man would have found impossible. Of those early years, Tamaru has this to say:

> For the first ten years at Dentsu, Yoshida kept me so busy I didn't have a minute to myself. I got to wondering why he always subjected me to those aggravating situations. But looking

back on it all now I can see that he was whipping me into shape so I could get on an even footing with those Dentsu managers who had started with the company much earlier than I. Now I feel grateful for what he did.

Tamaru's perseverance paid off. During the ensuing years he worked in nearly every department, learning the business from the ground up. When it was announced that he would become the seventh president of Dentsu, however, the news came as a surprise to his many friends who know him by his affable and unpretentious manner. Indeed, Tamaru himself remembers the event as the shock of his life.

Reflecting his early experience as a teacher, Tamaru's leadership of Dentsu proceeds with the well-ordered discipline of an academician. Tamaru is usually one of the first to arrive at the Dentsu building near Tokyo's Ginza district, and the last to leave. He exercises daily to keep fit and prepare himself for the arduous task of running the company. Reading is his favorite hobby, much of it centering on business and economics. Whenever possible though, he returns to the classics of Japanese literature and particularly the lyric "Manyoshu" poetry that dates from the eighth century, a subject in which he is keenly interested and knowledgeable.

percent of persons of French, Italian or Polish ancestry reported speaking a language other than English at home. Most of the Asian population living in the United States speak a language other than English at home: 93 percent of the Vietnamese, 81 percent of the Chinese, and 44 percent of the Japanese speak a language other than English at home. Seventy-nine percent of Koreans, 68 percent of Filipinos, and 69 percent of Indians said they speak other than English at home. Curiously, 58 percent of all Americans who speak a language other than English were born in the United States.

To reach such people there have been foreign-language papers for years. At the height of U.S. immigration in the 1920s, there were 500 foreign-language papers published in this country. Today there are about 200. In Chinatown, New York City, there are 10 Chinese papers. Michigan may have the largest Arab population in the country. In Detroit alone there are three Arab papers. The fastest growing segment of the population is Hispanic. According to the U.S. Census Bureau there are about 16 million Hispanics, many of whom are likely to turn to Spanish-language newspapers for their news. Their numbers make them an attractive market. In fact there are now 18 Spanish-language weeklies and four dailies published in the United States. Advertisers are beginning to realize that to reach this audience, they have to place ads in the Spanish press.

There are some widely accepted generalities about Hispanics in the United States: They are younger; they have larger households; they are more loyal to church and brands. Although they are poorer and less educated than the population as a whole, they represent buying power. A survey by Yankelovich, Skelly & White reported that 50 percent of Hispanics in the United States think of themselves as Hispanic first, American second.[4] Los Angeles, after Mexico City, is the second largest Spanish-speaking city in the Northern Hemisphere. U.S. Hispanics also see important differences among themselves. It would be similar to the way an Englishman and an American would identify themselves if they both lived in France. They would be similar, but different.

Changing Television Habits

It was not so long ago that when a person was "watching television" it meant watching a program on network television. Today "watching television" also means watching a movie on the VCR or a how-to cassette brought home from the video store or the local library. Another interesting change is late-night viewing. Young viewers are watching more late-night television, the staple for which is repeats of defunct series. We can expect a string of revivals of vintage shows such as *Perry Mason, Peyton Place, Marcus Welby,* and other "new" old shows. The baby boomers, now middle-aged, enjoy watching the shows they enjoyed so much 20 years ago. The supply of old shows is virtually inexhaustible.

There are two kinds of television viewers—selective and nonselective. Selective viewers are light viewers who consciously limit the amount of television they watch. They tend to be better educated and more affluent. When they use a VCR, it is usually a supplement to other entertainment such as reading a magazine or going out to a movie. The nonselective viewers are people who watch seven or more hours daily and do not give much thought to

---

[4] *Advertising Age,* March 21, 1985, p. 13.

Bahamas Tourism

All the Caribbean islands, including the Bahamas, are seen as more or less the same, offering sun, sand, and sea — a warm-weather vacation. The attitude of the local people is perceived by many as ranging from disinterested to unfriendly. Why then select the Bahamas rather than any other Caribbean island?

It is estimated that there are over 9 million prospects for a warm-weather vacation — upscale, educated people. The opportunity lies in convincing these prospects that the Bahamas had everything that anyone could desire in an island vacation — sun, sand, sea, sports facilities, night life, gambling, and the relaxed pace of life — and all better than the competition.

The fact is the Bahamas has a wide variety of experiences to offer most travelers — from the most relaxed to the very sophisticated. Extensive concept testing indicated that people want to know about the experiences and activities available to them in addition to knowing that they can enjoy the option of doing nothing at all if they choose to. This concept was the most appealing across all demographic levels to potential vacationers. From this the agency developed the theme "In the Bahamas, you never run out of things to do. Until you want to." From this positioning it developed distinctive advertising in national consumer magazines plus informative quick-response tactical price advertising for radio and newspapers.

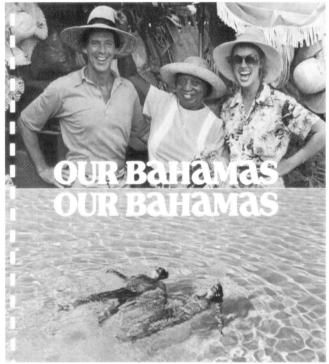

In The Bahamas, you never run out of things to do. Until you want to.

You really want to have some fun today? Good.
Spend a morning sailing on the clearest turquoise water in the world. Splash in it. Snorkel in it. Or scuba.
Have a quick lunch of conch fritters. Then stroll about town. Browse a Straw Market. Bargain for a hat. Play some

tennis before dinner. Then dig into a Bahamian lobster. Later, it's on to disco, baccarat and blackjack.
Tomorrow, let it begin at noon. Just the two of you on a beach. It's peace. It's tranquility. And it's all yours.
You can do it all. Or nothing at all. In one place, right here in The Bahamas.

For a brochure on your Bahamas, including the exotic Out Islands of Abaco, Andros, Eleuthera and Exuma, call your Travel Agent. Or toll free 800-327-0787. In Florida 800-432-5594. In Dade County 443-3821.

It's Better In The Bahamas.

what they watch. They don't watch by the program; they watch by the clock.

The fact is that VCR homes appear to watch more television according to Nielsen research. One study showed that VCR homes averaged 33.7 hours of viewing per week compared to 32.8 hours for non-VCR homes.[5] VCRs have created time shifts in audiences. Some viewers watch more prime-time shows than might otherwise be possible by taping some programs and watching them after the late news, the next morning, or on weekend mornings.

There have also been shifts in late-night viewing, and the audience is college-educated, single, professional/managerial. Some are working longer hours and watching later into the night.

Summary

What does the future hold for advertising? We can expect to see emphasis in two areas and we can expect to see interesting changes in advertising media. One area that will grow in importance is international advertising. As American marketers seek to expand their sales around the world, they will use advertising and promotion techniques developed in the United States but modified to suit different cultures, distribution channels, and media.

Another area that will probably grow in the United States itself is the advertising of services. As we become increasingly service-oriented, the advertising and promotion of services — housing, repair, entertainment, travel, financial — will offer new challenges. The intangible, perishable, and unstandardized nature of services makes their presentation difficult. Difficult, but not impossible. And at the same time we shall see a more extensive use of advertising by every level of government. The federal government, already a major advertiser, will find more opportunities to use advertising techniques to "sell" the American public on ideas and attitudes deemed necessary to fight inflation, reduce unemployment, and save fuel.

As for media, the number of electronic miracles still possible is incalculable. Barely 30 years ago, television was in its infancy. And now we have everything from portable, battery-operated sets with 7-inch screens to color television sets with 45-inch screens, videocassette decks, and cable connections. Will changing electronic technology affect an advertiser's media mix? Indeed it will. And advertisers in future, as they do today, must keep a careful watch on the changing demographics of the marketplace.

Questions for Discussion

1. What are some of the problems that face international advertisers?
2. Why is export business important to American industry?
3. What are some of the problems inherent in advertising services? How can they be overcome?
4. What consumer services do you think will improve most from an increase in service advertising?
5. What will be the future impact of cable tv on advertising?
6. What future changes in print media advertising can you envision?

---

[5] *ADWEEK*, March 18, 1986, p. 4.

Sources and Suggestions for Further Reading

"Advertising 'Round the World: Variations on Similar Themes." *Advertising Age* (August 29, 1977).

"Ad Week: An Ad in Any Other Land Is Not the Same." *Advertising Age* (September 4, 1978).

Bogart, Leo. "As Media Change, How Will Advertising?" *Journal of Advertising Research* (October 1973).

Chase, Dennis. "Global Marketing: The New Wave." *Advertising Age* (June 25, 1984).

Dichter, Ernest. "The World Customer." *Harvard Business Review* (July/August 1962).

Dillon, John, editor. *Handbook of International Direct Marketing.* London: McGraw-Hill, 1976.

"Growth Dots the Landscape," *Advertising Age* (January 17, 1985).

"Here Comes the Moving Poster," *ADWEEK* (January 28, 1985).

"Marketing to Hispanics." *Special Report, Advertising Age* (August 11, 1986).

McArthur, Edith. "What Language Do You Speak," *American Demographics* (October 1984).

Reece, Chuck. "Forget Yuppies — Here Come the 'Neds'." *ADWEEK* (May 5, 1986).

Schlosberg, Jeremy. "The Glittering World of City Magazines." *American Demographics* (July 1986).

Slater, Courtenay. "The (Business) Service Economy." *American Demographics* (May 1985).

Sonenklar, Carol. "Women and Their Magazines." *American Demographics* (June 1986).

Terpstra, Vern. *International Marketing.* 3rd ed. Hinsdale, IL: Dryden, 1983.

Unwin, Steve. "Advertising of Services, Not Products, Will Be the Wave of the Future." *Advertising Age* (May 27, 1974).

"Watch That Foreign Market — Everything Changes." *Advertising Age* (April 29, 1974).

Wayne, Leslie. "Services — the Star of U.S. Trade." *The New York Times* (September 14, 1986).

Weiss, E. B. "Advertising Nears a Big Speed-Up in Communications Innovation." *Advertising Age* (March 19, 1973).

"What Americans Can Learn from Europe — Market Segmentation." *Advertising Age* (February 16, 1976).

ILLUSTRATION CREDITS

Chapter 17
Page 411 Courtesy, Foote, Cone & Belding.
420 A & B Graphics, Inc., Hubert Baumgaertner/President.   **421** Courtesy Chicago Historical Society.   **423** Nancy Axthelm/Vice President, Production Group Head, Grey Advertising.
425 Sony Corporation of America.

Part 5
Page 428 Courtesy of Saatchi & Saatchi Compton, Bill Harris/Art Director, Jeff Wolff/Copywriter, Peter B. Kaplan and Joe Budne/Photographers.

Chapter 18
Page 433 Reprinted with permission of The Seven-Up Company, St. Louis, MO.
438, 439 Prepared by Foote, Cone & Belding for Sunkist Soft Drinks, Inc.   **445** Courtesy of Starch Ira Hooper, Inc.   **448** General Advertising Department, New York's Capitol Newspapers; Portland (ME) Newspapers.   **450** ITT Life Insurance Corporation.

Chapter 19
Page 454 Courtesy of Saks Fifth Avenue.
455 Courtesy of Alexander's.   **457** Courtesy of Neiman-Marcus.   **458** Chas. A. Stevens.
462 7 South 8th for HAIR.   **464–465** Courtesy The Syracuse Newspapers.   **466** Courtesy Lands' End.   **467** Courtesy Macy's.   **470** Sony Corporation of America.   **472** Courtesy Victory Shirt Company, Inc.

Chapter 20
Page 477 Courtesy of Diversitron Corp.
478 Courtesy of Walt Simson Associates, East Setauket, NY.   **479** Courtesy of RHG Electronics Laboratory, Inc.   **480** Pennwalt Corporation.
481 Courtesy of Multicore Solders.   **483** Courtesy of Networx, Dialight Corp.   **486** Courtesy of IBM.   **488** Courtesy AMF-American Division.
489 ITT Life Insurance Corporation.   **491** Courtesy of American Express and Ogilvy & Mather, Inc.   **492** Courtesy, Menley & James Laboratories.   **495** Courtesy National Yellow Pages Service Association.   **499** © US West, Inc.

Chapter 21
Page 506 Courtesy National Heart, Lung, and Blood Institute.   **507** Courtesy, Xerox Corporation.   **508** Distilled Spirits Council of the United States, Inc.   **509** Save the Children Federation, Inc.   **511** Courtesy of State of Florida, Dept. of Citrus.   **515** Courtesy GMAC.   **520, 521** American Association of Advertising Agencies.

Chapter 22
Page 528 Cadbury Typhoo Limited.   **530** Sony Corporation of America.   **531** Courtesy of Eastman Kodak Company.   **532** Used with permission, Kellogg Company.   **535** © 1985, American Express Travel Related Services, Inc.   **536** The Prudential Insurance Company of America.
537, 538 Courtesy Foote, Cone & Belding.
539 American Medical Association.   **541** Courtesy of Shopping Center Network; Campbell Soup Company.   **545** Courtesy of NW Ayer, Inc.

COLOR PLATES

Color plate 1 Oldsmobile Division, General Motors Corporation.   **2** Rolex Watch USA, Inc.
3 Reprinted by permission of Chesebrough-Pond's Inc.   **4** Courtesy of Hartmann Luggage and Leber Katz Partners.   **5** General Electric Co., Major Appliances Business Group.   **6** Cuisinarts, Inc.
7 Courtesy of Thom McAn, Carol Feinberg/Vice President, Marketing and Advertising.   **8** Courtesy of Foote, Cone and Belding.   **9** D'Arcy Masius Benton & Bowles.   **10** Prepared by Foote, Cone & Belding for the California Raisin Advisory Board.
11 Courtesy of The Upjohn Company, photography by Joel Meyerwitz.   **12** Courtesy of the American Dairy Association.   **13** Courtesy of Brock Musik, Inc.   **14** Courtesy of Wendy's International, Inc.
15 Courtesy of The Procter & Gamble Company.
16 Dun's Business Month.   **17** Courtesy of The Perrier Group.   **18** Toyota Motor Sales, U.S.A., Inc.   **19** Courtesy of Tangueray Gin and Smith/Greenland Inc.   **20** Courtesy of Riunite, Neil F. Trimble/Vice President, Advertising.   **21** Copyright © 1985 by The New York Times. Reprinted by permission.   **22** Reprinted with permission from PARADE Magazine: Copyright 1985 Parade Publications, Inc.   **23** Courtesy of Sports Illustrated © 1985 Time, Inc.   **24** Courtesy of Schwepps U.S.A. Limited.   **25** Shade Information Systems and Fallon McElligott Rice, Jarl Olsen/Writer, John Morrison/Art Director.   **26** 3M Company, Commercial Office Supply Division.   **27** Courtesy of Hyatt Corporation.   **28** Courtesy of Institute of Outdoor Advertising.   **29** © 1983 Stroh Brewery Co., Detroit, MI.   **30, 31** Courtesy of Institute of Outdoor Advertising.   **32, 33** Courtesy of Knauf Fiber Glass, Joe Whitman/Creative Director, John Bugg and Steve Cannon/Art Directors, Leslie Hunt-Davis/Copywriter.   **34** Courtesy of Canada Dry.   **35** Used by permission of Yves Saint Laurent

Parfums Corp., owner of trademark "Kouros."
36 Campbell Soup Company.   **37** Young & Rubican, Inc., Dan Sabatino/Art Director, Charles Gold/Photographer.   **38** Courtesy of Schenley Imports and Leo Burnett U.S.A.   **39** Revillon.
40 Courtesy of Miller Brewing Co.   **41** Courtesy of The Perrier Group.   **42** Courtesy of the Marschalk Company, Inc.   **43** Photo courtesy of Nike, Inc.   **44** United Airlines and Leo Burnett, U.S.A.   **45** Motor car photograph permission of Rolls Royce Motors.   **46** Cadillac Motor Car Division.   **47** Photo courtesy of Nike, Inc.
48 J.G. Hook, Inc.   **49, 50** Jockey International, Inc.   **51, 52, 53, 54, 55** Courtesy of Doyle Dane Bernbach, Inc.   **56** Sony Corporation of America.
57, 58 Courtesy of Leeming/Pacquin.   **59** Association of American Railroads.   **60** Neiman-Marcus.
61 Prince Manufacturing, Inc. and Waring & La Rosa, Inc.   **62** Fisher-Price, Division of The Quaker Oats Company.   **63** TIME Forum for Freedom and Livingston/Sirutis/Advertising.
64 TIME Forum for Freedom and Quinn & Johnson/BBDO.   **65** Courtesy of International Minerals & Chemical Corporation, Northbrook, Illinois, Dr. Lindsay Brown/Director of North American Marketing, Annette Degnan/Account Executive, Annette Bertelsen/Copywriter, Bill Winchester/Art Director.   **66** The Boy Scouts of America and Foote, Cone & Belding.   **67** Courtesy of General Motors Corporation and McCann-Erickson, Inc.   **68** Prepared by McCann-Erickson, Inc. for the Buick Motor Division.   **69** Reprint furnished courtesy of Quantas, The Australian Airline.   **70** Bermuda Dept. of Tourism and Foote, Cone & Belding.   **71** Courtesy of AT&T Communications.   **72** William Grant & Sons, Inc., importers of Frangelico Liqueur and Chiat/Day, Inc.   **73** South Dakota State Development.

INDEX

G

Gainesburgers, 364
Gallup, George, 18
   profile, 449
Gallup & Robinson ratings, 444
Gaze motion, 384, 386
General Motors, 7, 308
   Mr. Goodwrench, case history, 114, 115
Gillette Company, case history, 228, 229
Government advertising, 540
Gravure, 417
Gross impressions, 255
GRPs, 244, 253, 270
GTE Sylvania, 55

H

Halftones, 428
Headlines, 364–66
Heineken beer, case history, 328
HiFi color, 183
Hoffman, York & Compton, 78, 79
Holly Farms, case history, 376
Home Testing Institute, 105
Horizontal publications, 211
House agency, 82
House Beautiful, 194
House organs, 301
Houston Chronicle, 178
Houston Magazine, 198

I

Identification, product, 318
Illustration, 389, 391
Industrial
   advertising, 55, 476, 482
   advertising objectives, 484
   buying process, 482
   campaigns, 487
   copy, 485
   goods, 28, 477–81
   schedules, 487
Information for retailers, 459
Insertion orders, 156–57
Inserts, 196, 218, 488
Institutional advertising, 59, 61
Institutional publications, 215
International advertising, 526
ITT Life Insurance Corporation, case history, 450

J

Johnson, S.C., & Son, Inc., 43
Jolly Green Giant, 319

L

Lanham Act, 314
Lasker, Albert D., profile, 38
Layout, 381
   principles, 382
Leading advertisers, 19
Leading National Advertisers (LNA), 124, 125
Letterpress, 416
Licensing, 320
Life cycle, 50, 435
Life styles, 344
List broker, 294
List house, 294
Lithography, 416
Logotype, 320
Loss leader, 442
Lotteries, advertising, 540

M

MacPaint, 389, 390
Magazine space, 192
Magazines
   advertisers, 185
   city, 542
   top 10, 197
Mailing
   co-op, 298
   lists, 293
   solo, 298
Mail-order, 299
Major cities, U.S., 98
Malls, shopping, 541
Marketing
   concept, 26
   information for retailers, 459
   intelligence, 94–95
   intelligence reference guide, 118
   mix, 27
   objectives, 48, 49
   plan, 48
Marsteller, William A., 72
   profile, 227
Mass magazines, 189
Matched color, 195
Matrix organization, 73, 74
McCann, Harrison King, profile, 497
McGraw-Hill Research, 213
Media
   associations, 88
   buying services, 77
   changing, 540
   characteristics, 147
   international, 527
   mix, 151
   references, 166
   representative, 164
   research, 117
   for retailers, 463
   selection factors, 143